# THE PUBLIC SCHOOL
## MONOPOLY

# PACIFIC STUDIES IN PUBLIC POLICY

**Locking Up the Range**
Federal Land Controls and Grazing
*By Gary D. Libecap*
*With a foreword by Jonathan R. T. Hughes*

**Resolving the Housing Crisis**
Government Policy, Decontrol, and the Public Interest
*Edited with an introduction by M. Bruce Johnson*

## *FORTHCOMING*

**Impoverishing America**
The Political Economy of the Transfer Society

**Natural Resources**
Myths and Management

**Firearms and Violence**
Issues of Regulation

**Inflation or Deflation?**
Prospects for Capital Formation, Employment,
and Economic Recovery

**Water in the West**
Scarce Resource Allocation, Property Rights, and the Environment

**Forestlands**
Public and Private

**Rationing Health Care**
Medical Licensing in the U.S.

*For further information on the Pacific Institute's program and a catalog of
publications, please contact:*

PACIFIC INSTITUTE
for Public Policy Research
635 Mason Street
San Francisco, California 94108

# THE PUBLIC SCHOOL MONOPOLY

## A Critical Analysis of Education and the State in American Society

*Editor*
ROBERT B. EVERHART

*Foreword by*
CLARENCE J. KARIER

Pacific Studies in Public Policy
PACIFIC INSTITUTE FOR PUBLIC POLICY RESEARCH
San Francisco, California

BALLINGER PUBLISHING COMPANY
Cambridge, Massachusetts
A Subsidiary of Harper & Row, Publishers, Inc.

International Standard Book Number: 0-88410-383-8 (CL)
0-88410-388-9 (PB)

Library of Congress Catalog Card Number: 81-20635

Printed in the United States of America


**Library of Congress Cataloging in Publication Data**

Main entry under title:

The public school monopoly.

 (Pacific studies in public policy)
 Includes bibliographical references and index.
 1. Education and state—United States—History.
2. Public schools—Government policy—United States—History.
I. Everhart, Robert B. II. Series.
LC89.P8                379.73                81-20635
ISBN 0-88410-383-8                AACR2
ISBN 0-88410-388-9 (pbk.)

PACIFIC INSTITUTE
FOR PUBLIC POLICY RESEARCH

The Pacific Institute for Public Policy Research is an independent, tax-exempt, research and educational organization. The Institute's program is designed to broaden public understanding of the nature and effects of market processes and government policy.

With the bureaucratization and politicization of modern society, scholars, business and civic leaders, the media, policymakers, and the general public have too often been isolated from meaningful solutions to critical public issues. To facilitate a more active and enlightened discussion of such issues, the Pacific Institute sponsors in-depth studies into the nature and possible solutions to major social, economic, and environmental problems. Undertaken regardless of the sanctity of any particular government program, or the customs, prejudices, or temper of the times, the Institute aims to ensure that alternative approaches to currently problematic policy areas are fully evaluated, the best remedies discovered, and these findings made widely available. The results of this work are published as books and monographs, and form the basis for numerous conference and media programs.

Through this program of research and commentary, the Institute seeks to evaluate the premises and consequences of government policy, and provide the foundations necessary for constructive policy reform.

# CONTENTS

# ACKNOWLEDGMENTS

This work involved the cooperation and insight of a number of individuals who deserve recognition. Donald Erickson of the University of California, Los Angeles first suggested the idea of this book to me and assisted my working through various plans, one of which eventually launched the book into its present form. Don served as a patient counselor as I orchestrated the book to its conclusion, and to him I am most grateful. David Theroux, the President of the Pacific Institute for Public Policy Research, the organization which sponsored this project, was most supportive in providing the resources, confidence, and suggestions that helped move the book along smoothly. Estelle Jelinek provided useful editorial advice, and all of us benefited from her competency. Finally, the book represents the concerted efforts of fifteen individual authors, each of whom dealt with his topic in a competent and professional manner, all the while willing to recognize the constraints with which they had to live. I have been quite fortunate to work with scholars whom I respect so much. To all of them go my thanks.

R. B. E.

# FOREWORD

*The Public School Monopoly: A Critical Analysis of Education and the State in American Society* is an important work that challenges some of the basic assumptions undergirding American polity for over a century. Here, scholars from diverse fields question the right of the state to exercise monopoly control over education and analyze some of the instruments and consequences of this monopoly control. The essays in this volume are clearly reasoned, provocative in the subject matter they cover, and thoughtful in their conclusions. There is little doubt that the central focus of the book—the relationship between education and the state in American society—is a topic the examination of which is long overdue.

Yet its appearance at this particular time should not be too surprising as the book is indicative of the growing public dissatisfaction with the expansion of state power over the lives of more and more people, especially in the realm of education. This dissatisfaction has emerged not only because of the practical failings of the current educational system to deliver reasonable services but also because the political economy, which once provided the foundation for the public school ideology, has changed so much that the older faith is no longer credible.

The problem we face is historically rooted. Daniel Webster once defined public education as a "wise and liberal system of police, by which property and life, and the peace of society are secured."[1] With these words still resonating in their consciousness, such men as Horace Mann of Massachusetts, Henry Barnard of Connecticut, Calvin Stowe of Ohio, Caleb Mills of Indiana, and John Pierce of Michigan shaped the common school movement, which laid the foundation for what in the twentieth century grew into the educational state.

As the nineteenth century dawned in the grips of strong nationalistic fervor and considerable social and economic conflict, public power at both the state and federal levels of government began to grow. By the third and fourth decades of the century, state authority in education, especially in the Northeast and Middle Atlantic states, had grown to such an extent that a public school could be clearly defined as one which was publicly controlled and publicly financed. By mid-nineteenth century this distinction as to what constituted a public school as opposed to a private school was commonplace. Spurred on by the passions of nationalism, the social dislocations of the frontier, and the social and economic instability resulting from immigration and the early phases of industrialism, the common school, supposedly transmitting the common values of American culture, was realized as a government institution.

With that school development went a common school ideology which linked the political future of the new nation and the economic well-being of every citizen with the emerging educational system. It "never can happen," Mann argued, "that an intelligent and practical body of men should be permanently poor." The more formal schooling a population had, the less chance it had of being poor. The argument set forth in Mann's twelfth annual report to the Massachusetts Board of Education assumed not only that education would prevent poverty and thereby reduce class conflict through the process of everyone's getting some share of the wealth but that the very size of the pool of wealth to be distributed would steadily increase as a consequence of a more highly educated populace. Thus, Mann believed not only in education as the "balance-wheel of the social machinery,"[2] which disarmed the poor of their hostility towards the rich by preventing "being poor," but he had also clearly conceptualized a theory of human capital. As he put it: "Education has a market value. . . . It may be minted and will yield a larger amount of statutable coin than common bullion."[3]

The same year that Karl Marx wrote *The Communist Manifesto* (1848), Mann penned his last annual report to the Massachusetts Board of Education. In that report was embedded a theory of human capital, which conceptually linked schooling to economic and social growth within a presumed meritocratically organized social and economic class system. Here, then, was the rationale for public schooling which sustained the American nation for the next century. Implicit in that rationale was an ideology of competitive and possessive individualism packaged in the wrappings of equal opportunity for all, within a public system of locally managed schools under state authorization. Mann's Whig political-educational platform combined the earlier Hamiltonian respect for property with the Jeffersonian concern for equality, all set within the institutional framework of a presumed meritocratically governed public school system. The end product was a school system which taught not only how to read, write, and cipher but also Horatio Alger stories from which children learned the lesson that material rewards and riches come to those who have learned to work to achieve business success. And fundamental to the development of competitive capitalism in America was the development of a population well schooled in the virtues of such an economic system.

In the transcendentalist tradition, Henry David Thoreau argued that "the government is best which governs not at all." He further warned his fellow countrymen against the pending "age of the organization man." Thoreau was perhaps never so prophetic as when at Walden Pond he noted ominously that the sounds of the locomotive disturbed the idyllic peace and tranquility of his natural environment. By the end of the nineteenth century: "Things were in the saddle," as Emerson had earlier warned. To many, laissez faire capitalism,[4] which economically undergirded the ideology of nineteenth-century classical liberalism, had seemed to run its course in an age of "cut throat" competition and "robber baron" individualism. By the end of the century, in spite of the determined opposition of the populists, anarchists, radical classical liberals, and some socialist leaders, monopoly capitalism was conceived within the womb of the Progressive era-fashioned regulatory state.

The political progressives' solution to the many social and economic problems at the turn of the century was found in the idea of the regulatory state. This concept of state, as it was fashioned by such Wisconsin progressives as Richard Ely, John Commons and Robert LaFollette and later institutionalized by the national government, was historically rooted in the paternalistic Bismarckian state, which rationalized and regulated the political-social economy in the name of scientific efficiency and provided the broad social welfare legislation behind which monopoly capitalism grew. This idea, expressed in progressive legislation, emanated first from Wisconsin and then later was applied to the national arena. Like its forerunner the Bismarckian state, it was designed to ameliorate fundamental competition between competing economic and social interests. The positive liberal state was thus born out of the interest to regulate competition. As such, the regulatory state provided the protective shield behind which the phenomenal growth and consolidation of the corporate state occurred, which in turn was critical in establishing the cartelized American system of mass production, distribution, and consumption in the twentieth century. Charles Forcey reminded us of this phenomenal growth when he pointed out: "in 1897 the total capitalization of all corporations individually valued at a million dollars or more came to only 170 million. Three years later the same figure for total capitalization stood at five billion, and in 1904 at over twenty billion."[5] Massive accumulation of capital now was employed to underwrite the creation of assembly line mass production. Within decades, America became the leading producer of industrial goods. By the third decade of the twentieth century the Hoover Commission Report on the state of the economy pointed out that not only had worker productivity skyrocketed and the nation become the leading mass producer of standardized industrial goods, but in the future the nation would have to shift its capital investments to a correspondingly vast system of producing consumer goods and services.[6]

Mass advertising and mass education helped shape the values and desires of a consumer-oriented society. Within this context the nation was taught to live on credit and to use, waste, and consume as many goods and services as quickly as possible. Planned obsolescence became a standard part of American industry as corporations grew ever larger, relatively free of competition and protected by the bureaucratic workings of the regulatory state. The National Civic Federation, made up of representatives of big corporations, labor unions, banks, and government, played an instrumental role in creating the necessary legislation. Although much of this legislation *seemed* to protect the consumer against unfair pricing, it was also clear that much of the state regulations eliminated competition and effectively facilitated the development of even larger corporate units.

Along with the use of the state as a regulatory agency came the use of the state as a protective welfare agency, which, in exercising its power, extended its compulsory authority to nearly all aspects of life. The larger corporations as well as the larger unions found it to their financial advantage to support greater governmental regulatory authority. That same compulsory state authority which regulated commerce also came to regulate drugs, alcohol, tobacco, food, clothing, work, leisure time, transportation, communication, news, knowledge, research, medicine, child labor, social welfare, and education.

Within this context public secondary education rapidly expanded. By 1900 only 10 percent of American youth aged fourteen to seventeen attended a secondary school. Fifty years later approximately 90 percent of that age group were in secondary schools. Compulsory education had become a reality. The complex bureaucratic corporate structure now was matched with an equally complex bureaucratic educational structure, which helped prepare people for life in the new corporate state. By the closing decades of the nineteenth century the new university, modeled after the German university, dedicated to research and the production and dissemination of new knowledge, emerged as part of the educational state. By mid-twentieth century that institution was recognized not only as the chief producer and disseminator of new knowledge but also the chief institution for training the professional cadre who would staff the overall system.

The older, classical, liberal ideology, which had been rationalized on the basis of the earlier laissez faire political economy, no longer made sense within the context of an emerging monopoly capitalism created by the regulatory state. The older liberalism which had been espoused by Thomas Jefferson and others had to be reconstructed. George Herbert Mead and John Dewey played a major role in the reconstruction of American liberalism. A key feature in that reconstruction included a view of the function of the state, not in negative terms as the older classical liberals were apt to do, but rather with a positive view of the uses of state power. The state authority was now seen as an instrumental tool with which most social, economic, and educational problems could be solved. Although the overall reconstruction of modern American liberalism was considerably more complex and included a reconceptualization of human nature as well as the social order, a fundamental feature of that reconstruction was a reorientation toward state action.

By the third and fourth decades of the twentieth century there had clearly emerged not only a complex, widespread educational bureaucracy but also a cadre of professional experts who tended to accept many of the major tenets of the new liberalism, especially those which found state action in education acceptable. At its best the new liberalism of Dewey and others reflected the hopes and dreams of many for a more humane social order, although for these same people, at its worst, it tended to obfuscate the possibility of a significant critique of the social and economic order and thus prevented the practical realization of such dreams.

However one views liberalism, it is clear that within the last few decades it has come under significant criticism. Many of the key tenets of that faith which provided the basis for the public school educational ideology have come under serious question. Although some have laid the crisis of American liberalism to the rather sterile shadow cast over the minds of the post-World War II generation of young philosophers by past giants in the field, what seems more reasonable is to recognize that much of the crisis in the liberal faith in public education is intimately related to the same declining faith in the larger regulatory state. In this sense the thrust for deregulation of public utilities is not entirely unrelated to the argument for the deregulation of public schooling in America. While the exact consequences of such legislation may be difficult to predict and may be harmful to some and advantageous to others, the significant point is that it is seriously entertained at all. What is clear is that the liberal corporate state and its educational institutions which served this nation for a half-century are now undergoing some fundamental changes. What will take their place remains to be seen.

This book, then, addresses a variety of problems and issues emanating from the fundamental changes our society is currently undergoing. One may take issue with any one analysis or proposed solution, but the reader cannot help but come away better informed on the public policy issues involved in the production and control of education in modern day society. *The Public School Monopoly: A Critical Analysis of Education and the State in American Society* is significant not only because of the particular answers that are here proposed but further because it clearly reflects the extent to which the older faith in the corporate-liberal educational state has deteriorated and the extent to which serious scholars are searching for answers to the many political, social, economic, and educational problems which have ensued. Yet the book is important reading not just for its answers but for its beginnings. It represents the beginning of a serious dialogue, raising important questions which very much need public discussion if a more humane society is ever to evolve out of our current problematic world.

Clarence J. Karier
University of Illinois
Urbana, Illinois

## NOTES TO FOREWORD

1. Quoted in Clarence J. Karier, *Man, Society, and Education* (Glenview, Ill.: Scott Foresman, 1967), p. 51.
2. Quoted in Lawrence A. Cremin, *The Republic and the School: Horace Mann on the Education of Free Men* (New York: Teachers College Press, 1957), p. 87.
3. As quoted by Richard H. deLone, *Small Futures: Children, Inequality and the Limits of Liberal Reform* (New York: Harcourt Brace Jovanovich, 1979), p. 43.
4. American capitalism was really never purely laissez faire. Government land subsidies of railroads and canals as well as protective tariffs were all practices which ran counter to a truly free capitalism. Nevertheless, the overall orientation of the developing economic system in America for most of the nineteenth century tended toward a laissez faire situation.
5. Charles Forcey, *The Crossroads of Liberalism* (New York: Oxford University Press, 1961), p. xiv.
6. See *Recent Social Trends in the United States: Report of the President's Research Committee on Social Trends*, vols. 1 and 2 (New York: McGraw-Hill, 1933).

# INTRODUCTION

*Robert B. Everhart*

Though it may be somewhat of a shopworn phrase, there continues to be the "crisis in the classroom" of equal if not greater significance than that noted by Charles Silberman some ten years ago.[1] A recent issue of *Time* magazine, for example, noted that politicians, educators, "and especially millions of parents have come to believe that the United States public schools are in parlous trouble."[2] This growing lack of confidence in public education on the part of many is one of the central reasons behind the continuing enrollment gains in private schools throughout the nation and serves as a backdrop for the essays in this volume. It is our belief that without a serious reexamination and indeed even a possible reconceptualization of public education in the United States, this crisis of confidence will continue to grow and be manifested in a variety of conditions (both foreseen and unforeseen) evident in public schools throughout the nation.

What are some of the more obvious manifestations of this diminished confidence in public education? Financial stresses in our schools have grown to such epidemic proportions that, in many communities, school buildings are being boarded up and sold to real estate interests, and those buildings that remain rapidly deteriorate because of an absence of money to repair them. In those schools that remain open, educational materials are in such short supply that in some communities students are charged educational "fees" to pay for basic material necessities. Finally, we see the strains reflected in

1

the salaries paid to teachers, salaries falling further and further behind the rate of inflation. This problem is so severe that one study shows that teachers, on the average, have suffered a salary loss of 1.7 percent per year over the past ten years when inflation is taken into account.[3]

These conditions associated with diminishing confidence in public education have surfaced in areas other than those related to the material conditions within schools. Indeed, the lowered confidence in the ability of public education to produce demonstrable results appears to be associated with the growing sense of alienation from school on the part of many students. For instance, school violence now is of such epidemic proportions that Congress recently issued a major report on the causes and consequences of school violence.[4] In many urban schools, the presence of uniformed police officers throughout the school day now is an accepted fact. Yet student alienation from school can take other forms, not necessarily of a violent nature. In many schools, upwards of 30 percent of the student body is absent on any given day. In New York City, it is estimated that on a given day in half the schools, up to 50 percent of the students are absent from school, surely an alarming statistic by any stretch of the imagination.[5] In California, recent estimates of an average 20 percent nonattendance rate prompted one state legislator to suggest that school districts with nonmedically connected absentee rates above 5 percent should be ineligible for state funding for that proportion of students who exceed the 5 percent quota. Ostensibly, this would force districts to pursue more aggressively those that are deemed to be "truants" if the districts wished to receive state funds.

Finally, the diminishing faith in public education seems to have had an effect on the general propensity of many students not to take school as an intellectual experience as seriously as they once did, so much so that the pattern of "getting by" seems to be the accepted norm. Surely, when grade point averages have been increasing while standard test score averages are decreasing, then something is not quite right with the abilities of students, the criteria for grades, what the tests measure, or all three conditions. Yet those declining test scores could, again, represent as much a diminishing confidence in the effectiveness of schooling as they do a true decline in ability. Indeed, Christopher Jencks suggested a few years ago that the growing realization, on the part of many students, that top grades in school and possession of advanced education did not necessarily mean future economic and occupational success, may in fact be what is contributing to the disposition to take school less seriously and the consequent result of not doing as well on tests such as the Scholastic Aptitude Test (SAT).[6] Students may be viewing schooling as a continuing ritual more than as an opportunity for decided advancement.

Then there is the public, that strange thermometer of the present and barometer of the future. Certainly the above-listed manifestations are reflective, in part, of the public mood as well as symbolic, perhaps, of the general rootlessness—the "culture of narcissism" as Christopher Lash termed it, or that general lack of conviction that pervades our culture today. For whatever the reason, the public no longer holds out public education with the esteem it did even five short years ago. For example, when asked to grade the overall performance of their schools, respondents to the annual Gallup Poll on education who rated those schools as "excellent" decreased from 18 percent polled in 1974 to 8 percent in 1979; those rating those schools "good" decreased from 30 percent in 1974 to 26 percent in 1979. At the same time, those rating the schools as "poor" almost doubled, from 6 percent in 1974 to 11 percent in 1979. Perhaps most significant of the questions asked in the 1979 Gallup Poll was that which revealed that more than half of those polled felt that the schools their children attended were no better than or worse than those which they, as adults, attended when they were children. This is a dramatic reversal, for five years earlier, well over 50 percent of those polled felt that their children's schools were superior to those that they as adults had attended when they were youngsters.[7]

According to national polls, people more often than not see the public schools as increasingly ineffectual, less able to capably handle the educational problems of the day. Of course, the schools tend to be faulted for many things, so we must be aware of the tendency to blame many general social problems on the educational sector. Still, there does appear to be a growing public "crisis of confidence" in public education, seemingly generated by and within a system that all the while has grown increasingly resistant to changes, defensive to criticisms, and often less responsive to the aspirations of its constituents.

The essays here address the current erosion of confidence in the public school process by focusing on the role of the state in education and, most specifically, on the manifestation of that role in the predominant form of legitimized education—public schooling. We take this focus because it is public or state schooling over which the greatest concern seems to be expressed and in which the manifestations of diminished confidence are most obvious. We also feel that the relationship between the state and its dominant education system needs examination because of the seeming inability of the state to re-create confidence in the power and utility of schooling within its domain. Certainly we do not claim that to whatever extent there exists a growing incapacity of public schooling to solve educational problems that this incapacity is unrelated to the more general problems of the state in the areas of economics, political processes, and health and welfare. Indeed, we would claim that *the problems associated with state education are also problems that may be organic to the state itself.*[8] But the latter is a topic beyond the scope of this volume; hence we focus on the interrelationship between the state and education and, most specifically, public schooling.

The essays addressing this topic are quite diverse in content and approach but are united in their exploration of the relationship between education and the state in such a way that the forms and processes of state schooling are raised to a level of explicitness, hopefully permitting increased critical awareness. Specific alterations in the relationship between the state and education are neither proposed nor advocated as a "cure-all" to the current problems of public schooling. Still, the essays are united in their conviction that a critical reexamination of the relationship between education and the state is a necessary, although certainly not a sufficient, step toward a reanalysis of the purposes of education in our society and ultimately to a consideration of the specific forms that education should take. In this sense then, the relationship between the state and education has obvious policy implications.

Analytically, the essays approach the topic of the relationship between education and the state from a variety of viewpoints. First, as will become immediately clear, a number of disciplinary perspectives—anthropological, economic, historical, legal, philosophical, political, and sociological—are represented to provide the widest-ranging criticism possible. Second, one will find a range of epistemological systems standing behind these essays, among them those of free-market analysis, liberalism, and neo-Marxism, in addition to some positions that are not easy to classify. This diversity is intentional because of our conviction that a range of perspectives in juxtaposition to one another can provide the best potential for critical understanding. Finally, the essays differ in the manner in which their respective authors perceive the problem, that is, whether the current malaise of public schooling is a function *of* a specific role of the state in education, is associated *with* (but not necessarily caused by) the role of the state in education, or whether it is part and parcel of other issues or institutional forms as well, of which the structure of the state is but one compounding influence.

Before proceeding, however, we must examine two important concepts used, in one form or another, in every essay in this book in order to arrive at some basic understanding of their meaning. Discussion of these concepts is not meant to provide a rigid paradigm into which all the essays necessarily fit, but hopefully this review will provide a useful reference point, one from which new questions can be raised. These two concepts concern the nature of the state and the relationship between education and the state.

## THE STATE

To discuss the concepts of the state is to be aware of the dual meaning of the term and the manner by which historical context has influenced its usage. Historical and political context is crucial to understanding the role of the state in education.[9]

Generally speaking, the term "state" refers to the largest overall political organization of society. More specifically, its emphasis is twofold. In the first meaning, the term "state" focuses on the whole body of persons bound by one general political organization. Here, the term includes the citizenry in its total existence, ranging from cultural, social, and religious life, as well as economic and political life. In this use of the term, cultural and social factors are not seen as distinct from the specific organization of political activities. The state in this sense is much akin to the Greek term *polis*—the city-state within which *communitas* exist.

In the second and more modern sense, the term "state" is seen not so much as an organic collectivity but rather as a special *form* of association, deliberately organized into specific social groups that are distinguished from other social groups by purposes, the methods employed, territorial limits, and sovereignty. Here, the term "state" has a special and unique focus that is directly concerned with the maintenance and preservation of territorial integrity. In this sense, the state may be contrasted *with* its citizenry rather than emerging *out of* their associations. The emphasis in this definition of state is upon political organization to achieve a specified purpose unique to a given territory. This is contrasted with the first definition that emphasized the totality of interests (among them political organization) within a territory. It is, as we shall see later, the growth of the state as defined in the second sense that has greatly affected our view of education and its relationship with the state. Now let us briefly review the historical record to understand how the conceptualization of the state has emerged in its present form.

To the Greeks, the *polis* embraced a small territory but virtually all aspects of it—the cultural, religious, and social life. The *polis* was the idealized form of government to the Greeks because it entailed self-sufficiency necessary for social, economic, and political needs of that territory. There was little separation of social, political, and cultural aspects of the state because the state embraced everything and was the basic unit of Greek society. Of course, this entity had to be "governed," so political organization was considered. But this political organization was based upon "natural laws" or the inviolate laws seen to regulate the universe and meant "to be ruler over the rulers." The integration of all aspects of the society into the *polis* had as its purpose the discovery and application of these natural laws into the governance of the state. The Greek conception of the state emphasized its organic aspects—its interpenetration with the social fabric of the localized region. To talk of the state as external to the *polis* was virtually unknown.

The same basic principle of the state was followed in and through the height of the Roman Empire but with some important qualifications. The Roman *res publica* ("commonwealth") referred to the same self-sufficient entity as the *polis*, and conceptually this idea was adopted from the Greeks. But, practically speaking, such territoriality was limited by the tremendous expanse of the Empire, and intimate rule became difficult during its expansion to Europe, Northern Africa, and Asia Minor. Consequently, the Roman vision of the state also had associated with it, and in stronger fashion than the Greeks, a legal structure of political associations of Roman citizens. Here we see the first stages of the concept of the state as an association of administrative entities, the purposes of which were at least partly, if not primarily, legal.

The origin of the modern state had its fundamental and most explicit conceptual beginnings in *The Prince* (1512). Therein, Machiavelli, who certainly was not a political philosopher, put forward the absolute authority of the state vis-à-vis that of the Church, indeed, even that of "natural laws" as discussed by Saint Augustine and other philosophers up to the period of the Renaissance. Prior to the time of Machiavelli, the state was defined, and if necessary circumscribed, by the authority of the moral order—the cosmic, natural laws governing the universe. Machiavelli broke from this tradition when in his concern for the security and continuity of the state he noted that internal security may demand that the rulers' morality be put aside in favor of the continuity of rule. Of course, Machiavelli lived during a period of consolidation of feudal territories into larger civic units; therefore, his preoccupation with the stability of those units perhaps is understandable.[10]

So too was that of Thomas Hobbes who, in his *Leviathan* (1651), noted the now infamous statement, "war of every man against every man," in which there is "continual fear and danger of violent death, and where the life of man is solitary, poor, nasty, brutish, and short." To Hobbes, as to Machiavelli, this state of nature, wherein those natural laws whose origins were unclear and the operation of which was likely to be erratic and harmful to the social order they controlled, could not, indeed should not, regulate life in isolation from the will of a strong sovereign. Enter then the sovereignty of the state, with its authority absolute and undivided, dedicated to the protection of the individual from the brutish forces to which he would be subjected without the protection of the state.[11]

Such a monolithic conception of the state, common in the sixteenth and seventeenth centuries, evolved into a somewhat more limited conception in the seventeenth and eighteenth centuries with the emergence of "social contract theory," most specifically that of John Locke, Jeremy Bentham, and Jean-Jacques Rousseau. Locke did not favor the notion of absolute rule but instead proposed that all men had certain inviolate "natural rights," not subject to the capricious whim of the sovereign. These natural rights were those of "life, liberty, and property." To Hobbes the overthrow of the sovereign would mean the dissolution of the state; Locke saw the state as existing through a contract which outlined limited power "directed to no other end but the peace, safety, and public good of the people." Therein, the state existed because society itself is "inconvenient" and within which some natural arbiter must be found to intervene in disputes. Locke was clear to distinguish between the state—that source of authority within which there was a contract with the people of the state, and the government—that specific mechanism of the state whose source of authority was "trust." Should then the government fail to protect the citizenry, then the trust of the government by the people was absent, and this, in turn, justified a new government. The state, however, continued; it was simply a matter of finding a new bargaining agent.[12]

Bentham continued the idea of a limited state—a regulated state—through his espousal of what came to be called "utilitarianism." In his Introduction to the *Principles of Morals and Legislation* (1789), he supported the elimination of all natural law as a basis for the existence of the state, declaring that "the indestructible prerogatives of mankind have no need to be supported upon the sandy foundation of fiction." The role of government was not to *act* as much as it was to cease from acting—thereby to release the free choice of individuals and the play of market forces to create prosperity.[13]

In some ways, Rousseau's thoughts on the state represent a combination of those of Hobbes and Locke in their conception of the social contract. That is, Hobbes attempted to limit liberty for the sake of authority, and Locke severely constrained authority for the sake of liberty. But Rousseau proposed, as did the Greeks, that the law should express the "general will" of the citizenry. Because, in Rousseau's world, the law should be legislated directly by the citizens (not for them by representatives), it followed that in obeying the law, one was only submitting to those decisions that he himself had agreed to in the first place. Following the law was a free act, based upon the "general will," which was guided by a larger moral will aimed at the common good. To Rousseau, the legitimacy of the state existed because the state proclaimed only what its citizens proclaimed. As did the Greeks, Rousseau saw the state as an integration of the total life system of an area, united to produce a common good.[14]

The world envisioned by Rousseau, however, had ceased to exist (as it had for the Greeks), and by the eighteenth and nineteenth centuries, the expansion of the nation-state had become a trend of irreversible proportions. The modern state and the conceptions thereof reached their present form during the eighteenth and nineteenth centuries and were best represented philosophically in the work of Hegel. Hegel continued Rousseau's belief in the "general will," except that Hegel termed it the universal or "rational will." Accordingly, if man acts as a moral agent and in so doing his aims coincide with those of others, he does not think of pursuing self-interests but rather justice and the public good. Since there can be no conflict if people act "morally," their aims can be fully satisfied, resulting in total freedom. This freedom is possible only in a moral community, the highest form of which is the state. That Hegel should conceive this at the same time as the growing consolidation of the German state is, of course, no accident.[15]

Hegel, however, departed significantly from Rousseau's organic conception of the state by positing the presence of a "civil society" as that arm of the state that was necessary for the evolution of a state as a moral community. By the term "civil society" he meant those sets of institutions that met the needs of economic and political life and which regulated people's pursuit of private affairs. It was in the civil society that all of the "mundane business of administrative law" was to be carried out. The civil society was viewed as the antithesis of the family, which tended to pursue narrow and parochial interests. The synthesis of the family and civil society, and the highest form of organization was, to Hegel, the state. It was here too that Hegel departed significantly from utilitarians such as Bentham and social contract theorists like Locke, who saw the state as only a means to an end, namely, individual freedom. To Hegel, the state was the highest form of organization—an end in itself.

Hegel's work provided the foundation for the modern state as we know it today. As his "civil society" (in many respects an extension of *res publica*) became accepted and operationalized as an administrative arm of the state, certain key individuals envisioned the need to have this civil society be as efficient and productive as possible. German liberal jurists, such as Robert von Mohl and Rudolph von Gneist, advanced the notion that a proper and careful understanding of administrative science and law would bode well for the fulfillment and emergence of the state as a moral society. Through such ideas and their eventual implementation, especially in the form of a professional civil service and the scientific management of such, the importance and centrality of the civil society became unquestioned.

This unquestioned acceptance of the civil society had consequences not foreseen by the historical figures of the era. These consequences are with us still, and awareness of even their possibility should facilitate a more informed understanding of some of the major arguments found in this book.

One consequence seems to have been a growing concern with the administrative problems of the state which, as time progressed, overshadowed the constitutional dimensions of the public legal order. In other words, the civil society—what Hegel saw as a means to the state—became more important than the state as a moral society. This claim is made because, especially after the nineteenth century, the conceptual apparatus used to understand the state, as well as the specific operations under its auspices, are increasingly associated with the administrative mechanisms of government. Consequently, the manifestations of the state in the form of "administrative agencies" become accepted, and the moral order behind the state is taken for granted rather than a subject for considered debate.[16]

In organizational theory, such a process wherein means are substituted for ends is called "goal displacement."[17] As this substitution became regularized and modified, what came to be the state was not that of the *polis* of Plato, the "City of God" of Saint Augustine, or the organic whole of a Locke, a Rousseau, or a Hegel; rather it referred to the administrative machinery that regulated the basic (and accepted) system of social and political relations. Sometimes this is referred to as "government," a term which, as we shall discuss later, is too confining to describe the scope of state activities. The dominance of this form has led to our present view of the state as primarily a political unit that administratively regulates a given territory. The importance for education in this transition in the concept of the state will be addressed later in this section.

A second and related consequence of this means-ends transposition has been to see the civil society (what we call "the state") as distinct and separate from the moral society of the Greeks, the social contract theorists, indeed even that of Hegel. The state is not perceived primarily as the arm of society through which the moral order of society is expressed but, more importantly, is an efficacious way of administering the basic needs (justice, education, defense) of a given society in a relatively "objective" manner. This dimension of the state grew out of the nineteenth-century belief that social and formal organizations in the state could be administered effectively and rationally without prejudice. It is assumed that the system of justice "wears blinders" when it comes to individuals who come before it; that our system of state schools is "common" and thereby provides for the needs of all people regardless of race, creed, or national origin; and that our system of national defense is for defense not offense. In so viewing such institutions within the civil society as neutral and objective, they have, over time, been granted considerable autonomy to regulate the organizations and social relationships within their domain. Such objectivity, however, is a myth, as the essays in this volume discuss. A major focus of many of the essays centers on the existence of the state, specifically in the education of its youth, not as an "umpire" as believed in the nineteenth and early twentieth centuries, but rather as an active participant—indeed as a direct manager of educational activities. A number of authors argue that this specific role has lead to an educational system that serves the interests of the state (civil society) more than it does the interests of those educated.

## EDUCATION AND THE STATE

To this point, I have traced, albeit in a sketchy fashion, the conceptual development of the state in western thought. We have seen how the conception of the state shifted slowly but consistently from the Greek notion of *polis* to Hegel's "civil society," to the extent that the civil society has become the accepted vision of the state. Also, I have posited that this conception of the state has been accompanied by the relative autonomy of state institutions—the preferred and assumed separateness of the agencies of the state from the original moral purposes of the state itself. Such a shift, quite understandably, has paralleled similar shifts in views of education, a topic to which I now turn.

The conception of the educated person, the role of education in the context of the state, and most specifically the manner in which education is to be implemented in the state can be examined in conjunction with the changing conception of the state. In Hellenistic thought, for example, education was an integral part of the state since educated persons contributed toward the recognition and use of "natural laws" in conducting the business of society. Education to Plato was the chief method of reforming not only individual character but the state as well. In the *Republic*, II, Plato stated: "If you ask what is the goal of education, the answer is easy — that education makes good men act nobly and conquer their enemies because they are good."[18] In this respect the role of education is to produce the moral characteristics in individuals that enable them to "act nobly" so that, in turn, the state will be ennobled. Education serves the state and, in so doing, creates the conditions necessary for the discovery of natural laws and their application to the state. To quote Aristotle in *Politics*: "That which contributes most to the permanence of constitutions is the adaptation of education to the former government. The best laws, though sanctioned by every citizen of the state, will be to no avail, unless the young are trained by habit and education in the spirit of the Constitution."[19]

Of course, a similar perspective — that of education serving the state through the discovery and use of natural and divine law — prevailed throughout the Roman period and the Christian era that followed. For example, Plutarch believed that the essential responsibility of the sovereign was to educate the young "to the unity of the common model of virtue." This view stressed the applicability of natural laws to the governance of the state. Saint Augustine, in a somewhat different vein, saw education as the prime mode of achieving the "City of God," wherein the virtue and perfection that were part of the natural laws of God would become inherent in the lives of men. In both cases, education and the state were integrated to the extent that the existence of the state, that is, as the presence of the total culture of the society, was furthered by the knowledge of virtue and nobility gained through education.

Yet the nobility to be gained through education was not just that which was in conformance with natural laws, but rather natural law as sifted through the perceptual screen and needs of the sovereign. And so throughout the growth and expansion of feudalism and into the period of the consolidation of feudal empires into monarchies, those individuals who were to be formally educated would be educated in order to serve the regal prerogatives of the kingdom. Of course, that education which did occur was not necessarily formalized in the sense of schooling but rather consisted primarily of that understanding, through whatever means practicable, of the natural laws as interpreted by the Church which, in most cases during this time, was an extension of the sovereignty. Hobbes wrote in *Leviathan*: "It is annexed to the sovereignty to be judge of what opinions and doctrines are adverse . . . and what men are to be trusted withal in speaking to multitudes of people."[20] For Hobbes, to avoid the war of all against all, the sovereign must have the ultimate control of what doctrines to embrace, for if the authority for that decision lay not in the hands of the sovereign but could be individually determined by all, then in what way could the state be bound together? The educated person, cognizant of the needs of the sovereign and clearly supportive of his right to interpret and enforce divine right, would be a better subject, according to Francis Bacon in his *Treatise on the Proficience and Advancement of Learning*:

> for to say that a blind custom of obedience should be a surer obligation than duty taught and understood is to affirm that a blind man may tread surer by a guide than a seeing man can by light. And it is without all controversy that learning doth make the minds of men gentle, generous, malleable and pliant to government; whereas, ignorance makes them churlish, thwart, and mutinous.[21]

The divine right of kings became limited over time through the rise of constitutional forms of government. Consequently, and fueled in part by the ideas of social contract theorists such as Locke and Rousseau, the control over the educational process by those being educated was an issue that entered into the debate about the role of education in state systems. No longer was it necessarily acceptable for the individual citizen to accept the form and content of education parceled out by the sovereign under the guise of divine rights. Rather, the point of view that it is the individual himself who should be the primary arbiter of education—that individuals should choose that education that best fits their particular ends—became more apparent in philosophical circles. This did not mean that the state had no interest in the education of its citizens; far from it. The state did have a compelling interest in ensuring an educated citizenry. That, however, it should have a compelling interest in determining *how* that education was to occur was less clear. Accordingly, Adam Smith in *Wealth of Nations*, indicated that the state, to improve the morals of the society, could require that its public officials and professionals be well educated in the sciences and philosophies. Yet rather than providing salaries to teachers hired by the state, those salaries "making them negligent and idle," Smith felt that as long as the state required particular qualities of education of its citizens, that it should be left to the citizens themselves to determine how they best could acquire those qualities; as Smith said, people "would soon find better teachers for themselves than any whom the state could provide for them."[22]

A philosophy based upon the role of individual choice to determine the means of education led to other utilitarian philosophies, exemplified most dramatically by John Stuart Mill. Following up on the ideas of Jeremy Bentham, who believed that the role of the state was to free individuals to utilize market forces that were part of a natural cycle of society, Mill espoused education as a necessary function of the state but resisted fully the idea that the state should *direct* that education. One argument which Mill advanced resembles very much a current educational trend—the competency movement— except on a wider basis. Mill argued that qualified people should be judged on the basis of successfully completing exams "in defensible subjects" that did not cover values or beliefs, such that the state might control them. Control of thought stood out quite prominently in Mill's ideas. In fact, the main obstacle he saw in the dominant role of the state in the educational process was the very "molding" of people to the needs of the state. As he said in *On Liberty*: "A general state education is a mere contrivance for molding people to be exactly like one another; and as the mold that cast them is that which pleases the predominant power in the government . . . it establishes a despotism over the mind, leading to a natural tendency to one over the body."[23] Mill believed that to the degree that education by the state did exist, it should exist only "among competing experiments" to the extent that each such experiment served as a control on the others.

Reaction against the use of education by the state for furthering its narrow interests was a relatively novel belief that increasingly became a topic addressed by many thinkers of the eighteenth and nineteenth centuries, and with good reason. It had become clear by then that the "state" of Plato, Saint Augustine, and Rousseau—that organic community furthering a moral existence within the boundaries of moral will and natural laws—no longer existed, if indeed it ever had. Instead, that peculiar extension of the state—what Hegel came to call the "civil society"—came to dominate as an administrative agency *sufficient unto itself.* Further attached to this agency was an educational system, which, over time, became integrated into the state administrative machinery so that the organizational regularities of schooling were indistinguishable from those of the state. Indeed, in Britain, by the latter part of the nineteenth century, public tax-supported grammar schools were national policy, as they were also earlier in the United States. Tax-supported schools were followed in short order by compulsory attendance laws both in Britain and the United States and eventually in all the "developing countries." Such laws, while admittedly weak and unenforced for years, were symbolically important in establishing the right of the state to determine the *form* of education to be legitimated by the state. All the while, thoughtful critics like Mill rallied against this process, disclaiming the predominant orthodoxy they saw developing. So too did individuals at the opposite end of the political spectrum, who, like Marx in *The Manifesto*, rebuked those who opposed communist influence in education:

> And your education! Is that not also social, and determined by the social conditions under which you educate, by the intervention of society, direct or indirect, by means of schools? The communists have not invented the intervention of society in education; they do but seek to alter the characteristic of that intervention and to rescue education from the influence of the ruling class.[24]

By the time of Marx and Mill it was, so it seemed, "too late." The state as civil society had already emerged as the predominant form within which political choices were carried out. In the "age of capital," as Eric Hobsbawm has called it, the quest for economic expansion and political stability seems to have gone hand-in-hand, and the granting to organizational forms regulated by the state the autonomy for carrying out major tasks that once had been managed in formal and social settings largely outside the domain of the state grew to be more acceptable.[25] Of course, this shift in activities to the arena of the state has not been without its benefits, for many of the injustices of the relatively unregulated society have led to demands by disaffected groups for more intervention by the state. Certainly it would not be difficult to convince many families of the late nineteenth century, for example, that the intervention of the state into child labor was a much-needed intervention. Still, the contradictions present in the success of such interventions stand out, for it appears that the genre of questions raised by the Greeks and by political philosophers through the Middle Ages as to the basis of the state and educational processes within it appeared, in many respects, closed by the later part of the nineteenth century.

With the diminishing of explicit concern about the nature and scope of the state, there was a parallel and growing confidence in the power of the civil society—government—to be the fundamental embodiment of the state. Especially important has been the deference to state agencies their role as impartial arbiters of the political society. Yet what goes unrecognized in such a conviction, as represented in the form of administrative units, judicial organizations, legislative bodies, and executive agencies, is that the state does not make solely independent and objective political decisions but actively intervenes as well in the social, economic, and cultural life of society. In so doing, the state system often is more than "government" but is also a symbolic representation of interests and values outside its apparent jurisdiction. In other words, the business of the state is affected strongly by dominant persuasions in the economic, social, and political world. The term "state" then has to be seen in relation to the active presence of ideological interests, whatever their origin and whatever their role in the polity. We have to assume that the conceptions of "government" and "civil society" are but the tip of the iceberg and that the networks that influence the state in its daily operation are wide-reaching. As Ralph Milibrand has said: "Officials and administrators cannot divest themselves of all the ideological clothing in the advice which they tender to their ideological masters . . . nowhere do these men not contribute directly to the exercise of state power."[26]

"Moral will" then in the modern state is exemplified mostly in the accumulation of objects and materials, and to the degree the state facilitates such possessions, it is successful and supported. The present era continues to be a period of social engineering that stretches for over a century into the past, and in the expansion of the empires of Western Europe and within the United States, the question about the basis of empire was put aside in favor of the maintenance and growth of it. National economies have expanded to the international market and nation-states organized to meet those demands. International competition has led to national market control, economic concentration, and manipulation. It is the age of what David Landes has called "the new imperialism," wherein the civil society works hand-in-hand with majoritarian interests.[27] We have lived with that legacy for the past century, and it is only through the contradictions so generated that we now return to readdressing those questions of the nature of the state and its effects on, and the way it is affected by, educational processes.

In many ways, we arrive at this reassessment because the conception of the state, formulated in part by German jurists a century ago, appears to be inadequate to the times. Likewise, as many of the authors in this volume claim, so has the educational system that is part of that state. In this sense, the thoughts of von Mohl and von Gneist and the liberal perspectives engendered relative to an efficient state—somewhat neutral but progressive, goal-oriented, and governed by norms of universalism—may be seen as a myth of German idealism rather than as a real practice within society. To think that the Weberian bureaucracy, for example, could serve to rationalize education, make it more productive, and serve the needs of all rather than primarily those of special interests now seems somewhat naïve. Yet such beliefs certainly served as the basis of a movement in education toward administrative reform, bureaucratization, and consolidation of American education  that has been described so graphically by historians such as David Tyack, Diane Ravitch, and others.[28] It now appears that the rationality and objectivity of that educational system is a myth (a central point of many essays here) because the state and its respective agencies (such as schools) are not merely umpires arbitrating among conflicting interests in order to adjudicate impartially. Indeed, the state generates its own morality, and those who control it attempt both to consolidate their position as well as to involve themselves in actions that, in the end, convince those subservient to them that the state, continuing in its present form, is in everybody's best interests. This is not done so much by the conscious design within the apparatus of the state, marshaling its forces to further (in the case of the United States) the glories of corporate capitalism, for such blatant exercise of raw power is associated mostly with the past, the days of Jim Hill, Cornelius Vanderbilt, and the "robber barons." Instead, it is through the channels the state creates and within which communication occurs, that a livelihood is made, an education is conducted, and justice is meted out in which the aims of the state are reenforced and extended rather than challenged and questioned. To the extent that the state organizes public education in such a way that it severely restricts and curtails the rights and liberties of its citizens, thereby effectively precluding optimal self-determination, to that extent the educational system itself is representative of the state in its current metamorphosis. The nature of that representation in this place and in this time, and how it has come to achieve the form which it does, is the major focus of the essays in this volume.

## PLAN OF THE BOOK

This introduction has presented a perspective on education and the state so that the reader may evaluate these essays against a bench-mark of considerable validity. Yet, as noted earlier, we do not wish to "force" the argument of all the essays into this framework, for it was not a standard used in their selection.[29] Indeed, the actual role of the state in education is an empirical question that should remain open as one reads these essays although the topic will be addressed again in the conclusion.

These essays examine the relationship between the state and education in a manner that does not necessarily assume the state to be a monolithic entity that forces and regulates its will on an unsuspecting citizenry. We have tried to avoid a deterministic perspective about the state because we believe this perspective is a simplistic reification—one that is not very helpful for policy analysis. Instead, we much prefer what in political science perspectives may be termed the "descriptive theory" of the state. In this approach, one examines political processes and decision making related to a given domain and then asks the question: To what degree does "the state" fit into this paradigm? In educational circles we can examine processes and products of education as they exist and inquire about the role of the state in those processes. This permits us to view the role of the state in relation to other institutions in society such as the family, organized religions, political organizations, and interest groups; it permits us to ascertain how the state affects education in relationship to these other dimensions of society.

A key question for examination becomes the following: To what extent does the state, through its control of educational resources and its regulation of formal schooling, attempt to monopolize power in order to dominate formalized education in relation to other educative agencies? Said differently, we may inquire about the extent to which state-controlled public schooling (the dominant form of legitimate public education) constitutes a "predominant orthodoxy" about the nature of formal education, the acceptance of which limits our conception of education and the forms it may take. This leads us to examine the sources and consequences of the distribution of power within society, and to identify those factors that contribute to institutional domination of processes such as education.

The essays are divided into four basic sections. In Part I, "Historical Perspectives on State Schooling," four authors trace the historical roots of the deepening involvement of the state in education through state schooling. Part II, "The Elements of State Control," provides a reexamination of the assumptions that underlie state education. Here, two authors focus on these assumptions through a philosophical and legal understanding. In Part III, "Educational Consequences of the State School Monopoly," three authors provide an in-depth understanding of the actual operation of state education, speaking to this issue from anthropological, political, and sociological points of view. In Part IV, "Alternatives to Monopoly Schooling," five authors of diverse perspectives discuss various plans to "deregulate" the involvement of the state in schooling. In the Conclusion, I attempt to integrate the themes in these fourteen essays, particularly those relevant to educational policy.

## NOTES TO INTRODUCTION

1. Charles Silberman, *Crisis in the Classroom* (New York: Random House, 1970).

2. "Help! Teacher Can't Teach," *Time*, June 16, 1980, p. 54.

3. Allen Ornstein, "Teacher Salaries: Past, Present, and Future," *Phi Delta Kappan* 61 (1980): 667–669.

4. *Challenge for the Third Century: Education in a Safe Environment—Final Report on the Nature and Prevention of School Violence and Vandalism* (Washington, D.C.: U.S. Government Printing Office, 1977).

5. Beatrice F. Berman and Gary Natriello, "Perspectives on Absenteeism in High Schools," *Journal of Research and Development in Education* 11 (1978): 30.

6. Christopher Jencks, "Why Test Scores Are Declining," address before the Center for the Study of Democratic Institutions, Santa Barbara, Calif., March 1978.

7. George Gallup, "The Eleventh Annual Gallup Poll on the Public Attitude Toward the Public School," *Phi Delta Kappan* 6 (1979): 33–47.

8.  See, e.g., James O'Connor, *The Fiscal Crisis of the State* (New York: St. Martin's Press, 1973); and Alan Wolfe, *The Limits of Legitimacy* (New York: Free Press, 1977).

9.  One political theorist comments on the fact that there hardly has been any major political discourse on the state in the twentieth century, indeed since Marx. Liberalism, the basic political philosophy of the West during the past century, "does not so much explain the state as defend its purpose." It is ironic, Wolfe says, that "as more and more aspects of social life become located within the province of the state, the term itself begins to disappear from the language of political discourse"; Wolfe, *Limits of Legitimacy*, p. ix. See also Ralph Milibrand, *The State in Capitalist Society* (New York: Basic Books, 1969).

10. Niccolo Machiavelli, *The Prince* (New York: New American Library, 1952).

11. Thomas Hobbes, *Leviathan* (New York: Collier Books, 1975).

12. John Locke, *Two Treatises of Government* (London: Cambridge University Press, 1967).

13. Jeremy Bentham, *Introduction to the Principles of Morals and Legislation* (London: Athlone, 1970).

14. Jean Jacques Rousseau, *The Social Contract* (New York: E.P. Dutton, 1927).

15. Georg Friedrich Hegel, *The Philosophy of Right* (Oxford: Clarendon Press, 1949).

16. Milibrand argues that the unarticulated theories about the state held by most political sociologists "takes as resolved some of the largest questions which traditionally have been asked about the state, and makes unnecessary, indeed almost precludes, any special concern with its nature and role in Western type societies"; *State in Capitalist Society*, p. 2.

17. See Amitai Etzioni, *Modern Organizations* (Englewood Cliffs: Prentice Hall, 1964), p. 10.

18. Plato, *The Republic* (New York: New American Library, 1956), p. 173.

19. Richard McKeon, ed., *Introduction to Aristotle* (New York: Random House, 1947), p. 568.

20. Hobbes, op. cit., p. 77.

21. Francis Bacon, *Advancement of Learning and Novum Organum* (New York: Wiley Books, 1944), p. 58.

22. Adam Smith, *An Inquiry Into the Nature and Causes of the Wealth of Nations* (New York: Random House, 1937), p. 624.

23. John Stuart Mill, *On Liberty and Other Essays* (New York: Macmillan, 1926), p. 121.

24. Robert C. Tucker, ed., *The Marx-Engels Reader* (New York: W.W. Norton, 1978), p. 487.

25. Eric Hobsbawm, *The Age of Capital* (New York: Charles Scribner, 1975).

26. Milibrand, *State in Capitalist Society*, p. 51. See also Harry Eckstein, "On the 'Science' of the State," *Daedalus* 108 (1979): 1–20.

27. David Landes, *Unbound Prometheus: Technological Change and Industrial Development in Western Europe from 1750 to the Present* (Cambridge: Cambridge University Press, 1969).

28. David Tyack, *The One Best System* (Cambridge, Mass.: Harvard University Press, 1974); and Diane Ravitch, *The Great School Wars* (New York: Basic Books, 1975).

29. Indeed, a framework that argues against the role of the state as "interventionist" to the extent such intervention supports majoritarian interests is "interest group" theory, which argues that policy is set as the result of competing forces, all of which have access to equivalent resources. See Robert Dahl, *Preface to Democratic Theory* (Chicago: University of Chicago Press, 1956).

# PART I

# HISTORICAL PERSPECTIVES ON STATE SCHOOLING

In this first part, four essays provide a historical picture of the manner in which the state, through the expansion of state schooling, has become involved in education and some consequences of that relationship. The lead essay by Charles Burgess, entitled "Growing Up Blighted: Reflections on the 'Secret Power' in the American Experience," covers a wide canvass, on which the subtle but steady progression toward democratic totalitarianism is painted. The major role of state schooling in this march is graphically outlined. Borrowing from Tocqueville, Burgess chronicles the presence and continuation of the "secret power" that dulls people's ability to resist "the allures of uniformity that, in turn, fosters strong, paternal, central governments." He emphasizes the nineteenth- and twentieth-century development of the state as an administrative arm that has become *the* legitimated political arena and that has acted in coalition with ever-expanding industrial conglomerates and corporate monopolies. It was during this historical period (as noted in the Introduction) that the existence of the state as an administrative agent to promote "economy stimulating politics" became accepted as a central part of American life. Herein the central question became not *whether* to but *how* to include the state "as a legitimate member of the burgeoning corporate family."

Burgess shows that the movement toward the "secret power" has its origin in the changing roots of personal allegiance from local community to national community and ultimately to supranational community, illustrated most dramatically in the multinational corporation. This process began innocently and was benignly crystallized by the beliefs of those such as Horace Mann who wished to foster the state as a "willing helper" in local education. Yet once established, the involvement of the state as a "willing partner" grew, and local participation became less voluntary, more mandatory, expanding to expected allegiance to the nation-state. It was this trend that even Lincoln, at the height of national divisiveness, questioned as one possibly "too strong for the liberties of its own people." But grow it did, through the expansion of *parens patriae*, beyond concern with not only the lives of infants, children, and youth but also into the domain of the family, the world of work, and forging still more into the political sphere. All the while, a main generating force in the steady expansion of the state was the ideal of *e pluribus unum*—the movement toward a national identity, a national society, hammered together from diverse sources.

Marching in step with this amalgamating process has been the systemization of public education, an institution which itself has become more standardized and less tolerant of diversity from within and from without. All the while, says Burgess, the intentions of school people have hardly been malevolent. Indeed, he feels that had we ourselves lived in the late nineteenth century, many of us too would have encouraged the growing incursion of schooling into the lives of children, just as today many well-meaning people praise that capstone of nationalized education, the Department of Education. The issue is not as clear as we would like to think it is, for "doing good" is not the issue but doing good on whose terms? In the end, Burgess asks us to reconsider a greater emphasis on the *pluribus*, with perhaps less attention to the *unum*.

In "The Evolving Political Structure of American Schooling," Joel Spring examines in some detail the emerging structure and ideology pertinent to the control of American schooling by the state. Noting the aversion by many intellectuals of the seventeenth and eighteenth centuries to state-controlled schools, he traces the manner by which this aversion became muted and was replaced by acceptance, during the nineteenth century, of state-controlled schools. In his focus on the twentieth century, Spring discusses how the imperatives of such acceptance have turned into a somewhat disguised but nonetheless more powerful advocacy of state domination through such diverse arenas as growing professionalization, the expansion of educational research, and accountability theory.

Spring, like Burgess, sees the process by which the state controls schooling usually not developing as a diabolical plot on the part of those whose vested interests are tied to state control but rather oftentimes as a subtle process wherein well-intentioned reforms turn into tools that serve the state. That these tools take on different forms during varied historical periods is important to note, and Spring explains in some detail how the move toward professional and democratic education has had an especially profound effect on cementing the domination of the state in formal education.

A particularly important consequence of the rise of professionally run and state-controlled education has been the creation of a school system in tune with a managed political and social system. With the rise of professional and state control of schools came similar control in other fields—public administration, government, corporate enterprises, and health, just to name a few. That there was little client control in state schooling simply reinforced the domination of the state in all aspects of public life and led to the production of "apolitical citizens who would accept a managed political and social system." Spring sees it as no accident that such a trend is borne out in political socialization literature which evidences the minimal knowledge students have about the exercise of political power. Equally important, the acquiescence of political power to the state by the citizenry is demonstrated by the steady decline in voter participation rates.

George Smith's essay, "Nineteenth-Century Opponents of State Education: Prophets of Modern Revisionism," develops an issue raised in Spring's paper, namely, the nature of the earliest opposition to state schooling and the intellectual basis of that opposition. While Spring focuses upon that opposition as it was transported and developed in the United States prior to the control of schooling by the state, Smith presents a detailed examination of that opposition as it flourished in England in the nineteenth century in reaction to (rather than in anticipation of) the growing power of the state in formal education.

Smith places the discussion of opposition within the context of present-day revisionism, for example, the work of Clarence Karier, Michael S. Katz, and Joel Spring, among others. Such revisionists, Smith argues, "emphasize education as a form of social control and the use of state education to indoctrinate and mold a compliant citizenry." Noting that most revisionists usually are sympathetic to the politics of the left, Smith then proceeds to describe the beliefs of the "Voluntaryists" of nineteenth-century England, themselves proponents of free-market systems. What is so revealing is that these free-market advocates accurately predicted many of the failures of state-controlled education about which revisionists currently complain.

A fundamental theme of the Voluntaryists was the need for diversity in education. Fearful of the dulling conformity that a state education would produce and the resultant mediocrity that would be evident in the education of the citizenry, Voluntaryists advocated that no one agency should have the power to determine the scope or content of education and that the interference of the government in education, no matter how noble the cause, could result only in the enhancement of the values of special interests to the detriment of freedom for all. As a result, the best guarantee of liberty was for the state to foster no directives in education but rather to allow market forces to permit such diversity to exist that best met the needs of all citizens. As many of the arguments of the Voluntaryists are echoed today not only by revisionists but also by reformers, Smith's essay provides a useful vehicle through which we can examine many of the assumptions raised by those who, in the past and into the present, advocate a severance of the relationship between education and the state.

In the final essay in this section, C.H. Edson, in his "Schooling for Work and Working at School: Perspectives on Immigrant and Working-Class Education in Urban America, 1880–1920," focuses on much the same period of history as does Burgess (late nineteenth and early twentieth century). Edson addresses the merging of a number of simultaneous movements, among them: (1) the changing system of social relations in the workplace, (2) heightened demographic changes in the nation—exemplified by the immigration of southern and eastern Europeans, and, finally, (3) the professionalization of education as it occurred in increasingly centralized state-supported educational bureaucracies, an issue discussed at length by Spring. That these movements can illuminate trends present in education today and that these same movements are the raw material for the structural and ideological alliance between political and economic interests should alert us to the "stuff" of which the state is made and reconstituted throughout history.

Edson begins by chronicling changes in the social relations of production because of increased industrialization and changing conceptions of how work was to be performed. Since production lines and increasing specialization of function were predominant, educators sought, in quite "humanistic" fashion, to shelter children from the "exploitive realities of work" while providing more time for the development of appropriate work skills and attitudes conducive to the requirements of the new shops. Hence, the growth of secondary schools to keep children in school longer and the rise of vocational education as a means to provide a greater articulation between school and the realities of the workplace. Although these liberal motives are the type we would applaud today, Edson argues that such a position on the part of educators directed attention away from the structural problem of work and focused instead on how, not if, schools should prepare children for work.

Exemplified especially in the vocational education movement, proponents felt that the new education (vocational education) would instill proper attitudes toward work, thereby preparing the prospective worker for work life as well as providing for a more finely tuned, harmonious industrial sector. Of equal importance was the development in prospective workers of an attitude that work was something continuous—a series of interconnected jobs—a career. Acceptance of this credo, Edson proposes, would benefit the young in that they might avoid permanent acceptance of low-paying, dead-end jobs. It would also benefit employers who suffered continual turnover of employees, many of whom saw jobs as temporary rather than as stepping stones to better positions. The purpose of schooling, through vocational education became both to integrate pupils into the world of work as well as to imbue them with the idea of their future as "a career of ascending stages of activity."

Yet there were problems, foremost of which were the blinders that leaders in the educational system wore as they conceived of problems and solutions. These blinders prevented those who were at the forefront of establishing educational policy from seriously considering that not everyone viewed work and schooling in the same manner and that to people of different ethnic origins, prolonged schooling and the "life-career motive" might be seen as a problem more than a solution. Edson demonstrates the consequences of the vocational education "reform" for southern Italian immigrants in the nation. While educators homogenized all immigrant groups as needing the same solutions as did white Anglos, the world view of the southern Italian did not support education beyond minimal schooling, and certainly not schooling outside the mores of the family. In addition, work, for the southern Italian families, was something not to be delayed but rather to be begun as soon as possible. As a result, the beliefs of southern Italians toward work and schooling worked in opposite directions from the dominant movement occurring in public education—to use schools as a place to prepare children for work but still to substitute schooling for work until the child was ready to leave secondary school. As Edson concludes, by prolonging schooling and fostering the "life-career motive," educators "helped to establish class and culture-bound relations between work and schooling that rapidly became part of the predominant orthodoxy in American education."

In sum, the essays in this part point to the growing movement of the state toward greater management of education and of those citizens who, in increasing numbers, fell under its domination. Although many believed this to be "best" for the nation and for those so affected, thoughtful critics—philosophers as well as commoners—resisted such an incursion of the state into their lives. That such resistance was, in fact, present speaks of the extent to which people were aware of their liberties and their rights for self-determination. That today we so infrequently propose our own rights on this subject speaks, perhaps, to the extent to which we too have been managed and now unquestioningly accept the parameters of "the one best system."

## SUGGESTED READINGS

Avrich, Paul. *The Modern School Movement: Anarchism and Education in the United States.* Princeton: Princeton University Press, 1980.

Briggs, John W. *An Italian Passage: Immigration to Three American Cities, 1890–1930.* New Haven: Yale University Press, 1978.

Covello, Leonard. *The Social Background of the Italo-American School Child: A Study of the Southern Italian Family Mores and Their Effect on the School Situation in Italy and America.* Edited with an introduction by Francesco Cordasco. Totowa, N.J.: Rowman and Littlefield, 1972.

Curti, Merle. *The Roots of American Loyalty*. New York: Columbia University Press, 1946.

Ehman, Lee H. "The American School in the Political Socialization Process." *Review of Educational Research* 50 (1980): 99–119.

Erickson, Donald A. *Super-Parent: An Analysis of State Educational Controls*. Chicago: Illinois Advisory Committee on Nonpublic Schools, 1973.

Gutman, Herbert. *Work, Culture, and Society in Industrializing America*. New York: Alfred A. Knopf, 1976.

Lazerson, Marvin, and W. Norton Grubb, eds. *American Education and Vocationalism: A Documentary History, 1870–1970*. Classics in Education, No. 48. New York: Teachers College, Columbia University, 1974.

Nisbet, Robert A. *Community and Power*. New York: Oxford University Press, 1962.

Rodgers, Daniel. *The Work Ethic in Industrial America, 1850–1920*. Chicago: University of Chicago Press, 1978.

Rubenstein, Richard L. *The Cunning of History: The Holocaust and the American Future*. New York: Harper & Row, 1975.

Rushdoony, John Rousas. *The Messianic Character of American Education*. Nutley, N.J.: Craig Press, 1963.

Scott, William G., and David K. Hart. *Organizational America*. Boston: Houghton Mifflin, 1979.

Spring, Joel. "Anarchism and Education: A Dissenting Tradition." In Clarence Karier, Paul Violas, and Joel Spring, *Roots of Crisis*. Chicago: Rand McNally, 1973.

Spring, Joel. *Educating the Worker Citizen*. New York: Longmans, 1980.

Tyack, David B. *The One Best System: A History of American Education*. Cambridge, Mass.: Harvard University Press, 1974.

Wirth, Arthur G. *Education in the Technological Society: The Vocational–Liberal Studies Controversy in the Early Twentieth Century*. Scranton, Pa.: Intex Educational Publishers, 1972.

Wise, Arthur E. *Legislated Learning: The Bureaucratization of the American Classroom*. Berkeley: University of California Press, 1979.

# 1 GROWING UP BLIGHTED
## Reflections on the "Secret Power" in the American Experience*

*Charles Burgess*

## INTRODUCTION

It was a warm July midnight in Budapest, 1978. On the street in front of our hotel a young Hungarian man sobbed quietly as he slowly sliced the flesh of his bare left arm with a jagged piece of glass. Three or four American teenagers in our party saw him and unhesitatingly intervened. One or two talked to him in sign and soothing tones, gently working to calm him, to distract him from his mission of mutilation. Meanwhile, the others rushed in to the night clerk to ask him to call for the police and an ambulance.

The clerk knew clearly what was happening on that quiet street in front of the Hotel Royal; but he stonily refused to "bother" the authorities with a matter of such indifference. And, "no," the man could not be brought into the hotel. The entreaties for professional help continued, the voices more insistent. Finally, the clerk reached the end of his forebearance. Registering impatience and disdain, he reached beneath the counter and brought up a roll of tape and a wad of gauze. "Here! Take care of him yourself if you want to!

*Many colleagues and students read various drafts of this paper, here challenging and there encouraging my line of thought. Especially detailed criticisms were provided by Edward Beauchamp, Merle Borrowman, Patricia Burgess, Merle Curti, Robert B. Everhart, Clarence J. Karier, Donna H. Kerr, Marvin Lazerson, William Schill, Charles E. Strickland, and David Tyack. My grateful thanks to them all.

That's the trouble with you Americans! You have nothing better to do with your lives!" The bandages were relayed to the street. There the teenagers, having already calmed the young man, bound his crazy-quilt wounds and watched him walk unsteadily into the darkness and disappear. He would face at least one more dawn.

"That's the trouble with you Americans! You have nothing better to do with your lives!" Those words and that scene have more than once come to mind, inviting reflection on the fine line that distinguishes helping from meddling. At what point does caring become doting? When should outsiders inject themselves and when should they resist the impulse? Under what circumstances should one "take care of him yourself" rather than call in the authorities? Could it have been that the clerk knew this fellow as one who, when full of "bull's blood" wine, routinely ended his drinking bout by doing superficial damage to himself? Could it have been  that this was an example, totally beyond the cultural experience of our party, of the exercise of an established private right? Or could it have been that the clerk was not indifferent to human suffering, as I had first assumed, but was scornful because our first—and most persistent—request was for authorities to come and assume responsibility for the situation? If my neighbor is disturbing my sleep with a rousing party, and I can tolerate it no longer, do I call him and ask for consideration, or do I call the police—and wait half an hour, moaning in the shadows of merriment, for the authorities to save me?

When one considers the extent to which we have given ourselves to the care and attention of professionals and institutions, the extent to which our personal sense of helping, sharing, and behaving responsibly has been drained off in the mindless rituals of paying the tax, calling the authorities, and giving at the office, a jarring question about our freedom and self-worth may insinuate itself into our consciousness. Are we transforming ourselves, as some believe, into a population of fundamentally humane but socially immature and ineffectual dependents? Are the successes of the United Way also measures of our failures as individuals and as potential members of voluntary associations? Do our investments in low-cost housing for the elderly strip us of the power to care as much as they promote socially responsible behavior?

Our expert agencies of help and relief have fostered an excessive sense of dependency and permitted us to make light of our personal lapses into social indifference and irresponsibility. Many of our social agencies thereby show themselves to be possessed of an ethic alien to the American heritage or cut off from the code of ethics that traced its way so centrally through the American past. Belatedly, we realize that we have entered an age in which the sense of personal responsibility has been largely displaced by a patterned paternal social service in permanent and pervasive institutional form. The fields of personal goodwill go uncultivated. They lie fallow in the towering shadow of organized paternalism.

The displacement of the personal element was rapid. Just sixty years ago George Santayana observed:

> If it were given to me to look into the depths of a man's heart, and I did not find goodwill at the bottom, I should say without any hesitation, You are not an American. But as the American is an individualist his goodwill is not officious. His instinct is to think well of everybody, and to wish everybody well, but in a spirit of rough comradeship, expecting every man to stand on his own legs and be helpful in return. When he has given his neighbor a chance he thinks he has done enough for him; but he feels it an absolute duty to do that.

The goodwill has by no means vanished; but it now staggers under the weight of officiousness. Santayana further believed: "It will take some hammering to drive a coddling socialism into America"; but he did not consider the ease with which a reverence for the ideals of the expert society and a gradual shifting of that "absolute duty" to full-time professionals could quietly sap the sense of personal responsibility he so admired in 1920.[1] Nor, in particular, did he detect in the extremes of individualism the seeds of the very officious collectivism he decried.

Those young men and women in our Budapest group had reacted to an emergency in what has come to be a standard of responsible American behavior. They recognized a problem and sought to call the proper authorities to deal with it. On home ground that would have been the acceptable limit of their responsibility. But they were not on home ground—and the authorities could not be summoned—so they reacted by rising to meet those former standards of which Santayana had spoken with such fondness. With the consent of the Hungarian lad and the availability of bandage materials (both important considerations), they themselves bound his wounds and, in a spirit of goodwill, let him stand on his own legs and go his way. The Budapest incident was a more extreme—and more potentially dangerous—illustration than Santayana presumably had in mind. But, for an instant in time, perhaps the only one such in their lives, these American youth had acted in concert, in voluntary association, and, with no one to tell them to let the authorities handle the matter, had demonstrated that their capacity for mature initiative had not yet withered away.

When responsibility for others is permanently lifted from the individual and particular problems of intimate daily life are placed upon professional shoulders, a tyranny of "professional helpers" becomes a threatening possibility.[2] The one great release is in the direction of "doing your own thing." The heart of our contemporary darkness, Philip Slater has argued, lies precisely in individualism run amok.[3] That we could experience the press of paternalism and rampant individualism at the same moment in time seems to defy reason. Our common disposition has held that it was the individual who stood as the arch opponent of the state and its excesses. The twentieth-century version of liberalism as preferred by John Dewey and his allies, indeed, sought to modify individualism by arguing that in an inescapably collectivistic age the "new" individualism would have to depend on a sense of personal initiative linked to united action. In voluntary associations, among persons who recognized a common purpose in the name of personal liberty and human dignity, lay the future of individualism. The idea of individualism as the guardian against Santayana's "coddling socialism," meanwhile, approached the crossroads: individualism would either become atomized and the prey of paternalism or find in local association and personal initiative the means to protect individual worth and dignity.

In spite of continued rhetorical reverence for local initiative and individualism, it has been a steady tendency in America to reduce opportunity for citizens to function in a face-to-face world as useful participants in the work and play and caring of community life. Even as we properly salute the spirit of initiative and goodwill that still characterizes Americans, we realize that we have become organized economically, politically, and ecologically in ways and around principles that require "others" to care for increasing numbers of the citizenry who have been channeled into passive roles as dependents and excess persons. The rules of our system require acceptance of the staggering notion that perhaps a majority of our people must sit outside the system. These are all children and youth, many of the aged, the handicapped of all sorts, the blacks, Spanish-speaking peoples, Native Americans—the dependent poor, males and females of all racial and ethnic backgrounds. The bulk of the rest of us, the more or less affluent, are mere employees. And most of our bosses are also hired hands. Gone are most of the small farms, the once rich options for self-employment, and encouragement to promote effective local community organizations. To borrow the title of David Tyack's splendid study of American urban education, we have let ourselves become, in nearly every sphere of endeavor, devoted to the idea that there is "one best system" whose management belongs by right to professionals.[4] But that system is remarkably exclusionary and its agents officious and paternal.

The inspired promotion of professionalism and system in America has brought its blessings; but it has also brought presumptuous and self-righteous impatience with those who preferred alternative ideals and lifestyles. From the social dislocations of the Age of Excess (as Ray Ginger characterized the late nineteenth century), we have carved a new order. We now live in an age in which most citizens have been diminished and many have themselves become excess persons. We have dutifully tried to adjust ourselves to the system; we have not tailored our notions of system or limited our reverence for those notions to fit our prudential sense of individual initiative, worth, and dignity. Instead, that prudential sense has been sacrificed at the altar of the bureaucratic and technocratic symbols of system. It brings only temporary comfort to note that in the main the desire to do good, not malice or sinister intent, has directed this change.

How has this come to pass? Critics at the far right and far left have full-blown historical-ideological explanations and prescriptions for our current condition. Others, ranging in the wide territory between, have been inclined to explain that our current predicament is owing to "accident" or "mindlessness." Michael Harrington thus characterized the last generations as the "accidental century." And a Charles Silberman, a Richard Rubenstein, and a Paul Goodman, although in emphatic disagreement about how we might best extricate ourselves from our mire, all agreed that we got there by traveling the road of "mindlessness."[5] An uncomplimentary and none too instructive assessment, "mindlessness" does have merit as an eleventh-hour invitation to reflective thought and spirited action.

If mindlessness means a collective failure to note certain disastrous side effects of "progress" in America, Alexis de Tocqueville's metaphor for mindlessness becomes useful. Writing about the dynamics in the relationship between the individual and the state well over a century ago, Tocqueville maintained that there was "a secret power" that numbs people's ability to resist the allures of uniformity that, in turn, foster strong, paternal, central governments. Stealthily this "secret power" touches the human heart, unfelt it slowly constricts the vital organ, and finally it stills the pulse altogether.[6] To combat this power it is not enough to refuse to worship uniformity. One must treasure diversity and "secondary powers" in society. One must promote local initiative and elevate the notion of cultural diversity to the level of national purpose.

Over a generation before Tocqueville mentioned the "secret power," Wilhelm von Humboldt reached much the same conclusions:

> The very variety arising from the union of numbers of individuals is the highest good which social life can confer, and this variety is undoubtedly lost in proportion to the degree of State interference. Under such a system, we have not so much the individual members of a nation living united in the bonds of a civil compact; but isolated subjects living in a relation to the State, or rather to the spirit which prevails in its government—a relation in which the undue preponderance of the State already tends to fetter the free play of individual energies. . . . [I]n proportion as State interference increases, the agents to which it is applied come to resemble each other, as do all the results of their activity. And this is the very design which States have in view.[7]

Where Humboldt saw conscious intent on the part of the agents of the state to promote uniformity, Tocqueville implied that the impulse for uniformity originated in the populace. Others, such as Abraham Lincoln, suspected that uniformity was an unintentional possible result of a state seeking to perpetuate itself. During the fiery first months of civil war among the American states, Lincoln pondered the predicament of the republican state. Is there, he asked, an "inherent weakness" in all republics? "Must a government of necessity be too *strong* for the liberties of its own people, or too *weak* to maintain its own existence?"[8]

These three men, living in the economic worlds of mercantilism and laissez faire, represented those who thought of uniformity as a political problem. Not until after the Civil War, after all three had died, did the idea of the state undergo expansive redefinition. Especially after 1880 and continuing over the last century, the meaning of the state has grown in popular consciousness; it has come gradually to suggest a coalition of economy-stimulating politics promoting technology, industrial expansion, and corporate monopolies. Since the Civil War it has been the corporate order that has grown as a central agent of uniformity. The untapped potential of the political state had earlier been viewed suspiciously as the idling engine of individual repression. Now it stirred hope in many hearts as the one plausible way to tether the corporate drive for wealth and power to a strong precorporate moral code.

The corporate order itself was not at issue for most Americans; the policing of it was the question. Hoping to promote ideals of human dignity regnant in the late nineteenth century, an American majority gradually accepted the idea of the state as a legitimate member of the burgeoning corporate family. We now live in a nation-state grown more comfortably aligned with the interests of its corporate fellows than with those humane ideals that contributed so hopefully to its massive growth. Where a Humboldt was predisposed to see such developments as the weaving of a crafty design and a Lincoln might have called it the unfortunate working out of a congenital dilemma of the state, the common contemporary frustration with the nation-state holds mindlessness to be the culprit; and Tocqueville construed such mindlessness as the secret power.

The following reflections are not aimed at determining who might have the best of the argument. Rather, they are meant to serve as an exploratory consideration of selected conditions and social arrangements that have helped carve the modern state. The largely unconscious fostering of alienation, helplessness, and public paternalism—the side effects of the long-standing reverence for large-scale "system"—is in evidence throughout society. These side effects are especially clear in the sphere of education. Selected features of the history of American attitudes and activities in the worlds of childhood, youth, schooling, and community loyalties afford an angle of vision for tracing a critically important line in the development of the nation-state, the development of what in retrospect has been ruefully labeled mindlessness, of what in its inchoate state Tocqueville sadly called a secret power.

As one who has worked long in the worlds of childhood and schooling, I am not about to discredit indiscriminately those associated with formal education. I have come to know and admire far too many associates who have been intelligently and productively dedicated to children and learning to permit that broad-brush misunderstanding to arise. But the educational system itself deserves no such exemption from criticism. At its inception it was a frail creature made by many diverse hands and promoted by popular consensus. It seemed ideally suited to promote appropriate learning and loyalty. But it has since grown stronger; and communities of loyalty have since shifted. The educational system, then as now, is whatever the dominant community of loyalty would have it be; and the dominant community of loyalty is now the nation-state. The following, then, will sketch some of the more dubious features of the relationship between the growth of the educational system and the atomization of the individual in the modern state.

## SUBNATIONAL COMMUNITIES OF LOYALTY

The ways in which a social group interacts and educates its children are instructive measures of the vitality of life within that group. For present purposes all social groups will be referred to as "communities" (although the members of the group are no more than "familiar strangers," as David Riesman once put it). Some legitimate communities are strangely invisible to outsiders. To most of the residents of Portland, Oregon, for example, the Burnside district is seen only as an area where winos, inexpensive sex salons, and sometimes elegant eateries, the gray tones of poverty and occasional glitters of opulence, lie side by side as an off-beat invitation to a night on the town. To those who live there, however, the area is "Community! The word is crucial for understanding Burnside both yesterday and today," as Mark Beach pointedly observed. "For a century and a quarter people have been born as well as died there. They have been students, parents, and worshippers. They have been craftsmen, salesmen, and entertainers. Most important, they have lived together, whether sharing meager wealth, helping in the transition from immigrant to citizen or easing the pains of loneliness, poverty, or commercial risk. As good neighbors, they have been good friends."[9] The presence of community is often hidden from the eyes of those who cannot see the legitimacy of lifestyles foreign to their own.

The term "community" will also stand for a sense of shared allegiances to purposes and ideals that stand beyond the local community in the geographic sense. Asking the term to carry these varied meanings permits me to allude to several major communities that have vied for the loyalty of Americans, communities that have pulled and propelled Americans to educate children in sometimes disparate ways for varied purposes and allegiances. The major communities that have laid claim to American loyalty include one's family, the local community, the individual state, the national state, and, lately, supranational calls to form a world economic community as a force superior to the "obsolescent" state. One's loyalty might well have become divided among two or more of these several communities, but not necessarily. (Lost in this progression of loyalties was the sense of a region as a community of loyalty. Josiah Royce's call for promoting provincial differences and provincial loyalties to counter-act American standardization and uniformity went unanswered.)

No community of loyalty has had more historical persistence than has the pull of local community ties—the sense of being part of common interests and concerns in a particular locale. Secondary allegiances there might have been, but the stronger and more stable ties of localism made the deme, the home village, the "city on a hill," and the native township the historic heart of human loyalty. Not surprisingly in the American experience, when the local community has served successfully as one's primary community of loyalty, one's "love of country" has often reached towering heights. For those who enjoyed that one place on earth—a community "home"—where a sense of worth and belonging had been fostered, fond feelings toward "country" have not been difficult to elicit. It is natural to impute to the "country" the values of one's immediate world. "But in great communities," John Stuart Mill noted, "an intense interest in public affairs is scarcely natural...."[10] In communities great or small, however, the value-laden lessons of daily life often become the attributes of the faceless, far-flung "country."

In early nineteenth-century America, the sentiment of loyalty to country commonly found expression in affection for local community rootedness. But there were also influential voices, Noah Webster's and Mason Locke Weems's among them, urging Americans to devote even greater loyalty to the new nation itself. And in growing numbers, admirers of Henry Clay's American system of economic growth believed that the country (or the individual state) ought to command greater loyalty from each community. Promoters of higher loyalties joined in working against the exclusive stress on local community prerogatives. Some worked especially to develop loyalty to the individual state as an essential step in the elevation of loyalty to the national level.

In the 1830s and 1840s, Horace Mann symbolized the Whig enthusiasm for economic growth and broad-based social manipulations in the service of lofty moral codes. As Robert Church and Michael Sedlak observed, he spoke for those who looked to the individual states to enlighten and share loyalty with the local communities.[11] Mann's career as secretary of the State Board of Education in Massachusetts amounted to a quest for power concentration, for greater loyalty toward the entire state as a rightful participant in the theretofore jealously guarded realm of local prerogatives in education. From rudely bustling Boston, where the sense of community had come under seige, to the most placid and contented village in the commonwealth, Mann sought allies in the effort to convert schooling into a state-supervised activity that would, by implication, raise all children in conformity with the rules of the science of education and thereby enable children to transcend familial and local purposes in order to become more enlightened loyalists of the entire commonwealth.

Moved by the eloquent example of Mann, leaders in other states launched similar campaigns over the question of loyalty. While the Whig impulse in the world of trade involved widening the sphere of influence for the federal government, in the world of education the pull was primarily toward acceptance of the individual state as the proper overseer of all community educational endeavors in the interests of learning and solidarity. And unerringly it was seen that with the question of the control of schooling rested the best hopes for enhancing a desired acceptance of the authority of the state. As Michael Katz has noted, it was not a question of state-supervised schooling versus no schooling at all. Voluntary associations were at work; and the spirit of democratic localism had already demonstrated that communities could properly school their children.[12] But state-supervised education served as an ideal lever by which to ease the local burdens—and move the community of loyalty in the direction of the individual state.

Mann (and his counterparts in other states) did not blind local community leaders with dazzling rhetorical tricks. He did not dupe them into relinquishing an important element of local autonomy. He offered, rather, what was considered a reasonable measure of relief to those communities whose coherence had weakened, a reasonable measure of encouragement and support to those who shared his faith in education. He offered his state as a willing helper, prepared to share in the sacrifices schooling demanded. His offer came at a time when people, especially in larger communities, were found less willing themselves to make local institutions work. He spoke to the differences to be acknowledged between the happy sentimentality of localism and the more sober willingness to make sacrifices at the local level. Mann and his fellow reformers did not seek to destroy the home town as a community of loyalty, only to gain a share of that loyalty for the individual state. But uniform standards did become ideals of state-level enterprise; and sketchy outlines of a vertical network of supervisors in education did begin to form. An "incipient bureaucracy," appearing at first as only a modest participant in the crusade to improve children's education, did begin to cloud local options and undermine competing forms of voluntarism. But even state-level reform was based on voluntaristic principles. Had those principles been sustained and had there not been still other levels of community loyalty that bid for attention, the individual states and the local communities therein might have continued to foster a simple sense of shared loyalty based on geography and shared aspiration.

Primarily because the next half-century would see compulsion replace voluntarism do we look at Horace Mann's world and see there the laying of the groundwork for conditions that would undermine local communities of loyalty. In Mann's age shared ideological commitments to schooling and widespread esteem for voluntarism actually expanded the compatible realms of loyalty for most Americans. All participants understood that what was given voluntarily in exchange for some presumed good could be withdrawn. The providers of the presumed good knew well who their clients were. They knew the rules of the trade-off. When schooling became compulsory, on the contrary, loyalty was no longer dependent upon choice and sentiment. It is in the legislation of loyalty that the "secret power" began to grow.

## THE NATION AS COMMUNITY OF LOYALTY: *PARENS PATRIAE*

If individual states could legitimately participate in local schooling, could the same be said of the nation-state? Throughout all the states, but especially in the South, could be found rock-hard pockets of fond attachment to the notion of the sovereignty of the individual states. Here the Whig drive for centralization collided with the obdurate democratic preference for local option. The old Articles of Confederation plainly declared that each state retained sovereignty. The

Constitution had stood stonily silent on the question of state sovereignty; but neither did it mention the word "nation" or express an opinion of the several states as an organic whole. Among the naysayers, liberty and union were not inseparable; and the right to secede and the doctrine of nullification were, by the more daring few, declared open options, however unlikely the foreseeable cause to invoke them. With the fuzzy illusion of individual state sovereignty and guarantees of the Tenth Amendment to the Constitution, then, the state-sovereignty adherents held that the major arena of loyalty-sharing rested snugly at the subnational level.

But the Constitution did speak of the desire to form a "more perfect Union." And the questions of sovereignty and education involved cultural as well as political implications. In cultural terms the ante-bellum American warmed to the prospect of being a citizen in the most advanced and enlightened nation in the world. The Enlightenment ideals of an elevated quality of life, guided by informed leaders possessed of generous vision, had begun to blossom in the soil of the New World as a national symbol of the destined place of the American venture in the progress of civilizations. By the mid-nineteenth century, throughout the Western world, nationalism was becoming the prime political force.

Touched by this sentiment, many Americans who might otherwise have limited themselves to the fostering of loyalty to the individual state felt moved to hail the nation itself as yet another desired partner in promoting education. Earlier dreams of a national university had failed to materialize, but dreamers continued to promote ideals of national education as essential to a hoped-for American culture.[13] In 1865, subnational and national sentiment met at last. America, from sea to shining sea, came to be seen as a nation on a hill. With the question of state sovereignty settled, would the nation-state now become "too *strong* for the liberties of its own people," as Lincoln had feared?

The Civil War settled all questions about the nation as supreme community of loyalty. Carl Sandburg somewhere noted that the Civil War was fought over a verb. Prior to the war references to the United States had taken the plural form: "The United States are . . ." and "The United States have. . . ." Since then the cultural grammar has taken the singular form: "The United States is . . ." and "The United States has. . . ." The Union proved to be not only indivisible but the indisputable senior community of loyalty. Following the Civil War, the American mood grew remarkably nationalistic. Merle Curti's landmark study of the *Roots of American Loyalty* provided an instructive reminder of the fervor of nationhood as the first centennial years rolled in. Oratory, parades, public celebrations, the blarney, ballyhoo, and bloody shirt of politicians, the popular textbooks in American schools, and the reams of more reflective and reverent commentary made it clear that one community of loyalty towered over the others: the nation. The United States had become an organic whole. The new histories of the American experience gloried in the "sense of nationality" and gave prominent place to such leaders as Daniel Webster for declaring: "I am an American, and I know *no locality* in America: that is my country. . . . I was born an American; I will live an American; I shall die an American."[14]

The idea of the state, of nationhood, carried with it the promise of "moral goals that had eluded mankind for thousands of years."[15] With the preservation of the Union and the promise of "a new birth of Freedom," the unbroken historical record of oppression, ignorance, and suffering might at last be snapped. A new majoritarian mood favored the creation of national standards of taste and national agreement on the meaning of Americanism. Science and technology, commerce and efficiency, justice and equal opportunity—prominently displayed among the symbols of nationhood—could contribute to the mystique of the state only to the extent that Americans would accept the idea of the expert society and agree to cede powers of state prerogative and popular initiative to centralized professional deliberation in the interests of public improvement. Appalled as many were by the rise of the business corporation and pleased as they were by the trust-busting forays of Theodore Roosevelt and William Howard Taft, the standards of corporate activity nonetheless gained firm place in the American mind. Corporate abuses meant that corporate policing agencies were needed. Bigness here required bigness there. The power of private consolidations and combinations required a corresponding presence of agencies designed to promote and protect public purposes.

In the reordering of dominant American values, national loyalty overshadowed more intimate communities of loyalty. Expert leadership gained at the expense of local and individual initiative. The accomplishment and promise of large-scale operations made small-scale ideals seem inept and embarrassingly amateurish legacies of a dimming past; and the promotors of these inchoate collectivist values grew increasingly jealous of all competing loyalties. Kinship, region, local community—all came to be seen through a new set of state spectacles. And the secret power, its tracks now clear, began to high-ball into the twentieth century.

In the sphere of education, progressive reformers labored to bring local schools into the fold of the individual state governments. Unlike the reformers of Horace Mann's era their views now carried the potential force of law. Long since set aside was the belief that a child's attendance at school depended upon the will of the parents and the persuasive influence of the local community. By 1918 compulsory attendance was not only on the books in every state in the Union, but to the surprise of those who believed such laws were toothless, enforcement of compulsory attendance laws became common. It went hand-in-hand with enforced child labor laws. With new labor-saving machinery, boatloads of immigrant labor, and humanitarian concern for child welfare, children and youth were of diminished use to the leaders of production. The states, especially through their county offices, were becoming parents on a grand scale. And the federal state, too, began to feel the stirrings of parental responsibilities.

The state had traditionally functioned as a parent in a limited sense. It had long served as *parens patriae* in dealing with children under the age of seven whose persons or property had been violated. But by the dawn of the present century the world of childhood—and the reach of *parens patriae*—extended far beyond those first fragile years of life. Babies born into the twentieth century were to remain under the hand of *parens patriae*, and be consigned to the world of childhood and dependency, until they reached mid-teens at least. Where the state as parent had once been a modest chancery court activity reserved for pre-school-age children, the state now claimed that children of school age were within the reach of *parens patriae.* All dependents and members of the world of childhood were entitled to but one right: the right to proper custody. The state claimed for itself the right to determine the definition and arrangements for proper custody. And the courts were unanimous in their belief that the state could claim a legitimate right to the shared custody arrangements found in compulsory attendance laws. All parents, in effect, were thereby prejudged incapable of arranging for their own children's education.

In a 1901 landmark test case the Indiana Supreme Court worked like an alchemist to make the traditional and limited doctrine of *parens patriae* support compulsory attendance laws. Nodding in the direction of the older version of *parens patriae* the court observed: "The natural rights of a parent to the custody and control of his infant child are subordinate to the power of the state, and may be restricted and regulated by municipal laws." In that sentence the court set forth the ancient view of the state as parent. Did the court intend to rule against compulsory attendance? After all, the question before the court had to do with children and youth who were too old to be dealt with under the limited, traditional doctrine of *parens patriae*. Instead, and in the very next sentence, the court worked its magic and converted school-agers into "infants." "One of the most important natural duties of the parent is his obligation to educate his child, and this duty he owes not to the child alone, but to the commonwealth. If he neglects to perform it or willingly refuses to do so, he may be coerced by law to execute such civil obligations. The welfare of the child and the best interests of society require that the state shall exert its sovereign authority to secure to the child the opportunity to acquire an education."[16]

The court's reasoning might have been a bit shaky, but it was sufficient unto the day. And as the rise of the juvenile court and the hosts of child agencies would soon attest, "infancy" did indeed blur in meaning. The period of dependency and the paternal reach of *parens patriae* were to become whatever the majoritarian ethic decreed. It might have been psychologically comforting to think of compulsory attendance in terms of infant protection. Similarly, it served to soften the heart to speak in favor of child labor laws when the major consequence of such enactments was to limit employment opportunities for youth rather than children.[17]

Infants, children, youth—all became subject to the doctrine of *parens patriae*. All became classified as dependents. All became relieved of the full discretionary powers of parents and guardians. The newly formed juvenile courts also removed most dependents from the reaches of criminal justice. The juvenile courts did not adjudge "crimes." They conveyed to the child the impression that a question of proper custody was the central issue. If institutionalized for delinquent behavior, children were not adjudged "guilty" of a "crime" and sent to a "punitive institution"; rather, as *Bryant* v. *Brown*

(1928) explained, where they were sent was "in no sense a prison, but . . . an educational, industrial institution, designed for the training of immoral, delinquent, incorrigible or abandoned children—to cause them to become moral and industrious. Its purpose is a beneficent one, often transforming a vicious and criminally inclined child into a moral, industrious, and useful citizen."[18]

The process of criminal justice had been available to children and youth through most of the nineteenth century. But now they were no longer to have the right to confront accusers and cross-examine witnesses, to refrain from self-incrimination, to expect trial by jury, to have counsel, to receive a transcript of proceedings, and to have the right of review. In protecting children and youth from these proceedings in which "crimes" had been committed, their misbehaviors came to be called "delinquencies." Delinquent behavior raised the question of proper custody for the offender. The juvenile court made that determination. It came to represent the state as parent. And the state ruled, in effect, that the Bill of Rights and the Fourteenth Amendment no longer applied to children or youth.[19]

In effect, if not by design, the juvenile courts became public syphons. They expeditiously removed troublesome children and youth from society and placed them in state-sanctioned custody. Juvenile judges enjoyed a growing set of custodial options for their delinquents. Industrial and reform schools, mental institutions, foster homes, orphanages, facilities for the handicapped—all under state jurisdiction or directly managed by government—formed an array of options designed to demonstrate the responsible behavior of the state as parent. The custodial arrangements guaranteed the proper care of abused, abandoned, and neglected children, the proper rehabilitation or restraint of truants, the disobedient, the sex-drink-and-drug offenders, thieves, runaways, the mentally disabled and physically handicapped, and incorrigibles. Usually it was left to the wisdom of the juvenile judge to match the offender and the offense with the proper facility. Not surprisingly, the major recipients of juvenile justice were to be the poor, the minorities, and the unorthodox ("deviants").

The juvenile courts were pure expressions of the spirit of progressive reform. They presumptuously declared that in every case there existed "a nonadversarial relationship between the state and the client" and "that only the state could make the individual free."[20] A remarkable declaration, it was matched only by the unaccountably wide sweep of public acceptance that greeted it. It was, as well, a testimonial to the secret power.

In the early years of the present century Americans groped for new definitions of childhood and for public policy anent child custody. But their gropings, taken collectively, began to form a coherent pattern. From the federal heights of the U.S. Children's Bureau (1912) to the offices of public authorities in the several states came evidence that Americans had given at least tacit assent to the idea that the state was a primary custodian of all children and youth. By conscious intent and indifferent acquiescence, Americans allowed the child to undergo an exchange of masters, partial in most instances, total in others. Almshouses, orphanages, foster homes, reform schools, industrial and military schools, institutions for the handicapped, parochial and private schools—and the impressive machinery of public education—became an increasingly integrated network of alternative options open to the state as parent. Laws of compulsion left natural parents and their children no alternative avenues. The public day school, the most visible form of state guardianship, represented only a partial change of masters. But when day school and informal constraints failed to produce desired social results, there stood a full garrison of alternative custodial arrangements, most of them requiring around-the-clock treatment under state supervision and federal guidelines with their grant-in-aid inducements.[21]

I could well have been among those Americans who believed the blessings of education to be great enough to warrant enforced compulsory school attendance. Had I been one of the American majority at that time I might have thought such laws to be essentially harmless confirmations of my own behavior as a parent. After all, I would have sent my children to school anyway. Every parent should be similarly inclined. The persuasive talk of a coming expert society and the obvious rise of new professions with their educational credentials might well have encouraged me to join in the promotion of the public high school and enforced school attendance for teenagers. Civic education in the schools would only reinforce family teaching in my home; but it would be a blessing to us all if a potentially destructive lot of religious and ethnic minorities and latecomers to America could be so instructed in our schools. Why not make them attend? We are, after all, entering a new era. More and more we are becoming a nation of employees. The expectation of self-employment in island communities in some bucolic hinterland is at end. Our future loyalty lies with an industrial order, urban, nationally interconnected. A new "great chain of being" has been forged. Order, control, system, efficiency, punctuality, discipline—these are keys to our tomorrow. Compulsory school attendance is no price at all to pay; it is ennobling to us all and serves as insurance against the breakdown of democratic life in a technological society. I would probably have supported the juvenile court and been impatient with precious criticisms of the encroaching state. I would likely have felt none of its pinch. My family circle, I might well have erroneously concluded, is yet intact and inviolate. I would have been predisposed not to see beyond my local day school to the complex network of state custody and control of American children and youth in an urban and industrial age. National laws and standards were essential. Had I heard a public official insist, as one did, that "the children belong to the state and the state should see that they are educated," I might have let the first part of the statement pass as a bit of slightly overheated rhetoric and given hearty endorsement to the second part.[22] Reactions and beliefs similar to these, at any rate, must have been popular. Few were alarmed by the presence of the secret power in this new era. One heard remarkably little criticism of such a momentous personal sacrifice at the shrine of nationhood and the modern state.

Reasonably, the professional and corporate worlds sought their trained elites out of this reservoir of ordinary "learning." As machinery and efficiency made mass labor less necessary, the interests of the budding expert society made compulsory school attendance an ideal solution. Humanitarians, educators, and others far removed from the interests of corporate expansionism, speaking the idiom of patriotism and enlightenment, agreed. Further urbanization, industrialization, and mechanization multiplied the need for elites in the service-and-expertise "industries."

Through it all, the paternal impulse seemed at first too modest and unambitious, on the one hand, and too well-meaning, on the other, to threaten the health of the other communities of loyalty. By degrees, nonetheless, the family—and the intermediate communities of loyalty—continued to erode. Rochelle Beck, in tracing the record of the White House Conferences on Childhood, provided an instructive hint of the great paternal thirsts of professionals and experts. The first conference, in 1909, and the second, in 1919, drew only two hundred participants each time; and the topics were of limited range and consequence. The third conference, in 1930, was vastly different. Three thousand participants probed all over the range of childhood, youth, and the American family. Families and family life became one of the "problems" for professional consideration. The rural family was a special cause of impatience. It was berated for being stubbornly tight-knit and resistant to management! "An interesting feature of all researches on the family is the resistance of the rural family to change. A recent study has shown them to be disinterested in money matters, antagonistic to change, and staunch in the maintenance of older ideals of family life. . . ." Noting further that rural children had a pronounced difficulty adjusting to consolidated, urban-inspired care, the delegates were invited to ask themselves whether there were "aspects of the older family pattern which *should be changed.*"[23]

Where the 1930 conference had remained a bit hesitant about setting the limits of family prerogatives, the 1940 conference had grown fully confident. In that momentous fourth conference, delegates placed "major responsibility for meeting children's needs on a centralized public school system." And as for the family? Largely relieved of responsibility for transmitting central values, for advancing patriotism, democratic ideals, and the public interest, a redesigned set of "basic" responsibilities now fell upon the constricted family hearth: "Giving the child food, shelter, and material security is the *primary* task of the family."[24] In one century Tocqueville's "secret power" had been transformed from a subtle, potential force into the animating inspiration of the nation-state.

The expanded meaning of *parens patriae* converted most American children and youth into dependents and rose in opposition to the family as a community of loyalty. But the paternal energies of the state did not remain concentrated on children and youth. They were being spent in the adult world also.

## ATTRIBUTES OF A SECRET POWER

If a society is to be free, the evidence of its freedom must lie in the richness and diversity of the loyalties its members claim. The paternal effectiveness of the state in the twentieth century, however, hinged upon discrediting and crippling all other levels of community loyalty. It is in the interest of a free society that individual initiative and voluntary association link with local communities and state-level communities to promote ends that are locally and regionally sensible. Under local auspices the caring impulse remains a more appropriately personal expression of concern for another's material and spiritual well-being, usually more sensitive of the preservation of individual dignity, and suspicious of the expert who would make of caring a professional career. Under the hand of the modern state the common paternal pattern is compulsory, expert, even-handed, and impersonally rational above all else. It thereby transforms the idiosyncratic concern for individuals in a given locale into a systematized concern for groups of individuals everywhere.

In the sphere of paternalism the state acts in loyalty to the principle that in fundamental respects all humans are alike. Its administrative agencies, bureaucratically organized, are designed to behave according to the notion that "fair" treatment of citizens means "uniform" treatment. Where citizens seem divided in their appreciation of the treatment, the bureaucracies must be guided by what they understand to be the enlightened view and override the dissidents. To behave otherwise would be to violate the mandate to be rational, systematic, and uniformly fair to all. Deprived of the freedom to define fairness themselves, members of face-to-face communities are commonly required to bend their own senses of fairness into shapes determined by outsiders.

The common state treatment is to provide material elements of "happiness" with little sensitivity to liberating people's powers "and engaging them in activities that enlarge the meaning of life."[25] It amounts to "belly liberalism." The modern state enhances the role of the expert and works in effect to reduce large segments of the population to a condition of helplessness before the awesome scope of the domestic problems the state proclaims to be busily solving in behalf of its citizenry.

Robert Nisbet has cogently outlined this tendency of the nation-state in his provocative study of *Community and Power.* If we would understand the propensities of the nation-state, Nisbet noted, we must disabuse ourselves of several dangerous misconceptions. Its tendency to authoritarianism is not axiomatically conservative; it is commonly driven by liberal ideals. Nor does it ordinarily resort to force and terror. Neither is it true that the state is enemy of the cowering masses in most instances.[26] Nor is it an irrational force. It is supremely rational, orderly, and expert. In the authoritarian and paternal schemes of things,

> there is no single intellectual image intrinsic to the . . . design. There is no single spiritual or cultural value inherently incapable of being made into the

central image. . . . It can as well be racial equality as inequality, godly piety as atheism, labor as capital, Christian brotherhood as the toiling masses. What is central is not the specific image held up to the masses but, rather, the sterilization and destruction of all other images and the subordination of all human relationships to the central power that contains this image.[27]

Authoritarianism posits the existence of one supreme and exclusive community of loyalty. It cannot be understood, Nisbet argued, "except in terms of the weakening and destruction of earlier bonds, and of the attachment to the political State of new emotional loyalties and identifications." All other communities of loyalty, from family to voluntary associations, are undermined. The great triumph of the state comes with the atomization of individuals, with no dependable alternative communities of loyalty, in a psychological vacuum which the state fills as "the new and final enclosure for human life and purpose."[28] The common notion of the individual versus the state is dangerously wrong-headed. In reality, the course of the state is to reduce every member to the level of an individual, to remove from the individual the support found in other communities of loyalty, and thus render each separated person helpless and dependent. "Even constitutional guarantees and organic laws dim to popular vision when the social and cultural identities of persons become atomized, when the reality of freedom and order in the *small areas* of society become obscure."[29]

Nisbet's is a modern reminder of the great historic problem in government: to prevent the strongest power from becoming the only power. It is a reminder, as well, of Tocqueville's remarkable warning to democratic peoples everywhere and especially to Americans. Writing about the America he had studied in the 1830s, Tocqueville judged them unlikely to fall prey to a tyrant. Rather, it was likely that they would become ruled by paternal guardians. Under such rule, local and intermediate communities of loyalty wither. Voluntarism gives way to compulsion. The shadows of estrangement and aloneness deepen.

Meanwhile, standing above these helpless, alienated, and estranged souls is the state, doting on its citizens. But its parental care is ultimately destructive. It is not like that parent whose object is

to prepare men for manhood; but it seeks on the contrary to keep them in perpetual childhood. . . . For their happiness such a government willingly labours, but it chooses to be the sole agent and the only arbiter of that happiness: it provides for their security, foresees and supplies their necessities, facilitates their pleasures, manages their principal concerns, directs their industry, regulates the descent of property, and subdivides their inheritances—what remains, but to spare them all the care of thinking and all the trouble of living? After having thus successively taken each member of the community in its powerful grasp, and fashioned them at will, the supreme power then extends its arm over the whole community. . . . The will of man is not shattered, but softened, bent, and guided: men are seldom forced by it to act, but they are constantly restrained from acting: such a power does not destroy, but it prevents existence; it does not tyrannize, but it compresses, enervates, extinguishes, and stupefies a people, till each nation is reduced to be nothing better than a flock of timid and industrious animals, of which the government is the shepherd.[30]

Tocqueville here traced the course and sketched the consequences of the "secret power."

Americans in the late twentieth century might have reason to heed these lines with vastly more concern than did their forebears nearly a century and a half ago. The centralizations in business, government, and education, the bloated state of *parens patriae*, the life-sustaining paternalisms represented in the massive deployment of federal agencies, the marginal and helpless condition of so many citizens "softened, bent, and guided" to welcome the even greater expansion of the paternal and centralizing community of the state: these are the critical signs of the progress of the "secret power." Taken collectively, the powers that accrued to the state as the primary community of loyalty cast an enervating ray of realization that modern totalitarianism is no historical aberration. Rather, it is "closely related to the very trends hailed as progressive in the nineteenth century."[31] As Henry Jacoby put it in his study of *The Bureaucratization of the World*, "the bureaucratic limitation of freedom has been brought about largely by the freeing of individuals and the loosening of all social ties associated with that process. . . ."[32]

## THE SUPRANATIONAL COMMUNITY OF LOYALTY

The modern possibilities of authoritarianism now reach far beyond the essentially nationalistic—and territorial—limits of progressivism, for the political state is no longer the sole great organized power. There now stands a competitive organized power whose elites are untouched by the atomizing tendencies of the state. Theirs is a functional rival community of loyalty unto itself. Over the last half-century the great global corporations and conglomerates, through their elites, have come increasingly to dictate to federal regulatory agencies, to influence foreign policy, and to exert enormous influence over legislation and the administration of public policy. In his examination of *The Powers That Be*, G. William Domhoff identified this elite as the "ruling class." Through its control of the processes as well as the legislative results of government, "the ruling class has been able to dominate government and the underlying population throughout the twentieth century."[33] But only since the 1950s, Robert Heilbroner observed, have we come to see in this elite its multinational and global pretensions.[34]

Richard Barnet and Ronald Muller, in their instructive study, *Global Reach*, have identified "the most powerful human organization yet devised for colonizing the future." It is not the nation-state; it is the corporation. The so-called multinational corporations have already ushered in "a new stage in world capitalism." They have demonstrated "the power to transform the world political economy and in so doing transform the historic role of the nation-state. . . . In the process of developing a new world, the managers of firms like GM, IBM, Pepsico, GE, Pfizer, Shell, Volkswagen, Exxon, and a few hundred others are making daily business decisions which have more impact than those of most sovereign governments on where people live; what work, if any, they will do; what they will eat, drink, and wear; what sorts of knowledge schools and universities will encourage; and what kind of society their children will inherit."[35]

Global corporations are by no means an exclusively American phenomenon. In the mid-1970s, non-U.S. corporations owned "more than 700 major manufacturing enterprises . . ." in America.[36] American-based companies, however, are well ahead of others in the development of the global economy. Regardless of the countries in which the global corporations originally grew, its leaders reportedly see themselves as members of a new world community.

The corporate idea of world management has been advanced with rhapsodic promises of peace and prosperity everywhere. Its notion of sovereignty is not limited by geography; it rises above territoriality and sees itself as a force in contest with the obsolescent nation-state. The new global visionaries behold a world with no borders —

that, or at worst, a world dominated by the transcendent unity of the economic globalists in which a limited and internationally orchestrated role has been carved for once-sovereign nation-state.[37]

The nation-state could once trust its corporations to be loyal to ideals of home and territoriality, could encourage industrial expansionism with the expectation that corporate international holdings would not adversely affect the relationship between the state and the domestic economy. But such is no longer the case. The global corporations do not see "home" operations as distinguished from "adjunct" operations; they identify all operations as part of one planetwide economic unit. They are not prisoners of geography, nor are they any longer content to support the idea of territorial sovereignty so important to the nation-state. Nationalism, in the idiom of the global corporations, is "irrational," "obsolescent," and, in the widely shared estimate of Jacques Maisonrouge of International Business Machines, "woefully out of tune with technological progress. The critical issue of our time . . . [is the] conceptual conflict between the search for global optimization of resources and the independence of nation-states."[38]

The global corporations logically seek a more stable international order. In their quest for political legitimacy they promote themselves, with some justice, as devotees of peace and accord. In their proposed "global shopping center," to use Peter Drucker's admiring phrase, they would lead all people peacefully to adopt the same tastes and habits of consumption. To promote their political legitimacy, the global corporations promise worldwide "rationalization," "commonization," "uniformity," "quality control," and "centralization"; to promote their ideology, they offer stability and peace. Maisonrouge spoke for the new order in identifying "irrational nationalism" as the obstructionist enemy. As Drucker put it: "we need to defang the nationalist monster."[39]

The directorate of the global corporations looks with fine impartiality upon all nations. It is equally at home wherever it has an operation. Its nonnationalist character helps disentangle it from identification with any foreign power and reduces risks of political retaliation. Corporations with older, national names quietly phase in new nonnationalist titles: U.S. Rubber becomes Uniroyal and American Brake Shoe becomes Abex, for example. "All this," Barnet and Muller note, "is designed not only to blur images but to change loyalties. . . . It is now commonplace in corporate speeches that management must not put the welfare of any country in which it does business above that of any other, including the United States."[40]

Have we reached a point where the nation-state, having helped the corporations outgrow their dependence upon territorial sovereignty, has itself become the target of manipulation by the corporations? The nation-state has allowed its regulatory agencies to serve the corporations, has made splashy shows of taxing them and bailing them out, but it seems incapable of cutting the corporations free to reenter the world of competition or of breaking them up, even though the protection of its own sovereignty calls for such action, even though the inability to do so leaves only its power to herd the citizenry and to make war at its sovereign disposal. The militarist power is sovereignty at its worst. But the corporations have undercut sovereignty-at-its-best: as found in the nation-state's primary domestic functions—fairly raising revenue and maintaining sound currency, helping its citizens become useful contributors to the economy, expanding the opportunities for a sense of social maturity and self-worth.

A central purpose of the League of Nations—and, later, of the United Nations—was to diminish nationalist emphasis on military power. A central consequence of the work of the global corporations has been the enhancement of militarist power. Ironically, in both cases, the goal is a peaceful world. Strip the notion of peace of its implied potential to enhance the personal and cultural dimensions of life, and redefine peace as the absence of armed conflict among nations and tightened control of the citizenry within each nation. Then view each useful citizen in every diminished country as a dutiful producer and consumer. The result is the new peace promised by the global corporations.

Their present power owes a massive debt to the success of the nation-state in becoming the central community of loyalty. The ambitions of nationalism, at one with the subsequent goals of global corporatism, fragmented competing communities of loyalty. The processes of centralization loosened or severed all competing bonds of affection and association. They atomized individuals and reduced increasing numbers of them to a condition of helplessness. In the process, nation-states formed close alliances with corporate and military leadership. At nearly every step modern nations pursued a course that now conveniently feeds the ambitions of the global corporations. It remains for the world corporations to perfect the art of taming nation-states to serve a chastened supporting role in their hoped-for new order. One should not expect schooling to be a matter of indifference to the corporate planners of this new order. Even now, often indirectly, their daily decisions are more influential than those of many sovereign nations in shaping curricula, political values, and children's perceptions and prospects.

The sovereignty of the nation-state is seriously contested. It is being pulled in one direction by the structured power of the global corporation and in the opposite direction by the ill-organized, historically rooted tug of local and intermediate communities of loyalty. Both forces seek to diminish the prerogatives of that sovereignty. One force seeks, at whatever cost, to make the state submissive to supranational goals; the other seeks to reestablish equity and the idea of sovereignty in its finest sense.

Faced with the awesome rivalry of the global corporation, the state must deal with the complexity of its own ability to regain its finest sense of sovereignty—and to save itself from atavistic militarism—which hinges upon the revitalization of local and intermediate communities of loyalty within its territorial limits. Unless such revitalization begins, we who comprise the American citizenry will be further stripped of our birthright by paternal drift in a global supermarket.

The nation-state, unless it has already slipped too comfortably into the company of the global corporations, could do well to encourage us in the effort to restore greater reaches of local action and self-determination. In our age of quantification it would be a blessing to have a set of magic calipers by which we could measure the costs borne by local and intermediate communities of loyalty in allowing the state to become such an attentive parent. In our more utopian imaginings we might see an awareness of the atomizing mission of the state becoming apparent to leaders of all ethnic and racial groups in the land. Then, instead of fighting for ever-greater consideration from the paternal machinery of national government and elbowing one another aside while standing in line for help, we might be able more clearly to see that there is greater hope for freedom, dignity, and the restoration of caring in uniting against the corporation-serving inclination of the state to reduce citizens to the level of helpless, useless dependents.

While reading Bill Russell's memoir, *Second Wind*, I was struck, as he was, by two moments in his life that gave him a sense of the need for such united vigilance against the state. In the first instance the police power's color blindness arrested his attention. "When I was young," Russell began, "we had the pushers in the slums, selling heroin and marijuana. By the time I was a little older the pushers were in the suburbs and the penthouses. It took about twenty years, but it happened." Then, he continued: "In the Watts riot of 1965 the National Guard shot down blacks in the ghetto, and in 1970 the Guard was shooting white college kids at Kent State; it took only five years. The forces against freedom always spread, but whites don't see that the same forces that attack blacks will one day turn on them." The whites were not watchful; but neither were the blacks, as Russell suggested in the second instance. It had to do with Russell's indifference to the uproar over the witch hunting of Senator Joseph McCarthy. Why should he, a black, care one way or the other how a bunch of whites worked out their differences over *their* freedom? He counted as valuable the reply of his friend: "Bill, if whites aren't free, you know damn well that the blacks aren't going to be either, no matter what else happens. That's why you should care."[41]

Our glide toward paternal corporate governance is more difficult to deal with, more likely to be pushed from mind, because we have continued to believe we were working to sustain the ideals of *e pluribus unum*. But we have been vastly too lax in protecting *pluribus*. We have permitted ourselves to deplete the riches of cultural diversity and have, in other spheres of activity as well as in education, concentrated our attention on the building of that "one best system." We have been system building for a century and a half. The American penchant for uniformity troubled Tocqueville. "The Americans hold," Tocqueville said:

> that in every state the supreme power ought to emanate from the people; but when once that power is constituted, they can conceive, as it were, no limits to it, and they are ready to admit that it has the right to do whatever it pleases. They have not the slightest notion of peculiar privileges granted to cities, families, or persons: their minds appear never to have foreseen that it might be possible not to apply with strict uniformity the same laws to every part, and to all the inhabitants.[42]

A fascinating observation: that we were incipient bureaucrats long before we developed our fulsome bureaucratic structure. And we developed that structure while dominated "by the nineteenth-century rationalist's conception of society as a vast aggregate of unconnected political particles." The erosion of our pluralisms, of our local, intermediate, and voluntary communities of loyalty—in short, of our freedom—"is not the inevitable consequence of the democratic ideal of power vested residually in the people," Nisbet argued. "It is the consequence of the system of public administration which we have grafted onto the democratic ideal."[43]

The centralization of power by way of a vast network of experts pigeonholed in bureaucratic hierarchies has delivered the United States into what Johan Galtung has identified as a "structural fascism." We now have

> a system that in its consequences is destructive of particular groups of individuals, like people of other races or other classes, . . . but with no fascist ideology, attitudes, personality syndrome, or anything of that kind. One way of building up such a system is through a technocracy based on highly alienated technocrats and scientists who only carry out very limited jobs without asking questions.[44]

By our conciliatory slavishness, mystification at the complexity of our difficulties, and essentially honorable desire to live according to law, Paul Goodman once observed, "we drift into fascism. But people do not recognize it as such because it is a fascism of the majority." And in essential agreement with Bertram Gross and Noam Chomsky, Clarence Karier noted: "given all the problems America faces today and will face in the near future, we are on the road to a friendly kind of American fascism. . . ."[45] There are those in the world of global corporations who note approvingly that the road leads as well to a more stable nation-state, one better suited to support the world economic unit.

I am not competent to call our drift "fascist"; nor am I convinced that the future is so grimly clear. "Fascism" may be anachronistically unfit to describe the drift of the American state in the late twentieth century, although the term does have utility in suggesting the conditions of a cozy relationship between the political-military arms of the state and multinational corporation leadership. Unlike the era of the brown- and black-shirts, however, the "structural fascism" of contemporary parlance is civil and civilian, rational and paternal; it is, in a word, friendly. And again, unlike fascism of record, it is a fragmented power, riddled with internal inconsistencies.

Other analysts, seeking to describe the liaisons among the state, the military, the corporations, organized labor, and other acknowledged power blocs, see the authoritarian outline taking form as syndicalism on a large scale. William A. Williams, for example, identified the emerging corporate state as a syndicalist oligarchy promoting the internationalization of American business and developing a pattern of paternal custody of the domestic population at-large.[46] Whatever term one gropes for in the day of the global corporation, it must posit, among other things, an acquiescent populace, politically helpless, socially immature, presided over by an officious bureaucracy and the long shadow of the multinationals. It is still the "secret power" at work, but with twists even beyond the imagination of Tocqueville.

Somewhere along the line of progress into the twentieth century the old call to "eternal vigilance" lost its animating force. The heady sense of nationhood, the redefinition of *parens patriae* as a massive concession to paternalism, the erosion of voluntary association and intermediate communities of loyalty, economic expansionism, the enforced impatience with those who preferred not to walk with those committed to national collectivism, and the attendant encroachment of the state into the local, intimate, and small matters of our lives—all in the name of human welfare—have contributed to the creation of an order that is still peculiarly American ("friendly"), but fraught with great dangers to our remaining allotment of liberty.

## EDUCATION AND SURPLUS

The study of education in culture offers but one of many lines by which to trace our movement away from freedom. But that line is of singular importance. It stands at the center of wider considerations of freedom versus servitude. Education has become a chief wedge used by the state to encroach upon the local, intimate, and small matters of community life. The ante-bellum state-level protobureaucracies that formed to promote voluntary attendance had a most modest effect on individual initiative and local communities of loyalty. One hundred and fifty years later, however, that bureaucracy has become national, massive, propelled by the condition of compulsory attendance and capped by a Department of Education that reaches into every classroom and deems schooling to be an arm of the state and a means of social reform.[47]

Under these auspices, modern schools have become training grounds for individual acquiescence in the wisdom of management by experts in American society. They have promoted the passive ideals of efficient social, economic organization; and they have minimized an appreciation of the political dimensions of democracy while dilating upon democracy "as a social system which provides equality of opportunity for all people."[48] The students studied by Edgar Friedenberg believed government to be fair and benign, guided by professionals who worked impartially to promote the people's interests. The students believed that what we adults might have thought of as rights were merely privileges granted—and susceptible of being withdrawn—by government. The years since Friedenberg's study have witnessed no new rush to teach political rights, to promote individual control and power, or to advance the public dimensions of individual life. Such aims continue to be lost in the teaching of passive acceptance of the state as custodian of public matters.[49] Indeed, the second National Assessment of Educational Progress studies in social science and citizenship found, in the years from 1969 to 1976, that thirteen- and seventeen-year-old students showed a marked "decline" in their knowledge about government structure and function as well as in their understanding of and capacity to participate in political processes.[50]

As Joel Spring has noted, the school "teaches people not to make choices and it teaches them not to participate in the development of society."[51] It also teaches them that schooling is the key to individual advancement and social reform. Social problems are problems of education or the lack of education. Racial inequities? Children are bused to integrated schools—and the social-economic community structure is left intact. Employment? Vocational and career opportunities are added to the curriculum—and the world of underemployment in adult society remains no less constricted; and perpetual percentages of unemployment become acceptable nationally. Dropout problems? The requirements for employment are artificially inflated to induce greater numbers of youth to stay in school longer. So the poor and minorities stay in school, obtain their high school "credentials," and find that the job-entry credential requirements have meanwhile risen even further. "It is in fact the case," Karier has observed: "that the percentage of blacks who have completed high school has increased. It is however also a fact that the percentage of blacks unemployed from 1960 has also significantly increased. While the educational level of a significant segment of America's minority has increased, the opportunity of that population to be gainfully employed has consistently decreased."[52]

Especially for the students who become losers (but in effect for nearly all but the elites' children), the use of schools as agents of social reform tends to stress two lessons, according to Spring: first, that the school exists to help each student find a place in the adult world; and, second, that poverty is the result of educational deficiency and if a student fails to make a living after leaving school, it will be because he or she failed, while in school, to take full advantage of the opportunity freely given. The student is being prepared for the role of the atomized individual establishing a personal relationship with the state. There are surely—perhaps in the hinterlands—schools and communities in which lessons of political rights, individual action, and local association are not only taught but represent the conduct of public life in the local community. But the metropolitan world, in general, as the stronghold of the educational bureaucracy, should not be expected to promote political doctrines that would be critical of the roles of state and federal governments in education. Nor, as Spring noted, should schools be expected to downplay the place of schooling in the solving of social problems. Rather, it is patently "in the interest of this educational bureaucracy to support political doctrines that emphasize big government manned by professional experts who . . . work to develop social and educational programs to improve the quality of life."[53]

Children and youth should have ready access to schools as places of learning. But there is no longer a substantial educational rationale for schooling as a compulsory activity. What rationale that remains is mostly economic and political. Three generations of Americans have now passed through our schools under compulsory auspices. And in that relatively short time, the schools have become the delivery system of national ideals that demean or even ignore local community, voluntary action, and the legitimate expression of local purpose. They have become increasingly the voice of a vast interlocking bureaucratic order that stands ready to entertain the standardization of education on a national scale. Even as late as 1930, with an American population of less than 123 million people, local schools largely under local control were a reality. There were roughly 262,000 public schools in about 128,000 districts. Fewer than 10 percent of all pupils were bused. By 1977, with a nearly doubled American population, the consolidation of schools and districts and the centralizing of bureaucratic organization had reduced our schools in number to roughly 87,000 in about 16,000 districts. And now over half of all the students are bused. Over that time, state and federal agencies proliferated. Consolidators' promises of greater economy, efficiency, and quality have proven to be a major miscalculation and embarrassment; but the reorganizational work has been done.[54]

The federal cabinet-level Department of Education came into life talking out of both sides of its mouth about the future course of education in America. "The establishment of the Department of Education shall not increase the authority of the Federal Government over education or diminish the responsibility for education which is reserved to the States and the local school systems and other instrumentalities of the States," read the Organization Act of the Department of Education. At the same time, however, the act charged the new Department to "strengthen the Federal Commitment to ensuring access to equal educational opportunity for every individual, . . ." and to encourage "the increased involvement of the public, parents, and students in Federal education programs. . . ."[55]

During those long months of lobbying for the department, the "buzz" word in Washington, D.C., was "monolithic." Again and again, the promoters of the Department of Education, in meetings with concerned leaders from across the country, saw fit to volunteer emphatic assurances that the hoped-for new department would not be "monolithic." Increased efficiency and improved research and service would come, but without producing or even promoting greater uniformity in American education. Proponents predicted that the new department would best serve as a center for collecting and disseminating data about schools and schooling. (Data shuffling was the prime activity of the federal Bureau of Education a century ago; and federal involvement has long since moved well beyond that useful, and docile, activity.) The more prophetic promoters of the department were those who called for the development of a "coherent" national policy in education and demanded "integral" and "comprehensive" guidance of learning. Those were the persons who also best understood the nature of bureaucracy.[56]

The Department of Education is liberally represented by able, even brilliant, men and women. At all levels of education, among our related bureaucracies at the state and municipal levels, are to be found intelligent minds concerned with schooling. The problem is not that we simply need more intelligent management of education in the nation. The problem is rather that our talent is increasingly being mobilized around prescriptive mandates. And prescriptions, to be "fair," must ignore local peculiarities and local options and strive for greater uniformity. On the face of it, such a paternal penchant is misguided intellectually. In terms of learning alone it will harm even as it attempts to help. But it is consistent with state interests—and the "secret power"—to deal evenly with all as indistinguishable one from the other—and to promote the idea of schools as an essential reform agent of the state.

Educational experts might reasonably be encouraged to ponder the processes of education, but their prescriptive voice should be muted and their mission be limited to standing on call to provide advisory services to the classrooms. The quest for "one best system" should be abandoned and more encouragement given to ethnographic inquiry. Different designs and different policies, tailored to different local conditions, might make a bureaucrat uncomfortable; but they should also make learning success more likely and the local community of loyalty more lively. If we would restore the idea of public education as a public good, we must restore public education to its local publics. And in one small, local, intimate field of human endeavor the secret power would be frustrated. Additional gains could accrue through the restoration of voluntarism to schooling, the removal of excessive roadblocks to youth employment, and the return of the safeguards of criminal justice to the juvenile courts.

These are not breezily simple propositions. To work to restore a sense of local and regional autonomy is to invite confusion, frustration, and even suffering. There is a cost to be borne. Earlier generations created arrears; and the bills have come due in ours. The "freedom to grow up blighted," Henry James predicted nearly eighty years ago, may be "the only freedom in store for the smaller fry of future generations."[57] The blight is here. Voluntary groups and families *have* failed to meet their responsibilities. The distribution of wealth *has* left large sections of the population below even the lowest conceivable American living standard. Welfare groups *have* had nowhere to turn but to Washington. The fears and insecurities in an anonymous, vast, Big Society, will not magically subside through efforts to restore wider reaches of autonomy. Richard Sennett, a hard-headed urbanist, pointedly observed that the removal of the Linus blankets of government will create local difficulties and conflict but that the temperamental and intellectual ability to accept such disorder is vastly preferable to the paternal state. "Take conflict in the public arena away, and you revert to the idea that a broad swatch of urban society can have its best interests 'managed' for it by impersonal bureaucratic means." The opportunities for the restoration of voluntary association and individual initiative are present in abundance: in city administration, the police, in housing, as well as in schooling.[58]

Local determination in these endeavors is not as tidy as massive centralization; but it is essential to freedom and is technically feasible. The choice has really very little to do with the popular questions of efficiency or economy. It has to do with the lifeblood of democratic values in our culture and the noblest meaning of sovereignty in our nation. Pluralism is not merely a question of unity versus diversity or small versus large; it has to do with the essential vitality of communities of loyalty beyond the paternal reach of the state.

The restoration of local initiative, voluntary association, and spirited debate in the face-to-face world should not be seen as a likely way to secede from the larger body politic. The network of interdependencies is too complex. Nor should the guiding vision be to restore the local community as a base from which to reform the larger society in the image of the local community. Rather, the chief gain should be taken at face value, as reviving activities essential to the sense of personal worth and social responsibility at the local level. Individual dignity is delicate. One of the threads that holds it aloft is that of being recognized by others as a person with a rightful claim to social responsibility. "Person" in this sense is already too little honored. Were this a century of chronic underpopulation (and labor shortages), the point might be silly. But the twentieth century has been one of overpopulation (and chronic unemployment). Anonymity has come easily. Facelessness—the enemy of civility and individual dignity—has come easily. Perhaps the grimmest aspect of this century of the modern state and the rise of the global corporation has been the emergence of surplus people—surplus in the sense that they are totally unnecessary to a job-displacing technology and to the unimaginative purposes of the state and, moreover, unable to survive without the state acting as parent. We have managed to remove the bulk of the surplus from daily view, but we have never been able to put them completely out of mind. Their presence further enervates us and persuades us to ride with the drift. The threat of being consigned to the world of the surplus and the attendant fear of poverty has placed one foot, then the other, in a bucket of wet cement.

One of the beliefs that remained alive and well after the Civil War was that the right to belong was open to all who were willing to work. Only the exceptionally ignorant and the lazy were expected to be among the jobless. The "drones" and the "dullards" were out of work owing either to laziness or malevolent genes—in which case they might grumpily be excused. To sustain the belief in the potential usefulness of every citizen, however, required even then that there be several blind spots. Two of them will illustrate: first, one had to ignore the paper claims of the Native American and the newly emancipated Negro to inclusion among the citizenry; and, second, one had to reject the profound lesson of the depression of the early 1890s. In the first instance, the Native American and the Negro were quite invisible. With them removed to the distant reservations and hidden in the rural South, majoritarian sensibility could be dulled to their claims for more fair consideration.

But that depression, in the second instance, made its point with telling effectiveness. It emptied coal buckets and larders and closed shops and factories in full view of the shaken majority. Compared with the later quake of the Great Depression, it was only a tremor. Compared with panics Americans had then known, however, the depression of the 1890s left old certitudes stained with new doubts. In city after city from one end of the country to the other, and echoing in the hinterlands, hints of an uncongenial new truth could be heard: a person could be moral, intelligent, God-fearing, Anglo-Saxon, ambitious—and still be unable to work, unable to sustain a family, unable to survive. It was incredible. With national recovery came the time-honored reaffirmations of the hallowed belief that anyone who would work could work, that no one need be poor except the lazy or that surprisingly large minority upon whom nature had allegedly played genetic tricks. But the amen chorus was a bit more tentative and uncertain. Doubt had been planted. The memory, especially of the dark winter of 1892–1893, could not be erased. The widespread acceptance of the new and nettlesome truth would come in the 1930s. Then would the famous bum put his neopuritan antagonists to route with the question: "How the hell can I work when there's no work to do?"

In some immeasurable but important way the depression of the 1890s helped American labor get right with capitalism, colored the air in the crusade for child labor restrictions and enforced school attendance, greased the road toward professionalism in welfare and social services, and converted the condition of poverty into something to be despised as well as feared. The appearance of fear and hatred was not only novel in its national scope, as William James saw it; it was alarming. America's visible poor roused the twin sentiments of fear and hatred. "We despite anyone who *elects* to be poor in order to simplify and save his inner life," James lamented in 1902. "When we of the so-called better classes are scared as men were never scared in history at material ugliness and hardship; when we put off marriage until our house can be artistic, and quake at the thought of having a child without a bank-account and doomed to manual labor, it is time for thinking men to protest against so unmanly and irreligious a state of opinion." Beyond the presumed spiritual blessings found by some in the life of voluntary poverty there were social blessings as well. But too often "the desire to gain wealth and the fear to lose it are our chief breeders of cowardice and propagators of corruption. There are thousands of conjunctures in which a wealth-bound man must be a slave, whilst a man for whom poverty has no terrors becomes a freeman." Who will be left to fight for unpopular causes in America? James asked. Fear of poverty makes us sheep; we hold our objections back; we go along with the powers that be. We worry, fearing that "our stocks might fall, our hopes of promotion vanish, our salaries stop, our club doors close in our faces. . . ." Who but people unafraid of poverty, who see as well its liberating potential, can have unbribed souls? The appearance of such a pervasive, numbing fear of poverty in a society so excited by material gain—and so in need of unbribed souls—loomed in James's mind as "the worst moral disease from which our civilization suffers."[59]

Poverty never visited William James; but what he understood as a fear of poverty was real. From his secure perch he thought the fear no more than a flaw of character. He did not see that the fear of poverty masked an even more sinister prospect—the possibility that one could be permanently cast out as an unwanted, unnecessary—surplus—human being. An ugly new form of dependency, poverty was beginning to carry the added threat of being branded "useless." The marginal American risked not just poverty but ostracism. H.G. Wells was among the first of the well-placed to link unemployment and poverty to the notion of surplus. In 1939 he observed: "All the civilized communities suffer from a sort of cancer of irrelevant, useless, energetic young people. Their lack of function is a purely disintegrative force. We seem to have no better employment for them than to turn them over to war preparation, which must lead at last to their consumption in war." (Here one may well leap past World War II to consider the huge standing peacetime armed force we now maintain). Continuing, Wells asserted: "Human life has stalled; its organization is clogged with a *growing surplus of human beings* it can neither interest or use. And it seems *incapable of adapting its organization* to the new demand upon it." In just three or four decades, this condition "has rushed upon us and become *the major problem that faces mankind.*"[60]

Some economists will see no warrant for these references to a "surplus" population. They might take issue with Wells and prefer to think of this condition as merely a "variation in labor markets." But "surplus" as used here is not strictly economic in its meaning. The condition it describes also involves psychological and political anguish. Phrases like "labor market variations" and "chronic unemployment" have utility in the impersonal, antiseptic world of economic analysis. But they mask the ugliness of the condition. They lack the evocative power to reveal the basic genocidal tendency of the modern world: the creation of surplus persons. Corporate efficiency and technology, linked to Tocqueville's feared paternal government, have consigned peoples to the trashheap of the redundant.

It is still realistic for some persons to sleep the grand dream of becoming self-sufficient. For most people it may be the comforting vision of being gainfully employed at some worthy task that dances in that last sleep before the dawn. These are the warm visions of those who have claim to a sense of personal worth. Most persons— but by no means all—are spared the twisted, cold-sweat dream in which the hope of finding a place has vanished altogether. In the nightmare of nothingness one finds oneself huddled, herded, helpless, fenced off in a fog-draped land of surplus peoples who have been shunned over the last century. The Native Americans are there in large number. There are those blacks who walked one Freedom Road or another only to find that they had been detoured into this listless land of the unneeded. Through the dim one also sees the gypsies and Jews—the stateless and surplus people of Hitler's Europe—the Armenians and the hordes of potentially surplus victims of the Stalinist purges. Skin tones range from cadaverous white to ebony black. There are the losers in the Great Depression and the Japanese-Americans of World War II, the convicts and the aged, women in great number, the poor of many lands and diverse ethnic backgrounds, the deranged and handicapped, the Cambodians and the boat people, and, just coming into view, ever so many of our own children.

One knows that the sufferers encountered on that plain belong in that dark dream. History records them as surplus. But the nightmare edge to this scene comes with finding oneself lost among them. The recurring veiled vision of the surplus souls—the "victims of oceanic economic and social movements entirely beyond their control"— worms itself even into our dreams of well-being; and in our more reflective moments, we see that we too may be eligible for consignment to the trashheap of the surplus. Older employees who are incessantly reminded that they are eligible for early retirement, who are encouraged to feel guilty if they do not step aside, may sense the stage-one hint of the sensation of surplus. Under other conditions aging brings wisdom of a keener sort.[61]

Had we a government genuinely interested in conserving human values rather than in creating a sense of life-long dependence, Richard Rubenstein noted, it

> would seek to protect every citizen willing and able to work from the threat of economic redundancy. It is absurd to pretend that government has a responsibility to protect its citizens from theft and physical assault but has no responsibility to defend them from the infinitely greater violence perpetrated, often mindlessly, by institutions and policies that render millions of human beings literally useless. There is no private right or privilege that ought to be permitted to subvert the right of every person to a place of dignity and social utility within his or her community.[62]

But the modern state has not proven itself to be genuinely interested in such life-affirming conservation. Persons are routinely denied places of dignity and utility. They are routinely atomized with no semblance of a community in which to demonstrate that dignity and sense of social utility.

In this context, note the regularity with which some of our well-placed and observant contemporaries have come to see that our own children are being treated as useless. Allan Pifer of the Carnegie Corporation recently noted that our educational system functions "as if substantial numbers of youngsters can be considered expendable." In our civilization, Joseph Featherstone remarked, our children "are a distinct luxury." In the judgment of Joan Lipsitz, Americans reflect "a deep mistrust or even dislike of young people in the formative years of their lives." Peter Stearns noted: "Quietly, we seem to be entering an era in which young blood declines both in quantity and value."[63]

Albert Hirschman, in his *Exit, Voice, and Loyalty*, concluded that the deterioration and slack in education is inescapably linked to the fact that we now have "surplus" students, children and youth who are redundant in terms of the world of work that lies ahead.[64] Reminding us of a condition that has long been troubling, Urie Bronfenbrenner observed that we have made our children judge *themselves* to be useless "because we never let them do anything much more important than taking out the garbage."[65] Puzzled by what he senses to be our general attitude toward young people, Pifer said: "One would think that, in the face of the steady decline in the numbers of young people being born today, we would be more favorably disposed to do our best by those we have." He calls it an "irony" that "the opposite seems to be the case: as the numbers have declined, public attitudes have turned to indifference or even outright antagonism."[66]

In one sense it is an ironic situation. But we might ask ourselves if we have not been steadily drifting to this unexpected moment. Is it not likely that the sometimes soft, sometimes grinding erosion of family sanctity, local control of schools, and neighborhood schools plus the steadily widening sweep of the bureaucratic arm of the state with its use of the schools for purposes of reform and impersonal uniformity has begun to wrench the idea of the school away from the public heart? A great measure of that public indifference and outright antagonism is the result of what the state as parent has had a major hand in bringing to pass. In terms of the limited and limiting purposes of the corporations and the modern state, in terms of their custodial view of *parens patriae* and the prospects of corporate retrenchment across the nation, large numbers of our children shall in fact become lifelong burdens. They shall not fit in. We are coming ever closer to a public awareness of the course charted by the corporate order and the modern state and the attendant condition of uselessness in the human family.

As for young people in our probable future, Pifer offered a dismal prospect: "Young people will probably continue to be seen as economic burdens . . . , they will be given little chance to play a constructive role in the nation, and they will be regarded essentially as a threat to the comfort and security of adults."[67] He did not say what he thought they would become as adults; but in one forlorn forecast, all our children were seen as a negative force in American society. Pifer's hopes were for better things; but he laid long odds against their realization. And not only our children, but our entire society would thereby be at last atomized and dependent.

If the state is permitted to define and deal with our so-called "surpluses" as it alone sees fit, its paternal arm can only grow. In a climate of unchecked corporate globalism, its autocratic control over surplus populations will further cloud and impersonalize its deliberations affecting the lives of those who remain, momentarily, among the "useful." The state would then be totally unchecked in the wielding of that secret power.

Our options are not clean, but they are clear. As Barnet and Muller see it, we need to make the corporate giants publicly accountable; we need to promote "job-creating rather than job-displacing technology." The economy itself should be decentralized "so as to curb oligopoly power." Local communities should become aware of their situation as akin to that of underdeveloped countries and view global corporations accordingly, perhaps buying technical services rather than allowing the corporations to control local industry. Small-scale technology and "the development of strong neighborhoods" is a bewilderingly difficult but essential task. In short, human development must become the purpose of social organization, argue the authors of *Global Reach*.[68]

Theirs is pointedly the same argument advanced by others who did not think in terms of the multinational corporate world, but who thought more exclusively in terms of the nation-state as the sole great organized power. From such diverse angles of vision do we find contemporary agreement with Tocqueville. Once again the essential principles of freedom are contrasted with the practices of absolutism. Once again the call goes out for the restoration of local and intermediate communities of loyalty (*pouvoirs secondaires*) and the removal of the heavy government hand from matters local, personal, and intimate. Should the call go unanswered, it now seems clear that increased centralized control in a bureaucratized, exclusionary world awaits us and our children.

The roadblocks to reformation may seem hopelessly unmovable. But that is a judgment bred of despair. The central tendencies of our present drift took over a century to produce wide concern. The machinery of government, like the mill of the gods, grinds exceedingly slow but fine; and the reversal of its engines is not likely to be sudden, nor is it apt to produce a miracle of immediate salutary effects. At all levels of government—and especially at the local levels—we can take heart in every successive step, however small, away from our present course. If we can ask for a great deal over a long haul and not be morally crushed by the glacial weight of the obstacles before us, we might thereby capitalize on those precious freedoms we yet enjoy and contribute to the restoration of those we have squandered.

How do we proceed? David Rothman raised questions of the sort that bedevil us in the quest for reviving local and intermediate communities of loyalty. "Will we as a society be able to recognize and respect rights and yet not ignore needs? Can we do good to others, but on their terms?" And, one might add, can we do good *with* others, but on their terms? Can local communities of loyalty be renewed and restored? Can we afford not to try? "These are the right questions to be confronting," Rothman concluded, "even if the record of American reform gives little reason to be confident that we will answer them well."[69]

But we have every reason to be confident that the state, if left to its own purposes, will not even confront these questions. And that could promise a spreading blight of withered prospects for ourselves and our children.

## NOTES TO CHAPTER 1

1.  George Santayana, *Character and Opinion in the United States* (Garden City, N.Y.: Doubleday Anchor Books, 1956), p. 106.

2.  John Holt, *Escape From Childhood* (New York: E.P. Dutton, 1974), pp. 83–84.

    The nightmare state of the future, if it comes, and it is well on its way, will be above all a tyranny of "professional helpers," with an unlimited right and power to do to us or make us do whatever they (or someone) considers to be for our own good. It should not surprise us that the Russian police state now puts in "mental hospitals" those who strongly and publicly object to its way of doing things and there subjects them to "treatment" until they think or act as they are supposed to. Or that the miniature police states of our schools are more and more using strong drugs such as Ritalin on those children who do not, or will not, fit smoothly into its regime. (p. 84)

3.  Philip Slater, *The Pursuit of Loneliness* (New York: Alfred A. Knopf, 1961).

4.  David B. Tyack, *The One Best System: A History of American Urban Education* (Cambridge, Mass.: Harvard University Press, 1974).

5.  See, e.g., Michael Harrington, *The Accidental Century* (Baltimore: Penguin Books, 1965); Charles Silberman, *Crisis in the Classroom* (New York: Random House, 1970); Richard L. Rubenstein, *The Cunning of History* (New York: Harper & Row, 1975); and Paul Goodman, *Utopian Essays and Practical Proposals* (New York: Vintage Books, 1964).

6.  Alexis de Tocqueville, *Democracy in America*, trans. Henry Reeve, intro. John Stuart Mill (New York: Schocken Books, 1961) 2: 358-59.

7.  Wilhelm von Humboldt, *The Limits of State Action*, trans. J.W. Burrow (Cambridge: Cambridge University Press, 1969), pp. 23-24.

8.  *A Compilation of the Messages and Papers of the Presidents, 1789-1902*, ed. James D. Richardson (Bureau of National Literature and Art, 1904), 6: 23.

9.  Kathleen Ryan, *Burnside: A Community*, Mark Beach, text (Portland, Oregon: Coast to Coast Books, 1979), p. 3.

10. John Stuart Mill, "Introduction," in Tocqueville, *Democracy in America*, 1: xxxii.

11. Robert L. Church and Michael W. Sedlak, *Education in the United States* (New York: Free Press, 1976).

12. Michael B. Katz, *Class, Bureaucracy, and Schools: The Illusion of Educational Change in America* (New York: Praeger, 1975), pp. 3-55.

13. David Madsen, *The National University: Enduring Dream of the U.S.A.* (Detroit: Wayne State University Press, 1966).

14. Merle Curti, *Roots of American Loyalty* (New York: Columbia University Press, 1946). Webster quoted in Arthur Gilman, *A History of the American People* (Boston: Estes and Lauriat, 1883), p. vii, emphasis mine. See also Ruth Miller Elson, *Guardians of Tradition* (Lincoln: University of Nebraska Press, 1964).

15. Robert A. Nisbet, *Community and Power* (New York: Oxford University Press, 1962), pp. 175-76. Nisbet carries a great share of the load in this section of the paper.

16. *State* v. *Bailey*, 157 Ind. 324 (61 NE 730) 1901, pp. 731-32.

17. Daniel J.B. Mitchell and John Clapp, "The Effects of Child Labor Laws on Youth Employment" (Washington, D.C.: Brookings Institute, 1979), pp. 181-213.

18. *Bryant* v. *Brown*, 118 So 184 (151 Miss 398) 60 A.L.R. 1325.

19. See *In re Gault*, 87 S. Ct. 1428 (1967), *Supreme Court Reporter*, vol. 87A (St. Paul, Minn.: West, 1968), pp. 1428-72; and Anthony M. Platt, *The Child Savers: The Invention of Delinquency* (Chicago: University of Chicago Press, 1969). Since *Gault* criminal justice has gradually begun to reach into the juvenile courts.

20. David J. Rothman, "The State as Parent: Social Policy in the Progressive Era," in Willard Gaylin et al., *Doing Good: The Limits of Benevolence* (New York: Pantheon, 1978), pp. 74, 77; see also Donald A. Erickson,

*Super-Parent: An Analysis of State Educational Controls* (Chicago: Illinois Advisory Committee on Nonpublic Schools, 1973); and Robert B. Everhart, "From Universalism to Usurpation: An Essay on the Antecedents to Compulsory School Attendance Legislation," *Review of Educational Research* 47 (1977): 499-530.

21.  Charles Burgess, "The Goddess, the School Book, and Compulsion," *Harvard Educational Review* 46 (1976): 199-216.

22.  *Fifth Biennial Report of the Superintendent of Public Instruction of the Territory of Washington* (Olympia, Wash.: C.B. Bagley, 1883), p. 59.

23.  Rochelle Beck, "The White House Conferences on Children," *Harvard Educational Review* 43 (1973): 658, emphasis mine.

24.  Ibid., p. 659, emphasis mine. For a superb assessment of the plight of the family, see Christopher Lasch, *Haven in a Heartless World: The Family Besieged* (New York: Basic Books, 1977).

25.  John Dewey, *Human Nature and Conduct* (New York: Modern Library, 1922), pp. 293-94.

26.  Nisbet, *Community and Power*, pp. 194-98.

27.  Ibid., p. 193.

28.  Ibid., p. 164.

29.  Ibid., p. 201.

30.  Tocqueville, *Democracy in America*, 2: 380-82.

31.  Nisbet, *Community and Power*, p. 191; see also Rothman, "State as Parent."

32.  Henry Jacoby, *The Bureaucratization of the World*, trans. Eveline Kanes (Berkeley: University of California Press, 1973), p. 221.

33.  G. William Domhoff, *The Powers That Be: Processes of Ruling Class Domination in America* (New York: Vintage Books, 1979), p. 200. William G. Scott and David K. Hart have recently analyzed the remarkable fusion of the public and private sectors into an organizational scheme presided over by a "ruling elite" in America, an elite they see leading us into totalitarianism unless "extraordinary efforts to avoid it" are exerted. See their *Organizational America* (Boston: Houghton Mifflin, 1979), pp. 164, 211. See also Gabriel Kolko, *The Triumph of Conservatism* (Chicago: Quandrangle Books, 1963).

34.  Discussed in Richard J. Barnet and Ronald E. Muller, *Global Reach: The Power of the Multinational Corporations* (New York: Simon & Schuster, 1974), p. 478.

35.  Ibid., pp. 363, 15; see also Bradford C. Snell, *American Ground Transport*, presented to the Subcommittee on Antitrust and Monopoly of the Committee on the Judiciary, U.S. Senate (Washington, D.C.: U.S. Government Printing Office, February 26, 1974).

36.  Barnet and Muller, *Global Reach*, p. 27.

37.  Ibid., p. 21.

38. Quoted in ibid., p. 19.

39. Quoted in ibid., p. 55.

40. Ibid., pp. 56–57.

41. Bill Russell and Taylor Branch, *Second Wind: The Memoirs of an Opinion-ated Man* (New York: Random House, 1979), pp. 207, 229.

42. Tocqueville, *Democracy in America*, 2: 352.

43. Nisbet, *Community and Power*, pp. 259, 271.

44. Johan Galtung, *The European Community: A Superpower in the Making* (London: Allen & Unwin, 1973), p. 189.

45. Goodman, *Utopian Essays*, p. xvii, Clarence J. Karier, "The Quest for Orderly Change: Some Reflections," *History of Education Quarterly* 19 (1979): 164. See also Karier's "Testing for Order and Control in the Corporate Liberal State," in Clarence J. Karier, Paul C. Violas, and Joel Spring, *Roots of Crisis: American Education in the Twentieth Century* (Chicago: Rand McNally, 1973), pp. 108–37.

46. William Appleman Williams, *The Contours of American History* (Cleveland: World, 1961), p. 448.

47. Joel Spring, "Education and Political Control," *Gadfly* 1 (1978): 2–12. See also his *Sorting Machine: National Educational Policy Since 1945* (New York: David McKay, 1976).

48. Spring, "Education and Political Control," p. 7.

49. Edgar Z. Friedenberg, *Coming of Age in America* (New York: Vintage Books, 1963).

50. *Changes in Political Knowledge and Attitudes, 1969–76*, Citizenship/Social Studies Report No. 07–CS–2 (Denver: National Assessment for Educational Progress, January 1978), as cited in Lee H. Ehman, "The American School in the Political Socialization Process," *Review of Educational Research* 50 (1980): 99–119.

51. Spring, "Education and Political Control," pp. 7, 9.

52. Karier, "Quest for Orderly Change," pp. 163–64. Speaking of the credential system in which everyone competes for positions, Randall Collins pointedly observed:

> Even if ethnic differences were completely to disappear today, this institutional structure would still be with us and still occupy a central place in our stratification. The fact that ethnic diversity *does* still exist and that Chicanos, Puerto Ricans, blacks, Asians, and various white ethnic groups . . . make demands for precedence within the credential system today merely *accelerates* the pattern of development of that system in channels laid down several generations ago." (*The Credential Society: An Historical Sociology of Education and Stratification* [New York: Academic Press, 1979], p. 103)

But not all minority members make demands. In some cases the minority sees the majority as using education to destroy what sense of community they yet had. One black student looked at the old lost neighborhood school and said, "It was almost all black back then and we had a good school. We worked together, we cared—the teachers cared. But now I feel as though I could drop dead right in this spot and no one would care what happened to me!" And another black student noted, "There is all this talk about equality of educational opportunity but all I can say is that I've got a bus ride." Jacqueline Scherer and Edward J. Slawski, "Color, Class, and Social Control in an Urban Desegregated School," in *Desegregated Schools: Appraisals of an American Experiment*, ed. Ray C. Rist (New York: Academic Press, 1979), p. 151.

53. Spring, "Education and Political Control," p. 6; see also James G. Anderson, *Bureaucracy in Education* (Baltimore: Johns Hopkins University Press, 1968).

54. For a ringing indictment of rural consolidation, see, e.g., Jonathan P. Sher and Rachel B. Tompkins, *Economy, Efficiency, and Quality: The Myths of Rural School and District Consolidation*, pamphlet (Washington, D.C.: National Institute of Education, July 1970). E. G. West further scored the basic economic assumptions underlying public schooling altogether in his *Education and the State*, 2nd ed. (London: Institute of Economic Affairs, 1970).

55. U.S. Department of Education Organization Act (Public Law 96–88 — October 17, 1979), 20 USC 3402, 3403.

56. The Department of Education officially opened its doors in May 1980, with its army of employees aiming most of their budget at the objective of equalizing educational opportunity. See Arthur E. Wise, *Legislated Learning: The Bureaucratization of the American Classroom* (Berkeley: University of California Press, 1979).

57. Henry James, *The American Scene* (Bloomington: Indiana University Press, 1968), p. 137.

58. Richard Sennett, *The Uses of Disorder: Personal Identity and City Life* (New York: Alfred A. Knopf, 1970), p. 198. See also E. F. Schumacher, *Small Is Beautiful: Economics as If People Mattered* (New York: Harper & Row, 1977); and his *Guide for the Perplexed* (New York: Harper & Row, 1977). Even the master of prediction and control, B. F. Skinner, has backed away from his earlier support of monolithic controls. In his *Science and Human Behavior* a quarter century ago, he scorned diversification of control. But Skinner has recently reconsidered his earlier position. "Counter control" might, after all, be useful! It is a "primitive device," unfortunately; but "if we are to make sure that no individual or small group will emerge to use despotically the power conferred by a science of behavior, we must design a culture in which no one *can* emerge in such a position." Skinner continued to be enthusiastic about designing large-scale cultures, but his new-found sense of caution deserves note. B. F. Skinner, "Answers for My Critics," in *Beyond the Punitive Society*, ed. Harvey Wheeler (San Francisco: W. H. Freeman, 1973), p. 266.

59. William James, *The Varieties of Religious Experience: A Study in Human Nature* (New York: Modern Library, 1902), pp. 359–61, emphasis mine.

60. [Statement of] H.G. Wells, *I Believe: The Personal Philosophies of Certain Eminent Men and Women of Our Time*, ed. Clifton Fadiman (New York: Simon & Schuster, 1939), pp. 421–22, emphasis mine.

61. Throughout this consideration of surplus I have drawn heavily upon Rubenstein's *Cunning of History*, a remarkable study; the quotation here is from that work, p. 86.

62. Ibid., p. 96.

63. Allen Pifer, *Perceptions of Childhood and Youth*, Report of the President, Carnegie Corporation of New York, 1978, pamphlet, p. 9; Joseph Featherstone, review of *Children and Youth in America*, in *Harvard Educational Review* 44 (February 1974): 163; Joan Lipsitz, *Growing Up Forgotten* (Lexington, Mass.: D.C. Heath, 1977), p. xvi; Peter N. Stearns, "The Fading of Youth," *Newsweek*, July 23, 1979, p. 15. Stearns's observations relate particularly to the "larger decline in our belief in progress, change, and education" (p. 15).

64. Albert O. Hirschman, *Exit, Voice, and Loyalty: Responses to Decline in Firms, Organizations, and States* (Cambridge, Mass.: Harvard University Press, 1970), pp. 5–15.

65. Quoted in Mildred George Goertzel et al., *Three Hundred Eminent Personalities* (San Francisco: Jossey–Bass, 1978), p. 342.

66. Pifer, *Perceptions of Childhood*, p. 7.

67. Ibid., p. 10; also see Edgar Z. Friedenberg, "Children as Objects of Fear and Loathing," *Educational Studies* 10 (1979): 63–75.

68. Barnet and Muller, *Global Reach*, pp. 377, 387, and ch. 13.

69. Rothman, "State as Parent," p. 95.

# 2 THE EVOLVING POLITICAL STRUCTURE OF AMERICAN SCHOOLING

*Joel Spring*

Fear of government-operated schools as an instrument of control and domination was often expressed by the ideologists of the American Revolution. The concern was that those who controlled the state would use government-operated schools to teach political and social ideas that would perpetuate their power. By the middle of the nineteenth century this argument was forgotten as the champions of the common school movement argued that local control with democratic elections would keep government schools from becoming instruments of power and ideological control. But there were inherent problems in that argument which have increased in the twentieth century as state and federal governments extended their power over local educational systems. This paper proposes to examine the phenomenon of government-operated schools as an instrument of state control and focuses specifically on the shifting mechanisms of control from the early nineteenth century to the present.

The critical issue lies in discerning whether or not the shifting patterns of control of government schools in the United States have resulted in the schools functioning as instruments of control and domination of the intellectual life of the nation. On the surface this would *not* appear to be the case because federal and state intervention has been justified in terms of correcting discriminatory actions by local school systems against minority groups and the poor. What should be noted about this justification for federal and state intervention into local schools is that the intervention itself is an admission that the political structure of local school systems did, in fact, result in one group using the schools as an instrument of control and power over another group. The most obvious example has been the segregation of minority groups within school systems and the providing of unequal educational opportunities.

If local schools systems have functioned in this manner, what can be said about the present political arrangements in education? To answer this question this essay will first explore the original objections to government-operated schools and then trace the history of the shifting patterns of political control to the present time. The concluding section argues that the present control of education has resulted in an educational ideology which, while sometimes operating in subtle ways, still is part of a more general political philosophy that justifies the continuation of bureaucratic control under different banners. In other words, those who control the schools use the schools to perpetuate an ideology which justifies their control.

## THE AMERICAN REVOLUTION AND THE FEAR OF IDEOLOGICAL DOMINATION

Freedom of speech and thought was of primary concern in the many pamphlets written and distributed in England and the American colonies before the Revolution.[1] It was these pamphlets that provided the intellectual justification for the Revolution and for the first time in Western history presented the argument that the progress of society depended upon freedom from government intervention in the control of ideas and their expression. Freedom of the press, assembly, and speech were considered essential for the establishment of a libertarian society.

As part of this belief in the necessity of freedom of ideas was a fear that the establishment of government-operated schools would seriously abridge the free development of ideas. One of the earliest statements of this concern can be found in Robert Molesworth's *An Account of Denmark as It Was in the Year 1692*. The theme also appeared in the work of two of Molesworth's friends, John Trenchard and Thomas Gordon. They wrote a series of essays in London in the 1720s that became known on both sides of the Atlantic as *Cato's*

*Letters.* It was *Cato's Letters*, which circulated through the coffee houses in England and the colonies, that provided the popular justification and intellectual underpinnings of the American Revolution. As Bernard Bailyn, the famous historian of the intellectual origins of the American Revolution, has written: "So popular and influential had *Cato's Letters* become in the colonies within a decade and a half of their appearance, so packed with ideological meaning, that . . . it gave rise to what might be called a 'Catonic' image, central to the political theory of the time. . . ."[2]

Molesworth linked the problem of government schools to the relationship between religion and government. In these terms, separation of church and state also meant separation of schools from the state. In his study of tyranny in Denmark he identified as a key element in the perpetuation of existing power the gaining of absolute obedience of the people by the operation of schools by state-supported religious groups. Molesworth argued that these religious groups preached and taught a doctrine of submission and obedience to both heavenly and earthly rulers.

Molesworth wrote: "'tis plain, the education of Youth, on which is laid the very Foundation Stones of the Publick Liberty, has been of late years committed to the sole management of such as make it their business to undermine it. . . ." In this context the problem was that the schoolmasters or religious orders served primarily the interests of those in control of the government. Or, as he stated: "enslaving the Spirits of the People, as preparative to that of their Bodies; . . . those Foreign Princes think it their Interest that Subjects should obey without reserve, and all Priests, who depend upon the Prince, are for their own sakes obliged to promote what he esteems his Interest." Molesworth believed that the primary thing that schools under a tyranny taught was obedience to the state and authority. The major service that religion through education of youth performed for the state was "to recommend frequently to them what they call the Queen of all virtues, Viz. Submission to Superiors, and an entire blind Obedience to Authority. . . ."[3]

John Trenchard and Thomas Gordon in *Cato's Letters* gave a broader defense of freedom of ideas and learning by declaring them essential for the economic and social development of a nation. In making the link between social progress and freedom, they were able to give their defense in concrete terms rather than in an appeal to abstract justice. They argued that a country needed freedom because without freedom there would be no growth in human wisdom and invention and, consequently, no progress in economic development. Tyranny and slavery stopped social development and improvement in human well-being whereas freedom and liberty led humans down the road of progress and happiness. They wrote: "Without Freedom, there can be no such thing as Wisdom; and no such Thing as public Liberty, without Freedom of Speech: Which is the Right of every Man, as far as by it he does not hurt and control the Right of another. . . ."[4]

In this context freedom of thought and speech was essential for the general well-being and progress of society. This meant an absolute and not a selective freedom of thought because knowledge was so complex that no person or groups of persons could determine before the investigation what areas of thought should be limited. "The least Cramp or Restrain upon Reasoning and Inquiry of any kind," they wrote, "will soon a mighty Bar in the Way of Learning."[5]

There is a short passage in *Cato's Letters* which gives a forceful summary of what the authors considered as the interrelationship among freedom, liberty, and prosperity and considered in opposite terms, tyranny, slavery, and misery. "Ignorance accompanies Slavery, and is introduced by it. People who live in Freedom will think with Freedom; but when the Mind is enslaved by fear, and the Body by Chains, Inquiry and Study will be at an End." In this condition *Cato's Letters* claimed: "Men will not pursue dangerous knowledge, nor venture their Heads, to improve their Understandings. Besides, their Spirits, dejected with Servitude and Poverty, will want vigor . . . to . . . propagate Truth; which is ever High-Treason against Tyranny."[6]

As this libertarian tradition evolved in the seventeenth century, concern about freedom of thought and expression became specifically linked to opposition to government-operated schools. The most famous representatives of this libertarian tradition were Joseph Priestley, William Godwin, Matthew Boulton, James Watt, Erasmus Darwin, Samuel Galton, and Josiah Wedgewood.[7] These were men whose ideas, inventions and technological developments sparked the industrial revolution and increased interest in the application of science to the improvement of the human condition.

One of the clear and often stated concerns of this group was government systems of education. Education historian Brian Simon has written with regard to Priestley and this group of intellectuals: "In common with Godwin, however, and indeed all other dissenters, Priestley was adamantly opposed to education becoming a function of the state. Should it do so, it would not achieve the object he desired, on the contrary, it would be used to promote uniformity of thought and belief. . . ." The same regard for the importance of intellectual freedom permeated the thinking of this group as it had that of the previous generation of libertarians. Priestley declared: "Let all friends of liberty and human nature join to free the minds of men from the shackles of narrow and impolitic laws. Let us be free ourselves and leave the blessings of freedom to our prosperity."[8]

Historian Caroline Robbins summarizes Priestley's feelings regarding state provided education: "The chief glory of human nature, the operation of reason in a variety of ways and with diversified results would be lost. Every man should educate his children in his own manner to preserve the balance which existed among the several religious and political parties in Great Britain."[9]

Priestley's friend, William Godwin, considered national systems of education one of the foremost dangers to freedom and liberty. Godwin argued that the two main objects of human power were government and education. Of these two, education was the most powerful because "government must always depend upon the opinion of the governed. Let the most oppressed people under heaven once change their mode of thinking and they are free." If individuals can control the opinion of the people through education then they can control government. If education is made a function of government, then those who control government can use education to maintain and strengthen their control. Godwin gave warning to his generation and future generations in his study of government, *Enquiry Concerning Political Justice* (1793): "before we put so powerful a machine under the direction of so ambiguous an agent, it behooves us to consider well what it is that we do. Government will not fail to employ it, to strengthen its hands, and perpetuate its institutions."[10]

The writings of Godwin and Priestley contained the two major concerns that the libertarians of the eighteenth century had with government-operated schools. The first was that government schools would create a uniformity of thought that would hinder the evolution of science, technology, and political and social ideas. In this context, they believed that government-operated schools would slow the progress of society and the welfare of humanity. And, second, there was a fear that government-operated schools would teach a political orthodoxy that would be used as an instrument of political power.

## THE RISE OF THE COMMON SCHOOL

At the conclusion of the American Revolution there was no rush to establish government-operated systems of education. In fact, the common school movement, which is most often considered as the beginning of the present system of public schools in the United States did not occur until the 1820s and 1830s. There did exist at the time of the Revolution government systems of schooling in some of the colonies. The most famous of these was in Massachusetts, which had its origins in the early days of the colony in the sixteenth century. The schools in Massachusetts represent exactly what ideologists of the Revolution objected to in government-operated schools. The schools stressed a religious and moral orthodoxy and were designed to produce citizens who would be obedient to both the government and the Church. The most famous text in these New England schools was the *New England Primer*, a catechism and collection of moral homilies to be memorized by the student.[11]

There were proposals for government-operated schools at the end of the Revolution, but these proposals, except for those of Thomas Jefferson, emphasized the creation of a political and moral orthodoxy. These proposals reflected a concern with limiting freedom by controlling individual conscience. The most famous of these proposals were by Noah Webster and Benjamin Rush.

Noah Webster, the often-called schoolmaster of America, wanted to use education to stabilize the political system and to create a sense of nationalism. Both goals involved an emphasis upon the teaching of a political orthodoxy. This orthodoxy can be found in the pages of his famous *Blue-Backed Speller* completed in 1783, which sold one-and-a-half million copies by 1801, twenty million by 1829, and seventy-five million by 1875.[12] Webster's thinking on education was in sharp contrast to the freedom of thought emphasized by the libertarian tradition. He wrote: "good republicans . . . are formed by a singular machinery in the body politic, which takes the child as soon as he can speak, checks his natural independence and passions, makes him subordinate to superior age, to the laws of the state, to town and parochial institutions."[13] His spelling book contained a "Federal

Catechism" which required the memorization of specific answers to questions, such as "What are the defects of democracy?" The child was to memorize the answer: "In democracy, where the people all meet for the purpose of making laws, there are commonly tumults and disorders. . . . Therefore a pure democracy is generally a very bad government. . . ."[14]

Benjamin Rush shared the same desire to use government schools as a means of imposing a republican orthodoxy on future generations. In language which stressed submission and molding, he proposed that schools produce what he called "republican machines." He wrote: "Let our pupil be taught that he does not belong to himself, but that he is public property. Let him be taught to love his family, but let him be taught at the same time that he must forsake and even forget them when the welfare of his country requires it." For Rush good citizenship meant obedience to the law or as he explained in regard to the education of youth, "the authority of our masters be as absolute as possible. . . . By this mode of education, we prepare our youth for the subordination of laws and thereby qualify them for becoming good citizens of the republic."[15]

Thomas Jefferson was the other writer who, immediately after the Revolution, proposed a state system of education. But his proposals were different from those of Rush and Webster and did not reflect the moral orthodoxy of the Massachusetts school system. He proposed only that all children should receive three years of free education in reading, writing, and arithmetic and that political values were to be formed by the reading of a free press, for Jefferson was primarily concerned about using a system of schooling to select future republican leaders who would be sent on for college training. But even in this proposal he could not resist the temptation of assuring some form of political orthodoxy. Jefferson proposed to censor and control the political texts at the University of Virginia. His fear here was the possible teaching of his political enemy, federalism. He wrote, in reference to federalism: "It is our duty to guard against such principles being disseminated among our youth, and the diffusion of that position, by a previous prescription of the texts to be followed in their discourses."[16] Therefore, even Jefferson could not resist the temptation of using an educational system to perpetuate what he considered to be political truth. This was precisely what the libertarians had been warning against with regard to government-operated schools.

The legacy of the Massachusetts schools and the writings of people like Noah Webster and Benjamin Rush provided the backdrop for the common school movement of the 1820s and 1830s. It remained for this movement to receive its greatest impetus from Horace Mann, a former Calvinist-turned-phrenologist and lawyer-turned-educator. Mann served as secretary of the Massachusetts Board of Education in the 1830s and 1840s, and his reports to the board are considered the major ideological justification of the common school movement. When he left his law office for the schoolhouse, it was in pursuit of a utopian dream. He believed that government schools could shape the child into a moral and social creature whose actions would be free from conflict and evil intent. Mann wanted to create the good society not by changing its structure but by reforming the individual.

The theme that runs throughout Mann's writings is the necessity of creating a political community. From his perspective the greatest dangers faced by the United States were political strife resulting from universal suffrage and the struggle between social classes. He hoped to overcome the dangers of possible social class conflict by mixing the children of the rich and the poor in the same schoolhouse and using education to provide equality of opportunity. Education was to be the great balance wheel of society. The mixture of social classes in the schoolroom was to reduce the animosity between the social classes while equality of opportunity was to reduce the rigidity of the class structure.[17]

The political community was to be created by the mixing of all social groups in the schoolhouse and the teaching of common moral and political doctrines. The common school was to be common in the sense that all people attended and all were taught a common ideology. But in teaching a common moral and political doctrine, Mann was faced with the problem of differing religious and political opinions. He knew that if the schoolhouse became the center of religious and political strife that it would not survive. His solution was to teach only those political principles that all good republicans would agree upon and moral principles common to all religions. He warned teachers to avoid the discussion and teaching of any controversial doctrines.

Mann's solution was practical when one considers the problems of operating a government school in a democratic society where supposedly all citizens participate in governing. Any institution in this situation must steer a safe, middle course through the different waves of political and religious conflict. The practical merged with his dream of building a political community by creating a consensus of values that would hold society together as religious arguments and political debates continued. Political and religious strife was never to be great enough to tear society apart because of the consensus of values.

Mann's dreams, however, contained two major unresolved problems. One was that the practical solution of steering a safe, middle course could mean stripping political teachings of all content. As we shall see later, this continues to be one of the common complaints of contemporary political scientists, who argue that the schools are producing graduates who do not participate in the political process and have no awareness of major political issues and ideas.

The second problem focused upon who or what mechanism was to be used to determine common moral and political principles. In this regard, the political structure of education becomes the determining force. Obviously, if there really exist common principles shared by all people, then it is not necessary to have the schools teach them. If, on the other hand, one says that people should have common principles, then it is implied that people do not share common principles and that the schools will make some particular set of values common. In this case the political structure of the schools will determine what political and moral values will be taught as common values.

Yet the common school ideology, as exemplified by Mann, was only one force at work during the embryonic stage of development of government-operated schools in the United States. The other major force in creating common schools was a working-class movement for free government schooling in both England and the United States. It is important to understand that the goals of this movement were different from those of educational reformers like Horace Mann. The workers wanted the schools to provide them with the intellectual tools to gain power as opposed to the emphasis upon the schools teaching a common ideology.[18]

One of the interesting aspects of this popular movement for education by workers and the poor was that in England it opposed central government control of schooling, and in the United States it supported local control. The English working-class movement placed great stress on the importance of a free press as a means of education along with schools run by working-class organizations. English historian Harold Silver has written: "Education, for the working class political reformers, meant political education; the fight for education meant the fight for a free press and for parliamentary representation; the fight against ignorance meant the fight against the newspaper tax."[19] It was believed that government taxes on newspapers were making them too expensive for the poor and that the lack of cheap newspapers and not the lack of schools was retarding the political education of the working class.

Simon has summarized the feelings of the working-class movement in England in the 1830s: "education must be unsectarian, and, to prevent it being used to enhance the power of a despotic central government, it must be under the control of directly elected local representatives." Simon points out that there were objections within the working-class movement to the idea that education could teach political rights before the working class had actually gained all their rights. One working-class writer warned in 1838 that "any system of education which meets with the acquiescence of their foes, will have for its object the perpetuation of the people's slavery."[20]

The working-class campaigns for education in the United States in the 1820s and 1830s are often hailed as the beginning of a democratic theory of education. The theory is considered democratic because it saw public schools teaching people their political rights and arming them against the state and because the political control of schooling was to be in the hands of local people. It was to be working-class people through local control of the schools who were to determine the ideological content of schooling.[21]

Yet, as we shall see below, working-class control of education never became a reality. In fact, by the twentieth century labor unions were complaining that the schools were teaching an antiunion and antiradical political and economic philosophy.[22] It should also be noted that at least one historian believes that this was the only time in the nineteenth century that educational policies were influenced by a popular movement as opposed to being imposed by those in control of the educational structure. Silver considers the working-class movements of the 1830s the "only time when the popular movement came near to shaping educational provisions from below in the emergence of mass education in the nineteenth century. . . ."[23]

Besides the common school movement and the working-class campaigns for education, there were other internal reforms in schools that made possible the extension of the government school monopoly. One of the most important factors in creating a government school monopoly was the provision of free education for all children. The provision of free education was one of the important goals of the working-class movement in the 1820s and 1830s. This goal was based on the assumption of working-class control of the financial resources through local control of the schools. But if the working class did not control the schools, it would mean that they would be taxed to support an educational system which taught an ideology that was contradictory to their beliefs.

The importance of the free school issue can best be exemplified by considering some of the historical alternatives. First, government schools could have been provided without making them free. In this situation, all users would pay full cost. This would have meant that government schools would have been forced to compete with private or nongovernment schools. And, second, government schools could have been made free for only those who could not afford to pay full-cost tuition. A sliding tuition scale could have been used based on the income of the user. This situation is in contrast to the present method where those who can afford to pay full tuition receive a free government education.

The second alternative was in fact the method in practice during the first part of the nineteenth century in the form of rate bills where parents were charged a tuition to attend government schools based on their income. Historian and economist E.G. West has investigated the shift from rate bills to free public schooling in New York in the 1840s and has concluded that it benefited primarily the teachers and administrators who worked for government-operated schools. Now, it is important to remember that the issue was not free schooling for the poor who received it with rate bills but free schooling for all.[24]

West's argument is important in terms of later developments in the twentieth century. He is able to identify the early role of the professional educator in the political structure of education and also the economic advantages to some professional educators in the existence of a tax-supported free government school monopoly. West found in his investigation of the shift from rate bills to free schooling that professional educators objected to the collecting of payments from parents because it often caused a delay in paying teachers' salaries. He found that the actions of these professional educators fit an economic theory of democracy where those in the service of government tend to try to maximize their benefits on policies regarding their incomes. In West's words, the educator "may be prompted by the desire to help others as well as by the desire to help himself and his family. . . . And what people do is a better guide than what they say." West argues that there was no proof that free government schools would create public benefits like political stability and improved public morality. These arguments for government schooling and free tuition were rationalizations for an attempt to improve the economic advantage of those employed in government schools. West writes: "The suppliers of educational services to the government, the teachers and administrators, as we have seen, had produced their own organized platforms by the late 1840s; it was they indeed who were the leading instigators of the free school campaign."[25]

West believes that the interest of professional educators in government service was enhanced by the elimination of the problem of salaries dependent on the collection of rate bills and by the creation of a monopoly situation. Free government schools made it difficult for private schools to exist because even with rate bills, there was still some option available to parents to choose private schooling. With compulsory taxation providing free schools, private schools were hard-pressed to compete. As West demonstrates, the creation of free government schools led to a rapid decline in the number of private schools. It also turned private schools that had served a wide variety of the population into schools which primarily served the rich, who could afford to pay educational taxes and private school tuition.

The government school system that emerged from the common school campaign, the political actions of working-class parties, and the free school movement all tried to overcome the concern about ideological control as it was expressed in the eighteenth century by emphasizing local control of the schools. This political structure for education was supposed to avoid the dangers of providing a single institution with the power of transmission of political, economic, and social knowledge.

But local control of government schools, even if it were to survive, did not completely answer the problem of ideological domination. As even the working class was to learn, local control did not always work in their interests. For unions, local control in the nineteenth and first half of the twentieth century often meant that schools taught an antiunion philosophy. Even in the context of the common

school concern with teaching a common ideology, there was a problem of majority determination of what should be taught. Local control could mean that minority views would be suppressed by the control of the majority. In fact, the very growth of the Catholic school
system was a result of the feeling that a majority view of religion
and morality was being imposed through government schools that
was in opposition to the minority beliefs of Catholics.[26] Certainly,
majority determination of what political doctrines should be taught
as the common ideology could have a stultifying effect on the whole
evolution of political ideas. The concern with majority determination
of what should be taught in government schools began to lose meaning by the 1890s as local control began to mean elite control and
professional educators gained a stronger hand over the system.

## ELITE AND PROFESSIONAL CONTROL
## OF GOVERNMENT SCHOOLS

The political transformation of the schools in the latter nineteenth
and early twentieth centuries has been well documented during the
last decade by a variety of historians.[27] While there is disagreement
about the causes of the changes, there is no disagreement about the
nature of the structural changes. If one were to portray the range of
interpretations of these changes, they would be between a desire of a
powerful economic elite to use the schools for their own purposes to
a desire by a well-intentioned reform group to correct real problems
in the schools.

But no matter what the real causes were, the consequences were
structural changes which affected the nature of democratic participation in the schools and strengthened the role of professional educators. The story of these changes was similar from city to city. It
usually began with complaints that the schools were being used by
political groups or parties to dispense favors and strengthen political
power. The appointment of teachers and school administrators and
the awarding of school contracts, it was argued, were based on political affiliation or support. It was declared that the schools were being
victimized by political machines. The resulting reform cry was "Get
the schools out of politics!" by making school board elections nonpartisan and school boards small. These two changes had very important consequences for the meaning of local control of the schools.

First, consider the consequences of reducing the size of school boards. In most cities, members were elected from local wards or districts to school boards that ranged in size from about twenty to forty. Election by ward or district made it possible for a larger number of the population to run for the school board as opposed to running on a citywide basis. It took fewer financial resources to campaign in the limited geographical area of a ward or district as opposed to campaigning in an entire city. Also, election by ward or district made it possible for candidates to relate to their constituency on a more personal basis.

When school boards were made small, the method of election shifted from ward or district to citywide. This meant that the possibility of running for the school board was reduced for most citizens because candidates needed greater resources to conduct citywide campaigns. It also meant that school board members would represent the interests of citizens throughout the city rather than the interests of the citizens in a specific neighborhood. In concrete terms this meant a reduction of control of the average citizen over school policies because of the reduced possibilities of being on the school board or having one's interests represented on the school board.

Second, making school board elections nonpartisan eliminated the use of the machinery of political parties for nominating school board candidates and conducting campaigns. This vacuum was often filled by the very reform groups that worked for nonpartisan elections. These groups began to nominate candidates and conduct election campaigns. In some cities these organizations were formed by the participation of service clubs like the Chamber of Commerce, Rotary, and other social service organizations. The result was that school boards began to be dominated by elite members of the community. They were the ones that could afford to conduct citywide campaigns and who generally belonged to the new civic groups that replaced the political parties in the new nonpartisan elections. Every study of the social composition of school boards done in the twentieth century has found that in real terms they do not represent the social composition of the community but are primarily upper-income business or professional people.[28]

As these structural changes turned the meaning of local control into control by a community elite, professional educators began to demand greater control over the internal workings of school systems. Again the change was justified in terms of getting the schools out of politics. It was argued that elected school board members represented political concerns whereas school people represented the children or students. School administrators and teachers were pictured as disinterested professionals whose sole goal in life was to serve students. For school people, getting education out of politics meant putting it in the hands of professionals.

The model adopted by school administrators around the country was that of a corporation where the superintendent was managing head and the board of education represented company stockholders.[29] There was to be a clear distinction between the administrative staff and the board of education. Functions that had been the means to board of education control in the nineteenth century became administrative functions in the twentieth century. Probably the three most important functions in terms of influence over the ideology and quality of schooling were selection of textbooks, examination and licensing of teachers, and annual examination of students by members of the board of education.[30]

Obviously, the creation of small school boards, particularly in urban areas, resulted in a reduction of the actual tasks that could be performed by school board members. There were not enough members to participate in all the activities that had been the traditional functions of the school board. In addition, these new elite members were often busy professional or business people who were used to distributing work to an administrative staff. Therefore, the development of small school boards, coupled with a desire by educational administrators to gain control, resulted in a decline of power by school boards over local school systems. By the 1930s there were even suggestions that school boards should be eliminated. The very prominent professor of education Charles Judd argued that school boards blocked important educational reforms and were often tools of political bosses. He suggested that "a movement to abolish schools boards is in order and should be supported by all who believe in the simplification of government and in reliance on experts." Judd's colleague at the University of Chicago, political science professor Charles Merriam, supported Judd's approach to government with the argument that the professionalization of all administrative services of government would create a new era of political competence.[31]

As administrative power expanded in the schools, the development of curricula, the testing of students, and the selection of teachers became primarily a function of educational experts. The role of the school usually became that of approving decisions made by the administrative staff. The government of schools became a government of expert managers who were trained and licensed in colleges of education. It should be emphasized that educators like Judd argued that administrative control was preferable to democratic control.

The increased involvement of state governments in education also caused a diminution of local governing powers and an expansion of control by professional educators. Although state power expanded into areas of curriculum, the most interesting area, and possibly the most important in terms of quality of schooling, was the development of state licensing of teachers. The history of state licensing of teachers has varied from state to state, but it did become a function of most state governments by the 1930s and was generally made a function of course work in colleges of education as opposed to licensing by examination.

The licensing of teachers at the state level had important consequences for increasing the power of colleges of education. Traditionally, the selection of teachers by a local system required some form of examination by the local school board regarding knowledge of subject matter and ability to teach. Very often local school boards administered their own written examinations. This form of local licensing, while often including requirements for training in pedagogy, was primarily based on demonstrable knowledge and skills.[32] The transfer of licensing to the state level resulted in an emphasis on course work; a college degree and so many courses in education became the usual means of getting a license. This meant that it was to the advantage of colleges of education constantly to lobby at the state level to expand requirements in training in courses in professional education.

## THE IDEOLOGY OF PROFESSIONAL
## AND ELITE CONTROL

The changes that occurred in the political structure of education in the twentieth century were accompanied by a transformation of the basic goals of government schools and an ideology which justified the new goals and political structure. It will be argued later in the chapter that it is precisely this ideology which students in today's schools are being trained to accept.

The two key components of the new political ideology was that government should be controlled by expert managers and that equality of opportunity should be a function of the school rather than a function of the marketplace. These two things changed the meaning of citizenship from one that emphasized political power and rights to one that emphasized social cooperation and working for the public good. In the context of the new political ideology, social cooperation meant working well with others under the control of expert managers who would define the public good.

The most revealing document of this new political ideology in education was the 1918 report *Cardinal Principles of Secondary Education* by the National Education Association. This report was important not only for the ideology it expressed but also for its definition of the role of the high school in the twentieth century; it influenced the development of the high school as an institution for managing equality of opportunity. The *Cardinal Principles* report stated: "The purpose of democracy is so to organize society that each member may develop his personality primarily through activities designed for the well-being of fellow members and of society as a whole." This was a definition of the purpose of democracy which stressed the social organization of society and not the provision of political power and rights. It also stressed that citizenship was working for the public good. Consistent with this definition of the purpose of democracy, the report stated: "education in a democracy . . . should develop in each individual the knowledge, interests, ideals, habits, and powers whereby he will find his place and use that place to shape both himself and society toward ever nobler ends."[33]

The actual transformation of the high school outlined in the *Cardinal Principles* matched its definition of the purpose of democracy and a democratic education. The major change in the educational purposes of government schools in the twentieth century was the assumption of management of human resources. This meant the identification of individual aptitudes and interests in terms of the occupational needs of society, the separation of students into different curricula and ability groups in terms of some future occupational destination, and the creation of educational programs to meet social needs.

The means of accomplishing these goals were vocational guidance, standardized testing for interests and abilities, and the expansion of vocational education. These new developments, along with the restructuring of the high school, were to turn the educational system into one designed to shape individual talent in the schools to meet the needs of the labor market. This is what the *Cardinal Principles* meant by "he will find his place. . . ." Of course, it was to be the professional educator armed with the expert skills of testing and curriculum planning who was to guide the individual into his or her proper place in society. In this context a democracy was a social system, which, by allowing individual talent to match the needs of the occupational structure, created a more efficient social organization. This was the argument for equality of opportunity that had been inherited from the nineteenth century but given a new twist in the context of democracy viewed as a managed social system.

In the nineteenth century, equality of opportunity was to be a function of competition in the marketplace with education helping people to compete. In the twentieth century, equality of opportunity had been brought under the management of educational experts with equality of opportunity becoming a function of the internal workings of the school. With the transformation of the school, students no longer graduate with equal educations which allow them equal opportunity to compete in the labor market. With vocational guidance, vocational education, and the separation of students into different curriculum tracks, students graduate with unequal educations.

What equality of opportunity has come to mean is that the school should provide an equal chance for students to choose an education which leads to a particular job. Making equality of opportunity a function of the internal workings of schooling, as opposed to the marketplace, was and is justified as being fairer by allowing for more equality of opportunity. It was and is claimed that teacher ratings, vocational guidance, and standardized tests can provide equality of opportunity by placing a student in a program on the basis of ability as opposed to social background.

There was another idea in the *Cardinal Principles'* definition of the purpose of democracy and an education in a democracy. This was that each member should use his or her place in society "to shape both himself and society toward ever nobler ends." This was at the heart of the problem faced by the writers of the report. The problem was how to provide an education which trained people for specialized slots in society and at the same time developed a sense of social cooperation. The *Cardinal Principles* report resolved this problem by arguing that the separation of students into separate curricula based on their future occupational destinations should take place in a social setting which emphasized cooperation and group activities. The report argued that extracurricular activities like sports, clubs, student government, student newspapers, and assemblies should be the means for bringing all students together to develop a sense of social cooperation and a desire to work for the good of the social whole.

This was the transformation of the goals of the school which accompanied the transformation of the political structure of schooling. In most cases, the transformation conformed to the desires of the elite members of the school boards who wanted a disciplined and trained force.[34] It also justified the increased power of professional educators who were to command the supposedly scientific tools that would select and train students for the labor market.

The doctrine of equality of opportunity also helped to legitimize the increased power of professional educators by allowing them to claim to be the friend of the poor. It was the school that was supposedly going to find individual talent among the poor and promote them through the social system. It was the professional educator armed with scientific techniques who was going to help the poor by overcoming the effects of social background and the marketplace. Government school people would now wave the flag of helping the poor whenever the schools came under attack.

## DEVELOPMENT OF FEDERAL CONTROL OF EDUCATION

It was precisely because elite and professional control of education resulted in discrimination against the poor and minorities and a decline in the quality of schooling that the federal government began to expand its power over education in the decades following World War II. This did not mean an end to the doctrine of equality of opportunity and government by bureaucratic experts but an assumption of these goals by a higher level of government.

Two major reports published after World War II identified the central problems in educational policy for the next three decades. One was a sociological study by A. B. Hollingshead, *Elmtown's Youth* (1949), which provided the basis for future studies on the discriminatory nature of American schooling. *Elmtown's Youth* described the social life of adolescents in a small town in Indiana. What the study found in terms of local high schools was that the separation of students by curriculum tracks paralleled the socioeconomic status of the students. Rather than the high school functioning as a means of upward mobility, it was perpetuating and reinforcing social class differences.[35] This argument set the stage for federal intervention in the 1960s in the form of the War on Poverty.

The other study was Vannevar Bush's *Science—The Endless Frontier*, which had been written at the request of President Roosevelt and was issued in 1945 after the president's death. The purpose of the study was to outline federal science policy for the postwar years. One of its major proposals was to increase scientific manpower by supporting student interest in science and mathematics and by influencing local school curricula. One of the results of the report was the inclusion of these goals in the establishment of the National Science Foundation in 1950.[36]

*Science—The Endless Frontier* and the National Science Foundation became part of the Cold War policy of the United States. The key was getting the schools to produce enough scientists and engineers to win the technological race. Within this framework, Cold War policy became the major determiner of federal educational policy. The stress in the 1950s was not on how well the schools were winning the race with the Soviet Union but how the schools were failing to equip students with needed intellectual skills. Early in the 1950s history professor Arthur Bestor declared the schools to be antiintellectual and educational wastelands. Bestor went on to organize scholars into the Council for Basic Education to work for the establishment of intellectual rigor in the public schools. Hyman Rickover declared across the land that the schools were the weakest link in our defense against the Soviet Union. And Richard Hofstadter identified the schools as one of the central sources of antiintellectualism in American life.[37]

Critics of the 1950s were almost unanimous in identifying the villain as the professional educator, who, trained in the antiintellectual environment of colleges of education, went forth into the schools and turned teaching and curricula into studies of personal problems rather than of traditional intellectual problems. The Council for Basic Education believed that the only way to restore intellectual rigor to the schools was to take control of the curriculum from the hands of professional educators and give it to scholars in particular subject matter areas. Rickover believed that by their control of curricula and teacher certification laws, professional educators were bringing America to its knees before a superior Russian educational system.[38]

The attack on the schools and professional educators provided the backdrop for the first major federal intervention in the schools in the form of the National Defense Education Act of 1958 (NDEA). Although in previous years the federal government had been indirectly involved in the schools, the NDEA was the first major step in attempting directly to influence the curricula in local schools. It provided money specifically for foreign languages, science, mathematics, and vocational guidance and extra money to the National Science Foundation to develop and distribute new curricula to local school systems.[39]

One of the important features of the NDEA was the use of categorical funding as a means of controlling educational policy at the local level. In terms of the NDEA, categorical funding was considered a means of circumventing and overcoming control by professional educators. Throughout the 1950s educators had been asking for federal money to solve a severe financial crisis in local school systems. But their pleas were for general federal funds for salaries or buildings with actual determination of how the money would be spent left in the hands of local school systems.

This was precisely what the NDEA rejected. During congressional hearings on the NDEA, supporters stressed that the money should be earmarked for special categories like mathematics and science rather than its use being determined by professional educators. On the other hand, educators decried the development of federal control over local school systems. During the congressional hearings, William Carr, executive secretary of the National Education Association, bitterly opposed the passage of the NDEA because of its use of categorical funds, and thus its influence on local educational policy.[40]

The NDEA established the precedent for future federal control of local educational policies through categorical funding. Local school systems would be in a constant need of extra money, and whenever the federal government established a new program, local school systems would rush to embrace those programs as a means of getting needed funds. The promise of money became a means of persuading local school districts to adopt federal educational policies. The NDEA also represented the greatest fears of eighteenth-century opponents of government schooling because it made national educational policy a function of America's foreign policy. Discrimination against minority groups and the poor also highlighted the concern about the use of government schools as instruments of domination.

Elite and professional control of local school systems had resulted in the creation of segregated, in terms of race and income, school systems in both the North and South. In the South, segregated education was viewed as the key to maintaining a segregated society and the economic exploitation of blacks. State laws in the South requiring segregated schools were an important means of assuring white racial domination. In the North, elite school boards drew school district lines so that the school population was divided by race and social class. Inside the schools, professional educators armed with standardized tests that were biased against minority groups and the poor divided students into curriculum tracks and ability groups.[41] As Hollingshead had found in *Elmtown's Youth*, the schools rather than providing the poor and minorities with upward mobility had begun to lock them in place. The claim that the school could be fairer than the marketplace in providing equality of opportunity turned out to be false as educators and school board members turned their prejudice into educational policy.

It is important to understand that the discriminatory actions of local school systems were legitimized by claims of scientific technique and equality of opportunity. The claim of being scientific masked the biased use of standardized tests to categorize students. The claim of providing equality of opportunity masked the dividing of students into different curriculum tracks according to socioeconomic background.[42]

A major step in attempting to stop the use of schools as a means of domination at the local level was the 1954 Supreme Court decision declaring school segregation unconstitutional and its subsequent decision giving power of enforcement to local federal district courts. One of the problems with this approach was that local courts were often dominated by the same types that were on local school boards. Consequently, school desegregation did not progress at a very rapid rate until the passage of the 1964 Civil Rights Act which established a new means of federal control of education.

Title VI of the 1964 Civil Rights Act provided for the withholding of federal funds from institutions found discriminating on the basis of race, color, or national origin. This meant that federal policy could be implemented by either the giving of money or the threat of withholding money. What gave teeth to the 1964 Civil Rights Act was the passage of the 1965 Elementary and Secondary Education Act, which provided funds to local school systems to wage a war on poverty. The threat of withholding these funds proved a powerful influence in bringing about school desegregation in the South.[43]

Federal financing of research and development in education was still another means of shaping local educational policy. Certainly, the production of new ideas and their application to educational policy can have a powerful influence. This is particularly true when money is provided for particular categories of research. Scholars will do work in those areas because of the availability of funding. This can shape the whole evolution of intellectual development. Federal planners were quite clear that they viewed the financing of research as a means of changing local educational policy. The federal task force report which was responsible for the research section of the Elementary and Secondary Education Act declared: "We must overhaul American education." The key to this overhaul was to be educational innovation resulting from federally sponsored research. The report stated: "We now know, beyond all doubt, that, educationally speaking, the old way of doing things will not solve our problems. We are going to have to shed outworn educational practices, dismantle outmoded educational facilities, and create a new and better learning environment."[44] By 1965 the federal government provided more than 71 percent of the money for educational research in the United States.[45]

That federally sponsored educational research was to be directed toward the fulfillment of federal educational policies became quite evident in the 1970s with the establishment of the National Institute of Education (NIE). The NIE was originally conceived, as one of its earliest proponents, Daniel P. Moynihan, stated: "To bring 'big' science to bear on education, especially the problem of low achievement among students from low-income families."[46] The NIE began to establish priority areas for educational research which reflected the more general direction of federal educational policy. For instance, in 1977 the proposed program activities for the NIE specified a priority to the area of study of the relationship between education and work. The plan states: "Activities in this area of long-standing concern to the public will help students (a) make better choices in their careers, (b) improve their mastery of skills to enter and progress in jobs, and (c) leave and re-enter occupational education throughout their lives."[47] The specification of particular areas of research became another means of indirect federal control.

Categorical funding, the threat of withholding federal funds for discriminatory actions, and the financing of research and development are the major means by which the federal government has regulated education at the local level. These are the means by which it has attempted to overcome the discriminatory domination by professional educators and elites at the local level and to fulfill the goals of national policy. In the 1950s the major concern was the Cold War. In the 1960s it was poverty and unemployment, which led to an emphasis upon educational policy in the War on Poverty programs. In the 1970s it was concern with unemployment that led to an emphasis in federal education policy on career and vocational education.

## CONCLUSION—THE IDEOLOGY OF FEDERAL CONTROL

Federal involvement in education after World War II did not produce a rejection of the ideology of equality of opportunity but instead was an attempt to correct the negative features of that ideology as it appeared at the local level. In fact, federal policies in the 1950s and 1970s gave stress to the industrial efficiency component of equality of opportunity. In the 1950s America's position in the Cold War was to be improved by the channeling of youth into science, engineering, and mathematics. Here was a direct attempt to match what were defined as the labor needs of the economy with educational programs and students selected to go through those programs. During the 1970s federal sponsorship of career education was to get children thinking about careers at even younger ages. In fact, it was proposed by Commissioner of Education Sidney Marland that children in kindergarten begin thinking about their education in terms of some future career.[48] Career education combined with expanding vocational education programs was to bring the schools into closer alignment with the needs of the labor market.

The other component of equality of opportunity, aiding the social mobility and improvement of the poor, was expressed by federal policies in the 1960s with the funding of compensatory education and programs like Head Start. This has remained a consistent strand of federal policies up to the present time. But like the equality of opportunity argument voiced at the beginning of the century, it was to take place within the school and not in the marketplace. The attempt to bring the school into closer relationship to the labor market and to provide more specialized vocational training has provided even more unequal education, since vocational students are not getting the same education as college preparatory students. Equality of opportunity has become even more a function of the internal workings of the school.

The justification for federal involvement in local education was not that local educational systems were dominated by professionals and elites but that they were not achieving the two goals of equality of opportunity. Federal involvement added a new layer of professional control and removed the schools even further from the democratic process as it had been originally envisioned in the nineteenth century. In fact, the 1965 Elementary and Secondary Education Act not only resulted in the expansion of the federal bureaucracy but also provided money for expanding departments of education at the state level.[49]

The professional experts moved into these new bureaucracies with the same hope as previous generations of professionals, that science and proper management would achieve the two goals of equality of opportunity. But this new breed of professionals brought with them a new set of skills which would make the schools even more undemocratic. In addition to previous reliance upon testing and curriculum design, this new generation became wedded to behavioral psychology and statistical methods. Management by behavioral objectives, teaching by behavioral objectives, evaluation by behavioral objectives, and planning by behavioral objectives became the methods that would typify the new professional in control. The key to the new system of control by professionals at the state and federal levels was to force local school systems to write objectives so that they could be evaluated and controlled.

The ideology of federal control included a belief that control of the system should be in the hands of scientific managers. Nowhere is this made clearer than in the community control-accountability controversy in the early 1970s. The community control movement began in the late 1960s among minority groups who believed that they could remove racism from the schools if they could control the selection of teachers, determine the curriculum, and choose learning materials. Obviously, the community control movement threatened the power that professional educators and elite school boards had achieved in these areas. In fact, it was teachers' unions which put up the greatest resistance to the community control movement.[50]

Professional educators responded to the democratic thrust of the community control movement by proposing public accountability as opposed to public control. The accountability movement in education gave professional educators the role of reporting to the public the results of schooling rather than having the public control schooling. In this context the relationship between the schools and the public was placed in the hands of school administrators who reported test results to the public rather than have the public control their actions.

The book that popularized the idea of accountability was Leon Lessinger's *Every Kid a Winner: Accountability in Education* (1970). Lessinger, a former associate commissioner of education, called for the establishment of public auditors who would be called into schools to provide for public accounting of a school system's accomplishments. The tenor of the book was reflected in the title of a subsection, "Accounting for Competence as Well as for Cash." The individuals who were to be in control of the accountability process were "educational engineers." The source of this new profession was, according to Lessinger, the type of research sponsored by the federal government. Lessinger wrote: "Thus, over the past decade, an increasing amount of money in education has gone to people with expertise in such fields as systems design and analysis (for 'management by objectives'), quality control, operations research, instructional technology, facilities design, performance contracting, and accomplishment auditing."[51]

Lessinger placed the community control issue between attempts by professional educators to protect their prerogatives and an attempt to "throw open the process of governance to a populist chaos in which every citizen claims expertise about election on the grounds of having gone through school or of having a child there."[52] He dismissed the democratic arguments of community control as leading to "populist chaos." Using a medical analogy, he saw a middle road between professional defensiveness and popular control. We respect the skills of a surgeon, he argued, and do not rush into an operating room demanding democratic control. On the other hand, a patient can complain about inadequate delivery of services and incompetent surgeons. The decision on how to correct these problems is left in the hands of the medical professional. Translated into educational terms, this meant that the professional educator had a duty to account to the public regarding educational achievements, and the public had the right to complain about those achievements and other problems. The solutions were to be in the hands of the professional.

Thus, the proper role of the nonprofessional in education was not to control but to complain about inadequate delivery of services. In Lessinger's words: "To a somewhat greater extent than in an operating room, these critics of the school may even have ideas about how the problem might be solved; but in each case the professional has to do the work himself. If a surgeon needed technical help, he would consult not a layman but a specialist."[53]

The ideology of elite professional control was part of the new educational research community which gave birth to Lessinger's "educational engineer." Richard Dershimer, former executive officer of the American Educational Research Association, candidly wrote: "Every research and development support program in education launched by the federal government was initiated by a small handful of persons, in other words, by a professional-bureaucratic complex."[54]

Dershimer's major concern was with the conflict between the federal bureaucrat and the professional researcher. Dershimer does not even consider democratic or popular control a meaningful issue. In fact, his resolution of the problem, as he defined it, was for the research community to become more political. While affirming his belief in elite professional control, he wrote: "We need to grow our own crop of bureaucrats who understand the value systems, the vicissitudes, the foibles, and the aspirations of researchers, but who develop a sympathy for and an understanding of the political world. Only then will we have the basis for developing a really effective R&D complex."[55]

The above illustrations demonstrate how increased federal involvement in education has reinforced the twentieth-century pattern of professional control and the use of education to promote industrial efficiency. One of the striking things about these discussions of why professionals should control education is the lack of consideration of the political content of schooling. It will be recalled that there was originally a concern about the use of the school as an instrument of political control by the teaching of a dominant political ideology. The new breed of educators give no consideration to this issue.

Professional control depends on a citizen who is apolitical and willing to accept a social system governed by expert managers. In this context, the dominant ideology of the schools becomes one of producing citizens who lack knowledge of the political system and of issues of political control and individual rights. A political system dominated by professionals and bureaucrats depends upon a citizenry which does not desire to exert political power and defines citizenship in terms of obedience to the law.

Studies of political socialization find that this is exactly what is happening in the schools. Schools are, in fact, producing apolitical citizens who have little knowledge of the exercise of political power. The majority of studies on political socialization have found that schools are producing students who define good citizenship as obedience to the law and who have little knowledge about the exercise of political power other than that of voting. Studies have shown a steady decline over the last decade in the political knowledge held by American youth. This is matched on the national scene by a steady decline in voter participation rates.[56] For instance, Lee Ehman writes that the National Assessment of Educational Progress shows for thirteen- to seventeen-year-old students "declines in knowledge, attitudes and participation" with regard to the political process.[57]

It is in this manner that the political structure of education is reproducing itself in the political values and attitudes of its products. The warning in the eighteenth century was that government schools would be used to maintain the power of those who controlled the government. Although there was hope that this problem could be solved through representation at the local level, those hopes were defeated with the rise of elite and professional control in the twentieth century. There was hope in the nineteenth century that education would prepare people to protect their democratic rights. Those hopes disappeared as elite and professional control gave schools the major task of promoting industrial efficiency through emphasis upon career and vocational training. The new political structure of education stripped the schools of meaningful political content and directed their purposes toward the production of apolitical citizens who would accept a managed political and social system.

The history of schools in the last two centuries brings into clearer focus the problem of government-operated schools in a free society. The concerns of the eighteenth century are justified by the events of the twentieth century. It is now important for society to consider whether or not it wants to continue with government-operated schools which are used to justify the power of those who control the schools. The lesson of history is that a free society needs a system of schooling which is free from the control of those who control the government. A free society cannot afford to let schooling become an instrument of power.

## NOTES TO CHAPTER 2

1.  For a detailed study of these pamphlets, see Bernard Bailyn, *The Ideological Origins of the American Revolution* (Cambridge, Mass.: Harvard University Press, 1967).
2.  Ibid., p. 44.
3.  Robert Molesworth, *An Account of Denmark as It Was in the Year 1692* (Copenhagen: Rosenkilde & Bagger, 1976); all quotations are taken from the preface, whose pages are not numbered.
4.  John Trenchard and Thomas Gordon, *Cato's Letters*, 6th ed. 1755, ed. Leonard Levy (New York: Da Capo Press, 1971), 1: 96.
5.  Ibid., 3: 33.
6.  Ibid., 3: 32.
7.  For a general description of this tradition, see Caroline Robbins, *The Eighteenth-Century Commonwealthman* (Cambridge, Mass.: Harvard University Press, 1959).
8.  Brian Simon, *Studies in the History of Education 1780–1870* (London: Lawrence & Winhart, 1960), pp. 34–35.
9.  Robbins, *Eighteenth-Century Commonwealthman*, p. 350.
10. In Joel Spring, *Primer of Libertarian Education* (New York: Free Life Editions, 1975), pp. 13–33.
11. Paul Leicester Ford, ed., *The New England Primer* (New York: Teachers College Press, 1962).
12. Harry Warfel, *Noah Webster: Schoolmaster to America* (New York: Macmillan, 1936), pp. 71–75.
13. Ibid., p. 21.
14. "Noah Webster's Federal Catechism (1978)," in *Education in the United States: A Documentary History*, ed. Sol Cohen (New York: Random House, 1974), pp. 769–71.

15.  Benjamin Rush, "Thoughts upon the Mode of Education Proper in a Republic," in *Essays on Education in the Early Republic*, ed. Fredrick Rudolph (Cambridge, Mass.: Harvard University Press, 1965), pp. 5–17.

16.  Thomas Jefferson, "To Joseph Cabell," in *Crusade Against Ignorance: Thomas Jefferson on Education*, ed. Gordon Lee (New York: Teachers College Press, 1961), p. 133.

17.  Lawrence Cremin, ed., *The Republic and the School: Horace Mann on the Education of Free Men* (New York: Teachers College Press, 1957).

18.  Rush, Welter, *Popular Education and Democratic Thought in America* (New York: Columbia University Press, 1962), p. 48.

19.  Harold Silver, *The Concept of Popular Education* (London: MacGibbon & Kee, 1965), p. 175.

20.  Simon, *Studies in the History of Education*, pp. 260, 268.

21.  Probably the best material on the Workingmen's movement is being gathered by Professor William Russell at the University of Louisville. He has found no emphasis on secularism, political rights, and control.

22.  See Joel Spring, *Education and the Rise of the Corporate State* (Boston: Beacon Press, 1972), pp. 126–48.

23.  Silver, *Concept of Popular Education*, p. 210.

24.  E.G. West, "The Political Economy of Public School Legislation," in *Studies in Education*, no. 4 (Menlo Park, Calif.: Institute of Humane Studies, 1977); originally published in *Journal of Law and Economics*, October 1967.

25.  Ibid., pp. 19, 20.

26.  See Vincent Lannie, *Public Money and Parochial Education: Bishop Hughes, Governor Seward, and the New York School Controversy* (Cleveland: Case Western Reserve University Press, 1968).

27.  The following books are in general agreement about the changes in the political structure of American education: Spring, *Education and the Rise*; Joseph Cronin, *The Control of Urban Schools* (New York: Free Press, 1973); and David Tyack, *The One Best System* (Cambridge, Mass.: Harvard University Press, 1974).

28.  The following are the major studies of the social composition of school boards from the early part of the century to 1980: Scott Nearing, "Who's Who in Our Boards of Education?" *School and Society* 5 (January 20, 1917): 89–90; George Counts, *The Social Composition of Boards of Education* (Chicago: University of Chicago Press, 1927); Harmon Zeigler and Kent Jennings, *Governing American Schools* (North Scituate, Mass.: Duxbury, 1974); and Kenneth Underwood et al., "Portrait of the American School Board Member," *American School Board Journal*, January 1980: 23–26.

29.  See Tyack, *One Best System*.

30.  The best available history of professionalization of teaching in relationship to these issues is still Willard Elsbree, *The American Teacher: Evolution of*

*a Profession in a Democracy* (New York: American Book Company, 1939).

31. Cronin, *Control of Urban Schools*, p. 138.

32. Elsbree, *American Teacher*, pp. 178–92, 336–60.

33. *Cardinal Principles of Secondary Education* (Washington, D.C.: U.S. Bureau of Education, 1918), p. 35. For a detailed discussion of this document, see Spring, *Education and the Rise*, pp. 108–26.

34. See Paul Violas, *The Training of the Urban Working Class* (Chicago: Rand McNally, 1978); Marvin Lazerson and W. Norton Grubb, eds., *American Education and Vocationalism* (New York: Teachers College Press, 1974), pp. 1–57; and Joel Spring, *Education and the Rise*, pp. 1–108.

35. A. B. Hollingshead, *Elmtown's Youth* (New York: Wiley, 1949).

36. Vannevar Bush, *Science—The Endless Frontier: A Report to the President* (Washington, D.C.: U.S. Government Printing Office, 1945); Dorothy Schaffter, *The National Science Foundation* (New York: Praeger, 1969).

37. Arthur Bestor, *Educational Wastelands* (Urbana: University of Illinois Press, 1953); Hyman Rickover, *Education and Freedom* (New York: E. P. Dutton, 1959); and Richard Hofstadter, *Anti-Intellectualism in American Life* (New York: Random House, 1962).

38. See James D. Koerner, ed., *The Case for Basic Education* (Boston: Little, Brown, 1959); Rickover, *Education and Freedom*, pp. 45–192.

39. For a discussion of the NDEA, see Spring, *Sorting Machine*, pp. 93–139.

40. "Statement of William G. Carr, Executive Secretary, National Education Association," *Science and Education for National Defense: Hearings Before the Committee on Labor and Public Welfare United States Senate Eighty-fifth Congress Second Session* (Washington, D.C.: U.S. Government Printing Office, 1958), p. 475.

41. For a study of the development of the testing movement and its relationship to racial bias, see Clarence Karier, "Testing for Order and Control in the Corporate Liberal State," in Clarence J. Karier, Paul C. Violas, and Joel Spring, *Roots of Crisis* (Chicago: Rand McNally, 1973), pp. 108–38.

42. See Caroline Persell, *Education and Inequality* (New York: Free Press, 1977).

43. See Gary Orfield, *The Reconstruction of Southern Education: The Schools and the 1964 Civil Rights Act* (New York: Wiley-Interscience, 1969).

44. Quoted in Richard Dershimer, *The Federal Government and Educational R&D* (Lexington, Mass.: Lexington Books, 1976), p. 64.

45. See Lee J. Cronbach and Patrick Suppes, eds., *Research for Tomorrow's Schools* (London: Collier-Macmillan, 1969), p. 205.

46. Daniel P. Moynihan, "Can Courts and Money Do It?" *New York Times*, January 10, 1972; reprinted in Miriam Wasserman, *Demystifying School* (New York: Praeger, 1974), pp. 167–94.

47. National Institute of Education, *Preliminary FY 1977 Program Plan Executive Summary* (undated).

48.  See Spring, *The Sorting Machine*, pp. 233–37.

49.  See Eugene Eidinberg and Roy Morey, *An Act of Congress: The Legislative Process and the Making of Education Policy* (New York: Norton, 1969).

50.  For a study of the community control and union resistance, see Miriam Wasserman, *The School Fix: NYC, USA* (New York: Outerbridge & Dienstfrey, 1970), pp. 185–391.

51.  Leon Lessinger, *Every Kid a Winner: Accountability in Education* (New York: Simon & Schuster, 1970), pp. 23–41, 119.

52.  Ibid., p. 128.

53.  Ibid., p. 129.

54.  Dershimer, *Federal Government*, p. 2.

55.  Ibid., pp. 138–39.

56.  The following are the major studies of political socialization in the schools: Robert Hess and Judith Torney, "The Development of Political Attitudes in Children," in *Political Socialization*, ed. Edward Greenberg (New York: Atherton Press, 1970; M. Kent Jennings and Richard G. Niemi, "Effects of the High School Curriculum," in *The Political Character of Adolescence: The Influence of Families and Schools* (Princeton: Princeton University Press, 1974); Dean Jaros, *Socialization to Politics* (New York: Praeger, 1973); Richard Dawson and Kenneth Prewitt, *Political Socialization* (Boston: Little, Brown, 1969); and Lee H. Ehman, "The American School in the Political Socialization Process," *Review of Educational Research* 50 (Spring 1980): 99–119.

57.  Lee H. Ehman, "The American School in the Political Socialization Process," *Review of Educational Research* 50 (1980): 99–119.

# 3 NINETEENTH-CENTURY OPPONENTS OF STATE EDUCATION
## Prophets of Modern Revisionism

*George H. Smith*

## REVISIONISM AND AMERICAN EDUCATION

The historian Bernard Bailyn, writing in 1960, argued that American educational historiography was sadly deficient. There was little effort to link the history of education to broader social developments, and the discipline itself was controlled by education professionals with strong vested interests. The typical history of education course found in universities, Bailyn noted, had become "a form of initiation" for those in the teaching profession—a means to illustrate the purportedly glorious achievements of public schools. History of education texts were "the patristic literature of a powerful academic ecclesia," and the entire field "displayed the exaggeration of weakness and extravagance of emphasis that are the typical results of sustained inbreeding."[1]

Educational history has changed dramatically since Bailyn's critique. The rosy picture of state schools[2] drawn by conventional historians, such as Ellwood Cubberley,[3] which depicted the victory of state schooling as a triumph of humanitarian reform, has been demolished by a new wave of historians. These historians, commonly referred to as "revisionists," have told an altogether different story. The battle for tax-supported compulsory schooling was a recurring story of political power, social control, and the growth of a powerful, unresponsive bureaucracy. Revisionists have emphasized that the welfare of the child (teaching literacy skills, for example) was a relatively minor concern of those reformers who pushed for increased state intervention. Instead, various social goals were foremost in the minds of reformers—such as "Americanizing" immigrants, teaching a proper respect for government, and inculcating the values of the dominant class.

Radical revisionism[4] penetrated the academic community with the publication of Michael Katz's *The Irony of Early School Reform* (1968), followed by his *Class, Bureaucracy, and Schools* (1971).[5] Katz stresses the need for a historical perspective as a framework to understand the current problems besetting school reform. The present school system is a legacy of the past; by 1880 the state system "had acquired its fundamental structural characteristics, and . . . they have not altered since." State schools have a bureaucratic structure, and "the result has been school systems that treat children as units to be processed into particular shapes and dropped into slots roughly congruent with the status of their parents."[6]

Katz traces the evolution of the school bureaucracy during the nineteenth century; and he maintains that the bureaucratic model applied to schools served primarily the interests of those within the bureaucracy itself, just as the same bureaucratic structure serves powerful interests today. "It serves the interests," to cite just one example, "of the educators by providing career lines and regulating entry." In opposition to alternative models of school organization, such as democratic localism, the proponents of centralized bureaucracy won the day with their version of a solution for "the cultural divisiveness inherent in the increasing religious and ethnic diversity of American life."[7] The bureaucratic solution, not coincidentally, also served to insulate teachers and administrators from the consumers of education;[8] and it provided a sanctuary from change that threatened the status quo. Bureaucracy, Katz emphasizes, "inhibits reform." "Its potent informal organizations mobilize resistance and frequently sabotage innovations. Bureaucrats counter reformist arguments by changing their own goals, replacing earlier extravagant claims with much more limited objectives, and asserting that critics misunderstand their purposes."[9]

Katz's general conclusions about the imposition of a bureaucratic school system and its harmful effect on the consumers of education— children—have been supported by a number of more recent studies.

David Tyack's *The One Best System* explores why the victims of state schools were frequently the "poor and dispossessed" and, moreover, why this victimization was "predictable and regular—in short, *systematic*." He concludes, in a manner similar to Katz, that the bureaucratic structure is largely to blame. "The search for the one best system has ill-served the pluralistic character of American society." In addition, bureaucratization "has often perpetuated positions and outworn practices rather than serving the clients, the children to be taught."[10]

Similarly, William Bullough points out that school reformers of the late 1800s "often defined education as an agency of control" and that this control was imposed through the mechanism of bureaucracy.

> Schools in American cities may yet be paying the price for the successes of turn-of-the-century reform. The highly structured educational systems which emerged from that period remain essentially intact, increasing the difficulty of evolving programs and institutions relevant to the demands and needs of a constantly changing urban society and frequently impeding the flow of communications between the schools themselves and the public they serve.[11]

Revisionism, of course, is not cut from a whole cloth, and revisionists disagree among themselves on important points. Among revisionists not mentioned thus far—Joel Spring, Clarence Karier, Paul Violas, Colin Greer, E.G. West, David Nasaw, and others[12]—one finds a wide spectrum of opinion. Nevertheless, certain themes run throughout virtually all revisionist writings. Revisionists emphasize education as a form of social control and the use of state education to indoctrinate and mould a compliant citizenry. They tend to analyze educational bureaucracies in terms of how those bureaucracies further the interests and goals of those who control the system. They point out the tendency of state education to repress diversity—whether cultural, religious, or ideological—and they agree on the deleterious effects of the attempt to impose a uniform system of education. These are among the important lessons of revisionism.

## THE BACKGROUND OF VOLUNTARYISM

Before the advent of revisionism, nineteenth-century opponents of state education (or "Voluntaryists," as they were known in England, and as I shall refer to them here) were scarcely mentioned at all, or they were portrayed in a highly unfavorable light.[13] Those who warned against the dangers of state education, and who desired an educational free market instead, were summarily dismissed as doctrinaire laissez faire advocates who stubbornly resisted social improvement. Their commitment to the free market was brushed aside as "ideological" — ignoring the fact that pro-state education theorists of the last century were as ideological as their opponents. Horace Mann, Sir James Kay-Shuttleworth (Mann's English counterpart), and many lesser-known champions of state education were fully committed to their principles, and they wished to see these principles implemented through systems of national education.[14] Indeed, the nineteenth-century conflict over state education was an ideological clash of the first order. Rarely does one see a debate with such well-defined principles on both sides — or with such momentous practical consequences.

The opponents of state education are of particular interest when viewed in the context of revisionism. Many of the things that they predicted would happen under a state system of education are the very things that revisionists now complain about. This is ironic when one considers that Voluntaryists were free-market advocates whereas most revisionists display little sympathy for laissez faire.[15] Of course, I do not suggest that the predictions of Voluntaryists, however accurate, prove the theoretical principles on which those predictions were based. But I do maintain that the perspicacious analysis of the Voluntaryists qualifies them for more serious attention than they have hitherto received.

In this essay I shall examine the ideology of Voluntaryism, with special emphasis on those areas where Voluntaryist predictions have turned into revisionist facts. My main focus is on Voluntaryism in England, because this is where it flourished, but I shall begin with a brief overview of some American representatives (without intending this list to be exhaustive). After delineating the major figures in American and English Voluntaryism, I shall turn to some arguments and principles of Voluntaryism.

The relation between school and state in American individualist thought has a checkered past. Many traditional heroes of American individualism, such as Thomas Paine and Thomas Jefferson, upheld some role for the state in education, however minor that role is by today's standard. Even William Leggett, the radical "loco foco" and laissez faire advocate who opposed nearly all kinds of government intervention, made an exception in the case of education.[16] Voluntary education was not an integral part of republican individualism in America.

Radical individualism, however, which generated American anarchism, is another matter. Josiah Warren, often regarded as the first American anarchist, warned in 1833 that national aid to education would be like "paying the fox to take care of the chickens";[17] and he feared the consequences of placing control of education in the hands of a single group. The Voluntaryism of Warren was adopted by most American anarchists in the nineteenth century. Benjamin Tucker's *Liberty*—the foremost individualist journal of its day—consistently opposed all forms of state education.[18] Some followers of Tucker, such as C. L. Swartz and Charles Sprading, carried the anarchist teaching into this century, sometimes preferring to call themselves "mutualists."[19]

Some limited government individualists also opposed state education. Gerrit Smith—radical abolitionist, supporter of John Brown, and admirer of Lysander Spooner—upheld the separation of school and state. "It is justice and not charity which the people need at the hands of government," Smith argued. "Let government restore to them their land, and what other rights they have been robbed of, and they will then be able to pay for themselves—to pay their schoolmasters, as well as their parsons."[20]

There were Voluntaryists to be found among the American admirers of Herbert Spencer. William Youmans, editor of *The Popular Science Monthly*, favored leaving education to "private enterprise." The Spencerean John Bonham vigorously attacked "the one true system" of Horace Mann that would impose a dulling uniformity and extirpate diversity.[21]

We see, therefore, that there were numerous Voluntaryists in nineteenth-century America. But their impact was limited. Although education was important to American libertarians—as witnessed by their persistent efforts to establish schools of their own[22]—they had little influence on American politics. Most political battles centered not on whether the state should educate at all, but on whether state aid should go to sectarian schools, whether attendance should be compulsory, and so forth. Voluntaryism—consistent opposition to *all* state aid and interference—never achieved the dimensions of a national movement in America, as was the case in England.

For two decades Voluntaryism in England was a force to be reckoned with. An explanation for why this movement blossomed in England, whereas there existed no comparable movement in the United States, is not hard to find. After the Restoration of Charles II in 1660, "Dissenters" or "Nonconformists" (technically, any Protestant who refused to subscribe to the Thirty-Nine Articles of the Anglican Church) found themselves persecuted and saddled with severe legal disabilities. Oxford and Cambridge were effectively closed to them,[23] as were other conventional channels of education. The notorious Act of Uniformity (1662) was but one in a series of acts that subjected Dissenters to considerable hardship (although repressive measures were not always enforced to the letter). The Act of Uniformity decreed that "every Schoolmaster keeping any public or private school, and every person instructing or teaching any youth in any house or private family as a tutor or schoolmaster" must conform to the liturgy of the Church of England.[24]

As a consequence of repression, a good deal of Nonconformist education went underground, so to speak. Even when political conditions became more favorable, Dissenters often preferred to patronize their own educational institutions. The eighteenth century saw the rise of Dissenting Academies, described by one historian as "the greatest schools of their day."[25] Renowned for their innovation and scholarship, these academies even attracted Anglicans who preferred them to Oxford and Cambridge.

Thus Dissenters had a long tradition of independent education of which they were justly proud. Moreover, Dissenters constituted the core of libertarian activists in eighteenth-century England. Caroline Robbins praises the Dissenters for "the gradual enlargement of the idea of liberty, and . . . the maintenance of the ideal of a loyal diversity of belief and practice. . . ." "No one, indeed," writes Albert Goodwin, "in eighteenth-century England, could claim the title of 'friends of liberty' . . . with more justification than the Dissenters, for they were enamoured not only of their own liberty in matters of religious conscience but also of secular causes resting on the inherent rights of human personality, wherever they were in question."[26]

Joseph Priestley (1733–1804), the famous chemist and Dissenting minister, was among the first to speak out against state education in *An Essay on the First Principles of Government*. From 1761 to 1767

Priestley lectured at the Warrington Academy, and throughout his life he prized the freedom and diversity that educational liberty, in his view, would bring. William Godwin (1756–1836), often cited as the first anarchist, was vehemently opposed to state education. Although he later abandoned his religious beliefs, he was educated for the ministry at Hoxton Academy. David Williams (1738–1816), another foe of state education, was an educational innovator and entrepreneur of considerable merit; and, not surprisingly, he also hailed from a Dissenting background.[27]

Herbert Spencer (1820–1903), the leading libertarian theoretician of the nineteenth century and an ardent Voluntaryist, was educated in Dissenting causes by his father and uncle. "Our family was essentially a *dissenting* family," he wrote in later life, "and dissent is an expression of antagonism to arbitrary control." Much of Spencer's first political article, which he published in *The Nonconformist* at the age of twenty-two, was devoted to a critique of state education, and it possibly influenced the birth of the Voluntaryist movement in the following year.[28]

Other Dissenters who campaigned for Voluntaryism in the nineteenth century included Joseph Sturge (1793–1859), a prominent Quaker pacifist who was instrumental in the antislavery movement, Samuel Morley (1809–1886), Andrew Reed (1787–1862), Henry Richard (1812–1888), Edward Miall (1809–1881), and Edward Baines, Jr. (1800–1890). Among these Miall and Baines were the most important. Edward Miall founded and edited *The Nonconformist*, one of the most important Dissenting periodicals of its day; and he was a tireless campaigner for Church disestablishment. Edward Baines, Jr., for many years editor of the influential *Leeds Mercury*, was the driving force behind Voluntaryism after 1843. Through his many pamphlets and articles, which combined cogent argumentation with detailed statistics, the case for Voluntaryism reached a wide audience.[29]

Until 1833 English elementary education progressed without state aid or interference. Popular education on an ambitious scale was undertaken by Dissenters with the establishment, in 1808, of the British and Foreign School Society (originally called the Royal Lancasterian Society). Funded primarily by Dissenting congregations, it used the monitorial system to bring education to the working classes without government assistance.[30] Moreover, it spurred the birth of a competing group—the National Society for Promoting the Education of the Poor in the Principles of the Established Church (usually referred to as the National Society)—which was supported by Anglicans.

Not until 1833 did these two organizations receive government funds. Available to the two societies for the erection of new schools was 20,000 pounds per annum, with each pound from voluntary contributions to be matched by a pound of state funds. Because the National Society had considerably more voluntary support, it was soon receiving the lion's share of government funds; and Dissenters began to learn the hard way that government "aid" to education would serve the prevailing orthodoxy.

Even by 1839, however, when the Melbourne government proposed an increase in aid from 20,000 to 30,000 pounds, there was little opposition in the Dissenting community. Most Dissenters approved of state funding if it did not favor one religious group over another and if it did not entail state interference. The Dissenting Deputies, who were later to become firm advocates of Voluntaryism, supported the increased aid; and the one deputy who argued that education "is not a legitimate function of the government" could find no support among his peers.[31] A meeting of Dissenting ministers in 1840 expressed its "satisfaction" with plans of government aid to secular education.[32] And even Edward Baines, Sr., supported the government proposal in the House of Commons.[33]

Sir James Graham, home secretary under the Peel administration (1841–1846), changed all this. On March 7, 1843, he presented a bill before the House entitled *A Bill for Regulating the Employment of Children and Young Persons in Factories, and for the Better Education of Children in Factory Districts.* Among other things, this bill required factory children to attend school for at least three hours each day, five days per week; and it placed effective control of these schools (to be financed largely from local rates) in the hands of the Established Church.[34] "The Church has ample security," wrote Graham to William Gladstone, "that every master in the new schools will be a Churchman, and that the teaching of the Holy Scriptures, as far as the limited exposition may be carried, will necessarily be in conformity with his creed."[35]

The Dissenting opposition to Graham's bill was swift and severe. It "set the whole country on fire," according to one commentator.[36]

"From one end of the empire to the other," declared *The Eclectic Review*:

> the sound of alarm has gone forth, and the hundreds of thousands who have answered to its call have astonished and confounded our opponents. The movement has been at once simultaneous and determined. The old spirit of the puritans has returned to their children, and men in high places are in consequence standing aghast, astonished at what they witness, reluctant to forego their nefarious purpose, yet scarce daring to persist in the scheme.[37]

Thousands of petitions with over two million signatures were presented to the House in opposition to the Factories Education Bill, whereupon Graham submitted amendments in an effort to appease the Dissenters. But to no avail. Petitions against the amended clauses contained nearly another two million signatures, and the measure was withdrawn.

It was during this agitation that support by Dissenters for state aid to education (provided it did not favor the Anglican Church) was transformed into opposition to all such aid. Edward Baines, Jr., described the transition: "The dangerous bill of Sir James Graham, and the evidence brought out of the ability and disposition of the people to supply the means of education, combined to convince the editors of the *Mercury* that it is far safer and better for Government not to interfere at all in the work; and from that time forward they distinctly advocated that view."[38]

The Voluntaryist philosophy crystalized quickly. In meetings of the Congregational Union held in Leeds in October 1843, Baines articulated the basic arguments against state education that he was to expand on in the years that followed.[39] The Congregational Union officially declared itself in favor of voluntary education.[40] An education conference held at the Congregational Library in Leeds (December 1843) resolved that all government aid should be refused by schools supported from Congregational funds "and that all funds confided to the disposal of the central committee, in aid of schools, be granted only to schools sustained entirely by voluntary contributions."[41]

By 1846 the majority of Congregationalists and Baptists supported voluntary education.[42] Prominent Nonconformist papers and journals—such as the *Leeds Mercury*, *The Nonconformist*, and *The Eclectic Review* (which became radical when the Baptist Thomas Price became editor in 1837)—argued the case for Voluntaryism. Many

Voluntaryists were active in the Anti-Corn Law League, and they sought to apply the principles of free trade to education. The younger Baines constantly disputed reports which purported to show the deplorable condition of voluntary schools, especially in the manufacturing districts;[43] and other Dissenters accused government committees of distorting facts in order to buttress their case for government interference.[44]

Not all Dissenters supported Voluntaryism, of course, and the Voluntaryists found themselves attacked by other Nonconformist journals, such as *The British Quarterly Review* (edited by Robert Vaughan).[45] In addition, some Manchester free-trade advocates (Richard Cobden being the most notable example) were active in the movement for state secular education, creating a serious rift among the classical liberals. Indeed, in 1848 Cobden remarked that "education is the main cause of the split amongst the middle-class Liberals."[46] Manchester became a center of agitation for state education whereas Leeds was the stronghold of Voluntaryism. "In Leeds the question was whether the State should intervene at all, while in Manchester it concerned the form that intervention should take....Leeds imposed a proscriptive ban upon state education per se; Manchester sought to define the proper goals of a state education scheme that was both necessary and desirable."[47]

We cannot here relate the political fortunes of Voluntaryism after its birth as a distinct movement in 1843, except to note its dissolution in the 1860s.[48] It had become apparent that state education was on the march in England, and many Voluntaryists, preferring not to go down with what they saw as a lost cause, abandoned Voluntaryism and began to fight for the particular form of state education most congenial to their beliefs. Richard, Morley, Miall, and even Baines abandoned the sinking ship. Henry Richard, a contributor to the best collection of Voluntaryist essays, later called not only for state education, but for compulsory attendance as well.[49] Samuel Morley, who was so impressed with Spencer's attack on state education in *Social Statics* that he financed its publication as a separate pamphlet, abandoned a twenty-five year commitment to Voluntaryism in favor of state education on a wide scale.[50] Edward Miall reluctantly endorsed state education, using the extension of the suffrage in 1867 as rationale.[51] And even Edward Baines, the soul of Voluntaryism, declared himself a "practical man" in 1867 who is "compelled to abandon the purely voluntary system."[52] Three years later Edward Baines, Jr., former Voluntaryist and now Edward Baines, M.P., endorsed the Forster Education Bill of 1870.[53] This mass desertion was indeed "the most astounding volte-face of the century."[54]

A few Voluntaryists continued to swim against the tide. Herbert Spencer remained steadfast to the end. "[F]rom my very earliest days down to the present time," he wrote in 1897, "I have been a persistent opponent of all State-education." Auberon Herbert, an admirer of Spencer and a leading English libertarian, wrote articulate attacks on state education in the latter part of the century, and some other libertarians followed suit. As late as 1903 Spencer's article on "National Education" (excerpted from *Social Statics*) was reprinted by "The Society for the Liberation of Education from State Control." And in 1910 the treasurer of this society, Ernest Pomeroy, wrote a scathing attack on compulsory schooling.[55]

With the preceding outline of the Voluntaryist movement, we shall now turn to the principal arguments advanced by Voluntaryists. Their case was two-pronged: empirical and theoretical. On the empirical side, the English Voluntaryists argued at length that the progress of voluntary education in England had been satisfactory and that there was no need for state interference. On the theoretical side, Voluntaryists used their moral, social, and economic principles to build a formidable case against state education. Unfortunately, the former aspect, although important, is beyond the scope of this discussion. We shall focus exclusively on the latter, specifically, we shall concentrate on those areas where the concerns of yesterday's Voluntaryists overlap with the concerns of today's revisionists.

## EDUCATION AND LIBERTY

Political liberty was a basic concern of all Voluntaryists. Dissenters saw themselves in the tradition of Sidney, Locke, and other "Commonwealthmen," defenders of individual rights and foes of oppressive government. Religious liberty in particular—freedom of conscience—was viewed as the great heritage of the Dissenting tradition, any violation of which must call forth "stern and indomitable resistance."[56]

Liberty should not be sacrificed for a greater good, argued the Voluntaryist Richard Hamilton. "There is no greater good. There can be no greater good! It is not simply means, it is an end."[57] Education is best promoted by freedom; but should there ever be a conflict, "liberty is more precious than education." "We love education," Hamilton stated, "but there are things which we love better."[58] Edward Baines agreed that education is not the ultimate good: "Liberty is far more precious." It is essential to "all the virtues which dignify men and communities."[59]

The preservation of liberty, according to most Voluntaryists, is the only legitimate function of government. The purpose of government, wrote Herbert Spencer in "The Proper Sphere of Government," is "to defend the natural rights of man—to protect person and property—to prevent the aggressions of the powerful upon the weak; in a word, to administer justice."[60] Edward Miall agreed that government is "an organ for the protection of life, liberty and property; or, in other words, for the administration of justice."[61]

Government, an ever-present danger to liberty, must be watched with vigilance and suspicion. "The true lover of liberty," warned *The Eclectic Review*, "will jealously examine all the plans and measures of government."

> He will seldom find himself called to help it, and to weigh down its scale. He will watch its increase of power and influence with distrust. He will specially guard against conceding to it any thing which might be otherwise done. He would deprecate its undertaking of bridges, highways, railroads. He would foresee the immense mischief of its direction of hospitals and asylums. Government has enough on its hands—its own proper functions,—nor need it to be overborne. There is a class of governments which are called paternal. . . . They exact a soulless obedience. . . . Nothing breathes and stirs. . . . The song of liberty is forgotten. . . . And when such governments tamper with education, the tyranny, instead of being relieved, is eternized.[62]

Government is "essentially immoral," wrote Spencer in *Social Statics*, and with this many Voluntaryists agreed. The government has only those rights delegated to it by individuals, and "it is for each to say whether he will employ such an agent or not." Every person, therefore, has "the right to ignore the state."[63] The source of political authority is the people, argued Hamilton, and the people may revise or even "outlaw the State."[64] There was a consensus among Voluntaryists that education exceeded the proper boundaries of government and that to vest such power in government is to endanger liberty.

This hostility to government is reflected in the work of Thomas Hodgskin, who developed a libertarian theory in the 1820s and 1830s. A near-anarchist and an enthusiast for laissez faire, Hodgskin defended the right of self-ownership and the right to property on Lockean principles:

> ... I look on *a right* of property—on the right of individuals, to have and to own, for their own separate and selfish use and enjoyment, the produce of their own industry, with power freely to dispose of the whole of that in the manner most agreeable to themselves, as essential to the welfare and even to the continued existence of society.

Government, for Hodgskin, is a parasite and a threat to social order. "Government, as such, produces nothing, and all its revenues are exacted by violating the natural right of property. This I put down as the first point aimed at by all laws." Hodgskin condemned the "legislative classes" who use the state to enhance their power and ill-gotten gains. Taxes were a special target of Hodgskin's attack. All politicians, whatever their differences, "unite one and all, heart and soul, to uphold" the legitimacy of taxation. The first aim of government must be to "bestow a sufficient revenue" upon itself. "Who can enumerate the statutes imposing and exacting taxes? Who can describe the disgusting servility with which all submit to be fleeced by the demands of the tax-gatherer, on all sorts of false pretences ... ?"[65]

Government should not interfere in money or banking. Private industry is better able to provide public works, such as roads. Hodgskin even suggested that police duties should be taken out of state hands and placed in the private sector.[66] Given this attitude, it is not surprising that Hodgskin joined the Dissenters in their hatred of state education. In editorials appearing in *The Economist* (of which he was a subeditor), Hodgskin defended free-market education. "We advocate laissez faire in education ... as in trade," he wrote. The state, which "certainly has the art of contaminating that which it touches," should leave education alone to develop unmolested. Indeed, "for the State to meddle with education, is to bring education somewhat into discredit."[67]

The concern of Voluntaryists for liberty can scarcely be exaggerated. Schemes for state education were denounced repeatedly as "the knell of English freedom," an "assault ... on our constitutional liberties," and so forth. Plans for government inspection of schools were likened to "government *surveillance*" and "universal *espionage*" that display "the *police spirit.*" Compulsory attendance was described as "child-kidnapping." Educational freedom is "a sacred thing" because it is "an essential branch of civil freedom." "A system of state-education," declared Baines, "is a vast intellectual police, set to watch over the young at the most critical period of their existence, to prevent the intrusion of dangerous thoughts, and turn their minds into safe channels."[68]

Contrary to later historians, who were to portray Voluntaryism as a battle for narrow sectarian interests, the Voluntaryists insisted that crucial principles were at stake. "The crisis involves larger interests than those of dissent," stated *The Eclectic Review.* The threat that government education poses to liberty is sufficient ground to "take up a position of most determined hostility against it."[69] In support of this view, Voluntaryists often drew parallels between educational freedom, on the one hand, and religious freedom, freedom of the press, etc., on the other. "We cannot violate the principles of liberty in regard to education," Baines noted, "without furnishing at once a precedent and an inducement to violate them in regard to other matters."

> In my judgment, the State could not consistently assume the support and control of education, without assuming the support and control of both the *pulpit* and the *press.* Once decide that Government money and Government superintendence are essential in the schools, whether to ensure efficiency, or to guard against abuse, ignorance, and error, and the self-same reasons will force you to apply Government money and Government superintendence to our periodical literature and our religious instruction.[70]

Baines realized that a government need not carry the principle inherent in state education to its logical extreme, but he was disturbed by a precedent which gave to government the power of moulding minds. If, as the proponents of state education argued, state education is required in order to promote civic virtue and moral character, then "where, acting on these principles, could you consistently stop?" "Would not the same paternal care which is exerted to provide schools, schoolmasters, and school-books, be justly extended to provide mental food for the adult, and to guard against his food being poisoned? In short, would not the principle clearly justify *the appointment of the Ministers of Religion, and a Censorship of the Press?*"[71]

Baines conceded that there were deficiencies and imperfections in the system of voluntary education, but freedom should not be abrogated on this account. Again he pointed to the example of a free press. A free press has many "defects and abuses"; certainly not all the products of a free press are praiseworthy. But if liberty is to be sacrificed in education in order to remedy deficiencies, then why not regulate and censor the press for the same reason? Baines employed this analogy in his brilliant rejoinder to the charge that he was an advocate of "bad schools."

> In one sense I am. I maintain that we have as much right to have wretched schools as to have wretched newspapers, wretched preachers, wretched books, wretched institutions, wretched political economists, wretched Members of Parliament, and wretched Ministers. You cannot proscribe all these things without proscribing Liberty. The man is a simpleton who says, that to advocate Liberty is to advocate badness. The man is a quack and *doctrinaire* of the worst German breed, who would attempt to force all mind, whether individual or national, into a mould of ideal perfection, to stretch it out or to lop it down to his own Procrustean standard. I maintain that Liberty is the chief cause of excellence; but it would cease to be Liberty if you proscribed everything inferior. Cultivate giants if you please; but do not stifle dwarfs.[72]

To the many state-school advocates who pointed to the Prussian system as a model, Baines retorted: "Nearly all the Continental Governments which pay and direct the school, pay and direct also the pulpit and the press. They do it consistently."[73] This was the "despotism" that Baines loathed.

Freedom of conscience was precious to Dissenters, and they feared government encroachment in this realm, even in the guise of "secular" education. *The Eclectic Review*, using arguments similar to those of Baines, stressed the relation between religious freedom and educational freedom. Advocates of state education claimed that parents have the duty to provide their children with education and that the state has the right to enforce this duty. But parents have a duty to provide religious and moral instruction as well. "Are we then prepared to maintain . . . that government should interpose, in this case, to supply what the parent has failed to communicate? . . . If sound in the one case, it is equally so in the other. . . ."[74] The same journal reiterated this basic principle several years later:

> The educational question involves, to a considerable extent, the same general principles as those of religion. Let government interference be admitted in the

one case, and it will be tenfold difficult to withstand it in the other. . . . Admit the right and the necessity of government interference with mind, and the whole province of man's inner self will be claimed as the legitimate subject of human legislation. The arguments advanced on behalf of the one, will, with slight modification, equally avail on behalf of the other. They constitute the thin point of the wedge, and our only safety is in refusing its insertion. Here is the real contest. Here, therefore, our stand should be taken.[75]

We should not suppose that English Voluntaryism was based on religious sectarianism, as some critics have charged. Voluntaryists based their case for educational liberty on a defense of liberty in general; and they offered religious freedom as an example of civil liberty which paralleled the desired freedom in education. Education, according to the Voluntaryists, necessarily involves the shaping of moral character (and in this they agreed with their opponents). Education, because it involves the inner life of the individual, should remain beyond the reach of the state. Government should concern itself only with outward acts, specifically, with acts of injustice. The state cannot move beyond this and trench upon the inner life without violating a sacred domain. Freedom in education, like freedom in religion, means a policy of laissez faire by the state. Just as government has no right to interfere in religion, so it has no right to interfere in education. The principle of liberty applies in both cases.

## THE PROBLEM OF INDOCTRINATION

A common prediction of Voluntaryists was that government would employ education for its own ends, especially to instill the habit of obedience in its subjects. William Godwin expressed this clearly: the "project of a national education ought uniformly to be discouraged" he wrote, "on account of its obvious alliance with national government. . . . Government will not fail to employ it, to strengthen its hands, and perpetuate its institutions."[76]

With the consolidation of Nonconformist opposition to state education in 1843, the Godwinian warning was repeatedly stressed:

It is no trifling thing to commit to any hands the moulding of the minds of men. An immense power is thus communicated, the tendency of which will be in exact accordance with the spirit and policy of those who use it. Governments, it is well known, are conservative. The tendency of official life is notorious, and it is the height of folly, the mere vapouring of credulity, to imagine that the educational system, if entrusted to the minister of the day, will not be employed to diffuse amongst the rising generation, that spirit and those views which are most friendly to his policy. By having, virtually, at his command, the whole machinery of education, he will cover the land with a new class of officials, whose dependence on his patronage will render them the ready instruments of his pleasure.[77]

Government education, this writer feared, would produce "an emasculated and servile generation." A possible advance in literacy would be purchased at the price of man's "free spirit." Elsewhere *The Eclectic Review* compared state schools to "barracks" and their employees to "troops." "The accession of power and patronage to that government which establishes such a national system of education, can scarcely be gauged."[78] Teachers paid by a government will owe allegiance to that government.

What a host of stipendiaries will thus be created! and who shall say what will be their influence in the course of two generations? All their sympathies will be with the powers by whom they are paid, on whose favour they live, and from whose growing patronage their hopes of improving their condition are derived. As constitutional Englishmen, we tremble at the result. The danger is too imminent, the hazard too great, to be incurred, for any temporary stimulus which government interference can minister to education. We eschew it as alike disastrous in its results and unsound in its theory—the criminal attempt of short-sighted or flagitious politicians, to mould the intellect of the people to their pleasure.[79]

For Edward Baines indoctrination is a basic feature of state education. State education proceeds from the principle that "it is the duty of a Government to train the Mind of the People." If one denies to government this right—as defenders of a free press and free religion must logically do—then one must deny the right of government to meddle in education. It "is not the duty or province of the Government to train the mind of the people,"[80] argued Baines, and this "principle of the highest moment" forbids state education.

Herbert Spencer articulated the belief shared by many Voluntaryists that government education, by its very nature, entails indoctrination.

For what is meant by saying that a government ought to educate the people? Why should they be educated? What is the education for? Clearly, to fit the people for social life—to make them good citizens. And who is to say what are good citizens? The government: there is no other judge. And who is to say how these good citizens may be made? The government: there is no other judge. Hence the proposition is convertible into this—a government ought to mold children into good citizens, using its own discretion in settling what a good citizen is and how the child may be molded into one.[81]

Indoctrination was an issue that troubled even proponents of state education. A case in point is William Lovett, the Chartist radical who is often heralded as an early champion of state education. In his "Address on Education" published in 1837, he maintained that it is "the duty of Government to establish *for all classes* the best possible system of education." Education should be provided "not as a charity, *but as a right.*" How was government to discharge this duty? By providing funds for the erection and maintenance of schools. Lovett desired government financing *without* government control: "we are decidedly opposed to placing such immense power and influence in the hands of Government as that of selecting the teachers and superintendents, the books and kinds of instruction, and the whole management of schools in each locality." Lovett detested state systems, such as that found in Prussia, "where the lynx-eyed satellites of power . . . crush in embryo the buddings of freedom." State control of education "prostrates the whole nation before one uniform . . . despotism."[82]

Several years later Lovett became less sanguine about the prospect of government finance without government control. While still upholding in theory the duty of government to provide education, he so distrusted his own government that he called upon the working classes to reject government proposals and "to commence the great work of education yourselves." The working classes had "everything to fear" from schools established by their own government, so Lovett outlined a proposal whereby schools could be provided through voluntary means, free from state patronage and control.[83]

We see a similar concern with indoctrination in the work of J. S. Mill. Mill contended that education "is one of those things which it is admissible in principle that a government should provide for the people," although he favored a system where only those who could not afford to pay would be exempt from fees.[84] Moreover, a parent who fails to provide elementary education for his child commits a breach of duty, so the state may compel a parent to see that his child receives instruction. Where and how a child is taught should be up to the parents; the state should simply enforce minimal educational standards through a series of public examinations. Thus did

Mill attempt to escape the frightening prospect of state control. At this point he begins to sound like an ardent Voluntaryist:

> That the whole or any large part of the education of the people should be in State hands, I go as far as any one in deprecating. . . . A general State education is a mere contrivance for moulding people to be exactly like one another: and as the mould in which it casts them is that which pleases the predominant power in the government . . . in proportion as it is efficient and successful, it establishes a despotism over the mind, leading by natural tendency to one over the body.[85]

Dissenters who favored state education were also alive to the prospect of indoctrination, but they thought either that the state could be kept at a distance or that by confining state schools to "secular" subjects the trouble could be avoided. The Voluntaryists disagreed, and they repudiated all attempts at compromise. Government aid, however small and innocent, was bound to be followed by government strings. Government aid is "a *trap* and a *snare*," declared *The Eclectic Review*. It is "a wretched bribe" which, if accepted, "will have irretrievably disgraced us."[86] The question is not, "How can we obtain Government money?" wrote Algernon Wells, "but, How can we avoid it?" Dissenters

> must ever be equally free to act and speak. They must hold themselves entirely clear of all temptation to ask, when their public testimony is required, —How will our conduct affect our grants? The belief of many Independents is that, from the hour they received Government money, they would be a changed people—their tone lowered—their spirit altered—their consistency sacrificed—and their honour tarnished.[87]

Perhaps Edward Baines best summarized the sentiment of the Voluntaryists: "When Governments offer their arm, it is like the arm of a creditor or a constable, not so easily shaken off: there is a handcuff at the end of it."[88] The lesson was clear. Educational freedom is incompatible with state support. If government control and manipulation of education is to be avoided, financial independence and integrity must be maintained.

## THE NEED FOR PLURALISM

A fundamental theme in Voluntaryism was the need for diversity in education. Voluntaryists warned that state education would impose a dulling uniformity that would result, at best, in mediocrity. This was a primary concern of the eighteenth-century Dissenter Joseph Priestley.

Priestley argued that education is an art, and like any art it requires many "experiments and trials" before it can approach perfection. To bring government into education would be, in effect, to freeze the art at its present stage and thereby "cut off its future growth." Education "is already under too many legal restraints. Let these be removed." Priestley viewed the perfection of human nature as the goal of education. The purpose of education is not simply to preserve "the tranquillity of the state," but to produce "wise and virtuous men." Progress in this area requires "unbounded liberty, and even caprice. . . ." Life requires diversity in order to improve, and this is especially true of human life. Variety induces innovation and improvement. "From new, and seemingly irregular methods of education, perhaps something extraordinary and uncommonly great may spring." The "great excellence of human nature consists in the variety of which it is capable. Instead, then, of endeavouring, by uniform and fixed systems of education, to keep mankind always the same, let us give free scope to everything which may bid fair for introducing more variety among us."[89]

Priestley abhorred uniformity ("the characteristic of the brute creation") and reveled in diversity ("the glory of human nature"). One kind of education, he maintained, "would only produce one kind of men," so it is imperative to "relax the bonds of authority, rather than bind them faster."[90] The opposition to uniformity and the defense of diversity as essential to progress were to become important weapons in the Voluntaryist arsenal.

We see similar concerns expressed by Godwin. State institutions resist change and innovation. "They actively restrain the flights of mind, and fix it in the belief of exploded errors." Government bureaucracies entrench themselves and resist change, so we cannot look to them for innovation and progress. State education, Godwin argued, "has always expended its energies in the support of prejudice."[91]

The opposition to uniformity became a preeminent concern of Herbert Spencer, who developed a theory of social progress based on increasing social heterogeneity. National education "necessarily assumes that a uniform system of instruction is desirable," and this Spencer denied. Unlimited variety is the key to progress. Truth itself—"the bright spark that emanates from the collision of opposing ideas"—is endangered by imposed uniformity. The "uniform routine" of state education will produce "an approximation to a national model." People will begin to think and act alike, and the youth will be pressed "as nearly as possible into one common mould." Without diversity and competition among educational systems, education will stagnate and intellectual progress will be severely retarded.[92]

It is because individuals vary widely in their capacities, needs, and skills, Spencer argued, that we need a variety of educational systems from which to choose. The flexibility of competing systems allows the individual to find something suited to his individual requirements. This is provided in a free market where teachers are answerable to the public. In a state system, on the other hand, where teachers are "answerable only to some superior officer, and having no reputation and livelihood at stake to stimulate them," there is little motivation for them to consider individual needs. Education becomes uniformly gray. Hence "in education as in everything else, the principle of honourable competition is the only one that can give present satisfaction or hold out promise of future perfection."[93]

This theme was argued constantly by Voluntaryists. The uniformity of state education, Baines warned, obstructs improvement. It will serve to "stereotype the methods of teaching, to bolster up old systems, and to prevent improvement." If we leave education to the market, we will see continual improvements. "But let it once be monopolized by a Government department, and thenceforth reformers must prepare to be martyrs." Wells made a similar point:

> How to teach, how to improve children, are questions admitting of new and advanced solutions, no less than inquiries how best to cultivate the soil, or to perfect manufactures. And these improvements cannot fail to proceed indefinitely, so long as education is kept wide open, and free to competition, and to all those impulses which liberty constantly supplies. But once close up this great science and movement of mind from these invigorating breezes, whether by monopoly or bounty, whether by coercion or patronage, and the sure result will be torpor and stagnancy.[94]

*The Eclectic Review*, protesting that the "unitive design" of state education "would make all think alike," continued with a chilling account of uniformity:

> All shall be straightened as by the schoolmaster's ruler, and transcribed from his copy. He shall decide what may or may not be asked. But he must be *normalised* himself. He must be fashioned to a model. He shall only be taught

particular things. The compress and tourniquet are set on his mind. He can only be suffered to think one way. . . . All schools will be filled with the same books. All teachers will be imbued with the same spirit. And under their cold and lifeless tuition, the national spirit, now warm and independent, will grow into a type formal and dull, one harsh outline with its crisp edges, a mere complex machine driven by external impulse, with it appendages of apparent power but of gross resistance. If any man loves that national monotony, thinks it the just position of his nature, can survey the tame and sluggish spectacle with delight, he, on the adoption of such a system, has his reward.[95]

Auberon Herbert also cautioned against the "evils of uniformity." Like his mentor Herbert Spencer, he thought that "all influences which tend towards uniform thought and action in education are most fatal to any regularly continuous improvement."[96] Imagine the effect of state uniformity in religion, art, or science. Progress would grind to a halt. Education is no different. "Therefore, if you desire progress, you must not make it difficult for men to think and act differently; you must not dull their sense with routine or stamp their imagination with the official pattern of some great department."[97]

Herbert was especially sensitive to the difficulty of implementing change in a bureaucratic structure. A free market, he argued, encourages innovation and risk taking. An innovator with new ideas on education can, if left legally unhampered, solicit aid from those sympathetic to his views and then test his product on the market:

> But if some great official system blocks the way, if he has to overcome the stolid resistance of a department, to persuade a political party, which has no sympathy with views holding out no promise of political advantage, to satisfy inspectors, whose eyes are trained to see perfection of only one kind, and who may summarily condemn his school as "inefficient" and therefore disallowed by law, if in the meantime he is obliged by rates and taxes to support a system to which he is opposed, it becomes unlikely that this energy and confidence in his own views will be sufficient to inspire a successful resistance to such obstacles.[98]

The American Spencerean John Bonham applied the Voluntaryist critique of uniformity to Horace Mann and his ideal of the Common School. Mann, wrote Bonham, postulated "that a system of uniform teaching, from uniform books, by uniform methods, was necessarily beneficial and civilizing." Mann's system—"a process of mind-cramming with uniform books"—was touted by its defenders as "the one true system" for the betterment of mankind. "Mann was ready to employ the power of government to carry out his system, in its application to human intellect, to its logical conclusions. If he had been possessed of the surgical power necessary to mould human faculty into exact unity, he would have produced a fine uniformity—but what would have become of civilization?"[99]

## A FREE MARKET IN EDUCATION

Voluntaryists, as we have seen, prized social diversity (or what we call today a "pluralistic society"), and they were convinced that state education would impose the dead hand of uniformity. Rather than giving to government the power to decide among conflicting beliefs and values, they preferred to leave beliefs and values to the unfettered competition of the market. One must appreciate this broad conception of the free market, which includes far more than tangible goods, if one wishes to understand the Voluntaryists' passionate commitment to competition and their unbridled hatred of government interference. English libertarians had a long heritage of opposition to state patronage and monopoly reaching back to the Levellers of the seventeenth century; and the Voluntaryists, with the bitter struggle to repeal the corn laws fresh on their minds, were convinced that government interference in the market, whatever its supposed justification, actually served special interests and enhanced the power of government (thereby furthering the goals of those within the government). The various struggles against government, therefore, were seen by Voluntaryists (and by many others as well) as battles to establish free markets in religion, commerce, and education. It was not uncommon to find the expression "free trade in religion" among supporters of church-state separation; and when the editor of the *Manchester Guardian* stated in 1820 that religion should be a "marketable commodity," he was expressing a view widely shared.[100]

When fellow free-traders, such as Richard Cobden, supported state education, the Voluntaryists took them to task for their inconsistency. Those who embrace free trade in religion and commerce but advocate state interference in education, argued Thomas Hodgskin, "do not fully appreciate the principles on which they have been induced to act." "We only wonder that they should have so soon forgotten their free-trade catechism," wrote another Voluntaryist, "and lent their sanction to any measure of monopoly."[101]

Before free-traders ask for state interference in education, Hodgskin pointed out, "they ought to prove that its interference with trade has been beneficial." But this, by their own admission, they cannot do. They know that the effect of state interference with trade has always been "to derange, paralyse, and destroy it." Hodgskin maintained that the principle of free trade "is as applicable to education as to the manufacture of cotton or the supply of corn." The state is unable to advance material wealth for the people through intervention, and there is even less reason to suppose it capable of advancing "immaterial wealth" in the form of knowledge. Any "protectionist" scheme in regard to knowledge should be opposed by all who understand the principle of competition. Laissez faire in education is "the only means of ensuring that improved and extended education which we all desire." [102]

*The Eclectic Review* posed the basic question: Can education "be best produced by monopoly or by competition?"—and it came down unequivocally on the side of competition. Education is a "marketable commodity," and demand for it is "as much subject to the principles and laws of political economy, as are corn or cotton." Government intervention, in education as elsewhere, leads to market distortions:

> How will it affect the balance between the demand and the supply; disturb the relations of the voluntary teacher, and misdirect the expectations and confidence of the market? Let a private teacher attempt to come into competition with such accredited and endowed agents of an incorporate system ... and he will find himself in the same state with a merchant who ventures to trade without a bounty in competition with those whose traffic is encouraged by large public bounties. [103]

Voluntaryists predicted that state aid to education would drive many voluntary schools out of business. Market schools would find themselves unable to compete with schools financed from taxes, and philanthropists who had previously contributed to education would withhold their funds, believing that, since the state would provide education anyway, there was no need for charitable support. As state aid increased, therefore, market education would diminish, and this would be used to support the contention that voluntary education had failed. Thus the educational bureaucracy, however tiny at its inception, would grow rapidly. An educational orthodoxy, with employees answerable to the state, would emerge. Costs would increase, and productivity would decrease. "Public servants are sustained at the largest cost, and always are subject to the least responsibility." The principle of the market, to produce "the best article . . . at the cheapest price," would disappear in a state system. In an educational free market, on the contrary, a "real and effectual discipline" is exercised over educators by consumers.[104] Free-market schools must either satisfy their customers or go out of business.

In calling for laissez faire in education, Voluntaryists squared-off against the major economists of their day, all of whom saw some role for the state.[105] Mill, for instance, opposed leaving education to the market. "In the matter of education," he wrote, "the intervention of government is justifiable, because the case is not one in which the interest and judgment of the consumer are a sufficient security for the goodness of the commodity."

> The uncultivated cannot be competent judges of cultivation. Those who most need to be made wiser and better, usually desire it least, and if they desired it, would be incapable of finding the way to it by their own lights. It will continually happen, on the voluntary system, that, the end not being desired, the means will not be provided at all, or that, the persons requiring improvement having an imperfect or altogether erroneous conception of what they want, the supply called forth by the demand of the market will be anything but what is really required.[106]

The Voluntaryists responded impatiently to this elitist argument. In their crusade for church-state separation (a campaign, in effect, for a free market in religion), the Voluntaryists had encountered the same argument many times. With man's eternal soul at stake, defenders of a state church argued that religion was simply too important to be left to the untutored judgment of the masses. "It is the old dogma," Wells said, "the people can know nothing about religion and it must be dictated to them."[107] Wells contended that the argument from incompetence, if used to support state education, must also justify state religion. The fact that fellow liberals failed to see the ominous implications of the incompetency argument obviously annoyed the Voluntaryists.

Spencer dismissed Mill's argument as "a worn-out excuse" which has been used to justify "all state interferences whatever." "A stock argument for the state teaching of religion has been that the masses cannot distinguish false religion from true. There is hardly a single department of life over which, for similar reasons, legislative supervision has not been, or may not be, established."[108]

Spencer questioned whether parents are as incompetent to assess education as Mill alleged. Parents are solicitous for their children's welfare, and even uneducated parents can seek advice from others whom they trust. Even granting problems in this area, however, it does not follow that the state should intervene. As a market for mass education developed, Spencer believed that consumers would gain experience and become more sophisticated in their choice of products. Social improvement takes time, and Spencer thought that "this incompetence of the masses to distinguish good instruction from bad is being outgrown."[109]

Spencer contended that Mill's argument is based on a false premise. Even if the interest and judgment of consumers are insufficient to guarantee educational quality, Mill must assume "that 'the interest and judgment' of a government *are* sufficient security." Mill must believe in an identity of interests between rulers and subjects, a proposition that Spencer ridiculed. The English government desired "a sentimental feudalism," a country where "the people shall be respectful to their betters," and an economy "with the view of making each laborer the most efficient producing tool." The interests of the state are quite distinct from the interests of the people, and "we may be quite sure that a state education would be administered for the advantage of those in power rather than for the advantage of the nation." Hence, even if we concede some inadequacies in market education, the inadequacies of state education are far more serious— and dangerous.[110]

As for the possible rejoinder that Spencer's argument may apply to governments of his day but not necessarily to an ideal government that may someday exist (where the rulers would presumably have the interests of their subjects at heart), Spencer retorted that Mill's argument relies on the people "as they now are," not on the people as they might be in an ideal market. Therefore, we must consider Mill's alternative—government—"as it now is," not as it *should* be in a hypothetical paradise. Spencer was inviting Mill to descend from the clouds of political theory to the real world of governments. All things considered, Spencer argued, in matters of education "the interest of the consumer is not only an efficient guarantee for the goodness of the things consumed, but the best guarantee."[111]

## CONCLUSION

We have surveyed revisionism and Voluntaryism in order to highlight some of their similarities. Of course, those revisionists who blame the problems of American education on "capitalism"—that ever-popular boogeyman of restless intellectuals—will dismiss the possibility that the ills they complain about stem from the absence of a free market in education.[112] But for those historians who have immersed themselves in the depressing rhetoric of pro-state educationists of the nineteenth century—and who have wearied of the constant references to social control, moulding good citizens and workers, putting Catholics and immigrants in their place, and so forth—the unconventional (and largely unexplored[113]) ideas of Voluntaryism may prove a refreshing and suggestive change.

## NOTES TO CHAPTER 3

1. Bernard Bailyn, *Education in the Forming of American Society* (New York: Norton, 1972), pp. 8-9.

2. In this essay I use the terms "state schools" and "state education" primarily to designate systems of education financially supported, in whole or in part, by government funds. Such systems may or may not involve government interference on a substantial scale, compulsory attendance, etc. Therefore, in speaking of proponents of state education, I am referring to any person who believes that education is a proper function of government. There are obvious differences among state educationists, but it is the *principle* that is important here.

3. It is difficult to believe that Cubberley's influential books failed to disturb people before the revisionists came along. There is, for example, his notorious discussion of immigration to America after 1882, which he described as consisting mainly of Southern and Eastern Europeans who, being largely "illiterate, docile, lacking in initiative, and almost wholly without the Anglo-Saxon conceptions of righteousness, liberty, law, order, public decency, and government . . . served to dilute tremendously our national stock and to weaken and corrupt our political life." Government education, of course, was supposed to combat this "serious case of racial indigestion"; *Public Education in the United States* (New York: Houghton Mifflin, 1919), p. 338. Then there is his priceless observation: "Our schools are, in a sense, factories, in which the raw materials (children) are to be shaped and fashioned into products to meet the various demands of

life"; *Public School Administration*, rev. ed. (Boston: Houghton Mifflin, 1929), p. 512.

4.  The line separating "radical" from "moderate" revisionists is somewhat blurred. The contention of Diane Ravitch that radical historians argue "that bureaucracy was purposely chosen to institutionalize racism and social class bias in the schools" is simply untrue; *The Revisionists Revised* (New York: Basic Books, 1978), p. 47. And her suggestion that radical revisionists, despite their differences, "argue that the overall direction of American history has *not* been towards a more just society" (p. 32) is so vague as to be virtually useless as a criterion. Radical revisionists seem to differ from moderate revisionists not so much in terms of their historical conclusions but in terms of their policy recommendations. Radical revisionists are generally skeptical of reform from within, and they call instead for a radical restructuring of the present system. The specific recommendations vary, of course, depending on the political beliefs of the revisionists. These political beliefs range from Marxist (e.g., Samuel Bowles and Herbert Gintis) to libertarian (e.g., Joel Spring).

5.  Michael Katz, *The Irony of Early School Reform: Educational Innovation in Mid-Nineteenth Century Massachusetts* (Boston: Beacon Press, 1970); and his *Class, Bureaucracy, and Schools: The Illusion of Educational Change in America* (New York: Praeger, 1971). An excellent revisionist work that preceded the outpouring of revisionist studies in the 1970s is Rousas John Rushdoony, *The Messianic Character of American Education* (Nutley, N. J.: Craig Press, 1963). This superb examination of the ideology of American state educators has been ignored by the revisionist community, possibly owing to Rushdoony's strident Calvinism and his opposition to state education.

6.  Katz, *Irony of Early School Reform*, pp. xix, xviii.

7.  Katz, *Class, Bureaucracy, and Schools*, pp. xxiii, 39.

8.  The sociologist Lester Frank Ward recommended state education precisely because it would protect professional educators from "the caprices" of "heterogeneously minded patrons."

    > The secret of the superiority of state over private education lies in the fact that in the former the teacher is responsible solely to society. As in private, so also in public education, the calling of the teacher is a profession, and his personal success must depend upon his success in accomplishing the result which his employers desire accomplished. But the result desired by the state is a wholly different one from that desired by parents, guardians, and pupils. Of the latter he is happily independent. (*Dynamic Sociology*, 2nd ed. [New York: Appleton, 1897], 2: 589–90.

9.  Katz, *Class, Bureaucracy, and Schools*, p. 57.

10. David B. Tyack, *The One Best System: A History of American Urban Education* (Cambridge, Mass.: Harvard University Press, 1974), pp. 4, 11.

Tyack, it should be noted, dissociates himself from the radical revisionists (pp. 9–12), but his research clearly lends support to their work.

11. William A. Bullough, *Cities and Schools in the Gilded Age: The Evolution of an Urban Institution* (Port Washington, N.Y.: Kennikat Press, 1974), pp. 9, 13.

12. For some important revisionist works, see Joel Spring, *Education and the Rise of the Corporate State* (Boston: Beacon Press, 1973), and his *The Sorting Machine* (New York: David McKay, 1976); Clarence J. Karier, *Shaping the American Educational State: 1900 to the Present* (New York: Free Press, 1975); Paul C. Violas, *The Training of the Urban Working Class* (Chicago: Rand McNally, 1978); Clarence J. Karier, Paul C. Violas, and Joel Spring, *Roots of Crisis: American Education in the Twentieth Century* (Chicago: Rand McNally, 1973); Colin Greer, *The Great School Legend: A Revisionist Interpretation of American Public Education* (New York: Penguin Books, 1976); E. G. West, "The Political Economy of American Public School Legislation," *The Journal of Law and Economics* 10 (1967): 101–128; David Nasaw, *Schooled to Order: A Social History of Public Schooling in the United States* (New York: Oxford University Press, 1979). For an overview of revisionism, see Sol Cohen, "History of Education as a Field of Study: An Essay on Recent Historiography of American Education," in *History, Education, and Public Policy*, ed. Donald Warren (Berkeley: McCutchan, 1978), pp. 35–53.

13. See Francis Adams, *History of the Elementary School Contest in England* (London: Chapman & Hall, 1882). This work was heavily relied upon by later historians, and it typifies the treatment that English Voluntaryists were to receive. Adams claims that Voluntaryism "was assumed rather in defence of sectional interests than on account of any fundamental objections in principle" (p. 125). The Voluntaryists, in opposing state education, "made a great mistake" (p. 127). The "Voluntaryists were fighting not for the rights and duties of parents, but for the control of education by religious denominations" (p. 129). "The law of supply and demand . . . had conspicuously failed. . . . It was evident the Voluntaryists did not rely upon the law of supply and demand, but on sectarian and party rivalry and zeal . . ." (p. 129).

14. Sir James Kay-Shuttleworth is an example of an educational reformer whose luster has begun to tarnish. His early biographer Frank Smith (*The Life and Times of Sir James Kay-Shuttleworth* [London: John Murray, 1923]) treats him with the admiration one would expect. More recently, Trygve R. Tholfsen (*Sir James Kay-Shuttleworth on Popular Education* [New York: Teachers College Press, 1974]), though insisting that Sir James deserves our admiration, is clearly troubled by Kay-Shuttleworth's desire to use state education as a means of keeping the working class in its

place. Disturbed by recent Chartist uprisings, Kay-Shuttleworth complained that the working classes "have never yet been sufficiently educated to frame rational wishes and to pursue them by rational means"; Sir James Kay-Shuttleworth, *Four Periods of Public Education* (London: Longman, 1862), p. 229. Lest they fall prey to Chartism—"an armed political monster" (p. 230)—the government must educate the working classes "to guard them against pernicious opinions" (p. 232). Like most utilitarians, Kay-Shuttleworth saw state education as a means of preventing crime—an inexpensive form of police protection.

15.  Two notable exceptions are Joel Spring and E. G. West.

16.  See *A Collection of the Political Writings of William Leggett*, ed. Theodore Sedgwick, Jr. (New York: Taylor and Dodd, 1840), 1: 80-1.

17.  Quoted in William O. Reichert, *Partisans of Freedom: A Study in American Anarchism* (Bowling Green, Ohio: Bowling Green University Popular Press, 1976), p. 70. On Warren see also William Bailie, *Josiah Warren: The First American Anarchist* (1906; rpt. New York: Arno Press, 1972); and James J. Martin, *Men Against the State* (Colorado Springs: Ralph Myles, 1970), pp. 1-87.

18.  See, e.g., A. W. Wright, "The State and Education," *Liberty* 12(11) (1897): 6-7. Cf. Tucker's article on education in *Educational Review* 15 (1898): 6-10.

19.  See Clarence L. Swartz, *What Is Mutualism?* (New York: Vanguard Press, 1927); and Charles T. Sprading, *Freedom and Its Fundamentals* (Los Angeles: Libertarian, 1923).

20.  Quoted in Octavious Brooks Frothingham, *Gerrit Smith: A Biography* (New York: Putnam's, 1878), p. 184.

21.  *Popular Science Monthly*, May 1887, pp. 124-27; John M. Bonham, *Industrial Liberty* (New York: Putnam's, 1888), pp. 286-326.

22.  For an account of anarchist education in America, with special emphasis on the Ferrer movement, see Paul Avrich, *The Modern School Movement: Anarchism and Education in the United States* (Princeton: Princeton University Press, 1980).

23.  Admission to Oxford required one to subscribe to the Thirty-Nine Articles. Dissenters could be admitted to Cambridge but must declare themselves members of the Church of England in order to take certain degrees. See H. McLachlan, *English Education Under the Test Acts* (Manchester: Manchester University Press, 1931), p. 1.

24.  C. Stephenson and F. G. Marcham, eds., *Sources of English Constitutional History* (New York: Harper, 1937), p. 545.

25.  Irene Parker, *Dissenting Academies in England* (Cambridge: Cambridge University Press, 1914), p. 45. Cf. McLachlan, *English Education Under the Test Acts*; and Anthony Lincoln, *Some Political and Social Ideas of*

*English Dissent, 1763–1800* (Cambridge: Cambridge University Press, 1938), pp. 66–100.

26.  Caroline Robbins, *The Eighteenth-Century Commonwealthman* (Cambridge, Mass.: Harvard University Press, 1959), p. 221; Albert Goodwin, *The Friends of Liberty: The English Democratic Movement in the Age of the French Revolution* (Cambridge, Mass.: Harvard University Press, 1979), p. 66. For an overview of the literature in this area, see Isaac Kramnick, "English Middle-Class Radicalism in the Eighteenth Century," *Literature of Liberty* 3 (2) (Summer 1980): 5–48.

27.  Burton Pollin points out that Priestley later acknowledged some role for government in education, albeit grudgingly; *Education and Enlightenment in the Works of William Godwin* (New York: Las Americas, 1962), p. 137. On Godwin and education, see ibid.; the best work on Godwin's political philosophy is John P. Clark, *The Philosophical Anarchism of William Godwin* (Princeton: Princeton University Press, 1977). On Williams see W. A. C. Stewart and W. P. McCann, *The Educational Innovators, 1750–1880* (New York: St. Martin's Press, 1967), pp. 35–52.

28.  Herbert Spencer, "The Filiation of Ideas," in *The Life and Letters of Herbert Spencer*, ed. David Duncan (London: Williams & Norgate, 1911), p. 537. Spencer's article, "The Proper Sphere of Government," appeared in *The Nonconformist* in twelve parts beginning June 15, 1842. Did this article contribute substantially to the Voluntaryist movement? According to Raymond Cowherd: "Spencer constructed a new political platform to combine economists, Radicals, and Dissenters. . . . The political events of 1843, seeming to confirm Spencer's conclusions, impelled the Dissenters toward a more extreme voluntaryism"; *The Politics of English Dissent* (New York: New York University Press, 1956), pp. 157–58. Cf. G.I.T. Machin, "The Maynooth Grant, the Dissenters and Disestablishment, 1845–1847," *English Historical Review* 82 (January 1967): 66. Machin agrees that Spencer "provided the extreme Voluntaries with a political philosophy." Unfortunately, neither Cowherd nor Machin provides documentation to show that Spencer's early writing had a significant impact on the Voluntaryist movement. Spencer indicated that Edward Miall (editor of *The Nonconformist*) was impressed enough to say that "if the *Nonconformist* had had a more extensive circulation he should have been happy to have offered me a share in the editorship"; Duncan, *Life and Letters*, p. 38. Miall recommended Spencer to Thomas Price as a possible contributor to *The Eclectic Review*, to which Spencer contributed an article on education. (This was accepted but never published.) Thus it is safe to say that the young Spencer was admired by leading Dissenters who were to become prominent in the Voluntaryist cause. I have been unable to find any proof of direct influence, however.

29.    In 1845, when the Committee of the British and Foreign School Society decided to continue accepting government aid, Sturge withdrew his support, stating that "a small annual Government grant may make the recipients subservient to the State"; see Henry Richard, *Memoirs of Joseph Sturge* (London: S. W. Partridge, 1864), pp. 336–39. On Miall, see Arthur Miall, *Life of Edward Miall* (London: Macmillan, 1884); William H. Mackintosh, *Disestablishment and Liberation* (London: Epworth Press, 1972); and David M. Thompson, "The Liberation Society," in *Pressure from Without*, ed. Patricia Hollis (London: Edward Arnold, 1974), pp. 211–38. On the younger Baines, see Derek Fraser, "Edward Baines," in *Pressure from Without*, pp. 183–209. Cf. Derek Fraser, *Urban Politics in Victorian England* (Leicester: Leicester University Press, 1976).

30.    For a history of the British and Foreign School Society, see Henry Bryan Binns, *A Century of Education* (London: J. M. Dent, 1908).

31.    "The Protestant Dissenting Deputies consisted (and consist) of two members chosen annually from each congregation of the 'three denominations, Presbyterian, Independent and Baptist' (to use their time-honoured phrases) 'in and within twelve miles of London' (originally ten miles) 'appointed to protect their civil rights' "; Bernard Manning, *The Protestant Dissenting Deputies* (Cambridge: Cambridge University Press, 1952), pp. 2, 339.

32.    R. W. Dale, *History of English Congregationalism* (London: Hodder & Stoughton, 1907), p. 652.

33.    Edward Baines [Jr.], *The Life of Edward Baines* (London: Longman, 1859), p. 216. The elder Baines, like his son, later became a Voluntaryist.

34.    See J. T. Ward and J. H. Treble, "Religion and Education in 1843: Reaction to the 'Factory Education Bill,' " *Journal of Ecclesiastical History* 20 (1) (April 1969): 79–110. A thorough account of this bill is also contained in Dale, *History of English Congregationalism*, pp. 654–59.

35.    C. S. Parker, *Life and Letters of Sir James Graham* (London: John Murray, 1907), 1: 344.

36.    Dale, *History of English Congregationalism*, p. 655.

37.    *Eclectic Review*, n.s. 13 (January–June 1843): 698.

38.    Baines, *Life of Edward Baines*, p. 171.

39.    Dale, *History of English Congregationalism*, pp. 659–60.

40.    R. Tudur Jones, *Congregationalism in England, 1662–1962* (London: Independent Press, 1962), p. 212.

41.    Dale, *History of English Congregationalism*, p. 661.

42.    This was the opinion of Dale (ibid., p. 663), a prominent Dissenter who was opposed to Voluntaryism. An article in *The British Quarterly Review* (probably written by Robert Vaughan) questioned whether Voluntaryism was as widespread among Dissenters as its supporters claimed. "We doubt much if there will be a single county union of Congregationalists in Eng-

land that will not present considerable difference of judgment in reference to this question. . . ." Among the supporters of state education Vaughan lists "Churchmen in England and Scotland; Free churchmen and Methodists in both countries; the bulk of Dissenters north of the Tweed, and a considerable number south of it; together with the whole body of British Catholics;—all our great political parties, moreover,—Tories, Whigs, Radicals, and the Chartist and Working Classes . . ."; 6 (August–November 1847): 544–45.

43. See Edward Baines, Jr., *The Social, Educational, and Religious State of the Manufacturing Districts* (1843; rpt. New York: Augustus M. Kelly, 1969); his *Letters to the Right Hon. Lord John Russell . . . on State Education*, 3rd ed. (London: Ward, 1847); and his "On the Progress and Efficiency of Voluntary Education in England," in *Crosby-Hall Lectures on Education* (London: John Snow, 1848), pp. 2–47.

44. See, e.g., the excellent article by Henry Richard, "On the Progress and Efficacy of Voluntary Education, as Exemplified in Wales," in *Crosby-Hall Lectures*, pp. 171–224.

45. See 4 (August–November 1846): 444–508.

46. John Morley, *The Life of Richard Cobden* (London: T. Fisher Unwin, 1906), p. 495.

47. Fraser, *Urban Politics*, p. 272.

48. For accounts of the complex political entanglements during this period, see Norman Gash, *Reaction and Reconstruction in English Politics, 1832–1852* (Oxford: Oxford University Press, 1965); and G. I. T. Machin, *Politics and the Churches in Great Britain, 1832 to 1868* (Oxford: Oxford University Press, 1977).

49. Dale, *History of English Congregationalism*, pp. 676–77.

50. The reprint of Spencer's article was entitled *State Education Self-Defeating* (Duncan, *Life and Letters*, p. 60). For Morley's later views on education, see Edwin Hodder, *The Life of Samuel Morley* 2nd ed. (London: Hodder & Stoughton, 1887), pp. 331ff.

51. See Miall, *Life of Edward Miall*, pp. 273–74.

52. Quoted in Fraser, "Edward Baines," p. 202. Baines recanted before a meeting of the Congregational Union on October 11, 1867: "Ought we to cripple and destroy our schools rather than accept those payments? I honour the motives of those who reply in the affirmative; but my own deliberate and revised judgment answers in the negative"; quoted in Smith, *Sir James Kay-Shuttleworth*, p. 159, n. 1.

53. See Baines's speech before the House in *Hansard's Parliamentary Debates*, 3rd series, vol. 202, cols. 831–35.

54. J. Briggs and I. Sellars, *Victorian Nonconformity* (London: Edward Arnold, 1973), p. 121.

55. Duncan, *Life and Letters*, p. 404. See Herbert's article from *Fortnightly Review* (1880), "State Education: A Help or Hindrance?" reprinted in *The Right and Wrong of Compulsion by the State, and Other Essays by Auberon Herbert*, ed. Eric Mack (Indianapolis: Liberty Classics, 1978), pp. 53–80; cf. Auberon Herbert, ed., *The Sacrifice of Education to Examination* (London: Williams & Norgate, 1889), pp. 174–97; for another libertarian critique of state education during this period, see A. E. Hake and O. E. Wesslau, *Free Trade in Capital* (London: Remington, 1890), pp. 204–22 (chapter entitled "The Persecution of the Child by the State"). Ernest Pomeroy, *The Education Tyranny: The Education System Examined and Exposed, Together with Practical Aids for Persecuted Parents* (London: J.G. Hammond, 1910).

56. *Eclectic Review*, n.s. 13 (January–June 1843): 576.

57. Rev. Richard Winter Hamilton, *The Institutions of Popular Education* (London: Hamilton, Adams, 1845), p. 266.

58. Richard Winter Hamilton, "On the Parties Responsible for the Education of the People," in *Crosby-Hall Lectures*, p. 77.

59. Baines, *Letters to Russell*, p. 76.

60. *Nonconformist*, June 15, 1842, p. 411.

61. *Nonconformist* (1843), quoted in Briggs and Sellars, *Victorian Nonconformity*, p. 62.

62. *Eclectic Review*, n.s. 20 (July–December 1846): 291.

63. Herbert Spencer, *Social Statics* (1851; rpt. New York: Schalkenbach, 1954), pp. 185–86.

64. Hamilton, "On the Parties Responsible," p. 82.

65. Thomas Hodgskin, *The Natural and Artificial Right of Property Contrasted* (1832; rpt. Clifton, N.J.: Augustus M. Kelly, 1973), pp. 24, 49, 50.

66. Thomas Hodgskin, *Travels in the North of Germany* (Edinburgh: Archibald Constable, 1820), 2: 108.

67. Thomas Hodgskin, "Shall the State Educate the People?" *The Economist*, April 3, 1847, pp. 379–81. Given Hodgskin's extreme individualism, it is surely ironic that most commentators persist in referring to him as a "Ricardian Socialist." On Hodgskin see Elie Halévy, *Thomas Hodgskin* (London: Ernest Benn, n.d.).

68. *Eclectic Review*, n.s. 13 (January–June 1843): 581; *Eclectic Review*, n.s. 21 (January–June 1847): 507; Baines quoted in ibid., p. 363; Baines, *Letters to Russell*, p. 124; *Eclectic Review*, n.s. 20 (July–December 1846): 303; Baines quoted in *Eclectic Review*, n.s. 21 (January–June 1847): 363; and Baines, *Letters to Russell*, p. 72.

69. *Eclectic Review*, n.s. 21 (January–June 1847): 507.

70. Baines, *Letters to Russell*, pp. 73–74.

71. Ibid., p. 8.

72. Baines, "On the Progress and Efficiency," p. 39.

73. Baines, *Letters to Russell*, p. 8.

74. *Eclectic Review*, n.s. 13 (January–June 1843): 579.

75. *Eclectic Review*, n.s. 21 (January–June 1847): 125.

76. William Godwin, *Enquiry Concerning Political Justice and Its Influence on Morals and Happiness*, 3rd ed. (1797), ed. F. E. L. Priestley (Toronto: University of Torontd Press, 1946), 2: 302.

77. *Eclectic Review*, n.s. 13 (January–June 1843): 580.

78. *Eclectic Review*, n.s. 20 (July–December 1846): 291.

79. *Eclectic Review*, n.s. 21 (January–June 1847): 359.

80. Baines, *Letters to Russell*, pp. 7, 10.

81. Spencer, *Social Statics*, p. 297.

82. *Life and Struggles of William Lovett*, ed. R. H. Tawney (New York: Alfred A. Knopf, 1920), 1: 139, 142, 143.

83. William Lovett and John Collins, *Chartism: A New Organization for the People* (1840; rpt. New York: Humanities Press, 1969), pp. 63 ff.

84. J. S. Mill, *Principles of Political Economy*, 5th ed. (New York: Appleton, 1899), 2: 574.

85. J. S. Mill, *On Liberty*, ed. David Spitz (New York: Norton, 1975), pp. 98–99.

86. *Eclectic Review*, n.s. 20 (July–December 1846): 297–98.

87. A. Wells, "On the Education of the Working Classes," in *Crosby–Hall Lectures*, p. 65.

88. Baines, *Letters to Russell*, p. 120.

89. *Priestley's Writings on Philosophy, Science, and Politics*, ed. John A. Passmore (New York: Collier, 1965), pp. 307–08, 306, 309.

90. Ibid., p. 311.

91. Godwin, *Enquiry Concerning Political Justice*, 2: 298–99.

92. *Nonconformist*, October 19, 1842, p. 700.

93. Ibid. Spencer's contempt for uniformity remained with him throughout his life. In 1892 he complained of "a mania for uniformity, which I regard as most mischievous. Uniformity brings death, variety brings life; and I resist all movements towards uniformity"; Duncan, *Life and Letters*, p. 315. In 1897 he again referred to "mania everywhere for uniformity," and he argued that "Competition in methods of education is all essential and anything that tends to diminish competition will be detrimental" (p. 404).

94. Baines, "On the Progress and Efficiency," pp. 42–43; italics omitted. Baines, *Letters to Russell*, p. 53. Wells, "On the Education," p. 60.

95. *Eclectic Review*, n.s. 20 (July–December 1846): 290.

96. Herbert, *Sacrifice of Education*, p. 191.

97. Herbert, "State Education," p. 68.

98. Ibid., pp. 68–69.

99. Bonham, *Industrial Liberty*, pp. 297–98.

100. Quoted in Gash, *Reaction and Reconstruction*, p. 64, n. 1.
101. *Eclectic Review*, n.s. 22 (July–December 1847): 598.
102. Hodgskin, "Shall the State Educate the People?" p. 380.
103. *Eclectic Review*, n.s. 22 (July–December 1847): 592, 596, 607.
104. Ibid., pp. 609, 611.
105. On the classical economists and education, see William L. Miller, "The Economics of Education in English Classical Economics," *Southern Economic Journal* 32 (3) (January 1966): 294–309; Mark Blaug, "The Economics of Education in English Classical Political Economy: A Re-Examination," *Essays on Adam Smith*, ed. A. Skinner and T. Wilson (Oxford: Oxford University Press, 1975), pp. 568–99; and E. G. West, *Education and the State* (London: Institute of Economic Affairs, 1965), pp. 111–25.
106. Mill, *Principles*, 2: 573, 577.
107. Wells, "On the Education," p. 77.
108. Spencer, *Social Statics*, p. 300.
109. Ibid., p. 302.
110. Ibid., pp. 303–04.
111. Ibid., p. 301.
112. Revisionists Samuel Bowles and Herbert Gintis throw everything except the proverbial kitchen sink at the feet of capitalism, including "drugs, suicide, mental instability, personal insecurity, predatory sexuality, depression, loneliness, bigotry, and hatred . . ."; *Schooling in Capitalist America* (New York: Basic Books, 1976), p. 276. This is alarming news, indeed, but it is at least good to know that these problems do not exist in noncapitalist societies.
113. Some articles on Voluntaryism have appeared in recent years. See, e.g., Joel Spring, "Anarchism and Education: A Dissenting Tradition," in Karier, Violas, and Spring, *Roots of Crisis*, pp. 215–31; and Robert H. Chappell, "Anarchy Revisited: An Inquiry into the Public Education Dilemma," *Journal of Libertarian Studies* 2 (4) (Winter 1978): 357–72.

# 4 SCHOOLING FOR WORK AND WORKING AT SCHOOL
## Perspectives on Immigrant and Working-Class Education in Urban America, 1880-1920*

*C. H. Edson*

## INTRODUCTION

Between 1880 and 1920 a relationship was established between work and schooling that became permanently embedded in both the structure and ideology of American public schooling. This relationship—manifested in a new belief that public schools could, and indeed should, prepare youth for work—rapidly became a part of the predominant orthodoxy that continues to shape and limit educational thought and practice today.

During the four decades surrounding the turn of the nineteenth century, patterns of work and schooling underwent dramatic changes. Through increased mechanization, minute subdivision of labor, centralization of large industrial organizations, and scientific management, the industrial transformation inexorably altered patterns of work and upset prior assumptions about the great moral benefits of work. Likewise, with the phenomenal growth of public high schools, youth aged fourteen to seventeen began attending school in ever-increasing numbers rather than following former patterns of going to

*Some of the research for this chapter was made possible through a grant from the National Institute of Education, Department of Health, Education, and Welfare; however, the content does not necessarily reflect the position or policy of that agency, and no official endorsement should be inferred. Appreciation is gratefully extended to David Tyack who made many contributions to the initial writing of this essay.

work at age fourteen. Partially in response to the needs of industry for a skilled, disciplined, and regularized workforce and partially in response to solving internal school problems through encouraging school attendance and completion, turn-of-the-century educators articulated a new and close relationship between work and schooling.

The fundamental characteristic of industrialism was not technological innovation and mechanization but rather the reorganization of the social relations of production whereby control of the production process shifted from the hands of the workers to the hands of the employers. Scientific management and the minute subdivision of industrial labor expropriated both the workers' technical knowledge of the manufacturing process as well as their traditional rights to set their own hours of labor and establish their own production schedules. As most, but not all, industrial jobs tended toward less skilled types of work, industrialists and managers became less concerned with the technical abilities of their workers and expressed a growing preoccupation with the work habits and work attitudes of their employees. The reorganization of the social relations of production, therefore, required that workers be educated to a new industrial reality—a reality at once quite different from the preindustrial past, yet one carrying many of the moral prerogatives of an earlier time.

The transformation of public schooling—especially public secondary schooling—between 1880 and 1920 was, in part, a direct response to the changes in the organization of industrial work. Advocating a closer articulation between the world of work and the world of public schooling, turn-of-the-century educators largely accepted the industrialists' definitions of the educational nature of the problems that were besetting work in America and responded in ways consistent with the changed demands of the workplace. First, to restore the dignity and the moral preeminence of work for people performing monotonous, repetitive, and minutely subdivided tasks, educators taught about the larger industrial order and illustrated how each basic task and every worker performing those tasks made a significant contribution to industrial production. Second, to meet the changed demands of the workplace for skilled workers, clerical and white-collar personnel, and disciplined production workers, educators incorporated vocational and technical subjects into the traditional high school curriculum and stressed the importance of promptness, order, and following instructions as behavior necessary for success in industrial work settings. Third, to alleviate growing problems of labor militancy, high job turnover rates, absenteeism, and a lack of vertical job mobility, educators sought to imbue future workers with a sense of loyalty to their jobs, convey an individualistic and often antiunion work ethic, and teach a sense of career that would lead to permanence and stability in the workplace. Indeed, as James Gilbert concludes: "The responsibility for a positive response to modern industrial and social alienation in America fell upon education rather than upon politics or economic reorganization. . . . In the United States education and not politics was the principal arena in which the issues of modern industrial capitalism were joined."[1]

The educational response to the problems of modern industrialism, however, was not simply one of passively acceding to the labor demands of industrial capitalism. Rather, educators discussed the problems affecting the workplace in a forthright, if not always consistent, manner. Aware of the evils of child labor, sensitive to the many problems troubling the workplace, and concerned about the high rates of school elimination and grade retardation (especially among immigrant children), school personnel sought to alleviate what they perceived to be a growing disjuncture between work and schooling. Educators, however, recognized the inconsistencies between their visions of proper work preparation and the realities of the workplace. Specifically, their goals of equipping children with habits and skills that would lead to occupational success and of imbuing in them a life career motive that would goal-orient their work activity and lead to occupational persistence and mobility simply did not match the reality of the subdivided, monotonous, and low-skilled industrial jobs that were seldom organized into ascending stages of reward and responsibility.

Although educators recognized and actively discussed the problems of industrial work, their solutions blurred the debate between work and schooling. Unable to wholly reconcile their vision of a proper work preparation with the realities of industrial jobs, educators advocated prolonging school attendance beyond the normal school-leaving age of fourteen. They believed that universal secondary schooling for all youth would at least shelter children from the exploitative realities of industrial work, while giving them the time and opportunity to develop appropriate work behaviors, industrial skills, and career instincts that would prevent them from going to work as unskilled and immature wage earners. In short, by advocating prolonged school attendance for all youth, educators directed their attention away from the structural problems of industrial work and focused their energies on the ways in which schools *could* prepare youth for work.

Finally, although the evolution of the belief that public schools should prepare youth for work must primarily be seen in terms of changes in the organization of industrial work, it did not emerge solely as a result of impersonal economic forces. Such a static, one-way correspondence between changes in work and changes in schooling fails to account for the ways in which individuals actively responded to, and in turn helped to shape, new patterns of both work and schooling. Responses of educators, for example, stemmed from internal attendance and curriculum problems as well as from external demands of the capitalist economy. Likewise, industrial workers, immigrants, and their children—populations that received the primary attention of educators concerned with work and schooling—responded to new patterns of work and schooling as much in accordance with their own unique class and cultural traditions as in accordance with the demands of the industrial economy.

Thus, avoiding a correspondence theory that posits a direct, one-way relationship between the changing patterns of work and the changing patterns of schooling, the following essay first examines the transformation of work in nineteenth-century urban America. The second section explores the perceptions and strategies of turn-of-the-century American educators concerning the changes in work and schooling, both in terms of external economic forces and internal organizational forces. The third section analyzes the emergent ideology that schools could prepare youth for work in terms of how educators viewed working classes and their children—populations that educators felt suffered most from what they perceived to be a growing disjuncture between the worlds of work and schooling. The fourth section discusses those traditional southern Italian attitudes toward work and schooling that helped to shape their work and school behaviors after arriving in the United States. Finally, the last section explores the conflicts between educators and southern Italian immigrants in terms of their differing attitudes toward work and schooling. The essay concludes that by failing to appreciate how powerful class and cultural continuities continued to shape the work and school behaviors of diverse working-class and immigrant populations, educational reformers remained blinded to the cultural and social limitations of what they thought were universal and comprehensive solutions to the problems besetting work and schooling.

## THE TRANSFORMATION OF WORK

In the second half of the nineteenth century, huge factories began to replace small workshops and farms as the dominant mode of production in the leading sectors of the U.S. economy.[2] Unlike earlier and smaller manufacturing enterprises, in which skilled workers largely controlled the process of production, the new, highly mechanized factories expropriated the workers' technical knowledge through minute subdivisions of labor, and a new breed of "scientific managers" came to control the production process. This transformation of industrial work into monotonous, specialized tasks challenged former commitments to the moral primacy of work and created labor problems that industrialists and managers seemed unable to control.

To increase factory output and to centralize control of the production process according to the principles of scientific management, factory managers of the 1880s and 1890s broke up the production process into component procedures that made obsolete many of the skilled trades. A skilled shoemaker in the early nineteenth century, for example, would probably be a factory machine operative by the 1880s, performing only one of some thirty or forty subdivided tasks that he earlier performed alone. Likewise, in a Cincinnati clothing factory, the task of making a pair of men's pants—formerly the job of a single tailor—had been divided into seventeen different occupations by 1859.[3] Not all industrial jobs suffered skill degradation. Mule spinners in textile factories and heaters and rollers in the steel industry required high levels of technical skill; nevertheless, as most factory jobs required decreasing levels of skill, most skilled craftsmen saw their trades so subdivided that they became mere appendages to the machines they operated. Overseen by growing ranks of technical and supervisory personnel and regulated by new factory clocks, workers lost their traditional rights to set their own hours of labor and their own production schedules. Thus, although increased mechanization, subdivision of labor, and scientific management had pushed the United States past all other nations in industrial production by 1900, disturbing and unsettling currents of criticism and protest began to be heard from many sides.

In one sense, the new factory system represented a triumph of the work ethic. Through an immense amount of hard work, America had become the industrial giant of the world. Indeed, by 1910, industrial production in the United States nearly doubled that of its nearest rival, Germany. But, as Daniel Rodgers observes, there was considerable irony in that triumph. In their headlong pursuit of industrial development, Rodgers writes, "Northerners so radically transformed work that the old moral expectations would no longer hold." [4]

The new industrial transformation tore apart work and work ideals in the early twentieth century, upsetting prior assumptions about the moral preeminence of work. Formerly, most believed that hard work and a will to succeed brought economic success and independence — everyone could get ahead if they tried. On the other hand, massed wage earners, assembly lines, increased mechanization, and minutely subdivided labor brought such beliefs into question. By subdividing the work process, workers no longer needed to learn the multiple skills that had earlier led to mobility and status in the occupational hierarchy. Now as factory operatives, they were trapped with little expectation of vertical occupational or economic mobility. In the past, working for wages was not considered wage slavery because of the ever-present promise of mobility; however, when fifty-year-old production workers were likely to earn the same wage they made when they were twenty, that promise seemed hollow indeed.[5] In short, hard work and a will to succeed no longer insured either economic success or economic independence.

Equally disturbing in terms of beliefs about work were certain nonmaterial consequences of the industrial transformation. The minute subdivision of labor largely destroyed such worker intangibles as creativity, self-expression, satisfaction with a completed product, and individual identity taken from the work a person performed. Work had not only been an avenue for self-expression but was believed to build moral character as well. New industrial work often did not allow for such individual needs, and rather than identifying themselves with a particular product or skill, many workers became solely identified with the machines they operated. Changing patterns of work, therefore, had shattered the long-cherished belief about the close relationship between work and morality.

If the industrial transformation challenged earlier conventions about the moral primacy of work, it also brought open opposition and resistance to new patterns of work.[6] Acutely conscious of the problems in the workplace and concerned with growing union membership, increasing strike activity, and the swelling popularity of socialist candidates at the polls, turn-of-the-century industrialists and managers knew they faced serious problems. Factory laborers actively resisted the new industrial discipline by reporting to work irregularly, participating in work slowdowns and work restrictions, and by restlessly moving from job to job. Although all these forms of worker unrest increased manufacturing costs and kept production down, the extraordinarily high rate of labor turnover was of greatest concern. Studies between 1905 and 1917 showed that the majority of industrial workers changed jobs at least every three years, and yearly turnover in individual enterprises often exceeded the total number of workers. The Armour meat packing plant in Chicago, for example, reported a 100 percent turnover in 1914; likewise, turnover rates in the woolen industry between 1907 and 1910 ranged between 113 and 163 percent. Finally, in 1913 alone, Ford Motor Company reported an astonishing turnover rate of 370 percent.[7]

Largely accustomed to seeing laborers in terms of interchangeable parts of a machine rather than as individuals seeking to upgrade their positions through job hopping, managers and industrialists were perplexed by such worker instability. Efficient industrial production required a hard-working, stable, and regularized workforce. The managers believed that education could adjust the worker to this new industrial reality. To overcome tardiness and absenteeism, workers needed to learn habits of promptness and loyalty to the company. To alleviate the monotony and isolation of highly subdivided, machine-paced tasks, workers needed to learn that their work was a part of something larger and intimately connected with the wider industrial community. And to discourage high turnover rates that brought havoc to systematic industrial production, workers needed to think about work in terms of permanent or long-term commitments rather than as a random series of unrelated jobs. In their call for workers educated to this new industrial reality, however, managers and industrialists often misunderstood the complexity of the problems they faced and frequently increased the tension between the worker and the factory.

## VOCATIONAL EDUCATION: EDUCATORS'
## PERCEPTIONS OF WORK AND SCHOOLING

As industrialists articulated their fears and problems to the nation at large, they captured the ears and the imagination of a new breed of urban educational managers—people who were as intent on building their own professional empires as the industrialists had been in erecting theirs. Although urban educational reformers of the early twentieth century translated industrial problems into specific educational strategies such as vocational education, those strategies stemmed from internal curriculum and attendance problems as much as from external demands of the industrial economy. To investigate the origins and evolution of the belief in the close relationship between work and schooling, therefore, both external and internal forces require examination. Initially, however, brief mention must be made of the changes taking place in public schooling during the four decades surrounding the turn of the nineteenth century.

In the nineteenth century, the chief goals of public education were to develop good moral character and teach the basics. Many believed that basic training in reading, writing, and arithmetic provided all that was necessary for continued self-education after leaving school.[8] According to William Wood, temporary chairman of the New York City Board of Education in 1869, the 3-R's "was all that was required in this free country to succeed in life, and nothing more should be taught in the public schools."[9] Seldom was schooling seen as a preparation for work; indeed, a widespread belief in the culture of self-help militated against establishing a close relationship between work and schooling. Secondary education in the nineteenth century was a minority institution. In the words of the National Education Association's Committee of Ten in 1893, the high school was designed "to prepare for the duties of life that small proportion of all children in the country—a proportion small in number, but very important to the welfare of the nation—who show themselves able to profit by an education prolonged to the eighteenth year, and whose parents are able to support them while they remain so long in school."[10]

Vocational training was not a major function of the high school; in fact, some late-nineteenth-century critics argued that continued schooling beyond the elementary years might actually inhibit youth from assuming responsible work. In 1879, one of the architects of the Portland, Oregon, public schools warned that extended schooling might "graduate whole regiments of sickly sentimentalists: young gentlemen unused and unfit to work."[11] "The maintenance of free high schools is unwise," proclaimed the Massachusetts paper manufacturer James P. Munroe in 1892, "because it offers to boys and girls wholly unfit for secondary education, a temptation to exchange the actual benefit of remunerative work at fifteen years of age for the doubtful advantage of a training that can have no direct bearing upon their life work, and which, at the time of life it occurs, may do decided harm."[12]

In an age when there were few educational requirements for available jobs, a majority of the population felt that occupational success bore little relation to secondary schooling. Such beliefs were reflected by a businessman in 1880 who stated: "a child who has a good English education, if he has any snap about him, will succeed better than the average graduate of the high school who knows a little of everything."[13] Yet, in spite of these reservations about the relationship between work and schooling, the high school rapidly became a mass institution: one that soon embraced the majority of American adolescents.

The growth of public secondary education around the turn of the century was phenomenal by any standard. Between 1890 and 1920 new high schools opened on the average of over one per day, and student enrollments increased by 812 percent compared with a nationwide population increase during the same period of only 68 percent. Most important, however, were figures reflecting the percentage of youth, ages fourteen to seventeen, enrolled in public high schools: from 4 percent in 1890, the figures swelled to 28 percent by 1920, and to 47 percent by 1930. This rapid expansion of the high school constituted an unprecedented shift in the occupations of youth. Now, for the first time in history, millions of young people were going to school rather than following the normal pattern of going to work. Statistics on the labor force participation of youth underline the dramatic shift. Between 1900 and 1930, the percentage of working males, aged fourteen to eighteen, dropped from 43 percent to 12 percent; for females, the decline was from 18 percent to 5 percent.[14] It was rapidly becoming apparent that schooling was replacing work as the normal "career" of youth.

Educators were acutely conscious that the shift from work to school violated long-held values and folkways, and they attempted to find a moral equivalent for productive employment within the school. In the hope of smoothly meshing the high school and the occupational order, school officials sought a social, political, and economic justification for schooling youth rather than employing them.[15] Vocational education provided those needed rationales and established structures that fundamentally altered the ways in which people viewed the relationships between work and schooling.

A combination of external economic forces and internal organizational forces catapulted vocational education into the mainstream of American public education between 1906 and 1917. Turning first to external economic forces, public schools in the early twentieth century faced new demands to increase industrial productivity by producing workers fitted to the urban-industrial environment. Although educators remained critical of many of the consequences of industrialization, they largely accepted the changes in the organization of work and used them to justify extending the schooling of youth beyond fourteen years of age. The architects of vocational education believed that industrialization had separated work and life by removing the locus of work from home to factory; therefore, the school had to offer the vocational training once provided by other social agencies. The industrial transformation, explained Stanford University professor Ellwood Cubberley in 1909, made the home an inadequate place to prepare youth for work:

> Along with these changes there has come not only a tremendous increase in the quantity of our knowledge, but also a demand for a large increase in the amount of knowledge necessary to enable one to meet the changed conditions of our modern life. The kind of knowledge needed, too, has fundamentally changed. The ability to read and write and cipher no longer distinguishes the educated from the uneducated man. A man must have better, broader, and a different kind of knowledge than did his parents, if he is to succeed under modern conditions.[16]

In addition, with the invention of cash registers, pneumatic tubes, telephones, and a host of assorted office machines, many jobs for urban twelve- to sixteen-year-olds—cash boys and girls, office workers, messengers, and telegram delivery boys—became obsolete.[17] Chicago social settlement workers Edith Abbott and Sophonisba Breckenridge observed in 1917 that at the present time "there is so little demand for the labor of children under sixteen years of age that it is impossible for more than a small percentage of the children who leave school at the age of fourteen or fifteen to find employment."[18]

Finally, as many jobs had suffered skill degradation, growing numbers of unskilled, "dead-end" jobs awaited the uneducated youth. As Norton Grubb and Marvin Lazerson argue, the fracturing of vertical skill ladders through the increasing subdivision of labor made the threat of "dead-end" jobs a reality—providing further justification for prolonged school attendance and vocational training.[19] Changes in the nature of work, therefore, had not only resulted in demands for more highly skilled workers but had also reduced the number and quality of jobs available to youth. Urban educational reformers responded to these changing economic conditions with programs of vocational education.

Along with providing new technical knowledge and work skills to meet external industrial demands, advocates of vocational education saw their programs instilling first, appropriate work behaviors and second, proper attitudes toward work. First, echoing the desires of industrialists and managers, school reformers sought to teach appropriate work behaviors that would lead to success in the industrial world. By stressing the importance of regular school attendance, punctuality, and classroom order, educators felt they could mitigate the problems of absenteeism, tardiness, and lack of discipline that plagued many industries. Regular school attendance established habits of regularity and persistence that directly translated to the workplace. Given the changing nature of work, many feared that the workplace was no longer the best environment for learning good work habits. Among others, many of whom also came from rural backgrounds, John Dewey argued that children needed protection from city work: "The kinds of work in which the young can engage, especially in cities, are largely anti-educational. That prevention of child labor is a social duty is evidence on this point."[20] And according to A. E. Winship, editor of the *Journal of Education* in 1900: "the boy who leaves school and goes to work does not necessarily learn to work steadily, but often quite the reverse."[21] As David Cohen and Marvin Lazerson suggest, some educators felt that appropriate work behaviors were better learned in school than at work.[22]

Second, educators sought to develop programs that would convey proper attitudes toward work that would enable youth to cope with the problems of industrial labor. Again, influenced by the concerns of industrialists and managers about the monotony and isolation of highly subdivided industrial labor, educational reformers, such as Harvard University President Charles Eliot, believed that the state of mind of the worker was more important than the job he or she performed.[23] Jane Addams, the founder of Hull House, believed that an "informing mind" would produce these proper work attitudes. In 1909 she wrote:

> If a child goes into a sewing factory with a knowledge of the work she is doing in relation to the finished product; if she is informed concerning the material she is manipulating and the processes to which it is subjected; if she understands the design she is elaborating in its historic relation to art and decoration, her daily life is lifted from drudgery to one of self-conscious activity, and her pleasure and intelligence is registered in her product.[24]

In schools, therefore, children should learn that all tasks—however minute or unimportant they may appear to those performing them—were intimately connected with the wider industrial community and contributed to the progress of the nation. Among others, Cubberley felt that extended schooling with a more explicit industrial focus could address these demands. "As our industrial life becomes narrower and its processes more concealed," Cubberley wrote in 1909,

> new and more extended training is called for to prepare the future worker for his task, to reveal to him something of the intricacy and interdependence of our modern, social and industrial life, and to point out to him the necessity of each man's part. With the ever-increasing subdivision and specialization of labor . . . the task is thrown more and more upon the school of instilling into all a social and political consciousness that will lead to unity.
> . . .[25]

Through the proper kind of extended schooling, therefore, the problems of monotony and isolation that not only characterized the workplace, but according to some, the entire society, could be alleviated.

Finally, the proponents of vocational education justified extended schooling for youth in order to fully develop a "life career motive" in every child. To enable young people to avoid the dead-end, low-paying, nonskilled, and dangerous jobs they so often performed, they not only needed to be sheltered from the workplace but also needed a longer period of schooling to develop career instincts. In 1910, Charles Eliot deplored the inadequate work preparation of youth: "At present we are permitting the great majority of American children to go out into the world as unskilled laborers, without having chosen any trade or other occupation requiring skill and without having felt in their school work the motive of the life-career."[26]

Eliot's solution was to increase the hours of schooling, per day and per year. Depending on the age of the pupils, he advocated extending school time from twenty-five hours a week to between thirty-three and forty-four hours and felt that summer vacations should be "much reduced."[27] Cubberley also advocated longer periods of preparation for youth: "Child life is everywhere experiencing to-day a new lengthening of the period of dependence and training. In proportion as our social life becomes broader and more complex, a longer period of guidance becomes necessary to prepare the individual for active participation in it."[28]

As educational reformers developed their notions of career preparation, they once again reflected the external concerns of the workplace. High turnover rate and an apparent lack of commitment by workers plagued industrial production. According to industrialists and managers, workers failed to think about their work in terms of long-term commitments that suited both their individual aims and abilities; therefore, without sufficient information to make job decisions wisely and without any apparent goal beyond wages for immediate daily survival, workers aimlessly drifted from job to job. Workers without a career motive—one that led to sustained, goal-oriented activity and the possibility of occupational mobility—hurt themselves as much as they hurt industrial output.

For their part in improving the industrial process, public schools would imbue future workers with a "life career motive." "The world in which most of us live," Dewey stated in 1899, "is a world in which everyone has a calling or occupation."[29] To discover that career, however, meant that young people had to be sheltered from the world of work for a period of time sufficient to develop their natural talents and instincts. With proper guidance and training, career choices could be made intelligently and scientifically and lead to a preestablished pattern of work activity that, through persistence and merit, would result in upward mobility. A career of ascending stages of activity meant that individuals should no longer think of work in terms of a random series of jobs. If schools, through vocational guidance and counseling, could teach children to think in terms of careers rather than jobs, everyone would benefit. Turn-of-the-century educators felt confident that schools were capable of responding to these external economic concerns of the workplace.

Not only did advocates of vocational education feel that extended schooling would alleviate external industrial problems by integrating youth more smoothly into the economy, but they also felt that vocational education could solve internal problems that were plaguing the schools. The traditional high school as constituted, however, was poorly equipped to meet either the changed educational demands emanating from the workplace or the pressing problems coming from within.

School surveys and studies of school dropouts appeared to confirm the need for an educational reform that would reduce the disjuncture between work and schooling. Urban school systems were plagued by high dropout rates in the early twentieth century. In an inquiry into why children left high schools in such large numbers, the Massachusetts Commission on Industrial Education concluded in 1906: "It is the dissatisfaction of the child which takes him from the school . . . the lack is in the system, which fails to offer the child of fourteen continued schooling of a practical character."[30] This theme was reiterated seven years later by the editor of *Manual Training Magazine*: "children leave school because they don't like to go to school, because the work is distasteful to them and offers them little or nothing that they may conceive to be of value in their lives."[31] "Moreover," stated Eliot, "from lack of interest they acquire while in school a listless way of working."[32] Finally, Theodore Roosevelt joined the chorus of critics in his annual message to Congress in 1907:

> Our school system is gravely defective in so far as it puts a premium upon mere literacy training and tends therefore to train the boy away from the farm and the workshop. Nothing more is needed than the best type of industrial school, the school for mechanical industries in the city, the school for practically teaching agriculture in the country.[33]

In short, the traditional literary curriculum of the high school—in which 49 percent of the total students still enrolled in Latin as late as 1910—was accused of being irrelevant, bookish, and undemocratically fitted to the bright, college-bound child.[34]

"[T]he only way our schools can be made truly democratic," proclaimed the Superintendent of Boston schools in 1908, is "to begin industrial training in the public schools." "Until very recently," he continued, "they have offered equal opportunity for all to receive *one* kind of education, but what will make them democratic is to provide opportunity for all to receive such education as will fit them *equally well* for their particular life work."[35] In the minds of many reformers, the high schools around the turn of the century had been exclusively serving the interests of the upper classes. With the belief that the high school should serve the children of all social classes, Eliot stated that "the educational publicist must keep in mind the interests of the 95 percent of the children, rather than those of the 5 percent."[36] Eliot and others believed that the professional and managerial classes were well taken care of and that now the schools must see to the needs of the common people. In short, the conception of the school had changed, and according to Cubberley, "Industrial and vocational training is especially significant . . . [for] the classes in society which the school is in the future expected to serve."[37] Thus, vocational education would keep the students in school because they would be interested in the curriculum and would benefit from both the skill training and career guidance they would receive. Finally, vocational education would restore the promise of American education and American democracy by serving the needs of *all* pupils, not just those of the elites and the college-bound.

In 1918, the year following the passage of the Smith-Hughes Act, which provided federal support for vocational education, the National Education Association's Commission on the Reorganization of Secondary Education (CRSE) published its influential report that confirmed the shifting climate of opinion in support of a closer link between work and schooling. Entitled the *Cardinal Principles of Secondary Education*, the report duly noted the many changes which had taken place in American life that affected the integration of youth into the economic order. In addition to health, command of fundamental processes, worthy home membership, citizenship, worthy use of leisure and ethical character, vocation was one of the seven objectives that were to guide the future course of secondary education. "Vocational education should equip the individual to secure a livelihood for himself and those dependent on him, to serve society well through his vocation, to maintain the right relationships toward his fellow workers and society, and, as far as possible, to find in that vocation his own best development."[38] In the quarter century between the *Report of the Committee of Ten* (1893) and the *Cardinal Principles of Secondary Education* (1918), high schools in America had been endowed with the new task of preparing youth for the world of work.

In the early years of the century, school reformers argued against a dual system of education on the grounds that providing separate schools for vocational training or continuation schools for working children would polarize class divisions and necessitate a costly duplication of administrative machinery. Seeking both to preserve the egalitarian values of American schooling and to satisfy the skill and behavior requirements of the workplace, school reformers successfully advanced the idea of the comprehensive high school, a school that would provide *both* vocational and liberal education.

By combining liberal and vocational education in the comprehensive high school, however, a structure emerged that blurred the debate about the proper relationships between work and schooling. The questions of whether the schools would merely adapt workers to the existing industrial society or would help workers to see the full dimensions of their work in the hopes of ultimately transforming the workplace became submerged. Dewey saw the dangers better than most:

> Any scheme for vocational education which takes its point of departure from the industrial regime that now exists, is likely to assume and to perpetuate its divisions and weaknesses, and thus to become an instrument in accomplishing the feudal dogma of social predestination. . . . But an education which acknowledges the full intellectual and social meaning of a vocation would include instruction in the historic background of present conditions; training in science to give intelligence and initiative in dealing with material and agencies of production; and study of economics, civics, and politics, to bring the future worker into touch with the problems of the day and the various methods proposed for its improvement.[39]

Although a segregated school system was rejected, the acceptance of a differentiated curriculum represented a radical departure from nineteenth-century common school ideology. That ideology, espoused by educators from Horace Mann to William Torrey Harris, insisted that all children, regardless of class or future occupation, should receive the same education. The emergent ideology, according to the *Cardinal Principles of Secondary Education*, recognized "individual differences in capacities and aptitudes among secondary school pupils" and sought to provide an education for all children commensurate with their abilities and probable occupations.[40]

To meet the goal of fitting students for their life work, it became necessary, as Eliot noted, to sort students "by their evident or probable destinies."[41] This critical process of selection should not be done haphazardly by the classroom teacher. Rather, selection should be achieved objectively through scientific testing and vocational counseling. Intelligence test pioneer Lewis Terman stated in 1923:

> Intelligence tests can tell us whether a child's native brightness corresponds more nearly to the median of (1) the professional classes, (2) those in the semi-professional pursuits . . . or (5) unskilled labor. This information will be of great value in planning the education of a particular child and also in planning the differentiated curriculum here recommended.[42]

The use of scientific means for selection, claimed the National Society for the Promotion of Industrial Education's (NSPIE) Executive Secretary Charles Prosser, would "adjust boys and girls for life by having them undergo varied experiences in order to uncover their varied tastes and aptitudes and to direct and to train them in the avenues for which they display the most capacity." Such a program, Prosser concluded, "would require a differentiation of the course of study for pupils between *twelve and fourteen years of age.*"[43] Vocational education, therefore, not only made educational testing and vocational guidance fundamental to the operation of the schools but also lent support for an entirely new structure in American education, the junior high school.

The emergent ideological consensus that schools could prepare youth for work, therefore, stemmed from both internal demands on public schooling as well as from external economic forces. Yet by advocating prolonged school attendance for all youth, educators largely avoided the structural problems attending the reorganization of work and helped to establish the belief that work preparation was primarily an educational matter to be dealt with in the public schools. Furthermore, as educators largely failed to appreciate that different groups of people viewed patterns of work and schooling differently, they frequently misunderstood the educational problems they faced and often misinterpreted the wide range of responses from different ethnic and social groups. As educators remained blinded to the cultural and social limitations of what they thought were universal and comprehensive solutions to the problems besetting work and schooling, it soon became apparent that the predominant orthodoxy was ill-equipped to deal with the increasing diversity and complexity of twentieth-century American society.

## SCHOOLING FOR WORK: EDUCATORS' PERCEPTIONS OF IMMIGRANTS AND WORKING CLASSES

The arrival of twenty-three million immigrants between 1880 and 1919 accompanied the dramatic changes taking place both in the workplace and the public school. These immigrants—largely from eastern and southern Europe—settled primarily in the urban areas of the industrial Northeast and Midwest. In many cities these new arrivals and their children outnumbered citizens of native-born fathers. As early as 1880, for example, immigrants and their children made up over 80 percent of the population of cities such as Cleveland, New York, Detroit, Milwaukee, and Chicago. The large numbers of immigrants among the working classes led the clergyman Samuel Lane Loomis to observe in 1887: "Not every foreigner is a workingman, but in the cities, at least, it may almost be said that every workingman is a foreigner."[44]

Similar to the industrial workplace, many urban public schools became dominated by immigrants and their children. By 1908, for example, the U.S. Immigration Commission found that 58 percent of the school children in thirty-seven cities across the country had foreign-born fathers. New York led all the large cities with 72 percent of its students reporting foreign-born fathers, followed by Chicago with 67 percent, Boston with 64 percent, and Cleveland with 60 percent.[45] Thus, in many of the large cities around the turn of the century, immigrants dominated both the factories and the public schools; nevertheless, those individuals largely responsible for articulating the new relationships between work and schooling— educators, business leaders, social reformers—failed to understand the complex cultural and social worlds of their workers and pupils. Their cultural insensitivity and class-bound notions about work and schooling, however, did not stem from a failure to recognize immigrant differences but rather from a belief that these differences detracted from individual and national progress. Through proper education, they reasoned, these class and cultural differences could largely be overcome.

The apparent insensitivity to cultural differences on the part of educational reformers came primarily from their beliefs in assimilation. In Darwinian fashion, most believed that through a natural, evolutionary process the foreign element—all those who did not fit the Anglo-American mold—would largely disappear. Their unswerving faith in unlimited economic and social progress, however, depended upon maintaining what they believed to be a rational and scientific order. All parts of society needed to fit together like parts of a machine in order to be efficient and productive. Regarding anything that did not mesh with that perceived order as going against the goal of social advancement, reformers viewed religion, language, and cultural traditions as distractions to improving the American standard of living and furthering American progress. In short, ethnic backgrounds and national loyalties were not paramount. "The immediate duty which the community has to perform for its own protection," stated the social reformer Jacob Riis in 1892, "is to school the children first of all into good Americans, and next into useful citizens."[46]

In a similar but not always consistent fashion, school reformers remained insensitive to class as well as cultural considerations. The middle-class ideal of a "life career motive," for example, seldom matched working-class behaviors or working-class realities. An ideology of professional careers had become pervasive in the occupational order in the late nineteenth century. Just as growing numbers of universities and professional schools began to certify professionalism, careerism, and expertise, so too did more and more states begin to license professionals such as pharmacists, dentists, and physicians. Imbued with what Burton Bledstein labels a middle-class "culture of professionalism," upwardly mobile school reformers also thought of work in terms of a career rather than a random series of jobs undertaken for immediate physical survival.[47] People who performed the dull, monotonous, and low-paying factory jobs, they concluded, were either lower on the evolutionary ladder and lacked the innate ability to undertake more complex work, or they did not have the proper education and guidance when they were young. That some working-class families objected to the extended schooling required to develop these career instincts and skills—either for reasons of custom or necessity—perplexed middle-class professionals. "I can only stand lost in wonder at the objections [to career training]," Dewey stated in 1899. "It sometimes seems to me," he concluded, "that those who make these objections must live in quite another world."[48] For many educational professionals, working-class realities were indeed of another world.

Believing that issues of ethnicity and class obstructed evolutionary progress, turn-of-the-century educators tended to homogenize southern and eastern European immigrants who came from widely different social and national backgrounds. That these immigrants lacked Anglo–Saxon, middle-class habits and values was of *far greater concern* to the reformers than were the differences immigrants had among themselves in terms of past experiences, traditions, and aspirations. As Paul Boyer argues, reformers believed that a single moral standard was necessary and attainable, for only through a secure cultural consensus could a harmonious community life, one that had been torn apart by immigration and the industrial transformation, be restored.[49] Blinded to the ways in which ethnic differences mediated immigrant assimilation into American society, educators sought to treat these newcomers in the same manner. In 1909, Cubberley detailed the dangers the country faced and the task that lay ahead for educators:

> These southern and eastern Europeans are of a very different type from the north Europeans who preceded them. Illiterate, docile, lacking in self-reliance and initiative, and not possessing the Anglo-Teutonic conceptions of law, order, and government, their coming has served to dilute tremendously our national stock, and to corrupt our civic life. . . . Our task is to break up these groups or settlements, to assimilate and amalgamate these people as a part of our American race, and to implant in their children, so far as can be done, the Anglo-Saxon conception of righteousness, law and order, and popular government, and to awaken in them a reverence for our democratic institutions, and for those things in our national life which we as a people hold to be of abiding worth.[50]

As Cubberley clearly illustrated, issues of class and ethnicity merged in the minds of many educational professionals. Thus, in their attempts to reduce the disjuncture between work and schooling, educators often mistook class-related patterns of work and school behavior as resulting from the immigrant's lack of Anglo-Saxon habits and values. For example, rather than interpreting the high labor turnover rates as a response by immigrants to maintain a steady income in an industrial economy characterized by high seasonal employment followed by unemployment, educators felt most immigrants drifted from job to job because they had failed to develop a "life career motive" or that they lacked the cultural persistence and moral discipline necessary for occupational success. Likewise, educators attributed low school attendance and achievement rates among some immigrant families to a similar cultural and moral deficiency. As David Hogan points out, however, patterns of school attendance often directly related to working-class concerns over home ownership. "To immigrants in Chicago," Hogan states, "home ownership was a safeguard against irregular employment, illness, death, low wages, and all the vicissitudes of life in a wage labor society."[51] Youth who could contribute to that goal of economic survival by working, rather than attending school, were assets that could not be ignored. Thus, by believing that public schools should impose a universal and undifferentiated moral order on the chaos of immigrant school and work patterns, educators fundamentally misunderstood the nature of the problems they faced and often erected unbridgeable cultural and class barriers between the schools and their immigrant clientele.

Although school reformers homogenized southern and eastern European immigrants when discussing their commonly shared deficiency of Anglo, Protestant, middle-class values, they were acutely aware of differences between immigrant nationality groups as assessed by standard measures of intelligence, school achievement, and occupational mobility. Yet after recognizing these differences, educators continued to apply universal, undifferentiated solutions that stood in sharp contrast to the complexity of the immigrants' cultural and social worlds. Through limited understanding and homogeneous treatment of their immigrant clientele, conflicts arose that should have brought into question their middle-class myopia; however, without specific knowledge or appreciation of the social and cultural experiences of immigrants prior to arrival, educators were largely unable to see how these experiences mediated their work and schooling patterns in America. An examination of the divergent views of reality held by southern Italian immigrants illustrates how educators' attempts to establish a close and uniform relationship between work and schooling conflicted with the complex educational traditions of a particular immigrant population.

## SOUTHERN ITALIAN ATTITUDES TOWARD WORK AND SCHOOLING

Traditional southern Italian attitudes toward work and schooling were varied and complex, stemming from long-held beliefs, social experiences, and educational traditions.[52] Traditional education in southern Italy took place largely within the confines of village life, as both the physical isolation of the south Italian town and an intense regionalism tended to restrict external interaction with the world beyond the village. More precisely, education took place within *la famiglia*—the inclusive social unit of south Italian society. Because of its central importance in defining, legitimating, and integrating peasant existence, it was only natural that the family was the central institution for educating the young. Education taking place outside the home environment, on the other hand, threatened the stability of traditional society and was, therefore, viewed with suspicion.

Traditional education in southern Italy focused on two themes: first, the moral and social, and, second, the practical. The moral content of education, while broadly designed to maintain the stability of south Italian society, was specifically directed toward preserving family tradition and honor. Largely within the context of the home and primarily through the medium of folklore, children learned the moral and social beliefs and behaviors supportive of the familially oriented social system. Numerous proverbs and formal sayings stressed the following themes: *male superiority*, "A thousand females don't make a male," and "Women are long in the hair and short in the brains"; *the authority of the family head*, "The law was made for the city. Here the father rules the roost"; *parental respect*, "He who does not respect his parents comes to a bad end"; and *family loyalty*, "Family members should be 'all united like the fingers of the hand,'" and "Dust was never swept beyond the threshold of the door."[53] Finally, the moral theme of education appeared universal in south Italian society—as applicable to nonpeasant classes as it was to peasants. Speaking of his father, a lawyer's son recalled: "He taught us many Latin and Italian proverbs, dealing primarily with outward conduct and good manners. . . . He was anxious that we should bear ourselves honorably in life, mainly emphasizing obedience and good behavior as well as respect toward authority and to the aged."[54]

The practical content of education, customarily transmitted by the family through adult imitation, was specifically directed toward family welfare. In a society where physical survival for many depended on hard work, and social standing depended largely on material wealth, each member had to learn to contribute to the family welfare as soon as was physically possible. Thus, from a very early age, children learned the skills, habits, and attitudes that enabled and encouraged them to work, whether in the fields, at home, or in a shop. Three interrelated themes characterized the transmission of work attitudes to the young: economic necessity, family duty, and early maturity.

The agricultural economy of southern Italy made it necessary for everybody to work—even young children. The economic contribution of children, however small, often provided the margin necessary for family survival. Peasant children began work at an early age. Although widespread throughout Italy, child labor was most pronounced in the South. In 1911, for example, of the approximately two and a half million children in Italy between the ages of ten and fifteen, one and a half million were gainfully employed.[55] The proportion of working children in the South, however, was probably higher, for agriculture, unlike some industry, provided numerous tasks such as weeding or removing stones from the fields that required little strength or skill. Unequal enforcement of national laws regulating child labor and compelling school attendance also contributed to a higher incidence of child labor in the South. Because of the absolute necessity of child labor and the inaccessibility of many regions, these national laws had little practical significance in southern Italy.[56]

Because of economic necessity, children learned positive and unambiguous attitudes toward work almost from infancy. "Young as he might be in age," recalled an Italo-American, "he had to learn the most important lesson in life, 'that he who does not work does not eat,' or 'he who eats must toil.'"[57] Work also defined play activities, and, in many cases, the only games children were allowed to play were those imitative of adult work activities. Tradition prohibited play for mere pleasure or recreation, and children quickly learned that to play in this manner was "to wear out shoes, undermine health, and waste time."[58] "Our children work and work hard," the mayor of a small town in Basilicata concluded. "They don't go around playing, I can assure you. They begin to know life from an early age...."[59]

The theme of economic necessity was seldom a sufficiently compelling reason for learning positive attitudes toward work—especially for children too young to understand such complexities of survival as rents, taxes, and interest payments. Consequently, in teaching the young respect for work, parents also appealed to the theme of family duty. As family membership in peasant society required everyone to earn *la spesa* (the necessary self-sustaining contribution), both boys and girls were duty-bound to begin work soon after the period of infancy. The bond between work and family duty was strong: "From the moment of birth you had to learn to assume your responsibility in the life of the family. . . . You had a purpose in living and that was to work and be of service."[60] Likewise, an agricultural laborer from Ventimiglia, Sicily, remembered working with his father in the fields "almost from infancy [as] every pair of hands could contribute something to the family's welfare."[61] Finally, Pascal D'Angelo spoke of his Abruzzi boyhood: "Both my parents worked out in the fields. . . . And I too had to help them intermittently from the time I was very young." At seven, D'Angelo had the responsibility of watching the family's sheep and goats as his father could not afford to hire an older boy. "I can safely say," D'Angelo concluded, "that work rather than school was the important element in my boyhood."[62]

Added to the closely related themes of economic necessity and family duty, the transmission of positive work attitudes to the young received further support from the theme of early maturity. As the assumption of substantial and responsible work denoted maturity in southern Italian society, parents taught children that early employment brought adult respect and status. Although the assumption of adult work roles resulted in newly acquired rights and responsibilities within the family, early maturity had a wider social significance as well. In addition to participating with their respective adult groups on the streets or at the fountain, boys and girls also underwent certain outward changes. Girls discarded their childhood braids and wore the scarf of womanhood about their shoulders; likewise, the usually barefoot boys proudly wore the mocassins (*scarponi*) that signified the doing of man's work. Children of artisans also assumed responsible work at an early age. Rather than in the fields, however, the artisan boy worked as an apprentice, and by the time he was twelve assumed adult work roles and received wages for his labor.

Customarily, the onset of puberty signaled the end of childhood and a time to assume adult work and responsibility. A Sicilian adage taught, "When hair begins to grow between the legs, one is fit to marry and work."[63] By the time boys reached twelve and girls ten, they generally had assumed adult work. At these ages, boys were sufficiently mature and strong to till the earth, and girls were fully capable of cooking, sewing, and helping in the conduct of the household. A man from a small fishing village near Palermo, Sicily, recalled that early passage to the rights and responsibilities of adulthood was a major force in transmitting positive work attitudes: "When I was fourteen I became a regular member of the [fishing] crew. . . . I felt very proud of being a man and did my best to hold up my end."[64]

In conveying positive attitudes toward work, the theme of early maturity had an added significance for women in southern Italian society. As industriousness and respect for work enhanced marriage prospects, girls were taught to eschew laziness and idleness. Two Sicilian proverbs warned: "Lazy girls do not catch husbands," and "If out of the window she idly stares, she's not a girl for whom anyone cares."[65] Early assumption of work by girls (both in the fields and in the home) was a subject of communal interest as well, for good work behaviors indicated fine marriage qualities. Communal expectations, therefore, reinforced an exacting regimen of work for girls: "There was never an idle moment for girls or women. We all wanted to earn the reputation of being good workers."[66]

Themes of economic necessity, family duty, and early maturity, therefore, characterized the transmission of work attitudes to the young. Children learned respect for work in simple and absolute terms: to survive one must toil, to maintain family membership one must contribute, and to gain early access to the rights of adulthood one must assume responsible work at an early age.

Although the content of education in southern Italy was predominantly moral and practical in nature, a third category—the intellectual—was conspicuously absent. Intellectual pursuits were economically and socially impractical for the majority of southern Italians. Not only did intellectual attainment fail to contribute to economic survival, neither did it serve as an important determinant of social standing. More often than not, the acquisition of learning was more a result of wealth and status than a cause. In south Italian society, status meant material wealth: "Learned men were respected, but their wealth was more important than their mere wisdom."[67]

Because of its economic and social impracticality for most peasants, education with an intellectual content was considered appropriate only for the upper classes. A peasant remarked: "The earth is hard but safe. Education is for the sons of gentlemen."[68] In addition to impracticality, intellectual pursuits were often viewed as threats to traditional ways of life. Proverbs warned children of the dangers of deviating from the accepted content of education: "He who leaves the old way for the new, knows what he leaves but knows not what he will find," and "He who changes the old for the new changes for the worse!"[69] Finally, too much learning of an abstract or intellectual nature was considered dangerous to one's health, as an Italo-American from Campania suggested: "One man in Scala . . . had secured an outside education, and therefore [was] believed to be crazy by the more ignorant. . . ."[70]

The goal of education was embodied in the term *ben educato*. Differing from the term *ben istruito* meaning "well learned" or "well instructed," *ben educato* referred to an individual who had internalized and who displayed the familial and communal behavior patterns supportive of traditional south Italian society—in short, an individual of good character, including such virtues as parental respect, obedience to elders, and family duty, being well educated did not "include categories of school learning, book learning, or knowledge in general."[71] Being well educated, therefore, was defined as acquiring all the social, cultural, and moral values designed to perpetuate traditional southern Italian ways of life.

Traditional goals of education were often at variance with the demands of public schooling, and few southern Italians ever went beyond the first three years of elementary education. Indeed, the majority failed to complete the full three-year elementary course and many children spent their entire three years in the first class. Widespread age-grade retardation and high attrition rates characterized the Italian public school system. Of the little over three million students enrolled in public elementary schools in the 1907–1908 school year, 42 percent were in the first class, 29 percent were in the second class, 20 percent in the third, 6 percent in the fourth, 3 percent in the fifth, and a mere half of 1 percent were in the sixth class.[72] The high attrition rate following the first three years of schooling was particularly important as the compulsory school attendance laws had been extended from three years (ages six to nine) to six years (ages six to twelve) in all communes of over four thousand inhabitants in 1904.

As attitudes toward public schooling in southern Italy varied by class, nonpeasant attitudes must be examined separately from peasant attitudes. Relationships between public schools and nonpeasant populations of southern Italy embodied a paradox that stemmed from the rigid social structure of the south Italian town. In principle, the nonpeasant segment of the population (*galantuomini*) opposed universal public schooling, regarding it as a "leveling force" that would upset the status quo. In practice, however, the *galantuomini* desired the benefits that schooling brought both to their children's futures and to their own social standing. To reconcile these ambivalent attitudes toward the national system of compulsory public schooling, the *galantuomini* actively attempted to insure that public schools in southern Italy served their needs—to the exclusion of the peasant (*contadino*) class, if necessary.

According to Luigi Villari, ruling-class opposition to popular education was based on "the specious pretext that any ignorant working man is more submissive."[73] A Calabrian mayor around the turn of the century, for example, warned of the dangers that an educated peasantry presented: "the illiterate *contadini* are docile, the truly dangerous individuals are the semi-literate who believe themselves to be something extraordinary because they can read and write."[74] Some local officials withheld their support for public schooling fearing an erosion of their political power base. A southern Italian mayor in 1908 administered the exam given at the end of the third elementary class "with great precaution" because those who passed the exam were entitled to vote in elections. As the cost of buying votes in an election was already over three hundred lire, he explained, it was important not to unduly increase the size of the electorate.[75]

To allay the fear that an educated peasantry might upset the social order, local *galantuomini* often denied peasant children access to schools through the manipulation and even the destruction of school registers.[76] Flagrant violation of compulsory schooling laws, however, was only one of numerous manifestations of upper-class opposition to universal public schooling. More frequently, local ruling cliques registered their opposition to universal schooling by actively discouraging peasant children from regular school attendance. For example, as a representative and usually a member of the *galanuomini* class, the teacher often dissuaded peasant children from attending school with derogatory remarks such as, "Of what use is school to you anyway? You'll always be a peasant."[77] Similarly, an Italo-American recalled: "When a boy was absent from school for a few days, the teacher would question the boys about the absentee. A boy would state that the family had put him to work on full time.

The teacher would remark: 'Well, his hand is better adapted to hold the *zappa* (hoe) than the pen.' "[78]

Upper classes regarded elementary schools as exclusive organizations. An Italo-American who grew up near Palermo, Sicily, related:

> In our town of Altavilla which had a population of a little over 4,000 people, there were two elementary schools with about 200 pupils (boys and girls) in each. Practically none of these children were of peasant class but belonged to the families of the local *galantuomini*, shop keepers, officials, landlords, etc. . . .
>
> In the school I attended we were all children of the *proprietario* (propertied) class and realized that the school was established for us and not for the *contadinò* children who had no business in school at all; they were supposed to work in the fields and help their parents at home.
>
> I distinctly remember a case when a peasant's son came to our school and the outcry of the parents: "*Per Bacco!* (By Heaven!) Things are going too far. We pay the taxes, we rent the building, we support the teacher, so it is up to us to decide whether a *cafone* [low brow] needs the school."[79]

The elementary curriculum, decreed from Rome, prepared upper-class children for the entrance examinations to the classically oriented secondary schools and seldom offered the type of instruction that would have been of immediate practical value to the peasants. Thus, public schools were avenues for social and economic advancement for the sons of nonpeasant families who would become notaries, druggists, doctors, lawyers, and engineers. Stefana Miele, born in Biano, near Naples, recalled the importance of schools in fulfilling family expectations:

> My folks were of the middle class; and like most Italians above the peasant class, they were willing to spend money to educate their children. Each family is ambitious that its sons should be professional men; each desires to have a lawyer, a doctor, and a priest. I was to be a lawyer. I was sent to school, and then to college.[80]

The benefits of public schooling for women, on the other hand, were not seen in terms of career preparation. Indeed, extended schooling for females was considered wasteful and even detrimental to their future roles as wives and mothers. "What was the purpose of schooling in the life of a woman?" queried a native of Basilicata. "Would it help her to bear a child? Raise a family?"[81] Nevertheless, the daughters of the *galantuomini* attended the elementary schools for the basic education that befitted their social position. In part, the practice of sending both boys and girls to elementary school was a means of gaining social status in the eyes of the community. As material wealth was a primary determinant of social standing, ability to afford the expense of sending all one's children to school was a conspicuous sign of high economic status. In this sense, schooling was not a virtue in itself but rather something the *galantuomini* supported as a symbol of their place in society.

Although complex patterns of support and opposition characterized the relationships between the public schools and the nonpeasant population, the peasants generally opposed the practice of compulsory public schooling. The conflict between the peasant population and the public schools resulted, in part, from the successful efforts of the *galantuomini* to direct and sustain the system for their own benefit. Despite national legislation requiring universal attendance in elementary schools, peasants were disposed to believe that schools were not open to their children. "So great was the chasm between the *contadino* class and the ideals and purposes of schooling that he was afraid to enter the school. It awed him because of its alien character."[82] Peasant opposition to the alien character of public schools, however, was only partially attributable to class considerations. Regional differences between northern and southern Italy and traditional family mores of the peasants provided two further sources of peasant opposition to public schooling.

Regional opposition to compulsory schooling stemmed from geographic, economic, and cultural differences between northern and southern Italy. As politicians from the northern and central provinces directed both the government and the schools, the national system of education tended to be based on northern cultural norms. The school year, for example, based on the climatic and occupational conditions of the North, did not conform to the agricultural cycle of the South. As planting and harvest time arrived much earlier in southern Italy and as the marginal agricultural economy required the labor of peasant children as well as adults, many young people simply could not attend school for the entire year.

> When harvest time came late in September, while school was already officially in session, we all lent a hand in gathering grapes. Everybody pitched in from the youngest to the oldest. The family job took priority over school attendance, and no one would deem it possible, but even reprehensible, to return to school until the harvest was over.[83]

Not only was the school year out of phase with southern Italian peasant life; so was the curriculum and the language of instruction. Public school offerings were largely irrelevant to the peasant classes of southern Italy. Studies concerning female employment (such as in the needle trades) and male occupations (such as agricultural studies) were almost totally unknown in the public schools. Furthermore, the literary Italian that children learned in school was an alien language in those villages where intense regionalism served to perpetuate the use of native dialects. Children found literary Italian unfamiliar, awkward, and of little use in an environment where only a native vernacular was spoken. In addition, parents unable to understand the strange tongue were suspicious of the knowledge their children learned that they, themselves, could not comprehend. Finally, because teachers were seldom from the local village and were thus unfamiliar with local dialects and customs, they often exacerbated both the students' difficulty of learning in a strange language and the parents' suspicion of the moral content of what was being taught.

A second source of peasant opposition to public schooling stemmed from the family mores of the peasants. As the family was the inclusive social unit in south Italian society, other social institutions, such as public schools, were potential threats to the primacy of the family mores. Specifically, the public school threatened the fundamental familial concept of solidarity and endangered the transmission of those social, cultural, and moral values that perpetuated the traditional way of life.

The public school threatened family solidarity in numerous ways. Socially, while parents limited their children's circle of acquaintances primarily to siblings and cousins to strengthen family identification, public school attendance broadened the opportunity for social intercourse and made random associations outside the family group, if not inevitable, at least possible. Physically, the public school often threatened family solidarity in a direct and compelling manner. Physical proximity of family members was essential to family unity; yet because of inadequate public school provision in southern Italy, attendance beyond the first several years often required children to leave the family dwelling and reside in a nearby community that had more complete school facilities. Few peasants, even if they could afford the expense of maintaining their children outside the home, were willing to voluntarily dissolve the physical bond that held the family together. Finally, peasants believed that the public school threatened family solidarity by detracting from the prestige and authority of the *capo di famiglia* ("family head"). "I hear you promised the teacher to send your boy to school again in the fall. Well, it's not my affair, but surely you realize that it does no good to the boy. Your son already now 'talks back' to you. What will he not do if he goes one year more? If one cannot educate his boy at home, no school can be of help."[84] Whether real or only perceived, the peasants resisted such threats to family solidarity and often prohibited their children from attending public schools.

The public school also threatened the primacy of family mores by endangering the proper education of youth. The peasants generally mistrusted what their children learned in public schools and felt that the schools did not prepare their sons and daughters for the early assumption of adult roles. Adulthood for girls meant early marriage, for boys, early assumption of responsible work. In both cases, public schooling prolonged the period of social infancy and threatened the character of their training.

Prolonged schooling for girls delayed early marriage, for "If a girl did not marry by the time she was twenty, there was little hope of her fulfilling her traditional role except with some less desirable mate."[85] Likewise, school attendance threatened the ambition of every mother to see her daughters *sistemate* (settled) before her death.

> Every girl's place sooner or later is in a man's home. The earlier she marries the less worries there are for her relatives. . . . Three daughters of mine are well placed. My youngest is seventeen. With God's help, I hope she will not disappoint me by going to school. In that case I may never be able to see my happy day when all my daughters are married and I don't have to worry any more.[86]

School attendance also threatened the character of a girl's preparation for early marriage. As chastity insured marriageability, southern Italians traditionally attempted to restrict communication between girls and boys, especially between those of marriageable age. Indeed, many believed that even a rudimentary knowledge of reading and writing would enable, and even encourage, a young girl to correspond with her sweetheart and, in doing so, jeopardize her future. "My mother explained to me the reason for her illiteracy. In her case it was the fear of my grandparents that she would write love letters to young men in the town and thus would trespass against the decorum of a well brought up Italian girl."[87] As the importance of female chastity took precedence over the demands of compulsory schooling, peasants often kept their daughters at home. An Italo-American from Castelbuono, Sicily, recalled how her grandmother restricted her mother's schooling: "She let her daughter attend school through the fourth grade and then because she grew up very fast and looked older than she really was, she had to leave school and stay at home and be a good young lady."[88] The young lady married at fifteen.

Prolonged schooling for boys had more serious social implications. By delaying the early assumption of responsible work, school attendance postponed social maturity and thus undermined family tradition and structure. The pattern of male dominance dictated that mature boys (denoted by the assumption of work) take an active role in family affairs and oversee the conduct of their sisters. School attendance, however, prevented boys from undertaking such responsibility and consequently eroded the tradition of male superiority.

Most importantly, public schooling threatened the character of a boy's preparation for work. The public school not only removed the boy from an environment where he could learn to work but failed to offer training that had practical value in his life.

> Well, he has gone to school. He has learned to make a few scrawls on a piece of paper. He can read *zoppicando* (haltingly) out of a book. Now that this has been done, what good is it to him or anybody else? He has not only wasted time but the family has had to go to the expense of buying blank books, primer, pen, pencil and paper, and what has the family gotten out of all this? What use can we get out of going to school?[89]

As few peasants entered professional careers, the public school was seen as a place for developing intellectual interests rather than preparing for work. Although peasants were aware of the benefits that came with a basic knowledge of reading, writing, and arithmetic, they considered that too much intellectual training threatened a boy's preparation for work, encouraged poor working habits, and imbued them with "crazy" ideas: "Schooling? Certainly till the age of seven, enough to learn to sign our names. . . . After seven, it was time to go to work. My father was of the opinion that too much school makes children lazy and opens the mind for unhealthy dreams."[90] In similar fashion, an Italian educator stated: "Mother believed you would go mad if you read too many books."[91]

For many peasants, the world was finite, familiar, and relatively satisfactory. Abstract categories of knowledge, therefore, had little place in preparing boys for adult roles and only served to challenge the traditional mode of peasant life. "Now suppose I know something that I did not know before. Of what use would it be to me? It would only spell a radical change in my traditional methods, a change which I probably cannot face. I have faith in the old method which is proven and good."[92] These peasants perceived public school education and book learning as alien pursuits, apart from the real world and remote from everyday experience. " 'School isn't life, my dear Don Benedetto,' Concettino interrupted. 'At school you dream, in life you have to make adjustments. You come up against a reality older than yourself, to which you have to adapt yourself.' "[93] To properly prepare their sons for work, and thus for life, therefore, peasants resisted singular promotion of intellectual interests and, in doing so, solidified their opposition to public schooling.

In summary, southern Italian opposition to compulsory public schooling was widespread. The nonpeasant segment of the population opposed the principle of universal public schooling for its "leveling" tendencies; however, in practice, they restricted school access and directed the content of schooling to serve their own ends. Thus, to the *galantuomo*, the public school was "sort of a private club where you received certain things for which you and your parents paid . . . strictly an affair of a selected group of people."[94]

Peasant opposition to public schooling was less ambiguous. In the first part of the twentieth century, a Florentine society formed to support popular education in Calabria summarized peasant opposition to public schooling:

> because the public school doesn't exist; because the public school is at an inconvenient distance; because during the harvest the parents prefer to send their children to evening school, and the public evening school after 1904 was reserved for adult illiterates only; because in the periods in which there is no agricultural labor to be done, the private masters take the children all day not for just a few hours; because the private schools remain open in the months in which the *contadini* do not have to work, while the public schools have vacation exactly when the *contadini* is disposed to go to school; and because the teacher or teachers in the public schools do not teach well.[95]

Interestingly, however, the society found that many southern Italian peasants were willing to incur the expense of having their children study in private schools or under private tutors rather than patronize the free public schools.

## THE PREDOMINANT ORTHODOXY IN CONFLICT

Traditional southern Italian attitudes toward work and schooling stood in sharp contrast with the emergent belief of American educators that public schools—especially public high schools—could and should prepare youth for work. By advocating prolonged school attendance and vocational training in order to develop a "life career motive," promote good work habits, and instill moral discipline, educators helped to establish class and culture-bound relationships between work and schooling that rapidly became part of the predominant orthodoxy of American education. However, the rational, evolutionary model that educators developed to define and solve problems relating to work and schooling failed to account for the complexities of southern Italian social and cultural reality. Their educational prescriptions, therefore, often conflicted with southern Italian immigrant life in the United States.

When compared with other immigrant nationality groups such as English, German, Swedish, and Russian-Jewish, American educators found that southern Italian school children were more often in grade levels below those considered normal for their ages. In addition, they also discovered that southern Italian children had poorer records of grammar school continuation and completion, and lower rates of high school entry, continuation, and graduation.[96] Without specific knowledge or appreciation of the social and cultural experiences of southern Italians prior to arrival, however, turn-of-the-century educators were largely unable to understand this apparent maladaptation of southern Italian children to the patterns of schooling in America. Furthermore, educators failed to see that southern Italians responded to new patterns of work and schooling as much in accordance with their own class and cultural traditions as in accordance with the demands of the American public school and the industrial economy.

Prolonged schooling to protect children from dead-end jobs and vocational training to develop career instincts conflicted with the educational traditions of many southern Italian immigrants. First, as we have seen, southern Italian parents attempted to limit their children's friends to siblings and cousins in order to strengthen family identification. School attendance, on the other hand, made associations outside the family possible, if not inevitable. Second, prolonged schooling was at variance with southern Italian educational traditions that disparaged intellectual tasks and demanded close family supervision of females. Third, because the integrity of the south Italian family depended on children assuming their respective adult roles at an early age (early marriage for girls, early assumption of responsible work for boys), prolonged school attendance challenged family mores by extending the period of social infancy and dependence. Fourth, because of the importance placed on family responsibility and reputation, southern Italian mothers rarely left their homes to work unless supervised by relatives or friends. School attendance, by removing young males from income-producing jobs, threatened the economic survival of the family and made it necessary for southern Italian women to forsake low-paying work done at home and seek higher-paying jobs in industry and domestic service.[97] In short, acting in accordance with strongly held cultural traditions, many southern Italians kept their children out of school to preserve the integrity of the family.

Prolonged schooling and vocational training also ran counter to the aspirations and the working-class realities of many southern Italian immigrants. The ideology of a "life career motive," for example, conflicted with work and schooling attitudes of many southern Italian immigrants who thought of work in terms of jobs rather than ascending career stages that brought greater responsibilities and rewards. Given the lack of vertical mobility in most unskilled factory work or common manual labor, many southern Italian immigrants may have made more accurate assessments about their life chances than the educators who felt that they had a truncated sense of their own possibilities.

Finally, prolonged schooling—even of a vocational character—also failed to match the aspirations of many immigrant Italians who were intent on making money and returning to Italy to buy land. Each year between 1907 and 1911, an average of seventy-three southern Italians repatriated for every one hundred that arrived.[98] For those immigrants, ones who did not aspire either to permanent settlement or a career in the United States, prolonged schooling was viewed as a waste of energy and a detraction from income-producing activity.

Thus, by prolonging school attendance beyond the normal school-leaving age of fourteen and by introducing vocational subjects to benefit and interest the children, educators felt they had arrived at a comprehensive solution for reducing the disjuncture between work and schooling. The comprehensive high school, they believed, would embrace youth of all social classes and provide a differentiated curriculum which would prepare children for a wide spectrum of occupational futures. Their class and culture-bound perceptions of work and schooling, however, often conflicted with the views of those they sought to serve. Blinded to the ways in which cultural continuities and adaptations shaped the work and school behaviors of diverse working-class populations in the United States, educators failed to perceive the cultural and social limitations of what they thought were comprehensive solutions. Indeed, so convinced were educators of the correctness of their solutions that as the problems of industrial work and universal secondary schooling continued to persist into the second and third decades of the twentieth century, they remained unable to think about work and schooling in alternative ways.

## A POSTSCRIPT FOR THE 1980s

In the past two decades, growing concerns about work in America have again focused national attention on the relationships between work and schooling. Increasing alienation, absenteeism, alcoholism, and drug abuse among workers, growing underemployment and unemployment (especially among teenage youth), and gloomy predictions about the future of the economy captured in such titles as *Business Civilization in Decline* and *The Twilight of Capitalism*, have contributed to a growing uneasiness that something is fundamentally wrong with work in America.[99] Today, as in the past, these troubles affecting the workplace and the economy are largely viewed as educational problems requiring educational solutions. Often ignoring the structural problems of industrial work and the multiple realities of the workplace, educational policy makers today are paying greater attention to the vocational preparation of youth.[100] Lacking historical understanding of the structural and ideological legacies of the past, however, policy makers are often unable to examine certain assumptions about the relationships between work and schooling. As a consequence, they may be expending boundless energy reinventing an ideology and structure ill-equipped to solve the urgent problems that command our attention.

Many observers today view the increased interest in vocationalism as a response to liberal education policies of the 1960s that failed to adequately prepare youth for adult employment.[101] More accurately, perhaps, this renewed interest in vocationalism may be seen as a delayed response to recent demographic shifts that have greatly increased the proportional representation of youth in American society. As James O'Toole explains, between 1960 and 1976, the number of young people aged fifteen to twenty-four in the workforce increased by 100 percent.[102] These young men and women, born during the boom years of 1945 to 1955, will constitute nearly 50 percent of the labor force by 1985. The result has been an increase in the total size of the workforce of about 50 percent over the last twenty-five years. As the economy strains to provide enough jobs for a surfeit of youthful labor, debate escalates about how schools can prepare youth for work. "What must be recognized," O'Toole states, "is that there has never been a problem of 'fitting education to the world of work' during periods of labor shortages."[103] For example, lack of specific job training in schools did not prevent youth—even minority youth—from getting entry-level jobs during World Wars I and II.

Today, we are entering a period during which the number of young people as a percentage of the total workforce will rapidly decline. It is probable that public and professional concern about preparing youth for the world of work will diminish as youthful workers find employment more easily. It is ironic that vocational programs stimulated by the demographic impact of an age cohort now twenty-six to thirty-six years old will share the credit for the decline in youth unemployment when demographic changes may make such shifts inevitable. Reminiscent of turn-of-the-century educators, proponents of vocationalism continue to assume that school reform will solve the problems besetting work in America.

The nature of the relationships between work and schooling, however, remain elusive. Today, advocates of vocational training in the public schools often assume what was problematic around the turn of the century. As we have seen, during that era many people questioned the advisability of extending the years of schooling beyond age fourteen. In addition, many believed that public schools were not proper places for vocational training. However, by combining liberal and vocational education in the comprehensive high school, educators fashioned an ideology that work preparation was a matter for the schools to address and, in the process, blurred the debate between work and schooling. By accepting without question the predominant orthodoxy that schools can and should prepare youth for rapidly changing work requirements, policy makers today tend to narrowly focus their attention on the ways in which, not *if*, schools can prepare youth for work.

Finally, present notions of work and schooling remain as class and culture-bound as they were in the past. Middle-class ideals of a "life career motive" continue to be at variance with many working-class people who view work not in terms of ascending career stages but rather as a series of jobs undertaken for immediate economic survival. Likewise, little attention is paid to how ethnic differences continue to shape work and schooling attitudes among increasing numbers of foreign-born Americans. Today, in addition to refugee populations from Cuba and Southeast Asia, close to half a million immigrants legally enter the country each year—a figure which underreports the actual increase of the foreign-born as it does not include illegal immigrants nor Puerto Ricans who are American citizens. Therefore, if advocates of increased vocationalism fail to investigate the complexity of immigrant cultural and social reality—an inquiry that would enable them to examine their own culture and class-bound notions of work and schooling—it is likely that their policy formulations will prove inadequate in solving the wide range of problems affecting both the school and the workplace.

## NOTES TO CHAPTER 4

1.  James B. Gilbert, *Work Without Salvation: America's Intellectuals And Industrial Alienation, 1880–1910* (Baltimore: Johns Hopkins University Press, 1977), p. 110.

2.  For analyses of the changing nature of industrial work, see Harry Braverman, *Labor and Monopoly Capital: The Degradation of Work in the Twentieth Century* (New York: Monthly Review Press, 1974); and Daniel T. Rodgers, *The Work Ethic in Industrial America, 1850–1920* (Chicago: University of Chicago Press, 1978).

3.  Rodgers, *Work Ethic*, p. 23.

4.  Ibid., p. xii.

5. Joseph F. Kett, *Rites of Passage: Adolescence in America, 1790 to the Present* (New York: Basic Books, 1977), p. 151.

6. For an excellent discussion of worker resistance to new patterns of work, see David Montgomery, *Workers' Control in America: Studies in the History of Work, Technology, and Labor Struggles* (Cambridge: Cambridge University Press, 1979).

7. Rodgers, *Work Ethic*, p. 163; Montgomery, *Workers' Control*, p. 41; see also Daniel Nelson, *Managers and Workers: Origins of the New Factory System in the United States, 1880-1920* (Madison: University of Wisconsin Press, 1975), p. 86.

8. William Torrey Harris, "Elementary Education," in *Monographs on Education in the United States*, ed. Nicholas Murray Butler (Albany, N.Y.: J. B. Lyon, 1900), pp. 79-139.

9. Diane Ravitch, *The Great School Wars: New York City, 1805-1973* (New York: Basic Books, 1974), p. 95.

10. Edward Krug, *The Shaping of the American High School, 1880-1920* (Madison: University of Wisconsin Press, 1969), p. 64.

11. David Tyack, "Bureaucracy and the Common School: The Example of Portland, Oregon, 1851-1913," *American Quarterly* 19 (1967): 489.

12. Krug, *Shaping of the American High School*, p. 179.

13. Tyack, "Bureaucracy and the Common School," p. 489.

14. W. Norton Grubb and Marvin Lazerson, "Education and the Labor Market: Recycling the Youth Problem," in *Youth, Work, and Schooling: Historical Perspectives on Vocational Education*, ed. Harvey Kantor and David Tyack, report of a conference on the Historical Study of Education and Work, Boys Town Center, Stanford University, December 1979, p. 185.

15. For an insightful examination of the debate about work and schooling, see Arthur Wirth, *Education in the Technological Society: The Vocational-Liberal Studies Controversy in the Early Twentieth Century* (Scranton, Pa.: Intext Educational, 1972).

16. Ellwood P. Cubberley, *Changing Conceptions of Education* (Boston: Houghton Mifflin, 1909), pp. 18-19.

17. Selwyn Troen, "The Discovery of the Adolescent by American Educational Reformers, 1900-1920: An Economic Perspective," in *Schooling and Society: Studies in the History of Education*, ed. Lawrence Stone (Baltimore: Johns Hopkins University Press, 1976), pp. 241-43.

18. Ibid., p. 243.

19. Grubb and Lazerson, "Education and the Labor Market," pp. 188-89.

20. John Dewey, *Democracy and Education: An Introduction to the Philosophy of Education* (New York: Free Press, 1966), p. 196.

21. David K. Cohen and Marvin Lazerson, "Education and the Corporate Order," *Socialist Revolution* 2 (1972): 51.

22.  Ibid.

23.  See Rodgers, *Work Ethic*, p. 238.

24.  Jane Addams, *The Spirit of Youth and the City Streets* (New York: Macmillan, 1909), p. 122.

25.  Cubberley, *Changing Conceptions*, p. 55.

26.  Charles W. Eliot, "The Value During Education of the Life-Career Motive," in *Readings in Vocational Guidance*, ed. Meyer Bloomfield (Boston: Ginn, 1915), p. 8.

27.  Ibid., pp. 10–11.

28.  Cubberley, *Changing Conceptions*, p. 55.

29.  John Dewey, *The School and Society* (Chicago: University of Chicago Press, 1971), p. 23.

30.  *Report of the Massachusetts Commission on Industrial and Technical Education* (Boston: The Commission, 1906), pp. 86–87.

31.  Sol Cohen, "The Industrial Education Movement, 1906–1917," *American Quarterly* 20 (1968): 98.

32.  Eliot, "Life-Career Motive," p. 1.

33.  Krug, *Shaping of the American High School*, p. 225.

34.  Leonard Ayres, *Laggards in our Schools: A Study of Retardation and Elimination in City School Systems* (New York: Charities Publication Committee, 1909), p. 5.

35.  Marvin Lazerson, *Origins of the Urban School: Public Education in Massachusetts, 1870–1915* (Cambridge, Mass.: Harvard University Press, 1971), p. 189.

36.  Cohen, "Industrial Education," p. 108.

37.  Cubberley, *Changing Conceptions*, p. 53.

38.  National Education Association, *Cardinal Principles of Secondary Education: A Report of the Commission on the Reorganization of Secondary Education*, U.S. Bureau of Education, *Bulletin*, no. 35 (1918), p. 7.

39.  Dewey, *Democracy and Education*, p. 318.

40.  *Cardinal Principles*, p. 2.

41.  Charles W. Eliot, "Industrial Education as an Essential Factor in Our National Prosperity," National Society for the Promotion of Industrial Education, *Bulletin*, no. 5 (1908), p. 13. Eliot later advocated postponing "the actual training for a specific trade or occupation till at least the sixteenth year, because in most cases the body is not sufficiently developed before that age to undertake the real work of a trade"; "Life-Career Motive," p. 6.

42.  Clarence Karier, "Testing for Order and Control in the Corporate Liberal State," in Clarence Karier et al., *Roots of Crisis* (Chicago: Rand McNally, 1973), p. 121.

43.  Wirth, *Education in the Technological Society*, p. 102; emphasis added.

44. Herbert Gutman, *Work, Culture, and Society in Industrializing America: Essays in American Working-Class and Social History* (New York: Alfred A. Knopf, 1976), p. 40.

45. U.S. Immigration Commission, *The Children of Immigrants in Schools* (Washington, D.C.: U.S. Government Printing Office, 1911), 1:14–15.

46. Ravitch, *School Wars*, p. 123.

47. Burton J. Bledstein, *The Culture of Professionalism: The Middle Class and the Development of Higher Education in America* (New York: Norton, 1977).

48. Dewey, *School and Society*, p. 23.

49. Paul Boyer, *Urban Masses and Moral Order in America, 1820–1920* (Cambridge, Mass.: Harvard University Press, 1977).

50. Cubberley, *Changing Conceptions*, pp. 15–16.

51. David Hogan, "Education and the Making of the Chicago Working Class, 1880–1930," *History of Education Quarterly* 18 (1978): 236.

52. For an expanded discussion of traditional southern Italian attitudes toward work and schooling, see C.H. Edson, "Immigrant Perspectives on Work and Schooling: Eastern European Jews and Southern Italians, 1880–1920," unpublished Ph.D. dissertation, Stanford University, 1979.

53. Ignazio Silone, *Bread and Wine*, trans. Gwenda David and Eric Mosbacher (New York: New American Library, 1946), p. 172; Giovanni Verga, *The House by the Medlar Tree*, trans. Eric Mosbacher (New York: Grove Press, 1953), p. 62; Silone, *Bread and Wine*, p. 132; Leonard Moss and Walter Thompson, "The South Italian Family: Literature and Observations," *Human Organization* 18 (1959): 37; Moss and Thompson, "South Italian Family," p. 36; Leonard Covello, *The Social Background of the Italo-American School Child*, ed. and intro. Francesco Cordasco (Totowa, N.J.: Rowman and Littlefield, 1972), p. 156.

54. Constantine Panunzio, *The Soul of an Immigrant* (New York: Macmillan, 1921), p. 14.

55. Covello, *Social Background*, p. 230.

56. Phyllis Williams, *South Italian Folkways in Europe and America* (New York: Russell and Russell, 1969), p. 21; Covello, *Social Background*, p. 230.

57. Covello, *Social Background*, p. 270.

58. Leonard Covello, with Guido D'Agostino, *The Heart Is the Teacher* (New York: McGraw-Hill, 1958), p. 11.

59. Covello, *Social Background*, p. 254.

60. Covello, *Heart Is the Teacher*, p. 6.

61. Paul Radin, *The Italians of San Francisco: Their Adjustment and Acculturation*, abstract from SERA Project, 2–F2–98: Cultural Anthropology, July 1935, p. 138.

62. Pascal D'Angelo, *Pascal D'Angelo, Son of Italy* (New York: Macmillan, 1924), p. 22.
63. Covello, *Social Background*, p. 229.
64. Radin, *Italians of San Francisco*, p. 66.
65. Covello, *Social Background*, p. 231; Verga, *House by the Medlar Tree*, p. 18.
66. Covello, *Social Background*, p. 265.
67. Ibid., p. 89.
68. Silone, *Bread and Wine*, p. 255.
69. Covello, *Social Background*, p. 257; Verga, *House by the Medlar Tree*, p. 160.
70. Radin, *Italians of San Francisco*, p. 126.
71. Covello, *Social Background*, p. 261.
72. John Walker Briggs, "Italians in Italy and America," unpublished Ph.D. dissertation, University of Minnesota, 1972, p. 54.
73. Covello, *Social Background*, p. 248.
74. Briggs, "Italians in Italy and America," p. 63.
75. Ibid.
76. Covello, *Social Background*, p. 248.
77. Ibid., p. 252.
78. Ibid., pp. 252–53.
79. Ibid., p. 249.
80. Hannibal Duncan, *Immigration and Assimilation* (Boston: D. C. Heath, 1933), p. 561.
81. Covello, *Heart Is the Teacher*, p. 16.
82. Covello, *Social Background*, p. 256.
83. Ibid., p. 251.
84. Ibid., p. 259.
85. Williams, *South Italian Folkways*, p. 83.
86. Covello, *Social Background*, p. 200.
87. Ibid., p. 264.
88. Radin, *Italians of San Francisco*, p. 136.
89. Covello, *Social Background*, pp. 257–58.
90. Radin, *Italians of San Francisco*, p. 85.
91. Fred Strodtbeck, "Family Integration, Values, and Achievement," in *Education, Economy, and Society*, ed. A.H. Halsey, Jean Floud, and C. Arnold Anderson, (Glencoe, Ill.: Free Press, 1961), p. 316; see also Williams, *South Italian Folkways*, p. 129.
92. Covello, *Social Background*, p. 254.
93. Silone, *Bread and Wine*, p. 15.
94. Covello, *Social Background*, p. 255.
95. Briggs, "Italians in Italy and America," p. 66.

96. Michael R. Olneck and Marvin Lazerson, "The School Achievement of Immigrant Children: 1900–1930," *History of Education Quarterly* 14 (1974): 453–82.

97. Virginia Yans McLaughlin, "Patterns of Work and Family Organization: Buffalo's Italians," *Journal of Interdisciplinary History* 2 (1971): 35–41.

98. Thomas Kessner, *The Golden Door: Italian and Jewish Immigrant Mobility in New York City, 1880–1915* (New York: Oxford University Press, 1977), p. 28.

99. Robert Heilbroner, *Business Civilization in Decline* (New York: Norton, 1976); Michael Harrington, *The Twilight of Capitalism: A Marxian Epitaph* (New York: Simon & Schuster, 1975). For the crisis in work, see Studs Terkel, *Working: People Talk About What They Do All Day and How They Feel About What They Do* (New York: Random House, 1974); U.S. Department of Health, Education, and Welfare, *Work in America* (Cambridge, Mass.: MIT Press, 1973); Braverman, *Labor and Monopoly Capital*; Grubb and Lazerson, "Education and the Labor Market."

100. See, e.g., Sidney P. Marland, Jr., *Career Education: A Proposal for Reform* (New York: McGraw-Hill, 1974); James S. Coleman et al., *Youth: Transition to Adulthood: Report of the Panel on Youth of the President's Science Advisory Committee* (Chicago: University of Chicago Press, 1974); National Commission for Manpower Policy, *From School to Work: Improving the Transition* (Washington, D.C.: U.S. Government Printing Office, 1976).

101. See the discussion in W. Norton Grubb and Marvin Lazerson, "Rally 'Round the Workplace: Continuities and Fallacies in Career Education," *Harvard Educational Review* 45 (1975): 451–74.

102. James O'Toole, "Education Is Education, and Work Is Work — Shall Ever the Twain Meet?" *Teachers College Record* 81 (1979): 6.

103. Ibid., p. 15.

# PART II
# ELEMENTS OF STATE CONTROL

Part II is directed toward a reexamination of some of the assumptions underlying the nature of education and its practice under the auspices of the state. The two essays here provide a foundation for inquiry into some of the unexamined and/or accepted modes by which education occurs, how that education commonly is translated into state schooling, and finally some consequences of that relationship between education and the state.

Michael Katz, in "Critical Literacy: A Conception of Education as a Moral Right and a Social Ideal," focuses on the presence of "critical literacy" as the main criteria by which the adequacy of educational opportunity should be evaluated. By "critical literacy" Katz means the ability of individuals to think for themselves—to be influenced by thought and to understand the social basis of thought. He outlines the conditions under which he feels state-sponsored education should foster critical thought.

First, Katz makes the distinction between the right to education as an "entitlement" and as a "principle." As an entitlement, we can conceive of education as a right to attain economic and social self-sufficiency (that is, in the form of an adult capable of being independent or interdependent rather than dependent) and as a right to be schooled (in the sense that schooling most often is the legitimated operational definition of education). In Katz's terms, education as a

189

right to attain self-sufficiency would have to provide the attainment of critical thinking skills (as well as the ability to make a living) so that one is prepared to ask questions about the work one does as well as to actually do it. Yet the right to schooling as an entitlement does not ensure the development of critical thought, for the individual may not wish to possess such skills, which may not necessarily be attained at the school. The best that schooling can provide is the opportunity to develop critical thinking skills.

Since it is not clear that schooling can develop critical thought, Katz argues that it is preferable to think of the "right to education" as an "ideal directive"—a moral principle rather than a rule. This distinction is fundamental because rules set out the conditions for application whereas principles do not regulate conduct but provide direction and establish criteria. Using the case of *San Antonio Independent School District* v. *Rodriguez* as an example, Katz explains that seeing education as a rule leads to a facile and oversimplified determination of whether education is adequate whereas viewing it as a principle (as did Justice Thurgood Marshall) allows education to be viewed in the same frame of reference as are other constitutionally protected rights (such as free speech). In so doing, education can be viewed much more broadly, thereby permitting greater flexibility and self-determination.

The role of the state in affecting what form education takes is, of course, powerful. In his final section, Katz examines the conceptual relationship between the state and the development of critical thinking skills. There, he argues that conceptually and practically the state controls critical thought through "dominance," that is, by direction and command. In so doing, it: (1) establishes its own goals for teachers and students, thereby minimizing democratic problem solving processes, and (2) minimizes alternative actions that may emerge from its own regulated educational system. Katz urges us to pay careful attention to the concepts of "right to education" and the notion of universal education as necessary steps in the reexamination of educational policy.

The essay by Stephen Arons and Charles Lawrence builds upon Katz's notion of education as a legal principle. In "The Manipulation of Consciousness: A First Amendment Critique of Schooling," the authors claim that schooling is little more than value inculcation (as is religion), and since religious choice is protected under the First Amendment, why should schooling be viewed as any different?

The fundamental argument by Arons and Lawrence is that the interpretation of First Amendment issues must be expanded beyond the protection of only the *expression* of belief and cover as well the *formation* of belief and opinion. This is the case because to the extent that the state can regulate the development of ideas and opinion through information exposure, freedom of expression is a meaningless ritual. The authors then outline how schooling, as presently constituted, does in fact regulate information flow and belief formation through the teaching of skills and the existence of the "hidden curriculum." This is a special problem for racial and ethnic minorities, who always have been disproportionately the victims of consciousness manipulation by majoritarian interests. And although Supreme Court decisions have acknowledged the presence of value inculcation in schooling, the Court has restricted its vision only to religious values and has not seen as important the role of nonreligious values in the formation of world views. Arons and Lawrence place this value inculcation process directly in the middle of a constitutional interpretation, seeing it applicable not only to the issue of free exercise (First Amendment) but also to that of the right of individuals to participate in the political process (Fourteenth Amendment).

The authors then discuss the manner in which public schooling can be viewed as a violation of First Amendment rights and, thus, why schooling needs to be seen as a legal principle (see Katz). Since few clients (save the wealthy) can opt out of schools that are not of their choice, those so dissatisfied are confronted with the tough choice of "giving up [their] basic values as a price of gaining a 'free' education in a government school, or paying twice in order to preserve their First Amendment rights."

What solutions might reconcile these constitutional dilemmas? One solution might be educational vouchers or tax credits wherein racial minorities could gain more control over their schools and thereby possibly lessen the coercive socialization experienced by their children in state-controlled schools. Would such plans work? Cautiously, the authors conclude that, at the legal level, and with some additional safeguards, parental choice and racial equality can be compatible. Still another solution focuses upon remedies within the state school, such as the abolition of standardized tests, greater degree of community control of the schools, and the reeducation of teachers about the role of belief systems in their teaching. Yet as the authors perceptively conclude, there is a big difference between legal possibility and political reality. The history of the nation does not provide a tradition of optimism to indicate that legal reform, even if instituted, would be followed in practice. The history of the school prayer decision is ample evidence of that. Similarly, the special interests representing the testing industry and elements of the educational bureaucracy are so highly organized that reform within will be exceedingly difficult. In the end, political power on the part of the disaffected, fueled by the continuing contradictions within the state educational system, seems to be the only tool that can bring about change. In this regard, interested readers should be sure to follow the arguments found in other essays in this volume, especially those by Laurence Iannaccone, Robert Everhart, and Michael Apple.

In Part II, we have raised critical issues, the answers to which help define the state/education relationship. What, for example, does it mean to have a "right to education"? To what extent does the exercise of freedom of expression in state schools provide true freedom? Does the process of belief formation that occurs in state schools run counter to the rights of racial, ethnic, and class groups? Does the minimization of involvement by the state in regulating education necessarily constitute the presence of liberty? These issues, while admittedly difficult to answer, are addressed again in subsequent essays.

## SUGGESTED READINGS

Arons, Stephen. "The Separation of School and State: *Pierce* Reconsidered." *Harvard Educational Review* 46 (1976): 76–104.

Coons, John E., and Stephen D. Sugarman. *Education by Choice: The Case for Family Control.* Berkeley: University of California Press, 1978.

Crittendon, Brian. "Education as a Human Right." *Proceedings of the Philosophy of Education Society*, 1971. pp. 60–78.

Deardon, R. F., P. H. Hirst, and R. S. Peters, eds. *Education and the Development of Reason.* London: Routledge & Kegan Paul, 1972.

Dewey, John. *Democracy and Education.* New York: Free Press, 1944.

Emerson, Thomas. *Toward a General Theory of the First Amendment.* New York: Random House, 1966.

Freire, Paulo. *Pedagogy of the Oppressed.* New York: Herder & Herder, 1970.

Green, Thomas F. *Predicting the Behavior of the Educational System.* Syracuse: Syracuse University Press, 1980.

Scheffler, Israel. *Reason and Teaching.* Indianapolis: Bobbs-Merrill, 1973.

Siegel, Harvey. "Critical Thinking as an Educational Ideal." *Educational Forum* 45 (1980): 7–23.

# 5 CRITICAL LITERACY
## A Conception of Education as a Moral Right and a Social Ideal*

*Michael S. Katz*

## INTRODUCTION

Do people have a right to education? If so, what is it they are entitled to? Should education as a minimal personal entitlement be distinguished from education as a social ideal? And what implications does the ideal of universal education have for the state control of education in a democracy? This essay explores these questions; in so doing, it aims to shed light upon how we might profitably understand education both as a moral right and as a social ideal in a democracy.

In the first section, I present and criticize two plausible ways of considering education as a moral right: (1) education as a right to be prepared for adult life, that is, the right to learn (in school or elsewhere) the skills necessary for formal social and economic self-sufficiency; and (2) education as a right to formal schooling. I suggest

*My thanks to Harvey Siegel and Martin Friedman for their critical reactions to the ideas expressed in this essay. Nicholas Burbules, Robert Heslep, Ralph Page, and Richard Western provided critical commentary on an earlier and somewhat different version. Maxine Greene, Betty Sichel, Hollibert Phillips, and Tom Cole also reacted critically to an earlier draft. Karen Garver gave editorial criticism on the preliminary drafts and Judith Timberg gave detailed editorial suggestions on the final draft; to her I owe a special debt of gratitude. Finally, I want to thank Robert Everhart for his criticism and for his patience in allowing substantive changes in the argument.

that both views need to take greater account of one central goal or function of education—enabling people to acquire "critical literacy," the capacity and inclination to think critically and act on the basis of informed judgment.[1] I suggest that if formal education is to be conceived of as a right in a democracy, it should be conceived of as the right to those educational opportunities that are necessary to develop critical literacy. The state cannot provide the necessary and sufficient conditions for the achievement of universal critical literacy in its citizens, but it can provide the educational opportunities that are necessary to enable people, if they have the ability and the will, to become critically literate.

In the second section, I suggest that the moral right to education is not a specific entitlement, but that it functions like other general (and rather vague) rights, such as the right to life or the right to liberty—as a general principle. Principles can guide but not prescribe specific policy decisions. It is beyond the scope of this essay to provide an adequate philosophical justification of this principle of critical literacy, but such a justification would have to make reference, I believe, to a coherent conception of a just society and the good life. Nevertheless, one can plausibly claim that a democratic society is committed, in theory, to enabling people to achieve the kind of intellectual self-sufficiency necessary to experience a fulfilling sense of personal and political liberty. This theoretical commitment gives meaning to the ideal of universal education.

Later in the second section, I consider how universal education might function as a guide to both schooling policy and to other educational features of the general culture. It is suggested that critical literacy extends far beyond schooling itself and depends, in part, upon the liberty to pursue an understanding of the world in ways that are reasonably free from government-influenced efforts to distort such an understanding. Being entitled to opportunities to develop critical literacy, I believe, is a principle which should function as a critical guide to schooling policy and other governmental efforts. In the concluding part of this section, the central conceptual distinction drawn between viewing the right to education as a specific rule-like entitlement and the right to education as a guiding principle is employed to inform our understanding of an important constitutional law case, *San Antonio School District* v. *Rodriguez*. In this case, the majority based its decision, in part, on the belief that there is no constitutional right to education. My own view is that the majority interpreted "the right to education" as a rulelike entitlement to formal schooling rather than as a vaguer entitlement to educational opportunity.

In the third and concluding section, I suggest rather tentatively how the fostering of critical literacy may be related to state control of schooling. First, drawing upon Israel Scheffler's conceptual distinction between two kinds of "control," what he calls "dominance" and "causal planning,"[2] I suggest that state control most often takes the form of dominance. In this regard, there seem to be at least two ways in which state control (as dominance) can undermine the fostering of critical literacy.

My overall purpose is to invite others to join in rethinking the ideal of universal education and in reestablishing it as a meaningful guide for educational policy in the decades ahead. An adequate and realistic vision of what is desirable can inform both our beliefs about what is possible and our conviction about what is no longer tolerable in American education.

---

The idea of universal education is the idea of the moral right to education, writ large. As a social ideal, the commitment to education for every citizen has been connected to diverse intellectual visions, including those of Jefferson, Mann, and Dewey. Indeed, vigorous discussion over how this ideal should be translated into institutional arrangements was widespread during the nineteenth century when the state expanded its role in assuming control of formal education and began to compel parents to send their children to school. It is important to examine the ideal of universal education, then, when we engage in critical dialogue over the possibilities and limitations of formal schooling, over its directions and purposes, and over the state's role in providing, regulating, and legitimating educational experiences. We can judge the success of education, in part, through how well it realizes its basic goals and purposes.

Since the middle of the nineteenth century, the ideal of universal education in the United States has been interpreted as, and implemented through, a system of universal schooling. As Thomas Green has so forcefully pointed out, the system of universal schooling has developed a political, economic, and cultural dynamic of its own, one that functions independently of philosophical considerations about what constitutes a good education.[3] Schooling policy and practice have a momentum of their own, and it is naïve to think they will be easily changed by philosophical reflection on the ideal of universal education or the moral right to an education. Nevertheless, such reflection can illuminate the dynamic tension that is inevitably built into systematic efforts to create an educated citizenry—a tension between the state's conservative inclination to preserve and maintain the status quo and the interests of many individuals (primarily students, parents, and teachers) in developing each person's critical and creative capabilities as fully as possible.

In translating the ideal of universal education into an ever-expanding system of universal schooling, rarely have we questioned whether a universally educated citizenry would be brought about merely by extending the opportunities for schooling. Even more rarely have we entertained the possibility that schooling could, in some forms, either fail to educate or militate against the development of educated people.

However, recent events have prompted a reexamination of the taken-for-granted association between schooling people and educating them. In spite of increased financial expenditures on schooling, our faith in the educative powers of schools has been seriously challenged. Newspaper headlines have dramatized falling college board scores as well as high percentages of daily absenteeism in urban schools, increased vandalism and violence by students, and outbreaks of racial violence over desegregation efforts. Moreover, scholarly analyses of schools, both historical and sociological, have dramatized the gap between our elevated hopes for formal education and the realities of mass, compulsory schooling. Revisionist historical scholarship, in particular, has shown how the emergence of large, centralized bureaucratic school systems has reflected the state's conservative tendency to reinforce the status quo.[4] In this view, schools have emphasized preparing students to accept and conform to the existing social order; conversely, schooling practice has not emphasized the liberating possibilities of teaching students to think critically about history, contemporary events, or social policy.[5]

At this point it remains unclear what the ultimate effects of the widespread disillusionment with the quality of public schooling will be and whether an enlightened debate over the purposes of education will develop to inform educational policy. Legislative pressures to make schools more "accountable" have already begun to be felt, and the state's role in the regulation of education seems to be expanding as a result of the increased attention upon fiscal restraint. In addition, concern has arisen that high school diplomas have limited educational currency; one reflection of this concern has been a national movement for minimum-competency-based testing, a movement that has swept through a majority of the states.[6]

One might have hoped that legislative debates over "minimum standards" for high school diplomas would have yielded a philosophically enlightened reexamination of the state's responsibility in educating its citizens. Instead, we have seen the emergence of various formulations of what "minimally educated" or at least "minimally competent" high school students should be able to do. The dominant conception of minimal education (or competence) has been a narrow, conservative idea of functional literacy in the "basics"—mathematics, reading, and writing. The capacity of students to think critically for themselves is seldom acknowledged as a legitimate concern of the schools.[7] As a result, I have concluded that an enlarged conception of universal education as a social ideal has not guided recent state schooling policy.

Although I have suggested that the time is ripe for a philosophical reconsideration of education as a moral right and as a social ideal, I do not believe that one must justify philosophical considerations of central educational questions in light of contemporary events. In this regard, a few disclaimers are in order. I do not want to suggest that my own interpretation of universal education as a social ideal is the only one or the best one possible. The ideal of universal education may have both a minimal and maximal form as well as various sensible versions. I shall concentrate on what I regard as a minimal form of universal education and a narrow version. I shall not focus upon a more elevated ideal of universal education although I have an intuitive sense of what one might look like. It would be a society characterized primarily by liberally educated persons, individuals who not only had the capacity and inclination to think critically but who possessed breadth of knowledge, aesthetic sensitivity, and moral understanding. The elaboration of such an ideal would require a different essay than this one or perhaps several additional ones. Moreover, I do believe that, by and large, the state's compelling interests in providing education are minimal rather than maximal although its regulation of education may be more maximal than minimal.[8]

This is a speculative, interpretive essay, rather far-ranging in its ambition to cover a lot of ground in a short space. Its purpose is to invite others to join in bringing the discipline of philosophy to bear on questions of educational policy, for the eternal philosophical question "What is an educated person?" is hardly remote or abstract. It is a question legislators are asking and answering, with serious consequences for the public good.

## THE RIGHT TO BE PREPARED FOR SOCIAL AND ECONOMIC SELF-SUFFICIENCY

My purpose here is to examine critically the idea that there is a right to education and that it consists in the entitlement to preparation for becoming socially and economically self-sufficient. Such an idea is intimately connected to an older notion of education as proper child rearing and to each society's efforts to insure that its distinctive way of life is transmitted to future generations through its arrangements for young people to pass from a state of helpless dependency to a condition of independence or interdependence.

Before the nineteenth century, "education" meant "training or bringing up."[9] Implicit in the notion of education was an assumption that children must be brought up properly. Employing the older sense of education, one could plausibly argue that children had a moral right to be brought up properly. What constituted proper child rearing was culturally defined. Puritan parents were expected to bring up good Puritans. Upper-class colonial Virginia parents were expected to bring up proper Anglican ladies and gentlemen. The duty to educate children was primarily a parental duty, part of the special moral relationship existing between parents and children.[10] Although in practice the duty to bring children up properly often meant schooling them, there seemed to be no logical relationship between educating children and schooling them in the seventeenth, eighteenth and early nineteenth centuries in the United States.

Although parents had the moral responsibility to educate their children in the sense of bringing them up properly, the state also had compelling interests in insuring that they were so brought up. According to Thomas Green, these interests were and still are that each individual become economically independent and that each grant minimum obedience to the laws of the state. As Green puts it: "we could say, in more colloquial terms, that the compelling interests of the state are that children grow up so that they are neither on the dole nor in prison."[11] Clearly these interests, although compelling, are minimal.

The cultural correlative to child rearing is initiating a society's young into its distinctive patterns of adult life and thus transmitting this way of life to them. Conceived of broadly from this societal or cultural perspective, education is society's effort to transmit itself to succeeding generations. As Dewey wrote:

> Education, in its broadest sense, is the means of . . . social continuity of life. . . . Mere physical growing up, mere mastery of the bare necessities of subsistence will not suffice to reproduce the life of the group. Deliberate effort and the taking of thoughtful pains are required. Beings who are born not only unaware of, but quite indifferent to, the aims and habits of the social group have to be rendered cognizant of them and actively interested. Education, and education alone, spans the gap.[12]

The survival of distinctive forms of social life, then, depends upon effective methods of transmitting the skills, aims, understanding, and practices of the society to successive generations. Education, broadly conceived, consists of the formal and informal methods of societal transmission.

One's right to be educated can thus be conceived of as a right to learn the skills and understanding required for independent survival in society. Put another way, an individual is entitled to instruction in how to be socially and economically prepared for adult life.

The Puritans and the Amish provide two examples of societies assuming the responsibility of insuring that children were prepared for adult life. In both, education consisted of religious and economic socialization; and in both, the right to education was compatible with a limited state role and was distinguishable from the right to schooling.

The Puritan Commonwealth assumed the responsibility for trying to insure that parents lived up to their moral responsibilities by passing compulsory education laws in 1642 and 1648—laws that spelled out what it meant to be minimally educated, that is, raised properly to be prepared for adult responsibilities. All Puritan children were expected to acquire the ability to read, an understanding of the principles of Puritanism and the laws of the Commonwealth, and vocational training. No standardized means to these outcomes were required of all parents. In passing these laws, the Puritans translated the child's moral entitlement to an education into specific legal form and transformed the parental obligation to educate into a legal requirement; in the process the Commonwealth moved to legitimize its own formal responsibility for education.[13]

In the twentieth century the old-order Amish obtained an exemption to schooling beyond the eighth grade on grounds of religious freedom, persuading the Supreme Court that their own approach to socializing their adolescents was a form of legitimate education. Although the Amish offered no formal instruction to their children beyond the eighth grade, the Court in *Wisconsin* v. *Yoder* accepted the testimony of Amish witness Professor Donald Erickson that the Amish "system of learning-by-doing" was an "ideal system" of education for preparing Amish children for life as adults in the Amish community. The Court also cited approvingly Erickson's judgment that the Amish "do a better job in this than most of us do" and the "self-sufficiency of the community is the best evidence . . . [that] whatever is being done seems to function well."[14]

Whether he did so deliberately or not, Chief Justice Warren Burger accepted the notion of education as "the preparation of people for adult life" in his majority opinion. This criterion for education was used to defend the Amish claim that additional years of compulsory schooling were not necessary. Thus, Burger asserted:

> Respondents' experts testified at trial, without challenge, that the value of all education must be assessed in terms of its capacity to prepare the child for life. It is one thing to say that compulsory education for a year or two beyond the eighth grade may be necessary when its goal is the preparation of the child for life in modern society as the majority live, but it is quite another if the goal of education be viewed as the preparation of the child for life in the segregated agrarian community that is the keystone of the Amish faith.[15]

The view that education is the moral right to be prepared for social and economic independence is especially compatible with culturally homogeneous societies with stable adult roles. The duty to educate in the sense of bringing children up properly or in the sense of preparing them for adult life is not nearly so vague in these settings as to be nonoperational. Moreover, it would, under these conditions of cultural homogeneity and stability, be a reasonably manageable problem to determine if a person's right to education was being violated.

## Some Qualifications

There is much to recommend the view that the right to education consists of the right to preparation for social and economic independence in adult life. It conforms to a broad and meaningful sense of education as something more extensive than schooling. It connects well with the shared responsibilities of parents and the state in aiding youth in their transition into adulthood. It seems to fit the variety of socialization patterns employed by different societies.

Nevertheless, this view has its problems. In traditional form, it offers little help as a guideline for policy makers living in a rapidly changing society. On what basis, for example, would one consider a person prepared for life twenty, thirty, or forty years hence in this society? This is not to suggest that no meaningful conception of being prepared for life may exist for societies in which change is a constant feature. Dewey's conception of education provides one stimulating model for considering the task of preparing people for life. In Dewey's view, education consists essentially in the transformation of uninformed, routine habits of thinking and acting into informed, enlightened habits of reflective inquiry—habits that would be infused with concern for social cooperation and scientific thoroughness.[16]

The Deweyan model emphasizes what our first conception of education as a right may not—the capacity and inclination to think critically for oneself, that is, "critical literacy." Education as society's preparation of the child for adulthood can clearly have its liberating and nonliberating forms. On its conservative, nonliberating side, one finds significant social pressures toward insuring that children conform to the existing status quo, neither challenging it nor reflecting critically upon it. Such an emphasis on adapting to the existing social order, if carried too far, militates against the kind of thoughtful participation in social-political life that is demanded of citizens in a democracy. In this regard, P. A. White warns of the dangers of an educational process aimed at conformity:

> We must . . . guard against children coming to think that anything which is in fact valued in any given society ought to be so valued, by developing in them a rational stance toward what is highly regarded in their society. This is demanded by the value put on the development of men as rational beings in a democracy and by the commitment to the desirability of individual ideals. To

support an education for conformity, for conformity's sake, is for a democratic society to allow itself to rot from within.[17]

An adequate notion of being prepared for self-sufficiency in adult life, then, must include the capacity and inclination to think critically for oneself. Indeed the notion of adult independence is impoverished if independence in thinking is not included within it. A life with some measure of autonomy demands independent judgment, thoughtful planning, the capacity to evaluate various courses of action, the ability to distinguish effective arguments from specious reasoning, and the ability to learn from one's previous errors of judgment.

Philosopher John Passmore makes a very useful distinction, I think, between the skills of critical thinking and what he calls the "critical spirit." The skills of critical thinking are value-neutral; they can be used wisely or unwisely, to serve one's narrow interests or to illuminate the thinking of others. However, unlike critical skills, the critical spirit cannot be misused, for it is more like a character trait than a set of neutral skills. With critical skills one can make judgments about the achievement level of performances in which one has been trained to engage, but only with the critical spirit can one make judgments about the value of the performances themselves. "To exhibit a critical spirit," Passmore asserts, "one must be alert to the possibility that the established norms themselves ought to be rejected, that the rules ought to be changed, the criteria in judging the performances modified."[18]

Passmore's notion of the critical spirit points to the important possibility that one who is educated to this end is inclined to view the society in which he lives with a critical eye. Is it just? Are its leaders honest? Is its legal system fair? A sensitivity to moral principles, as well as to principles of logic, it is hoped will characterize the person who has come to be intellectually self-sufficient. Such a person will be concerned to distinguish right from wrong, both in intellectual reasoning and personal action; he/she will be concerned to work through moral as well as intellectual muddles.

## The Right to Schooling

The purpose of this section is to examine critically the idea that the right to education is a right for formal schooling. This view is both plausible and worth taking seriously since the state has legitimated educational achievements through its schooling diplomas and credentials and has made these credentials prerequisites for many employment opportunities. Not to attend school and not to graduate from high school clearly constitutes an educational liability for most people in American society.

That there is a right to education, and it involves the right to schooling, is enshrined in Article 26, section 1 of the U.N. Declaration of Human Rights. This section reads as follows: "Everyone has the right to education. Education shall be free, at least in the elementary and fundamental stages. Elementary education shall be compulsory."[19]

Since common sense readily suggests that attending school is neither a necessary nor sufficient condition for becoming educated, one needs to inquire into why the right to education would be conceived of as the right to schooling. One underlying reason is that formal schooling is necessary for a complex society to transmit itself to new generations and for children to learn the skills necessary for adult independence. Dewey was one thinker who recognized that education was a broader process than schooling and that special difficulties attended the transition from an emphasis on informal education to an emphasis on formal education; but he also explicitly recognized that increased significance would have to be placed on schools as the legitimate agencies of formal education. In Dewey's view, the more complex societies become, the more dependent they would be on formal education as the means of cultural transmission:

> Much of what adults do is so remote in space and in meaning that playful imitation is less and less adequate to reproduce its spirit. Ability to share effectively in adult activities thus depends upon a prior training given with this end in view. Intentional agencies—schools—and explicit material—studies—are devised. The task of teaching certain things is delegated to a special group of persons. Without such formal education, it is not possible to transmit the resources and achievements of a complex society. It also opens a way to a kind of experience which would not be accessible to the young, if they were left to pick up their training in informal association with others, since books and the symbols of knowledge are mastered.[20]

It seems reasonable to argue that a heavy investment in schooling remains strategically essential to the perpetuation of an industrialized, highly technological society. Mass schooling seems the best guarantee that society will generate a large pool of professionally trained workers necessary for the administrative, technological, and scientific jobs required to keep an industrial society functioning.

In providing mass schooling, the state has defined what is and is not a legitimate education. In fact, since the middle of the nineteenth century, and especially since the early twentieth century in the United States, state-controlled formal schooling has been virtually the only avenue for preparing for adult responsibilities. In this period, the notion of education as proper child rearing has acquired a secondary significance. Conversely, the notion of education as "the systematic instruction, schooling, or training given to the young in preparation for the work of life" has become dominant.[21] Over the years, ordinary usage has come to reflect the view that education is equivalent to schooling. Thus, it has become altogether common to ask of someone "Where did you get your education?" or "How much education have you received?" Efforts by such modern critics as Paul Goodman and Ivan Illich to make a radical distinction between education and schooling run counter to our own entrenched mental and linguistic associations.[22]

The state's interest in universal schooling is complemented by the individual's interest in schooling. His/her educational achievements, while intrinsically valuable in their own right, will acquire noneducational (social and economic) value only through recognition provided by the state—schooling credentials. For the most part, these credentials can be achieved only through a significant amount of school attendance. Of course, the distribution of social and economic rewards according to diplomas and degrees reflects an assumption that success in school corresponds to the attainment of intellectual skills, knowledge, and understanding.[23] The recent competency-based testing movement indicates the problem with such an assumption about the intrinsic value of our formal schooling.

The basis for claiming that there is a right to schooling, then, is twofold: (1) education is seen as equivalent to formal schooling in our society; if one is to be thought of as educated, one must go to school; and (2) the educational benefits associated with success in schooling are symbolized in school diplomas, certificates, etc., which are extremely important in the distribution of noneducational goods such as income, employment opportunities, status, and prestige. Not to have access to schooling opportunities is not to have the opportunity to earn these diplomas and compete in society for the noneducational goods available there.[24]

## The Right to Schooling: Some Problems

In spite of the plausibility of considering the right to education as the right to schooling, two problems are associated with this view and serve, I think, make it less than a fully satisfactory one: (1) there is some conceptual oddity in talking about the "right to schooling" in the context of the legal compulsion that requires children to attend school and parents to send them to school; and (2) if we define being minimally educated in terms of the ability and inclination to think critically for oneself, or even in other terms, then the question of how much schooling—or what part of it—provides educational opportunities remains open to investigation. These problems shall be considered in turn.

According to Hillary Rodham, on November 20, 1959, when the right to education was promulgated and associated with the right to compulsory schooling in the U.N. Declaration of Human Rights, one delegate reportedly asked how it was possible for a person to be given a right that he would be compelled to exercise.[25] Rights are usually associated with voluntarism rather than compulsion; they involve choices and the freedom that accompanies such choice. To call compulsory schooling the "right" to education smuggles in the notion of liberty where it does not apply.[26]

The second difficulty concerns the relationship between schooling and educational opportunities. One should not think about the right to education as the right to be an educated person, for arriving at that state is a complex achievement that presupposes effort and ability on the part of the person who becomes educated. Similarly, education is not usefully thought about as a commodity, like food or clothing, although it is sometimes talked about in this way. Education is not provided in the way that material goods are provided.[27] Nor is education simply a matter of one-way transmission since it does involve, as Dewey argued, a dynamic set of transactions between the student and his educational environment—transactions involving the student's active effort to learn.

We cannot provide education; at best, we can provide the opportunities that enable people to learn if they have the capacity and will to do so.[28] *If there is a right to education, then, it must be conceived of as the entitlement to those opportunities that would enable a person to become at least minimally educated.* What we are to count as an "educational opportunity," of course, depends upon our conception of "being educated."

If we think of being educated, at least in a minimal sense, as the ability and inclination to think critically for oneself, we would have some basis for considering what kinds of schooling opportunities could legitimately be regarded as "educational opportunities." It would still be an empirical question to determine more precisely what kinds of experiences contributed to the development of critical thinking; however, a reasonable conception of the capacity and inclination to think critically would go far toward helping us judge intuitively what kinds of schooling experiences constituted "educational opportunities."[29] In this view, to the degree that schools stifled curiosity, discouraged critical inquiry, and disparaged critical dialogue, they would not be providing educational opportunities but denying them. Similarly, to the degree that schools encouraged students to accept uncritically a wide variety of assumptions and dogmas rather than encouraging them to consider various views on their rational merits, schools would not be providing educational opportunities.

## THE RIGHT TO AN EDUCATION:
## A MORAL PRINCIPLE

Implicit in the criticisms of the previous two conceptions of education as a right is my own view concerning how education can profitably be viewed. Let me restate my two basic criticisms. First, it is not enough for a democratic state simply to prepare people for social and economic self-sufficiency since critical literacy, that is, the capacity and inclination to think for oneself, is essential to meaningful self-sufficiency. Second, it is not enough for the state simply to provide and require schooling because not all schooling opportunities can be regarded as "educational opportunities" for the development of critical literacy.

The right to education is clearly not like the right to park one's car in a garage, for parking one's car in a garage is a specific and clear entitlement. The right to education, on the other hand, remains vague. Nevertheless, we cannot dismiss those fundamental moral interests that are vague simply by saying that they are too vague to be rights. The Constitution itself enshrines several vague moral interests as legal rights—life, liberty, property, and due process among them.

Applying Joel Feinberg's scheme of rights, we may categorize "the right to education" as he categorizes "the right to life" or "the right to liberty"—as an ideal directive. Ideal directives, according to Feinberg, are endorsements of more or less vague ideals; they do not, by themselves, specify particular entitlements, that is, specific things one is allowed to do or have.[30] Rather, they function as guiding principles deserving to be honored and commanding us to do our very best for the cause that is built into the expression. Since a degree of vagueness is associated with it, we can regard the right to education as a moral *principle* rather than as a specific moral rule.

In ordinary language, we often talk about principles and rules as if they were interchangeable notions. However, as Ronald Dworkin has pointed out, principles can be usefully distinguished from rules in several subtle but important respects. A rule, according to Dworkin, sets out the conditions for its application and must be applied in an all-or-nothing manner; that is, a rule either applies to a situation or it does not. Rules, therefore, can regulate specific conduct by permitting or prohibiting this conduct. On the other hand, principles are more general; they do not regulate specific conduct, but they do have a dimension of weight which rules lack. In other words, if two principles were in conflict with each other, one would have to decide how much weight to attach to each principle in light of the circumstances. Principles function as important considerations to be taken into account in arriving at a decision, but they do not by themselves prescribe the decision to be reached.[31]

My own position is that the right to be minimally educated does not function like a specific entitlement but functions instead as a general principle, one that has weight and deserves to be taken into account in arriving at social policy decisions. The principle leaves the goals and content of education open to debate; however, I have suggested that one goal is central to being minimally educated—having acquired the inclination and ability to think critically.

A full-scale philosophical justification of this principle is beyond the scope of this essay, but I will sketch what I believe such a justification might look like. Any adequate conception of human rights requires, I believe, a view of the social ideal and a view of the nature of persons. It also requires a conception of human community. I believe that persons are endowed with potential rationality, free will, and moral agency. Robert Nozick suggests most usefully that these characteristics are best thought about in relation to each other and that their significance is clear: "a being able to formulate long-term plans for its life, able to consider and decide on the basis of abstract principles or considerations it formulates to itself and hence not merely the plaything of immediate stimuli, a being that limits its own behavior in accordance with some principles or picture it has of what an appropriate life is for itself and others, and so on." Nozick suggests this view adds an additional feature to human beings—"the ability to regulate and guide its life in accordance with some overall conception it chooses to accept."[32]

This conception of persons, with its central emphasis on rational autonomy, leads one to ask what persons are entitled to in the educational sphere? At the very minimum, one can argue for education as a negative right: the right not to be indoctrinated or brainwashed. Indoctrination does harm to the individual in his effort to develop the rational capacities necessary for living an autonomous life.

Strict libertarians might want to limit the right to be minimally educated to the negative right not to be brainwashed. Others might not want to posit such a right in the first place. Clearly, the position I am advocating—that an individual has a right to those opportunities necessary for the development of critical literacy—suggests more than a minimal negative right not to be brainwashed. In that regard, it seems connected to a broader vision of a democratic social ideal, one in which an individual is entitled to develop the integrity of mind and personhood necessary for living a thoughtful existence. It also seems connected to a system of social justice which does not deprive a child of positive developmental opportunities as a result of the arbitrary distribution of talents and social goods.

The question of how far a society must go in redistributing educational opportunities remains open to question, and one could argue whether compulsory schooling is a necessary condition of the application of the principle.[33] As I have previously indicated, it remains open to question whether all forms of schooling provide educational opportunities. Nevertheless, that question seems open merely in theory if society legitimates only schooling opportunities as its basis for distributing nonschooling opportunities for wealth, status, and prestige.

At what point one's entitlement to educational opportunities is fulfilled remains problematic, for, as I have indicated, such an entitlement is not specific and functions more like a principle than a specific right. A much fuller philosophical justification of "the right to critical literacy" seems necessary, and my own intuitions suggest that it be grounded in a full-scale theory of social justice as well as in a theory of persons.[34] Nevertheless, one can plausibly assert that the capacity and inclination to think critically lies at the heart of what it is that enables a person to experience a meaningful sense of personal and political liberty and to live a moral life, that is, a life lived in accord with moral rules and principles. Our own democratic society is committed, in theory, to such an ideal for all of its citizens. It is this commitment that gives meaning to the ideal of universal education.

## Universal Education as a Social Ideal

How might the ideal of a universally educated citizenry, capable of critical thinking, guide schooling policy?[35] First, it would provide a general basis for determining whether schooling policy and practice is seriously taking account of the value of critical thinking. The environments of schools characterized by a commitment to this value would be alive with the spirit of critical dialogue between teachers and students and among the students themselves. Various and diverse forms of intellectual inquiry, moreover, would be evident. Students in this environment would expect to receive serious and constructive intellectual criticism on their work so that they would be able to internalize the standards for making reasoned intellectual appraisals of their own thinking and that of other people.

On the other hand, schools that clearly did not take the value of critical thinking seriously might be ones that were dominated by rote memorization, routine drill, and passive, unquestioning acceptance of everything said by the teacher or written in the textbooks. Such schools would discourage students from questioning their teachers and expressing divergent views.

The ideal of critical thinking could also guide schooling policy judgments about the value of certain curricula, teaching methods, and various features of the schooling enterprise. Harvey Siegel puts it this way:

> Critical thinking is a regulative idea. It defines regulative standards of excellence, which can be used to adjudicate rival educational policies and practices.

... Of two educational practices, whichever tends to develop in students those habits, character traits, skills, and dispositions central to critical thinking is prima facie more desirable and ought to be chosen.[36]

Although the ideal of universal education as a citizenry educated to be critical thinkers would guide schooling policy, it would extend far beyond schooling itself. One recalls Jefferson's concern that critical judgment depends upon the liberty to pursue the truth in ways that are reasonably free from government-sponsored efforts to distort it or conceal it. Access to information and divergent, critical views in the press and in the street becomes essential in enabling one to interpret the world in an intelligent fashion and to think critically about what is happening and why it is happening. Official efforts at indoctrination are possible not only through schooling but through control of the press, television, and radio and by generally restricting access to information.

In many nondemocratic societies, education is viewed as a deliberate instrument of the state in its effort to inculcate into the minds of the ruled the dominant political doctrines and myths that make up the official ideology of the state. Even so-called democratic societies run the constant risk of moving toward such a posture. Education in such a scheme aims for the loyal, unquestioning acceptance of an official set of doctrines and myths. Such a conception diminishes the development of critical intelligence, open discussion and debate, and the subjection of ideas and public policies to rational scrutiny.[37] But democracy is predicated upon the rational consent of the governed. It places its faith in the capacity of its citizens to make intelligent decisions as they participate in the political process; in this regard, intellectual dependence must definitely be regarded as one of the most serious enemies of the democratic ideal. To the degree that people cannot evaluate critically what they hear and read, they remain dependent upon the authoritative pronouncements of others; foolishness disguised as the expression of official wisdom will be difficult to identify or expose. Democratic governments, then, are based upon the ideal of critical intelligence. If people are to be free to pursue the truth and make critical judgments, these governments must be on guard against efforts to conceal or distort information, provide one-sided accounts of events and controversies, and stifle dissenting views.

One cannot fail to recognize that it often serves the purpose of governments to have individuals believe what is not true; such belief may heighten loyalty to government policies and diminish criticism of official action. Administration denials of actual American military involvement in Cambodia for a lengthy period offer a recent example. It is not surprising that military coups in previously democratic countries often quickly involve the takeover of the media, the establishment of systematic censorship of the news, and the temporary closing of universities—all measures designed to control information and suppress public criticism. Social and political realities are often disturbing; thoughtful interpretations of these realities and simple truths about them can, and do, have unpleasant political consequences for the politicians and political party in power. Nevertheless, systematic efforts to conceal the truth and to distort reality militate against the kind of free, critical judgment that underlies an open society in which citizens and their representatives are called upon to express their political will.

Built into the right to educational opportunities essential for critical literacy, then, is the right to pursue critical understanding in a way that is reasonably free from government-sponsored efforts to distort or conceal the truth. Such a right functions not only as a general constraint on schooling efforts but also as a constraint on other government-influenced activities. The capacity and inclination to make critical judgments are influenced, for example, by all of the following: the nature of newspaper and television reporting, the tolerance of dissenting views in society, the access of people to libraries, the absence of unreasonable censorship, the respect accorded intellectuals in society, the quality of educational television and popular entertainment, and the nature of the political process. The development of critical thought is not something that can simply be assigned to the schools; rather it must be encouraged throughout the cultural life of a democratic society.

### Applying the Conceptual Framework of Education as a Right to the *Rodriguez* Case

The usefulness of viewing the right to education as a principle is evident in a consideration of the Supreme Court case *San Antonio School District* v. *Rodriguez*. Justice Thurgood Marshall, in his dissenting opinion, argued that the right to education is tied to constitutional rights in principle. In this view, the capacity to think critically is necessary if citizens in a democracy are to participate intelligently in the political life of the country and if other constitutionally protected liberties, such as freedom of speech, the freedom of association, and the right to vote, are to be meaningfully enjoyed. The inability to think critically is undoubtedly an extraordinary constraint in exercising one's liberties in a meaningful way. The inability of adults to make thoughtful choices, intelligent personal plans, and critical judgments upon public pronouncements clearly undermines the values of liberty and autonomy, upon which liberal democracies are based.

In this important case, Mexican-American parents of children attending schools in Edgewood Independent School District in San Antonio, Texas, charged that the Texas school finance scheme was unconstitutional because far less money was spent on their children than was spent on children in other San Antonio school districts, and, thus, they argued that the Texas financing scheme violated the equal protection clause of the Fourteenth Amendment. One of the issues in the case was whether education was a constitutional right or not; if education was to be deemed such, the Texas scheme would be subjected to strict judicial scrutiny, and a heavy burden of proof would be placed on Texas to show a compelling interest in its financing scheme.

The majority of the Court held that "education is not among the rights afforded explicit protection under the federal Constitution." "Nor," Justice Lewis Powell asserts, "do we find any basis for saying it is implicitly so protected." Although the majority of the Court concluded that there was no constitutional right to education, the content of this conclusion is not readily obvious. What was it that there was no constitutional right to? Moreover, what kind of right was being denied? First, the Court did not see itself dealing with a constitutional liberty, such as the right to free speech or the free exercise of religion. Rather, it viewed "the right to education" as a right to schooling. In this regard, Powell asserts:

> Even if it were conceded that some quantifiable quantum of education is a constitutionally protected prerequisite to the meaningful exercise of either right (the right to free speech or the right to vote), we have no indication that the present levels of educational expenditures in Texas provide an education that falls short.[38]

In Marshall's dissenting view, denying to education the status of a constitutional right oversimplifies and misrepresents the issue of its

fundamentality, for the Court had previously protected other fundamental interests that were not explicitly or implicitly spelled out in
the Constitution, including the right to procreate and the right to
access to criminal appellate processes. The fundamentality of education as an interest lies, according to Marshall, in the "nexus between
specific constitutional guarantees and the nonconstitutional interest." If this nexus is a close one, the nonconstitutional interest—in
this case, education—becomes fundamental. Marshall acknowledges
that "this Court has never deemed the provision of free public
education to be required by the Constitution." Nevertheless, his
argument does underscore the fundamental interest citizens have in
educational opportunities. According to Marshall, "the fundamental
importance of education is amply indicated by the prior decisions of
this Court, by the unique status accorded to public education in our
society, and by the close relationship between education and some of
our most basic constitutional values."[39]

Marshall's argument that the fundamental interest in education
provides a guideline in determining how much scrutiny Texas's
financing scheme deserves brings to light the distinction between
how the right to education would function as a rule or as a principle.
As a rule, the right to education would specify a particular kind of
entitlement, and one could easily determine whether the state was or
was not providing or honoring such an entitlement. As a principle,
the right to education would simply provide a general guideline for
examining whether the state was or was not fulfilling its obligation to
provide educational opportunities to people on a nondiscriminatory
basis. Marshall's argument points to the flexibility to be gained in
considering "the fundamental interest in education" not as a specific
entitlement to a certain amount of schooling or to schooling at all.

My own view is clearly sympathetic to Marshall's dissent. However, I do not think the dissent went far enough in suggesting why
the fundamental interest in educational opportunities qualified those
opportunities to be regarded as a right of all citizens (though clearly
not as the right to schooling; the right to educational opportunities
is a broader principle than a specific entitlement to schooling). The
justification for regarding the right to education as a legal principle
lies in its intimate connection with other constitutionally protected
values, including the right to free speech, the right to free association, the right to vote, and the general privilege of participating in
the political processes.

## STATE CONTROL OF EDUCATION AND THE
## DEVELOPMENT OF AN EDUCATED CITIZENRY

In this final section, I want to consider briefly the relationship between state control of schooling and the fostering of critical literacy. In regulating the practice of formal education, the state can determine who can teach, who is schooled and for how long, what will be taught, and what are acceptable levels of student performance for receiving degrees and other credentials. As Thomas Green suggests, the state's capacity for control is virtually unchecked: "Power does not impose its own limitations . . . the derived interests of the state can be extended to the most minute regulation of curriculum, school organization, support, licensing of teachers, and so forth. What is initially a concern with bare essentials can become all-inclusive in its reach."[40] Observers of the educational scene in America bear witness to Green's point. Increased concerns of fiscal restraint and school effectiveness have prompted legislatures, in recent years, to take a more active role in prescribing both the ends and the means of the schooling enterprise. Nevertheless, it remains an open question whether such control promotes or militates against fostering critical thinking and thus developing an educated citizenry.

The relationship between state control and the development of critical thought is both conceptual and practical. At the conceptual level, there are two senses in which we can speak of "control." In the first sense, control is "dominance." For example, one group of persons can be said to control others if (in relevant respects) the others' behavior is subject to its directions or commands.[41] When people are controlled in this sense, acting upon one's critical judgments can be risky, especially if those actions would challenge or undermine the commands of policies of the controlling group. An alienated "why bother" attitude may easily prevail among employees of a large organization if those in control seem punitive or especially insensitive to critical comment from below.

Another sense of control may be thought of as "causal planning." In this sense, a group would be said to control an event or phenomenon if it could intentionally produce the causal conditions for that event's occurrence. Control, in the sense of causal planning, seems to be value-neutral, at least on its face.[42] It might be employed to develop a conformist, anticritical orientation to society and thus be antieducational. On the other hand, it could be used to foster criticism and rational autonomy. If we think of control primarily as causal planning, there is no reason to believe that increased state control of schooling is necessarily a social evil, for it remains unclear how enlightened the state's policies will be. There is no logical impossibility in the state using its causal control of schooling toward developing citizens who can think and act intelligently for themselves.

In practice, state control most often takes the form of dominance rather than causal planning. In this form it presents two significant problems in fostering the education of critical thinkers: (1) in dominating the schooling enterprise, the state imposes its own goals upon teachers and students—it eliminates the process of democratic problem solving and decision making; and (2) one wonders how the intellectual criticism of ideas and arguments can be translated into thoughtful action in a setting characterized by dominance. Let me consider each of these problems briefly.

The first problem resides in the alienation of students and teachers from the educational decision-making process. This problem would be felt most strongly by those sympathetic to Dewey's views of schooling as a process in which critical thinking and social democracy can and should be harmonized. In Dewey's view, critical thinking involves teachers and students in identifying problems to be solved and in arriving at the means of solving them. Education as an ongoing process is not to be dominated by fixed ends or rigidly prescribed methods. Ends or goals are always problematic and depend upon the felt needs and interests of the students. As an active social-intellectual enterprise, then, formal education should involve teachers and students in determining the goals to be pursued, the "ends-in-view."

In a Deweyan view, it would be antithetical to the development of critical thinking in a democracy for teachers and students to experience themselves as instruments in a plan they had not conceived themselves. Ends imposed externally through the state's control of the schooling enterprise would constitute a form of dominance that was alien to the cooperative, critical, democratic ideal schools should exemplify. Dewey referred to such an alienated condition as the "vice of externally imposed ends." He described its alienating origins and effects as follows:

> The vice of externally imposed ends has deep roots. Teachers receive them from superior authorities; these authorities accept them from what is current

in the community. The teachers impose them upon children. As a first consequence, the intelligence of the teacher is not free; it is confined to receiving the aims laid down from above. Too rarely is the individual teacher so
free from dictation of authoritative supervisor, textbook on methods, prescribed course of study, etc., that he can let his mind come to close quarters
with the pupil's mind and the subject matter. This distrust of the teacher's
experience is then reflected in lack of confidence in the responses of pupils.
The latter receive their aims which are natural to their own experience at the
time and those in which they are taught to acquiesce.[43]

Dewey's model of critical thinking emphasizes both the intimate
relationship between thought and action and the essential connection
between freedom of choice and freedom of thought. His model alerts
us to the dangers of taking away from teachers and students the decisions that most concern critical thinking—decisions of curriculum.
For Dewey, what was to be learned and how it was to be learned
could not be decided in a way that was remote from the needs, goals,
preferences, interests, and abilities of the people who were learning—
students.[44]

The second problem with the state's practical domination of the
schooling enterprise lies in the subtle institutional pressures for conformity of thought and action placed upon the subordinates in the
system. One can get an intuitive feeling for these pressures by reflecting briefly on the following questions: Can a teacher, administrator,
or student easily challenge or resist statewide policies governing curriculum? Can a teacher or administrator concerned with a lifetime
career in education safely speak his/her mind and decry what he/she
regards as mindless state policies or other forms of institutional foolishness? In principle, the answer is "yes." In practice, the answer is
usually "no." The hidden message behind the state's detailed regulation of the schooling enterprise is the expectation that employees in
the system will obey the rules, follow the guidelines, and remain
loyal to their superiors.

State control of education takes many practical forms. Its most
extreme version resembles a model of depersonalized factory production—in this case production of certain student behaviors. The
effectiveness of schools, in such a model, is viewed in reductionist,
quantitative terms—standardized reading and mathematics scores.
While these scores are highly emphasized, less tangible features of
schooling, including critical reasoning, are deemphasized. The school-
as-factory model highlights the instrumental role of teachers as tech-

nicians and diminishes their role as catalysts for reflective inquiry. In turn, students are viewed as objects to be manipulated rather than as persons with intellectual curiosity and a capacity for critical judgment. Factory production may seem like a bizarre and inappropriate model for conceiving of the human enterprise of formal education. Yet it fits well with both the language and the form of much state control of education, a control that takes the form of "dominance" rather than "causal planning" for rational autonomy in students.

That state control of education seems most often in practice to violate our idealistic sense of what education should be does not mean we must give up our ideals nor reduce our efforts to speak to the purposes of education. However, if our efforts to redirect the nature of the educational enterprise are to be more successful, we must know of what we speak. As Donna Kerr said: "Often the hardest errors to recognize are those that regard not what we think about, but the way we think about it."[45] The way we think about education may broaden or constrict our sense of possibilities for reform.

---

The purpose of this essay has been to urge us to reexamine the way we conceive of the right to education and the ideal of universal education, for such a reexamination may illuminate our fundamental goals and our most important ideals. Education, as William James reminded us, "enlarging as it does our horizon and perspective, is a means of multiplying our ideals, of bringing new ones into view."[46] In James's view, ideals by themselves are not worth much. However, when combined with courage, pluck, and "the sterner stuff" of virtue, ideals are what make a life significant. They are, moreover, what give a society its direction and sense of purpose.

The ideal of universal education is integrally connected to the kind of democratic ideal in which people can aspire to think and act intelligently for themselves and can continue to develop their own potentialities through creative effort. Such an ideal needs to be reinvigorated and given new substance as a guiding ideal of educational policy, broadly conceived as that which affects educational opportunities, not merely schooling opportunities. To those who would dismiss this invitation to idealism as a fanciful dream, it is useful to remember the lines from Thoreau: "If you have built castles in the air, your work need not be lost; that is where they should be. Now put the foundations under them."[47]

To the degree that the ideal of universal education remains vague, we need to clarify it and give it substance. We need to relate it to the existing realities of the world we live in. To the degree it remains a castle in the air, there is work to be done. The foundations are yet to be laid.

## NOTES TO CHAPTER 5

1. I am indebted to my colleague Harvey Siegel for the term "critical literacy." See his "Critical Thinking as an Educational Ideal," *Educational Forum* 45 (1980): 7-23. One might just as easily have used the term "critical thinking" instead of "critical literacy," for there is no effort here to suggest how the ability to think critically is both involved in, but extends beyond, the skills of reading and writing that are suggested by the notion of "functional literacy." It is also *not* my intention to extend the contemporary fashion of legitimating educational interests by attaching the term "literacy" to them.

2. Israel Scheffler, "Science, Morals, and Educational Policy," in *Reason and Teaching*, ed. Israel Scheffler (Indianapolis: Bobbs-Merrill, 1973), pp. 97-115.

3. Thomas F. Green, with the assistance of David P. Ericson and Robert H. Seidman, *Predicting the Behavior of the Educational System* (Syracuse: Syracuse University Press, 1980). Green's provocative work seeks to develop a theory of the educational system, conceived of as a rational system guided by rational arguments.

4. See Michael B. Katz, *Class, Bureaucracy, and Schools: The Illusion of Educational Change in America* (New York: Praeger, 1971); and David Tyack, *The One Best System* (Cambridge, Mass.: Harvard University Press, 1974). The term "revisionist" is not used in a pejorative sense.

5. I confess to having my own skepticism about the extent to which expanded schooling has fostered habits of critical thinking but admit that such skepticism rests on intuition rather than on research. For a contrasting perspective based on an ambitious program of research into the lasting effects of schooling on critical understanding of values, see Herbert H. Hyman and Charles R. Wright, *Education's Lasting Influence on Values* (Chicago: University of Chicago Press, 1979). Even the skeptic may find Hyman and Wright's findings impressive.

6. For a provocative critique of the competency testing movement, see Walt Haney and George Madaus, "Making Sense of the Competency Testing Movement," *Harvard Educational Review* 48 (1978): 462-84.

7. However, it must be admitted that it would be hard to argue that schools in the United States have been successful in suppressing individuals' ten-

dency to be critical as adults. That there is a widespread inclination to be critical is manifested in numerous polls assessing the public's confidence in our public institutions as well as in much ordinary discourse. This point was made forcefully to me by Martin Friedman.

8.   Green, *Predicting the Behavior*, p. 24. What the role of the state should be in providing for, or guaranteeing, fundamental human interests is a central problem in social and political philosophy. The seminal work of John Rawls and Robert Nozick has contributed to a burgeoning philosophical literature in this area. See John Rawls, *A Theory of Justice* (Cambridge, Mass.: Harvard University Press, 1971), and Robert Nozick, *Anarchy, State, and Utopia* (New York: Basic Books, 1974). Both books present contrasting critiques of classical utilitarianism, but Nozick's in particular argues for a limited state role. Unfortunately, it is beyond the scope of this essay to connect my own conception of education as a right to this significant body of recent scholarship.

9.   R. S. Peters, "Education and the Educated Man: Some Further Reflections," in *Education and the Education of Teachers*, ed. R. S. Peters (London: Routledge & Kegan Paul, 1977), p. 11.

10.  See Frederick A. Olafson, "Rights and Duties in Education," in *Educational Judgments*, ed. James F. Doyle (London: Routledge & Kegan Paul, 1973), pp. 173–95. Olafson argues that education is a "generational right" that is derivable from the special relationship existing between parents and children.

11.  Green, *Predicting the Behavior*, p. 22.

12.  John Dewey, *Democracy and Education* (New York: Free Press, 1966), pp. 2–3.

13.  M. S. Katz, *A History of Compulsory Education Laws* (Bloomington, Ind.: Phi Delta Kappa, 1976), pp. 11–13.

14.  *Wisconsin* v. *Yoder*, 406 U.S. 205 (1971) at 223.

15.  Id. at 223. For a critical analysis of the Amish court cases, see Michael S. Katz, "The Concepts of Compulsory Education and Compulsory Schooling: A Philosophical Inquiry," unpublished Ph.D dissertation, Stanford University, 1974, pp. 187–251; and Peter J. Riga, "*Yoder* and Free Exercise," *Journal of Law and Education* 6 (1977):449–72.

16.  M. S. Katz, "Two Views of 'Teaching People to Think,'" *Educational Theory* 26 (1976): 160.

17.  P. A. White, "Socialization and Education," in *A Critique of Current Educational Aims: Part I of Education and the Development of Reason*, ed. R. F. Dearden, P. H. Hirst, and R. S. Peters (London: Routledge & Kegan Paul, 1972), p. 119.

18.  See John Passmore, "On Teaching to Be Critical," in *The Concept of Education*, ed. R. S. Peters (London: Routledge & Kegan Paul, 1967), pp. 192–209, 197.

19.  "Universal Declaration of Human Rights," adopted and proclaimed by the General Assembly of the United Nations on December 10, 1948, in *Political Theory and the Rights of Man*, ed. D. D. Raphael (Bloomington: Indiana University Press, 1967), p. 147. There are some very useful philosophical discussions of "rights" in the Raphael volume.

20.  Dewey, *Democracy and Education*, p. 8.

21.  *Oxford English Dictionary*, Compact Edition (1971), p. 833.

22.  Paul Goodman, *Compulsory Mis-Education and the Community of Scholars* (New York: Alfred A. Knopf, 1962); and Ivan Illich, *Deschooling Society* (New York: Harper & Row, 1970). To their credit, radical critics of schooling raised the important possibility that all forms of schooling were not necessarily educational.

23.  Green, *Predicting the Behavior*, p. 48.

24.  As Martin Friedman pointed out to me, a society could be unjust to use schooling credentials as "part of its process of distributing employment benefits unless it can show that there is an exceptionally strong relationship between these symbols and competence in employment." It is not clear that such a strong relationship exists.

25.  Hillary Rodham, "Children Under the Law," *Harvard Educational Review* 43 (1973):494, n. 19.

26.  Advocates of compulsory schooling in the late nineteenth century were fond of talking about "the right to education." Nevertheless, the philosophical literature on rights, albeit expressing diverse conceptions of what constitutes a "right," suggests that one is generally not compelled to exercise one's right.

27.  See Brian Crittendon, "Education as a Human Right," *Proceedings of the Philosophy of Education Society 1971*, p. 68.

28.  Ralph Page has pointed out that some educational opportunities presuppose that previous educational opportunities have been provided and taken advantage of; see his "Opportunity and Its Willing Requirement," *Proceedings of the Philosophy of Education Society 1976*, pp. 304–5. See also Nicholas C. Burbules and Ann L. Sherman, "Equal Educational Opportunity: Ideal or Ideology," *Proceedings of the Philosophy of Education Society 1979*, pp. 105–14; and Thomas F. Green, "Response to Burbules and Sherman," *Proceedings of the Philosophy of Education Society 1979*, pp. 115–20. Most of the literature on equal educational opportunity, I believe, has not usefully integrated clear conceptions of "opportunity" and "education."

29.  See Hyman and Wright, *Education's Lasting Influence*, and Siegel, "Critical Thinking." Siegel's emphasis lies primarily, I believe, with the criticism of arguments and claims, that is, with deductive reasoning; my own point of view, although not sufficiently elaborated here, attaches more importance to practical reasoning than his does. It should also be pointed

out that there seem to be forms of criticism that are closely linked with particular disciplinary fields or areas of discourse. See Stephen Toulmin, *The Uses of Argument* (Cambridge: Cambridge University Press, 1958). See also Robert Ennis, "Presidential Address: A Conception of Rational Thinking," *Proceedings of the Philosophy of Education Society 1979*, pp. 3-34.

30.    Joel Feinberg, *Social Philosophy* (Englewood Cliffs, N.J.: Prentice Hall, 1973), p. 71. In general, I find Feinberg's typology of rights quite useful. A voluminous philosophical literature on rights awaits one inquiring into this topic. See, for example, Wesley Newcomb Hohfeld, essay, in Walter Wheeler Cook, ed., *Fundamental Legal Conceptions* (New Haven: Yale University Press, 1923); A. I. Melden, *Rights and Right Conduct* (Oxford: Blackwell, 1959); Nozick, *Anarchy, State, and Utopia*; and Rawls, *Theory of Justice*. See also, Stuart Brown, "Inalienable Rights," *Philosophical Review* 64 (1955): 192-211; Martin Golding, "Towards a Theory of Human Rights," *Monist* 62 (1968): 521-49; H. L. A. Hart, "Are There Any Natural Rights?" *Philosophical Review* 64 (1955): 175-91; Robert E. Ladenson, "Two Kinds of Rights," *Journal of Value Inquiry* 13 (1977): 161-73; H. J. McCloskey, "Rights," *Philosophical Quarterly* 15 (1965): 115-27; *Political Theory and the Rights of Man*, and Samuel Scheffler, "Natural Rights, Equality, and the Minimal State," *Canadian Journal of Philosophy* 6 (1976): 59-76. Two recent works deserve thoughtful consideration: Ronald Dworkin, *Taking Rights Seriously* (Cambridge, Mass.: Harvard University Press, 1978), and Charles Fried, *Right and Wrong* (Cambridge, Mass.: Harvard University Press, 1978).

31.    Ronald Dworkin, "The Model of Rules," *University of Chicago Law Review* 35 (1967): 25-7. Dworkin's full-scale critique of legal positivism can be found in his *Taking Rights Seriously*; in ch. 12, Dworkin presents an argument against the popular position that there is a "right to liberty."

32.    Nozick, *Anarchy, State, and Utopia*. See also Golding, "Towards a Theory of Human Rights."

33.    The issue of legal compulsion seems much less important than the range of social and economic configurations in which educational opportunities might be provided. For a very provocative conceptual analysis of diverse schemes for providing education, ranging from purely voluntaristic arrangements to governmentally coercive structures, see Stephen D. Sugarman and David L. Kirp, "Rethinking Collective Responsibility for Education," *Law and Contemporary Problems* 39 (1975): 144-225. I share Sugarman and Kirp's concerns for increasing parental liberty while not diminishing the equitable distribution of educational opportunities. Sugarman and Kirp provide an analysis which draws heavily on concepts and understandings derived from welfare economics, but some of the philosophical points made in this essay are foreshadowed in their article,

although I discovered it after drafting my own argument. Their article concludes with a strong critique of governmentally controlled schooling and thus is quite relevant to the theme of this volume.

34.  I am intrigued by Samuel Scheffler's alternative conception of natural rights in which he posits the idea that every person has a natural right to a sufficient share of every distributable good whose enjoyment is a necessary condition of a person's having a reasonable chance of living a decent and fulfilling life; see his "Natural Rights, Equality, and the Minimal State." What would constitute a sufficient share of "educational opportunities" is a difficult question to answer; moreover, whether they should be equitably distributed remains to be determined.

35.  A fuller analysis of the logical relationship between ideals, principles, and rules would enhance my own argument. At bottom, I am claiming that the ideal of universal education is a central dimension of an adequate democratic ideal; moreover, it is my belief that a meaningful conception of the ideal of universal education would have at its conceptual core the principle of each person's entitlement to those educational opportunities necessary, if that person had the ability and the will, to become critically literate. It might be argued that no social ideal by itself will be the basis of social reform unless it is conceptually linked with principles, rules, and facts.

36.  Siegel, "Critical Thinking," pp. 11-12.

37.  I am indebted in this section to Israel Scheffler's thoughtful piece, "Moral Education and the Democratic Ideal," in *Reason and Teaching*, pp. 136-39.

38.  *San Antonio School District* v. *Rodriguez*, 411 U.S. 1 (1972) at 30; at 33-34. It should be noted that attorneys for Texas frankly admitted that they could not show a compelling interest in Texas's financing scheme.

39.  Id. at 111.

40.  Green, *Predicting the Behavior*, p. 24. The state's capacity for control operates within a monopolistic condition wherein the government has assumed primary responsibility for formal education. As Sugarman and Kirp put it: "While it does not formally preclude families from voluntarily doing more, the education that it provides is meant to be both sufficient and, in fact, largely preemptive." "Rethinking Collective Responsibility," p. 192.

41.  Israel Scheffler, "Science, Morals, and Educational Policy," in *Reason and Teaching*, p. 111. I do not intend to suggest by the term "dominance" any conspiratorial conception of the state.

42.  Ibid., p. 111.

43.  Dewey, *Democracy and Education*, p. 109.

44.  One can be committed to the principle of critical literacy without being committed either to Dewey's conception of critical thinking or to his view of students' role in curriculum development.

45.  Donna Kerr, "Thinking About Education with a Strict Typology of Rights," *Educational Theory* 28 (1978): 165.

46.  William James, "What Makes a Life Significant," in his *Talks to Teachers on Psychology and to Students on Some of Life's Ideals* (New York: Dover, 1962), p. 142.

47.  Henry David Thoreau, *Walden* (Princeton: Princeton University Press, 1971), p. 324.

# 6 THE MANIPULATION OF CONSCIOUSNESS
## A First Amendment Critique of Schooling

*Stephen Arons and*
*Charles Lawrence III*

### INTRODUCTION

Schooling is everywhere and inevitably a manipulator of consciousness—an inculcator of values in young minds. This essay addresses the school's imposition of values and its relation to the system of freedom of expression articulated in the First Amendment to the Constitution. Some of the practical implications of the First Amendment critique of schooling are discussed. The emphasis, however, is upon examining the ways in which First Amendment rights are threatened by the structure and ideology of American schooling, not upon the evaluation of particular strategies for change.

In the first section of this essay, we reevaluate the nature of First Amendment protections, applying one of the amendment's central themes to the structure of contemporary education. In the second section we examine in greater detail some of the conflicts between this view of the First Amendment and the present educational system. In the last section we examine racism as a constitutional and practical problem raised by a view of the First Amendment which calls for greater family liberty in choosing schools and greater family control of value inculcation within schools.

The problem of racism commands our attention (1) because the poor and working class are disproportionately the victims of consciousness manipulation in government schools and because member-ship in this group is in turn overrepresented by racial minorities; (2) because one of the clear implications of our argument about the schools' infringement of First Amendment rights is the provision of equal choice in schooling for all families; yet family choice has his-torically been a code word for the preservation of racially segregated and stigmatizing schools; and (3) because racism has been the most persistent and pernicious flaw in the consciousness and structure of American schooling.

Throughout we deal with problems that have traditionally been understood as questions of equality in the social order or of due process of law. We do not dispute these traditional understandings; but we try to refocus the problems in terms of their relationship to the operation of the system of freedom of expression which is cen-tral to the constitutional order.

> Men cannot be truly human apart from communication, for they are essen-tially communicative creatures. To impede communication is to reduce men to the status of "things."
>
> Paul Freire,
> *Pedagogy of the Oppressed*

> Congress shall make no law respecting an establishment of religion, or prohib-iting the free exercise thereof; or abridging the freedom of speech, or of the press; or the right of the people peaceably to assemble, and to petition the Government for a redress of grievances.
>
> First Amendment to the
> U.S. Constitution

## FIRST AMENDMENT PROTECTION OF THE FORMATION OF BELIEFS

### The Traditional First Amendment Conception

This section will outline a general understanding of the relation of First Amendment protections to the problem of manipulation of belief and opinion by schools.[1] In this context we view the First Amendment not only as a collection of interconnected personal rights but as the lynchpin of a system of free expression[2] and open political decision making. The need to examine and further develop a theoretical understanding of the First Amendment is accentuated by the problem of applying the amendment to social institutions which neither existed nor were contemplated at the time the Bill of Rights was enacted. Among all the institutions which have arisen since the end of the eighteenth century, perhaps the most complex and problematical one for First Amendment analysis is universal, compulsory schooling.

It has been observed that the various First Amendment rights are reflections of a single intent and understanding on the part of the framers.[3] Expressed in terms of the traditional understanding of politics and personality, this central conception regarded the individual as the central unit of political and social being, free to develop in his or her own way, to express himself, and to engage in the struggle to mold social institutions and public policy without government interference. The First Amendment is thus a statement of the dignity and worth of every individual, of the value of a "single human soul,"[4] of the fact that the government exists for the benefit of the people and not the people for the benefit of the government.

The particular freedoms of press, speech, assembly, and other freedoms that have been inferred from them are part of the system which guarantees individual and group expression and ensures that opinions and beliefs shall be freely given and exchanged in a marketplace of ideas. Self-expression, which is an end in itself, and the fair and reliable making of public policy are both served by these protections. Religious freedoms likewise protect ways of expressing personality and of sharing and changing basic human values and perceptions.

### Belief Expression and Belief Formation

To implement this conception of the First Amendment in the world of universal, institutionalized education requires broadening the amendment's traditional protection of *expression* of belief and opinion to cover *formation* of belief and opinion. As will be seen in applying First Amendment principles to institutionalized education, expression and formation are not as separate in human interaction as they have been analytically.

Free expression makes unfettered formulation of beliefs and opinions meaningful and possible. In turn, free formulation of beliefs and opinions is a necessary precursor to freedom of expression. If the government were to regulate the development of ideas and opinions through, for example, a single television monopoly or through religious rituals for children—freedom of expression would become a meaningless right. To the degree that government regulation of belief formation interferes with personal consciousness, fewer people conceive dissenting ideas or perceive contradictions between self-interest and government sustained ideological orthodoxy. If the system of freedom of expression did not protect the development or formulation of ideas and world views, totalitarianism and freedom of expression might be characteristics of the same society.

Connecting the theme of the dignity of the individual with an understanding of how personal development may be influenced by a pervasive child-rearing institution such as schooling suggests a new formulation of First Amendment principles: the development as well as the expression of those beliefs, opinions, world views, and aspects of conscience which constitute individual consciousness should be free of government manipulation. The notion of manipulation here refers not to the effectiveness of any particular technique of value inculcation but to government control over what values are taught. The individual ought to control his or her own education, or where the individual is too young to make an informed, intelligent, and voluntary choice, his or her parents ought to control it. This formulation of the modern meaning of the First Amendment suggests a protection of individual human consciousness from coercion by the state whether that coercion takes the form of religious indoctrination,[5] the involuntary administering of psychoactive drugs,[6] the elimination of nonpublic schooling,[7] or a government monopoly of television broadcasting. In modern times the attempt to manipulate consciousness precedes and may even obviate the attempt to manipulate expression.

The effect of dispensing with individual consent or of sacrificing individual control to government-sponsored manipulations of consciousness is to render individual expression a mere game of mirrors. But more important to the First Amendment's position as the lynchpin of constitutional democracy is the effect which consciousness manipulation has upon the political process and the sovereignty of the political individual.

Alexander Meiklejohn has articulated a useful understanding of individual consciousness and the First Amendment by focusing on the realm of political action. According to Meiklejohn, the First

Amendment is meant as an absolute protection for individuals in exercising their electoral power, not simply in voting, but in all those activities of thought, communication, and belief formation which inform the electoral power of the individual or are part of the right of self-government guaranteed by the Constitution. Any exercise of freedoms of speech, press, assembly, or petition is protected from any government abridgement "whenever those activities are utilized for the governing of the nation."[8] Meiklejohn's enumeration of the freedoms necessarily related to the exercise of governing power under the First Amendment is expansive, including public discussions of public issues, together with the spreading of information and opinion, literature and the arts, the achievements of philosophy and the sciences in creating knowledge and understanding, and education in all its phases. Any activity is protected if it can reasonably be described as related to thought or expression, which ultimately is part of the governing role of citizens.

According to Meiklejohn's theory, although some regulation of communication may be permitted under the amendment (chiefly regulation of the incidents of speaking or other freedoms, not their content), no regulation of belief can be tolerated:

> A citizen may be told when and where and in what manner he may or may not speak, write, assemble, and so on. On the other hand, he may not be told what he shall or shall not believe. In that realm, each citizen is sovereign. He exercises powers that the body politic reserves for its own members.[9]

The logic of Meiklejohn's formulation suggests that the society which can utilize institutional power to reduce an individual's control over the development of personal consciousness has made that individual politically impotent. Under these conditions the government becomes a kind of political perpetual motion machine, legitimizing its policies through public opinion the government itself creates. The protection of the governing powers of the individual through the First Amendment is a necessary part of a system which relies upon the just consent of the governed. Every citizen must participate in making these decisions, not out of loyalty to some idealized notion of democracy but out of a sense of self-preservation. The right to vote, the freedoms of expression and belief enumerated in the First Amendment, the legitimate formation of political majorities and public policy all are knit together in making the dignity and political powers of the individual meaningful.

Those who are prevented from making themselves felt or whose participation in public affairs is stilted or contorted by government intervention are not only stunted and warped in personal development and human interaction; they will also find themselves victims of others who are better able to understand and express their self-interest or their personal version of the general welfare. Although the meaning of the First Amendment begins with specific freedoms of expression, it ultimately involves in the deepest sense the capacity to be human and the ability to participate in political action, to acquire and produce knowledge, and to make it into power affecting the conditions of daily life.

## Schooling and Belief Formation

There is a reciprocal relationship between schooling and a modernized view of the First Amendment. The application of the amendment to schooling suggests ways of rethinking the amendment's meaning; the revised understandings of the amendment shed new light on the function and effect of American education.

It is commonplace to recognize that schools, as institutions which occupy a substantial portion of a child's waking life, ought to respect the First Amendment rights of students. While the law has recognized that teachers and students do not "shed their constitutional rights to freedom of speech or expression at the schoolhouse gate,"[10] most cases have dealt with the right of the individual to be free of specifically imposed restrictions of expression. It is also commonplace to hear that by teaching basic skills of communication as well as knowledge and patterns of thought, the schools are preparing children to exercise those political freedoms which are at the core of democratic activity. What is not recognized in either of these two statements is the pervasiveness of value transmission in the schools and that the choice of appropriate values to be transmitted lies not with the child or the child's family but with the political majority or interest group in charge of the school system.[11] Once this is recognized, it becomes possible to argue that certain restrictions on freedom of press or speech imposed upon children by school authorities are merely the most obvious and superficial examples of restrictions on First Amendment rights embedded in schooling. It also becomes possible to see that the rhetoric of "training for democracy" only obscures the interference with First Amendment principles prevalent in contemporary schooling. Even when a school bends over backwards (as it almost never does) to provide all points of view about ideas and issues in the classroom, it has barely scratched the surface of value inculcation in a child-rearing institution.[12] It must still confront its hidden curriculum—the role models teachers provide, the structure of classrooms and of teacher–student relationships, the way in which the school is governed, the ways in which the child's time is parceled out, learning subdivided and fragmented, attitudes and behaviors rewarded and punished. Even in those areas concerned with basic skills, it is clear that teaching is never value-neutral, that texts, teachers, subject matter, atmosphere, all convey messages about approved and rewarded values and ideas.[13] It is unlikely that any amount of "equal time" will reduce this effect.[14]

Most parents of children about to begin school want to know whether their children will be helped to learn to read or do mathematics or develop physical dexterity, but hardly anyone stops with these questions. How are the skills to be taught? Will children learn to respect the values their parents try to preserve at home? Will they accept inferior social and political roles for women? Will they perceive themselves as dependent upon the group, or will they act on the assumption that their own welfare can be achieved at the expense of others? Will they learn to look down on manual work? Will they become alienated from learning itself as the price of attaining technical certification? What will they internalize about the proper relationship of individuals to power and authority; about mysticism, emotion, and art as part of social life; about God, communal living, achievement, violence, personal inadequacy, and pleasure; about people's relation to the natural environment and the manipulation of other human beings? Whatever their values, most parents seem to recognize that a good deal of child rearing will take place at school and that the school is a social environment from which a child may learn much more than what is the formal curriculum. The effect of the school on children's consciousness is to alter their concept of reality and, therefore, their perception of and reaction to all things.

The Supreme Court has recognized that value inculcation is inherent in schooling. Thus far, however, the Court has found such value inculcation to be unconstitutional only in its more overt forms or when the values involved are religious.

In the landmark cases of *Pierce* v. *Society of Sisters* and *Meyer* v. *Nebraska*, the Court placed limits on the power of the state to promote homogeneity in its schools. In *Pierce* the Court invalidated a state statute which required all students to attend public school. In striking the law down, the Court noted that "the child is not the mere creature of the state" and ruled that the Constitution "excludes any general power of the State to standardize its children by forcing them to accept instruction from public teachers only."[15] A central concern of the Court seems to have been preserving the right of the family to direct the upbringing of its children without unreasonable interference from the political majority. In *Meyer* the Court held unconstitutional a statute prohibiting the teaching of modern languages to young children, finding this an impermissible means of fostering "a homogeneous people with American ideals. . . ."[16]

In *West Virginia Board of Education* v. *Barnette*, the Court held invalid under the First Amendment a statute which compelled public school students to salute the flag. Writing for the Court, Justice Robert Jackson noted that the pledge was a form of utterence which required "affirmation of a belief and an attitude of mind." He went on to point out that the case did not turn solely on the religion clauses of the First Amendment but was based on the amendment's broader protection of nonconformists' belief. Perhaps in the Court's most absolute declaration of the freedom of individual consciousness, Jackson said: "If there is any fixed star in our constitutional constellation, it is that no official, high or petty, can prescribe what shall be orthodox in politics, nationalism, religion, or other matters of opinion or force citizens to confess by word or act their faith therein. . . ."[17]

As the next section of this essay will argue, the current system of education forces students "to confess by word or act" in a variety of ways that have not been attacked by courts or legislatures. Nevertheless, *Barnette* remains a powerful formulation of the unconstitutionality of state-imposed orthodoxy and of the intimate relationship between holding and expressing beliefs.

In *Abbington School District* v. *Schempp*,[18] the Court recognized the existence and unconstitutionality of attempts at value orthodoxy involving Bible readings or the recitation of prayer. The Court stressed the need for government neutrality with respect to all "orthodoxies." The Court's wall of separation of church and state as applied to school prayer seeks to prevent religious factionalization of political institutions and to preserve the government neutrality toward religion which is part of First Amendment doctrine.[19]

In recognizing the danger of religious value inculcation or establishment in schools, the Court has failed to consider the First Amendment implications involved when equally basic but nonreligious values form a part of the world view established by a school and communicated to its students.[20] Perhaps the clearest example of how the law has ignored the similarities of religious and secular socialization is *Wisconsin* v. *Yoder* in which the Amish community of Wisconsin was granted a constitutional exemption from compulsory high school attendance. The Court ruled that attendance at a high school would impose value conflicts and alienation, which would destroy the Amish religious community and violate their First Amendment right of free exercise of religion. In making its ruling, the Court enumerated Amish objections to high school socialization, which, although religiously based for the Amish, are equally important to parents with no religious affiliation or background:

> The high school tends to emphasize intellectual and scientific accomplishments, self-distinction, competitiveness, worldly success, and social life with other students. Amish society emphasizes informal learning-through-doing, a life of "goodness" rather than a life of intellect, wisdom rather than technical knowledge, community welfare rather than competition, and separation rather than integration with contemporary worldly society.[21]

The Court thus recognized that socialization is an integral part of schooling and at the same time limited the constitutional impact of that recognition to religious issues.

### The First Amendment and the Fourteenth Amendment: Twin Guardians of the Political Process

While value inculcation under the present structure of public education threatens the debate in the marketplace of ideas which the First Amendment seeks to ensure, we must not overlook the fact that schools influence the quantity and quality of that debate not just by the transmission of values contrary to those of many families but by inequalities in the transmission of skills and knowledge. Not only are the values of the more powerful groups in our society embedded in the official and invisible curricula of our public and private schools, but the children of these who share those values have greater access to the skills and information that are necessary to the effective articulation of their interests. Segregation, suspensions, and expulsions; standardized tests and tracking; and unequal resource allocation all operate to deprive some students (and these students are disproportionately minorities and the poor) of skills, information, and attitudes which would enable them to speak and act more effectively.

Such problems have traditionally been thought to involve questions of equality rather than of free expression. It is not suggested that they are problems which no longer require active redress under the equal protection clause. Rather, it should be recognized that such practices conflict with both the First and the Fourteenth Amendments, which stand as twin guardians of the democratic process. Just as one aim of the First Amendment is to foster intelligent self-government, the Fourteenth Amendment is directed in part at protecting the right to participate in the political process. Because education is vital not only to the effective exercise of the ballot but to effective participation in the political process that precedes and follows the election, the First and Fourteenth Amendments are both implicated by inequalities in the educational system.

As will be discussed in the second section, the constitutional problems raised by unequal access to educational opportunity are intertwined with those created by value inculcation. To the extent that schools provide minority and poor children with fewer skills and less information, they will be relatively less able to hold their own in a political debate that involves the increasingly complex issues of our technocratic society. But in addition to being well informed, effective participants in the political process must understand what is in their own self-interest. If the schools expose children only to those values and ideas which buttress the status quo and legitimize the position of those in power, it is unlikely that those who are presently oppressed will learn the cause of their oppression or how to overcome it.

Similarly, effective political participation requires a positive self-identity, a sense of self-worth that enables one to believe that one deserves to be treated well and that one is capable of doing something about being treated badly. If the values expressed in our schools convince minority children that they are worthless, then they are deprived of that quality most essential for political self-preservation: the desire to preserve oneself.

In *Brown* v. *Board of Education* [22] the Supreme Court found that segregated schools stigmatized black children and that the resulting sense of inferiority made it more difficult for them to learn. The Court held that this cause-and-effect relationship made segregated schools inherently unequal. The same stigma operates to minimize any minority child's ability to be an effective self-interested participant in the political debate. Because the segregated individual is labeled as inferior to his fellow citizens, his thoughts and words will be given less weight when affairs of the body politic are discussed. If he accepts the stigma, he may mistrust his own ideas and perceptions and feel that his interests deserve less protection. The stigma of segregation restricts the ability of blacks to participate in the political process and thus impairs First as well as Fourteenth Amendment rights.

The refocusing of First Amendment principles from communication to formation of ideas, and from self-development to political power, is meant to deepen rather than reject other formulations of the importance and meaning of the first freedom. But in so doing, a revised understanding of the First Amendment raises new problems of interpretation and of conflict with other aspects of the Constitution. Attempting to apply a modernized understanding of the amendment to schooling creates an opportunity to explore some of these problems and to test the usefulness of invoking the Constitution to protect individual consciousness. This application will also point the way to some new understandings of the nature of schooling and education policy.

## SCHOOLING AND THE MANIPULATION OF CONSCIOUSNESS

### The First Amendment and Family Choice of Schools

Government-run schooling, universal, compulsory, and publicly supported, has traditionally been viewed by most Americans as an essential democratic institution. According to this view, schooling teaches skills necessary to the exercise of citizenship rights, is required for survival in our economic system, and inculcates in the rising generation those values and attitudes which support democratic institutions. In their more rapturous moments, the teaching profession and educators have claimed not only that schooling is the bulwark of democracy in America but that the schools are the nation's primary agency for eliminating social ills, inoculating against anti-Americanism, and perfecting personal and national character.[23]

This ideology, which correlates the American school system with social democracy and personal liberty, may be more self-serving than self-evident. In fact, American schooling is structured in a way that undercuts the most basic freedoms of democracy. At the heart of the American school ideology is the belief that schooling decisions, like most governmental decisions, are the proper province of the political majority.

The commitment to majoritarian control over what basic cultural and political values are institutionalized in public schools is made tolerable to some parents because they are constitutionally guaranteed the right to choose a nonpublic school for their children. It is made tolerable to others because they can afford to move their homes to those school districts in which they feel their aspirations, beliefs, and style are reflected in the schools their children attend. These escape hatches exist for the very few whereas the poor and working class are saddled with schooling decisions they often neither effectively control nor basically agree with. It is significant in this regard that so few people have expressed the belief that school decisions are so personal in origin and meaning that they ought to be classed along with religion and freedom of speech and press as beyond the reach of the majority. Majoritarian control of the transmission of personal belief, conscience, and world view through schooling is a problem whose magnitude is equaled only by our massive public refusal to discuss it.

The Supreme Court has eliminated religious indoctrination in public schools. We argue here that the imposition of secular values may constitute as significant an interference with First Amendment values as the imposition of religious beliefs. Nevertheless, except when dealing with overt instances of value inculcation such as the compulsory flag salute in *West Virginia Board of Education* v. *Barnette*,[24] the Court has left the establishment of other ideologies untouched.

Government neutrality in imposing values and influencing the formation of beliefs, essential to preserving First Amendment freedoms, is thus achieved by allowing families to inculcate their own values by choosing other than public schools.[25] The neutrality consists in being neutral as to school choices made by families, not in the vain attempt to create neutrality in the public school itself and not in the elimination of compulsory schooling.[26] Keeping the government or political majority from intervening in family choice of schools would prevent the essentially political process of school governance from being overburdened by the mutually exclusive value preferences of parents.[27] Whenever a political majority establishes some set of values as central to a school, a dissenting family ought to be able to send its child to another more suitable school. Schooling decisions do not have to be resolved by choosing for one value against another or by creating an artificial compromise which respects neither value. On a personal level this policy respects the dignity and the personal and cultural values of individuals. On a political level this policy ensures that no group or political majority can use school socialization to maintain or extend its ideology or political power. The democratic process of formulating public policy is preserved.

This entire argument might simply prove that a majoritarian school system is consistent with the tenets of political democracy and individual dignity as long as it provides that dissenting families may attend nonpublic schools. But many, perhaps most, families are too poor to afford private schools. We have in effect created a system of school finance which provides free choice for the rich and compulsory socialization for the poor and working class. The present structure of American schooling—its method of finance and control—discriminates against the poor and working class and even a large part of the middle class by conditioning the exercise of First Amendment rights of school choice upon an ability to pay while simultaneously eroding that ability to pay through the retrogressive collection of taxes used for public schools only.[28] The arrangement seems no more defensible than denying a man the right to vote because he cannot afford the poll tax.[29]

The present method of financing and controlling schooling in America is neither accidental nor unchangeable. Because we assume that the majority may rightfully dictate what values school children will learn, we do not permit the dissenting family to have the benefit of tax dollars collected from every citizen. The family which wishes neither to have its children learn a set of values it finds abhorrent nor to suffer the conflict and alienation which result from competing efforts to control the child's learning must pay private school tuition as well as a public school tax. In effect, we confront the dissenting family with a choice between giving up its basic values as the price of gaining a "free" education in a government school or paying twice in order to preserve its First Amendment rights.

Naturally, the burden of forced choices between economic survival and the preservation of personal and cultural values falls most heavily upon the poor, the working class, and those minorities which are overrepresented among the poor and working class. Unresolvable, self-consuming conflict or unnatural passivity in the face of schooling "experts" is often the result. And all the while our present school ideology tells these same poor and working-class persons that the present structure of school is their best hope for an equal place in a sane and equitable society. It is natural that those who are least able to resist should be most systematically deprived of their ability to dissent in the molding of their children's minds.

A change in government created school-financing mechanisms suggests itself as a direct means of rectifying the abridgement of First Amendment rights of the poor and equalizing the right of all families to choose schools. Such a program would make real for the majority of families what is now only a hollow constitutional right to avoid government schooling by making use of alternative schools.

### The First Amendment Inside the School: Conditioning Access to Education on Confessions of Belief

Children whose families cannot exercise their constitutional right to obtain alternative schooling have no escape from the values of the public school which they must attend. Despite the ringing words of Justice Jackson in *West Virginia Board of Education* v. *Barnette*, children who wish to succeed *in* school are forced to offer confessions of belief in various subtle and not so subtle ways. Few ever realize that the Constitution protects their right to be different. It is questionable how many students are even aware of their constitutional right to avoid the flag salute. Most children are homogenized into the dominant cultural-political ideology without appreciating the changes worked upon their values.

Value inculcation, however, is only one aspect of the challenge to First Amendment guarantees posed by the system of schooling. Those students who do not share the majoritarian values of the educational establishment may be denied access to the knowledge and skills necessary for them to participate in the political process. Alienation from the dominant value structure may generate discipline problems or cause poor showings on standardized tests, as discussed below. In either case, educational doors will close.

To make effective schooling available to disssenting students only upon compromise of their First Amendment freedoms violates the general rule that government benefits may not be conditioned on surrender of constitutional rights.[30] More pointedly, to do so runs counter to the teaching of *Barnette*. In that case the Court stated:

> The sole conflict is between authority and rights of the individual. The State asserts power to condition access to public education on making a prescribed sign and profession and at the same time to coerce attendance by punishing both parent and child. The latter stand on a right of self-determination in matters that touch individual opinion and personal attitude.

In its holding the Court clearly rejected the state's asserted power to make education available only to those who would tolerate the school's invasion of "the sphere of intellect and spirit which it is the purpose of the First Amendment to our Constitution to reserve from all official control."[31]

*Disciplinary Action as a Form of Belief Coercion.* School discipline is not always an easily recognized form of value inculcation. Children are usually disciplined for behavior which is antisocial in any cultural context. But often the disciplined behavior is merely the tip of the iceberg—the aimless striking out of a young person forced to accept a system of values which denies his humanity.

In a case several years ago, a sixteen-year-old student had been expelled from school for fighting. He was one of nine black students who had been expelled from school for their participation in a race riot which had occurred at a recently integrated high school. No white students had been asked to leave the school. At first blush this seemed a typical due process case, with equal protection overtones. But as the case unfolded, it became apparent that the disciplinary problems were a result of a clash in values between the formerly all-white, largely upper-middle-class school and the newly arrived poor black students.

In order to remain in the good graces of their teachers, this student and his friends would have had to accept a set of attitudes and corresponding behavioral requirements which would have restricted their self-realization and development as full human beings and as effective participants in the body politic. The school demanded that they walk and talk and wear their clothes in a way that made their white teachers comfortable. They were expected to remain silent while teachers blamed their poor performance on their lack of intelligence or the conditions of their homes and neighborhoods. When they came to class, they were ignored or ridiculed because, unlike their upper-middle-class white classmates, they did not sound like their teachers when they spoke. When they cut class to avoid embarrassment, they were suspended. If they refused to assimilate, they were ostracized as misfits or patronized as underprivileged charity cases.[32]

The response of these young people to the school's hostile environment was increased hostility of their own—a hostility that expressed itself in the kind of antisocial behavior which provided a rationale for their expulsion from school. The requirement that the schools' attitudes be accepted with silent consent was no less a coercive ritualistic confession than a flag salute. It was not less a denial of these students' First Amendment rights. They were being trained to be passive, docile, self-denying individuals, a process which restricted their First Amendment rights of individual development and participation in the political process. If they resisted that training, they were denied the right to remain in school where the skills and knowledge necessary for the exercise of those same rights were available.

*Testing and Tracking as Forms of Belief Coercion.*  Each year thousands of black and Latino children are judged by our schools to be mentally retarded because of low scores on standardized I.Q. tests.[33] Allan Bakke was found to be "better qualified" for admission to medical school than minority students who were admitted via a special admissions program mainly because of his score on the Medical College Aptitude Test. In South Carolina, California, and other states, hundreds of black teachers, many of whom have been successful teachers, are being denied employment due to their scores on the National Teachers Examination. Standardized testing has become an integral part of our educational system with devastating impact on blacks and other minorities.

While the most obvious form of bias in the standardized tests which permeate our educational system is the bias of language, there is often a cultural and ideological bias as well.[34] Dr. Asa Hilliard has noted that "the only way that many Europeans or European-Americans have been able to observe Africans or African-Americans has been as a perceived deviation from a European or European-American 'norm.' "[35] He refers to this form of assessment as the "Type I" question. It takes the form, "Do you know what I know?" Type I questions are the type of questions which characterize almost all standardized testing. A Type II question begins from an entirely different point. It takes the form, "What is it that you know?" The Type I question, which typifies the standardized test, is not only an inaccurate measure of the minority individual's intelligence or ability to learn, it is also a tool of belief coercion. In order to score well on the test, the test taker must "confess belief" in the values and world view of the tester.

The National Teachers Examination, for example, affects the lives of hundreds of thousands of black children and tens of thousands of black teachers. It has already resulted in the denial of employment to many competent black teachers and in legitimizing the "competence" of many teachers who have not been able to produce educational gains in black children. Educational Testing Service measures the knowledge they claim as "basic to successful teaching" by using items devised from what they call a "standard" curriculum. Implicit in their claim is the assumption that there is a standard curriculum for teacher preparation nationwide. No such curriculum exists. Nor has there been any attempt to demonstrate that it does. But to the extent that there is a common or universal content to the curriculum of American education, it is a curriculum permeated with European-American ethnocentrism. Again, Hilliard has pointed out that such a test *must* be biased against Afro-Americans since it is based on over four hundred years of academic bias in scholarship.[36]

Increasingly, the ability of individuals from minority subcultures to gain access to effective education in grade school and high school, not to mention admission to college, professional school, or professional certification, is dependent upon their ability to succeed on examinations which adopt the values of their oppressors.[37] Our educational system in general and the ubiquitous use of standardized tests in particular force those without power in society to accept the values of the powerful or punish them for holding beliefs that are unacceptable to their oppressors and may well be essential to their own survival.

*Literacy, Value Inculcation, and the Seeds of Revolution.* In to-day's society literacy is a requirement for effective participation in the political process. But if our schools require that poor young people adopt the beliefs and behavior of those who oppress them as a price for obtaining that skill, it should not be surprising that they reject the process and cling to their humanity.

A 1975 Office of Education study indicated that 22 percent of Americans over seventeen are illiterate and another 32 percent are only marginally literate. James Harris, past president of the National Education Association, noted in 1975 that 23 percent of all school children fail to graduate from high school and that a large segment of those who do graduate are functionally illiterate.[38] While the situation is dismal for all American school children, it is even worse for minorities who are disproportionately represented in these illiteracy rates—rates more than twice that of the population as a whole. Eighty-five percent of black students read less well than the average white student. In 1975, 87 percent of the elementary and junior high school students in Central Harlem failed their standardized tests in reading.

Functional illiteracy is generally defined by educators with reference to an individual's ability to read instructions, fill out forms, and perform other everyday reading and writing tasks which are vital to one's independence and well-being. In First Amendment terms, however, an individual is functionally illiterate if he does not have the skills necessary to understand what is happening in the political system and effectively to participate in that system by making his views known. If illiteracy were measured as a function of one's ability to participate in the political process, it would be apparent that the problem is even graver than has been imagined.

This initial level of recognition of the effect of illiteracy on the process which the First Amendment is designed to protect is important. Without the skills necessary to gather information or communicate one's ideas and beliefs, an individual is denied even minimal participation in the political debate. There is another way, however, in which the fact of widespread illiteracy acts to hinder the free flow of ideas. Those who are unable to participate in the governing process because of the inability to recognize or articulate their self-interests or the nature of their oppression become dehumanized. When individuals are deprived of all control over their own destiny and are treated as objects by the rest of society, they come to believe they are less than human and therefore unworthy of participating in the political process.[39]

Educators will surely respond that they are not responsible for these First Amendment deprivations. After all, they have offered these young people an opportunity to read. It is not their fault that their offers have been rejected. But, as has been argued, the offer was not made without substantial conditions impossible for these young people to accept. The teachers of ghetto minority children who refuse to learn typically believe that the children's world is dirty, ignorant, and immoral and accept a view of the world that says that these children and those they love are at fault. The school's value system labels their fathers as lazy deserters, their mothers as immoral whores, and their older brothers and sisters as criminals. Those who profess to educate them accept no responsibility for their condition other than to ask them to reject it.

These young people who refuse to learn to read provide us with the most basic understanding of the conflict between our present modes of schooling and the command of the First Amendment. When alien values are imposed upon an individual, that individual gives up his identity. He is required to abandon that which is most crucial to his sense of selfhood: his own unique view of the world around him. The purpose of the First Amendment is to protect the individual in society from governmentally imposed uniformity. When each person is free to bring his or her own view of the world to the self-governing process, the vitality of that process is protected.

The application of a First Amendment protection of the development of belief to the world inside schools indicates that it is not only in the absence of parental choice that families, especially minority families, suffer manipulation of their children's consciousness. Practices, such as standardized testing, and policies which fail to recognize and respect cultural differences in the name of discipline or literacy all contribute to a broad denial of First Amendment freedoms for children and families. In considering any proposed set of mechanisms for restoring equality of First Amendment liberty to American education, it is essential to recognize all the means by which denial of First Amendment rights have been and could continue to be accomplished. The provision of parental choice alone would still leave standardized testing and other practices as forceful denials of First Amendment liberties.

## FUTURE DIRECTIONS: RECONCILING LIBERTY AND RACIAL EQUALITY

This essay has focused upon an understanding of the First Amendment as a protector of individual consciousness and upon the application of this understanding to schooling in America. We have sought to demonstrate ways in which the structure, ideology, and operation of our school system constitutes a massive infringement of the First Amendment; but we have neither analyzed nor advocated any particular solution to this problem. We have avoided possible solutions in part because of our fear that the attempt to identify and discuss the basic First Amendment problems of schooling might have been lost in an attack upon any proposed solution.

Throughout our discussion of value transmission and cultural conflict in schooling, our underlying concern has been with the power of individuals and families over the formation of belief and with the unfettered access of these same persons to the political debate protected by the First Amendment. Whenever the problems of power and political access are raised in the context of schooling, the question of racism must also be addressed. History, law, and politics impose this dilemma upon us. Because there are in fact several conceivable solutions to First Amendment problems in schooling and because these solutions would have effects on racism as well as the distribution of liberty, we have chosen to examine directly the implications of our First Amendment concerns for racial equality.

There are two broad groups of remedies which might be suggested to ameliorate the infringement of First Amendment rights by schools as described in this article: (1) those remedies which provide families with increased choice among schools and which therefore imply a conflict between family choice and racial equality, and (2) those remedies which reduce the imposition of values within schools and therefore imply that liberty and racial equality are not in conflict. Our discussion of these two groups of remedies will not be exhaustive since we wish to preserve our emphasis upon the seriousness of First Amendment problems in a school system. Our purpose is to suggest the direction of thinking which needs to be done to reconcile educational liberty and racial equality once the crucial importance of these two principles has been recognized.

### Where Educational Choice and Racial Equality Conflict

A number of plans have been suggested or are conceivable which would arguably have the effect of substantially increasing the ability of all families to choose the schools their children attend without suffering additional school tax or tuition burdens. Under these plans the choice exercised by families would remove or substantially lessen the coercive socialization of children with values not in harmony with those of the family. The question is whether such plans can be compatible with racial equality in schooling.[40]

Although we have suggested that the First and Fourteenth Amendments are twin guardians of the political process, history indicates that these two broad principles of constitutional order may be at odds where racial equality is concerned. When choice among schools is the issue, the First and Fourteenth Amendments may appear to be in direct and unreconcilable conflict. Such a conflict was suggested during the early resistance to school desegregation when the claim was made that a white family's rights of free association were of equal importance to a black family's right to equal education opportunity and an end to segregated schooling. The history of the attempt to create racially equitable schooling supplies more evidence than necessary to prove that schemes for free choice in schooling can easily become methods for preserving forced separation of the races, the denial of equal educational resources, and the stigmatization of minorities. White privilege has often come at black expense in the sorry history of the races in America.

*Overview of Racism and Family Choice Since 1954.* After the Supreme Court declared school segregation unconstitutional in 1954, the resistance of some school districts to eliminating racism took the form of tuition vouchers or grant-in-aid plans which had the effect of preserving white-only schools. In a Louisiana statute passed in 1962, the purpose of providing tuition reimbursement was described as aid to

needy children enrolled in private schools in the state whose parents choose not to enroll children in public facilities because they are mindful . . . that the parent, not the State of Louisiana, shall be the determining force which shall decide the type of education ultimately received by the child.[41]

The plan had provided tuition expenses to all children attending state-approved private schools. When the Court in *Poindexter* v. *Louisiana* invalidated the scheme for its effect as well as its design, it said: "The inevitable effect of the tuition grants was the establishment and maintenance of a state supported system of segregated schools for white children, making the state a party to organized private discrimination."[42]

In an even more blatant attempt to circumvent an order of the federal courts, Prince Edward County, Virginia, eliminated its public schools altogether and provided "scholarships" for those children attending the white academies in the county. The plan was ruled illegal after several years but not before it had contributed to the notion that parental choice is synonymous with racial discrimination.

Even without using tuition or scholarship aid, states and school districts have attempted to preserve discriminatory patterns in schooling by appealing to the notion of free choice and the natural desire of parents to have significant influence over the education of their children. In 1968, the Supreme Court's ruling in *Green* v. *County Board* made it clear that while "freedom of choice" plans might not be unconstitutional in and of themselves, they are unacceptable so long as there are other methods which promise "speedier and more effective conversion to a unitary nonracial school system."[43]

When school systems include racially identifiable schools, the existence of such schools may be cited as evidence of invidious discrimination in school policy. But parental choice may also lead to racially identifiable schools, and the battle of choice and racial equality is thereby joined.[44]

The history of the relationship of racism and parental choice does not encourage the view that First and Fourteenth Amendment principles are compatible where school choice is the issue. But suppose the public and especially poor and working-class minorities were to realize the importance of eliminating economic discrimination in the exercise of First Amendment schooling rights and to demand the creation of a system in which every parent had an equal ability to choose his child's school. Would the result simply be a return of racism in schools? Can choices which are racist be prohibited while at the same time preserving the general operation of the First Amendment principle of parental liberty in school choice? In another society and at another time it might not be necessary to single out some family choices for prohibition; but the fact of American history simply is that whites have so persistently and systematically victimized blacks that we must resist the accumulated and institutionalized racism of the past with specific safeguards and remedial actions in the present. The question must be whether existing legal and political protections against racism in an independent school system would be strong and reliable enough to insure that family choice and racial equality are not incompatible.

*Existing Protections Against Racism.* There are three basic protections against racial discrimination in admissions and the distribution of school benefits. The Fourteenth Amendment, as has been discussed, prohibits such discriminatory practices wherever it can be shown that the government (or the public) is intentionally involved in perpetuating or condoning such practices. Relying upon private persons to ferret out and file suit about discriminatory admissions or distribution of benefits, however, may not be the most practical way of eliminating such practices, especially considering the cost, in time and money, of litigation. But it does seem clear that to the extent that school tax funds are used at nongovernment schools pursuant to family choice, sufficient state action would be found to prohibit racial discrimination.

A second source of protection against discrimination lies in federal legislation, especially Title VI of the Civil Rights Act of 1964 which provides that no organization shall discriminate on the basis of race (among other grounds) in the distribution of federal benefits. Insofar as nonpublic schools chosen by families received federal funds, Title VI would apply. Federal aid to nonpublic schools is not substantial, however, and the same problems of private enforcement make Title VI weaker than it might appear.

Finally, there is the denial of nonprofit tax status to discriminatory schools by the Internal Revenue Service. A recent attempt by the Internal Revenue Service to promulgate rules which would make the enforcement of nondiscrimination requirements through denial of tax-exempt status more effective has been at least stalled by vigorous resistance by much of the private school sector.[45]

The Supreme Court has consistently rejected the argument that the First Amendment requires government to assume a neutral stance vis-à-vis privately initiated racial discrimination. In *Norwood* v. *Harrison* the Court held unconstitutional a Mississippi program in which textbooks were purchased by the state and loaned to students in both public and private schools, including private schools with racially discriminatory policies. Chief Justice Warren Burger speaking for a unanimous court noted that

> although the Constitution does not proscribe private bias, it places no value on discrimination as it does on the values inherent in the Free Exercise Clause. Invidious private discrimination may be characterized as a form of exercising freedom of association protected by the first amendment, but it has never been accorded affirmative constitutional protections.[46]

*Teaching Racism.*   The most difficult aspect of the conflict between First and Fourteenth Amendment principles arises from the teaching of racist doctrine or values in schools operating under a parental choice system. It might be expected that under a family choice plan children would attend any particular school voluntarily and that families would have an increased and more intimate influence over the values taught at their child's school. But even if families had the energy and time to exercise this influence, other schools may choose to foster racism. Some parents will wish to exercise their right of government-subsidized family choice in education to send their children to schools teaching racism at public expense. These schools may get away with such policies more easily because the victims of their ideology do not attend the school and no one has to face the human reality of their twisted thinking. In such a circumstance, a minority group has lost any semblance of control or even influence over an ideology which directly victimizes them. The stigma which is generated through the teaching of racism is attached to its victims even if they do not attend that particular school. More fuel is added to a fire which burns only a minority of the population.

If a school taught some other set of attitudes or values than racist ones—for example, if it taught collective rather than competitive living, or exploratory rather than authoritarian learning—an enlightened public would not be moved to intervene. Certainly, the concept of individual rights of freedom of expression and belief articulated in the first section of this essay argue against any such intervention by the majority. Each person and group has a right to hold, share, communicate, and teach whatever values it pleases. Yet the history and present reality of racism are so vicious and dehumanizing that one sees the ideas and practices as inseparable and wants them eliminated.

The First Amendment tells us that no matter how odious a majority may find the existence or expression of an idea to be, no matter how apparently corrupt or twisted that idea may be, its expression cannot be suppressed. Such ideas may be argued against, exposed, ridiculed, attacked verbally, or subjected to widespread public disfavor, but the power of the state may not be used to suppress them. Where the Thirteenth and Fourteenth Amendments clash with the First Amendment, this absolute position needs reexamination.

In *Runyan* v. *McCrary*, a case holding that a federal civil rights law prohibits private, commercially operated, nonsectarian schools from denying admission to blacks, the Court indicated that its earlier holding in *Norwood* had not raised the question of whether the First Amendment protected the teaching of racially discriminatory subject matter or values in private schools. But the reasoning in *Norwood*, *Poindexter*, and other cases extending the equal educational opportunity principle of *Brown* v. *Board of Education* to private schools receiving government support would seem to require the same result where admissions are made on a nondiscriminatory basis but the curriculum remains racist. The advocacy of white supremacy in a school subject to the mandate of *Brown* or statutes designed to achieve its goals is an example of speech which is inseparable from forbidden conduct. Such advocacy is not simply expression but teaching and urging, which are acts of racism in themselves and which pose the clear and present danger of creating the stigmatization forbidden by the Thirteenth and Fourteenth Amendments. A discriminatory admissions policy violates *Brown* because segregation stigmatizes the black child and thereby denies him/her an equal educational opportunity. Clearly a school which imposes the stigma even more directly, by teaching its students that blacks are inferior, is also in violation of the command of the equal protection clause. It is also apparent that the obvious and foreseeable result of a school's teaching of racially discriminatory subject matter and values will be the deterrence of attendance by black children. Such transparently coercive "free choice" has been firmly rejected by the Court.

An alternative approach might be used in considering the constitutionality of government regulation of teaching racism in schools. If the government's purpose for the regulation is seen not as the suppression of racist speech but as realizing the constitutionally compelled goal of avoiding state-sponsored stigmatization of blacks or segregation, then the regulation may be characterized as one which places an incidental burden on speech. The ban on racist expression in schools would be a side effect of achieving the Thirteenth and Fourteenth Amendment goals of removing the stigma of slavery and achieving full citizenship for blacks. Such a ban would not constitute an effort to suppress racist ideas per se but would only involve their restriction in those places (such as schools) where the government deemed it necessary to achieve non-speech-related goals. The courts have analyzed this form of speech abridgement by balancing the First Amendment claims against the government interest involved.

Here the government interests are extremely weighty. The same Constitution, which it has been argued here ensures an economically equitable right of family choice in schooling, also forbids stigmatization and the denial of rights and benefits on the basis of race. The Thirteenth, Fourteenth, and Fifteenth Amendments express the constitutional commitment that whatever choices individuals, families, or groups may be entitled to make, they are not entitled to inflict racist conditions upon others. Certainly the preservation of racism is not among the rights secured by the First Amendment.

Furthermore, racist speech would not be wholly suppressed. Private citizens would still be free to express racist ideas outside of the schools. Finally, while the Court has generally condemned discrimination among ideas as forbidden censorship, it has also valued some speech more highly than other speech and therefore protected it more scrupulously. Thus, while libel and pornography are not excluded from the First Amendment's protection, their regulation appears to be more easily justifiable than speech which is viewed as more highly valued. The commitment to racial equality articulated in the Thirteenth and Fourteenth Amendments necessarily implies that racist speech is of little value to the political system that the First Amendment seeks to protect and that like pornography and libel it should be given less weight when placed in the balance against competing societal interests.

When all these factors are considered, there seems little doubt that the balance should swing in the direction of the government's protection of equality. If a commitment to making racist teaching unlawful were added to the existing protections against racial discrimination in all forms of schooling, it might be possible to conclude that on the legal level parental choice and racial equality can be compatible. The problem then will be whether it is politically realistic to believe that these antidiscrimination protections will in fact be enforced.

### Where Education Liberty and Racial Equality Are Not in Conflict

The second broad category of school reforms which might vindicate First Amendment rights calls for reducing the imposition of values within schools rather than increasing choice among schools. Here the target is any mechanism which aids the powerful in imposing beliefs, attitudes, or ideologies upon the powerless.

These reforms assume that most children will continue to go to public schools. They are based on the premise that even incomplete remedies which move in the direction of increasing respect for First Amendment freedom of consciousness are important. These partial remedies may not provide the comprehensive protection for minority values which equal choice of schooling promises. But they have the benefit of advancing racial equality along with parental liberty. This is so because, as the discussion of confession of belief, discipline, and functional illiteracy has indicated, the failure to respect the culture and values of the minority student will lead to consequences which are condemned by both the First Amendment and the Fourteenth Amendment. Racism and the repression of parental liberty are two sides of the same coin to many families; and minority families are a disproportionate share of the victims of the imposition of consciousness in government schools.

Three possible remedies which are aimed at the mechanisms of imposing belief within schools are the abolition of standardized testing, the creation of decentralized community control of schools, and the retraining of teachers concerning the imposition of values.

*Abolition of Standardized Testing.* The discussion in the second section above made clear the need to abolish standardized testing as a means for determining who will have access to knowledge and power. Just as there is no such thing as value-neutral education, there is no such thing as a value-neutral test. Forward-looking educational psychologists have already begun to devise nonstandardized methods of evaluation, diagnosis and prognosis which will provide educators with the information they need to determine how to best teach their students. Job-related measures of performance should replace tests like the National Teachers Examination. When classification devices are laden with values which are unrelated to one's ability to acquire knowledge or perform the job in question, they impinge upon rights protected by the First Amendment and should be abandoned.

*Community Control of Schools.*    The community control movement was at its peak in the late sixties. At its root was the realization among black parents that the schools were not likely to be responsive to their wishes nor serve the needs of their children unless they controlled the purse strings and the decision-making process with respect to hiring, firing, and educational policy.

The struggle by minority communities for control of the schools was important not simply because it represented a first step toward a more generalized shift in the power relationships of the ghetto but because control of one's children's education meant control of the vehicle for transmitting the ideas and values which would allow them to view the world from their own perspective.

If people who are otherwise excluded from the political process are allowed to determine what and how their children will be taught, they will regain control of a necessary ingredient in achieving effective participation in the political process. In other words, they will take an important step toward recapturing their First Amendment rights.

Supporters of proposals to remove the schools from the public sector have argued that support of their proposals will result in greater parental influence over the schools their children attend. In theory this is true. But in any school system those who control the school will teach and promote values and ideals which best serve their own interest. So long as schools are controlled only by groups who can command substantial financial resources and flex political muscle, they will reflect the interests of those groups. Meaningful choice among schools will be maximized only when the diversification of control or power to run the schools is maximized. Parental choice must also involve parental control.

But community control of schools for those who have been excluded from the political process involves a conscious and vigorous effort to destroy barriers to the involvement of heretofore powerless people. Those who profess to advance such a goal must be willing to insure that these barriers are done away with and that the advances made in the transfer of control are protected in reality as well as in theory.

*Reeducating the Educators.* Most educators, while professing neutrality, impose their values upon their students in an almost self-righteous fashion. This is because most fail to recognize that they are transmitting beliefs and self-interested values rather than objective truths. The teacher who has been taught a Eurocentric version of history has no reason to believe that his imposition of that history upon a black child is belief coercion. This means that a necessary first step toward the preservation of First Amendment freedoms must involve the reeducation of educators to help them recognize their own values and sensitize them to the values of others. A teacher who is well aware of his own values and teaches them as possible alternatives is preferable to a teacher who sees his values as value-neutral objective truth. This reeducation of educators must also involve teaching them that diversity of values is valuable for the whole, that it is necessary for the health of the political process, and that it is the First Amendment's purpose to protect it.

Of course, this would itself lead to teaching school children values some parents reject. Many parents believe that their values are objectively true (for example, ordained by God or history); they would object to their children being taught that values are relative and a matter of personal choice. Some parents even object to the democratic values of tolerance, free expression, and diversity; they would object to their children being taught these. The First Amendment protects freedom of thought even for those who reject freedom of thought. If parents have a First Amendment right to determine what values their children will learn, then even intolerant parents have that right and teaching their children tolerance denies it. Nor do efforts to give equal time to differing views dispose of the subtler biases of the hidden curriculum. The best that can be said for more tolerant teacher attitudes is that in the public schools such attitudes would infringe fewer people's rights and infringe them less severely than would intolerant propagation of any narrower official doctrine.

## Legal Solutions, Political Realities

It is important to think politically as well as constitutionally about the significance of remedies for government-controlled school socialization. Although reforms in the areas of testing, parental participation, and teacher attitudes within the public schools do not bring conflicting constitutional values into play, they are likely to encounter strong political resistance. The testing industry has strong economic interests at stake, which it will not easily relinquish. Nor will those who are advantaged by present test bias be eager to give up that privilege. As noted earlier, the Supreme Court has turned a deaf ear to constitutional attacks on standardized tests based on the equal protection clause. It is unlikely that the Court will be more sympathetic to challenges based on a less well-established First Amendment theory.

The massive resistance of professional educators to the participation of poor and minority parents in school governance was documented during the struggle for community control in New York City schools. There is little reason to believe there has been substantial change in the self-interested politics of predominantly white teachers' unions located in predominantly nonwhite school districts. It is equally unlikely that a series of sensitivity training sessions will significantly change the attitudes of these teachers toward their students.

Given the experience of minority communities in their struggles to eradicate racism within the existing public system, it should not be surprising that one encounters skepticism about the ability of existing constitutional and statutory provisions to resist the racism which may well accompany innovations designed to maximize school choice.

Freedom of choice plans first manifested themselves as schemes for avoiding court-ordered desegregation in the South. There is the continuing suspicion among minorities that what is most valuable to white parents is the status and privilege which accompanies their whiteness and that they will make their choices accordingly. What minority parents see is that inner-city schools have become increasingly segregated because white parents can afford to take their children to the suburbs or send them to private schools. It is hardly surprising that they are opposed to making white flight more affordable. Supporters of proposals aimed at maximizing school choice have argued: (1) that segregated schools are illegal and will remain so, (2) that privately run schools cannot be much more segregated than the present publicly run ones, (3) that black parents will now have the resources to follow the white parents in their flight from the public schools, and (4) that safeguards and incentives will be built into the new legislation to insure that segregation in our schools will not increase.

But the Supreme Court's reaffirmation of the applicability of *Brown* v. *Board of Education* to private schools not withstanding,[47] that same Court has been increasingly reluctant to apply provisions of the Fourteenth Amendment to even the most heavily regulated private institutions. It is similarly easier to get legislatures and public administrators to take responsibility for the actions of public entities than for private ones. The only appropriate response to the argument that "things can't get much worse" is that they can. Furthermore, once segregation is cloaked in the honorific rhetoric of First Amendment freedom, the damage that is done will be even harder to rectify.

The experience of minorities and the poor with the private sector has taught them to be extremely skeptical of those economic theories which tell them that given an equal number of dollars they will have equal purchasing power and thereby have access to the same or equivalent educational opportunities. The same dollars buy them poorer food and housing. Why should it be any different with education? Minorities have had even less success in influencing the values and actions of landlords, merchants, and money lenders in their neighborhoods than they have had with the public schools.[48]

Finally, while the authors of various free choice proposals promise that special attention will be given to measures to guard against further segregation of our schools, minorities have little confidence that such measures will survive a political climate dominated by proposals to balance the budget, suits claiming "reverse discrimination," and legislation designed to prohibit busing to achieve racial balance.

The suggestion that we remove the schools from government control has come at just the point when blacks and other minorities are gaining control of government at the local level where most school decisions are made. They are being asked to abandon majoritarian decision making when they have finally become, in many localities, a significant and effective political majority. There is little evidence that the forces which have kept minorities from acting in their own self-interest where they have been and are a majority will disappear once schools are isolated from the democratic process. There is in fact some evidence that once isolated from that process those forces will become even more firmly entrenched.

In the final analysis it would appear that where racial minorities and the poor are concerned, the question is not so much how to protect the minority from the imposition of majority values as how to protect those who are relatively powerless from having the values of the powerful imposed upon them. If a financing system which provides maximum choice can do no more than provide minorities a choice among schools controlled by those persons who presently control the private sector, the choice offers little more than the opportunity to leap from the frying pan into the fire. And if majority opposition to ending standardized testing, establishing community control, and reeducating teachers continues, those who leap back into a system of government schools will not thereby escape either racism or the manipulation of consciousness.

One is tempted to conclude, therefore, that while the legal protections against racism in schools could be sufficient to insure that increased parental liberty would not mean increased racial discrimination, legal protection and political reality are not necessarily the same. The First Amendment is massively abused by the present structure and ideology of schooling. Changes enhancing family choice and taming the forces of conformity in schools are needed. It is politics which will determine whether these changes are achieved for the equal benefit of all families or simply as instruments for perpetuating the status quo in a new form.

## CONCLUSION

Throughout this essay we have focused on a variety of ways in which the ideology and structure of schooling infringe upon First Amendment rights and undercut the political process. We have sought to transform a complacent American assumption into a serious question of public policy. Through the First Amendment analysis we have tried to add another dimension to the traditional understanding of how poor, working-class, and minority families are victimized by their lack of power over schooling decisions. Although "practical" people may find it disconcerting, we have pointed to a problem without offering a solution.

At bottom we conceive this problem as a power issue—how is the power to use the schools' inevitable value-inculcation process distributed among those for whom access to the political process is at stake? Whether the power of involuntary school socialization is held by the political majority, a governmental entity, an interest group, or a private organization intimately involved with the education business, the damage to the individual's formation and expression of belief is the same, and the threat to the health of the First Amendment and the political system is as great. We have offered a broad interpretation of the modern meaning of the First Amendment and value inculcation in schooling which requires a broad understanding of how inequitable allocation of power distorts the system of freedom of expression.

We suspect that those who focus solely upon the separation of school and state that might be accomplished through a voucher system or tax credits will find that they have failed to address powerful forces which will continue to effectively deprive parents of control over value inculcation in schools. The presence of standardized testing in admission or promotion decisions or the misunderstanding of discipline problems may render family choice among schools a mere illusion.

We suspect also that those who, in the name of opening up the system of freedom of expression and the political process, advocate changes in schools such as the elimination of standardized testing or the reform of conformist teaching will eventually discover that their goals are thwarted by an absence of equal family choice among schools. In matters as personal as the formation of conscience there will always be dissenters; and if the First Amendment has any meaning, it is that dissenters may not be subjected to majority coercion no matter how enlightened the values of the majority may become.

If this essay contributes to an understanding of the ways that schools damage the political process and increases skepticism about school reforms which do not take account of value inculcation, it may be regarded as useful. If this essay contributes to an increased public discussion of the First Amendment and schooling, it will have satisfied its authors' best intentions.

## NOTES TO CHAPTER 6

1.  Alexander Meiklejohn, *Political Freedom* (New York: Oxford, 1965); Alexander Meiklejohn, *Free Speech and Its Relation to Self-Government* (New York: Harper & Row, 1948); Alexander Meiklejohn, "What Does the First Amendment Mean?" *University of Chicago Law Review* 20 (1963): 461; Alexander Meiklejohn, "The First Amendment Is An Absolute," *Supreme Court Review* (1961): 245. See also William Brennan, "The Supreme Court and the Meiklejohn Interpretation of the First Amendment," *Harvard Law Review* 79 (1965): 1; cf. "Comment: By Any Other Name: Meiklejohn, The First Amendment and School Desegregation," *Connecticut Law Review* 3 (1971): 299.

2.  See Brennan, "The Supreme Court." A major exploration of First Amendment theory is found in Thomas Emerson, *Toward a General Theory of the First Amendment* (New York: Random House, 1966). Also see Thomas Emerson, David Haber, and Norman Dorsen, *Political and Civil Rights in the United States*, 4th ed. (Boston: Little, Brown, 1976).

3.  Meiklejohn has best described the existence of a core meaning in the minds of the framers of the amendment: "Apparently all they could make their words do was to link together five separate demands which had been sharpened by ages of conflict and were being popularly urged in the name of the 'Freedom of the People.' And yet, those demands were, and were felt to be, varied forms of a single demand" (Meiklejohn, "What Does the First Amendment Mean?" pp. 461, 463).

4.  *Gillette* v. *United States*, 401 U.S. 437, 469 (1971) (Justice William O. Douglas dissenting).

5.  *Abbington School Dist.* v. *Schempp*, 374 U.S. 203 (1963).

6.  *Rogers* v. *Okin*, U.S.L.W., CA. 75-1601-T, District Court of Massachusetts. In ruling that a mental patient is entitled to refuse treatment in nonemergency situations, Judge Joseph Tauro relied not only upon the patient's right to privacy but upon his First Amendment rights:

    The First Amendment protects the communication of ideas. That protected right of communication presupposes a capacity to produce ideas. As a practical matter, therefore, the power to produce ideas is fundamental to our cherished right to communicate and is entitled to comparable constitutional protection (slip opinion p. 68).

7.  *Pierce* v. *Society of Sisters*, 268 U.S. 510 (1925).

8.  Meiklejohn, "The First Amendment," pp. 257-58.

9.  Ibid.

10. *Tinker* v. *Des Moines Independent Community School Dist.*, 393 U.S. 503 (1969); *Pickering* v. *Board of Education*, 391 U.S. 563 (1968); and *Healy* v. *James*, 408 U.S. 169 (1972).

11.  This problem was perceived one hundred years ago by J. S. Mill when he wrote:

> state-sponsored education . . . is a mere contrivance for molding people to be exactly like one another; and the mold in which it casts them is that which pleases the predominant power in the government, whether this be a monarch, a priesthood, an aristocracy, or the majority of the existing generation, in proportion as it is efficient and successful, it establishes a despotism over the mind . . . (*On Liberty* [Parker & Son, 1959], pp. 190–191).

12.  Social science research examining value inculcation in schools includes the following: on sex-role stereotypes, see Terry N. Saario, Carol Kehr Tittle, and Carol Nagy Jacklin, "Sex-Role Stereotyping in the Public Schools," *Harvard Educational Review* 43 (1973): 286–416. On political ideology and cognitive structure, see Sara Lawrence Lightfoot, "Politics and Reasoning: Through the Eyes of Teachers and Children," *Harvard Educational Review* 43 (1973): 197–244; and Patricia Minuchin, Barbara Biber, Edna Shapiro, and Herbert Zimiles, *The Psychological Impact of School Experience* (New York: Basic Books, 1969). On individualism, achievement, and the categorization of persons, see Robert Dreeben, "The Contribution of Schooling to the Learning of Norms," *Harvard Educational Review* 37 (1967): 211–37; Paul E. Breer and Edwin A. Locke, *Task Experience as a Source of Attitudes* (Homewood, Ill.: Dorsey, 1965); and David C. McClelland, *The Achieving Society* (Princeton: Van Nostrand, 1961), esp. pp. 453–74.

13.  Value inculcation is an extremely complex phenomenon which cannot be judged or detected simply by looking for children whose values match those of the school. Some children will react by swallowing whole the values which are put forth didactically or in the hidden curriculum. Others will "fake it," confessing beliefs and acting as if they complied with the prevailing orthodoxy but internally suffering anything from personal alienation to confusion and loss of identity. Still others may rebel against the proffered values, but even their consciousness has been manipulated since, as every lawyer knows, the power to determine which questions someone else must answer is much more significant than the power to answer those questions. In any case, children are being asked to choose among reactions which interfere with their self-development and may clash with their family values. The variety of such reactions is explored in the setting of "total institutions" in Erving Goffman's *Asylums* (Chicago: Aldine, 1962). As with religious ceremonies in public schools, the threat to the Constitution is not judged according to the number of true believers turned out by the ceremony but by the institutionalized favoring of some forms of consciousness over others.

Perhaps the most direct way of explaining the offensiveness and operation of value inculcation in schooling is by analogy to the flag salute prohibited by *West Virginia v. Barnette*, 319 U.S. 624 (1943), as "confession of belief." Taken together, the structure, curriculum, texts, teacher expectations, and operational rules of schools form a structure of order to which the young student must adhere in order to gain the available rewards (e.g., grades, recommendations, approval) and avoid punishment (e.g., poor grades, suspensions, lower "tracks"). This structure of order, the subject of school board policy making (see, e.g., *Tinker* v. *Des Moines*), is based upon and expresses the beliefs, values, and attitudes of those who formulate or seek to control it. The inevitable requirement that students adhere to this institutional structure of order exacts from students, through their everyday behavior, confessions of belief which may be abhorrent to them or their families. The *Barnette* court did not base its ruling upon the efficient production of student jingoism; and the recognition of value inculcation as a problem in schooling cannot be based upon how much school graduates resemble the superintendent in whose institution they have been schooled.

14.   It may be argued of course that the principle behind "equal time" — that children should be exposed to differing and conflicting values and beliefs — is primary to the present arrangement of schools. As policy this may be desirable, but it was not sufficient to justify the requirement that all children attend public school only; *Pierce* v. *Society of Sisters*. Moreover, there is something perverse in the idea that young children are benefited as much as adults by being caught in an emotional and intellectual crossfire. Undoubtedly there is a point in the development of young people at which they not only can benefit from conflict between authorities and among values and beliefs, but are entitled to be exposed to such conflict regardless of what would-be censors might think. Most people have seen examples, however, of children confused, frustrated, and psychologically damaged by conflicts between the authority figures in their lives. In some communities children may be susceptible to this problem even into their teens; see testimony of Donald Erickson in *Wisconsin* v. *Yoder*, 406 U.S. 205 (1972), where the issue was the preservation of the Amish community against the worldly influence of high schools.

Finally, the advocates of adversarial forms of nurture for young children ought to check out their local schools. Anyone who sees them as a marketplace of ideas and a pluralistic culture in which all values are respected has probably not been inside a school in this century; see Jonathan Kozol, *The Night Is Cold and I am Far from Home* (Boston: Houghton Mifflin, 1975).

It is clear that it is in the nature of childhood that some institutions and/ or persons will have the primary influence over the formation of values in the young. If the choice for such primary influence is between the family and the state, common sense and case law favor the family. Some case law suggests in general that the family is a favored institution even though the definition of family is not agreed upon. See *Wisconsin* v. *Yoder* and

*Moore* v. *City of East Cleveland*, 97 S. Ct. 1932 (1977). For purposes of this essay, family choice and individual rights are used interchangeably. This reflects the need to understand the coercion applied in schools and leaves for another essay the generation of principles capable of resolving contests between the child and the family over value choice and schooling decisions.

15. *Pierce* v. *Society of Sisters*, at 535.

16. 262 U.S. 390 (1923), at 402.

17. *West Virginia* v. *Barnette*, at 633; id., at 642. See also *Wooley* v. *Maynard*, 430 U.S. 705 (1977). In *Wooley*, the Supreme Court upheld a district court order enjoining the state from arresting or prosecuting two Jehovah's Witnesses for covering the "Live Free or Die" motto on the New Hampshire license plate. Although the Maynards claim that their moral, religious, and political objections to the motto were based on the free exercise clause, the language of the opinions seems equally applicable to a free speech claim:

> The First Amendment protects the right of individuals to hold a point of view different from the majority and to *refuse to foster* . . . any idea they find morally objectionable (emphasis added; *Wooley*, at 715).
> However, where the State's interest is to disseminate an ideology, no matter how acceptable to some, such interest cannot outweigh an individual's First Amendment right to avoid *becoming the courier* for such messages (emphasis added; *Wooley*, at 717).

18. *Abbington School Dist.* v. *Schempp*.

19. Paul Freund, "Comment: Public Aid to Parochial Schools," *Harvard Law Review* 82 (1969): 1680.

20. See *U.S.* v. *Seeger*, 380 U.S. 163 (1965); and Lawrence Tribe, *American Constitutional Law* (Mineola, N.Y.: Foundation Press, 1978), section 14–11.

21. *Wisconsin* v. *Yoder*, at 211.

22. 347 U.S. 483 (1954).

23. A historical review of the ideology supporting compulsory schooling may be found in Robert Everhart, "Compulsory School Attendance Laws," *Review of Educational Research* 47 (1977): 499. See also Michael Katz, *Irony of Early School Reform* (Cambridge, Mass.: Harvard University Press, 1968), David Tyack, *The One Best System* (Cambridge, Mass.: Harvard University Press, 1974), and David Nasaw, *Schooled to Order* (New York: Oxford, 1980).

24. 319 U.S. 624 (1943).

25. Describing the right of choice as a family right creates obvious problems of the rights of children to be free of the imposition of both family and state. Justice William O. Douglas discussed this in his dissent in part in *Wisconsin* v. *Yoder*, at 244–245, and the policy issue of children's autonomy and state regulation of family school decisions has been the subject

of considerable thought. See, e.g., Joel Spring, *A Primer of Libertarian Education* (New York: Free Life, 1975) and John Coons and Stephen Sugarman, *Education by Choice* (Berkeley: University of California Press, 1978). Our position is that the primary issue is between family and government and that a First Amendment resolution of this issue would create a proper context for examining the educational, legal, and developmental rights of children within families or against the state.

26. The elimination of compulsory schooling has been suggested (William Rickenbacker, ed., *The Twelve-Year Sentence* (La Salle, Ill.: Open Court, 1974) on a number of grounds, but even this would leave the government in the position of conditioning the provision of a government benefit (tax-supported schooling) upon the sacrifice of First Amendment rights. See *Sherbert* v. *Verner*, 374 U.S. 398 (1963).

27. *West Virginia* v. *Barnette*, at 641:

> As governmental pressure toward unity becomes greater, so strife becomes more bitter as to whose unity it shall be. Probably no deeper division of our people could proceed from any provocation than from finding it necessary to choose what doctrine and whose program public educational officials shall compel youth to unite in embracing. The ultimate futility of such attempts to compel coherence is the lesson of every such effort. . . . Compulsory unification of opinion achieves only the unanimity of the graveyard.

28. The problem of choice is to be distinguished from the problem of per capita school expenses which depend upon accidents of district tax base, as litigated in *San Antonio Independent School District* v. *Rodriguez*, 411 U.S. 1 (1973), and more successful state cases such as *Serrano* v. *Priest*, 5 Cal. 3d 583, 487, P. 2d 1241 (1971); and *Robinson* v. *Cahill*, 303 A. 2d 273 (N.J. S. Ct. 1973). The assertedly fundamental right to education rejected by the Court in *Rodriguez* is not the same as the accepted fundamental rights of the First Amendment which we argue includes school choice. See *Sherbert* v. *Verner*.

29. *Harper* v. *Virginia Board of Elections*, 383 U.S. 663 (1966).

30. The doctrine of "unconstitutional conditions" holds that the government may not condition the receipt of its benefits upon the nonasserting of constitutional rights: *Pickering* v. *Board of Education*; *Keyishian* v. *Board of Regents*, 385 U.S. 569 (1969); and *Sherbert* v. *Verner*. This rule that the state may not accomplish indirectly what it is forbidden to do directly is if anything even more inviolate when, as here, the benefit involved is arguably another constitutional right—the Fourteenth Amendment right to equal educational opportunity. See *Brown* v. *Board of Education* and *Goss* v. *Lopez*, 419 U.S. 565 (1975).

31. *West Virginia* v. *Barnette*, at 630; id., at 642.

32. The experiences of these students are not atypical. See *Hawkins* v. *Coleman*, 376 F. Supp. 1330 (N.D. Tex. 1974); *Rhye* v. *Childs*, 359 F. Supp. 1085 (N.D. Fla. 1973); Children's Defense Fund (The Washington Re-

search Project, Inc.), "Children Out of School in America" (Washington, D. C., 1974), ch. 20; Children's Defense Fund, "School Suspensions: Are They Helping Children?" (Washington, D.C., 1975), ch. 4; Southern Regional Council and the Robert F. Kennedy Memorial, "Student Pushout: Victims of Continued Resistance to Desegregation" (Washington, D. C., 1974), p. 6. These studies rely largely upon data collected by the Office of Civil Rights (OCR) of the U.S. Department of Health, Education, and Welfare in the fall of 1973. As part of its National School Survey of Public Elementary and Secondary Schools, OCR surveyed almost three thousand school districts, accounting for over 50 percent of the total enrollment in American public schools and about 90 percent of all minority students; brief for Children's Defense Fund of the Washington Research Project, Inc., and the American Friends Service Committee as Amici Curiae at 20, *Goss v. Lopez*. School districts were asked to reveal the total number of students suspended and expelled during the academic year, the cumulative number of suspension days out of school, and the racial and ethnic breakdowns of those figures. See generally, Phillip Jackson, *Life in Classrooms* (New York: Holt, Rinehart, and Winston, 1968); Herbert Kohl, *36 Children* (New York: New America Library, 1967); Charles Silberman, *Crisis in the Classroom*, (New York: Random House, 1970), ch. 4; Sara Lightfoot, *Worlds Apart: Relationships Between Schools and Families* (New York: Basic Books, 1978); Ray Rist, *The Invisible Children: School Integration in American Society* (Cambridge, Mass.: Harvard University Press (1978); Tom Cottle, "Dying a Different Sort of Death: The Exclusion of Children From School," *School Review* 83 (1974): 145.

33.   Asa Hilliard, "Standardization and Cultural Bias as Judgments to the Scientific Study and Validation of Intelligence," *Journal of Research and Development* 12 (1979):47.

34.   There is a considerable body of research exploring racial, cultural, and class bias in standardized testing. These studies present evidence that demonstrates that standardized tests are uniformly poor predictors of performance for the population as a whole and thus arguably an irrational means of classification. See David White, "Culturally Biased Test Scores," *Harvard Civil Rights/Civil Liberties Law Review* 14 (1979) 100 n. 40–42. There is also substantial evidence that the vast majority of standardized tests employed by our school systems are specifically biased against racial minorities and the poor. See *Larry P. v. Riles* opinion, dated October 16, 1979 (N.D. Cal.); not yet reported. But the bias measured by these studies presents only the tip of the iceberg, as they do not even touch upon the issue of the cultural bias of the test content discussed by Hilliard. In considering racial or class bias in standardized tests, educational psychologists have limited their inquiry to determining the presence of statistical bias or predictive validity. E.g., the researcher will ask whether the Law School

Aptitude Test (LSAT) underpredicts the performance of blacks in their first year of law school while it is relatively more accurate in predicting the grades of white students; see Asa Hilliard, "Standardization and Cultural Bias as Impediments to the Scientific Study and Validation of 'Intelligence,'" *Journal of Research and Development in Education* 12 (1979): 219–50. What this question does not take into account is the fact that the researcher is measuring the bias, or lack thereof, of the test by its ability to predict performance in an equally biased setting. To the extent that the LSAT is a valid predictor of first-year grades in law school, it is because the test is designed to measure the applicant's ability to perform on first-year law exams. The exam's supporters will of course argue that that is exactly what it should be measuring. But our present methods of teaching and evaluation are not given. Moreover, it has never been shown that the traditional law school curriculum and examination process either teaches or measures those qualities which are most essential to good lawyering; for an excellent discussion of the history of the use of standardized tests as barriers to the legal profession, see David White, "The Definition of Legal Competence: Will the Circle Be Unbroken?" *Santa Clara Law Review* 18 (1978):641. It will doubtless be argued that this type of cultural test bias merely requires the examinee to state the facts or give the answer the examiner expects and that belief need not be affected. Although this may well be true in theory, there is a considerable body of literature on operant conditioning which documents the ability of teachers to control children's behavior and ultimately their values by the granting or withholding of rewards and punishment. Furthermore, social scientists have long recognized the destructive nature of environments which require the individual to constantly act out or confess to one value system while maintaining belief in another; see Stanley Elkins, *Slavery* (Chicago: Chicago University Press, 1969); William Burghardt Dubois, *Souls of Black Folk* (New York: New America Library, 1969), pp. 16–17.

35.    Asa Hilliard, "Standardized Testing and African-Americans: Building Assessor Competence in Systematic Assessment," position paper presented to the National Institute for Community Development, National Task Force on Standardized Testing, August 1978, pp. 6–7.

36.    Ibid, p. 20:

> African-Americans have the right as citizens and the human right not to be required to become "expert achievers" in test content which may well be biased against African-Americans. For example, a test of general information and history which failed to treat the activity of Toussaint L'Overture, Marcus Garvey, Edward Wilmont Blyden, Carter G. Woodson, Paul Robeson, Ira Aldredge, and others who have been heroic in the struggle for the liberation of African-Americans, would represent gross misinformation for African-American people. In reading the questions on the *NTE*, the College Boards, the Iowa Test of Educational Development, and other standardized tests of achievements, one would get the impression that

African–Americans were non-existent and that the condition of slavery and other forms of oppression were unimportant for an educated person. Indeed, to be judged as a competent teacher by the *NTE* in South Carolina no less, or elsewhere, some African–Americans would have to commit cultural suicide.

The implications of Hilliard's observations about the ethnocentrism of the *NTE* and other standardized tests go far beyond an argument for the exclusion of a few obviously biased history questions and the inclusion of a few items dealing with "black history." The "standard" curriculum upon which these tests are based are gathered from history books written to justify American racism and imperialism. Social science scholarship has portrayed black family life and culture as pathological (see Sara Lightfoot, *Worlds Apart: Relationships Between Families and School* [New York: Basic Books, 1978]) and curriculum in language and literature which ignores the literary contributions of blacks and characterizes their language as an underdeveloped dialect—and therefore proof of their inferiority.

It is the cumulative effect of required curricula and examinations which are based on a world view and supporting scholarship designed to rationalize a history of oppression and exploitation which required the minority individual to learn to mouth the "perpetrator perspective" in order to receive the educational system's stamp of approval. For additional indications of biased scholarship, see Leland H. Carlson and George A. Colburn, *In Their Place: White America Defines Her Minorities* (New York: Wiley, 1972); Allan Chase, *The Legacy of Malthus: The Social Costs of New Scientific Racism* (New York: Alfred A. Knopf, 1977); Thomas F. Gossett, *Race: The History of an Idea in America* (Dallas: South Methodist, 1968); Robert Guthrie, *Even the Rat Was White* (New York: Harper & Row, 1976); John L. Hodge, Donald K. Struckman, and Louis D. Frost, *Cultural Bases for Racism and Group Oppression: An Examination of Traditional "Western" Concepts, Values, and Institutional Structures Which Support Racism, Sexism, and Elitism* (Berkeley: Two Riders, 1975); Leon Kamin, *The Science and Politics of I.Q.* (New York: Halstead, 1974); Dan Lacy, *The White Use of Blacks in America: 350 Years of Law and Violence, Attitudes and Etiquette, Politics and Change* (New York: Atheneum, 1972); William Stanton, *The Leopard's Spots: Scientific Attitudes Toward Race in America* (Chicago: University of Chicago Press, 1960); Alexander Thomas and Samuel Sillen, *Racism and Psychiatry* (New York: Brunner, 1972); Cedric X. (Clark) "The White Researcher in Black Society," *Journal of Social Issues* (special issue) 1 (1973): 29.

37.    The benefit or right to education is conditioned upon one's performance on standardized tests; see *Hobson* v. *Hansen* 327 F. Supp. 844, *Larry P.* v. *Riles*, and *U.C. Board of Regents* v. *Bakke* 438 U.S. 265. Because standardized tests contain content which is biased in favor of the world view of those who control our political and educational institutions, blacks and

other oppressed minorities must sacrifice their own beliefs and confess to the majoritarian ideology if they wish continued access to the benefit of education:

> In January 1977, the Maryland State Department of Education expressed an official philosophy of education in two . . . policy statements [which] broaden the concept of minimum adult competence far beyond mastery of "basic skills" . . . and include . . . "citizenship," "survival skills"—including "inter-personal skills" and "parenting"—and the "world of work." In the fall of 1977, a draft list of approximately 600 competencies was generated by advisory panels of professional educators and laypersons at the initiative of Maryland's Project Basic staff. Grouped and identified with each of the five human activity areas, the competencies expressed as "behaviors" were then winnowed down to 321 "possible prerequisites for graduation." . . . Numerous items on the draft list probed the highly sensitive areas of feeling and opinion, although none of these items may survive the next stages in the development of the state's competency tests. In late July of 1978, the Maryland Board of Education approved a "Declared Competency Index." . . . Although many of the value-loaded items on the draft list distributed for public validation have or may be discarded, they nonetheless serve as useful illustrations of the kinds of competencies which, if transformed into mandatory test questions, may raise first and fourteenth amendment challenges."

("Change, Competency Testing, and Potential Constitutional Challenges," *Catholic Law Review* 28 [3] [1979]:469–509.

38.  Nat Hentoff, *Does Anybody Give a Damn?* (New York: Alfred A. Knopf, 1977) p. 55. Functional literacy refers to the application of reading, writing, and mathematical skills to "routine tasks of the adult world" such as reading a menu or a job application; see Baratz, "Policy Implications of Minimum Competency Testing," paper presented at the Second Annual American Education Research Topical Conference in Washington, D.C., October 12, 1978.

39.  An anology may be drawn between the situation of contemporary ghetto youth and of slaves in states where it was forbidden to teach slaves to read or write. The master who forbade his slaves to learn to read did so to inhibit their ability to communicate. But he also sought to dehumanize the slave by denying him information about the world around him and limiting his ability to control that world; see Leon Higginbotham, *In the Matter of Color*, vol. 1 (New York: Oxford, 1978); Richard Kluger, *Simple Justice* (New York: Alfred A. Knopf, 1975); Lerone Bennett, Jr., *Before the Mayflower* (New York: Penguin, 1966), p. 129; Frederick Douglass, *Life and Times of Frederick Douglass* (Hartford, Conn.: Park, 1881) p. 76. Today, oppressed illiterates are heavily concentrated in our urban ghettos. Their condition has been described as the "culture of silence"; Paolo Freire, *Pedagogy of the Oppressed* (New York: Herder & Herder, 1970) p. 13. In many of the country's core cities, youth gangs occupy and control whole neighborhoods. They have been described by the media as "animals" and "totally without morals." They describe themselves as

"survivors"; Joel Dreyfus, "Black Progress, Myth, and Ghetto Reality," *Progressive* 41 (1977): 21–5.

These young people have rejected the public schools and with them the American dream of equality of opportunity for all. They believe that there is no future for them, that they have been classified as expendables by an affluent society. Because they understand that the dominant society's value system has stamped them as surplus, they have refused to recognize the rules of that society. They have formed their own societies, clubs, and gangs with their own, often destructive, values and standards of behavior. As functional illiterates they are nonentities in the normal political process. They have been denied the First Amendment right to participate in that process; so they create their own process in order to remain human.

40.  There are of course other serious questions about the desirability of family choice plans even when they are seen as vindicating First Amendment rights to be free of government-sponsored manipulation of consciousness in schools. These questions fall into six broad categories: (1) religious domination—the fear that family choice in schooling is simply a cover for attempts by the Catholic Church and a few other sects to gain control of large parts of the public treasury; (2) civil liberties—the fear that those most likely to take advantage of an equalized right of school choice are those least likely to support civil liberties and most likely to seek to spread intolerance; (3) need for social cohesion—the belief that public schools attended by almost all children and controlled by the majority provides one of America's only forums for creating a cohesive society able to define and meet national goals; (4) balkanization—the fear that if all families and subgroups can equally pursue their own values, the society will become hopelessly fragmented, probably on the basis of class, economic status, religion, and political persuasion, as well as race; (5) expertise—the belief that only education experts have the knowledge and ability to create a good education and that more parental control will undermine the objective quality of education; and (6) technocracy—the belief that the technocratic and inequitable values often found in public school bureaucracies are so pervasive in other American institutions such as television and school text industries that a family may not be able to noticeably increase its influence over child rearing through school choice.

Each of these problems deserves serious consideration and analysis, which will be forthcoming only after recognition of the threat to the First Amendment posed by economic discrimination in availability of school choice. But because the "color line" continues to be America's most fundamental dilemma, the problem of racism and liberty in schooling must command further attention here.

41.  LSA-R.S. 17: 2951–59.

42. *Poindexter* v. *Louisiana Financial Assistance Commission*, 275 F. Supp. 833, at 845 (E.D. La. 1967), affirmed per curiam, 389 U.S. 571 (1968).

43. *Green* v. *County School Board of New Kent County*, 391 U.S. 430 (1968), at 441.

44. Along with the opposition to systems which permit "black" or "white" schools has been a commitment to integration as the only justifiable expression of racial equality in schools. It is possible, however, that the formulation of schooling issues in such absolute categories ignores reality. Opposition to freedom of choice for all families may in part be fabricated by a disingenuous appeal to racial equality, just as support for some tuition voucher plans has been fabricated in part by a disingenuous appeal to parental liberty. Racially identifiable schools are not necessarily providing poor education or promoting racism, and integrated schooling may in some instances be a violation of the rights of equal education of minority families; see *Moss* v. *Stanford Board*, 350 F. Supp. 879 (D. Conn. 1972); *Brice* v. *Landis*, 314 F. Supp. 974 (W.D. Cal. 1969); but also see *Norwalk Core* v. *Board of Education*, 423 F.2d 121 (1970); *Parris* v. *School Commission of Medford*, 305 F. Supp. 350 (D. Mass. 1969). The fact that a minority family may choose a racially identifiable school, thereby perpetuating the school's identifiability, does not mean that the education provided there is inferior or that the family has been denied its rights under the Fourteenth Amendment. The education of children within a culturally supportive atmosphere may be an important quality, both to the child's education and to the family and subgroup's ability to preserve its unique heritage and values. In fact, a blind pursuit of racial integration, without attention to the values and desires of minority parents, may be as offensive a form of racism as coercive separation and stigmatization of minority parents.

45. The Senate voted to postpone the enforcement of these regulations for at least a year from September 6, 1979. The vote followed an earlier Senate decision to cut off the use of federal funds by the IRS to end discriminatory schools' tax exemptions; see 125 *Congressional Record*, section 11, pp. 978–87 (daily edition, September 6, 1979).

46. *Norwood* v. *Harrison*, 413 U.S. 455 (1973), at 464–65.

47. *Norwood* v. *Harrison*; *Poindexter* v. *Louisiana Financial Assistance Commission*, 275 F. Supp. 833 (E.D. La., 1967), affirmed 389 U.S. 571 (1968); and *Runyan* v. *McCrary*, 427 U.S. 160 (1976).

48. David Caplovitz, *The Poor Pay More* (New York: Free Press, 1967): "Merchants," ch. 2, pp. 12–31, and "Credit Patterns," ch. 7, pp. 94–104; Michael Harrington, *The Other America* (New York: Macmillan, 1962): "On Slums," ch. 8, pp. 139–57.

# PART III

# EDUCATIONAL CONSEQUENCES OF THE SCHOOL MONOPOLY

The three essays in this part provide a more complete understanding of how the state educational monopoly operates and some consequences of that dominance. Their purpose is to provide a multifaceted examination of the interrelationship between the state as the political representative of majoritarian interests and those educational activities legitimated by the state, most specifically public schooling.

Thomas La Belle's "A Comparative and International Perspective on the Prospects for Family and Community Control of Schooling" is an anthropological study of the family and community control of schooling. The author attempts to answer the questions how and when family control of schooling might be possible, if it has happened elsewhere, and under what conditions. (Readers will want to be sure to read the essays in the next part, for they elaborate on many of La Belle's points.)

To provide answers to the above questions, La Belle first gives an overview of the role of the state in schooling as it pertains to cultural continuity and discontinuity. He sees that all societies sort out social groups into subordinate and superordinate positions and that historically schools have played an active role in that process. As others in this volume stress (for example, Edson), this sorting is a dynamic process that continues over time and often is well-intentioned and benevolent. La Belle states that this integrative process involves largely centripetal forces while there may exist, at the local unit level, provision for structural centrifugation as well (as in the use of language dialects).

La Belle argues that state schools manifest primarily centripital forces but that there are differences among state-supported schools (a factor which, as is pointed out in the Introduction, should caution us against too standardized an interpretation of the state and its role in education). Utilizing the centripetal-centrifugal continuum, the author illustrates differences among schools in four nations—South Africa, Great Britain, the United States, and Switzerland.

Despite the differences among state schools in different cultures, the general nature of state schooling is to circumvent "the interests and goals of local groups, especially those organized around family and kinship ties" (a positive attribute to Hegel in his support of the "civil society"), a point illustrated by history. In this regard, state schools always have supported national socioeconomic and political structures (as noted by Burgess, Spring, and Edson) while, at the same time, they have been at some variance with the interests of many individuals and groups. This variance is most clear within schools operated by subordinate groups since it is those schools which most threaten majoritarian interests. Yet local and subordinate groups do initiate their own schools. La Belle proceeds to describe such schools in his discussion of the kibbutz of Israel, Argentine family schools, and schools in the United States—those of the Amish and Black Muslims. The conditions within these schools illustrate the manner in which family and community-controlled schools might exist within the mandate of superordinate, state-regulated education.

Laurence Iannaccone examines the same general movement of changing power balances noted by La Belle through his focus on the changing political configurations *within* specific state educational units in the United States. Iannaccone's essay, "Changing Political Patterns and Governmental Regulations," examines the political ideologies that have developed over the past century, these ideologies leading to, "policy assumptions" that eventually "disappear beneath the surface of political controversy, their acceptance taken for granted as the way things are and are supposed to be." Iannaccone spells out how the development of beliefs about public education has led to myths which go unexamined, all the while the operational world of schooling demands reappraisal of those "policy assumptions."

Iannaccone's beginning point is the municipal reform era of the late nineteenth and early twentieth centuries, and here his discussion parallels that of Spring. This general period evidenced the rise and predominance of three major "doctrinal tenets" relative to education. First was the belief that education and politics could be separated, that, indeed, the state could establish an educational system that was independent of moral choice. Second, and certainly related, was the belief in the neutrality of the professionals who operated the system of state schools. It was widely held that administration could be a science that was value-free and that administrators themselves could serve as referees who exercised only objective decisions. Finally, there was the view of the unitary community, a point noted already by Edson and others. This view spurred the emphasis on consensual politics, on state bureaucracies, and on the movement toward uniform policies for a unitary society.

Yet such an ideological system often did not "fit" the reality of American schooling, and Iannaccone adroitly points out that the ideological basis of municipal reform did not square with the non-hierarchical structure of American schools, within and between which many points overlap and ambiguity exists. Because of this, there exist multiple fissures or "cracks" at the federal, state, and local levels where pressure can be placed to affect decisions. Therefore, decisions were affected but in a different form. As Iannaccone states, municipal reform "did not eliminate or suppress politics in education" but facilitated political decisions by those who knew best how to chart a course through these fissures—the social and economic elite, influenced by organized professionals.

All of this has had a profound impact on the past twenty years. Iannaccone traces the impact of federal intervention in education vis-à-vis such issues as desegregation, poverty programs, and major curricular innovation. The failure of such interventions is examined within the context of the ideological assumptions of the past and the loosely coupled nature of public schools. There is little doubt, as Iannaccone notes, that the "increased politicization of education . . . is to be expected into the next decade" as the state struggles with the contradictions generated from within.

The last essay in this part examines the relationship between the state and educational innovation in schools. Robert Everhart, in his "Institutional Parameters and the Purposes of Schooling: State Regulation of Educational Innovation," utilizes a sociological perspective on school organization to discuss the conditions under which change occurs in state schools and the types of changes one might expect.

First, Everhart makes the distinction between innovations based upon distributive criteria and those based on constitutive criteria. Changes based on distributive criteria, he argues, have to do with the allocation of agreed-upon educational services to previously unaffected groups whereas those based on constitutive criteria raise the very issue of how educational knowledge comes to exist and how it is defined. In a brief review of the literature on organizational change in schools, the author concludes that most change has focused on distributive issues and that the disillusionment on the part of many about the nature of schooling (as summarized in the Introduction) is based in part on the unreal expectation that significant organizational change can be made outside the context of values, beliefs, and political choices. Distributive-based change predominates because it does not question as overtly the role of values and political choice in education, a position that Arons and Lawrence claim is myopic if not unconstitutional.

What is the role of the state in this process? Through what Everhart calls "institutional parameters," the state effectively regulates educational changes by controlling the limits within which change may legitimately occur (see the similar argument made by La Belle). Everhart then describes the nature of the "common school" and compulsory school attendance to illustrate how state-regulated schooling channels educational process in a manner supportive of the state. Again, this is not done necessarily maliciously or even intentionally but as a natural consequence of education as it occurs in a monopolistic framework.

The author argues that to change the relationship between education and the state, political action must be seen as a natural part of educational change since all schooling is in fact politically based (see Arons and Lawrence, La Belle). He feels it is unrealistic continually to support educational change as primarily a technological process when, in fact, values and beliefs are so fundamental to education. As he states: "schooling must be seen as part of a system of beliefs and actions that perpetuates the state and not just as a technical process objectively operated by and/or for professionals who operate that process removed from the world of moral choice." This point is detailed more fully by Michael Apple in the last part.

The essays in Part III point to the ubiquitous presence of the state in education and suggest that to seek for its absence is unrealistic both historically and culturally. The question then is not *if* but *how* the state will control education and the consequences of that control as a function of the context within which it occurs. In this regard, all three authors point to the changing nature of the state/education relationship and discuss some of the factors affecting such changes. That contradictions generated within the state itself become the most powerful catalyst for directed change of education is a point that should not be overlooked.

## SUGGESTED READINGS

Apple, Michael W. *Ideology and Curriculum.* London: Routledge & Kegan Paul, 1979.

Callahan, Raymond E. *Education and the Cult of Efficiency.* Chicago: University of Chicago Press, 1962.

Cohen, Yehudi A. "The Shaping of Men's Minds: Adaptations to the Imperatives of Culture." In Murray L. Wax et al., eds. *Anthropological Perspectives on Education.* New York: Basic Books, 1971, pp. 19–50.

Collins, Randall. *The Credential Society.* New York: Academic Press, 1979.

Everhart, Robert B. "From Universalism to Usurpation: An Essay on the Antecedents to Compulsory School Attendance Legislation." *Review of Educational Research* 47 (1977): 499–530.

Firth, Simon, and Paul Corrigan. "The Politics of Education." In Michael Young and Geoff Whitty, eds. *Society, State, and Schooling.* Sussex: Falmar Press, 1977.

Halperin, Samuel, and George R. Kaplan, eds. *Federalism at the Crossroads: Improving Educational Policymaking.* Washington, D.C.: Institute for Educational Leadership, 1976.

Iannaccone, Laurence, and Peter J. Cistone. *The Politics of Education.* Eugene: ERIC Clearing House on Educational Management, University of Oregon, 1974.

La Belle, Thomas. "Cultural Determinants of Educational Alternatives." In John Goodlad, ed. *The Conventional and the Alternative in Education.* Berkeley: McCutchan, 1975, pp. 165–88.

La Belle, Thomas. "Schooling and Intergroup Relations: A Comparative Analysis." *Anthropology and Education Quarterly* 10 (Spring 1979): 43–60.

Mitchell, Douglas E., and Laurence Iannaccone. *The Impact of California's Legislative Policy on Public School Performance.* California Policy Seminar

Monograph No. 5. Berkeley: Institute of Governmental Studies, University of California, 1980.

Mosher, Edith K., and Jennings L. Wagoner, Jr. *The Changing Politics of Education.* Berkeley: McCutchan, 1978.

Ogbu, John. *Minority Education and Caste.* New York: Academic Press, 1978.

Scribner, Jay D., ed. *The Politics of Education.* The Seventy-Sixth Yearbook of the National Society for the Study of Education, Part 2. Chicago: University of Chicago Press, 1977.

Tyack, David B. *The One Best System: A History of American Education.* Cambridge, Mass.: Harvard University Press, 1974.

West, E. G. *Education and the State.* London: Institute of Economic Affairs, 1970.

Wolfe, Alan. *The Limits to Legitimacy.* New York: Free Press, 1977.

# 7 A COMPARATIVE AND INTERNATIONAL PERSPECTIVE ON THE PROSPECTS FOR FAMILY AND COMMUNITY CONTROL OF SCHOOLING

*Thomas J. La Belle*

This essay explores the prospects for implementing a system of family and community control of schooling, a system that is intended to place educational decision making in the hands of smaller, more intimate groups, principally the family and community, where the best interests of children are said to be known and understood. The issue of greatest interest here concerns the potential for altering the role and function of both the state, as it begins to share its position of being the principal provider of publicly supported education, and the local community, group, and/or family, as these units assume a greater share in the authority over the choice of schools which their children will attend. This is not, however, a treatise on the values and beliefs associated with the appropriate amount of authority that should be assumed by the state and the local unit. Instead, the questions to be addressed here concern the viability of a decentralized policy of family and community choice in education, given the use of schools by groups in this and in other countries. Specifically, is it feasible for the state to subsidize a range of private and public educational alternatives which may undermine its authority and challenge its ideological orientations? And from an international perspective, to what extent have nation-states permitted ethnic, class, political, and other groups the opportunity to initiate educational programs of their own which might challenge the direction and authority of the state?

275

Educational anthropologists are attracted to the study of school control because of the school's role in maintaining the culture and because of its contribution to social selection and stratification. The goals and methods of schooling offer an arena in which the general maintenance and changes of aspects of the wider culture can be studied. Here the educational anthropologist might look to the continuities and discontinuities in cultural learning among children from different segments of society over time as the children interact with each other as well as with the school's curriculum and its staff. In addition to the role of schools in maintaining the wider culture, the educational anthropologist is concerned with the use of schools as a mechanism for channeling youngsters into particular occupational and career patterns. Who gets educated, what type of education is imparted, the relation of that education to socioeconomic pursuits, and so on, are among the questions that are often raised.

In analyzing the contribution of schools to maintenance and stratification, one must account for the changing relations among social and cultural groups in a society, including both their respective access to power and resources as well as their interests and goals. It is then possible to study the use of schools as a mechanism to adapt or change the relationship among groups, especially as schools are presumed to affect a group's achievement of sought-after cultural and structural goals.

## EDUCATION AND SOCIETAL INTEGRATION

All societies are characterized by group differences and segments which function as frames of reference for members of the society. These societal groupings are based on both cultural and structural attributes which serve as a basis for defining, interpreting, and assessing one's own experiences and the experiences of others. Cultural segments, or ethnic groups, represent an attributed or self-proclaimed identity that involves certain religious, linguistic, or other collective symbols or representations. Structural groups, or social classes and castes, on the other hand, are based on the group's relative access to or possession of political and economic power or resources. Typically, these cultural and structural characteristics are intertwined in such a way that certain ethnic groups occupy either subordinate or superordinate class or caste positions relative to other groups in society. As societies sort out their social groups into super-ordinate and subordinate positions based on cultural, political, and economic characteristics, the result is a differential form of societal participation in accord with cultural and structural group member-ship. Schools, as one institution where this participation takes place, would reflect both the groups' positions in society as well as the cultural and structural goals that these groups expect formal education to achieve.

Following R. A. Schermerhorn, I will use the terms "dominant" or "superordinate" to signify: "that collectivity within a society which has preeminent authority to function both as guardians and sustainers of the controlling value system, and as prime allocators of rewards in the society." The term "subordinate" will be used to indi-cate those groups which lack such authority. How these groups inter-act within the bounds of a single society or political entity can be broadly termed as integration. According to Schermerhorn, there is an emphasis on the *dynamic* nature of integration; it is not a state of being but rather: "a process whereby units or elements of a society are brought into an active and coordinated compliance with ongoing activities and objectives of the dominant group in that society."[1]

For purposes of this discussion, the integration process rests on an assessment of the overall aims or goals of both the superordinate and subordinate groups in a society. Schermerhorn argues that these aims are typically either centripetal or centrifugal in nature. A centripetal tendency refers to a trend toward common, societywide lifestyles and institutional participation whereas a centrifugal tendency in aims refers to a group's attempts to retain and preserve unique cultural attributes as well as to seek greater political and economic auton-omy. In schooling, for example, a superordinate population may wish to use the school to achieve societal consensus through mandat-ing the use of a particular language of instruction or requiring all students at a certain level to pass a standardized examination to com-pete successfully for a job or for further education. At the same time, a subordinate group may seek to use its own language as the instructional idiom and to abolish standardized examinations because they are biased in favor of the background and experiences of the dominant group. If the superordinates and subordinates share a modal tendency, whether centripetal or centrifugal, an agreed-upon form of integration is likely to take place. If the modal tendencies differ as above—for example, one group seeking greater uniformity while the other seeks greater autonomy—the integrative process is likely to be conflictual in nature.

In analyzing these centripetal and centrifugal tendencies for integration, one must identify a group's *separate* structural and cultural aims. Herbert Kelman argues that the legitimacy of a nation-state in the long run is derived from its reflection of the ethnic-cultural identity of the population as well as its ability to meet the needs and interests of the population.[2] These two aspects of legitimacy can be seen in the cultural and structural attachments that link an individual to the larger society. A cultural or "sentimental" attachment involves an internalization of values, an attachment to group symbols, and an obedience to the state's authority. Potentially, schooling serves these cultural ends by socializing youngsters to accept and behave in accord with a particular set of principles and goals. A structural attachment to the nation-state will be found in an individual who believes that the system is a vehicle for achieving his/her own ends or the ends of other members of the system. It is a structural commitment to the existence of certain social roles, and a commitment to law and order and to system maintenance in general. Structurally, the schools serve to define and to transmit appropriate roles and statuses, the nature of acceptable political and economic participation, and the skills to gain access to the socioeconomic structure. The greater the attachment in both these areas—cultural and structural—by all groups, the greater the overall centripetal tendency in the society. Although these attachments must exist to some degree for a nation-state to survive, the extent to which they are present and the predominance of one type of attachment instead of another will depend on the orientations of both the superordinate and subordinate populations.

Another reason that it is important to distinguish between structural and cultural aims within centripetal and centrifugal tendencies is that in an analysis of the control of education it permits an accounting of what often appear to be contradictory trends. On the one hand, for example, a policy of cultural centrifugation might encourage each group's language to be used as the instructional idiom at the local level. Simultaneously, however, the standards for proceeding through the educational system and the mechanisms for decision making might be quite uniform and centrally coordinated or controlled. This latter policy would be an example of structural centripetalism, as the desire of the superordinate group would be to incorporate the school and its participants into the nation-state's economic and political spheres.

Although such orientations may or may not be seen as contradictory by policy makers, for analytical purposes it is well to remember that they do exist simultaneously. The issue that may be most important is the relationship between the orientation held by the superordinates as opposed to the subordinates with regard to these issues of centripetal/centrifugal tendencies and structural/cultural interests. Whether both groups share rather than differ in their orientations will not affect integration per se; the important difference between agreed-upon and conflictual types of integration is the greater ease of the former. That is, in either case there will be coordinated compliance with objectives of the dominant group, but where that compliance is voluntary, it will also be somewhat more predictable over time and will require less governmental effort to maintain.

Although the superordinate group generally establishes the goals of the educational enterprise in any given nation, alterations in the short-term policies governing schools reflect the ongoing interaction between superordinate and subordinate populations. This interaction between groups may result in the establishment of either common or conflicting goals for schools, which, in turn, reflect the vested interests of both superordinates and subordinates. Primary in this regard are issues of control or where the decisions governing various aspects of the educational enterprise reside. For example, there are usually concerns expressed over financial support; criteria for access, advancement, and completion; the curriculum; personnel training and recruitment; language of instruction; and so on. Each society and, in some cases, each province, county, and municipality differ in the extent to which these matters are centralized and ultimately under the control of the superordinate population or decentralized and hence become the responsibility of local groups and subject to the influence of subordinate populations.

In a recent analysis of educational policies and intergroup relations worldwide, Peter White and I have argued that the local level generally assumes responsibility for only those aspects of schooling delegated and/or sanctioned by the central authority. We contend that schools serve to maintain the society and culture on behalf of the dominant population through socialization, skill training, and social selection. Utilizing the concepts of centripetal and centrifugal tendencies discussed above, our focus has been on the educational policies of societies that are characterized as bi- or multiethnic. To place the educational policies and directional tendencies within a particular social, historical, geographic, and economic context, we inductively generated four types of intergroup relations. Specific countries were then selected to demonstrate the relationship between group membership and socioeconomic and participatory roles and group membership and cultural identity and values. Through a discussion of particular educational policies, we were able to describe the extent to which agreement and conflict among groups over the schooling process characterize the various types of intergroup relations.[3]

The most centralized and coercive type of intergroup relations we found is characterized by two or more groups whose differences along ethnic lines are highlighted and reinforced by the near monopoly of cultural prestige, political power, and economic power exercised by one group over the other group(s). The most striking example of this type of society is South Africa, where apartheid legislation is intended to guide a clearly centrifugal process of "parallel development" along racial lines. Two of the factors that engendered the apartheid idea include self-preservation by the white, especially the Afrikaaner, population and the threat of economic and political supremacy by the numerically greater black population. Educational policies operate in accord with the Bantu Education Act of 1953. Among the act's provisions, new curricula had to be devised to ensure the preservation and enrichment of "Bantu" culture, and black Africans had to be more involved in the administration of their schools through local school committees. The black South Africans did not, however, receive any control over teacher appointments, curricula, or classroom procedures. The principles of the act were fostered through complex white fears that unless the "Bantu" were schooled in and through their native culture, they would soon draw even with the level of competence of whites and eventually dominate the numerically weaker Afrikaaner-English civilization. Hence, the act, while technically providing equal educational opportunity, was really geared to a perpetuation of the lifestyle of the "Bantu" and to preventing black Africans from acquiring the skills which would make them competitive with the whites.[4] Control over education in South Africa is ultimately vested in the central government, and access to all levels of schooling coincides with ethnic and racial boundaries. The effect is to exclude most subordinate group blacks and to channel them into the low-status occupational sphere.[5] In sum, schooling in South Africa, through group-specific curricula, teachers, and language of instruction—especially at the elementary school level—supports the overall centrifugal goals of the dominant group to maintain group separation and subordinate group economic and political dependency.

Although we found that the majority of the cases of intergroup relations in the world do not engender the same level of coercive separation as in South Africa, most are nevertheless characterized by a division which favors one population over another. Here Great Britain is an appropriate example, as there exists ethnic group dominance—for example, whites over immigrant West Indians—but some structural permeability allowing selective socioeconomic mobility of individuals. The West Indians first came to Britain following the Second World War in response to labor shortages. By 1972 West Indians constituted the largest minority population in British schools. Although the language of instruction in schools is English (the West Indians speak an English patois) and the curriculum is said to be similar to that used in the West Indies, West Indian children do not do as well in school as dominant group children or other immigrant children. They are underrepresented in the selective schools, score lower on standardized tests, and are overrepresented in schools for the so-called educationally subnormal.[6] Overall, the dominant group in Great Britain evinces a generally centripetal tendency in its educational policies as it seeks to incorporate the subordinate populations into the social structure and into superordinate cultural patterns. Education assists this goal through administrative centralization and the adoption of curricula, language of instruction, tests, and so on, that reflect primarily the dominant culture. Hence, even though access to schooling is initially broad for all groups in a society like Great Britain, success requires considerable accommodation to the cultural criteria of the dominant group.

Schooling in the United States reflects a similar dominant group orientation. Although socioeconomic roles and ethnicity are partially overlapped in the United States and there is some prospect for participation by subordinate group members in higher-status positions, as in Great Britain such participation depends on an acceptance of superordinate cultural patterns. This means that even though there is some tolerance for group differences, it is dominant group criteria that are used for judging appropriate values and behavior and for determining access to higher socioeconomic positions. There criteria are manifested implicitly and explicitly through standardized tests, methods of instruction, and curricula. Large numbers of subordinate group members who do not meet such criteria for school success are typically tracked into curricula leading to lower socioeconomic roles and statuses in the wider society. Although there is increased awareness of ethnic group differences in schooling in both countries brought on by persistent demands by subordinate groups for group-specific curricula, teachers, and the like, the result is often a short-term adaptation in basically centripetal policies rather than significant change. Such is often the case, for example, with bilingual instruction, which permits the use of a subordinate group's language in the classroom. The dominant group may foster bilingual instruction as a more efficient way for subordinate children to learn the dominant group language and to practice more dominant group behaviors. In this instance, bilingual education may appear to accommodate to subordinate group desires for strengthening the subordinate group culture, but in reality it only masks the long-term strategy of subordinate group assimilation.

Another type of intergroup relations that White and I describe differs from the others in that continual conflict over schooling among groups is not a characteristic. In these instances the participating groups agree tacitly to the nature of the educational programs and to the locus of ultimate control. In Switzerland, for example, the population groups are roughly equal in prestige and political and economic power, and they participate in a single socioeconomic system that is not highly segmented by class divisions. This balance among groups reflects parity less than it reflects a series of structural and cultural trade-offs, as no one group is perceived as completely dominant or subordinate. There is typically shared governance of education between the nation at the central level and the various ethnic groups regionally. Here decentralization in decision making closely follows ethnic group boundaries, even though the central government intervenes to provide a common ideology and national goals. Typically, in areas of curricula, teacher training, and the school's language of instruction, a dialectic between centripetal and centrifugal policies emerges; for example, there is a tendency in Switzerland to employ group-specific practices at the elementary school stage whereas secondary and higher education institutions tend to reflect more common national and international content and practices.[7]

## STATE CONTROL OF SCHOOLS

These and other similar cases suggest that it is in the ultimate control of the state over the schooling process, primarily to ensure ideological consensus among population segments, where the arguments for family and community control of schooling appear the weakest. Whether consensus for both order and personal liberty in society will be enhanced through private choice rather than through compulsory public schooling is not clear. Although some argue that state-financed educational entitlements will diminish the threat of dissenting and antagonistic ideologies, such an assumption depends very much on the cultural and structural goals of the groups present in a given society. A society's strength may be derived from and fostered by the expression of subordinate challenges to superordinate positions, as is often argued by advocates of local control of schooling. But schooling supported by the state is not likely to be viewed by the superordinate populations as an acceptable forum for such challenges. While intergroup conflict may be inevitable and even lend strength rather than weakness to a society, state-sanctioned schooling is not an acceptable vehicle for ideological challenges to the existence of the state when the public education process is intended to promote consensus around cultural and structural attachments dominated by superordinate populations.

The control exercised by the nation-state determines to a considerable extent the sociopolitical unit for which a child is being educated. In this regard, Yehudi Cohen argues that the existence of the nation-state presumes active adult participation in the wider society and circumvents the interests and goals of local groups, especially those organized around family and kinship ties.[8] Such local groups utilize a particularistic form of cultural transmission for centrifugal aims to inculcate behaviors in children which underlie appropriate local adult activity. Whereas these behaviors arise under circumscribed conditions often addressing idiosyncratic goals, the state seeks to transmit behaviors which are more centripetal and, hence, universally oriented. Cohen characterizes these two forms of cultural transmission as socialization and education. At the local level, the process of socialization occurs around particular individuals—those who do the teaching—whereas at the state level the process of education is concerned with *what* is being taught without concern for who teaches it. The result is a potential conflict between the local group and the state about personnel, process, and content. The state's centripetal aims result in an inculcation of standardized and stereotyped knowledge, skills, values, and attitudes by means of standardized and stereotyped means. The school is the state's predominant institutional transmitter of this informtion, and standardized credentialing and testing are among the mechanisms used to ensure that the aims of the superordinate social system are met. In state-sanctioned schools it matters little who the teacher is since certification legitimates his or her role and since the major concern is with what and how something is being taught.

To ensure that children assume their adult roles and function in accord with superordinate expectations, the state typically takes two principal steps, both of which involve schooling. First, in the interest of legitimating its authority, a uniform ideology is established among the citizenry. Schools become an institutional mechanism by which a standardized and uniform set of cultural symbols—flags, pictures of culture heroes or rulers, slogans, standardized books—are transmitted, ensuring some conformity to the aims and imperatives of the state system. The second step interacts with the first as the state must be willing to subvert local sources of solidarity, loyalty, and authority to ensure that its own ideology can be established.[9]

History tends to support these propositions regarding the role of the state and the community in the control of schooling.[10] From the Middle Ages to the end of the eighteenth century in the West, for example, a tacit agreement between the church and the crown in the governance of society placed spiritual matters, including schooling, under the control of the church. This left the state with responsibility for both economic and political matters, including the military and police, whereas the church was charged with inculcating the official ideology through parishes, families, and schools. At the end of the eighteenth century, this monarchical-theocratic form of governance gave way to the nation-state. A new ruling class toppled the church/crown alliance and initiated its own form of institutions.[11] The French Revolution, for example, unified different groups in overthrowing the aristocracy, and France emerged as a nation-state under the control of the national bourgeoisie. The control of schooling was a major issue before and after the French Revolution, as many wanted to remove school control from the church and hence from the influence of the former aristocracy. The issue was resolved by initiating ministries of education and placing schooling under the direct jurisdiction of the state.[12]

In the establishment of the modern state, schools became enmeshed in the state organization along with other economic and political institutions. Schools expanded rapidly, and the initiation of compulsory education paralleled the development of the state.[13] The need was to overthrow the monarchic system and schooling figured prominently in the plans to secure popular support for the new ruling class. The concept of a nation-state drew the support of the masses, willing to fight for liberation, and provided a common cause around which loyalty could be expressed. The school assisted in undermining local vested interests while helping to create a common ideology and direction for the new state.[14]

Because of the strong relationship that typically exists between the aims of the dominant group and the aims of the nation-state, it is not surprising that schools operating under the state's jurisdiction in the long run are supportive of the national socioeconomic and political structure. In effect, state-sanctioned education assists in maintaining and facilitating the existing social order by reflecting the interests and concerns of the decision makers in power. It is for this reason that educational change—both the means and the aims—follows rather than precedes radical upheavals in a national system. Hence, the Soviet Union in the 1920s, Hitler's Germany in the 1930s, Mao's China in the 1950s, Castro's Cuba in the 1960s, Allende's Chile in the 1970s, and Pinochet's Chile and Khomeini's Iran in the 1980s are all examples of the use of education for reorienting the citizenry and challenging antagonists. They are reminiscent of the ways schools were used following the French Revolution.

## LOCAL CONTROL OF SCHOOLS

Although in most societies the state has a monopoly on the ultimate control of schools, there often exists in these same societies some space for local educational alternatives. A major issue, however, concerns the nature of these alternatives and the extent to which they are controlled by superordinate or subordinate groups. The most prevalent form of local control is that which occurs among superordinate populations as they privately fund and direct their own schools. The superordinate groups are able to exercise local control as an extension of the political power and economic resources that they hold at the national level. In effect, the wealthy and politically powerful offer little or no threat to the maintenance of the basic underpinnings of society and thus are able to take advantage of their resources to exercise educational choice.

Subordinates, however, often represent a potential threat to maintaining intergroup relations in their present form, and because subordinates lack the resources to exercise educational options, they are most often restricted to schools controlled directly or indirectly by the superordinates. If subordinates seek greater cultural or structural autonomy by creating their own schools and this conflicts with superordinate aims, their efforts may be ignored or undermined, but they are seldom supported. In cases where the subordinate group's alternatives are small and relatively insignificant in size and visibility, they are often permitted to remain. If they become too visible, however, the schools might well be found to be in violation of certain legal guidelines in the areas of health, personnel, facilities, curricula, and so on, requiring their modification or even closure. Less directly, the subordinate group schools can be stereotyped as being of such low quality that the graduates are able to enter the job market at only the lowest levels. These and other options are available to the superordinate population if it seeks to stifle and obstruct subordinate groups from successfully implementing educational alternatives. In effect, subordinate populations seeking to exercise options, especially radical alternatives that conflict with the overall centripetal or centrifugal aims of the superordinates, are seldom successful as they are viewed as a threat to the status quo and because they lack the political and economic resources to legitimize and sustain the alternatives for very long.

This is not to say that local groups have not initiated and sustained their own schools.[15] In most instances, however, such schools are generally isolated, and the economic and political conditions under which they exist are often unique. Typically, and most important, there is an implicit or explicit agreement between the community initiators of the schools and the government to permit the schools to persist. Such an agreement is often accompanied by guidelines or rules, which are monitored and enforced by the state. A second characteristic of such schools is centered in the socioeconomic resources of the community and its cultural and religious heritage.

Probably the best-known example of such a community-initiated alternative in the world is the Israeli kibbutz. The kibbutzim are collective settlements first established in the early twentieth century by Zionist immigrants. Each kibbutz has responsibility for the economic, social, and cultural welfare of its members and, as with other social groups, uses education to preserve its community way of life. Formal education in the kibbutz is viewed as a mechanism for preserving the kibbutzim way of life. Schooling is designed to inculcate a sense of community membership and responsibility as well as to prepare the student for productive work. Not only is education closely tied to the wider community, it is in and of itself a community. Children live, work, and play in collective children's homes. They are part of an age group that advances through the nonselective educational system as a unit. The prestige and political influence of the kibbutz in Israel has enabled each of the four kibbutzim federations in the country to retain considerable autonomy over its schooling. Each federation has an education committee which supervises the organization and operation of the kibbutzim schools and each kibbutz has its own teacher and parent committee which administers the school program, selects and assigns teachers, and takes responsibility for the guidance, placement, and psychological adjustment of each child.

A second example of community-initiated schools is the Argentine family schools, based on a French model, begun in 1970 by third- and fourth-generation Italian immigrants in the northern section of Argentina. Nearly all of the residents of the area are members of socioeconomic cooperatives with a history of community organization and a desire to become involved in their children's education. The schools operate on the principle of creating interaction between life outside of schools and the school curriculum, with students engaged in independent study and problem solving at home. Each family school has a team of four or five monitors who work with a council of parents and students to operate the school. The schools offer the first three years of secondary school. Twenty to thirty male and female students attend for one week, during which time they live in and do all the upkeep with the exception of cooking. Then they return home for two weeks. Thus, the school can be used for all grades on a rotating basis. The curriculum, as the leadership points out, is based on questions not answers; there exists an aversion to the encyclopedic teaching/learning process of traditional schools.

There is also a belief that life outside schools is more important than that inside schools and that the family must be central to and responsible for the school. Although there has been some friction between the government and the family schools involving the Argentine government's desire to influence the operation and direction of the schools, thus far the interference has not resulted in the closure of any schools.

Even though there are other community-initiated schools, some characterized by local control (for example, Harambee Schools of Kenya and National Campaign of Community Schools of Brazil) and others by central government control (for example, China, India, and Tanzania), two examples from the United States are perhaps closer to the community-initiated alternatives of the Israeli kibbutzim and the Argentine family schools and provide models of local educational initiatives. These are the schools of the old-order Amish and the Black Muslims.

The Amish are descendants of the Swiss Anabaptists who settled in Pennsylvania in the late eighteenth century. The Amish are typically organized in church communities and are often identified as the population that uses horsedrawn carriages, avoids using electricity, telephones, and automobiles, and forbids formal education beyond elementary school. The Amish place a high value on communal obligation and the development of a Christian character. J. A. Hostetler and G. E. Huntington identify five cultural themes which distinguish the Amish and are important for understanding their socialization practices: "separatism from the world, voluntary acceptance of high social obligations symbolized by adult baptism, the maintenance of a disciplined church-community, practice of exclusion and shunning of transgressing members, and a life of harmony with the soil and nature."[16]

The Amish establish their own schools and select their own teachers to foster these values and to provide a systematic way of preparing their children to live in an agricultural environment and church community which does not recognize worldly, external criteria of success. Amish children generally aspire to occupations needed by the community, and because the community is able to offer occupational opportunities through its own agricultural resources, children are prepared in schools for a generally secure and predictable future.

A second example of a community-initiated school in the United States among subordinate populations is that initiated by the Black Muslim community. The Muslims are a separatist religious organization based on principles of black nationalism and the teachings of Islam. They believe that the black man is the original man, that he is part of Allah, and that he is divine and supreme. They advocate the segregation of white from black and the practice of a strict moral code, which includes abstaining from alcohol, gambling, profanity, and drugs.[17] They also adhere to a strict diet akin to that of Orthodox Jews. The Muslims' most essential goal is economic independence, an objective they feel will foster both freedom and power and ensure a continuous segregated life cycle.

The Muslims want schools that separate boys and girls and that are taught and administered by people who adhere to black Muslim values of righteousness, decency, and self-respect. The objective of a Muslim education is "to re-educate the so-called Negro, who has been the victim of centuries of mis-education . . . to attain his rightful place in the sun as a Black man . . . to give the students a feeling of dignity and appreciation of their own kind."[18]

The common elements in the kibbutzim, old-order Amish, Black Muslim, and Argentine family school communities are several, and they assist in explaining the survival of these community school efforts. Importantly, all of these initiatives emanate from unique cultural conditions involving strong ethnic traditions and relatively homogeneous populations. Furthermore, each community is characterized by considerable experience in community organization for religious, political, and economic ends. The members of each group share similar values, and they seek cultural autonomy to enculturate their children with those values. These locally initiated, and in a majority of cases privately financed, schools are also characterized by their existence in communities that are relatively autonomous economically. In each instance, the particular group owns and controls sufficient production capacity, typically in the form of land for agriculture or ranching, such that they are not dependent upon outsiders for employment or for access to basic commodities or services. This economic self-sufficiency enables each community to guarantee the succeeding generations an opportunity for access to employment and job security. The combination of these cultural characteristics in the form of religion, language, and values with the ability to be relatively autonomous economically enables these communities to control much of the basic life cycle of their members.

Because these communities exist within nation-states, however, they are faced with the need to create a viable and functional relationship with the legal and political mandates of the state. All of these communities have evolved such a set of understandings regarding their schools, or they are engaged in attempting to do so, thereby acknowledging the ultimate control over the schooling process held by the state. The Argentine government, for example, has attempted to alter family school curricula, and in Israel the kibbutzim have a long-standing set of agreements with the government, which sanctions their existence and persistence.[19] In the United States, the relations between the government and the old-order Amish represent a long history of litigation over such issues as compulsory schooling, teacher credentialing, required curricula, and so on. As to the Black Muslims, they, among all of the communities mentioned, probably represent the greatest threat to the interests of the superordinates. Consequently, their activities have often been closely monitored by U.S. law enforcement agencies.

The experience of these community-initiated and oriented schools suggests that, irrespective of sponsorship, the control of schools will ultimately remain with the superordinate population but that there is some space for families and communities to share in the educational decision-making process. Most of the family and community participation in educational decision making, however, is likely to fall within generally accepted philosophies of education rather than in radical alternatives that seek to challenge superordinate economic and political structures. Although this rather conservative type of decision-making space will continue to satisfy the superordinates as well as a majority of the rest of the population in their attempts to socialize their children in particular ways as a variant of the norm, it is assumed that many others will emerge to challenge the values that provide the foundation for the current socioeconomic system. These groups are not likely to be similar to the basically ethnic-oriented community initiatives just discussed but will probably represent a range of specific issues and points of view that confronts those who align themselves with superordinate interests. Although many of these alternatives will prove acceptable, including humanistic, religious, and environmentally oriented schools, many will not. The proponents of these other schools are likely to be characterized as racist or unpatriotic, and the superordinates will find them unsuitable and threatening to the stability and orientation of the wider community and the state.

Schools under the control of organizations aligned with racist ideologies such as Nazism or the Ku Klux Klan and economic and political ideologies such as Marxism will prove most difficult for the state to justify its continued funding under a local community control plan. Some separatist religious ideologies, like the Black Muslims, will probably also confront superordinate values and belief systems and be difficult for the state to support. Given the recent trend toward multicultural education and the growing acceptance of the importance of cross-cultural and international understanding, however, such areas as group language, history, identity, and so on, will likely be tolerated with little or no difficulty, especially as they receive attention within more traditional and acceptable state-sanctioned school curricula.

## CONCLUSION

Advocates of local community and family control of educational choice in the United States will be confronted with addressing the potential conflict between superordinate centripetal tendencies toward homogeneity and, at least on the radical fringes, some subordinate group centrifugal tendencies in cultural and structural aims. In those instances where subordinate groups seek to use schools as more efficient vehicles of social mobilization with the intent of enabling group members to become involved more effectively in the wider society, alternatives will represent acceptable schooling patterns and will most likely range from an emphasis on basic skills to a concern for identity and interpersonal relations. Even when subordinate groups choose to foster cultural pluralism through modest centrifugal tendencies, there will probably be tolerance from superordinates. Potential conflict is likely to arise, however, in the use of public monies to support subordinate group aims which undercut the centripetal tendencies and lifestyles of superordinates. If such separatist and/or confrontation moves threaten to take away from the superordinates the use of schools as a principal mechanism for controlling and shaping the nature of the relationship between groups and the rate of change in society, conflict will probably be heightened.

Such conflict during the implementation of family and local control of a schooling system will enable some family choice advocates to see their hypotheses put to a test regarding the strength of a society emanating from dissent and conflict. Thus far in the United States superordinates have generally been able to adapt the schooling process to the interests of subordinates without challenging the basic means and ends of publicly sanctioned schooling. Some parents, for example, have been able to send their children to religious and other private schools, and others have kept their children in public schools while fostering greater equality in the treatment of subordinate populations. Although there is little reason to believe that the superordinates will be confronted with the need to change as opposed to adapt the schooling process in the face of a local control system, it will be of interest to see what kinds of adaptations will result while ensuring sufficient space for local initiatives.

It is entirely possible, for example, that in the long run the use of public funds for the support of education will be linked to such adaptations as standardized examinations, teacher certification, textbook approvals, and so on, which, while permitting what will appear as basic change through experimentation, will ensure that superordinate centripetal tendencies will be fostered. It might further be anticipated that accreditation agencies will be called upon to judge the educational quality of various schooling enterprises and to gather information on the educational process and the treatment of children. Combined, these long-term actions mean that radical school alternatives linked to political ideologies with centrifugal structural aims will be at risk relative to state support. Such schools will be scrutinized because they will challenge the state's ultimate control over the political and social education of children and will challenge its goal of assimilating subordinates to the lifestyles of the superordinates.

## NOTES TO CHAPTER 7

1.  R. A. Schermerhorn, *Comparative Ethnic Relations* (New York: Random House, 1970), pp. 12, 14.
2.  Herbert C. Kelman, "Patterns of Personal Involvement in the National System: A Social-Psychological Analysis of Political Legitimacy," in *International Politics and Foreign Policy*, ed. J. N. Rosenau (New York: Free Press, 1969).

3. Thomas J. La Belle and Peter S. White, "Education and Multi-Ethnic Integration: An Inter-Group Relations Typology," *Comparative Education Review* 23(2) (1980): 155-173.

4. Monica Whately, "Educating the Bantu for Serfdom," *America* 93(26) (1955): 618-19.

5. H. Bernstein, "Schools for Servitude," in *Apartheid*, ed. A. La Guma (London: Lawrence & Wishart, 1972), pp. 43-79.

6. John Ogbu, *Minority Education and Caste* (New York: Academic Press, 1978).

7. See C. A. Gilliard, *A History of Switzerland* (London: George Allen, 1955); W. R. Keech, "Linguistic Diversity and Political Conflict in Switzerland," *Comparative Politics* 4(3) (1972): 387-404.

8. Yehudi A. Cohen, "The Shaping of Men's Minds: Adaptations to Imperatives of Culture," in *Anthropological Perspectives on Education*, ed. Murray L. Wax, Stanley Diamond, and Fred O. Gearing (New York: Basic Books, 1971), pp. 19-50.

9. Ibid.

10. Thomas J. La Belle and José Da S. Goncalves, "Control and Service of Schools: The Community and the State," *Compare* 10(1) (1980): 3-15.

11. See D. A. Dallari, *Elementos de teoria geral do estado* (Sao Paulo: Edicao Saraiva, 1972); A. Hussain, "The Economy and the Educational System in Capitalist Societies," *Economy and Society* 5(4) (November 1976); H. Lefebvre, *De l'état: De Hégel à Mao*, vol. 2 (Paris: Union Générale d'éditions, 1976); and N. Poulantzas, *Pouvoir politique et classes sociales*, vols. 1 and 2 (Paris: Petite Collection Maspéro, 1975).

12. Val D. Rust, *Alternatives in Education* (London: Sage, 1977).

13. See ibid.; and Hussain, "Economy and the Educational System."

14. See Dallari, *Elementos de teoria*; Lefebvre, *De l'état*; Cohen, "Shaping of Men's Minds"; Poulantzas, *Pouvoir* and *politique*; Frederick Engels, *The Origin of the Family, Private Property, and the State* (New York: International, 1975).

15. See Thomas J. La Belle and Robert E. Verhine, "School-Community Interaction: A Comparative and International Perspective," *Communities and Their Schools*, ed. Don Davies (New York: McGraw-Hill, 1980).

16. J. A. Hostetler and G. E. Huntington, *Children in Amish Society: Socialization and Community Education* (New York: Holt, Rinehart and Winston, 1971), p. 4.

17. Louis E. Lomax, *When the Word Is Given* (Cleveland: World, 1963).

18. C. E. Lincoln, *The Black Muslim in America* (Boston: Beacon Press, 1961), p. 126.

19. A. E. Kleinberger, *Society, Schools, and Progress in Israel* (Oxford: Pergamon Press, 1969).

# 8 CHANGING POLITICAL PATTERNS AND GOVERNMENTAL REGULATIONS

*Laurence Iannaccone*

For more than two decades, both national and state governments attempted to reform the American school. In fact, their efforts sometimes exacerbated the educational problems they sought to address. One outstanding consequence of these interventions was clear by the end of the 1970s. Whatever the pedagogical successes or failures of these centralized policy efforts, the delicate systems of balances which for some sixty years had guided educational managers in reducing internal conflicts within the profession and which had buffered the schools from external political attacks were no longer functioning adequately. The delicate balance between lay and professional influence and that between teacher and administrator power had been disrupted. Not as obvious but just as true, the ideological underpinnings of the system appropriate to the preceding sixty years were ill suited to the new circumstances.

Three basic ideological contradictions are now embedded in American educational policies and its policy system. First, two conflicting philosophies of government have coexisted as inherent in the American system of educational government since early in this century. One is the creed of federalism; the other, the tenets of municipal reform. Aspects of each were woven into both the public ideology and governmental structures of public education as it emerged from the first decade of municipal reform's political victories, 1910–1920.[1] Municipal reform's tenets became the predominant orthodoxy of the system's policy making and guided its natural development within the constraints of federal realities. Federalism was sheltered by American constitutional structures. This loose-coupled structure cushioned the natural process of incrementalism in policy making so that the gradual but steady strengthening of the predominant orthodoxy at the expense of federalism did not direct widespread national attention to basic philosophic contradictions in the system.

A second contradiction lies in the definition of the public school's mission to produce a single cultural type consistent with other aspects of the enterprise. The most recent reforms have injected significantly different instructional task definitions into an organism of domestic policy which was designed specifically to reject similar task definitions over half a century ago. Thus, the host organism has a strong tendency to reject these as inimical to its proper development and functioning, and the new implants have a tendency toward destroying their host. Finally, less apparent is the difference between the weakness of the decaying ideological roots of the educational policy system and its seemingly flourishing new growth. The natural developmental tendencies of the educational policy system toward expansion, centralization, and professional bureaucratization have been markedly stimulated by governmental interventions since 1965. Many of its secondary doctrines have been carried toward their logical ends. Other ideological aspects, however, especially its root tenets, have lost much of their credibility. This growing imbalance is likely to produce some of the system's most severe conflicts in the next decade.

Edith Mosher and Jennings Wagoner, Jr., point out that "when . . . profound questions are raised about the meaning and significance of widespread political controversies over education, then it is necessary to probe the ideological underpinnings of the whole system."[2] This approach is necessary because the normal incremental policy-making process rests to a significant degree on ideological assumptions "introduced into policy analysis as though they were settled fact."[3] Policy assumptions are an organized set of interlocking generalizations or principles about the organization of a public service. Even a loosely organized set of mistaken beliefs can serve to guide the incremental policy-making process of an organization, so long as they meet the requirements of two tests. First, they must have a consensus-building character; they must be accepted by the society as representing the authoritative articulation of societal beliefs to guide the action of individual groups and governmental units. Second, they must have developed the characteristic of a myth. That is, their public acceptance must be such that they are no longer seen as political issues. Instead, they must disappear beneath the surface of political controversy, their acceptance taken for granted as the way things are and are supposed to be. Then they have been introduced as settled fact to guide policy formation. Probing the ideological underpinnings of a policy system raises two key questions. What foundation beliefs provide the point of departure for its natural developmental tendencies? Toward what ends is it inclined to move? These questions asked about the American educational enterprise focus attention, first, on the basic doctrines upon which the twentieth-century public school system rests, especially the educational policy system, and, second, on its natural developmental proclivities.

## THE MUNICIPAL REFORM IN EDUCATION

The watershed of public conflicts which saw municipal reform's doctrines translated into a dominant political myth may be found between approximately 1890 and 1920. The 1896 national election has been identified as a national turning point election.[4] The turn of the century municipal reform movement developed in a climate of corruption in the urban political machine and the city boss. The result was a loss of credibility about all government services and a developing tax-saving ideology. The reform was also a response to a new set of social, economic, and technological conditions in American life. Most significant among these changes was the transition between 1900 and 1910 of America from a rural and agricultural society to an urban and industrial one. The predominant nineteenth-century philosophy of democratic government, a Jacksonian interpretation of Jeffersonian thought, supported individualism above collective action, frequent changes in office, and laymen over continuance and professionals and was suspicious of government. This political creed combined with the post–Civil War corruption, especially of the largest cities, was attacked by the municipal reform movement with a new philosophy of government. The reform's image of government was a rejection of the nineteenth-century federal decentralized and diffused power conceptualization of democratic government. It was, instead, modeled on the corporate government of the newer developing industrial organization of the turn of the century. It was also, as Dwight Waldo said: "a reinterpretation of the meaning of democracy for America, one for the new, urban America."[5]

The reform provided in a single package a political and administrative program. One of the influences shaping that politico-administrative paradigm was the image of the business executive appropriate to what is now considered a traditional industrial organizational model, one hierarchically structured to produce highly centralized policy making and control. The reform's program advocated the concentration of power and the professionalization of public services walled off from grass-roots client and political influences. Its stated aims were equality, efficiency, and strong, honest government. Its means were the centralization of domestic services managed by professionals trained in the use of scientific methods, for example, the city manager, who was accountable to small lay groups similar to the industrial corporations' board elected by the short ballot, preferably in at-large, nonpartisan elections. Consistent with its ideology, the movement was manned primarily by financial and professional leaders, including college professors and school superintendents. The movement aimed at cutting the city machine's roots. However, the reformers also, as Samuel Hays pointed out: "deplored the decentralized ward system in large part because it empowered members of the lower and lower-middle classes (many of whom were immigrants)."[6] Thus, municipal reform reveals a social class bias both in the composition of its leadership and in its political ideology. The same class bias characterized its educational reform membership, and its ideology of educational governance reflected the same corporate model. Its administrative image aped that same business executive, and its delivery system was based on factory analogies.

The specific problems which triggered the educational aspects of similar political conflicts also had their roots in the cities. Joseph Rice's assessment of the urban schools in 1893, the Coleman Report of that era, shocked people by its indictment of both the lack of quality and equality within the existing system. Rice's analysis focused public attention on political machine intervention in the schools. His solutions reflected the political ideology of municipal reform as it applied to the governance of education. His report added ammunition to a conflict which had been developing for years between school superintendents and school boards. In 1895 occurred the eruption of battles which R. E. Callahan described as: "the boldest attack ever made by school administrators as a group upon school boards."[7] Had it succeeded, a superintendent's tenure in office would have been assured. Boards would have become advisory to professional administrators, who would have run the schools. Despite their defeat in 1895, the struggle continued. Many aspects of the professional school's agenda were incorporated in the reforms that were made in education during the next decades. Municipal reform's political myth in education rests upon three major doctrinal tenets and their operational corollaries. All three had the manifest purpose of destroying the political corruption of the urban boss system and its impact on education. Briefly, the three major tenets are the separation of public service from politics, the belief in professionalism, and the view of the community as unitary.

## The Separation of Politics and Education

The separation of politics and education was seen as necessary for order, efficiency, and effectiveness as well as for equality in the delivery of educational services. The belief that politics and public education ought to be separated assumes that providing one of the largest and most pervasive public services in the society can be apolitical. The political slogan was manifestly an attack on the city machine. The muckrakers' exposés had set the stage for freeing the educational governance system from the political machine, its ward bases, and their bosses. The political machine's representational base was rooted in ethnic neighborhood politics. The reform aimed at eliminating or at least depressing the political power of these neighborhoods. The historical evidence, however, indicates that the reform's bias went far beyond a desire for honest government to clean up the corruption of the ethnic and Catholic political machines. Hays points out that the reformers' intention was not simply to turn out bad men to be replaced by good ones; their purpose was to alter the occupational and class origins of the policy makers. David Tyack, following Hays's lead, found this to be true in education too: "Underlying much of the reform movement was an elitist assumption that prosperous, native-born Protestant Anglo-Saxons were superior to other groups and thus should determine the curriculum and the allocation of jobs."[8]

Governmental mechanisms, especially at the local level, were fashioned to operationalize the doctrine of the separation of education from politics. These were to (1) reduce the political machine's hold on schools, (2) change the social composition of school boards, (3) decrease the influence on schools of neighborhoods with their ethnic and class variations, (4) increase the accessibility of educational decision-making centers to upper-middle-class and professional interest groups, and (5) refashion the school's policy-making system along the lines of the corporate model. Significant structural changes used to separate the educational policy-making and administrative system from the established political system included the separation of the time of local school district elections from other local elections, the development of local school districts deliberately drawn with boundary lines not coterminous with other local governments wherever possible, and the reduction of the size of school boards to conform to the corporate model.

A more significant governmental mechanism for cutting the machines' roots was the recruitment of school board members through nonpartisan, districtwide, at-large elections. This mechanism almost guarantees the election of socially visible, upper-middle-class candidates. This was precisely the virtue proclaimed for this pattern by one of its most effective advocates, Ellwood Cubberley, professor of educational administration at Stanford early in the century. Cubberley was an omnipresent consultant to innumerable school districts for much of the early part of this century. His textbook, *Public School Administration*, first published in 1916 and reprinted several times, dominated that field's training. It is an example of economic class prejudice as much as prejudice against the urban ethnics. The central doctrine of separating schools from politics with its inferred mechanisms of the corporate model was intended to keep the "wrong" people from influencing school policy. It made educational policy less vulnerable to the political machine. Cubberley was quite consistent when he wrote: "The larger the city the more important that the ward system be abandoned."[9]

These doctrines are negative operational correlates that are needed to implement the primary doctrine of keeping politics out of education. The central governmental feature embodying this doctrine at both state and local district levels, the corporate board, is ill suited for public debate and deliberation. It is, instead, a design for general oversight and prudential control. Its natural ethos is public trustee-

ship rather than representation; its internal norms are toward consensus building; its natural external political function is symbolic
reassurance. Leadership, the initiation of action, and the public debate of issues, which, in democratic societies normally precede
action, are foreign to its fundamental character. Nor did the educational reformers intend otherwise. Certainly Cubberley understood
this, as his statements about the desirable boards for both states and
local districts indicate. A true board of education, the most desirable
type of educational board in his words, "is the small appointed
board, composed of citizens of the state, acting as a board of direc-
tors of a corporation would act and exercising general control over
the appointed executive of the board." What is meant by "exercising
general control" is indicated clearly by Cubberley's fuller description
of the local board advocated by the reform:

> A reduction in size to a body small enough to meet around a single table and
> discuss matters in a simple, direct and business-like manner, under the guid-
> ance of a chairman who knows how to handle public business, and then take
> action as a whole, is very desirable. With such a board, long evening meetings
> are unnecessary. If the board confines itself to its proper work, an hour a
> week will transact all of the school business which the board should handle.
> There is no more need for speeches or oratory in the conduct of a school
> system than there would be in the conduct of a national bank.[10]

So much for public debate about educational issues!

## Professional Neutral Competence

A dominant political paradigm must contain as one of its key elements a leadership rationale or else it will not predominate. Ruling
class theory has provided an apologia for power in most societies.
The reform's functional equivalent was supplied by its administrative doctrine of professional neutral competency. This is the belief
that professionals operating as technical experts in their public service area make decisions which are value-free and apolitical. The
apolitical aspect of this image was supported by the corporate model
of government. The value-free decision aspect was the apologia for
the superintendent's leadership influence in the schema of policy
making and administration. It rested upon the society's new religion
in public life, science. School administrators had appealed to the
Social Darwinism of Herbert Spencer in their struggles against the

boards and the nineteenth-century politics of pluralism from at least 1890.[11] From 1895 on, the business-industrial analogy was increasingly used by school administrators in their continued struggles to reform educational government.[12] The emergence in 1910 of the scientific management movement, a strand of reform, combined the virtues of science with those of the business-industrial analogy for the school reformers' agenda.[13] It made a value-free science of administration believable. Scientific management is primarily associated with the work of Frederick Taylor. His scientific bent was almost entirely naked empiricism. His goal and that of the scientific management movement, as described by Waldo, was: "to discover the One Best Way to perform complex human operations . . . the dream of making social science really scientific."[14] The claims made by advocates of Taylor's system for efficiency, financial savings, and scientific management were used by school administrators to support their view of educational administration and its leadership function in the new political schema.

## The Myth of the Unitary Community

The third major municipal reform doctrine, perhaps the most important, underpinning and shaping the educational enterprise was the conceptualization of the school district as a single social entity, the school community. This doctrine and the meaning of the term is that:

> regardless of ethnic, racial, religious, economic, or political differences and group conflicts in other arenas of urban life, education need not, and should not if it could, recognize or legitimize those differences. Education is a process that must not be differentiated according to section or class. Learning is the same phenomenon, or should be, in every neighborhood.[15]

One appealing element of this view is its redefinition of egalitarian democracy toward sameness. Since differentiating programs of the day were clearly unequal, it was easy to assume undifferentiated ones would be equal. A second appeal of this view was its reflection of the romantic in Western culture. "A consensual, integrated, organic community was and is an abiding standard for many American intellectuals."[16] The conceptualization also supported the separation of education from politics. It furnished an additional argument for nonpartisan, at-large board elections. Not only should the appropriate governmental structure of reform break the school district's elections from the established political machine, but the unitary community value required that it should also recruit a lay aristocracy, the "best" people, to man its central representative agencies, local and state boards. So, for example, one of Cubberley's justifications of the small board elected at large was the doctrine of the unitary community with its inherent social class bias:

> The tendency of people of the same class or degree of success in life to settle in the same part of the city is matter of common knowledge. The successful and the unsuccessful; the ones who like strong and good government, and the ones who like weak and poor government; the temperate and the intemperate elements; and the business and the laboring classes. One of the important results of the change from ward representation to election from the city at large . . . is that the inevitable representation from these "poor wards" is eliminated, and the board as a whole comes to partake of the best characteristics of the city as a whole. The members represent the city as a whole, instead of wards; they become interested in the school system as a unit, instead of parts of it. . . . Better men are almost always attracted to the educational service when election . . . at large . . . is substituted for ward representation.[17]

This view of the school district as a single community, a whole, a united organic entity easily leads to a view of the school system as a unit, a single giant machine. This view in turn justified the struggle of school superintendents for unit control in the administration of school districts. The struggle continuing into the 1930s focused most often specifically on the unification of two offices, the superintendent for business and the instructional superintendent, into links in a chain of command. The term more generally meant the combination of all administration into a single hierarchical pyramid responsible to a chief school officer, the superintendent, who in turn was the sole officer reporting directly to the board. Independent reporting to boards by other central officers or school principals was viewed as inefficient and bad management. It was also seen as improper meddling by boards in professional matters. Thus, the unitary community doctrine added support to the educational adaptation of Taylor's "one best way" of scientific management.

The reform doctrine also ideologically reinforced the thrust for consensual politics and policy making that was built into the corporate board, scientific management, and the rational bureaucratic system. The school community view of the district as unitary regardless of its size or social complexity functioned as a criterion reference to distinguish legitimate from illegitimate issues as well as participants. Educational issues stated in terms which violated this unitary community picture, for example, concepts which had as their reference, racial, ethnic, religious, or social class differences, were obviously considered illegitimate. Controversies involving particular neighborhoods were labeled as "special interest" politics and therefore illegitimate. So too, public debate over handling of a particular school building's problem was seen as inimical to the pursuit of the best interests of the school community. Such problems are viewed as internal organizational issues to be dealt with by the rational organization's professional bureaucracy, its expertise, and its specialized methods.

As a matter of course, the reform needed to cope with the reality of the pedagogical problems which had led to it. The stubborn realities beneath these were the expansion of education through compulsory education laws, the wave of immigration, and the rapid movement of populations off the farms into the cities. The most important doctrinal correlate of the unitary community tenet was the melting pot definition of the school's mission. The educational program also was viewed as unitary, and the melting pot philosophy became the dominant thrust in the curriculum. The reformer's mandate was to implement an elite education system for all. The needs and values of ethnic or class neighborhoods different from the dominant ones were ignored or considered to be hostile to good education. Rather than using these categories to define educational policy making, its goal was to eliminate, suppress, or, at least, to overlook them. Issues which singled out parts of the district for different attention were perceived as inherently divisive and wrong thinking. Implied in the melting pot curriculum is the promise of upward social mobility through education. It was a special redefinition of equality different from its pluralistic Jacksonian predecessor. Implicit in this doctrine was a monocultural educational mission modeled on its definition of the "better" people. As Tyack said: "It was the mission of schools to imbue children of the immigrants and the poor with uniformly WASP ideals."[18] The educational delivery system's policy direction may best be seen in this melting pot curriculum. The differentiation of the pupil as a person with unique potential is not compatible with this curricular orientation. Individualized instruction in this context is conceptualized as a means—

never an end—for breaking pupils away from their cultural roots whether these were European ethnic, American rural, or urban lower-class cultures. Charles Silberman reports how Leonard Covello, the first Italo-American to become a principal in the New York City schools, described the impact of this educational delivery system: "We were becoming Americans by learning how *to be ashamed of our parents.*"[19] More subtle but no less real, this delivery system policy implies a docile learner worked on by a professionally trained teacher supervised by scientific managers. That work was viewed as going on in a mass production plant, the school building. The factory model became embedded in American thought about the school, with the pupil conceptualized as material to be worked on, not as a member of the organization. The melting pot mission adapted to the site level of education tended to do precisely what Mary Abigail Dodge had deplored in 1880: "The thing which a school ought not to be, the thing which our system of supervision is strenuously trying to make the school into, is a factory, with the superintendents for overseers and the teachers for workmen."[20]

The factory analogy used by schoolmen long before the reform might not accurately describe the reality of classrooms and school buildings, but this view of the organizational workplace of the industrial corporate model falls coherently in place within that conceptualization of the educational enterprise with its corporate board, professional administrative leadership, scientific management, and bureaucratic policy making. The addition of the unitary community doctrine to those of the apolitical nature of educational government and professional neutral competence provided a full underpinning for educational policy making. As E. E. Schattschneider wrote: "All forms of political organization have a bias in favor of the exploitation of some kinds of conflict and suppression of others because organization is the mobilization of bias."[21] The unitary community definition of issues provided the criterion reference to go along with the governmental structure and administrative orientation of the new educational policy system.

## A BASIC GOVERNANCE CONTRADICTION

The governance model of the reform sought to refashion the educational enterprise by fitting each of its units into a giant corporation

pattern. But throughout its subsequent history this consistent ideological system has been confronted by another set of governance
realities inconsistent with and often hostile to its basic nature —
American constitutional federalism and its political philosophy. The
coexistence of these two systems has shaped the character of the
educational enterprise as a whole. The reform's conceptualization of
educational policy making rests on the assumption that all powers
are (or should be) integrated into a single, monolithic, smooth-run-
ning unit, which, like a giant machine, would ensure realization of
the public good if the parts were just maintained in proper working
order. The ideology of municipal reform fostered a civics textbook
hierarchical cascade model of political control. This model assumes
that policy decisions flow from legislature to state department, to
local board, to central office, to school site. Each intervening structure is believed to be guided by goals sent from above and by specific
conditions found at lower levels in the cascade. At each level in the
policy system, the cascade framework expected policy goals to be
referred to education professionals for interpretation and application. That expectation, in turn, relies on two factors for its validity
and reliability: scientifically based expertise and professional norms.
The training of professional administrators and teachers rested on the
assumption of a scientific "one best way," guided by research, and
on the acquisition of appropriate norms for the use of expertise in
schools of education. The methods of scientific management require
centralization of authority and tight-linked hierarchical control by
supervisors of subordinates with definite, preferably measurable,
direction of all processes performed. In addition to business methods
of fiscal accountability, the development of the field of psychological measurement and standardized testing provided necessary tools
for tighter internal accountability structures. The time and motion
supervision of teachers in the 1920s was a logical product of scientific management.

Growth, centralization, professional bureaucratization, and autonomy became the principal development features of the new political
paradigm. These were the tendencies of the municipal reform movement. Those who commanded technical knowledge under these circumstances eventually controlled the system. This same doctrine
functioned as an ideological buffer against pluralistic values and
against political intervention except as this can be exerted through
the central boards. At the same time it fostered professional autonomy through leadership of these bodies under the policy rubric that

"boards make policies and school administrators carry them out" by assuring that the administration functioned as the board's central source of scientific information and policy proposals. At the state level, also, buffer mechanisms, for example, state boards and chief state school offices partly independent from elected state officials, were strengthened and new ones developed to protect state bureacracies from elected officials and lay interest groups. The political philosophy of reform is a big government with a centralizing ideology which justifies professional experts in hierarchically organized bureaucracies as the governors of the system. However, as D.W. Brogan pointed out:

> It is a dangerous and idle dream to think that the state can be ruled by philosophers turned kings or scientists turned commissars. For if philosophers become kings or scientists commissars, they become politicians and the powers given to the state are powers given to men who are rulers of states, men subject to all the limitations and temptations of their dangerous craft.[22]

The new structures created a new vulnerability.[23] The void left by the political party separation was filled by upper-middle-class social and economic interest groups. The research by G. S. Counts, published in 1928, on the social composition of school boards made it clear that the social groups which led the reform now sat on the boards. The resulting policy system's capacity to heed and respond to the needs of racial, ethnic, and social class neighborhoods that lacked board representation was markedly reduced. Less obvious was another fundamental change in educational policy making. The larger the school district, the more remote is its policy-making center from teaching/learning activities. As that distance increases, the probabilities are greater that policies will be universalistic and impersonal. Paradoxically, confronted with the realities of the intractable nature of teacher/pupil classroom relations, such policies result in the increased bureaucratic behavior of teachers and in the autonomous condition of the school site but with a decrease of accountability for pupil learning.[24] The reform's separation of education and politics results in the increase in the central system's accountability to those urban elites who take time for its governance but decreases the delivery system's accountability to its clients and the neighborhoods. An increase in universalistic and impersonal policies and regulations commonly results in an increase in worker routine, mindless behavior, and alienation—not unlike the effects of most large-scale industrial production systems on their workers.

This system was superimposed upon the constitutional structures of the American federal system of government, which is fundamentally nonhierarchical. Its salient feature is the brute fact of structural divisions of power and authority in the system's organization of governance units. In its educational government, the obvious structural divisions are those separating the system into levels: a four-tiered arrangement of national, state, and local school districts and site level attendance area units. Each of these displays its own decision-making centers, administrative structures, and norms related to their several peculiar governance processes. Almost as obvious as these horizontal separations are the vertical fissures or "cracks" in the system at the state and national levels, for example, the divisions of executive, legislative, and judicial powers. Less obvious, but nonetheless real, are those between central district subunits (for example, board, central office specialized units, and districtwide organized interest groups that are both lay and professional education groups) and those at the site level between teachers, administrators, and pupils within school buildings and around the site (for example, neighborhood and parent groups).

Only the political concept of sovereignty seems strong enough to express the degree to which local authority structures are independent of state level policy processes in education. Although state constitutions place sovereignty entirely at the state level, political citizenship by residents of local school districts is tremendously vital and effective. (Ask any school board member who has participated in a careless school attendance boundary change, the decision to close a building due to declining enrollment, or a school desegregation planning process.) Moreover, local school boards were at work organizing and monitoring the delivery of educational services before there were any state constitutions. These factors have created and been sustained by the "religion of localism," which sees sovereign control of school governance as lodged in the local district board. "Dual sovereignty"[25] is the first brute fact in school governance which must be understood to realistically appraise state and national policy effects. Although the state is constitutionally paramount, its sovereignty is clearly shared with local districts.

The problem of dual sovereignty in education is further complicated by the extent to which individual school sites are structurally and politically disconnected from the control and authority of school boards and central office managers. The school site is the basic unit of educational program development, the focus of loyalty for students and their parents, an expression of neighborhood identity and culture, and frequently a major social center providing opportunities for entertainment or enrichment. These factors, combined with structural reinforcement through PTA and various advisory group structures organized by school sites, have meant that control over school site operations through national intervention programs, state regulations, school board policy decisions, and/or central administration planning, budgeting, or evaluation activities is in many ways just as problematic as is control over districts by state level structures. Consequently, one needs to differentiate between *district* and *site* level governance structures as well as to differentiate between state and local district governance units.

The American school building organization itself simultaneously supports two dissimilar decisional systems. Both are needed to cope with the policy demands of higher authorities and the requirements of the person-to-person work of instruction and learning. The first, the administrative system, meets the bureaucratic needs of the organization and displays the formal hierarchical decision-making structure and processes of most governmental bureaus. The second is primarily concerned with the requirements of the instructional task of teachers working with pupils. It often is more creative, informal, and flexible. These two decisional systems interact and are mutually supportive much of the time. Sometimes they conflict. In general, local norms and understandings of participants govern which system has preeminence over what sorts of decisions. Effective policy development needs to be conscious of these internal normative systems for decision making, especially in dealing with crises, in order to avoid careless disruption of these customary decisional systems while dealing with solutions to specific crises.[26]

If the structural divisions between the various levels (site, district, state, and national) are viewed as "horizontal" fissures in educational governance, there are equally important "vertical" separations between functionally distinct units at each level. The division of power and authority in educational governance creates not just separate identities for its structures but also a broad array of "cracks" or fissures in the system where structural units are only loosely coupled to each other. The predominant orthodoxy stressed the hierarchical integration of the system through a rational organizational model of a careful subordination among units, a system of "checks and balances." Morton Grodzins, using the model of federalism as his frame of reference, emphasized the multiple "cracks" in the system as points of access for interested groups and individuals to exercise significant but limited influence over governmental operations.[27] Policy is the overall result of ongoing interactions between different substructures, each with limited powers and divergent interests.

Without the loose-coupled, structurally decentralized nature of federalism, the fuller implications of the reform probably would have been rejected. The establishment of a single national policy system for education or the abolition of the local school district did not appear feasible for a new group of reformers even after half a century of the gradual strengthening of American belief in the reform's doctrines.[28] Instead, precisely because the reform's ideology had to wend its way over time through the thickets of the federal structure, state by state, from local district to district, it was able to wage limited political conflicts, gradually occupying more ground after the turning point conflicts early in the century that established its doctrinal preeminence. These conditions of federalism, ill suited to the reform's idealized model, were, nonetheless, well suited to its political needs for limited conflicts and a consensual political style. Once the reformers were organized and their ideology articulated, the realities of federalism helped to contain the scope of political conflicts.

Control of the scope of conflict is the prime instrument of political conflict. The tactics of limiting or expanding political conflicts are influenced by the federal structure. Indeed, the American federal structure itself is the result of major strategic considerations for controlling the contagion of political conflict. One way to restrict conflict is to localize it as the federal structures of states and local districts do. Another form of restriction is the mobilization of bias through organizational structures and ideology. Schattschneider pointed out:

> One-party systems . . . have been notoriously useful instruments for the limitation of conflict and depression of political participation. This tends to be equally true of measures designed to set up nonpartisan government or measures designed to take important public business out of politics altogether.[29]

Many issues which had been rife in the public political turmoils of 1890–1910 were translated into private matters for board and administration policy making by the reform's ideology and progress. Privatization of conflict within social and economic elites and especially inside professional bureaucracies in educational politics is exactly what the structure of educational government resulting from the municipal reform and its political ideology support. Consequently, the politics of education have traditionally been the low-visibility politics of informal agreement and consensus building among educational interest groups. It has conferred special advantages on the insider.

> It is the politics of the sacred, rural rather than secular, urban community; a politics of the priesthood rather than the hustings. The two genres of politics are different in kind. The politics of the hustings are visible and thrive on conflict and its resolution. The colorful kaleidoscope and calaphonic calliope of the campaign is its milieu. The politics of the priesthood are hidden and shrouded in mystery. They subsist on the informal development of consensus prior to public debate. The whisper campaign and the etiquette of gossip are its social climates. The one functions best when confronted with a well-organized loyal opposition; the other, avoiding confrontations has produced educational politics devoid of a loyal opposition, lacking the power of self-criticism and amenable to the influence of minorities, particularly the educational professionals, until recently.[30]

The municipal reform's doctrines did not eliminate nor suppress politics in education. What they did was substitute a different, non-party, social, and economic elite interest group politics increasingly influenced by organized professionals for the pluralistic politics which had existed. Numerous research studies have documented the tendency through most of this century for education policy to be initiated by administration-led professional groups at each level of governance.[31] The myth is not apolitical. The reform's doctrine is a thoroughgoing apologia for the power of the strong, professional, bureaucratic state. In effect, the municipal reform papered over fundamental social cleavages for more than half a century by promising to solve the underlying problems, especially, though not only, in education. The reform's myth reduced conflict in education by redefining political issues and restructuring the educational policy-making system. The reform's doctrines became the ideological underpinnings of the educational enterprise's predominant orthodoxy, but the overall structure of federalism remained as its constitutional reality, and much of the ideology of federalism continued giving ground to the predominant orthodoxy stubbornly and slowly throughout most of this century.

By the mid-1950s the system was more centralized. Its operations and management had become strongly established in professional bureaucracies. It had come closer to producing universal schooling than had any large society in the history of the human race. It had functioned to a significant degree as a major route of social mobility for the children of many immigrants and people moving off the farms into the cities. It had successfully played a major role in preparing workers for an industrial society, including people for higher educational training in management and for the technical specializations of such a society. At the same time it had become more autonomous and increasingly detached from the political mainstream of American life.

All organizations, including special governments as in American education, tend to maximize different value preferences from those of the general society. The more insulated they are from general widespread controversies of the society and the longer that insulation continues, the greater the degree of divergence of value preference displayed by them in their decisions. That divergence does not continue endlessly without check from the larger society, however. Their authority for allocating values and distributing resources arises from a sort of benign neglect or direct legal authorization, often a combination of both, as is the case in the twentieth-century educational enterprise. Implicit in their exercise of authority is the assumption that their actions will not visibly clash with the dominant political beliefs of the society. Also implied is the assumption that they will adequately provide the services for which they were created. When the public perceives the service as inadequate or improperly delivered, even more when that exercise of authority is perceived as misused, controversies emerge which spread beyond the organization's privatized conflicts. The more prolonged and widespread they become, the more they come to be viewed as requiring the attention of political branches of government. They lose their private character and become public affairs. Persisted in long enough, such conflicts will disturb the dominant political paradigm, first by carrying it to its logical extreme and then by challenging it. This is what happened to the politics of education during the last two decades.

## AN ERA OF NATIONAL INTERVENTION

During the 1960s the educational enterprise came under increasing attack. At first, the specific target of these attacks was the educational establishment, especially its administrators, the leadership of its professional organizations.[32] Before the end of the next decade the traditional politics of education had been upset, every major unit of the system had experienced attacks, and the enterprise itself was challenged. In the words of Tyack:

> People on both ends of the ideological spectrum began to propose basic alternative structures of schooling—vouchers, performance contracting, radical decentralization, free schools, alternative schools within the public system—and even the abolition of compulsory schooling or the deliberate deschooling of society.[33]

The public discussion of such issues is an indicator that the ideological assumptions which had been introduced into educational policy analysis, as though they were settled fact over half a century ago, are no longer so considered. The process of demythologizing the ideological underpinnings of the educational enterprise is underway. This condition is in large part the result of over two decades of national intervention policies, a change in role relations between the national government and the other members of the family of educational governments.

The historic role of the national government had been to provide general aid within a few broad categories (for example, technical and vocational education) to states and local districts without significant policy-shaping restrictions other than the customary prudential financial safeguards. It also supplied technical information and assistance in response to state or local requests in specialized areas. One aspect of its changed role began modestly with the National Defense Education Act (NDEA) of 1958. The national government's grant-in-aid power was used to stimulate changes in educational policies through differential funding. Earmarked categories of funds provided financial incentives to fund curriculum projects and purchase specific services. The categorical grant instrument to shape educational policies in local schools was greatly expanded by the passage of the Elementary and Secondary Education Act (ESEA) of 1965. By the late 1970s at least four hundred programs in education were administered by some seventy different national agencies.[34] Many of these were lodged neither in the Bureau of Education nor even in the Department of Health, Education, and Welfare. Thus, through a continuous expansion of the intervention mechanism of fiscal incentives with categorical regulations, the national government has become a major source of new educational policies. A second aspect of the national government's new role is seen in the influence of the federal judiciary. No single public decision has had a greater effect on education than the Supreme Court's 1954 decision to desegregate the schools. The enormous expansion of the judiciary's role in desegregation cases and the direct administration of local schools subsequent to finding a condition of segregation are only part of the growing influence of this branch in educational policy making. Judicial influence now includes pupil discipline, records, bilingual programs, and the rights of the handicapped. The implementing mass of adminisrative guidelines, regulations, evaluation procedures, and forms to be filled out resulting from the combination of national legislation, categorical programs, and judicial decisions is nothing less than staggering. The impact upon state and local educational organizations and policies of this quantity of matter alone would have been enough to throw into disequilibrium the previously delicately balanced system. In addition, the policy accretion of more than two decades of intervention has resulted in an inharmonious mass of contradictory policies rather than a coherent program of reform.

The present dissonance in national intervention policies reflects the influences of significantly different, sometimes antithetical, ideological concerns of quite diverse constituencies. These range across a spectrum from Cold War enthusiasts to civil rights advocates. Their shifting, short-term, and shaky coalitions and equally fluid adversarial relations shaped many of the national intervention policies. Two events, the 1954 *Brown* decision and the 1957 Soviet launching of Sputnik, were political catalysts dramatically accelerating the extension of elements of the predominant orthodoxy toward some of their logical conclusions. The immediate fallout from Sputnik persuaded Americans that (1) their country was falling behind the Russions in the space race, (2) this was the result of losing the trained manpower race, and (3) the underlying blame for this state of affairs was to be found in the poor quality of American education. By the 1960s even as strong a former ally as James Conant had recanted his previous twenty-two-year support of what he now termed "the educational establishment."[35] Liberals who had defended the educational profession against the right-wing attacks in the early 1950s (for example, the curriculum conflict in Pasadena and the book-burning battles in Scarsdale) often joined leaders of the scientific, military, and centrist political establishments as critics of education. The passage of the NDEA in 1958 followed hard on the heels of

Sputnik. The speed of this response reflected the policy planning already underway in science and military establishments to refashion the school's curriculum toward what came to be known as the new math, the new physics, etc.[36] Their goal, as Silberman wrote: "was to construct 'teacher proof' materials that would 'work' whether teachers liked the materials or not or taught them well or badly."[37] This would certainly have been the high point of Taylor's "one best way."

Silberman's observations at the end of the 1960s on the classroom effects of these national programs were that "the schools themselves are largely unchanged."[38] His explanation for this failure was, in part, the reformer's ignorance of the realities of the federal nature of the system. "Because the reformers were university scholars with little contact with public schools or schools of education, moreover, and because they neglected to study earlier attempts at curriculum reform, they also tended to ignore the harsh realities of classroom and school organization."[39] Whatever the failures of these curriculum reform efforts, the intervention programs were not without effects. Whether from ignorance or hubris, these efforts to bypass teachers and to attack the educational establishment saw each of these three distinct constituencies claiming the rights of expertise, pitting against one another different referents of the doctrine of neutral competency in their political conflicts over the curriculum. Paradoxically, although the reformers extended the doctrine of neutral competency in their claims of expertise, they denied the legitimacy of its use by school administrators and teachers. Implicit in these political conflicts was a weakening of the doctrine of the separation of education and politics. These post-Sputnik curricular programs also pushed the unitary community correlate of the melting pot curriculum toward one of its logical implications. A dilemma becomes apparent when one asks what is the meaning of the goal of equality of achievement for all students with the same elite curriculum and criteria. The demand for more science, more math, and higher educational achievement was the equivalent of demanding equal elitism. The residue of these demands may be seen in the stress for additional standardization of the system. Modern testing packages, evaluation policies, and state assessment programs owe much to Sputnik. The packaged interventions to produce universal excellence reinforced the joy-killing, mindless, routinization of teaching/learning.

The educational policy effects of the *Brown* decision were slower in their unfolding but run both wider and deeper. By deciding that separate is not equal, the Supreme Court took a position consistent with the unitary community doctrine. Segregation was a blatant violation of the unitary community doctrine and the melting pot mission of the schools. The painfully slow but continuing pressure from the courts for desegregation in de facto as well as de jure instances is a continuing extension in application of that definition of the school's mission. Given the demographic realities of larger school districts, the use of busing to achieve the goals of equality as defined by de facto desegregation is a logical step, as is the use of formulas for racial balance in schools. However, the categories needed to operationalize racial balance create a cognitive map of the population that contradicts that of the unitary community underpinning the melting pot mission.

With the ESEA in 1965 the national government's policies used differentiated population categories to define intervention programs for producing equality. Compensatory education programs were developed to overcome what was seen as the cultural deprivation of minority pupils. The funds and efforts put into compensatory education have in general produced little increase in academic achievement. Tyack noted: "The actual funds that reached ghetto schools were often small, prompting the comment that pouring in funds at the top of school bureaucracies was like feeding a horse in order to feed the sparrows. Often large sums went to pay new middle-class bureaucrats to administer the new programs."[40] The resistance of professional educationists to desegregation and the failures of compensatory education efforts were part of the backdrop of demands by minority groups for community control of schools. Conflicts between minorities and professional groups led to the charge that keeping politics out of education was a dishonest smokescreen by white professionals to keep minority groups in place. The alternatives of cultural pluralism and community control increasingly commanding the support of minority populations are a dramatic contradiction of the early century's definition of the unitary community. Community control of local school sites is precisely what the reform sought to eliminate. National policies, which, through the courts, work to establish the melting pot definition of equality, are contradicted by other national policies seeking to provide equity through compensatory programs and pluralism. The alternative delivery system mission of cultural pluralism meets the criterion value of equity—at least one politically potent definition of it—but it destroys the doctrine of the unitary community in its most significant policy assumptions. The political symbolism of community control rests on a different concept of community, one which contradicts the old doctrine's key concept. Recent programs of intervention for bilingual and special education pupils depend upon the conceptualization of the enhancement of the individual as their goal. "Individualism" so conceptualized for program definition is the ideological antithesis of the term as suited to and used in the melting pot curriculum. Its referent in the older school's mission was a differentiation of means for adjusting the pupil to a single standard and a monocultural type. Now, its referent is a differentiation in outcome as well as means.

By the end of the first decade of intervention, a third political realignment with major implications for educational policy making had entered the politics of education. The New York City teachers' strike of 1960 had a catalytic effect within the educational professions akin to that of *Brown* and Sputnik on the general public. The professional ideological base of the teacher movement is consistent with the doctrine of neutral competency and its correlate of faith in the technical expertise of teachers against administrative and board claims. But this application of the professional neutral doctrine is pitted against the administrator's application of the doctrine, a central policy assumption in education for over fifty years. The labor contract is carrying the bureaucratization of schools toward greater centralization, its logical conclusion. The continued cleavage within the professional world demonstrates for all observers that there is nothing politically neutral about the culture of professionalism. There is little left of belief that education and politics are or should be separate.

Intervention policies interact. Intervention, which emerges as inconsistent but discrete, and unrelated programs in Washington become contradictory regulations which interact upon one another at their point of impact. Their interaction produces a Catch-22 regulatory world of contradictory prescriptions for those who must implement them in classrooms and school buildings. The frustration, for example, of trying to implement a strong academic curriculum in racially balanced classrooms achieved through busing inevitably produced political backlashes from teachers and parents. The tendency of federal monitors and national bureaucrats to write off such opposition as only hostility to integration is too simplistic. By the end of the 1960s the mounting resistance to national governmental intervention in local educational settings became part of a more widely spread and growing public hostility to centralized, big government interference in local affairs. The failure of centralized program initiatives to produce significant achievement gains had become painfully obvious by the late 1960s. Whatever the reasons, pupil achievement scores on standardized tests were declining. The gap between policy making and implementation was expanding with an increasing irresponsibility as one of its results.[41] Combined with the revulsion over the war in Vietnam, the disruption of the Democratic party in 1968, and the public reaction to Watergate, the "turkeys" produced by national education programs seriously threatened the credibility of national interventions in education.

Efforts to recover that loss of credibility shaped the national intervention efforts in education of the 1970s. The growing American suspicion of big government shaped the character of national intervention policies in this last decade toward a search for legitimacy above all else. This search took several different forms, reflecting pragmatic and often conflicting tactics rather than a coherently planned strategy. The closest approximation to a strategy which characterizes the national interventions of the 1970s as a whole was a shift in target emphasis. National intervention programs of the 1970s focused significantly more on the states than had those of the 1960s.

At least two factors produced this change in target emphasis. One was the awareness of program implementation failure. The strengthening of state policy-making capacities and of state educational bureaucracies was seen in Washington circles as a necessary solution to overcome local citizen and teacher resistance or the inability to implement national programs. A second factor was a growing political conflict between the state and national governments over the question of which should govern what aspects of education. The states were demanding that their place in the Constitution be taken seriously by the national government. Another aspect of the changed tactics was a movement toward combining the most narrow categorical grant programs into somewhat larger blocks with greater involvement of the state in their control and implementation. This tactic was designed both to diffuse complaints about the narrowness of national interventions and to get the states to share in the responsibility for their implementation, as well as to shoulder some of the political conflicts generated by the program regulations. A quite different search for legitimacy, and a second tactic, was the creation of multiple advisory structures to expand citizen participation in state and local program planning, grant proposal writing, and the evaluation of programs. This tactic created legal access structures for special interest groups and local building site councils to influence educational policy making. It was a partial alternative to the demands for community control.

A third tactic in this search for legitimacy satisfied the demands of the growing political influence of teacher organizations for a cabinet post in the executive branch. One of the major arguments for this structural change in Washington was the need for a single legitimate spokesman for education, especially to deal with Congress. Fred Burke, the New Jersey Commissioner of Education, pointed out that weaknesses in the legitimacy of educational spokesmen led to the influence of special interest groups on legislation and a simplistic legislative view that the sheer production of policies resolves problems. He added: "Washington will continue to be reactive until a legitimate and powerful educational spokesman can be developed."[42] A second argument was the need to pull together the wide range of educational programs in different national agencies. In fact, the new department did not do this. Its narrow definition of scope resulted from two factors: various congressional committee interests in retaining their pieces of the educational pie and the powerful National Education Association's interest in having monopolistic influence on the new department, which would have been diluted by the range of other organized interests with stakes in a more broadly defined department. In sum, the 1970s search for legitimacy to support national intervention policies took three major directions. It placed greater emphasis on the state's responsibility for the implementation of its interventions; it expanded participation through advisory structures for special and site level interests; and it further centralized the Washington educational bureaucracy into an executive department with a cabinet post.

The present meaning of these 1970s developments for educational policy making and policies and their probable future effects can be seen in a change in the tone of national interventions, the rapid growth of state regulations, and the effects of these on local districts.

Briefly, the tone of "federal legislation is increasingly preemptive, prescriptive and regulatory."[43] The expansion of national funds has ceased since its high point in 1972, but the expansion of regulations has increased. If the national government has learned that social problems cannot be solved by throwing money at them, it has not learned that these cannot be solved by throwing regulations at them. And these are becoming punitive in tone. The public reaction to the mass of national interventions is succinctly illustrated by a recent editorial question demanding a political explanation for "how a whole melange of social problems has expanded, rather than diminished, under the weight of increasing governmental intrusion into the home, the school, the neighborhood."[44]

The states, too, have expanded their legislative and regulatory output. To cite but a few of the most obvious examples, schools have been asked to make major changes (1) in their attention to disadvantaged and minority populations through compensatory and bilingual programs; (2) in their funding and taxing patterns through statutes and court decisions aimed at increasing equalization simultaneously with decreased economic resources; (3) in response to state management control policies and procedures including phases of Program Planning and Budget Systems (PPBS), statewide testing and assessment programs, early graduation exams and standardized graduation requirements, and, in some states, site-oriented accountability policies; (4) in their emphasis on achievement outcomes through the development of competency testing; (5) in the scope of client rights through new due process and court decisions; (6) in the traditional relationships among teachers, administrators, and school boards as a result of legislation on collective bargaining, credentialing, and staff development, and (7) in the nature and extent of parent/citizen participation in planning and governance through laws involving public disclosure, advisory committees, and, more recently, school site councils. In sum, the schools have faced more different policy demands from national and state governments and from all three branches of these—executive, legislative and judicial—during the last twenty-five years, and especially in the most recent decade and a half, than in any other similar period in American history.

Regulations interact. The local districts and school building targets of regulation have lost much of the discretion they used to have in educational policy making and implementation. The changes in governmental structures produced by the combined national and state interventions have centralized more policy-making power in reorganized national and state bureaucracies than ever before. At the same time, they have created more access points for organized constituencies of special interests around specialized programs. The most serious constraint on citizen influence at the local level may, however, result from the major changes in local governance structures produced by collective bargaining. The creation of a legally sanctioned negotiation structure to determine the largest portion of the school's budget and to define working conditions produces a contractual-based set of policies for the educational enterprise near its delivery units. The labor contract is the most immediate set of local school policies from which local citizen influence is even further removed than before. National and state categorical programs, especially those in bilingual and special education, have redefined the schools' mission in terms diametrically opposed to its common curricular assumptions, the melting pot curriculum. Thus, its present mission, too, is based on contradictory ideological assumptions. The present combination of contradictory structural arrangements and mission ideologies at the local level sets the stage for major political conflicts rather than the unification of the policy system.

## CONCLUSION

Even this brief summary of recent policy changes indicates the dramatic effects experienced by the politics of education and the turbulent state of the educational enterprise itself, especially its policy-making and management subsystems. As a result, (1) the consensual and low-visibility forms of political involvement, the traditionally preferred politics of pedagogues for most of this century, no longer works well. Indeed, it no longer characterizes many of the enterprise's sectors. (2) Faced with an avalanche of social change programs, the political conflicts spawned around these and its responses to them, the nature of the American system of educational policy making and governance is itself rapidly becoming a political issue. (3) Its ideological foundations defining for policy purposes its governance as apolitical, its decision-making functions as scientific, and, for instructional purposes, its school district as a single unitary monocultural community have lost much of their consensus-building power. (4) A number of severe ideological and operational

contradictions are now embedded in the American educational enterprise, its policies, and its system of policy making. The American
system for educational policy making is facing a decade of political
conflicts in the 1980s. The educational policy system might be expected to manage the conflicts produced by these contradictions by
means of its traditional stabilizing techniques. These include (1)
localizing controversies, thus limiting political conflicts; (2) redefining ideological contradictions by adopting their words while adapting their operational meaning to fit within its paradigm; and (3)
bending for a time until the pressure for change is relaxed. But the
necessary conditions for these techniques to work are missing. Their
previous successes were achieved in a benign environment consisting
of an expanding economy, a quiescent political order, and a supportive, stable, industrial technology. None of these conditions is
now present. Nor does it appear that they are likely to emerge early
enough in the decade of the 1980s to serve the stabilizing needs of
the educational policy system.

The political conflicts envisioned are already emerging. These
conflicts arise directly from and give increased saliency to inconsistencies in educational policies. American educational policy has now
become a dissonant mass of juridical decisions, laws, administrative
guidelines, policy directions, and regulations. It once was a reasonably coherent panoply of these. It then provided political defense
for a relatively closed, autonomous policy-making system, and a
serviceable though imperfect shield for the entire public education
enterprise. Now, instead, the new patchwork of disjointed policies
provide the ideological banners for political mobilization of conflicting interests, the stakes at issue, and the necessary structural arrangements to carry political conflicts into educational policy making.
Formal access mechanisms to policy-making units of governments
granted to identified special constituencies, realistically potential
economic and psychological benefits for particular social groups, and
politically valued slogans which can attract still larger segments of
the population are the fuel of self-propelling political controversies.
Examination of the educational policy system and of the disarray of
its policies leads, first, to the conclusion that a continuation of the
increased politicization of education with even more severe and pervasive political conflicts is to be expected in the next decade. A second conclusion results from probing beneath these conflicts and
laying bare their roots of public ideology and political philosophy.
The outcome of conflicts ahead will either be a fundamental redesign

of the educational policy system or a repeal of major aspects of recent school reforms.

## NOTES TO CHAPTER 8

1.  Raymond E. Callahan, *Education and the Cult of Efficiency* (Chicago: University of Chicago Press, 1962); David D. Tyack, *The One Best System* (Cambridge, Mass.: Harvard University Press, 1974); and Dwight Waldo *The Study of Public Administration* (New York: Random House, 1963).

2.  Edith K. Mosher, and Jennings L. Wagoner, Jr., eds., *The Changing Politics of Education: Prospects for the 1980's* (Berkeley: McCutchan Publishing Co., 1978), p. 1X.

3.  Charles E. Lindblom, *The Policy-Making Process* (Englewood Cliffs, N.J.: Prentice-Hall, 1968), p. 3.

4.  Walter D. Burnham, *Critical Elections and the Mainsprings of American Politics* (New York: Norton, 1970).

5.  Dwight Waldo, *Study of Public Administration*, p. 19.

6.  Samuel P. Hays, "The Politics of Reform in Municipal Government in the Progressive Era," *Pacific Northwest Quarterly* 55 (1964): 163.

7.  Raymond E. Callahan, "The American Board of Education," in *Understanding School Boards*, ed. Peter J. Cistone (Lexington, Mass.: Lexington Books, 1975), p. 27.

8.  David Tyack, "Needed, the Reform of a Reform," *National School Boards Association, New Dimensions of School Board Leadership* (Evanston, Ill.: National School Board Association, 1969), p. 35.

9.  Ellwood P. Cubberley, *Public School Administration* (New York: Houghton Mifflin, 1916), p. 93.

10. Ibid., p. 92.

11. Raymond E. Callahan, *The Superintendent of Schools: An Historical Analysis* (Washington, D.C.: Cooperative Research Branch, U.S. Office of Education, Department of Health, Education and Welfare, 1967), pp. 68-77.

12. Ibid., p. 92.

13. Callahan, *Education and the Cult of Efficiency.*

14. Waldo, *The Study of Public Administration.*

15. Robert M. Salisbury, "Schools and Politics in the Big City," in *The Politics of Education at the Local, State and Federal Levels*, ed. Michael W. Kirst, (Berkeley: McCutchan Press, 1970), p. 20.

16. Ibid., p. 21.

17. Cubberley, *Public School Administration*, pp. 93-95.

18. Tyack, "Needed, the Reform of a Reform."

19. Charles E. Silberman, *Crisis in the Classroom: The Making of American Education* (New York: Random House, 1970).

20. Mary Abigail Dodge, quoted in Tyack, *The One Best System*, p. 82.

21. E. E. Schattschneider, *The Semisovereign People* (New York: Holt, Rinehart and Winston, 1975).

22. Denis William Brogon, preface to Bertrand de Jouvenal, ed., *Power: The Natural History of its Growth*, trans. J. F. Huntington (New York: Viking Press, 1949).

23. Salisbury, "Schools and Politics in the Big City."

24. Laurence Iannaccone, "Increasing Irresponsibility in Education: A Growing Gap Between Policy Planning and Operation Groups," in *State School and Politics*, ed. Michael W. Kirst (Lexington, Mass.: D.C. Heath, 1972).

25. Laurence Iannaccone and Peter J. Cistone, *The Politics of Education* (Eugene, Ore.: Eric Clearinghouse on Educational Management, 1974), pp. 27–29.

26. E. Mark Hanson, "The Professional Bureaucratic Interface: A Case Study," *Urban Education* 11(3) (1973).

27. Martin Grodzins, *The American System*, ed. Daniel Elayar (Chicago: Rand McNally, 1968).

28. James B. Conant, *Shaping Educational Policy*, (New York: McGraw-Hill, 1964), p. 110.

29. E. E. Schattschneider, *The Semisovereign People*, p. 12.

30. Laurence Iannaccone and Frank W. Lutz, "The Changing Politics of Education." *American Association of University Women Journal* 60 (1967): 160-162; 191-192.

31. Iannaccone and Cistone, *The Politics of Education*.

32. James B. Conant, *Shaping Educational Policy*.

33. Tyack, *The One Best System*, p. 272.

34. Samuel Halperin, *Federalism at the Crossroads: Improving Educational Policymaking* (Washington, D.C.: George Washington University Press, 1976), p. 41.

35. Conant, *Shaping Educational Policy*, p. 7.

36. Frank G. Jennings, "It Didn't all Start with Sputnik," *Saturday Review*, September 16, 1967, p. 77.

37. Silberman, *Crisis in the Classroom*, p. 181.

38. Ibid., p. 159.

39. Ibid., p. 180.

40. Tyack, *The One Best System*, p. 282.

41. Iannaccone, "Increasing Irresponsibility in Education."

42. Fred G. Burke, "The Dragon in Washington: Paper or Real?", in *Federalism at the Crossroads: Improving Educational Policymaking*, ed. Samuel Halperin (Washington, D.C.: George Washington University Press, 1976), p. 24.

43. Halperin, *Federalism at the Crossroads*, p. 19.

44. *Santa Barbara News Press*, August 27, 1980, p. F-2.

# 9 INSTITUTIONAL PARAMETERS AND THE PURPOSES OF SCHOOLING
## State Regulation of Educational Innovation*

*Robert B. Everhart*

The legislature shall provide for a system of common schools by which a free school shall be kept up and supported by each district. . . .

*Constitution*, State of California
Article IX, Section 5

It is better that working men and working women should not be able to read and write or do sums than that they should receive education from a teacher in a school run by the state. It is far better that ignorance should debase the working classes than that eternal principles should be violated.

Karl Marx, *Political Indifferentism*

Plus ça change, plus c'est la même chose.

French proverb

## INTRODUCTION

The drive toward innovation in education has become so pervasive in the past twenty-five years that it is difficult to conceive of a time when conspicuous attempts at change were not accepted as commonplace. There is some mystical quality surrounding the ethos of inno-

*I acknowledge the insightful criticisms of C.H. Edson, Sarah Everhart, and Michael S. Katz, none of whom would let me get away with simplistic thoughts and solutions. To the degree those and other errors remain, I accept full responsibility.

vation that compels educational leaders to address how their school uses the latest curriculum package, "individualizes" the mathematics program, has reorganized the school into "pods," or how principals or superintendents remove themselves from an authority position and govern by consensus, thanks to the latest training by "organizational development" specialists. At one time, it seemed that the number of innovative programs that could be attempted were limited only by the number of schools waiting in line to demonstrate their "progressivism."

Yet the results of these educational innovations seem to have been meager at best, as many told us even at the peak period of experimentation.[1] Scores on standardized tests continue to drop (even to the point where students who score in the top percentiles of the Scholastic Aptitude Test [SAT] are being as mercilously recruited by colleges as are athletes). Disenchantment with discovery techniques and the "new math" has set in, and an era that saw the application of the social sciences in the secondary schools is being replaced by one where "regular" history again prevails. To many, the new math, questioning strategies, and other progressive practices are seen as partly to blame for the surprising number of children who complete school with the barest of reading or computational skills. For all the investment of time and money in new methods, new materials, new ways to organize our schools, and new ways to teach, discontent now abounds both on the part of the general public and educators as to the changes and innovations which our educational system has experienced. As *Newsweek* magazine stated, this disillusionment

> suggests that the U.S. education's so-called wave of the future has crested. The result is that all across the nation, parents, school boards and often the pupils themselves are demanding that the schools stop experimenting and get back to the basics—in reading, writing, and arithmetic and standards of behavior to boot.[2]

The same somewhat conservative pattern is evident in the emphasis of funding agencies—what they promote and decide not to promote. In the first place, agencies like the National Institute of Education have realized a loss in real funding for 1978–1980, as has the Office of Education (OE).[3] But even considering the money that is available, the nature of the programs funded has changed as well. We hear very little any more about large-scale experiments such as the Alum Rock voucher experiment, the Experimental Schools project, or new ventures such as the Teacher Corps. This reduced emphasis on experiments aimed at some semblance of structural change is borne out by the fact that the support level in OE for grants for innovation from 1976 to 1980 has increased from $170 million to only $197 million, an increase that does not keep pace with the rate of inflation.[4] Currently, money seems headed into areas such as basic skill development, education for the disadvantaged (up over 50 percent since 1976), bilingual education (up 350 percent since 1976), and education for the handicapped, a budget category in which funding has increased 400 percent since 1976. These general trends suggest that the movement in education is toward increased quantities of present, agreed-upon schooling treatments for members of targeted groups as well as for correcting educational deficiencies identified in these groups.

The assumption reflected in these recent funding trends is that the fundamental focus of educational agencies should be on an improved distribution of resources said to affect relatively predictable educational outcomes such as reading and computational skills, work operative skills, and the like. According to this line of thinking, school knowledge appears relatively set or predefined, and the consequent problems facing educators revolve around increased distribution of that knowledge to classes of students heretofore deprived of access to that knowledge, that is, minority students, the learning and physically handicapped, and former dropouts. Knowledge and skills emphasized in programs for such students—that is, knowledge that is relatively predefined, uniformly accepted, and whose value is unquestionably deemed to be worthwhile—is then merely applied through new delivery systems (technology) and/or to a new clientele (the disadvantaged, handicapped, etc.). Educational programs that foster such knowledge can then be said to focus primarily on *distributive* issues since their main point of concern is upon a more efficient diffusion of enduring forms of knowledge to the target population(s).

The type of knowledge and skills emphasized in programs characterized by distributive issues is qualitatively different from the knowledge and skills found in educational programs that raise to the level of explicitness that which is assumed in programs that are distributively oriented. Alternatively then, knowledge systems may emphasize multiplicity rather than uniformity, may examine the assumptions behind what is known rather than to take those assumptions for granted, and can require the structural alteration of the context of schooling (such as in organizational design, authority systems, decision-making processes) as a precondition to changes in how knowledge is transmitted and generated. Programs that emphasize knowledge in its phenomenological rather than normative form will foster fundamental concern with *constitutive* issues such as how knowledge is defined, who defines it as such, its form and applications, as well as its ultimate distribution. Constitutive issues are concerned with more than the efficient distribution of resources for learning; they are concerned with the very basis of what is known and how we come to know it.

Of course, constitutive issues are much more complex, vague, and difficult to assess than are distributive issues, for they make explicit the multiple functions of schools and the varied legitimate perspectives that can be brought to bear on any one educational issue. For example, on the simple question of who defines the basis of knowledge, one can propose such possibilities as the effect of the role of the person defining knowledge, that of the person who learns, the training of those writing curricula, the impact of the organizational position on how knowledge is defined—all among a host of other variables. Because of this complexity, constitutive issues normally involve the potential for large-scale organizational and institutional change because they call into question the fundamental processes of schooling, including (but certainly not limited to) distributive issues.

Fundamental concern with distributive issues, on the other hand, take the answers to such questions for granted and propose that what is of fundamental concern is the spreading of educational knowledge to recipients and the evaluation of the results of that effort on a standardized basis. Educational programs here are considered to be more consensual in the sense that agreement on means and ends is assumed. Distributive issues, in and of themselves, usually are indicative of relatively small-scale changes in the process of schooling because they take as given the purposes of schooling and focus instead on how the outcomes of schooling are to be allocated. In this way, the difficulty of knowing how, under what conditions, or by what criteria an educational program is said to be "successful" is normally ignored.

In so calling into question fundamental issues such as who, what, why, and how, programs that emphasize constitutive issues cannot avoid making manifest the value structures and ideology that underlie support for and against any one educational program. Lacking as we usually do wholesale and definitive proof that schooling is better under arrangement A than B—indeed, having to grope with the thorny issue of the criteria for "better" and the problem of "better for whom"—consideration of such issues inevitably raises for consideration the complexities of what we believe, what lies behind our articles of faith, the issues that cloud our vision, and the degree of tolerance we are willing to grant to others for their beliefs. Resolution of these issues is not easy, and it is much more expeditious to avoid than to confront them. In fact, as I will argue later, it is in the interest of certain sectors of our society that these issues be avoided, as confrontation stands to result in potential dissolution of a system of education that serves majoritarian interests.

We then arrive at the general thrust of this essay, which is that the present disillusionment with schooling reform and, most especially, disillusionment with constitutive type changes arises from an unreal expectation that the means of schooling can be uniformly stated and evaluated outside the context of values, beliefs, and political processes—an expectation which, because it cannot be met, leads to a preoccupation with distributive change. I will propose further that those very fundamental patterns that define schooling (what I later call "institutional parameters" and which are established by the state) directly influence the type of knowledge that permeates schooling and ultimately the range of changes that might be attempted in schooling. As I hope is clear by now, my effort is toward persuasion and possibility, not toward documenting incontrovertible truth.

I wish to make clear some assumptions on which my discussion about the nature of American schooling are based. First, many have claimed that schools are bastions of stability in a changing society and that their prime (and proper) function is cultural continuance more than cultural change. I do not argue with this position as it adequately describes historical patterns in this country and others. Nor do I take issue with the overall value of cultural continuity and stability, the belief that some dimensions of any society may be worthy of being conserved and transmitted across generations and that schools can play an important role in this purpose. Yet I do dispute that schools necessarily are agencies that conserve all knowledge in society rather than subjecting it to examination and possible change. I also dispute the position that the public school, representing as it does the political system of which it is a part (the state) and in its designated role as the agency of expertise concerning formal education, can best determine those dimensions of a culture that should be preserved in relation to those that may be subject to change. Yet the proper role of schools in society is not an argument I wish to debate here; nor do I wish to propose that change necessarily is preferable to stability. I do propose, however, that decisions about the proper role of schools must be made jointly, equally, and critically by constituents, clients, and educators and that such critical awareness and the power to implement decisions arising from that awareness is fundamental to affectuating decisions about the proper role of schools. I proceed on the assumption that determination by the constituents of schools about the function and operation of those schools is a social good that should be a significant basis for evaluating all educational change. I hold to this stance because education and schooling are complex processes that do not lend themselves to facile explanations, definitions, or assessments. Consequently, critical awareness and determination of those affected by schooling are fundamental to increasing the probabilities for that diversity in schooling which accurately represents the diversity of legitimate beliefs about the purposes of schooling. Hence, while I do not advocate that all change be constitutive, I do advocate that schooling can be so organized to more accurately reflect the predominance of constitutive issues.

A second assertion concerns the nature of the state, by which I mean simply the legitimized political entity within a given geographical entity, united by common obedience to a sovereign ideal or person. Within this political entity, maintained as it is by dominant groups and coalitions of groups who see that state as necessary and productive for their interests, certain social processes are supported that serve to continue that state and to legitimize the interests of dominant groups. In other words, the cultural continuity that exists within societies is manifested through the continuation of state-sanctioned political and social structures.

Such is no less the case in American society, as the cultural continuity within our society is carried out, in part, through and within political structures called schools, where the social processes tend to support the general social structure legitimized by the state. One may argue, however, that our own system of schooling was founded on the premise that, through varied world views being represented in one comprehensive school system, plurality of interests would be preserved within a common framework. I propose that this is the case only to a limited extent and that plurality of interests in and of schooling are subordinated to the dominant interests of those groups who support the state.[5] Translated into specific actions, the system of private enterprise in American society is supported and regulated by the state through state capitalism, which in turn leads to a proclivity by the state political structure to facilitate those social relations conducive to the continuance of state capitalism and to discourage those not so conducive. Schools are part of this political structure, and once knowledge that supports the continuance of the state has been defined, a momentum exists to maintain that type of knowledge. Given this condition, emphasis on changes in schooling will be upon distributive issues that do not call into question that which is known, and especially that which may challenge the dominant interests of the state.

Often there is conformity between state political structures and the social processes of schooling in other cultures, especially centralized state systems, such as Cuba and Iran; and my point is not to single out American society as unique in this respect. But that too is the main point—it is *not* unique; the ideological regulation that occurs in other societies is equally present in our own society, the pluralism of the public school system notwithstanding. Too often we ignore this facet of political life in our society, an issue that is critical when we examine the process of change within school organizations.

My purpose here is to discuss how the state necessarily limits constitutive changes in schooling and thereby limits multiple determination of the processes of schooling. I first advance the notion that most of the studies on how educational programs are decided and implemented in schools focus on factors that account for little of the variance on issues with which schools contend as they change. This is an important point because most of the literature on the adaptability of schools to changing conditions focuses on the technological capacity of schools as organizations to make changes in their purpose and processes, and it is my belief that to focus on this technological capacity is to misdirect our interest in change. Next, I propose that the crucial factors that do influence the school's determination of purpose and process are structural/political dimensions under the control of the state rather than organizational issues that can be manipulated by change agents. In the United States, these political dimensions present in schools are influential in helping to sustain the social and cultural processes that facilitate the continuance of state capitalism. To illustrate this point, I discuss the common nature of the public school and the issue of compulsory school attendance, particularly as these dimensions subvert pluralism to the continuance of state capitalism. I conclude that decisions about educational issues and the structure of and processes within schooling cannot be viewed as organizational engineering to be engaged in by educational technicians but rather must be seen as a political issue to be resolved first through political action.

## AN ANALYSIS OF RESEARCH ON CHANGE IN EDUCATION

There exist a number of compilations or reviews of literature on educational innovation.[6] With a few exceptions, however, these compilations reflect organizational change (that is, change in the operational dynamics of the state-supported public school) as an integral, natural, and desirable process within educational organizations. Such organizations within which change is not successful are viewed in a pathological perspective—such that identifiable dimensions of the organization are ill and need to be treated, and that it is the job of the organizational diagnostician—the change agent—to provide the needed remedy.

Yet too often this diagnosis is based on faulty assumptions, the basis of which preclude continued search for the root of the problem. Let me briefly review three areas in which we find forces said to be responsible for the lackluster success of change efforts; these areas focus on the inadequate preparation/training of teachers to become managers of educational change, the fact that most change efforts are poorly conceptualized and thus difficult to implement, and, finally, the fact that any organizational change, once introduced or implemented, produces results that were not anticipated in the beginning of the change effort. Attention to such organizational issues, dealing as most do with schooling in the distributive sense, is analogous to treating cancer as a surface wound.

## Teacher Preparation

One of the more frequently held tenets about the determinants of educational progress concerns the general predisposition of the teaching staff to work effectively with new educational ideas. This notion, related to the preparation of teachers, has been addressed in various ways. Some say, for example, that the archaic methods of teacher education do not constitute adequate preparation for the work of the profession, a problem especially problematical for beginning teachers.[7] John Goodlad and M. Frances Klein point out that "teachers, in the main, lack the pedagogical skills required to induce fully effective learning." Charles Silberman, in his broad-ranging attack on American schooling, *Crisis in the Classroom*, states that there is no reason why teachers cannot turn their schools around if they so desire. Attributing much of the problem to the "mindlessness" of educational personnel, Silberman proposes that if only teachers could envision educational goals instead of training goals and could continually ask questions of intent and purpose, then the grim statistics on the lack of success within our schools would not predominate.[8] Finally, some argue that teachers must be educated in the ways in which schools operate qua organizations and consequently in techniques to improve organizational health. Such an approach requires that teachers and administrators learn techniques of effective communication so as to identify the significant problems within the school and then to go about solving them.[9]

Although many researchers attribute the failure of educational innovation to poorly trained educators, others warn about placing too much faith in the role of teachers as the precipitators of educational change. For example, Dan Lortie, in his book *Schoolteacher*, indicates that teachers concentrate their energies on core teaching tasks and show little interest in organizational affairs.[10] They are, in turn, likely to delegate to administrators those "organizational affairs" not concerned with direct interaction with students. Furthermore, the ongoing world of the teacher is conceptually simple and intuitively based rather than predicated on the abstract rationality which usually is part of major efforts at organizational change.[11] Finally, as some have argued, even given superior training in undergraduate days, the socialization process of beginning teachers often erases a great deal of that idealism gained during the training period.[12]

Emphasis on teacher training as a way to institute change in educational processes usually ignores or minimizes the prevailing structural conditions of the classroom[13] and the role of teachers within that structure.[14] Accordingly, teachers must spend considerable time maintaining the instructional sequence and isolating themselves from the authority structure above them. Furthermore, the role of teacher as "ringmaster" demands complex coordination of inputs that are imprecise, yet which still demand considerable degree of closure. It is little wonder then that attempts to involve teachers in basic questions about the purposes of schooling often meet with resistance because of fatigue and teacher role overload.[15] Hence we witness the tendency for teachers to adopt those aspects of an innovation which can be incorporated into the ongoing patterns of instruction and to ignore those which cannot. According to Ernest House, who has studied a number of major educational innovations, "the teacher will reject or adopt a piece of it (the innovation) depending upon who sponsors it, personal values, and the existential situation."[16] Improved teacher education and training will do little to alter these organizational and role regularities.[17]

### Clarity of Purpose

Clarity of purpose is a second frequently mentioned barrier to change in schools. Oversimplification in the process of translating general guidelines into program regularities is a fundamental problem, and many educational programs fail because of "the fallacious assumption that a statement of general, abstract program values and objectives will easily be translated into new and appropriate behavior problems at work." Quite simply, if participants don't understand a program, then they can't implement it, thus "the clarity of an innovation to organizational members needs to be taken into account in conceptual schemes designed to explain the success or failure of implementation efforts."[18]

Part of the problem here is that most educational innovations carry a variety of interpretations about design and purpose rather than the standardized definition assumed by some.[19] Thus, the "formal doctrine," or that proclamation of the relationship between means and ends within any organization, can variously be interpreted when abstract program values never are sufficiently detailed.[20] Since most formal doctrines are exceedingly vague and ambiguous, they permit virtually any behavior to occur and to be justified within the far-reaching confines of the doctrine.

The implications of this concern with clarity of goals and objectives can be stated in the form of a proposition: if goals and objectives could only be made more clear, then innovations would stand a better chance of success. Yet careful analysis of this proposition reveals weaknesses, for it assumes that goal clarity, rather than being only a necessary condition, is a sufficient condition for successful change. The current advent of planning/decision-making models, educational competency plans, and the almost religious adherence to minute behavioral objectives in many educational programs suggests that, at least in the rhetoric of practice, clarity has become equated with successful change.[21] Yet we need to question the degree of faith that can be placed in the clear specification of objectives as the fundamental vehicle to accelerate change in our schools. The translation of educational objectives into "countable" and "measurable" qualities may so precisely define the permissible operations of an educational program that too narrow a range of actions results, thereby severely limiting the scope of the innovation. Perhaps more importantly, the casting of educational innovations into "objectives" can provide a false sense of rationality, often where one does not exist. A great hiatus exists between educational theory, the incantations of "educational objectives," and the relationship of these objectives to the actual operation of the school. Too often, objectives represent a cosmetic covering over day-to-day activities, as indicated by Aaron Wildavsky, reporting on the role of planning in the economic system of Nepal:

> Thus the American expert, come to spread the gospel of program budgeting, recommends that "major changes in these (the traditional society's) bureaucratic attitudes, habits, practices and procedures are essential; otherwise development efforts and project objectives will continue to be frustrated by administrative bottlenecks." The question can be turned around: why attempt to introduce a sophisticated system of analysis when elementary prerequisites are lacking? Or is it the purpose of program budgeting to discover that a government does not have what it takes, an apparently unnecessary

exercise? . . . Failing that, efforts at program planning will constitute window dressing, mere epiphenomena, designed to hide the fact that one is unwilling to attack the real problems.[22]

I do not wish to disregard totally the usefulness of clarity of goals and objectives in helping us to better understand the direction of schooling. Yet I am stating that for too long they have been held up as the soft spot that must be attacked in the belly of that demon called "barriers to change"; once this soft spot is punctured, the beast will die and change will be greatly facilitated. This line of reasoning represents too much of an oversimplification, for in our obsession with the articulation of goals and objectives as the prime vehicle to facilitate change, we often impose uniformity of purpose where such uniformity does not exist. We do this by taking for granted an understanding by participants of what the program is about, or, even more importantly, we assume that this artificial unit can be an understanding of what the program is/should be about. But organizations (and specifically goals in organizations) seem to be more sets of beliefs (often contrasting) than they are monoliths set apart from people.[23] Also, goals and objectives are more likely to "become,"[24] with the original goals serving only as a point of departure. To understand goal clarity as a way of facilitating the innovative process, it is necessary first to understand the complexity and diversity of the school as a means as well as an end—a place where people work out a host of interests and perspectives. The notion of goal clarity is not something that pertains just for the artifact called the organization but rather more fundamentally for clusters of people with like minds.

## Unintended Consequences

A number of major studies on why attempts to alter schooling do not succeed emphasize the unanticipated consequences of change efforts, the third area of change reviewed here. One such study focused on the attempts of an elementary school to change its organizational and instructional form in a very short period of time.[25] Noting the high level of uncertainty in such a radically changed environment, and the accompanying need for coordination by mutual adjustment, the authors identify the resultant low level of implementation as an unintended outcome. In such "alternatives of grandeur," system overload occurs when multiple changes are made in many components simultaneously, thereby exacerbating time constraints, resource availability, and the need to maintain stability while implementing change at the same time. The authors proposed an "alternative of gradualism" wherein changes are made more slowly and wherein risks are more moderate.

Other researchers adopt a similar approach when they state that any attempt to introduce change in a school affects some existing regularity; intended changes thus become submerged within ongoing regularities, producing unintended results. Unanticipated consequences therefore are better understood to the degree that the complexity surrounding the roles of educators is documented.[26] Accordingly, many change attempts made in schools are implemented without an understanding of the complexity of social roles—how people act, the factors leading to that action, or the meaning attached to the very acts themselves. Lacking such an understanding, change agents superimpose a foreign substance into the organism, leading to rejection in ways which often are unanticipated.[27]

One such study focusing on existing regularities and their effect on change is Ronald Corwin's study of the Teacher Corps, which examines unanticipated consequences that are a function of factors both within and beyond the school environment (teachers, administrators, and district committees) as well as those influential in shaping its environment (local universities, which served as training centers, and the Teacher Corps office in Washington). The Teacher Corps, however, established to break down local resistance to change, establish a network to facilitate ongoing educational reform in lower-income areas, and to insure goal adaptation necessary for survival, soon found itself the victim of the very focus it was attempting to change. As Corwin states:

> Ironically, whereas the program was intended to effect change, it became modified by the same principles and processes that had shaped the organizations it was trying to alter. The organizational character of this change agent . . . produced status dilemmas, conflicts in goals and roles, political constraints, local resistance, co-optation strategies, and other problems noted.

Corwin ends on a pessimistic note by proposing that most change efforts are forced to appease varied audiences, leading to a transformation of the innovation away from goal achievement and toward maintenance of the organization for its own sake. Without a clear recognition of the organizational factors that inhibit change, "modest approval is about all we can expect."[28]

Approaches that examine programmatic change as part of an educational "system" explain the complexities of change better than training and goal clarity because they take into consideration awareness of the school as an organization—guided and shaped by a multitude of forces existing both internally and within its immediate task environment.[29] Thus, change is inhibited not just because teachers are poorly trained or because goals are diffuse and/or transformed. Viewing the school as a system permits examination of, for example, its social and political context, subject to the same forces to which all institutions and organizations within the system are exposed. Accordingly, any change is multidimensional, affected by a host of factors that are related but not limited to such attributes of organizations as (1) the larger task structure of the organization; (2) status systems and status identities of members; (3) economic resources available to the organization and the way those resources are used; and (4) the use and distribution of power.

The problem with such studies of unanticipated consequences— indeed even those that recognize the school as part of a social system—is that key political and economic regularities are seen as given, varying only slightly in degree. This line of analysis assumes, for example, the permanency of political relations between local schools, state agencies, and the federal educational establishment. Likewise, unanticipated consequences regarding how the curriculum is used assume the constant relationship between the intents of the curriculum designers, the training of teachers, and the technology of teaching into which curricula must fit. Yet just as better teacher preparation cannot by itself facilitate structural alteration and just as goal clarification is a necessary but not sufficient condition for making decisions about program structure and process, so mere acceptance of the political, social, and economic parameters of schooling is a weak platform on which to build because it does not subject those parameters to critical examination. The fundamental problem with most attempts to understand how schools operate and why they make the kind of changes in structure that they do is that these attempts take for granted the forces that define the fundamental constitutive processes of schooling and proceed to examine change within that context. It is no wonder then that the more things change, the more they stay the same, for it is those forces defining the constitutive process of schooling that help make it so. Of utmost importance is the present uniformity in the structure of public schooling, which belies the fundamental complexity of educational processes and the values that permeate its practice, including those practices that illuminate the political nature of schooling. To ignore this fundamental political nature leaves unrecognized the critical dimensions that affect schooling and changes in its nature. Such an examination of the political/structural regulation of schooling constitutes the subject of the remainder of this essay.

## STATE SUPPORT OF INSTITUTIONAL PARAMETERS

A fundamental condition defines most efforts to modify the basic structures of schooling. The essence of this condition is located in those external dimensions whereby the state defines the type of educational system it will support. Consequently, internal changes in the operation of the school must be evaluated within the context of institutional parameters—those factors external to schools and/or educational systems that are most influential in shaping organizational structures and the ongoing processes within them. These institutional parameters act to regulate educational processes in such a way that they channel the proposed program and define the boundaries within which it must operate.

We know this limiting effect of such institutional parameters to exist in diverse but consistent ways. Richard Carlson has termed the public school a "domesticated" organization—one that does not compete for clients, that is cared for by the society that sponsors it and focuses on the mandate put forth by that society, that is immune from certain requirements (usually placed on other organizations) such as a clear indication of quality of performance, and that has little control over admission of members.[30] In the case of public schools, clientele are guaranteed because most children automatically are channeled into the public school from ages six to sixteen. Additionally, compulsory taxation guarantees schools a relatively stable level of financial support regardless of performance. Finally, schools carry out the general mandates of the society by adjusting their goals and procedures to "produce" a work force more in consonance with the needs of that society.[31]

Most critical, however, is not the presence of schools as domesticated organizations but the underlying relative stability that such domestication produces within the state political structures. The domestication of education, through schooling, serves both to further the purposes of the state system under which the school system enjoys its protected status as well as to regulate the range of changes that can occur within that system of schooling. Consequently, schools do not adopt innovations that call for major structural reorganization or for widely divergent educational outcomes, as may be called for by consideration of constitutive issues, because such changes may challenge the very state system that supports the school system.[32] In American society, this is illustrated most aptly by the manner in which the common public school and compulsory school attendance help perpetuate the relationship between schooling and the reproduction of processes supportive of state/corporate capitalism.[33]

## The Common Public School

The structure of common schools and the system of social relations that they encourage illustrate the reproduction and perpetuation of the predominant orthodoxy in American society. First and foremost, common schools evolved in our society to educate and train the population in skills (both technical and civic) and to socialize youth into a moral order. The claims for what a properly schooled citizenry could accomplish have been widely broadcasted and largely accepted, and over the past century schools have come to be seen as reform institutions, as "panaceas" within our society.[34] As the claims for schooling have expanded and because an educated citizenry was deemed necessary and in the best interest of the state, the common school has grown increasingly intertwined with the interests of the state, supported by public taxes and regulated by the state in the name of its citizenry.

The impact of the state on education in the United States is critical because, in addition to providing for skill development and some degree of intellectual challenge, critical dimensions of schooling have come to support the system of social relations and cultural patterns conducive to the relative stability of state capitalism. This continuance is achieved within the state-controlled school system, not by overt manipulation, explicit coercion, or even necessarily through conscious intent. Rather, it occurs and works through the very process of knowledge acquisition present in our democratic and pluralistic education system[35] and, ultimately, through the mechanisms for control and change that occur within the state-regulated system.

The symbiotic relationship between schools and the state occurs differently in different societies. In the United States, it seems to be embedded in the very dynamics of pluralism, said to be an important component in determining the purpose of the state public school system. Pluralism as practiced in our schools serves the state in a manner not immediately obvious. For example, radicals fault the schools for perpetuating social class inequities and supporting society as an institution of the status quo; to some radicals, schools must be disbanded. Liberals, on the other hand, claim that the schools are not "humanistically" oriented but rather are operated by people who, as Silberman termed them, are "mindless." Further along the continuum are the "traditionalists" who resent the schools doing more and more; they think schools should do less. For them, the schools should teach what they call the "basics" and drop all the "frills," which contribute to the yearly rise in taxes. Between and among these positions are a host of other specific issues with which to contend. Should the schools teach sex education? If so, how and with what constraints? Should the school set aside a room in which students can smoke? Should the school purchase textbooks that use profanity? What guidelines should be used to police the use of such books? Should schools support interscholastic athletes while only marginally supporting an intramural program which could potentially involve a larger number of students? How about driver education, environmental education, career education, discipline, dress codes? Should the school present points of view that could lead to radical changes in our social, political, and economic institutions? Who determines the worth of such topics? The list is endless. The school constantly must contend with such issues because of its common, public nature as an institution meant to serve the general public.

Yet in so processing the diversity of beliefs about schooling—its purposes, processes, and products—the diversity of beliefs is not represented in public school practice, but, rather, moderation and continuity are adopted because they represent the medium point between extremes. School officials are not likely to take positions that deviate much from what they perceive to be the zone of toleration granted to them by the community they represent. And if there are pressures all along the continuum of whatever the issue, since no one extreme can safely be chosen for fear of alienating those at the other extreme, the position that alienates the fewest, rather than satisfying the most, is the most logical choice. John Pincus points this out when he talks of schools in general:

> the public schools can be seen as more likely than private firms to adopt changes that do not require complex changes in management structure or organizational relations. Such innovations help to satisfy staff and client demands for change, without requiring from the organization the difficult task of self-renewal. . . . Such innovations also are safe . . . the innovating district, if it uses reasonable sense, is unlikely to get into trouble as a consequence of abandoning such innovations.[36]

The same "equilibrium" mentality carries into the curriculum field. Frances Fitzgerald, in her recent book on history textbooks, points to the immense pressure on textbook publishers to please everyone to the degree that "today, texts are written backward or inside out, as it were, beginning with public demand and ending with the historian. This system gives the publishers a certain security, since their books cannot be too far out of the mainstream."[37]

The dynamics of pluralism out of which stability may emerge and the effect of this dynamic on change are graphically illustrated even further in the now rather infamous Kanawha County, West Virginia, conflict in 1974. This conflict emerged ostensibly over objectionable materials present in county adopted texts used in the local public schools. During the first week of school in September, 3,500 coal miners, who supported the elimination of the objectionable materials in school books, engaged in a wildcat strike. The schools were boycotted, and public schooling in the county came to a virtual standstill while negotiations continued between the school board, the local teachers' associations, a citizen review committee, and those citizen groups that favored retention of the books and those who opposed the books. The school board vacillated through the fall, first reaffirming its vote to keep most of the books originally selected, but reversing itself a month later through the announced formation of a multimember committee to review material used in most major subject areas.

Yet in Kanawha County, as in many other areas of the country, the issue was not over textbooks per se but the values of disparate groups of people as these values focused on the schools, the education of their children, and the right of the schools as an arm of the state to effect change in those values. The anti-textbook groups drew their support from those community members who had lived in the area for long periods of time, who were from the more rural areas of the country, and who generally had fewer years of formal schooling. Many were of fundamentalist faith and were people who, for the most part, saw the incursion of liberal curricular material as a violation of their beliefs in literal biblical interpretations. The pro-textbook group generally was supported by the more cosmopolitan members of the urban community—people who had been somewhat more mobile during their lives, people with more years of formal schooling, people who believed in the power of reasoning and enlightenment rather than that of authoritative truth. The values of these two groups, in conflict before over sex education and issues with racial overtones, simply resurfaced over the use of textbooks in the school.

A recent countywide consolidation of schools, in which the rural schools had been incorporated into a countywide system under the guise of modernization and efficiency, exacerbated the conflict because of the requirement that the county school board adopt a set of books for all of its 45,000 students. In such uniformity, no allowances could be made for differences of belief, nor could those advocating their own strongly held belief redirect their energies into another option more to their liking. It was here that the power of the state became more pronounced in its rawest form, for those objecting to the books believed that their rights were not receiving full recognition. As one observer of the case said: "they [the protesters] do not insist that doctrine and arguments of fundamental Christianity be taught, or even alluded to, in the schools. They see the school as an executive arm of the state imposing, through its use of textbooks, a system of values antagonistic to their own."[38] Reaching a "settlement" over use of the books stopped neither the continuance of protest by anti-textbook groups into the ensuing years nor the charges by pro-textbook groups that the school board had capitulated to the anti-textbook forces.

The Kanawha County incident, as well as similar incidents that occur daily (religious freedom cases with the Amish, protests by cultural minorities for a greater degree of cultural sensitivity on the part of schools, demands by parents that their children be excluded from standard school practices such as sex education and psychological testing, etc.), illustrates the variety of beliefs that exist about educational processes and the range of issues with which the state educational monopoly must contend. Yet the public school system as presently constituted is ill equipped to adequately process such a wide range of issues—ill equipped in the sense that sufficient diversity of options does not exist within the state-controlled educational monopoly to permit resolution of these issues. This position is based upon a criteria of providing maximum determination by constituents over the products and processes of schooling while, at the same time, insuring that the citizens of the state are sufficiently equipped to function in the society as it exists. In no other institution whose outcomes are comparable with those of schooling (relatively ill defined, developmental, and somewhat diverse) do we grant to one organizational form unilateral and legitimized responsibility for preparation and training. It occurs less in the areas of religion, child rearing, and mental health. Yet in the case of schools, we seem convinced that one legitimate organizational form can best process the diversity of interests and beliefs about what constitutes a well-educated person. The pluralism that is said to be the hallmark of public education ends up serving state interests at the expense of the interests of subjugated minorities. No wonder that schools are known for stability, as pressures for change, in the long run, tend to cancel one another out. The continued domination by the state of public schooling provides primarily for the reduction of diversity and the control of change rather than the expansion of diversity and the facilitation of determination by those directly affected by schooling—parents and students.

### Compulsory Attendance

If establishment of a common public school system serves the state, then it also is in the best interest of the state that such a system, in order to operate in a noncompetitive framework with a relatively predictable level of resource inputs, be guaranteed a steady supply of clients. With a predictable supply of students, certain regularities serve to determine what those clients in the school must do to be classified as receiving a legitimate educational experience. Compulsory school attendance, the regularity most effectively serving this purpose, is another institutional parameter that constricts the variety of educational experiences available to students and further establishes the boundaries within with conformity occurs between schooling experiences and the system of social relations that are most supportive of the state.

Compulsory school attendance laws serve to reinforce the limited offerings of the common public school by channeling students into programs devised along very narrow lines. Since "clock time" in school—not attainment of an educational competency as jointly defined by parents, students, and educators—is the fundamental criterion of attainment, we rarely hear of students being permitted, for example, to learn reading at home rather than at school, even if there exists demonstrable evidence on the success of such a plan. Nor would the school countenance its students in auto mechanics class being permitted credit for learning from a local garage mechanic, even if the owner would agree to supervise them. Although Torsten Husen and others have pointed out that, in certain prescribed situations, there seems to be no necessary correlation between time spent in school and the achievement of students on school-defined educational outcomes, attendance still is mandatory.[39] Only in rare instances will the postulates of compulsory school attendance legitimize education beyond the scope of those experiences that are school-controlled and school-regulated.

Here then school attendance is equated with education. The literal definition of compulsory school attendance means attendance by a student at a school $x$ days a year for $y$ years, defined as necessary in order to be certified educationally competent. The education of this diverse population becomes defined as attendance at the school. Though educators admit the great amount that children may learn via television, newspapers, films, and through social interactions within their community, such counts little, for children don't receive diplomas watching television or reading outside of school; they receive them by doing what is required while they attend school the required time.[40]

Proposed changes in schooling must be considered within the framework set by compulsory attendance; that is, students must do most of their "work" in the school, they must do it during the school year, and they must do it in a chronological fashion until they reach the age at which they may voluntarily leave school. Any strategies for knowledge development at the constitutive level must follow accordingly. Because school attendance has become the official sine qua non of education, the public school is limited in what it can do to provide the diversity of possible educational experiences that might have a very positive effect on self-determination and even measurable outcomes. Yet consider those changes that might combat temporary student disinterest by eliminating the rigid chronological aspect of schooling and thereby permit some students the option of formal education outside the school, a proposal which might, in effect, extend the school "exit" a few years. Consider also those students who might learn to read more effectively by studying technical manuals while working on cars on the weekend rather than taking classes under Title I programs at school; the student who finishes a year's worth of math in seven months and who decides he or she would rather spend the rest of his or her time working in the mornings with the local little theater or students from politically active families who wish to do "vocational education"—one that builds toward education in and of the workplace.[41] These might all be considered "radical" educational options—changes which provide much greater self-determination on the part of students, parents, and educators but also those which, because of compulsory school attendance laws, are experienced, if at all, only by a privileged few in most school districts.

Compulsory attendance laws too are an important political regularity contributing to the tendency for schools to maintain the status quo even while being pressured to adapt to the demands by constituents for greater power in affecting those decisions. Consequently, individuals dissatisfied with their ability to affect the means of their children's schooling are left little recourse but to continue to send children to the school and thus perpetuate its supply of clientele. The individual parent or groups of parents, united by a dedication to a particular educational interest or philosophy that does not coincide with the mandates of school attendance, cannot threaten to withdraw their children from the school. They must continue to send their children to the school or find an "alternative" (private) school legitimated by the state. The school then does not face the ultimate threat—withdrawal of support—as a test of the worth of its product. Since students are obliged to attend for a specified and consecutive duration of time, the responsiveness of the school to countervailing pressures is limited. As long as it is the provision of the school to determine both educational ends (the definition of a sufficiently educated citizen) and means (the specific practices by which the individual will achieve that end) through school attendance, then outside options will be difficult to legitimate.

This forces the major responsibility for all formal education on the school, placing it in the position of having to be all things to all people. It seems ironic that the public school, in its quest to be responsive and to take on all tasks of formal education, is actually less responsive for having done so, for by necessity it must scale down and moderate changes so as to alienate as few constituents as possible. It seems ironic also that in a nation historically opposed to monopolization and restricted choice, particularly under the guise of "socialism," we continue to support compulsory school attendance, which offers little choice to the parents of children in their most formative years and which, in the end, rigidly defines the narrow boundaries of formal education.

## STATE CONTROL OF EDUCATIONAL CHANGE

Thus far I have argued that the state-controlled educational monopoly places severe restrictions on the school's adaptability to initiate or respond to issues that focus on the fundamental questions about schooling—its basic processes and how those processes are to be decided. Institutional parameters established by the state (two of which include the existence of a common public school system and compulsory school attendance) define the legitimacy of these dimensions to such a degree that basic constitutive issues usually are left unattended, even though such issues are of more critical importance than technical/organizational issues normally discussed in the change literature. I argue that such institutional parameters, rather than facilitating pluralistic interests and control within a common framework, subvert that potential for self-determination to the fundamental domination of the state.

The presence and effect of such institutional parameters is not random or happenstance—it is a fundamental regularity of state political systems. All state systems attempt to regulate the outcomes of schooling in any given society, this regulation controlling, to the greatest degree possible, the general outputs of educational experiences to those outputs that serve best for the continuance of the state. In our own society, and in Western societies in general, schooling perpetuates the system of social relations and cultural patterns that support state capitalism. Thus, state capitalism is extended to the degree schooling fosters and leaves unexamined the social relations of, for example, domination and subservience, competition and individualism, and cultural patterns that grow out of unexamined client resistance, the hegemonic functions of language, and the allocative results of schooling. These constitutive processes remain unaddressed in the schooling process, and when distributive issues rise to prominence, there is de facto acceptance on the part of educators and by those who are schooled of the relative impartiality of schools as the legitimate agency to certify attainment of skills needed for later personal and economic success. Despite evidence that schools do not necessarily foster equality of opportunity but rather perpetuate existing inequities[42] and despite a preponderance of data revealing that technical skills required in the employment market often are better learned at work than at school,[43] the assumed relationship between what is learned in school and the probabilities of subsequent economic (and thereby personal) success rarely is questioned. Yet if this contrary information—questioning as it does the manifest purposes of schooling—is so compelling, we must ask why the state resists most attempts to loosen the restrictions imposed on schools by such parameters as compulsory attendance at state-controlled schools.

This continuance of state control exists because a system of schooling that is relatively closely regulated by the state has greater impact on the noncognitive outcomes and processes of schooling than on cognitive outcomes. Accordingly, the interests of the state are not ultimately served as much by what schooling is *supposed* to achieve for the individual as much by the collective effect of schools on the gestalt of personal and social development and the ultimate acceptance of that development in such a way that the continuance of the state is served. For example, as a number of studies indicate, a stronger correlation exists between I.Q. and personality "type" than any other measure. Accordingly, children of parents in the poorest decile of families are only one-third as likely to end up "well off" (economically) later in adult life as children from families in the wealthiest decile, even holding constant educational attainment and I.Q.[44] Why this is the case is closely related to the behavioral patterns associated with class and not the technical skill said to be measured by I.Q. This phenomenon alone should alert us to the degree to which outcome measures such as I.Q. may be measures of behavioral disposition rather than accurate predictors of cognitive skills per se. The pioneering work of Basil Bernstein on language "codes" also reveals the extent to which schooling modalities that appear "progressive" are, in reality, often restrictive to children from lower-class backgrounds because the language-epistemological assumptions supported by those progressive programs are at odds with the epistemological systems of the child's family and community.[45] Because of the disparity and as children fail to adapt to the instructional patterns of the school, educators tend to "blame the victim" as students progress through school, all the while demonstrating increasing resistance to its patterns. This all contributes, as Bernstein points out, to a developing world view on the part of members of disaffected groups about the process of schooling, a view in which the individual ends up acknowledging the legitimacy of the school to so allocate the student's life chances. Yet there is no doubt that this allocative process does serve corporate/state capitalism in that it selects out "skill levels" and thereby feeds a differentiated wage-labor system.

The accumulation of these noncognitive traits in our society (relating to such issues as the legitimacy of institutions to allocate individuals to positions within the social structure, the presence of speech patterns the origin of which are class-based, and beliefs about social relations of the workplace) are important because of their concurrence with the continuity of state and corporate capitalism. Many of these noncognitive attributes pertain to what Pierre Bourdieu has termed "cultural capital" or the possession of social and behavioral attributes and dispositions commensurate with social position, and the congruence between those attributes and the reward structure that is present within institutional settings.[46] Bourdieu argues that the fundamental reason why students from lower economic groups and/or cultural enclaves tend to be less successful in school is because they lack the "cultural capital" necessary for success as reinforced by the dominant educational, political, and economic institutions in society.

Now all this is *not* to say that schools in the United States are intentionally rigged to reproduce the capitalist state, although that may be an appropriate description in some cases where "business values" are deemed important. It is not my purpose to argue for the *instrumental* effect that schools have on social and cultural reproduction. That is to say, I do not wish to propose a correspondence approach à la Bowles and Gintis, arguing that schools in American society are the tools of some reification we call "the capitalist state." Such instrumentality would require evidence of school processes as explicit and manifest instruments or devices of state reproduction, and I find little compelling evidence to support this point of view. More realistic, however, is the viewpoint that state control, as it currently exists and as it fosters social and cultural processes congruent to the stability of the state, has a *symbolic* effect—that is, as expressive of beliefs, values, and feelings of a particular sector of society as they are then manifested in a particular act, institution, or systemic regularity. The existence of these symbolic parameters (of which debates over and decisions about the purposes of schooling are one manifestation) reflect a belief system—they provide a symbolic representation—of what is hoped for, an expression of what should be.

To see schooling in its symbolic context is to make the distinction between *intent* and *consequence*. The proponents of public schooling, in advocating the preservation of the common school as a unifier of pluralistic beliefs, argue their case on the basis of the establishment and continuance of schooling within a common framework to which all will subscribe and which will best serve the collective interest. This is the classic liberal/progressive position which is, by the way, currently on the rebound in educational circles after a decade of disfavor.[47] Nowhere in this liberal argument do we see that the purpose of the school should be to perpetuate state/corporate capitalism and the privileges inherent in it. Yet, as I have argued thus far, the evidence strongly suggests that the perpetuation of state capitalism and its structural inequities is precisely what does occur through the continuation of the common school as currently structured in American society. The effect or consequence of the continuance of the common school within a pluralistic framework provides the symbolic manifestation of limited self-determination experienced by working people that has come to be the hallmark of state capitalism. Even more importantly, arguments about the unity of cultural tradition provided by public schooling are symbolic of the paranoia on the part of many people of an excessive diversity that might upset that social order which benefits majoritarian interests. This all suggests that it is not as important to understand the function of the common school as the drama that unfolds within it. The drama within the common school supports the predominant orthodoxy through which individuals in society come to accept the school's legitimate purpose of selecting, distributing, and "cooling out" individuals on criteria that are closely tied to class position. That class, more than race, may now have become the prime determinant of life opportunity for racial minorities is not insignificant, for fundamental acceptance of class differences on the part of students and families is much more easily attainable in our schools than is the acceptance of racial differences.[48]

To recapitulate, the current system of schooling serves the state by limiting changes in the process of schooling to distributive issues. The system assumes the permanence and inconvertibility of most school knowledge and, by not accepting as legitimate those constitutive issues relevant to the nature and purpose of schooling, thereby negates the very pluralism that the public school system is supposed to foster. It is because schooling serves the state in this almost clandestine fashion that fundamental change is so difficult to attain in schools, and that which does occur is of a ritual nature.

If one assumed that constitutive issues were legitimate for consideration and proceeded to institute commensurate change in schooling, then how might that schooling be different? This question can be answered in terms of two dimensions. First, in terms of the *products* said to be representative of schooling efforts, one would expect that since more varied client belief systems would be behind the structure of schooling, a greater manifestation of pluralism would be evident. Settings would be more diverse, practices within those settings more varied, and we would see a greater range of legitimate experiences constituting schooling activities. Certainly this would be more in keeping with democratic values, would foster greater national tolerance for differences between people, and would make schools truly "different." Yet the present constraint of state regulation through monopolization and overemphasis on requirements such as attendance precludes such products from being very diverse. Until such parameters are altered, we can expect most changes will continue to focus on distributive issues and that evaluations of those changes will continue to report that "no significant difference was found."

The legitimization of constitutive issues in educational change would also involve a *process* dimension that is equally as important as the product dimension. That has to do with students and parents being significantly involved in choosing the values and beliefs that represent, to them, the basic kind of society in which they wish to live, and then being able to choose the school (product dimension) that most closely puts into practice that belief system. In this sense then, self-determination, to the greatest degree possible, becomes a value in and of itself to the extent that it facilitates collectives of individuals being able to increase their chances of making themselves the kind of life they wish. Current educational options, dominated as they are by the paradigm of public, compulsory schooling, provide little self-determination and do not accurately reflect the multifaceted mosaic of belief about what contributes to the educated mind.

It is for these deep-seated, structural reasons that educational change qua organizational change is so ineffectual. The state system, through regulation of the range of educational practices, delimits what is legitimate, then compels attendance, facilitating the reproduction of cultural processes productive for the maintenance of the state. The system of state schooling is primarily a political structure in which educational processes roughly supportive of a particular political ideology are initiated, continued, and symbolically supported. Only secondarily is our system of public education an educational system meant to prepare people to be independent thinkers in a democratic society. To the degree that schooling is politically grounded, then educational change must be seen first and foremost as a political process requiring political knowledge and organization rather than as an organizational process dependent on technological sophistication. To accomplish change of this type, the pluralism that is part of our society must be used as the initial beginning point for change rather than as a condition to be subverted through the domination of schooling by the state.

## CHANGE AS A POLITICAL PROCESS

It seems more than unusual, given the times in which we have lived, to call for an educational agenda to be focused first and foremost on political dimensions. After all, we all were taught that the common school has been, in part, the "genius" of American education, as Lawrence Cremin once termed it—that institution within which the diversity of beliefs in a pluralistic society could at once be respected as well as solidified into a common purpose.[49] Yet more often than not, we have found this not to be true. Schools have not uniformly liberated the oppressed (although this is not to deny that there are those who have been so liberated). Rather they have permitted, indeed encouraged, through cultural reproduction, the accumulation of cultural capital by those groups who have, by and large, possessed it in the first instance, at the expense of those who lack it in the second instance. While this permits further social reproduction, it more significantly represents reproduction of a dominant belief and value system — a predominant orthodoxy — that goes unquestioned because the state so limits the conditions that facilitate diverse settings in which the purposes of schooling can legitimately be questioned. Because the continued existence of schooling in its present form grows out of expressions of ideology and political belief that most directly benefit those in the United States who control the means of production, so too is it that any change to benefit that larger proportion of the society that has minimal self-determination must be political as well.

But political in what sense? In the sense that first we must come to understand how the state, through the establishment and maintenance of institutional parameters such as the effectual monopoly of the public school and attendance in it, is not providing for critical thought and the facilitation of control by future citizens but, rather, perpetuates inequities and eventual student acceptance of them. In this way, we should come to see schooling not as neutral in its treatment of children but rather indicative of a political system that strains toward its own equilibrium through the manifestation of outcomes and dispositions most conducive to the continuance of the state. In this sense, then, schooling must be seen as part of a system of beliefs and actions that perpetuates the state and not just as a technical process objectively operated by and/or for professionals who operate that process removed from the world of moral choice.

Once some understanding of this issue is at hand, then the next most critical issue is a greater role by affected groups in determining the outcomes of schooling and the processes that are ongoing within it. Yet given the moral choices that are inherent in schooling, how are those choices to be made? The issue of control seems paramount. If we currently ask the question, "Who governs?" as Robert Dahl did twenty years ago,[50] we discover that it is the state, through its regulatory system, and professional educators through their training (in state-approved programs) and their representation in large, increasingly powerful, but increasingly distant professional associations, that govern formal education. Parents, children, and especially collectives of parents and children as ethnic, cultural, or class groups have relatively little determination over educational processes, to whatever extent they may wish that control or come to understand the need for it. What then is needed is control that maximizes the use of schooling for domination *by* clients rather than *of* clients. Such control means more than participation in school board decisions or a place as a representative on a school district curriculum committee. Control by clients must be institutionalized and ultimately legitimized in such a fashion that goals and beliefs about schooling can be implemented under the concept of "subsidarity"—that is, the minimal monopolization of schooling by the state. To this extent, we would have to see a major change away from increasing centralized control by professionals and bureaucrats and toward client-driven changes and the recomposition of institutional parameters to accommodate those changes. Control that operates under the pretenses of pluralism but then gives undue advantage (as now occurs) to technicians, managers, and power brokers in the larger society cannot continue to go unchallenged. Laurence Iannaccone, in this volume, indicates that such control by technicians no longer is uniformly accepted.

Of course, control itself means nothing in the absence of a critical understanding of that which is to be controlled. I am not, therefore, subscribing to the romantic vision that client control necessarily means more responsible schooling, that clients will want to make decisions about all aspects of their children's education, or even that the mechanisms of self-determination are universally understood by participants in all sectors of the society. These are tough issues that must be handled by each group depending upon the situation in which they find themselves. Yet radically inclined educators can go some way toward facilitating the development of what Gramsci called "organic intellectuals" or intellectuals whose origins are within and whose interests are focused upon traditionally disaffected classes.[51] Critical understanding of what is to be controlled can be helped through greater understanding of how specific groups and classes have been historically and systematically excluded from systems of social relations that are optimally self-determinative. To accomplish this critical understanding, we must be willing to engage in a critical dialogue with clients as to the purposes, functions, and consequences of schooling in U.S. society, the relationship of schools to the larger state/corporate society, and the extent to which schooling as presently constituted is a productive force. Clients must come to see that in their own participation in systems of social relations (many of which occur in schools), they too may be part of the very process of capital accumulation that ends up damning many to a life of subservience while others, through those very same social relations, continue to maintain control over their own lives as well as the lives of others.

It is quite evident that in focusing on issues such as control and critical understanding and in seeing schools as political organizations and schooling as a political process require a fundamentally different view of change than that set forth by the issues raised earlier in this essay—issues such as the training of teachers, clarification of intent, and awareness of consequences. These issues, technical in nature and assuming away as they do the political realities of schooling, fail to grapple with education as a practice of beliefs and ideologies that end up camouflaged as "learning" for one's own benefit. Values and beliefs in schooling will always be with us, and the purpose of schooling should not be to disguise them as it now attempts to do under the rubric of pluralism but rather to activate them in such a way that understanding about those beliefs can become a vehicle for educational determination. Neglect of the institutional parameters established by the state, accompanied by a continued faith in organizational change, serves only as a myopic solution to a fundamental problem. By not seriously addressing the constitutive nature of schooling through alteration of the political parameters that regulate it, we can continue to meander between schooling as Tweedledum and Tweedledee, remaining educators who, in Santayana's terms, "dispute the dogma but never question the revelation."

## NOTES TO CHAPTER 9

1.  John Goodlad and M. Frances Klein, *Behind the Classroom Door* (Worthington, Ohio: Charles A. Jones, 1970).

2.  "Back to Basics in the Schools," *Newsweek*, October 21, 1974, p. 87.

3.  Office of Management and Budget, *The Budget of the U.S. Government: Fiscal Year 1980* (Washington, D.C.: U.S. Government Printing Office, 1979), p. 424.

4.  Office of Management and Budget, *The Budget of the U.S. Government: Fiscal Year 1976–1980* (Washington, D.C.: U.S. Government Printing Office, 1976–1979).

5.  Randall Collins, "Functional and Conflict Models of Stratification," *American Sociological Review* 36 (1971): 1002-19.

6.  See Robert Chin and Loren Downey, "Changing Change: Innovating a Discipline," in *Second Handbook of Research on Teaching*, ed. Robert M. W. Travers (Chicago: Rand McNally, 1973), pp. 513-29; Michael Fullan, "Overview of the Innovation Process and the User," *Interchange* 3 (1972): 1-46; Joseph B. Giaquinta, "The Process of Organizational Change in Schools," in *Review of Research in Education*, ed. Fred N. Kerlinger (Itasca, Ill.: F. E. Peacock, 1973), pp. 178-208; Ronald Havelock, *Educational Innovations in the United States* (Ann Arbor, Mich.: Center for Research on the Utilization of Scientific Knowledge, 1973); Matthew B. Miles, *Innovation in Education* (New York: Teachers College Press, 1964); and Thomas Whiteside, *The Sociology of Educational Innovation* (London: Metheun, 1978).

7.  See Richard I. Miller, *Perspectives on Educational Change* (New York: Appleton-Century-Crofts, 1967).

8.  Goodlad and Klein, *Behind the Classroom Door*, p. 104; Charles Silberman, *Crisis in the Classroom* (New York: Random House, 1970).

9.  See Robert G. Owens, *Organizational Behavior in Schools* (Englewood Cliffs, N.J.: Prentice-Hall, 1969).

10. Dan C. Lortie, *Schoolteacher* (Chicago: University of Chicago Press, 1975).

11. See Philip Jackson, *Life in Classrooms* (New York: Holt, Rinehart and Winston, 1968).

12. See D. E. Edgar and Richard Warren, "Power and Autonomy in Teacher Socialization," *Sociology of Education* 42 (1969): 386-89; Wayne K. Hoy, "The Influence of Experience on the Beginning Teacher," *School Review* 76 (1968): 312-33; and Gertrude McPherson, *Small Town Teacher* (Cambridge, Mass.: Harvard University Press, 1972).

13. See Robert Dreeben, *The Nature of Teaching* (Glenview, Ill.: Scott, Foresman, 1970); and Jackson, *Life in Classrooms*.

14. See Philip A. Cusick, *Inside High School* (New York: Holt, Rinehart and Winston, 1973); Jacob Kounin, *Discipline and Group Management in Classrooms* (New York: Holt, Rinehart and Winston, 1970); and Louis M. Smith and William Geoffrey, *Complexities of the Urban Classroom* (New York: Holt, Rinehart and Winston, 1968).

15. See Louis Smith and Pat Keith, *Anatomy of Educational Innovation* (New York: Wiley, 1971); and Leila Sussman, *Tales Out of School* (Philadelphia: Temple University Press, 1977).

16. Ernest R. House, *The Politics of Educational Innovation* (Berkeley: McCutchan, 1974), p. 79.

17. See Seymour R. Sarason, *The Culture of the School and the Problem of Change* (Boston: Allyn and Bacon, 1971).

18. W. W. Charters, Jr., and Roland Pellegrin, "Barriers to the Innovation Process: Four Case Studies of Differentiated Staffing, *Educational Administration Quarterly* 9 (1975): 1–14; Neal Gross, Joseph B. Giaquinta, and Marilyn Bernstein, *Implementing Organizational Innovations* (New York: Basic Books, 1971), p. 196.

19. See M. D. Shipman, *Inside a Curriculum Project* (London: Metheun, 1974).

20. See Smith and Keith, *Anatomy of Educational Innovation.*

21. See Harry F. Wolcott, *Teachers and Technocrats* (Eugene: University of Oregon Press, 1977).

22. Aaron Wildavsky, "Why Planning Fails in Nepal," *Administrative Science Quarterly* 17 (1972): 527.

23. See T. Barr Greenfield, "Organizations as Social Inventions: Rethinking Assumptions About Change," *Journal of Applied Behavioral Science* 9 (1973): 551–74.

24. See Robert B. Everhart, "Patterns of Becoming: The Making of Roles in Changing Schools," *Interchange* 7(1) (1977): 24–33.

25. Smith and Keith, *The Anatomy of Educational Innovation.*

26. See Sarason, *The Culture of the School.*

27. See Paul Berman and Milbrey McLaughlin, "Implementation of Educational Innovation," *Educational Forum* 40 (1976): 345–70.

28. Ronald G. Corwin, *Reform and Organizational Survival* (New York: Wiley, 1973), pp. 350, 394.

29. Whiteside, *Sociology of Educational Innovation.*

30. Richard O. Carlson, "Environmental Constraint and Organizational Consequences: The Public School and Its Clients," *Behavioral Sciences and Educational Administration* (Chicago: National Society for the Study of Education, 1964).

31. See Michael W. Apple, *Ideology and Curriculum* (London: Routledge & Kegan Paul, 1979).

32. See John Pincus, "Incentives for Innovation in the Public Schools," *Review of Educational Research* 44 (1974): 113–44.

33. I have selected these two institutional parameters for analysis because they are, in my mind, most critical. Certainly other such parameters do exist, among them funding formulas and certification requirements.

34. See Henry J. Perkinson, *The Imperfect Panacea* (New York: Random House, 1978).

35. See Apple, *Ideology and Curriculum*; Robert B. Everhart, *The In-Between Years: Student Life in a Junior High School* (Boston: Routledge & Kegan Paul, 1982), and Paul Willis, *Learning to Labour* (Westmead, England: Saxon House, 1977).

36. Pincus, "Incentives for Innovation," p. 118.

37. Frances Fitzgerald, *America Revised* (Boston: Little, Brown, 1979), p. 69.

38. George Hillocks, Jr., "Books and Bombs: Ideological Conflict and the Schools—A Case Study of the Kanawha County Book Protest," *School Review* 78 (1978): 651.

39. Torsten Husen, "Does More Time in School Make a Difference?" *Saturday Review*, April 29, 1972, pp. 32–35.

40. Here I agree with those such as Lawrence A. Cremin ("Public Education and the Education of the Public," *Teachers College Record* 77 [1975]: 1–12), who point out the diversity of sources which can be considered "educative." My point, however, is that few of these sources are formally sanctioned as legitimate avenues of education whereas education via the school is both sanctioned and compulsory.

41. See Antonio Gramsci, *Selections from the Prison Notebooks* (London: Lawrence & Wishart, 1971).

42. See Samuel Bowles and Herbert Gintis, *Schooling in Capitalist America* (New York: Basic Books, 1976); and Christopher Jencks, *Inequality* (New York: Basic Books, 1972).

43. See Ivar Berg, *Education and Jobs: The Great Training Robbery* (Boston: Beacon Press, 1970); and Randall Collins, *The Credential Society* (New York: Academic Press, 1979).

44. Bowles and Gintis, *Schooling in Capitalist America*.

45. Basil Bernstein, "Social Class, Language, and Socialization," in *Current Trends in Linguistics*, ed. A. S. Abramson et al. (London: Mouton, 1973).

46. Pierre Bourdieu and Jean-Claude Passeron, *Reproduction in Education, Society, and Culture* (Beverly Hills: Sage, 1977).

47. See David B. Tyack, Michael W. Kirst, and Elisabeth Hansot, "Educational Reform: Retrospect and Prospect," *Teachers College Record* 81 (1980): 253–69; R. Freeman Butts, "Educational Vouchers: The Private Pursuit of the Public Purse," *Phi Delta Kappan*, September 1979, pp. 7–9; and R. Freeman Butts, *Public Education in the United States* (New York: Holt, Rinehart and Winston, 1978).

48. See William Julius Wilson, *The Declining Significance of Race: Blacks and Changing American Institutions* (Chicago: University of Chicago Press, 1978).

49. Lawrence A. Cremin, *The Genius of American Education* (Pittsburgh: University of Pittsburgh Press, 1965).

50. Robert Dahl, *Who Governs?* (New Haven: Yale University Press, 1961).

51. Gramsci, *Selections from the Prison Notebooks*, p. 35.

# PART IV

# ALTERNATIVES TO MONOPOLY SCHOOLING

In this concluding part, we present five essays that suggest possible directions beyond the monopoly of formalized education that occurs through state schooling. These essays consist of both theoretical arguments as well as those based upon empirical research. They are philosophically diverse as well, ranging from calls for market deregulation to arguments in support of increased power on the part of disaffected groups. They show the multiplicity of opinion about ways in which to disengage the state from excessive educational control and provide a beginning point for continued thought, research, and debate.

In the first essay, "The Prospects for Education Vouchers: An Economic Analysis," E. G. West utilizes a political economy model to analyze educational choices and why programs for choice have been more successful in Canada than in the United States. West first provides a general perspective of the political economy of schooling through an understanding of bureaucracies and the process of decision making in which bureaus engage to maximize economic resources and control. He argues that bureaus (and bureaucrats) attempt to maximize organizational or personal utility through a variety of means but primarily through manipulation in the presentation of political/economic choices to their constituency. Through explanation and example, West shows that according to the theories of political economy, bureaus attempt to minimize competition in agenda setting so as to maximize their attempts to present constituents with all-or-nothing proposals. In so doing, the bureau can dominate resources and thereby maximize its best interest in two crucial ways. First, as the bureau expands its domain, fewer choices are available to the bureau's clients. Second, the larger the bureau and the larger its constituency, the greater the apathy found in its constituents because constituents feel powerless to affect the agenda of the bureau. It is no wonder then that school districts favor consolidation, for the effect of individuals or power blocs is minimized in larger units. Herein, West provides an economic explanation for a trend noted by Burgess—that of school district consolidation.

All in all, then, public bureaus such as state school systems will attempt either to prevent competing systems (such as private schools) from expanding or will insist that any possible advantages that might be used by competing educational systems (such as public financing) be used within the system controlled by the bureau. The lesson here is clear: the bureau, if it is dominant, will do everything in its power to remain dominant.

West applies this general political-economic analysis to the attempts both in the United States and Canada to institute educational vouchers and explains why such movements have been more successful in Canada than in the United States, where, he claims, they have been "emasculated." West reviews the troubled career of vouchers in the United States, and the difficulty of implementing what amounts to an idea in search of a practice. The eventual (and sole) test of vouchers in the United States was at Alum Rock, California, but the experiment was so heavily compromised by the restrictions of local and federal bureaucracies that the outcome was hardly an adequate test of vouchers.

This seems not to have been the case in British Columbia, where a fascinating attempt in the demonopolization of schooling currently is ongoing (although prompted more by fiscal concerns than by motivation for educational experimentation). Here, the province subsidizes, at the rate of five hundred dollars per pupil per year, students who attend independent schools. The reasons for the quick passage of the legislation, the prospects for its future, and an analysis of similar attempts at voucher-type changes constitute the last part of West's essay.

Donald Erickson's essay, "Disturbing Evidence About the 'One Best System,' " is a natural sequence to West's, for in it Erickson presents early results from a study which he and his colleagues are conducting of that educational plan (described by West) now being carried out in British Columbia. By being present at the time that the British Columbia plan was being implemented and through data collection before its inception, Erickson has been able to trace the effect of public funds on the heretofore exclusively private schools.

Erickson first takes us back to the period before the 1977 legislation. British Columbia, some years before, had experimented with public support of some Catholic schools, and from those schools as well as schools totally privately funded, Erickson collected some initial data from parents and teachers. He found some striking differences along the lines of the perceived "special" nature of the totally privately funded schools. Informed by that exploratory study, he continued his line of questioning in the British Columbia schools, both public and private, as they entered the first year of the experiment described by West.

From these two studies emerged the concept of "commitment" as a useful descriptor separating the public and private schools. Commitment is a quality that emerges when people feel they have a "stake" in something and are willing to pursue their stake in it. Erickson concludes: "In contrast to public schools, as a whole, the private schools as a whole come through as places where people band together in committed fashion to achieve some special, agreed-upon goals."

In examination of additional data from parents of children in both public and private schools, collected shortly after the experiment had begun, those same differences seem to hold up. Parents of children in private schools feel strongly that the teachers are of higher quality, that they are more dedicated, and that there is better rapport between home and school. Contrary to what we might expect (often private schools are viewed as being elitist and parochial), parents of children in private schools, compared with those of children in public schools, feel their children have greater respect for minorities and are better able to think for themselves. (The following essay by Thomas Vitullo-Martin discusses some of these same points.) Yet additional data collected two years after inception of the experiment reveal a dramatic *decrease* in parental perceptions of school responsiveness. Why this is the case, according to Erickson, is directly related to the *form* which the public support of private education took, and Erickson discusses this issue at length.

Erickson's perspective is supported by the arguments put forth by Burgess, Everhart, and Iannaccone, among others. This is an important essay, providing useful information on a large-scale move to alter the role of the state in schooling.

West's essay addressed some underlying conditions and possible effects of a voucher program, that is, direct payment by the state to the family whose child attends a non-public school. Erickson provides additional data on a situation where a variation of that plan has been ongoing. The next essay discusses a variation of the voucher plan wherein the state can and does affect client choice of schooling. That fiscal variation is tax codes. In "The Impact of Taxation Policy on Public and Private Schools," Thomas Vitullo-Martin addresses the manner in which the state controls schools through various strategies—direct regulation, grants-in-aid, and tax codes. The last is of critical importance for general purposes pertaining to school choice as well as their consequence for "the social relations of different racial, ethnic, and economic group members and on the mobility of members of these groups to higher (or lower) status levels based on merit alone."

After reviewing the effects of direct regulation and grants-in-aid, Vitullo-Martin outlines why he feels that tax codes have the greatest effect on decisions about educational choice. This relationship exists because certain expenditures are tax-deductible expenses, serving to reduce the overall cost of those expenses to the taxpayer. Such deductions also cause the federal government, in effect, to subsidize those expenses at the rate of the deduction vis-à-vis the income bracket of the individual claiming the deduction. Since property taxes are legitimate deductions and as those taxes pay educational expenses at the local level, the federal government is subsidizing public education in those cases where individuals itemize deductions.

The author documents the consequences of this policy. He shows, for example, that in New York City and its suburbs the federal government in essence encourages movement of the more wealthy to the affluent suburbs because of the deductibility of the higher school taxes (property taxes) in the suburbs. At the same time, residents of New York City who wish to attain a comparable education for their children must pay private school tuition, an expense that is not deductible. If these same city families move to the suburbs to attain the same advantages as their suburban neighbors, the money they spent in the city is removed from circulation therein, further eroding the city tax base and exacerbating further the problems of the city public schools.

Vitullo-Martin turns to the tuition tax-credit proposal (Packwood/Moynihan) as a political solution to this phenomenon and focuses upon the objections raised against it along the lines of its fostering increased elitism and racial segregation. The information presented is revealing. The author contends that the most elitist schools generally are the suburban public schools, where enrollment is associated with neighborhood residence, which, in turn, is predicated on income level. He states further that there is no evidence to indicate that private schools, in general, are any more segregated than are public schools; indeed they probably are less so. Specific data from private schools in New York City is presented to support these points.

Vitullo-Martin concludes that the system of tax codes serves as an intervention by the federal government to regulate how people choose schools and, most importantly, which people are better able to make certain choices that are unavailable to others. Changes in the tax structure could make private schools even more egalitarian and public schools less segregated. Failure to address this issue eventually will price private education out of the reach of many lower and moderate income families and increase the growing disparity between urban and suburban public schools.

Roger Freeman, in "Educational Tax Credits," pursues the issue of tuition tax credits further. Noting that the constitutionality of tax credits seems to be the prime obstacle to their adoption, Freeman claims that the courts have been less than consistent and clear on their rulings pertinent to financial relief for those individuals choosing nonpublic education. Yet such inconsistency is not always related to the merits of individual cases but is somewhat comprehensible when one understands better the political context within which cases are decided. Freeman surmises, for example, that the mere fact that the deduction of tuition for private education affects but a small minority of taxpayers whereas the deduction of religious contributions affects a larger majority contributes to the direction of Supreme Court decisions, despite the absence of clear-cut constitutional differences between such deductions.

Yet the larger question remains whether or not tuition tax credits would be good public policy. Would they, in fact, lead to a mass exodus from the public schools? Would they amount to a "raid on the treasury"? Would they simply provide another large tax loophole for the wealthy? Freeman claims "no" on all counts. First, he feels that tuition tax credits would, indeed, lower the penalty for attendance at private schools but certainly not eliminate it. Thus, there is no automatic incentive for parents to pull their children from public schools and enroll them in private schools. Second, to the extent that educational tax credits withdraw funds from the treasury, they also save expenditures for public schooling. Freeman concludes then that tuition tax credits "are not a cost—they are a productive investment." Finally, the author discusses the creation of major loopholes by noting that the awarding of a five-hundred-dollar tax credit to each student currently enrolled in a nonpublic school would amount to only one-quarter of 1 percent of all nontaxable income—hardly a "major" loophole. Freeman concludes by suggesting ways in which tuition tax credits might be enacted given the past reaction to such attempts.

What are we to make of this movement toward the "deregulation" of schooling as described in these four essays? Should movements in this direction be encouraged? Will specific plans such as the tuition tax credit bill or educational vouchers produce the intended results? These are some of the questions tackled by Michael Apple in his "Education and Cultural Reproduction: A Critical Reassessment of Programs for Choice." Apple's essay addresses some consequences of deregulation to the essential relationship between the individual, education, and the state and the conditions under which we might expect to develop schooling that evidences greater "centrifugation," as La Belle might term it.

In Apple's socialist analysis, a fundamental issue is the consideration of the manner in which schools are "actors in the re-creation, and creation, of an effective dominant culture." This involves seeing the state (through schooling) as producing the conditions for its own continuation, certainly a theme in many other essays in this volume. Such reproduction, however, must be examined not as a random phenomenon but as the result of a system that "generates structurally based inequalities" (a point empirically documented by Vitullo-Martin). The concept of "class" then is involved not as an economic position alone but also in the larger relationship of the individual to the means of production and productive forces as well. "Class" refers not only to structural positions but is "lived" through social relations, power relations, language, and world view.

Such a perspective on the role of the state in education requires a complex understanding of how schools in fact do create the conditions of class-based cultural reproduction. Apple analyzes two recent ethnographic studies of adolescents in Great Britain and the United States. He points out that such reproduction does not occur because the schools are consciously attempting to inculcate youth into the social order. In fact, there exists considerable student resistance to the processes of schooling, and students find remarkably creative and culturally specific ways of adapting to these processes. The two studies point out that schools need to be seen as contradictory institutions, for they not only reproduce society but, in so doing, create the conditions that appear to contradict this reproductive process.

Yet student resistance in itself is contradictory. On the one hand, it illustrates, both practically and symbolically, student "penetration" of the demands of the state through schooling and student attempts to expose these perceived illegitimate demands. On the other hand, such resistance serves further to incorporate the students into the social structure of the state, and Apple explains the processes by which this occurs. Thus, contradictions serve both to identify class location to participants as well as eventually to institutionalize class patterns.

This backdrop provides the basis for pressures on the state to deregulate, for as confidence in state schools diminishes (see Introduction), fueled by the increasing generation of "opposites" in state schooling, various groups press to deregulate state schooling so that more control may be attained locally. Hence, the rise of tuition tax credits, voucher plans, and the like. Apple discusses these plans and the role of the state in them. He places special emphasis on the tendency for the state to set the conditions for cultural reproduction within the school and for the parallel interests of the state in legitimation and accumulation functions of schooling (discussed by La Belle in another context). Yet Apple suggests that the growing movement toward deregulation in general (see Iannaccone) and toward tuition tax credits and vouchers specifically (see West, Erickson, Freeman, and Vitullo-Martin) in itself reflects the contradictions of the state (see Arons and Lawrence), for while these plans do provide for some degree of greater self-determination, they may serve also to simply "export" the crisis of confidence in the education from one area of the state and deflect it to another—the state-dominated marketplace.

The essays in Part 4 propose a variety of solutions to the pervasiveness of the "predominant orthodoxy." Such solutions are characterized by various attempts to provide greater client control over educational decisions. The scant empirical evidence available (principally from Canada) suggests that some programs may in fact do that. Yet numerous questions still remain unanswered. Would the movement toward greater client choice result in greater diversity, or would clients choose that to which they were accustomed? Would the availability of diversity benefit all sectors of the society equally? What are the central criteria by which individuals and groups can decide whether educational deregulation can be truly beneficial? If deregulation is to occur, which of the several competing plans is preferable? Can sufficient unanimity about any one plan be created to serve as a potent political force to overcome entrenched vested interests? The answers to these and other such seminal questions will help determine future relations between education and the state.

## SUGGESTED READINGS

Apple, Michael W. *Ideology and Curriculum.* London: Routledge & Kegan Paul, 1979.

Bidwell, Charles E. "Students and Schools: Some Observations in Client-Serving Organizations." In W. R. Rosengren and M. Lefton, eds., *Organizations and Clients: Essays in the Sociology of Service.* Columbus, Ohio: Charles E. Merrill, 1970, pp. 37–70.

Carlson, Richard O. "Environmental Constraints and Organizational Consequences: The Public School and Its Clients." In Daniel E. Griffiths, ed. *Behavioral Science and Educational Administration.* Sixty-Third Yearbook of the National Society for the Study of Education, Part II. Chicago: The Society, 1964, pp. 262–76.

Cohen, David K., and Eleanor Farrar. "Power to the Parents? The Story of Education Vouchers." *Public Interest* 48 (Summer 1977): 72–79.

Coons, John E., and Stephen D. Sugarman. *Education by Choice: The Case for Family Control.* Berkeley: University of California Press, 1978.

Downey, L. W. "The Anatomy of a Policy Decision: B.C.'s Bill 33, The Independent Schools Support Act." Vancouver: University of British Columbia, September 1979.

Everhart, Robert B. *The In-Between Years: Student Life in a Junior High School.* Boston: Routledge & Kegan Paul, 1982.

Friedman, Milton, and Rose Friedman. *Free to Choose.* Harcourt, Brace, Jovanovich, 1980, especially Chapter 6.

Johnson, Richard. "Histories of Culture/Theories of Ideology: Notes on an Impasse." In *Ideology and Cultural Production,* edited by Michelle Barrett, Philip Corrigan, Annette Kuhn, and Janet Wolff. New York: St. Martin's Press, 1979.

Karabel, Jerome, and A. H. Halsey, eds. *Power and Ideology in Education.* New York: Oxford University Press, 1977.

Madaus, George F., Peter W. Airasian, and Thomas Kellaghan. *School Effectiveness: A Reassessment of the Evidence.* New York: McGraw-Hill, 1980.

O'Connor, James. *The Fiscal Crisis of the State.* New York: St. Martin's Press, 1973.

Tyack, David B. *The One Best System: A History of American Education.* Cambridge, Mass.: Harvard University Press, 1974.

U.S. House of Representatives, Committee on Ways and Means. *Hearings on Tax Treatment of Tuition Expenses.* 95th Cong., 2d Sess., 1978.

U.S. Senate, Subcommittee on Taxation and Debt Management of the Committee on Finance. *Hearings on Tuition Tax Relief Bills S. 96, S. 311, S. 834, S. 954, S. 1570, S. 1781, S. 2142.* 95th Cong., 2d Sess., 1978.

Vitullo-Martin, Thomas W. "New York City's Interest in Reform of Tax Treatment of School Expenses — Retaining the Middle Class in the City." *City Almanac* 13 (4) (1978): 1-16.

West, E. G. *Education and the State.* London: Institute of Economic Affairs, 1970.

West, E. G. *Education and the Industrial Revolution.* London: Batsford, 1975.

West, E. G. *Non-Public School Aid: The Law, Economics, and Politics of American Education.* Lexington, Mass.: D.C. Heath, 1976.

Willems, Edwin P. "Sense of Obligation to High School Activities as Related to School Size and Marginality of Students." In Donald A. Erickson, ed., *Educational Organization and Administration.* Berkeley: McCutchan, 1977, pp. 311-24.

Willis, Paul. *Learning to Labour.* Lexington, Mass.: Lexington Books, 1977.

# 10 THE PROSPECTS FOR EDUCATION VOUCHERS
## An Economic Analysis

*E. G. West*

The purpose of this essay is to apply modern tools of analysis in predicting the economic and political circumstances most likely to favor
the adoption of an educational voucher system. The term "voucher"
is used broadly to mean the use of publicly supplied funds in educating a child at the private or public school of the family's choice. The
strongest version of it is where the government provides a voucher of
a financial value equal to the average cost of schooling in government
schools to enable a parent to spend it in purchasing education. The
term "education," moreover, is so widely defined as to mean systematic instruction obtainable from among the largest possible variety of
sources.

Weaker versions of vouchers include those of a smaller financial
value than the average cost of government schooling. These versions
are also intended, in this discussion, to include arrangements where
the government funds do not pass through the parents' hands directly
but are paid by the authorities to the private school of the parents'
choice. In some cases, too, the range of schools eligible to receive
vouchers is restricted by administrative regulation, decree, or discretion. The present essay will take for its primary evidence the differential success of vouchers in the United States and Canada and will
discuss why they have been more successful to date in the latter
country than in the former.

In order to explain what is meant by "predicting" the success probabilities of vouchers, it will be necessary first to review the new change of emphasis in economic reasoning on education. This change will be shown to incorporate the new economics of bureaucracy and the economics of politics, that is, voting. The most interesting and fruitful part of the latter subject will be shown to be the strategic part played by what is called "agenda control" and the "reversion budget." Several important hypotheses emerging from this discussion will then be tested with evidence of voucher schemes in the United States and Canada. The major conclusion is that political institutions do make a difference. Vouchers stand a better chance of acceptance when there is more than one education bureaucracy, when U.S.-type school district referendum methods of budget determination are absent, and when governments are under unusual pressure to reduce taxes.

## THE POLITICAL ECONOMY OF SCHOOLING

### Positive Versus Normative Economics

For many years economists studied educational policy mainly by way of a search for the "correct" amount of resources that "should be" allocated to education in view of its beneficial externalities. This older argument stressed that when I educate my child, benefits are bestowed not only on my family but also externally on the neighborhood. Government should, therefore, encourage enough extra expenditure to capture the optimal amount of external benefits and to be responsible for what are unquestionably believed to be indivisible "public goods."

The present trend, however, is away from such normative study of what "ought to be" and toward the approach of positive economic analysis of "what is" in the real world. The latter usually incorporates two emerging branches of economics: the study of "public choice" and the "economics of politics."

In attempting to explain the world as it is, the newer approach does not begin with preconceived notions of an economy governed by philosopher-kings seeking to achieve "social optimality" through the "internalization of externalities." It starts with the realistic recognition that governments, for some not particularly obvious reasons, have taken over the supply of marketable *private* goods, the goods to which the externalities argument does *not* apply.[1] The long list of "private" services supplied by public "bureaus" includes garbage removal, libraries, housing, water, fire, hospitals, post offices, and the provision of fuel, transport, and recreation. These are all "private goods" in that their benefits are divisible among individuals who can be excluded from receiving the services if they do not pay a price. Such services, can be, and frequently are, marketed. Now there is no need to assume, a priori, that educational services are not also in this category. Whether education is a public, private, or "mixed" good, the interesting question remains as to why compulsory and "free" education is not matched by the compulsory and "free" clothing and feeding of children.

Once within the enclave of government supply, public choice analysts must focus among other things upon the economics of public bureaucracies. We shall proceed, accordingly, to a review of bureaucracy and voting theory as it applies to education. The degree of conformity of real world evidence with this theory will then be examined in the context of recent experiences in Canada and the United States. Our primary attention will be upon the chances of implementing voucher schemes in the face of bureaucratic constraints.

## The Economics of Bureaucracy

William Niskanen's seminal work in 1971, *Bureaucracy and Representative Government*, was structured on the assumption that a bureaucrat, like anyone else, maximizes his personal utility or that there are at least elements in his utility other than the general welfare and the interests of the state. In searching for some less abstract proxy for utility, Niskanen found it useful to borrow from modern theories of the firm that present managers as having a range of discretionary behavior within the objective of maximizing profit. Since the bureaucrat cannot directly appropriate (take home) the difference between the revenues and costs (profits) of the bureau, Niskanen contended that salary, perquisites of the office, public reputation, power, patronage, and output of the bureau were relevant elements (variables) that may enter the bureaucrat's set of preferred aims (utility functions). But each of these vary in a one-for-one relationship with the *size of the budget* of the bureau during the bureaucrat's tenure in office.

Four major predictions that came out of Niskanen's theory were: (1) The tendency of the bureau's expansion to squeeze most of the voter/citizen's consumers' surplus, (2) a momentum toward "bureaucratic imperialism"—continual expansion of the bureau's monopoly, (3) occasional alliances between a bureau and the factor supplies (such as labor) it employs, and (4) the bureau's all-or-nothing offer to what Niskanen calls a government review committee, for example, the education committee or the health committee. These consist of politicians selected because of their expertise. Usually this means that they are sympathetic to an expansion of supply in the relevant industries. The review committee thus becomes a "high demand committee."[2]

The theory has subsequently been modified to meet the criticism that it did not develop the conditions for a *precise* equilibrium output and that budget maximization was not necessarily consistent with utility maximizing by bureaucrats.[3] More reasonably, bureaucrats may (1) press for a maximum budget with services produced at cost, or (2) manipulate a "discretionary budget"—the difference between the full budget and the costs. In the latter case, the bureaucrat may take out his gains in the form of perquisites in his working environment, such as the use of lavish equipment and even leisure on the job. Costs will then not be lowest (the bureau will not be efficient).

The proof of any theory depends on whether the hypotheses developed are generally consistent with observed behavior. I shall demonstrate that Niskanen's theory *is* very illuminating and receives considerable empirical support when applied to the finance and organization of education. The discussion will not employ a sharp or consistent definition of the term "bureaucracy." While there should be no difficulty in distinguishing the specific meaning in context, sometimes it will simply imply a set of bureaucrats, and sometimes it will apply to the organizational structure and/or behavioral characteristics of bureaus. The term, used more commonly in North America, will obviously include local chief officers of education and to the U.S. Department of Education's full-time staff, but it will often be used in the broader sense to include all employees of the bureaucracy and especially schoolteachers and inspectors.

The phenomenon of "bureaucratic imperialism" is not difficult to document and will not receive much attention except for one or two observations. Bureaucratic growth in education has been going on in the Western world ever since the late nineteenth century. In England and Wales, for instance, the transfer of the administration of schooling from the old board schools to the municipalities was the first major step in increasing the size of the school district. Since then there have been expansions and mergers of local government areas. In Canada and the United States the increase of school district size has been especially rapid in recent years, and the process has been given the name "consolidation." Why have administrators, school principals, schoolteachers, and support staff in most countries all been leading supporters of the consolidation movement? The search for an answer to this question leads us to our second division of public choice that will receive much more scrutiny here.

### The Economics of Politics

*Competitive Agenda Formation Process.* Consider first the simplest of voting models: voting on single issues. Suppose, indeed, that education is the only issue. The size/amount of public education expenditures will meet the preferences of the median voter, the individual voter who is halfway in the range of voters, *provided there is a competitive agenda formation process.* (As will be shown later, the "Niskanen bureau" operates only when there is *monopolistic* agenda formation.)

A voter's utility is a function of the consumption of ordinary private goods (services) and the publicly provided good or service (which in our model is education). It can be transformed into a public sector preference map (function) as in Figure 10-1. The single peaked curve shows an ordering of alternative levels of the bureau's education budget by a given voter. The ordering shown in the curve is, of course, conditional upon given values of the voter's income, tax share, benefit share, and unit cost of the public sector good or service. The utility level from budget $Q_1$ is shown to be higher (because it is higher up the curve) at $D$ than at zero budget level (shown at $E$). $Q_0$ gives a higher level still (shown at point $C$). Because this budget level ($Q_0$) is, in fact, associated with the peak of the graph, it is called the voter's most preferred budget for the bureau. Note that a

Figure 10-1.

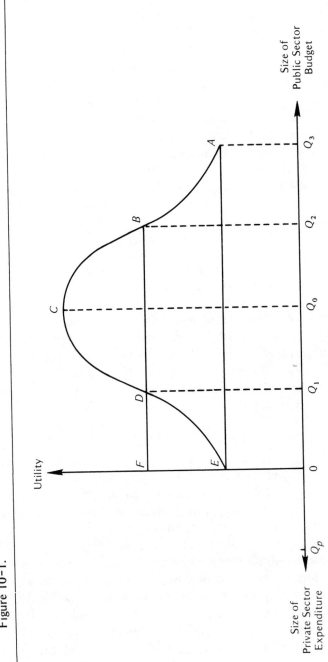

budget level of $Q_3$ gives the same level of utility as a zero quantity budget.

If we consider a simple model containing three voters, an illustrative diagram using the technique of Figure 10-1 requires *three* single peaked utility curves. This is illustrated in Figure 10-2. The most preferred budgets of three individuals $A$, $B$, and $C$, are shown to be $Q_A$, $Q_B$, and $Q_C$, respectively. Under competitive agenda formation, the equilibrium of the majority voting process is the median of the distribution of individual voters' most preferred budgets. This is shown here as $Q_B$. To see this, take $Q_B$ as the status quo, and pair it against several other alternatives. When it is paired against $Q_A$, voters $B$ and $C$ vote for $Q_B$ since they prefer that budget level to $Q_A$. When $Q_B$ is paired against $Q_C$, voters $A$ and $B$ vote for $Q_B$. Similarly, if we paired $Q_B$ with any other alternative—any other point on the horizontal axis of Figure 10-2—it is easily shown that $Q_B$ is the only alternative that can defeat all others. $Q_B$, therefore, is the equilibrium of the competitive voting process with competitive agenda formation. It follows that all candidates must promise to meet the

Figure 10-2.

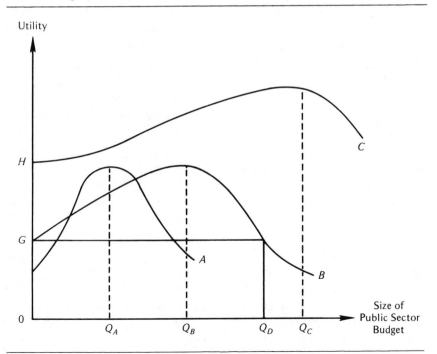

median voter's preferred budget if they are to stand a chance of election.

*Monopoly in the Agenda Formation.*    One important source of the monopoly power of the strong "Niskanen bureaucracy" is its domination of the public agenda or control over budget initiatives.[4] To ensure an all-or-nothing proposal the bureau, rather than the voters, must control the proposal generation process. To make a take-it-or-leave-it offer, based on a yes-no vote, the bureau's proposal *must avoid being paired against a multitude of competing proposals.* It could best do this if it could pair its proposal against a status quo, or reversion level, of nothing—that is, a budget of zero value. When maximizing expected returns to itself, the bureau will propose the largest budget that will obtain a majority. The choice facing the voter then becomes an all-or-nothing situation. It is this situation that is the trademark of the "Niskanen bureaucracy."

We now have some useful insight for our question as to why administrators, school principals, schoolteachers, and support staff have all been leading supporters of consolidation into large (merged) school districts. The more the population in a school district grows, the lower will be the probability of any single individual being the median voter. With a population of a thousand he has a one in a thousand chance. With a hundred thousand his chance is only one in a hundred thousand. This situation induces voter apathy, low participation rates in voting, and an erosion of the incentives for voters to obtain knowledge of the supply proposals on the public agenda. All this means reduced possibilities of agenda proposals competing with that offered by one single-minded bureau alliance comprising administrators, school principals, teachers, and support staff. Possibilities are reduced not only of alternative budget proposals in terms of quantity (size) but also of quality—whether, for instance, to have a given budget allocated differently using, for example, a system of vouchers.

In the extreme case the equilibrium quantity via the Niskanen bureaucracy occurs when there are *no* competing proposals on the agenda. It is shown in Figure 10-2 as $Q_D$, where the middle demander is almost indifferent between the budget proposed by the bureau and a zero budget. *Any* proposal between $Q_B$ and $Q_D$ will bring a winning coalition between $B$ and $C$ because they are both better off there than with the alternative zero budget. ($B$ is shown to be better off because all points on his utility curve between $Q_B$ and $Q_D$ are higher than $OG$, the utility level corresponding to a zero budget. Similarly, at all points between $Q_B$ and $Q_D$, voter $C$ has a higher utility than $OH$.)

The previous equilibrium was at $Q_B$ —the most preferred budget of the middle voter. It is a smaller budget than the Niskanen bureau budget by the amount of $Q_D - Q_B$. This is one measure of Niskanen's central finding that bureaus are "too large." With the ultimate appearance of Niskanen's bureau, "the median voter, instead of dominating the outcome in political markets, is viewed as solely a constraint on the expansionist tendencies of the bureau."[5]

It is true that in Niskanen's world the bureau has to bargain with a government committee—the review committee. But, as we have seen, this is a "high demand committee." It comprises one part of the large bureau alliance insofar as its politician members strongly represent education supply side interests such as teachers. Where, in Figure 10-2, the demand of this committee coincides with voter $C$, its optimal budget will also coincide with that of the bureau (at $Q_D$). Otherwise it will be between $Q_B$ or $Q_D$ and still be "too large."

### The Reversion Budget: The Crucial Item

We arrive now at a key point in the analysis. The only apparent way to reduce the bureau's power is to change the reversion level of the budget to something above zero. Refer again to Figure 10-1. Assume the utility curve shown to be that of the median voter. Suppose the status quo or reversion budget is not zero but $Q_1$. The largest budget the median voter will now approve in a referendum when paired against the status quo budget is $Q_2$. This gives him the same level of utility as that received from the status quo budget of $Q_1D$ $(OF)$. The Niskanen bureau's budget will still be "too large" but not as large as before.

This analysis suggests again why bureaus are jealous of *full* monopoly control of the agenda formation process, for *any* competitor (offering an alternative of, say, $Q_1$) will reduce the full expenditure level that the large bureau is capable of securing. The competitor could be a rival government, (for example, a local government versus a central government) or a rival bureaucracy within government. A dominant bureau, therefore, can be predicted to attempt to take over or swamp the rival whatever the form the rivalry takes. With competing government school districts, for instance, there will be a tendency toward amalgamation or take-over for noneducational reasons. The recent successful pressure in the United States for one monolithic department of education incorporating several subdepartments is consistent with this analysis.

But the rival may also be a private school system. Our median voter in Figure 10-1 may then have a preferred self-imposed budget of $Q_p$ corresponding to the peak of a utility curve starting at $E$ and rising to the left of it. (The size of the private budget can be measured on the horizontal ordinate leftward from the origin.) Suppose $Q_p$ is the same distance from the origin as $Q_1$ and produces the same utility level as $Q_1$ (namely, $Q_1 D = OF$). *The existence of a private school alternative is equivalent to a reversion budget of $Q_1$.* This again brings the maximum bureau budget down from $Q_3$ to $Q_2$.

The bureau can therefore be predicted to try to place as many obstacles in the path of private school development as possible. One example of this is the existent imposition of more stringent inspection standards for private schools than are applied to state schools. Furthermore, it can be expected that the established bureau will be hostile to schemes of subsidizing private schools finding a place on the agenda, for they will make the status quo budget larger, and therefore the size of the bureau's maximum budget is smaller still. Moreover, a private system is so outside the province of the bureau as to curtail the size of the *discretionary* budget and the accompanying perquisites. Thus, if there *is* pressure for a voucher system or experiment, the bureau will insist that the vouchers be spent only within the public system. Indeed, if a voucher "experiment" is to receive *additional* money to the public budget it will be welcomed by the bureau.

The pure all-or-nothing proposals may clearly work with public goods like defense. There can be either a government-provided missile defense system or nothing. Each voter cannot conceivably have his own separate and private missile. Education, however, is different. Consider a zero public budget proposal. This does not enforce zero education services.[6] A zero budget implies less need for taxation as well as rates and income taxes. The result is higher disposable incomes for *all*. And this means increased ability of all to purchase the alternative: private education. It is for this reason that $Q_p$ in Figure 10-1 is an available alternative to $Q_1$.

Suppose, next, that there is a marginal switch into private education following a voucher scheme such as that in British Columbia, where, since 1978, families have been enjoying up to five hundred dollars of public money annually directed to the (qualifying) private schools of their choice. The very experience of the private system by new users will oppose the restrictions on information that bureaus prefer. The additional information to the voter will reveal a truer comparative value of public-versus-private education. Such an information shift could move all the curves in Figure 10-2 to the left. To the bureaucracy, this would again have the undesirable result of severely reducing its maximum possible budget.

The argument of Robert Mackay and Carolyn Weaver contains no such information feedback.[7] Another unexplained issue is why the middle voter is ignorant from the beginning of the ultimate outcome of the bureaucrat's "game" while the latter is not. Perhaps the explanation lies in historical accident. Once a bureau is established, it may feel its way to the ultimate large budget. This could help resolve our earlier paradox that while education for children is free and compulsory, shelter, food, and clothing are not. The absence of an initial "threshold size" public bureau in the latter three commodities could explain a different course of events—contrasted with education.

Whatever the answers to these questions, it remains true that the analysis so far is rich in hypotheses on the structure of education. It is the special interest of this essay to focus on corollaries about bureau reactions to vouchers. Three major hypotheses that have emerged are (1) that the major education bureau in charge of government-provided schooling will be hostile to voucher schemes that include private schools, (2) voucher schemes stand a better chance when there are strongly competing bureaus, and (3) in view of the tendency to strong agenda control by the bureau, it will require something like a taxpayer revolution to dislodge it and to secure a voucher scheme through actual legislation. The first two hypotheses will be tested in broad terms by examining recent experience with vouchers in the United States. The third hypothesis will then be examined in the light of experience in Canada.

## THE POLITICAL ECONOMY OF VOUCHERS

### Bureaucracy and Vouchers:  The U.S. Case

It will be argued that a look at experience in the United States, where the voucher has now been seriously emasculated, will serve as an approximate test of the Niskanen theory. It is interesting to note that at the end of his book, where he searches for alternatives to a single bureau-dominated supply, Niskanen himself recommends vouchers as a promising system. For under it, "the role of the bureaucracy . . . is only to dispense the vouchers to the eligible group."[8] It will be contended here that Niskanen might have underestimated the strength of the bureaucratic Leviathan that his own analysis so vividly exposes.

Cohen and Farrar explain that vouchers appealed to U.S. intellectuals and reformers of all political persuasions in the late 1960s and early 1970s. All seemed at last united against the educational establishment. Yet right from the beginning, their idea was to implement a voucher system through *official* auspices. In retrospect nothing could seem to be more incongruous and contradictory:

> After all, the educational bureaucracy presumably was in charge everywhere, from Albuquerque to Xenia. Why should the established authorities tolerate an idea designed to diminish their power and make their lives much more uncomfortably competitive? The federal sponsors of the voucher test program never had a clear answer to this question. . . .[9]

An important fact for the purposes of our analysis is that at this time in the United States more than one bureaucracy was involved in the voucher controversy. The Office of Economic Opportunity (OEO), which in the late 1960s had been involved in heavily subsidized social programs, was under criticism for excess expenses and wastefulness. In the new era of entrenchment the emphasis was on modest experiments. On the left of the political spectrum the voucher system found advocacy in the sociologist Christopher Jencks. On the right was the economist Milton Friedman. Jencks's organization, the Center for the Study of Social Policy (CSPP), was awarded a grant by the OEO to study the feasibility of vouchers. The result was a report announcing that they were, indeed, feasible.[10]

For vouchers to gain a place on the public agenda, they must clearly have some fairly solid constituency in the political world.

Under the above rare circumstances the voucher system was initially espoused by a new bureaucracy, and this was competing with the old established one. The former, OEO, in need of public activities that would justify its continued existence, if not the expansion of its own budget, regarded the voucher system, at the time, as a suitable candidate. In the opinion of Cohen and Farrar the idea looked innovative, it had support from all political quarters, and the emphasis on the need for *experiment* gave it a "social scientific" and "trendy" appearance.[11] By 1969 the federal authorities had decided that the time was ripe for a test of the voucher system. But what happened next was a conflict between two bureaucratic "gladiators."

Obviously aware of the likely hostility to the plan by the biggest bureaucracy, the monopoly educational establishment, the smaller federal bureaucracy sponsoring the voucher test program attempted first to bring political pressure from below since the poor and minorities were receiving the worst educational treatment. The next sequence of events, according to Cohen and Farrar, was that the poor were difficult to organize into an active interest group; established black organizations, especially those with strong integrationist views, regarded vouchers as "a way out for whites"; and Catholics, among the most substantial minority groups in America, happened to prefer other avenues to church-school aid.

Since cooperation from below was thus difficult to find, the OEO and the CSPP turned to support from the top. Some individually interested administrators and school board members were located, and several school districts well outside the major cities seemed promising. But after they discovered the full implications of vouchers (and after much federal money had been spent), full cooperation began to lag. As the districts learned more about the plan, they were prompted to redefine it in such a way as to defeat its original purposes. As a result, by 1976 all the test sites in the United States had failed.

What little success there has been with vouchers has been associated with provisions at Alum Rock, California, in an experiment that continues to this day. The superintendent of the schools in that district was anxious for an internal reform by way of what he called "decentralization" of the (public) schools. His major obstacle was lack of funds since his was a poor area. After its failure in other states, the OEO bureaucracy, clearly anxious to justify its own existence, was most eager for a new volunteer for a voucher test. The

Alum Rock superintendent "quickly learned that OEO and CSPP needed him more than he needed them."[12]

From the beginning, both sides seem to have been somewhat at cross-purposes, the OEO requiring a test of consumer sovereignty, and Alum Rock requiring federal support for what it called a decentralization plan. The idea of the voucher plan was to bring back into education market incentives to increase student *achievement* (incentives that, in fact, are not reflected in the present pay methods/scales of teachers). Under competitive markets, education "firms" that are successful in meeting parental preferences and in increasing student achievement immediately enjoy expanded incomes via increased enrollments. But these incentives, while initially attempted in the Alum Rock experiment, were very soon blunted. And this occurred for three reasons. First, the teachers whose enrollments declined were given priority in assignments to other schools or were paid salaries by OEO while assigned to headquarters. Second, teachers whose efforts resulted in increased enrollments were not rewarded with higher salaries. Instead, their *school* would certainly receive more funds, but the money would be spent on more materials and more teachers. Third, parental demand was eventually restricted by making it impossible for the heavily patronized schools to expand, for teachers and administrators soon insisted that enrollment limits be placed on each school.

An equally important feature that led to the emasculation of the original voucher plan, one that contrasts strikingly with the present British Columbia scheme, was the official forestalling of *private* schools entering the voucher system. This fact supports our earlier hypothesis. An attempt by four teachers to start the only private school in the area proved abortive. The local certified employee council insisted that private schools meet most of the operating standards of the public schools. The new small-scale entrant was officially obliged to provide the same staff/student ratios, salaries, fringe benefits, and so on. It was thus doomed from the start.

The voucher system attempted by the OEO was of the Jencks's variety rather than the Friedman version. The Friedman voucher was intended simply to insure more efficiency in the spending of current amounts of government funds. The Jencks version weighed down the Alum Rock plan with other more complex objectives. It tried, in addition, to promote equality, to protect minorities and poor students from discrimination, and to protect consumers from "bad schools." Special fiscal incentives were provided for schools that enrolled poor children. There were detailed and complicated admission policies regulating the freedom of schools to choose applicants and applicants to choose schools; and there were even applicant lotteries.

It is interesting that Jencks's plan was designed to produce yet another bureaucracy, the Education Voucher Agency, to be independent of the participating schools, to distribute the vouchers, provide consumers with information to help them make "informed choice," and monitor the quality of schools. The actual Alum Rock system clearly reflected this aspect of Jencks's proposal. There was established an overall Education Voucher Advisory Committee (EVAC) run by both parents and professionals.

Although some observers have found it strange that parents did not take more advantage of the opportunities for gaining power through this organization, economists will *not* be so surprised. The opportunity costs, especially the costs of time facing parents, are high relative to expected benefits, in contrast with professional members. One cannot imagine an efficient market in which consumers have to spend valuable time on committees of supply on everything they buy. Usually they require only the power of choice—the power to dismiss this or that supplier by silently redirecting their custom and expenditure.

The American attempt to establish a voucher system thus seems well in accord with the Niskanen theory of bureaucracy. That theory, as we have seen, predicts that bureaucracies will use all means to expand and strengthen their monopoly power, to become the sole sources of the supply of information on desired quality of their services, to become political lobbies and voting constituencies in their own right, to monopolize the agenda process, and to discourage any new proposal, such as vouchers, where there is a danger of seriously reducing their longevity and budget, while encouraging it where the opposite prospects prevail.

### Buying Off the Bureau

Such a diagnosis might well appear depressing to many. They will see the present system as one that has become overpowerful, large, unimaginative, and grossly inefficient. The problem in economic terms may be diagnosed by some as one of entrenched monopoly. In formal welfare economic analysis, the primary defect of monopoly power per se is that it violates the necessary conditions for optimum efficiency or "pareto-optimality" in resource use.[13]

Theoretically, at least, this means that there must remain some unexploited "gains from trade" between the monopolist and his consumer-customers. James Buchanan and Gordon Tullock have asked the crucial question Why do we not also observe more efforts on the part of consumer-organized "cooperatives" to control monopoly firms through ordinary market purchase or acquisition? In the context of the public education monopoly, the question, more crudely expressed, is Granted that bureaucrats possess the equivalent of "property rights in monopoly power," why is it that the rest of society cannot buy them out? For this would be to the *benefit of all parties*—bureaucrats included.[14]

The Buchanan and Tullock theory relates to a simple monopoly. The monopolist's powers therein are restricted to raising prices (or reducing quality). This leads consumers to contract their demand so that ultimately lower quantities are traded. The purchaser loses some of his "consumer's surplus," some of it going as a transfer to the monopolist, and some of it disappearing as a dead-weight loss. It is the ability to recover the dead-weight loss that, theoretically at least, provides the motive to buy out the monopolist on mutually acceptable terms.

Although the buying out of simple monopolies may sometimes be feasible, it is important to note that the extreme type of "Niskanen bureaucracy" is of a different nature that does *not* lend itself to the Buchanan and Tullock solution. For this kind of monopoly does more than fix the price; it fixes quantities also. Consumers, in other words, are now *not* able to respond by contracting their demand. The Niskanen bureau operation is an "all-or-nothing" deal; it is an exchange of one lump sum quantity of service (output) for one lump sum payment. This price or payment has already squeezed from the consumer all of his surplus. Thus, there is no remaining dead-weight loss or consumer surplus with which to bargain.

Is the case of education close to the Niskanen model of monopoly? It clearly is insofar as there is control on quantities through compulsory laws, higher prices, and an all-or-nothing offer. One obvious conclusion, if pareto efficiency is to be the target, is the importance of concentrating on the prevention of monopoly. The monopolizing of education that started in the nineteenth century seems close to being irreversible. The recognition of this truth might at least offer some warning of the problems of further monopolization in other sectors of society. The statutory monopoly evidently promotes the most social waste and inefficiency.

The analysis so far has assumed that there are *some* initial gainers from the "game." These are the *original* bureaucrats who earn monopoly rents, a term expressing the "artificial" increase in their pecuniary and nonpecuniary incomes that stem from the ability to obtain for their education budget more total revenue from taxpayers. Eventually, however, resources will be invested by potential entrants to the bureaucracy with the aim of sharing some of the gains. Incumbent bureaucrats are led then to protect their profession by stipulating high qualifications for new entrants. Persistent entrants would eventually erode their potential monopoly gains because of the lifetime income costs of obtaining higher degrees. Under these circumstances, and in the long run, nobody gains from the present system, not even the current generation of bureaucrats. This is a classic case of political, not market, failure. The solutions are not obvious or easy. And they point to the need for *constitutional* revision, a process that returns us to basic *consensus* democracy, and not the simple majority form that seems hitherto to have opened traps, not doors.

## Constitutional Reform

The constitutional dimensions of politics *can*, nevertheless, be invoked, and without going to the extreme of formally rewriting the whole social contract. The Constitution is, itself, unfolding, and can be changed to suit dynamic changes. Reforms could concentrate on changing some particular rules of the game. They could, for instance, (1) increase competition among bureaucracies, (2) subsidize agenda proposal suppliers who are independent of the bureaucracy, (3) randomly assign elected politicians to review committees, (4) increase the minimum vote requirement to say 60 or 70 percent instead of the present 50 percent, and (5) increase private/public competition — as the British Columbia voucher promises to do.

In the United States more active use of existing constitutional avenues provide another facility for change. And "taxpayers' rebellions," such as the 1978 education tax revolt in Cleveland, Ohio, are easier to effect because constitutional educational bond issues have to be voted on by taxpayers. Proposition 13 in California is another example of this "facility of retaliation." In Canada there has been much discussion on procedures of voter-consultation-by-referendum on issues such as Quebec independence and the Trudeau government's proposed consideration of further uses of referenda that could be enshrined in the new Canadian constitution. Meanwhile, at the level of the Canadian municipality, voters in some provinces can petition to force a plebiscite challenging the spending intentions of elected leaders.

In U.S. education there has been another example of this kind of constitutional-style attempt at change in the recent Supreme Court judgments on the rights of parents.[15] Another instance of an attempt to challenge the bureau's monopoly of the agenda process has been the "audacious" endeavor in 1978 to pass legislation on tax credits for all levels of education, whether public or private.[16] This proposal would have attacked the heart of the public monopoly in education in an even more fundamental way than would vouchers. For it suggested emphasis on the truth that it is the individual's own money (contributed via direct or indirect taxes) that is being returned and that he is not receiving a grant from third parties in the shape of "public funds." Meanwhile, like vouchers, the tax credit creates the equivalent of a higher reversionary budget which curtails expansion.

The U.S. Senate Finance Committee passed the Moynihan/Packwood Bill almost unanimously early in 1978. Attempts were made later in the year to pass legislation on the floor of the House (the House of Representatives had similar proposals). Now we have seen that Niskanen's theory predicts hostility to such schemes from the major administration. There was, in fact, triumphant resistance from this quarter. President Carter and the secretary of Health, Education, and Welfare, Joseph Califano, declared solidly against the new proposal, the latter fearing a large-scale desertion from public schools—despite tax credits of up to five hundred dollars. Insofar as the fear was justified, it carried an implicit adverse parental judgment on the public schools. Anyway, it seems that the "cause" has now faltered in the United States. What then are the chances in Canada?

### The British Columbia Voucher Scheme

The most striking voucher scheme of all on the North American continent is contained in the legislation that was passed in September

1977 to allow grants of up to five hundred dollars per student at British Columbia independent schools (church schools included).[17] The budget for this measure was finally approved in April 1978, and it completed its first year of actual operation in the summer of 1979. Although the prevailing social credit government was responsible, other parties were not firmly opposed ideologically, and public opinion polls showed a majority in favor. A constitutional consensus on the demand side of politics thus seems to have taken place. The agenda initiative of the bureaucracy seems, in this instance, to have been severely challenged, and much of it appears to have been a personal triumph for one political leader who had upheld the principle of freedom of choice for many years.[18]

It is arguable that in the United States it is the availability of Proposition-13-type ballots that gives voter retaliation much more potential force in some of the states. But whatever the case, the mood of taxpayer resistance initiated there is now acknowledged to have spread across Canada. The British Columbia experiment *may* indeed be explained in this light; for if its provision of five hundred dollars per pupil per year has the effect of shifting many children from public to independent schools, the cost to the taxpayer, of public schooling which, according to the British Columbia Trustees' Association, averages at $1,653 per pupil for gross operating expenses alone, will drop by $1,153, although payment to those who would be private pupils anyway could offset this.

The argument that the need for significant tax reduction, rather than a desire for an experiment for purely educational reasons, was paramount in British Columbia's voucher legislation, has even stronger support on further scrutiny. For the scheme was made effective fairly quickly, which seems more in accord with rapid political responses to taxpayer rebellions. The earlier U.S. effort was hedged around with all kinds of qualifications. In the United States, as we have seen, the supporters had initially to wait upon an official feasibility study. Then there was a prolonged search for a suitable area for the experiment. Again the scheme was modified and remodified according to the Jencks version with its elaborate rules against discrimination. Most of all the experiments have been confined within the public system.

In view of the earlier account of the economics of bureaucracy, the outcome of the British Columbia voucher scheme is not immediately predictable. But the model of bureaucratic monopoly of agenda

control that we employed (using Figures 10-1 and 10-2) was originally, and ideally, applicable to a framework of direct democracy by
*referendum voting* on public expenditure, a practice that is peculiar
to the United States.[19] Budgets for primary and secondary education
reflect referendum outcomes in twenty-eight U.S. states, including
such populous ones as California, Illinois, Michigan, and New York.[20]
Typically, voters allow the bureaucracy to control the agenda and in
essence respond as "price-takers" to the bureau's supply offer. The
locally elected budget committee is certainly responsible in a formal
way for the proposals. But committee members are usually unpaid
and largely dependent on an interested bureaucrat, the superintendent of schools, for their proposals.

In contrast, in the parliament of the provincial government where
the British Columbia scheme was launched, the Canadian political
representatives, especially when under pressure to reduce taxation,
are obviously *not* always passive and lacking the capacity to initiate
alternative agenda proposals without being totally dominated by
departmental advice.[21] And it is significant, to repeat, that in British
Columbia there have been no extensive feasibility studies and no
complicated Jencks-type rules; the voucher has been introduced with
reasonable swiftness. There has, moreover, been no need for a search
for willing "guinea pig" areas. And the most important feature of all
is that the scheme has been directed, from the beginning, at an existing system of established private schools.

## CONCLUSION

The above analysis has been offered as a contribution to the major
theme of this volume: the consequences of state control of education. It has been shown that one major, if not dominating, consequence is the establishment of a self-interested bureaucracy. The
danger is that ultimately the original goals of public intervention will
become swamped by the objectives of the administration in alliance
with the organized teaching profession.

Insofar as this educational establishment has become entrenched,
it will be difficult to reverse the tide. The economics of bureaucracy
predicts that the establishment will organize itself to obstruct all
threats to its monopoly. Recent history shows, in fact, its open hos-

tility to novel methods of reintroducing choice, for example, by way of a voucher system.

But there are appearing some interesting "escape" attempts and stories. The Proposition-13-type voter seems now willing to organize himself into counteracting political "blocks." Much depends upon the nature of the Constitution, and the facility for public initiative in the United States seems to have been discovered, belatedly, as an avenue of substantial countervailing force.

Meanwhile, the "escape story" from British Columbia is another instance of the difference that the political configuration makes. But most Canadian supporters of vouchers for private education will have to watch for the future encroachment and attrition by established bureaucracies in *public* education. Nevertheless, it may be that British Columbia is now at the center of the voucher stage because of the fortuitous timing of the North American taxpayers' revolt, a revolt in which the tax-saving potential of a five-hundred-dollar voucher scheme, if sufficient numbers migrate from public to private schools, has made it suddenly attractive to political agents trying to accommodate the new public mood.

A unique opportunity now presents itself in British Columbia and in California of testing predictions that have accumulated from decades of debate about whether parents can exercise the responsibility of free choice in their children's education—once allowed the resources to do so. Whatever the long-run fate of the "stage plays" in these areas, when pitched against the likely obstacles that will ensue, there will be much work to do in recording the behavior of all the actors in it while the chance occurs.

## NOTES TO CHAPTER 10

1.  Some basic reasons for public supply of private goods are explored in E. G. West and Robert J. Staaf, "Limits on the Public Provision of Private Goods," *American Economic Review* 71 (1980): 461–65.

2.  William A. Niskanen, *Bureaucracy and Representative Government* (Chicago: Aldine, 1971), pp. 150–151.

3.  Earl Thompson, book review, *Journal of Economic Literature* 11 (1973): 950–53; Jean Luc Migué and Gerard Belanger, "Toward a General Theory of Managerial Discretion," *Public Choice* 17 (1974); and William A. Niskanen, "Bureaucrats and Politicians," *Journal of Law and Economics* 18 (1975): 617–43.

4.  Thomas Romer and Howard Rosenthal, "Bureaucrats vs. Voters: On the Political Economy of Resource Allocation by Direct Democracy," *Quarterly Journal of Economics* 99 (1979): 281–305.

5.  Robert J. Mackay and Carolyn Weaver, *Policy Analysis and Deductive Reasoning* (Lexington, Mass.: D.C. Heath, 1978), p. 148.

6.  Mackay and Weaver speak of "public sector goods" not "public goods." The latter (like defense) give equal shares of the service to all citizens. Mackay and Weaver develop their argument to show how bureaus can obtain still more "monopoly profit" by manipulating the benefit shares of voters with the object of price discrimination. Clearly, they have in mind "private goods publicly produced."

7.  Mackay and Weaver, *Policy Analysis.*

8.  Niskanen, *Bureaucracy*, p. 216.

9.  David K. Cohen and Eleanor Farrar, "Power to the Parents? The Story of Education Vouchers," *Public Interest* 48 (1977): 23–31.

10. Christopher Jencks, et al., *Education Vouchers: A Report on Financing Elementary Education by Grant to Parents* (Cambridge, Mass.: Center for the Study of Public Policy, 1970).

11. Cohen and Farrar, "Power to the Parents?"

12. Ibid., p. 82.

13. "Pareto-optimality" is a state where it is impossible to make *everybody* better off by reallocating resources.

14. James M. Buchanan and Gordon Tullock, "The 'Dead Hand' of Monopoly," *Antitrust Law and Economics Review* 21 (1968): 78–92; reprinted in James Buchanan and Robert Tollison, eds., *Theory of Public Choice: Political Applications of Economics* (Ann Arbor: University of Michigan Press, 1972).

15. E. G. West, "American Schools on Trial," *New Society* 43 (1978): 78–180.

16. My testimony before the hearings of the Senate Finance Committee in January 1978 is reproduced and extended in "Tuition Tax Credit Proposals: An Economic Analysis of the 1978 Packwood/Moynihan Bill," *Policy Review* 3 (1978): 61–75.

17. Although the government funds are directed toward qualifying independent schools, the system is equivalent to a voucher system because the money follows the individual student.

18. L. W. Downey, "The Anatomy of a Policy Decision: B.C.'s Bill 33, the Independent Schools Support Act," University of British Columbia, September 1979.

19. Romer and Rosenthal, "Bureaucrats vs. Voters," p. 1.

20. For a survey of U.S. school expenditure institutions, see E. O. Tron, "Fiscal Controls and Tax Requirements Imposed by States and Tax Options Available to School Districts," in *Selected Papers in School Finance 1976*,

U.S. Department of Health, Education, and Welfare (Washington, D.C.: U.S. Government Printing Office, 1977), pp. 267–82.

21.   According to Downey the forcefulness and resolution of one dedicated politician, the minister of education, had much to do with the success of the legislation despite the fact that "the whole concept of public aid to nonpublic education was an anathema to the minister's staff"; "Anatomy of a Policy Decision," p. 47.

# 11 DISTURBING EVIDENCE ABOUT THE "ONE BEST SYSTEM"

*Donald A. Erickson*

Some histories of American education depict our current general framework for schools as a triumph of good over evil.[1] These histories imply that most enlightened, well-intentioned citizens were rather quick to see the need for a universally available government-operated school system, entirely tax-supported and run by "professionals."[2] That "one best system" was delayed by the mean and unenlightened, by haughty elites and parochial interest groups. But through heroic efforts, the evil was overcome.

More recently, scholars have discredited that simple-minded view.[3] But the old ideology lives on, even in universities, our purported centers of open-minded scholarship. I still encounter deans and professors so dedicated to the "one best system" that they think no other arrangements should even be studied.[4] University advisors still dissuade students who propose theses and dissertations on private schools.[5]

At times it would be easy to believe that evidence on alternatives to the "one best system" is deliberately suppressed. For approximately a decade, two federal agencies (the Office of Economic Opportunity and, later, the National Institute of Education) spent millions of dollars attempting a limited experiment designed to reveal the consequences of education vouchers (which would permit parents to channel tax money to the schools of their choice, public or private). Only a handful of public school systems would even consider an experiment, and only one agreed to an experiment, and that one experiment was thoroughly subverted.[6] The Supreme Court has struck down every attempt by state legislatures to provide significant public aid to private schools. In response to my current research on the consequences of tax support of private schools, the British Columbia Teachers' Federation, whose members are expected to help youngsters search for the truth, asks its locals to urge their school boards to block us and suggests that members might well refuse their own questionnaires, throw them away, return them blank, or subvert the evidence by "choosing one number to circle consistently."[7] Fortunately, teachers in the public and private schools of Tacoma and San Francisco have seemed much more open-minded and cooperative when approached for highly similar evidence.

Accidents of Canadian history have made it possible to examine the effects on schools of public money (and the things that go with public money). Quite a few years ago Canada decided, in effect, to treat one single group of schools—the Catholic schools—in quite different ways in different provinces, giving them full tax support in some provinces and no support in others.[8] By comparing Catholic schools in the two situations, one can explore the effects of tax dollars, public regulation, and related influences. In the fall of 1978, the province of British Columbia began infusing public money into private schools of all kinds, none of which had experienced it before.[9] By examining schools *while the infusion occurs*, we can acquire unprecedented information.

Richard Nault and I began exploiting these opportunities early in 1977, under a grant from the Spencer Foundation.[10] The design of our early work was simple. We found parents and teachers (mostly the latter) in the five most westerly Canadian provinces who had moved from publicly supported Catholic schools to privately supported Catholic schools, and vice versa. We asked them what differences they noticed between schools of the two types. We checked their impressions against the impressions of leading Catholic educators in the same areas. If public money has profound effects on schools, parents, teachers, and key school officials should notice differences between schools that get the money and schools that don't. It was an advantage in this work that *all* the schools were Catholic, for differences among them could then not be attributed to differences in religious sponsorship.

To avoid putting ideas into people's heads, we began the interviews with parents and teachers by asking what differences, if any, they had noticed between the publicly and privately supported Catholic schools. Occasionally, parents and teachers asked what differences we had in mind. We always insisted that we had nothing in mind but wondered whether *they* had noticed anything significant.

I was apprehensive during the first interviews. I worried that teachers and parents might report nothing important or consistent in response to our open-ended probes. We would then regret such unstructured research and would be embarrassed to report how little we had accomplished with the Spencer grant.

My anxieties were unfounded. With consistency approaching unanimity, our respondents described parents as more committed in the privately supported than in the publicly supported Catholic schools. Most by far agreed that teachers were more committed as well. Many indicated that the privately supported schools were more "special" and enjoyed more consensus and collaboration. The interviews led us to suspect that public money had reduced commitment and produced other negative effects in the publicly supported Catholic schools, partly by destroying the jeopardy that seemed to make people feel needed, appreciated, and important in privately supported schools; partly by weakening connections between school and church; and partly through other mechanisms, discussed below.

While Nault and I were completing this work, some other colleagues and I seized the opportunity to study British Columbia's private schools longitudinally *while they were receiving their very first grants from the provincial government*. This research should provide the best evidence thus far on the effects of public money since the events can be observed in sequence rather than reconstructed from data gathered later.

It seems reasonable to anticipate that what happens in British Columbia as a consequence of aid to private schools could easily occur in many parts of the United States (and probably in other postindustrial nations) under similar circumstances. Cultural similarities between Canada and the United States are so pervasive that Canadian journalists seem perpetually seeking ways in which Canada is *not* like the United States. Of all Canadian provinces, the one most often accused, over many decades, of resembling its southern neighbor is British Columbia. Until 1978, the province whose funding policies for public and private schools were unquestionably closest to the U.S. norm was British Columbia.

In a baseline survey in the spring of 1978 we documented many characteristics of British Columbia's public and private schools *before* the new aid to private schools was introduced.[11] Comparisons between public and private schools in the baseline survey are exceedingly provocative and notably congruent with the earlier comparisons (mentioned above) between publicly and privately supported Catholic schools. Since the major influence common to both comparisons is public money, we are led to suspect (though we cannot yet be sure) that the money is a major explanation for the differences observed.

## THE BASELINE SURVEY

Since an extensive report of the spring 1978 baseline survey is available elsewhere,[12] only the most salient details need be specified here. The intended private school sample consisted of all eighty-five private schools (except those for exceptional students) then operating in British Columbia's largest population center (Vancouver and the lower Fraser Valley) and in one small hinterland city, Prince George. The intended sample of thirty-five public schools was drawn by stratified random procedures from a sampling frame created by matching each private school in the sample with the nearest public school of the same grade structure (excluding special-purpose schools). Since notable suspicion and hostility then surrounded the announced but not yet activated program of aid to private schools and since we were forced to proceed with unseemly haste, like many other scholars researching controversial issues we did not elicit the participation we wanted. We obtained usable parent questionnaires from eighteen public schools and forty-seven private schools, usable student questionnaires from fifteen public and forty-one private schools, and usable teacher questionnaires from fourteen public and forty-seven private schools. It is clear that we must be wary of possible sampling bias in all our interpretations. However, our efforts to uncover evidence of bias are thus far reassuring. It appears, for instance, that the nonparticipation of schools was mainly a function not of school characteristics but of timing, for we had generally excellent cooperation before some inflammatory news items appeared and very little afterward. Similarly, the nonparticipation of many individual teachers and parents seems to have affected our measures of school characteristics very little, for students, who responded in class and therefore provided response rates approaching 100 percent, had a strong tendency to agree with parents and teachers, whose response rates were often rather low. In all cases, there were statistically significant correlations among the measures which, though derived from different questionnaires (those administered to students, teachers, and parents, respectively), were designed to measure the same phenomena. The data behaved in a manner largely predicted in advance in terms of the ideas discussed below in this essay.

In the spring of 1978, when the baseline survey was conducted, many private schools in British Columbia were housed in rather antiquated buildings. Many were staffed by teachers paid about ten thousand dollars less than their public school confreres and were short of many material benefits, especially dollars. The future of the schools was in jeopardy. Our data show that the jeopardy was sensed by parents, teachers, and students. There was no indication that anyone loved the jeopardy per se. No one lauded leaking roofs, inadequate wiring, dog-eared books, meager wages, and a constant struggle to pay spiraling bills. With surprising consistency, however, parents, teachers, and students expressed affection for what they experienced within the *context* of the leaking roofs and meager wages. According to the reports of all three groups, the somewhat impoverished private schools were distinguished from the well-heeled public schools by superior commitment, consensus, community, accomplishment, and exceptionality.

The following examples illustrate the findings. We begin with data on commitment, which emerged as a major theme. Unlike some scholars, we define "commitment" as having a distinct affective component. It is a tendency to approach one's tasks and to relate to others in the enterprise with enthusiasm and concern. By this definition, committed people perform their tasks with verve and involvement. They "throw themselves" into the effort, are absorbed by it, and "self-actualize" by means of it, "going the extra mile" to do it well. Commitment, thus viewed, is different from completing defined units of work calculatively for defined units of remuneration. To be committed is to disregard, ignore, or supersede the units of work and pay, performing out of affection for the tasks, the enterprise as a whole, the shared goals of the enterprise, and the people who share those goals.

## Findings on Student Commitment

In the questionnaires administered to students in grades 8 through 12 in public and private schools, we included seven items on student commitment, developed and impressively validated in an earlier study by Richard Nault.[13] The following are representative:

*How willing would you be to*

(a) Work on a carwash held on a school holiday? The money you earned would be used to buy new equipment for the science department.

(b) Help some teachers for two nights after school put up a display of school awards in the window of a store in a nearby shopping centre?

(c) Take part in a program for new students to be held next fall during the five days before school starts? Your job would be to tell new students about school activities and to show them around the school.

The responses to Nault's seven items were strongly intercorrelated in our data. Their internal consistency, as a group, was impressive.[14] We obtained individual scores on this student commitment measure by summing each student's scores for the seven items.[15] Since the school was our unit of analysis, we then obtained the "school score" (the school mean) by averaging individual student commitment scores within the school. The school scores for public schools did not even overlap the school scores for private schools! The highest student commitment score for a public school was lower than the lowest private school score.[16]

## Findings on Teacher Commitment

Since we were particularly interested in teacher commitment, we probed it by means of three independent measures, a set of items in the teacher questionnaire (distributed to teachers in their classrooms), a set of items in the student questionnaire (administered in randomly selected classes), and a set of items in the parent questionnaire (administred by mail). We had responses from 1,096 parents,

408 teachers, and 7,066 students in the above-described public and private schools. The following items are illustrative:

[ *In the Teacher Questionnaire:* ]

What would you estimate as the approximate percentage of teachers in this school who throw themselves wholeheartedly into their work?

| | |
|---|---|
| All or nearly all | 1 |
| 60–80% | 2 |
| Around 50% | 3 |
| 30–40% | 4 |
| Less than 20% | 5 |

Some teachers in this school seem to have had the spirit and enthusiasm knocked out of them. [Negatively worded.]

Most teachers in this school seem dedicated to doing an outstanding job.

Some teachers in this school seem downright lazy. [Negatively worded.]

[ *In the Student Questionnaire:* ]

This teacher tries very hard to see that everybody learns.

This teacher really tries hard to do a good job.

I sometimes think this teacher is lazy. [Negatively worded.]

[ *In the Parent Questionnaire:* ]

This child's teacher seems to try very hard to do a good job.

When I see how dedicated many teachers are in this school, I feel I must do my best to help out.

Within each of the three measures of teacher commitment, the items are well intercorrelated.[17]

The parents, students, and teachers *agreed* in describing teacher commitment as higher in the private schools than in the public schools. The mean for all private schools is notably higher than the mean for all public schools in the teacher questionnaire measure, in the student questionnaire measure, and in the parent questionnaire measure.[18] The levels of statistical significance are rigorous.[19]

## Findings on Consensus and Exceptionality

We asked parents, teachers, and students whether their school had anything special about it, some agreed-upon, focused purpose around which people tended to band together. Our efforts produced four satisfactory measures, two from the teacher questionnaire and one each from the parent and student questionnaires.[20]

The teachers rather clearly differentiated the items (sampled below) dealing with "Social Cohesion" from those dealing with "Special, Agreed-Upon Mission":

*Social Cohesion* [*Teachers*] :

This school often seems like a big family; everyone is so close and cordial.

Parents often indicate that they appreciate the work teachers are doing in this school.

There isn't much group spirit in this school. [Negatively worded.]

*Special, Agreed-Upon Mission* [*Teachers*] :

I don't see anything very special about this school. [Negatively worded.]

Most people sending their children to this school seem to agree on what a good school is like.

This school offers students a number of unusual advantages.

The goals of this school are very similar to the goals most of our parents have in mind.

The parents spoke of agreement and cohesion as if they were the same phenomenon:

*Social Cohesion* [*Parents*] :

The school which this child attends often seems much like a big family; people are so friendly and agreeable.

The people who work together to make this school a success are a close-knit, friendly group.

There seems to be quite a bit of bickering among parents and teachers at this school. [Negatively worded.]

The students responded consistently to the items on exceptionality, such as:

*School Exceptionality* [*Students*] :

This school is no better than any other school. [Negatively worded.]

I feel it is an honour to go to a school like this.

Most of the time I think this is one of the best schools there is.

When teachers respond to the seven items on "Social Cohesion," when parents reflect on "Social Cohesion," and when students react to the items on "School Exceptionality," the private school means come out dramatically higher than the public school means.[21]

I cannot take space here to discuss our many other findings in any detail. But everyone examining the data is bound to reach the same general conclusion: the teachers, students, and parents in this sample unquestionably differentiate the private schools from the public schools in terms of commitment, consensus, community, accomplishment, and exceptionality. In contrast to the public schools as a whole, the private schools as a whole come through as places where people band together in committed fashion to achieve special, agreed-upon goals. That seems like an important advantage.

One must be careful in interpreting these indications. The picture is not black versus white, good guys versus bad guys. On most of our measures, there is overlap between public and private schools. A few public schools, for example, are described as enjoying more teacher commitment than a few private schools enjoy. Furthermore, there may be public school advantages, not measured in this study, which outweigh these private school characteristics. One could argue with some cogency that the technical skill of the teacher and the adequacy of the curriculum and equipment are more important than commitment, consensus, and the sense of doing something exceptional, although there is considerable recent evidence to the contrary.[22]

It is also possible, as I suggested earlier, that our data have been distorted by sampling bias and other as-yet-undetected influences. We are gathering evidence from other geographic areas and at different points in time and thus should soon be better able to determine whether the above-discussed reports of teachers, students, and parents are trustworthy and representative. For the moment, the data should at least be pondered seriously for their possible meaning. We have fairly impressive evidence of validity, as I have noted. The search for indications of sampling bias has been reassuring thus far. The trends in the evidence, far from being merely unanticipated but interesting happenstances from a single study, echo with surprising fidelity the conceptualization (summarized below) developed long before the data were gathered.

We also have some evidence gathered in the spring of 1979, after the private schools had been receiving public money for seven or

Table 11-1. Proportions of Parents Rating Their Children's Schools as "Excellent" in Seventeen Areas of Performance.

| Area of Performance | "Starters"[a] | | "Movers"[b] | |
|---|---|---|---|---|
| | Public Schools | Private Schools | Public Schools | Private Schools |
| 1. Helps students tell right from wrong. | 16.4% (12 out of 73) | 67.3% (134 out of 199) | 10.1% (10 out of 99) | 60.4% (102 out of 169) |
| 2. Has dedicated teachers. | 18.7% (14 out of 75) | 62.3% (124 out of 199) | 22.1% (23 out of 104) | 67.5% (110 out of 163) |
| 3. Encourages students to be respectful toward parents. | 12.5% (9 out of 72) | 54.8% (109 out of 199) | 8.8% (9 out of 102) | 54.5% (91 out of 167) |
| 4. Encourages students to be courteous and kind. | 20.5% (15 out of 73) | 61.7% (124 out of 201) | 14.2% (15 out of 106) | 63.9% (108 out of 169) |
| 5. Maintains morally safe conditions. | 19.4% (14 out of 72) | 58.0% (116 out of 200) | 11.7% (12 out of 103) | 51.8% (86 out of 166) |
| 6. Motivates students to do their best. | 16.4% (12 out of 73) | 54.0% (107 out of 198) | 16.7% (18 out of 108) | 54.4% (92 out of 169) |
| 7. Maintains good discipline. | 17.3% (13 out of 75) | 51.0% (102 out of 200) | 12.0% (13 out of 108) | 51.5% (88 out of 171) |
| 8. Develops a strong school spirit. | 18.9% (14 out of 74) | 49.0% (98 out of 200) | 19.6% (21 out of 107) | 52.7% (89 out of 169) |
| 9. Discourages prejudice against minorities. | 31.4% (22 out of 70) | 60.2% (118 out of 196) | 19.8% (19 out of 96) | 52.8% (85 out of 161) |

| | | | | |
|---|---|---|---|---|
| 10. Helps children get along well with each other. | 18.6% (13 out of 70) | 37.9% (75 out of 198) | 12.9% (13 out of 101) | 41.3% (69 out of 167) |
| 11. Encourages students to think for themselves. | 16.7% (12 out of 72) | 38.1% (75 out of 197) | 21.0% (22 out of 105) | 46.2% (78 out of 169) |
| 12. Has skillful teachers. | 18.7% (14 out of 75) | 40.4% (80 out of 198) | 19.6% (21 out of 107) | 42.3% (71 out of 168) |
| 13. Provides individual attention to students. | 18.7% (14 out of 75) | 38.0% (76 out of 200) | 13.0% (14 out of 108) | 38.1% (64 out of 168) |
| 14. Is responsive to parent complaints and suggestions. | 21.3% (16 out of 75) | 41.1% (81 out of 197) | 19.0% (20 out of 105) | 39.1% (63 out of 161) |
| 15. Has a competent principal (or headmaster or headmistress). | 37.3% (28 out of 75) | 54.8% (108 out of 197) | 29.1% (30 out of 103) | 52.7% (88 out of 167) |
| 16. Develops student self-confidence. | 17.6% (13 out of 74) | 32.3% (65 out of 201) | 15.0% (16 out of 107) | 40.2% (68 out of 169) |
| 17. Maintains physically safe conditions.c | 19.2% (14 out of 73) | 35.0% (70 out of 200) | 23.1% (25 out of 108) | 34.1% (57 out of 167) |

a. "Starters" are parents who had enrolled their children in the first grades of elementary and secondary schools.

b. "Movers" are parents who had recently moved their children from public to private schools, or vice versa.

c. The only difference in this table between public and private schools that is not statistically significant at the 0.0001 level.

eight months. It would still be too early, I would guess, for any dramatic impact of the public funds to be felt by parents, since both they and the schools had made most major arrangements for the 1978–79 school year before the precise nature of the provincial funding was known. Complex organizations like schools do not ordinarily change to any marked degree in such a brief period of time.

The 1979 data are from parents who had been interviewed by telephone in the fall of 1978 in an effort to determine how they decided whether their children would attend public or private schools. Since the vast majority of these one thousand parents said we could return for more information, we contacted the majority with mailed questionnaires in the spring of 1979, to see how they then felt about the schools in which they had enrolled their children seven or eight months earlier. The sample included nearly 250 public school parents and 250 private school parents who had recently enrolled their children in the first grade of elementary or secondary schools. It also involved nearly 250 parents who had recently moved their children from public to private schools, and 250 who had recently moved their children from independent schools.[23] The data discussed below concern *only* the parents who said the school of their choice was the one their child was now attending.

The parents were asked to evaluate their children's schools in the seventeen areas listed in Table 11–1, indicating whether they thought the schools were excellent, good, fair, poor, or very poor. Judging by the evaluations of these parents, the most pronounced differences between public and private schools, from among those listed, relate to helping students tell right from wrong (differences of 50 percentage points), having dedicated teachers (differences of around 45 percentage points), encouraging student respect toward parents (over 40 percentage points), maintaining morally safe conditions (around 40 percentage points), motivating students to do their best (around 37 percentage points), and maintaining good discipline (between 33 and 40 percentage points). The smallest (though still sizable) differences of a statistically significant nature relate to developing student self-confidence (14 to 25 percentage points), being responsive to parents (around 20 percentage points), providing individual attention (19 to 25 percentage points), helping children get along well with each other (19 to 28 percentage points), discouraging prejudice against minorities (28 to 33 percentage points), and developing a strong school spirit (30 to 33 percentage points).

## BEFORE-AFTER EVIDENCE

The evidence discussed above suggests, quite obviously, that privately funded schools are in many ways superior to publicly funded ones. However, the best evidence on this question would be longitudinal, or before-after evidence, showing that schools improved or deteriorated after the introduction or removal of public money. Fortunately, we now have such evidence, though as this essay goes to press it has not yet been completely analyzed.[24] But even at this early stage of our analysis, some stunning tendencies are emerging.

This body of evidence is from two surveys. One, already discussed, was done in the spring of 1978, before the public aid to private schools began to flow. The second survey was conducted two years later, in the spring of 1980, after nearly two years of experience with the new aid. If the aid has any pronounced effects, one would think they should start to manifest themselves after nearly two years. We may look for these effects by comparing data from the two surveys. The questionnaire items involved in the findings reported below were identical in the two surveys, and our analysis considers only the private schools that participated in both.

In both surveys, we asked parents to tell us the extent to which they viewed their private schools as responsive to their interests and suggestions. When we compare the comments in the two surveys, two years apart, we discover that our measure of responsiveness declined by more than 5 standard deviations (a *whopping* change) during the two years. When we compare parents' descriptions of the commitment of private school teachers, we find that our measure of that commitment declined by an almost equal amount. Our measures of social cohesion and of the school's desire and appreciation for parental help, as perceived by parents, declined by more than two standard deviations. Parents' judgments of their private schools' academic effectiveness declined by almost 2 standard deviations. Student responses in the two surveys indicated losses in enthusiasm for school work, a sense of being treated justly, affection for teachers and classes, and the belief that their private schools were in some way "special."

Teachers, most of whom had received exceptionally large salary increases (some salaries were more than doubled) as a consequence of the public aid, provided a more optimistic picture of social climate changes during the two-year period, particularly insofar as their own commitment was concerned.

Except for the data from teachers, who had good reason to view the aid and its consequences through rose-colored glasses, these findings from our before-after comparisons are mostly negative. The evidence, though still not conclusive, suggests, like the evidence discussed earlier, that public support may be *destructive* in schools. When we compared publicly supported and privately supported Catholic schools, in the work reported at the beginning of this essay, we encountered evidence of the superiority of the latter in important respects. Later, when we compared public schools (publicly supported, obviously) with private schools (then privately supported) in British Columbia, we found similar differences between the schools with and without public support. In the meantime another researcher, far away in Merced, California, has documented virtually identical differences between public and private schools.[25] And now, when we look at a group of private schools at two points in time, before and after the inflow of public money, we encounter highly similar differences associated with the presence and absence of public support. The evidence is beginning to accumulate in a consistent, persuasive fashion, to suggest that public support, or something that consistently accompanies it, has deleterious effects on schools.

I do not suggest that the evidence is conclusive. We need to complete our analysis of existing data and continue our investigations further. In the meantime, it may be useful to examine what I consider to be the most plausible interpretation of the evidence thus far presented—especially the telling evidence from our before-after comparisons.

### Effects of Jeopardy

When public money is not available to support a school, two immediate consequences seem obvious. First, its clients must support it (normally through fees), and, second, unless it obtains considerable access to private wealth, its future will be in doubt. This doubtful future is essentially what economists call "the discipline of the market." Everyone in the enterprise knows it will go out of business if it does not compete successfully for clients and their money, so normally everyone has an additional incentive to perform well. In our interveiews, many teachers and parents said their commitment to a school was enhanced when their efforts seemed badly needed and difficult to replace. Some teachers discussed the apparent benefits of understaffing in privately supported schools.[26] When there are barely enough *people* to keep the school running, apparently they value each other's contributions very highly and express appreciation often and intensely, thus reinforcing commitment. Similarly, when a private school is short of *money*, it appears that people pull together as a result. Teachers, viewing the financial sacrifices of parents and the conscientiousness of students, redouble their efforts. Students, knowing that their parents are doing without things to send them to school and seeing that their teachers work extra hard for ridiculously little pay, feel obliged to apply themselves to their work. Parents, noting that teachers do so much for so little and observing that their children apply themselves, are reinforced in their commitment. Some of our data suggest, on the other hand, that jeopardy has *opposite* consequences in schools supported entirely through taxation. Perhaps one common response when public schools run short of money is to curse the government and resent the citizenry. That is not a response likely to elicit high commitment or a close bond between school and community. The *source* of school money may be a critical factor, in addition to the amount. On the negative side, extreme deprivation seems likely to have negative effects in any school, producing discouragement more than commitment.

### Effects of Voluntarism

Patrons are more likely to affiliate *voluntarily* with privately supported schools than with publicly supported ones, for parents cannot be forced to pay school fees. There is some evidence to suggest that students who feel they have enrolled voluntarily in their secondary schools are more committed to several aspects of school life than are students who feel their affiliation was coerced.[27] Perhaps parents, too, will evidence higher commitment to schools that they have selected through a process of deliberate choice. The act of choosing may sensitize parents to special school benefits that would otherwise go unnoticed. Having made a choice, human beings do not like to be proven wrong and, hence, tend to demonstrate commitment by attempting to ensure that the choice turns out well. Freedom to choose may generate a sense of power that itself enhances commitment. Voluntary affiliation also means that a school cannot take its patrons for granted. It could lose them, along with the income they represent. Thus, voluntary affiliation contributes to the jeopardy mentioned earlier and indirectly to the effects of jeopardy on commitment. C.E. Bidwell argues that the relationship between client and professional is likely to be inferior if either party to the exchange lacks freedom to go elsewhere.[28] Voluntarism may be essential to the trust that helps make the teaching-learning encounter effective.

### Effects of Investment

Parents may often view schools which appear to cost them nothing as offering nothing special and thus warranting no special effort or thought. When parents must pay, one would expect them to affiliate more deliberately and with greater commitment. Fortunately, we have some recent data bearing on this issue (from the above-mentioned telephone survey of one thousand parents in British Columbia, conducted in the fall of 1978). Half of these parents were patronizing schools that extracted tuition fees and often additional contributions as well. The data from this survey seem unusually trustworthy. We did not run the risk of biasing the results by forcing parents to select from a list of predetermined answers in a questionnaire. Rather, we asked them an open-ended question, early in the interview, before we said anything to plant ideas in their heads. We asked why they had selected the schools their children were currently attending. The people conducting the interviews were instructed to write down exactly what the parents said, and if they had to summarize long answers, to do so by using phrases which the parents themselves had used. Subsequently, using a careful process that involved extensive cross-checking for accuracy, we sorted the parents' answers into categories.

Since we know that many parental choices are associated with income, education, and occupational status, we systematically controlled for those variables when comparing the answers given by parents in schools which *do not* extract fees (public schools) with the answers given by parents in schools which *do* extract fees (private schools). Table 11-2 controls only for parental education, but in other tables (not shown here) which control for income and occupa-

Table 11-2.  Number and Proportion of B.C. Parents Giving Each of Six Types of Reasons (first reason mentioned) for Selecting the Schools Their Children Currently Attend (as of Fall, 1978), Depending on Level of Parental Education and Whether School Affiliation is Costly or Free.

| First Reason Given | Parents Who Did Not Graduate from High School | | Parents Who Are High School Graduates | | Parents with Some Technical School or University Education | | Parents Who Are Graduates of Technical School or University | |
|---|---|---|---|---|---|---|---|---|
| | Affiliation is Costly | Affiliation is Free | Affiliation is Costly | Affiliation is Free | Affiliation is Costly | Affiliation is Free | Affiliation is Costly | Affiliation is Free |
| School program characteristics | 34 (25.6%) | 20 (15.2%) | 27 (23.9%) | 14 (14.0%) | 21 (20.8%) | 10 (12.3%) | 25 (20.5%) | 16 (25.4%) |
| School climate characteristics (religion, discipline, etc.) | 76 (57.1%) | 13 (9.8%) | 69 (61.1%) | 11 (11.0%) | 64 (63.4%) | 13 (16.0%) | 69 (56.6%) | 1 (1.6%) |
| School finances and facilities | 0 (0.0%) | 7 (5.3%) | 3 (2.7%) | 4 (4.0%) | 7 (6.9%) | 2 (2.5%) | 4 (3.3%) | 4 (6.3%) |
| Convenience, individual preference (proximity, less expense, child's preference, etc.) | 19 (14.3%) | 61 (46.2%) | 11 (9.7%) | 48 (48.0%) | 6 (5.9%) | 40 (49.4%) | 21 (17.2%) | 27 (42.9%) |
| Factors beyond family control | 1 (0.8%) | 20 (15.2%) | 1 (0.9%) | 15 (15.0%) | 1 (1.0%) | 11 (13.6%) | 2 (1.6%) | 12 (19.0%) |
| Other | 3 (2.3%) | 11 (8.3%) | 2 (1.8%) | 8 (8.0%) | 2 (2.0%) | 5 (6.2%) | 1 (0.8%) | 3 (4.8%) |
| TOTALS | 133 | 132 | 113 | 100 | 101 | 81 | 122 | 63 |

Source:  A telephone-interview survey of 1,000 parents conducted in British Columbia in the fall of 1978 (not all parents provided usable data of all three types, so this table does not total to 1,000).

tional status, the same results appear. The data in Table 11-2 show that parents who had chosen schools which levy fees and demand other contributions had a strong tendency to mention reasons concerning school climate—reasons having to do with religion, discipline, and academic emphasis, for example. These are not trivial considerations. In contrast, parents who had chosen schools entirely supported through taxation had a strong tendency to mention reasons which seem more superficial. Nearly half of them mentioned convenient location, the child's preference, or the fact that the school was attended by many of the child's friends. This evidence suggests (though it does not prove) that one way to elicit parental attention to the education of children is to make the choice of a school a costly or exacting one.

There may be other beneficial outcomes of requiring parents to make direct financial investments in the schools their children attend. One is that most parents will probably not invest in a school (if given a choice) unless they expect something extra in exchange for the costs. If they get something extra, or think they get it, they may feel obliged (committed) to reciprocate in some way. And people often follow their investments with efforts to help ensure a payoff.

Another is that some parents, having decided (for whatever reason) to shoulder the extra costs of a private school, may justify the costs by convincing themselves (in the absence of evidence, if need be) that the school does, indeed, feature special benefits. They may view the school through rose-colored glasses and respond to what they perceive with enhanced commitment. But one would not generally expect people either to shoulder the costs or evidence the commitment when there is nothing to suggest that the school does something extra. Schools with diffuse, unarticulated, or even contradictory goals probably inspire little commitment. It seems likely that most parents will respond apathetically to such schools and, if payment is involved, will decide the investment is not warranted. Privately supported schools may thus be expected to stress and preserve their signs of exceptionality in an effort to survive. Schools which charge no fees should not have as much need to appear distinctive.

### Effects of Homogeneity and Consensus

Since parents cannot be forced to pay school fees, it seems likely that only those who agree with a fee-charging school's special emphases will make the payments necessary to enrolling their children. Thus, privately supported schools are likely to have relatively homogeneous clienteles, composed of people who agree with the foci that these schools manifest. We suspect, in turn, that this consensus is a notable advantage to the school. When there is reasonable agreement on what a school should do, much energy that might otherwise be expended on managing conflict and trying to achieve too many different things simultaneously should be available for more productive tasks. When goals are more consistent and clearly focused, they should be easier to reach; there should be greater student achievement along the lines that the schools emphasize. The consensus should foster the development of cohesive social groups, characterized by norms of commitment to the common goals and by collective belief systems that reinforce the common commitment. Because of the internal consistency of such schools, students should feel they are treated in a more principled and consistent fashion, should believe they have more control over their destinies (because of the greater predictability), and should develop more self-confidence. Teachers should report that their intrinsic rewards are consistent and powerful, that their classroom efforts are generally successful, and that parents are supportive and trusting. To reiterate, consensus, in turn, seems a logical product of the screening effect of school fees and of the voluntary nature of the affiliation process.

There will obviously be some costs of permitting a school constituency to become homogeneous (or of any other freedom, for that matter). Some schools may elect to be homogeneous along racial lines, thwarting various attempts to obliterate racial injustice. Other schools may become distinctly parochial in emphasis, constricting student inquiry. In any logical consideration of public policy, both costs and benefits must be weighed. It seems, however, that the benefits of client homogeneity have been scandalously disregarded in many recent public policy choices.

## Effects of Transference

Consensus appears conducive to a mechanism that may be labeled "transference." The basic idea here is that relationships which apply in a familiar situation are often assumed to apply in new situations that look essentially similar. People seem to transfer attitudes from one situation to another on this basis. Transference may occur particularly often in church-related private schools. Teachers in these schools may exercise influence and authority on two bases—one's position and expertise as teacher and one's standing as a symbol of the church. Having noted the resemblance between church and school, the child may unconsciously transfer to the school the attitudes developed over many years of experience in the church. We speculate that transference also occurs, quite independently of the religious factor, in schools that enjoy a strong connection with any type of highly cohesive community, such as an ethnic community, or sometimes even a community defined primarily in terms of locale. One would expect the many pressures toward heterogeneity and disagreement in public schools, and many recent developments that sever school-community connections, to deprive public schools of the benefits of transference.

## Effects of Constituency Size

We encounter many comments from parents who consider small schools superior to large schools. For the moment, we will pass over the well-known arguments and evidence in favor of small schools.[29] A consideration generally overlooked is that when a school is small, at least in the private sector, the constituency over which the chief administrator and school board preside is also small—inordinately small as compared with the constituency of a large public school system. The relevant dynamics are easy to visualize. If a private school is patronized by fifty families, on the average each family can expect to have a discernible impact—approximately one-fiftieth of the constituency impact. As constituency size increases, the individual family's hope of being heard necessarily diminishes. In a constituency of one thousand, the average individual impact will be one one-thousandth. In a public school system serving half a million, it would be surprising if most school patrons did *not* feel relatively powerless. As the states and federal government assume more authority to govern schools, this powerlessness appears certain to increase. When a federal judge intervenes to affect the destinies of school systems in an entire metropolitan area, the average parent must feel enormously incapacitated. We strongly suspect, in turn, that the sense of being a helpless pawn is enormously destructive of commitment to the institution in which one is a pawn.

Even if one assumes that the "structural looseness" of school systems negates the control of school boards and superintendents in many areas of concern and, therefore, that the individual school is the important unit of governance in many respects, private schools, normally much smaller than public schools, still come out ahead on the question of constituency size. One would then still expect more sense of efficacy in school affairs among the patrons of private schools than among the patrons of public schools, and since sense of efficacy seems a logical source of commitment, more commitment as well. These ideas on constituency size constitute the one element of this conceptualization that we did not articulate before gathering our baseline survey data.

### Effects of Selective Admissions

In contrast to public schools, which are forced to serve virtually anyone who shows up at the door, privately supported schools may arbitrarily exclude would-be patrons who seem likely to create serious problems. Public funding per se need not affect selective admissions, the tendency of private schools to exclude people whom they do not want. But whenever public funding of private schools is considered or given, there is political pressure, as in British Columbia at present, to limit or obliterate selective admissions.

One great advantage of selective admissions is that schools may limit the range of problems with which they deal, thus probably achieving the greater cost-effectiveness that often comes with specialization. In fact, if a school manages to exclude a disproportionate share of difficult-to-educate students, it may achieve the appearance of greater effectiveness without really being more effective at all. When students and parents perceive access to a school as difficult to obtain, they may respond with greater commitment, feeling they have gained something special. Teachers may develop more positive attitudes toward their work when a school fends off the students who are serious "discipline problems." Selective admissions is one way of maximizing the homogeneity and transference mentioned earlier. Like voluntary affiliation, it may contribute to the trust between client and professional that helps make effective learning occur.

### Effects of Unorthodox Personnel Policies

Many distinctive characteristics in private schools may depend, more than is recognized, on unorthodox personnel policies. In most states, certification is not required of teachers in private schools whereas it is always required of teachers in public schools. As Milton Friedman argues, certification may artificially inflate the costs of running an institution and may deny the institution some capabilities that it badly needs.[30] This possibility may be especially pronounced in education, for the connection between certification and teacher competence is tenuous in the extreme.

Furthermore, if the training experiences demanded in most certification criteria have any impact at all, they may tend to standardize teachers, thus confronting schools which want to be distinctive with the dilemma of doing so with personnel who are *not* distinctive. Unorthodox personnel policies may be particularly important to transference. Transference may easily be destroyed if a school cannot be staffed by people who symbolize the authority of the church, the ethnic group, or a particularly cohesive community defined in other terms. If Nebraska is successful in its current effort to require certified teachers in all old-order Amish schools, it may destroy one fundamental explanation for the effectiveness of these schools, for the old-order Amish are forbidden by their religion to pursue a higher education, and thus could never qualify to staff their own schools.

## WHAT REALLY HAPPENED
## IN BRITISH COLUMBIA?

There seem to be many logical reasons, then, to anticipate that privately supported schools will be superior in numerous respects to publicly supported schools. It is not surprising, in the light of those reasons, that the reports of parents in British Columbia reflected several deleterious changes in private schools after nearly two years of public aid. But why did the teachers not agree with the parents in this regard? What happened in British Columbia, we suspect, was something like the following:

(a) Teachers have good reason to view British Columbia's aid to private schools through rose-colored glasses. Except in the few private schools in British Columbia that have access to wealthy clients, teachers must have experienced an overwhelming sense of relief, once the aid was given, for many of them had faced fiscal crisis after fiscal crisis, year after year. We know that the salaries of teachers in most private schools were considerably augmented as a consequence of the aid. Their jobs must now seem immeasurably more secure. We should not be surprised then, if teachers, flushed by this bright new era, are not yet cognizant of negative and less dramatic consequences of the aid. In fact, the thought of returning to endless financial emergencies may make it difficult for them to recognize negative consequences.

(b) Teachers, now much more secure in their positions, and looking forward to reasonably attractive remuneration, may be motivated to make a greater investment in collegial relationships, thus creating the enhanced social cohesion that they have reported. They may be unaware that parents are increasingly peripheral to the enterprise and thus perceive social cohesion as waning markedly.

(c) While the regulations attached to the provincial aid seem as yet mild and sympathetically administered, they may symbolize a powerful message: pay attention to the province's criteria of school adequacy, or you may lose your funds and suffer public disgrace. We have found much evidence of a desire to keep private schools above reproach in the view of provincial authorities, and ultimately, in the mind of the general public that relies on the provincial seal of good schoolkeeping. Perhaps the province need not wield a heavy hand to elicit a dramatic response from the private schools. They are strongly motivated to "keep their houses in order." In contrast, holding their clients is far less problematic in a day when demand far exceeds available student spaces in most private schools. Under these conditions, it would be surprising if the private schools were not becoming more responsive to the province (while simultaneously insisting that they will not be told what to do) and, as the parents are telling us, less responsive to parents. In effect, the private schools now have two masters, with two different criteria of good behavior, and under current conditions, displeasing the one master carries more serious consequences than displeasing the other. It is also not surprising, since provincial criteria of school adequacy are largely a reflection of the traditional standards of public schools, that students and parents are beginning to describe their private schools as less "special."

(d) The reported tendency for students to be somewhat more engaged in their schoolwork in spring 1980 than in spring 1978 may itself be evidence of the sensitivity of teachers to the expectations of provincial officials, since it is clear that the private schools will be judged in the future in terms of the performance of their students on standardized achievement tests. Teachers seem widely convinced that *time on task* is a prerequisite of student learning. This heightened teacher attention to student time on task, something directly evident to students but not to parents, may be one reason why students do not see teacher commitment as declining between 1978 and 1980, whereas parents do. Parents are probably responding to other indications of teacher commitment.

(e) Now that a large slice of each school's income (except in the few high-tuition schools) comes from the province, and each family provides an insignificant share, there is still another reason to be more responsive to the biggest client of all, and less responsive both to individual parents (who are less significant contributors and, under present conditions, easily replaced by other parents on the waiting list) and to parents as a total group (since the voice of the province is constant, whereas the sentiments of parents are difficult to register collectively). Furthermore, teachers, who want better salaries and fringe benefits, now compete for their share of the provincial dollar *against* parents, who want their school costs to be held down, or even reduced. Thus parents and professionals, who once worked together to raise funds, provide contributed services, and balance the budget, are drawn into opposition, in this respect at least.

(f) Now that the school is on a firmer financial footing, parents feel their contributions are less needed, and probably less appreciated. If the principle of paying people adequately for services becomes ever more firmly established, the private schools may reach the point where parents' contributed services are actually *resented*, since they reduce the need for teacher employment and overtime.

(g) To the extent that tuition fees and other costs for parents are reduced (allowing for inflation)—and some of this has occurred—and to the extent that the provincial funds are used to make private schools more attractive, these schools may be expanding to the limits of their capacity, and sometimes be increasing their capacity, at the cost of gaining clients whose motivations did not direct them to independent schools in the past. The inflow of these new clients, different in character from the old clients, may introduce dissonance into private schools, thus triggering the diminished sense of community (social cohesion) that parents' reports are indicating.

(h) Teachers, now with two masters (the province and the parent), with increasingly dissonant signals from the latter, and with new and unaccustomed reasons to take their own financial interests increasingly into account, may be torn in different directions and may act inconsistently in consequence. This inconsistency, in turn, may mean that students, finding the consequences of their actions less consistent and predictable, increasingly attribute their rewards and punishments to chance and injustice. Partly for this reason, they may become less enthusiastic about their schoolwork and find their schools, classes, and teachers less attractive.

One way of summarizing all these possible tendencies is to state that, in the wake of the introduction of provincial assistance, the typical British Columbia private school is ceasing to be a *Gemeinschaft* — a close-knit community in which people perform because of mutual commitment to special goals and to each other. This school is instead moving ever closer to the *Gesellschaft* — the complex "society" where relationships among people are segmented and specialized, where goals are divergent, and where people make their various contributions calculatively, in exchange for their own special incentives: teachers for salaries, parents for religious training or a more orderly school environment for their children, and children because they have little choice. If these tendencies continue, they may be self-reinforcing. As teachers focus more and more on extrinsic incentives, they may seem less and less committed to parents and eventually to students, they may be brought into increasing confrontations with parents and school boards, and they may exhibit numerous other attributes often subsumed under the term "union mentality." Parents, sensing more and more that their contributions and involvement are not only unneeded, but resented, may withdraw to the sidelines, perhaps eventually sniping at their schools in the alienated manner that has been so widely evident in recent years. Students, treated more like patients under treatment than members of a functioning community may perform ever more inauthentically, eventually exhibiting much of the hostility and disinterest that have been publicized of late. Eventually, private schools could lose all the social climate characteristics that once distinguished them from public schools.

## POSSIBLE IMPLICATIONS

We have examined evidence suggesting that commitment, consensus, community, accomplishment, and exceptionality are more pronounced in schools that are largely or entirely privately supported (normally, private schools) than in publicly supported schools (normally, public schools). It is not entirely illogical, we have discovered, to expect these tendencies. We have not proven anything. We need more evidence. But the possibilities deserve a hearing. In case these differences between public and private schools turn out to be generally observable facts, what do they imply about our prevailing modes of school finance and governance?

They do not imply that the way to improve a school is to lower all the salaries and ensure that the roof leaks, the fuses blow, and the instructional materials are meager. The most important possible implications *may* be that we have obtained a lot of material benefits for schools in a manner that often diminishes the things money cannot buy, such as commitment, consensus, community, accomplishment, and exceptionality. We are restructuring many public school sysems, I fear, in a manner that makes effective instruction more difficult to achieve. I suspect that no educational institution can function without a decent modicum of commitment, without reasonable consensus, without minimal mutuality with the home and other community institutions, and without some sense of respectable accomplishment. Like John Goodlad, I suspect that the best schools, public and private, seem exceptional to the people who inhabit and patronize them.[31]

Do our prevailing modes of finance and governance militate against these necessities? Is there any way of providing needed material benefits to schools without disastrous side effects? Would the attitudes of most teachers, students, and parents be fundamentally different if no schools were tax supported—if all parents paid fees at the schoolhouse door, and if the modest equality of opportunity now achieved were accomplished via a different mechanism, such as a negative income tax or education stamps for the poor? The evidence above suggests (though far from conclusively) that the attitudes would be different. If there is a serious possibility that public money has done much to ruin public schools, should we compound the problem by doing the same thing to private schools?

But these questions are perhaps too sweeping and simplistic. Public and private schools differ in many ways, not merely in source and liberality of financial support. Normally, they differ along many other lines, including their homogeneity and relative freedom from regulation. As we continue our longitudinal work in British Columbia, we hope to unravel the casual connections that explain the phenomena discussed in this essay, and many other phenomena as well. Some nuances in our data raise the possibility, for example, that the deleterious changes found in our before-after comparisons in British Columbia's private schools might not have occurred if the private schools had been "aided," not by grants given directly to the schools themselves, but by vouchers or tax credits to parents. As our work continues, we hope that Canada's experiments will provide clues for the improvement of all schools, public and private, in Canada and elsewhere. One thing seems clear — the available evidence raises serious questions about our current methods for financing and administering most schools in the United States, about the superiority of the "one best system."

## NOTES TO CHAPTER 11

1. See, e.g., Ellwood P. Cubberley, *Public Education in the United States*, rev. ed. (Boston: Houghton Mifflin, 1934).

2. David B. Tyack, *The One Best System: A History of American Urban Education* (Cambridge, Mass.: Harvard University Press, 1974).

3. Ibid. See also Lawrence A. Cremin, *The Genius of American Education* (New York: Random House, 1974); Bernard Bailyn, *Education in the Forming of American Society* (Chapel Hill: University of North Carolina Press, 1960); and Michael B. Katz, *The Irony of Early School Reform* (Cambridge, Mass.: Harvard University Press, 1968).

4. In my own experience, I have encountered resistance from deans (not in my current institution) to my research on private education. Colleagues working on my various studies have reported that their university peers often state or imply that research of this kind should not be done.

5. I have been contacted by many graduate students, in the initial stages of dissertation planning, who are interested in doing studies on private schools. After assisting them with the development of their ideas, we discover *in most cases by far* that they change to a public school topic, having been warned by their advisors that studies on private schools could "retard" the completion of work on their degrees.

6. See David K. Cohen and Eleanor Farrar, "Power to the Parents? The Story of Education Vouchers," *Public Interest* 48, 1977 (1), pp. 72–79; also Denis P. Doyle, "The Politics of Choice: A View from the Bridge," in *Parents, Teachers, and Children*, James S. Coleman et al. (San Francisco: Institute for Contemporary Studies, 1977), pp. 227–55.

7. Memorandum of April 24, 1980 to "local association presidents, geographical representatives, administrative staff, Tom McRae" from Al Blakey and Larry Kuehn, officers of the British Columbia Teachers' Federation, Vancouver, B.C.

8. Canada's constitution, the British North American Act of 1867, specified that the school rights which denominations enjoyed by law at the time of the entry of a province into confederation could never be taken away. Consequently, most provinces which maintained publicly supported Catholic schools at the time of confederation or later entry into it still maintain them, and the provinces which did not have such a tradition have not generally introduced similar arrangements.

9. Note that the schools known as "private" in the United States are called "independent" in British Columbia and other parts of Canada.

10. Donald A. Erickson and Richard L. Nault, *Effects of Public Money on Catholic Schools in Western Canada: Exploratory Interviews*, Final Report to the Spencer Foundation (San Francisco: Center for Research on Private Education, 1980).

11. Donald A. Erickson, Lloyd MacDonald, and Michael E. Manley–Casimir, *Characteristics and Relationships in Public and Independent Schools: COFIS Baseline Survey Interim Report* (San Francisco and Vancouver: Center for Research on Private Education, University of San Francisco and Educational Research Institute of British Columbia, February 1979).

12. Ibid.

13. Richard Nault, "The School Commitments of Nonpublic School Freshmen Voluntarily and Involuntarily Affiliated with Their Schools," in *Educational Organization and Administration*, ed. Donald A. Erickson, vol. 5 in the American Educational Research Series, *Readings in Educational Research*, Merlin C. Wittrock, series ed. (Berkeley: McCutchan, 1977), pp. 264–95.

14. The Cronback alpha was 0.86.

15. The response categories, along with the numerical values attached to them are as follows:

| | |
|---|---|
| Definitely would | 5 |
| Probably would | 4 |
| Don't know | 3 |
| Probably would not | 2 |
| Definitely would not | 1 |

16. The mean for private schools as a total group was more than 1.5 standard deviations higher than the mean for public schools as a total group.

17. The Cronback alphas are 0.87 for the teacher reports, 0.75 for the student reports, and 0.69 for the parent reports.

18. It is 1.1 standard deviations higher in the teacher questionnaire measure, 1.4 standard deviations higher in the student questionnaire measure, and 1.8 standard deviations higher in the parent questionnaire measure.

19. All multivariate and univariate probabilities shown in a multivariate analysis of variances are below 0.005.

20. The alphas are 0.83, 0.77, 0.71, and 0.72, respectively, for the four measures described below.

21. The difference between means is approximately 1.2 standard deviations. In addition, the differences between public and private schools illustrated by the above-discussed examples seem practically as well as statistically significant. In terms of the eta-squared calculation, of the variance in the student commitment measure, 59 percent is "explained" by the observation that some students are in public schools and others are in private schools. The proportions of variance thus explained are 0.39 for the student reports of teacher commitment, 0.65 for the parent reports of teacher commitment, 0.25 for the teacher reports of teacher commitment, 0.40 for the teacher reports of social cohesion, 0.53 for the teacher reports of special, agreed-upon mission, 0.59 for the parent reports of social cohesion, and 0.25 for the student reports of school exceptionality. For readers who prefer the omega-squared estimate of proportion of variance explained, the figures are 0.55, 0.37, 0.65, 0.22, 0.38, 0.51, 0.58, and 0.23, respectively. It appears that the differences between public and private schools on these attributes are considerable, even dramatic.

22. See e.g., George F. Madaus, Peter W. Airasian, and Thomas Kallaghan, *School Effectiveness: A Reassessment of the Evidence* (New York: Mc Graw-Hill, 1980); and Michael Rutter et al., *Fifteen Thousand Hours: Secondary Schools and Their Effects on Children* (Cambridge, Mass.: Harvard University Press, 1979).

23. After three follow-up mailings, the response rate was 75 percent.

24. For a somewhat more complete, but yet preliminary, report of the before-after comparisons, see Donald A. Erickson, "Effects of Public Money on Social Climates in Private Schools: A Preliminary Report," paper presented at annual meeting of the American Educational Research Association, Los Angeles, Calif., April 16, 1981.

25. Barbara L. Williamson, "A Study of Characteristics and Relationships in Public and Private Elementary and Junior High Schools in Merced, California," Ed.D. dissertation, School of Education, University of San Francisco, 1981.

26. Note the striking parallel here to the findings from studies of "undermanning" in high school extracurricular activities. See e.g., Edwin P. Willems, "Sense of Obligation to High School Activities as Related to School Size and Marginality of Students," in *Educational Organization*, pp. 311–24.

27. See Nault, "School Commitments."

28. C. E. Bidwell, "Students and Schools: Some Observations in Client-Serving Organizations," in *Organizations and Clients: Essays in the Sociology of Service*, ed. W. R. Rosengren and M. Lefton (Columbus, Ohio: Charles E. Merrill, 1970), pp. 37–70.

29. See, e.g., R. G. Barker and P. V. Gump, *Big School, Small School* (Stanford, Calif.: Stanford University Press, 1964).

30. Milton Friedman, *Capitalism and Freedom* (Chicago: University of Chicago Press, 1962), ch. 6.

31. John I. Goodlad, "Can Our Schools Get Better?" *Phi Delta Kappan* 60 (1979): 342–47.

# 12 THE IMPACT OF TAXATION POLICY ON PUBLIC AND PRIVATE SCHOOLS

*Thomas W. Vitullo-Martin*

The state quite properly influences the provision of basic educational instruction to its youth. It provides a legal framework for the organization of public and private schools, oversees the kinds of services they must offer, and, in varying degrees throughout the country, evaluates their performance. It requires all parents to ensure the instruction of their children and all students to complete specified periods of training or to achieve minimal levels of academic performance. It rewards those who complete their instruction successfully with access to higher levels of instruction or with opportunities in state-sponsored or licensed jobs. And, conversely, it punishes those who fail to participate in the instruction by denying certain kinds of jobs within its direct control, by sanctioning the denial of opportunity in jobs in the private sector, and even by direct punitive actions against the students or their families. Finally, the state provides services directly, or it offers incentives to schools to adopt specified programs. Thus, the state does not simply control every school in every detail through its coercive central power; it follows an array of policies—involving varying degrees of voluntaryism on the part of the schools—in its efforts to shape education.

Looking more closely, we see that "the state" is not one but three. Education policies are adopted separately by local, state, and federal governments, and these levels are as often in competition with one

423

another as they are complementary. The Elementary and Secondary Education Act, Title I, for example, represented a federal attempt to encourage local districts to turn from concentrating resources on schools in the wealthiest neighborhoods (which typically were the most politically important in supporting local systems and enjoyed the greatest success in their demands for higher quality or extra services) to schools in the poorest sectors. Subsequently, seventeen states adopted their own compensatory programs, which are modeled on the federal program; the states, too, attempt to encourage districts to alter their priorities.

The competition, however, is far more complex than a simple three-layer-cake analogy would suggest, for within any one level of government, several governmental units promulgate separate policies that shape schools. Only occasionally do these various units coordinate their policy efforts with one another. (Often there is more coordination of policy between units at different levels of government than between those at the same level.) Some of these units deliberately attempt to mold the schools for their purposes. Others, although they shape education, deliberately try to avoid responsibility for their effects on schools. The U.S. Department of Agriculture, for example, has been successful in turning schools into nutritional centers and—not incidentally—outlets for dairy and other agricultural surpluses. State labor relations boards, on the other hand, typically impose on public schools an industrial model of labor-management relations, unsuited to the character of activities and organization of elementary schools—in which teachers exercise professional judgments and, at least occasionally, operate as a collegial body in the management and direction of the schools. The labor relations boards take no responsibility for the way they inhibit this type of professional and collegial relationship between teachers and their school systems.

Most units of federal, state, and local governments implementing education policies distinguish between public and private schools in either the policies they follow or their mode of application. The more concerned the organizational unit is with the content of elementary or secondary education, the more exclusively it sees schools as its clients, and the more likely it is to treat public and private schools differently. Local fire departments treat public and private schools identically. The U.S. Office of Education does not. In the main argument of this essay, however, we will examine an exception to this rule. The Internal Revenue Service is fundamentally indifferent to the impact of its rules on education—in public or private schools. However, it treats the two types of schools in radically different ways, for what amounts to an accidental reason, and with socially damaging effects.

This essay brings some order to the question of how the state influences private and public schools. It considers a broader than normal range of state actions that influence schools, including some that are not primarily intended to affect education but nevertheless do, and is particularly concerned with the way the state's influence over schools affects the social relationships of students with different racial, ethnic and economic backgrounds and the quality and effectiveness of the instruction these students receive. The essay develops some startling conclusions about the net effect of federal and state intervention, after all actions are considered: On the whole, federal and state intervention encourages the economic, social, and therefore racial segregation of public schools and makes more difficult the economic and racial integration of private schools.

## STATE CONTROL: AN OVERVIEW OF DIRECT REGULATION, CATEGORICAL GRANTS, AND REDISTRIBUTIVE TAXATION

States and the federal government commonly use three methods to control or influence both private and public schools: *direct regulation*, *categorical grants* and other aid programs, and manipulation of *tax codes*.[1] In practice, the three affect public and private schools to different degrees. Perhaps because they receive general aid from the state, public schools are subjected to more, and more specific, *regulations* than private schools. This difference is, however, a matter of state policy, which could be reversed if a state or the federal government so desired.

Similarly, public schools are more influenced by *categorical grant programs* and other programs of specific aid than are private schools, principally because the largest educational programs exclude private schools from direct participation. Private schools do indirectly participate in most of the federal programs since their students are eligible to receive federally funded services from the public system. There is evidence that the private schools have been influenced by these federal programs in setting their own priorities, choosing programs, and designing their administrations. The nationwide record of public schools actually delivering these federally funded services to private school students is fair, at best. As this record improves and as the program of public school services to private school students matures, we can expect evidence of this influence over private schools' administrations and programs to increase.[2]

Because taxes provide the revenue for public schools and, to a limited extent, for private schools, they affect schools in a gross sense: the amount of revenue affects the size of the school's budget. But *tax policy* per se, at least until recently, has not been consciously used by the state to influence the behavior or social impact of schools. Nevertheless, both public and private schools are affected by tax codes in many ways that few observers—including many of the legislative designers of the tax system—have fully acknowledged. Both public and private schools are indirectly but strongly affected by the progressivity feature of the personal and business income taxation system when combined with tax deduction policies.[3] Both are also affected by the tax treatment of their capital costs. These features of the revenue codes indirectly affect the schools because they directly affect taxpayers who are the school's clients and whose decisions about schooling are influenced by the codes. They directly influence public schools by altering the market forces that establish the cost of their borrowed capital. And they directly affect private schools because these institutions have a potential tax liability and must abide by the rules which define and preserve their tax-exempt status—rules that have become increasingly concerned with the policies of the institutions.

I argue here that the state exerts its greatest influence over private schools through its tax codes. I shall describe the way the internal revenue system influences the choices of private or public schools, the socioeconomic patterns these choices encourage, and their import for social policies. The tax system reverses the flow of government aid from the poor to the wealthiest groups; it encourages the racial and geographic isolation of the highest-status groups in our society; and it hinders the provision of social and educational services to the lowest-income groups by increasing the difficulties of the urban governments, which are the principal suppliers of these services.

### Direct Regulation

In theory, state influence over schools is strongest through direct regulation. States regulate which institutions may call themselves schools; minimum standards for operations, programs, teachers; required courses and course hours for a diploma; and minimum standards for buildings and facilities. They can enforce the regulations with sanctions ranging from the withdrawal of a school's accreditation (which can block the school's students from entering higher-level educational institutions and may make public schools ineligible for public funds), to court-ordered closing of the schools, to fines and criminal charges of fraud against administrators and trustees. The state can also attack the clients of schools not meeting its requirements through the criminal penalties attached to the state truancy and juvenile delinquency laws. Students attending schools operating without state sanction may be sent to state reform schools; their parents and the school's teachers may be fined or jailed for contributing to the delinquency of a minor.

State regulations *can* be powerful shaping devices if they are clear and if they are enforced. After World War I, for example, several midwestern states prohibited public and private schools from teaching German (they even closed down a number of Lutheran schools). The prohibition was effective because the states enforced it. They were able to enforce it, first, because the public strongly supported it and, second, because violation of the regulation was clear.

However, in ordinary situations, enforcing regulations is much more difficult. Such clear standards separating schools violating regulations from those complying are rare. Consider the counting of credits for a high school diploma. States mandate how many credits a student needs in specific subjects to receive a diploma recognized by the state. But schools within a state—public and private—may differ widely on what they count as credits in a subject area. For example, students in a number of Pennsylvania public and private schools receive credits in agricultural or home economics courses for working on the family farm.

The problem that states face in enforcing their regulations is not only in ambiguous standards, but uncertain priorities. States normally show little enthusiasm for enforcing anything beyond minimum standards. State education regulators usually do not systematically review public schools, let alone private. Instead, they commonly respond to complaints about a school's practices from professional organizations, interest groups, parents, students, or other schools.

Whatever the potential of state regulations for public schools, the existing state-level codes and requirements do not appear to emanate from any core perception of what the schools should be like or what they should accomplish. Although general directives may mandate one kind of test or type of instruction, a certain number of hours of training for teachers, specified procedures for local school boards, and so on, the picture they paint is not of a detailed whole. It is more of a hodgepodge. This observation is consistent with the general findings of studies of state politics of education: that the education arena is marked by the presence of many groups interested in specific, narrow aspects of state schooling. Broadly interested education reform groups tend not to be active at the state level, or if they are active, they are short-lived.

The politics of state regulation of schools is quite similar to that of other areas of state regulative activity, like energy regulation, pollution control, land and water usage, and transportation. In fact, these areas share with schools a governmental invention of the late nineteenth century: a professional staff of advisers and administrators working with a legally responsible governing board made up of a small number of representatives of the regulated interests. Grant McConnell, in his classic study of regulative institutions, enunciated a dismal rule: regulative politics disproportionately serves the interests of those regulated. Although the regulative arrangement is nominally directed at advancing some grand, public-benefiting vision, in its operation it is typically directed by the self-interest of the most powerful forces contesting in the regulative arena.[4] The public good, says McConnell, becomes defined as a private good. In the formation of regulations, public goals are lost sight of. In a number of education policy matters, McConnell's general critique of regulative institutions seems to fit surprisingly well.

Most states are committed to a democratic concept of education: all students should have access to public schools of good quality; the schools are places where the wealthy and the poor "rub shoulders"; the privileged should not be separated from the underclasses—whether these be racial or ethnic minorities, the poor, the handicapped, women, or any other disadvantaged group; the disadvantaged ought not to be set off by themselves in isolation. Regulations should promote the highest quality in schools, offer students equal access, and foster the mixing of racial and economic groups in the classroom.

A school's quality is, at the least, a function of its teachers and their organization, its management, the clarity of its goals to teachers and students, and its resources. Ensuring that all students have access to schools of the best quality requires either that these elements of school quality be evenly distributed across schools or that students have equal access to the best schools that emerge.

The state regulative officials, with rare and sporadic exception, attempt to equalize neither quality nor access. The existing system of regulations does not apportion the best teachers equally across all school districts; rather, the apportionment of teachers is left to the marketplace of school districts. The regulations do constrain the supply of potential teachers. Only teachers receiving state teacher's certifications—controlled by the state teacher training institutions—need apply. The state does not in any serious respect equalize the resources the school systems have to attract prospective teachers, much less vary those resources in direct proportion to district needs. The only significant exceptions to this rule have been forced on states by court decisions and are not the result of state regulative initiative.

Even if it were impossible to devise and implement regulations which would permit schools to become comparable in quality, regulations could provide students with greater access to quality schools simply by permitting them to attend on an equal footing any school they wish, wherever it is located. Current district regulations restrict residents of neighborhoods to specific schools, irrespective of the school's quality. Even when a system adopts an "open enrollment" approach, as does New York City, it gives to residents of each school's "attendance area" preferential treatment in enrollment. No public systems accept "out of district" students for enrollment as a matter of right. No state regulations encourage, much less require, districts to offer scholarships to students who live outside their districts, in order to reach desirable racial and socioeconomic balances in the classroom.

A great deal of attention has been paid to the Supreme Court's failure to force integration across district lines. It is far more appropriate in a democratic community that the decision be made legislatively, in the state body that regulates the schools. There are no constitutional difficulties with a legislative determination that students have the right to attend any public school they choose on an equal basis, not subject to priority because of the location of their residence. Nor are there any difficulties with the requirement legislatively determined that racially and socioeconomically segregated districts be required to offer scholarships to integrate their schools.

The irony of current state regulations over public education is that they have produced schools that are undeniably at odds with the democratic ideology of public education. Today's public schools oppose the democratic ideal underlying the idea of free, public education. Instead of having a system giving students of all races and incomes equal access to the best education, we are developing high-spending public school districts with solely upper-income populations, with no minority or middle-income—much less lower-income—families represented. Public schools, particularly those serving the highest-income groups, have been moving toward becoming more racially and economically segregated. The education system the regulations are supporting undercuts the very objectives of free public education by its failure to counter this movement.

States have not successfully established their regulative controls over private schools. Private schools receive even less state attention—helpful or hindering—than public schools. Most states do not collect enrollment information on the private schools within their borders, and a number of states neither require private schools to register as schools nor compile lists of their names and addresses. Consequently, although direct regulation has the potential for powerful control of private schools, its potential is not developed. The enforcement of state regulations on private schools is not highly directive.

## Grants and Aid Programs

State governments support schools with basic education subsidies, state equalization payments, or other forms of state aid that are generally allocated to local districts by a formula and are available for the district's use on the same basis as the district's own tax revenues. The state generally avoids threatening the cutoff of these funds, even in the face of severe violations of state education regulations. For example, several states have found that local districts were guilty of racial segregation in their policies, but even then the states have not cut off the basic education grant to the districts. They have suspended the local boards of education and threatened board members with contempt-of-court actions. But states are loathe to tie the delivery of the basic education funds to compliance with the state's regulations. In most cases, the state education authorities lack the statutory authority to halt the funds and would have to seek court approval of their action.

But there are other categories of grants, most typically for categorical educational services like special education services, library services, enrichment programs, and the like, which require schools receiving them to use the funds on specific kinds of student problems, for specific kinds of educational programs. The awards of these grants typically take the form of contracts which are laced with regulations designed to ensure that the categorical objectives of the program are met by schools receiving the funds. Grant regulations have forced districts to adopt important changes in their policies, under threat of losing the government allocation. The sanctions are not criminal but rather the withdrawal of the benefit which the government has the right to withhold. Thus, the legal position of the enforcers of the regulation is quite different in the case of grants and contracts. In the case of regulations, ultimately the state must apply to the courts and prove its case that the penalties should be invoked, but with grants, the agency merely withholds or withdraws approval of the grant application until the school proves it is in compliance with the regulations. The school, if it wished to dispute the right of the agency to withhold the grant, would have to apply to the court and there prove the agency incorrect in its action.

Grants have proven to be quite effective devices for forcing local districts to comply with state or federal policies. For example, Title I of the federal Elementary and Secondary Education Act (ESEA— also known as the Compensatory Education Act) has regulations which have forced local districts to distribute basic education funds equally to all students. That is, the federal regulation limits how locally raised funds may be spent. Prior to Title I, most districts spent less per pupil in schools in poorer neighborhoods. State regulations failed to force districts to change their allocation patterns.

Title I grant regulations require the district to spend no less in a Title I school (which by definition is located in the poorer neighborhoods of the community) than in any other school in the system *before* federal funds could be spent in the district. Despite the magnitude of this change, its presumed interest to the dominant political support groups within local districts, and the fact that most districts in the country were affected by the change, the change appears to have taken place without political fights at the district level.

Grant regulations have forced many similar changes. Because they received federal and state education grants, public systems have been required to create new staff positions and to make changes in many areas of their operations, including accounting procedures, fund allocation to district schools, political relations with parents of school children, programs offered, teacher specializations, and relations with private schools in their districts. When private schools, such as schools for the handicapped, receive *direct* federal funds, they come under similar federal influence in the standards they maintain, the programs they offer, and the teachers they employ.

Grant regulations are effective because they immediately reward compliance and because they are simple to enforce. If the recipient school refuses to obey the regulations, it loses the grant. The school's officials must affirm that they have and will continue to comply with all regulations or be subject to criminal and civil penalties.

### Tax Regulation

Effective as grants are, tax regulations are even more influential in shaping private and public schools. They strongly influence taxpaying parents' choices of school—public or private, urban or suburban—by designating certain expenses deductible and others not. Most people know that, with rare exceptions, public schools are free and private schools are supported (at least in part) by tuitions or other family support. All other factors being equal, this gives the advantage to public schools. The tax system makes public schools even more attractive since it effectively increases the cost of choosing private schools. And because of the effects of inflation on our unindexed system of progressive income tax brackets, the weight of the influence of the tax system on parent choices has increased, especially in the past ten years. Many observers approve of this bias of the tax law on the grounds that racial and economic integration of schools is encouraged by discouraging private school attendance. I will argue, however, that the practical influence of the system is to encourage the economic and racial segregation of the private schools and of the public school communities—that is, their residential districts—which of course increases the segregation of public schools.

This adverse impact of the tax system on the integration of both public and private schools is enhanced by a little-remarked aspect of our income tax system, which permits the deduction of local taxation from individual and corporate state and federal income tax liability. The effect of this policy is, for corporations and wealthy families alone, to reduce federal and state taxation when local taxes are increased. Looked at from the perspective of a local taxing body like the school district, this provision of the tax law means that when the local district raises taxes, it in effect recaptures for itself some of the taxes that formerly went to the general revenue collections of the federal, state, and even local governments. It gets more revenue at proportionately lower effort of local residents than would be the case if this deduction system did not operate. Unfortunately for central cities and lower-income suburban districts, a standard deduction is taken by most of their citizens. (In New York, the Internal Revenue Service estimates that 90 percent of taxpayers take a standard deduction.) Therefore, increases in local tax levies are not offset by reduced federal taxation. Hence there is no significant pass-through of federal and state aid through the tax system to the lower-income districts, only to the wealthier. The tax system encourages the economic forces leading to the racial and economic stratification of the area and to the segregation, therefore, of the lower-income districts and of the private schools in those districts.

Both these arguments are involved and require a new view of taxation policy. Lowi, in fitting taxation policy into his schema of types of public policies, considers income taxation as "redistributive" policy, not because the tax brackets are progressive and require proportionately greater payments from the wealthy, but because taxation operates on "the environment of decisions," on the calculus of evaluating alternatives. In essence, taxation policy alters market calculations and market distributions, and the state can reach its policy ends without requiring, through police and penal coercion, the behavior it seeks.[5] With this view of taxation policy in mind, we must examine the role of the tax system in more detail.

From its original use as a simple revenue-raising device, the federal income tax system (and state systems modeled on it) has become a means of directing taxpayers' behavior. Tax incentives built into the federal system have encouraged families to own their own homes, the wealthy to buy municipal bonds, businesses to make investments in capital equipment, and so on. The system influences taxpayers' economic decisions through the mechanism of deductible expenditures, that is, expense items for designated purposes that can be deducted from gross income in calculating taxable income.

We can also view these deductions in another way: as government subsidies for those items designated tax-deductible. Thus, a businessman can buy office furniture that a homeowner would consider far too costly because the businessman's purchase is subsidized by tax savings. In a real sense, the furniture costs the businessman less than it would cost the homeowner, who cannot deduct the expense from gross income. Current tax laws also give incentives to businesses to educate their employees. Businesses can deduct expenses for employees' education related to the improvement of their job skills; individuals cannot.

In drawing up these tax rules, Congress and the Internal Revenue Service seem to have focused only on economic considerations, ignoring the impact of tax policies on schools. Two tax policies are of principal importance to education. First, the federal government permits taxpayers to deduct local and state taxes from personal and business income tax returns. Second, the federal government does not permit individuals to deduct the cost of elementary and secondary (or higher education) if paid for by any means other than local and state taxes.

Although families do not choose schools in the strict, economically rational fashion that investors choose bonds, a change in the tax policy will still normally affect a family's education decisions. The higher the family's income, the higher its tax bracket, the more valuable the tax deductions, and the more likely the family will be influenced by tax policy.

Suburbs—or any relatively homogeneous, wealthy government that takes on few public responsibilities but provides high levels of services in those few areas—offer several tax-related attractions to the high-income family; these attractions are enhanced and magnified by the tax codes. In contrast, more cities or older, aging suburbs with lower-income populations and a heavy burden of social services are substantially penalized by the tax laws. Using examples from New York City as the core city and its suburban areas as the wealthy suburbs will simplify a complicated discussion. However, the point of the New York example is not to show that the tax system damages central cities in comparison with their suburbs but rather to show that poorer jurisdictions providing a full load of public services are damaged in comparison with wealthier jurisdictions providing only a few high-quality services, including public schools.

In contrast to New York City, the typical affluent suburb has a wealthier tax base, fewer children per household, and, therefore, lower education expenses per household. The suburb can spend substantially more per pupil and still keep taxes relatively low because upper-income families seek few other public services. These families are able to provide more of what they need themselves; they live in low-density areas that require low capital investment and lower public service expenses. Local suburban governments principally provide the public services that wealthy families need and avoid the expense of those services used predominantly by lower-income families, such as welfare, parks, public transportation, and the like.

Central cities provide all these services and more. Wealthy families in the city must pay for such services even though they may make only minimal use of them. For upper-income families suburbs are more efficient since they tax for and deliver only those services their wealthy residents need. In the suburbs, affluent families bear only a small fraction of the cost of caring for the poor they would have if they lived in the city.

The federal tax codes enhance this natural advantage of the suburbs by permitting wealthy families to deduct local taxes from their federally taxable income. This deduction is, in effect, a subsidy to the affluent suburb by the federal government because the federal government foregoes a part of the taxpayer's normal tax obligation whenever the local government raises taxes. The significance of the deduction of local taxes is much greater in the affluent suburb, where most families are in high tax brackets, than it is in the central city, where most are in relatively low tax brackets. The proportion of the local budget refunded by the federal government through tax deductions of local taxes is therefore greater in affluent jurisdictions than in low-income suburbs or the central city.

Thus, it is doubly easy for the affluent suburb to raise its taxes and increase local revenues because (1) any given amount of tax revenue represents a smaller proportion of average family income in the affluent suburb than it does in the poorer central city ($4,000 property tax is a greater proportion of a city family's $20,000 annual income than of a suburbanite's $50,000 income), and (2) the federal government refunds a greater proportion of local taxes to the wealthy than to the poor.

## THE IMPACT OF TAX CODES ON PUBLIC AND PRIVATE SCHOOLS

### The Deductions as a Form of Public School Aid

Let us review this reasoning in greater detail: (1) the entire operating expense of local government—including local schools—is raised by state and local taxes and is deductible from personal income subject to federal taxation; (2) this deduction is, in effect, a federal subsidy of local expenditures; (3) in places where the average family income is relatively high, the average tax bracket is higher, and, consequently, the value of the average deduction is greater; (4) as a result, affluent suburbs receive a far greater per capita subsidy from the federal government than do central cities, and this federal aid covers a far greater proportion of all local expenditures in these wealthy areas; and (5) public school aid through the tax system far exceeds the direct programmatic aid the federal government gives to support education.

In 1980, state and local governments raised about $90 billion to support public schools. Although a precise calculation of the portion of these taxes refunded through federal income tax deductions—in other words the federal share of these local costs—is not available, $20 billion is a reasonable estimate—about three times the amount available from the federal government in its direct grant programs. Who does all this federal aid assist? At best, federal programs modestly skew the distribution of their benefits in favor of lower-income areas, but the tax refund benefits are much more heavily skewed toward wealthy areas. The net effect of federal intervention in education is to subsidize the wealthiest districts with the wealthiest families far more than the central cities or poorer towns and their residents.

To illustrate how this tax system aid benefits the wealthier districts disproportionately, we will turn to the example of two districts, New York City and one of its wealthy suburbs, Pocantico Hills, New York.

Pocantico Hills is a high-income, high-spending school district in Westchester County, New York. It operates its own elementary schools, and pays tuition for its high school students to attend schools out of district. Although 1980 census information on family income is not available at this time for the village, in 1970 its median family income was more than twice the national average and it has, if anything, become more affluent in the past ten years. We can conservatively estimate its median family income to be $45,000 for 1980. In the 1980–1981 school year, the school district spent $9,500 per pupil for the elementary schools it operated itself, and $4,500 per pupil in tuition to public high schools out of the district.[6]

New York City's residents have a median family income slightly below the national level, or approximately $20,000 in 1980. It spent approximately $3,200 per pupil for its elementary and intermediate-level students in 1980, and $2,700 for its high school students.

Federal aid through the tax system to these two districts is a function of the amount of expenditure locally raised (therefore deductible from individual and corporate taxable income), and of the tax brackets (and therefore tax savings from deductions) of the residents of each district.

Pocantico Hills receives only $10,800 from the federal government, for ESEA Title I and Title IV programs. Virtually all the $9,500 per pupil it spends in its elementary schools is raised by local or state taxes, and is deductible from the aggregate amount of taxable income in the district.

New York receives about $300 million in aid from the federal government, or about $300 per pupil. It raises locally about $2,800 of the $3,200 it spends in its elementary and intermediate schools.

To calculate the benefit of the tax deduction system to districts, and keep the main outlines of this argument from getting lost in a maze of detail, I will make some simplifying definitions and assumptions. First, I will regard as "direct tax system aid to a district" the savings in tax liability individual taxpayers realize as the result of deductions of local taxes. When local taxes go up, an individual's federal taxes go down a proportionate amount, and the exact proportion is determined by the individual's tax bracket. In effect, the local tax is passed through to the federal government. For example, if a taxpayer is in the 25 percent bracket (meaning that his or her last dollar of income is taxed at the 25 percent rate), an increase in local school taxes of $1,000 means a reduction of federal taxes by a little more than $250. The taxpayer has to come up with 75 percent of the new taxes because the federal government, in effect, shares the cost of the taxation by lowering its own bill. If the taxpayer falls into the 50 percent bracket, his or her federal taxes are reduced by a little more than $500. We can think of that $500 savings as a transfer payment from the federal government to the local taxing jurisdiction. Second, we will not go through the exercise of calculating the tax savings to each local resident and adding these up to get the district total of aid to the local schools through the tax system. All local expenditure that is locally raised is deductible on someone's tax return, and we will assume that the median income for the district gives us a reasonable approximation of the tax bracket for most of the residents, and is a reasonable basis on which to estimate the tax system aid to the district.

Pocantico Hills taxpayers are at about the 50 percent federal tax bracket, and this means that the tax system contributes about half the cost of educating the elementary school students, or about $4,750 per pupil. State and local income taxes follow the federal regulations both on tax rates and on deductions. Pocantico Hills residents have an approximately 15 percent additional income tax liability to state and local governments, for an aggregate tax rate of about 65 percent. Thus about $6,200 of the local expenditure of $9,500 per elementary pupil is aid through the tax system, and represents no additional burden on local taxpayers.

New York City residents are closer to the 15 percent tax bracket on federal returns, and 20 percent bracket for combined federal and state tax systems. Aid to the city system through the tax system amounts to only about $560 per elementary school student.

Unfortunately, this calculation substantially overstates the aid to the city through the tax system, because only 10 percent of city taxpayers itemize their deductions. Ninety percent of city residents use a standard deduction and obtain no additional tax savings from increases in local tax burdens. Thus when Pocantico Hills raises its spending per pupil by $1,000, as it has in each of the last two years, the increased burden on local taxpayers is only $350 per year. But if New York City schools had increased their spending by $1,000 per student for each of the last two years, the increased burden on local taxpayers would have been close to $1,000 per student each year.

Through the tax system, Pocantico Hills receives *eleven times* the aid per pupil that New York City receives. Even counting all federal aid together, we find that Pocantico Hills receives more than six times the aid per pupil than is given to New York. So Pocantico Hills is quite attractive to anyone who can afford to move into the district, and it will attract the wealthiest families from the city.

### Tax Disincentives for Using Private Schools

Upper-income New Yorkers are most likely to enroll their children in religiously affiliated or independent private schools that charge high tuitions because they are not heavily subsidized by a church, foundation, or other outside source. Tuitions range from $2,000 per year to $6,000, with an average charge of about $3,000. In addition, parents must bear the cost of school bus transportation and other fees and services normally borne by suburban governments or public school systems. The present tax system effectively doubles and triples these costs.

The amount of the penalty the tax system imposes is a function of the federal, state, and local income tax brackets into which the family's income falls. These, of course, vary with income. Representative federal tax brackets for 1980 for a married couple filing jointly are as follows:

| Taxable Income (in thousands) | Tax Bracket (%) | Taxable Income (in thousands) | Tax Bracket (%) |
|---|---|---|---|
| $ 8–12 | 22 | $52–64 | 53 |
| 16–20 | 28 | 76–88 | 58 |
| 24–28 | 36 | 100–120 | 62 |
| 32–36 | 42 | 140–160 | 66 |
| 40–44 | 48 | 180–200 | 69 |

In New York, state and city taxes average one-third of federal taxes. For the sake of clarity, let us take an extreme example, that of a family with a very high income. The line of argument, however, applies to all tax levels. A New York City family with a taxable income of $45,000 is in the 50 percent federal tax bracket. In addition, it is at approximately the 17 percent state and local bracket. After paying taxes ($14,700 federal and $5,500 state and local), the family has $24,800 remaining to pay nondeductible living expenses, such as food, clothing, rent, and tuition to private schools. Tuition and related education expenses for two children in private schools in the city would average about $8,000 per year, approximately one-third the family's after-tax income, leaving it with $16,800 for other expenses. Clearly, using private schools requires a deep commitment to living in the city since the public schools in the suburbs, as an alternative, often have a reputation for comparable quality.

If education expenses were deductible, as they would be if they were simply business expenses or religious contributions, the impact on the family would be quite different. An $8,000 deduction from a taxable income of $45,000 would bring the family down two tax brackets. It would pay $10,800 federal and $4,200 state and local taxes on its $37,000 taxable income. After all taxes and education expenses were paid, the family would be left with $22,000 or $5,200 more than it has today, without the tax deduction, for other expenses. The effect of a tax deduction of education expenses on the family would be to reduce the cost of private education by 65 percent.

Consider once again, but from a different angle, the present situation in which education expenses cannot be deducted. How much must the upper-income family earn in order to pay $8,000 per year in private education expenses? In its tax bracket, it would have to earn $24,000 in order to cover the $8,000 private school expenditure (assuming the $24,000 income is "earned income" and subject to a maximum federal tax of 50 percent and corresponding maximum state taxes). The federal, state, and local governments would be taking two dollars for every one dollar the family spent to educate its children in private school.

Our examples have substantially understated the economic incentives for the family to move from the city. The commitment to a private school is not a one-year commitment but stretches out over twelve to fifteen years of nursery, elementary, and high school. Tax consultants estimate the out-of-pocket expenses of a family using only private schools to be in the range of $40,000 to $60,000 per child, or $120,000 to $180,000 of pretax, earned income—if the education expenses cannot be deducted. If it remained in the city, the family with two children would have to spend $250,000 to $333,000 of its earnings for education in private schools.

At present, the alternatives are remarkably attractive. The same family could move to an exclusive suburban school district and invest in a home—a capital investment—the money it would have spent on private schools in the city. The home investment would produce tax deductions that allow the family to shelter a substantial portion of the $250,000 to $300,000 it has to invest over the fifteen years or so its children are in public schools. And the family may find its suburban home appreciate in value in that time.

In the suburb, the family can enroll both children in public schools, paying only the taxes on its property. Property taxes are a function of local tax rates and of the assessed value of the property and so cannot readily be projected. Let us assume that the family pays $3,000 per year in property taxes. Of this, 60 to 80 percent would be assignable to the costs of the public schools, or about $2,400 for both children. This amount would be deductible from the family's taxable income, lowering its tax bracket and saving it about $1,600 in taxes. Thus, the real cost to the family of the suburban public school education would be about $800, or $400 per child.

In summary, under the present tax system, the family must spend $24,000 of its gross income to remain in the city and use private schools, or $800 of gross income (which is the additional tax obligation the family must meet in the suburbs, after federal deductions are accounted) in the suburban public system.

Thus, the tax system has two notable damaging effects. It makes it almost certain that a family would choose suburban public schools over the city's private ones. If the family does opt for the suburbs, that choice also removes from circulation in the city's economy about two times the amount of money a resident family would pay to support private education for its children.

### The Tuition Tax Credit Debate

Any tax reform that removes some disadvantages private schools suffer under the revenue codes touches and ideological nerve in many Americans: the assumption that such a reform tries to skirt the First Amendment's prohibition of establishment of religion. During the 1978 congressional debate over tuition tax credits, this objection drew so much publicity that the actual impact of the proposed tax credits never really received careful attention. Opponents' use of a First Amendment argument stems from their confusing a taxation bill—which the tax credit proposal was—with a programmatic aid bill. The two are substantially different things. A tax credit is a form of standardized tax deduction. In the proposed bills, everyone would have been given the advantage of a deduction at the 50 percent bracket, and a "cap" would have been placed on total benefits per student.

It is the settled practice of Congress and the states to exempt religious organizations from taxation, and to allow individuals the deduction of religious and other charitable contributions in calculating their taxable income. Until the early 1960s, 80 percent of all private schools were virtually tuition-free because, as denominational schools, they were supported by contributions from churches and synagogues. These contributions were tax deductible even for the most sectarian of schools, and these tax deductions raised no First Amendment problems. Thus, as a practical matter, tax policy permitted parents to deduct the money that financed religious schools.

Although the internal revenue regulations did and do permit deductions of religious contributions, they prohibit the deduction of tuition payments except those made for direct business purposes. These tax regulations are not based on First Amendment principles. Their rational is purely fiscal.

Around 1963, partially in a futile effort to make themselves eligible for federal education funds and partially because of internal changes in their churches, the church affiliated schools began to charge and increase their tuitions, rather than rely on church subsidies to the extent they had. Not incidentally, the financing change permitted the church schools to open their doors to large numbers of non-church-members; the fact that previously only church members had supported the schools through their contributions to the church had been a barrier to the enrollment of non-members' children, since these "outsiders" would not be supporting the school. Ironically, as the church schools became less sectarian, their supporters became more adversely affected by tax policies. Any reform of the tax treatment of tuitions begins to restore these schools to the tax situation they enjoyed before the early 1960s, and the large increase in tuition-based financing.

Aside from the First Amendment arguments, the principal objections voiced during the debate on tax credits centered on the charge that the credits would help private schools prosper and that this was against the social interest. Such opponents to the measure as the Council of Great City Schools, the National Education Association, and the American Federation of Teachers argued that private schools (1) are elitist institutions, catering to wealthy clients who do not need aid; (2) are segregationist in their attraction to parents; (3) select the best students, leaving the public schools with the most difficult educational problems; and (4) weaken support for the public school systems.

The council itself argued that tax credits would result in private school children receiving more federal aid than public school children. The council claimed the 1977 distribution was $60 for private school students, $128 for public school students.[7] It believed that tax credits would tip the federal aid scale too heavily in favor of private school students. The council was also concerned that the bill would exacerbate the severe problem of declining enrollments in urban public school systems.

Other opponents echoed fears that tax credits would, in practice, mean fewer dollars for public schools and would encourage parents (presumably wealthy ones) to transfer their children to private schools. Some argued that the measure would help only the wealthy because the total potential aid (up to $500 in early versions of the plan) was too small to help lower-income families. Finally, the broadest opposition argument held that the strength of American public education rested on its being a monopoly and that the slightest encouragement of the competitive private sector would permit parents to indulge their most antidemocratic sentiments and turn against public schools.

We cannot discuss a change in the tax laws, then, without considering the reasonableness of these fears. Do the characteristics of the private school give grounds for them? Would federal appropriations for public education decline as a result of tax deductions for tuition expenses? And how would such a decline affect public schools? What democratizing aspects of public schools are threatened by encouragement given private schools? Would the wealthy benefit the most from the deductions or tax credits?

## Tax Credits and Fears About Private Education

The fears expressed by opponents of tax credits reflect serious concerns. We can judge the degree to which these fears are warranted only by examining them in the light of enrollment in private schools nationally. What proportion of all students do they enroll? What proportion of the wealthiest? Of the poorest?

*Are Private Schools Elitist?* In its 1976 *Survey of Income and Education*, the census bureau found that private schools enrolled 10 percent of all elementary and secondary students (or 4.8 million children), 17 percent of all students from families whose income was above $25,000, and 6 percent of all whose family income was below $10,000 (in 1975 dollars). Certainly private schools enroll a higher proportion of upper-income than lower-income students. Nationally, 58 percent came from families with above-median incomes, 42 percent from families with below-median incomes.[8] But the differences are hardly large enough to establish private schools as elitist.

Looked at from the public school side, the 1976 census data show that 83 percent of all students from the wealthiest families in the country take advantage of free public education. This would indicate great support for American democratic values *if* these students were in economically *integrated* schools. Certainly there is no great social advantage in providing free, *exclusive* educations to the wealthiest families in the country.

Unfortunately, the wealthiest students are disproportionately enrolled in public schools in places like Shaker Heights, Scarsdale, Marin County, Beverly Hills, Palo Alto, and Chevy Chase—exclusive districts with exclusive schools. A student can attend these schools only by living in the district, and to live in the district, the family must be able to afford housing that is among the most expensive in the country. Residence in such a school district requires that a family make a capital investment in a home, an investment typically equal to 25 to 40 percent of the cost of a luxury home.

The implications are startling: the most exclusive schools in America are suburban *public* schools. Enrollment in them is determined strictly by stringent economic criteria, that is, by the family's having enough capital to buy a house in a high-income school district. This economic requirement is surprisingly more severe than those set for admission to private schools serving families with comparably high incomes.

Private schools charge only tuition. In budgetary terms, this is an operating expense. It is far easier to cover this expense than it is to accumulate the capital needed to enter the best suburban systems.

Private schools purposely select a certain proportion of students from lower-income families to achieve some degree of socioeconomic mix in their student bodies, and they have scholarship funds for those whose families cannot pay tuition. In 1980, sixteen percent of the students in schools belonging to the National Association of Independent Schools (NAIS) receive scholarship aid, and most of these schools charge the highest tuition in the country.

Wealthy public schools, despite their financial resources, do not offer scholarships to low-income students from outside the district to achieve an economic mix in the student population. Instead, they treat residence in the district as an absolute requirement for admission to the school. Urban, selective, independent, high-tuition private schools provide a far more integrated education experience than their suburban public school rivals. Urban private schools, by removing one of the most powerful factors impelling middle- and upper-income white families to move to suburban districts, help keep the city economically and racially balanced.

*Are Private Schools Segregationist?*    Throughout the past decade, it has been the public school systems of the Northeast, Midwest, West, and some sections of the urban South that have become more segregated; the private schools are becoming increasingly integrated. For more than a decade, private schools have been increasing their enrollments of minority students. The movement has been totally voluntary and has occurred even though federal and state governments have offered no incentives to private schools to accept minority students. Federal income taxation policies have made the enrollment of minorities in private schools more difficult.

In 1969, only 4 percent of private elementary school students were black, but by 1979, 8 percent were black. If black students had been proportionately divided between public and private schools, these schools would have been 14 percent black in 1969 and 15 percent black in 1979, matching the percentage of blacks in the elementary-school-aged population (see Table 12-1). Private schools fell short of these goals, but made remarkable progress in closing the distance by almost doubling the proportion of blacks in their schools in the decade. The change in Hispanic enrollments is no doubt even more dramatic, but existing census data does not permit us to describe it.

Table 12-1.  Percentage Change in Black Enrollments in Private Schools, 1969-1979.

| Level | Percentage Black, 1969 | | Percentage Black, 1979 | |
| --- | --- | --- | --- | --- |
| | School-aged Population | Private Schools | School-aged Population | Private Schools |
| Elementary | 14% | 4% | 15% | 8% |
| Secondary | 12% | 5% | 15% | 7% |

Source:  U.S. Bureau of the Census, *Current Population Reports*, "Population Characteristics," Series P-20, no. 355, issued August 1980.

In any event, *perfect* distribution of minorities in private schools is an inappropriately high standard. First, each of the two largest private systems—Catholic and Lutheran—is run by a church whose membership is only about 2 percent black. To enroll black students, these church-operated schools—which account for about 65 percent of all private school enrollments—would have had to change traditional policies of orienting education services to members of their own religion. They have begun to do so—approximately 9 percent of Catholic school students are now non-Catholic—but the process is slow. Second, private schools are not evenly distributed throughout the country, but are concentrated in urban areas, especially cities in the Northeast and Midwest. Minorities are still concentrated in the rural areas of the South and the Southwest. While 55 percent of all minority students lived in the South and West in 1977, these regions enrolled only 35 percent of private school students. Hence, for private schools to enroll a perfect proportion of minority students, they would have to enroll higher proportions of minorities than the public schools in the areas where they are located.

Third, because no public subsidies exist for private schools, they must charge tuition or raise revenues from contributors. Most private schools do both. Minorities as a group have lower incomes and are more likely to be priced out of the private schools. Catholic schools raised average tuitions from $54 per year in 1969 to about $240 in 1980, an increase of almost 450 percent. Schools serving racial minorities raised tuition faster and to higher levels because they lacked the parish membership necessary to provide the kind of subsidies that permitted parish schools their traditionally low tuition.

Catholic schools serving blacks have average tuitions and fees closer to $500. Lutherans report similar tuition pressures.

Minorities should be increasingly priced out of the private schools, not enrolling in record numbers. Minorities are increasing their levels of private school enrollment because of the efforts of private schools to provide scholarship support and because minority parents are willing to spend a greater portion of their income on education — for private school tuition — than the average family is asked to spend.

These racial enrollment statistics understate the actual minority enrollments in private schools by leaving out nonblack Hispanics and recent European immigrants. Because of the way the census data has been gathered in the past, it is not possible to discuss the enrollments of these groups simultaneously with those of blacks and other racial minorities. The statistics collected by the private schools themselves provide a better picture, though unfortunately no system reports any information on European or other immigrant minority enrollments.

Between 1970 and 1980, Catholic elementary schools increased their minority enrollments from 11 percent to almost 20 percent, and secondary schools from 8 percent to 15 percent minority (see Table 12-2). Catholics enroll a higher proportion of Hispanics than the public schools, and the Lutheran secondary schools a higher proportion of blacks than the public schools.

The Lutheran Church, Missouri Synod, has reported comparably high concentrations of minorities in its schools. In 1978, its elementary schools were 12.5 percent minority (most of these were not Lutherans) and its high schools were 16.3 percent minority (14 percent black), a slightly higher proportion of blacks than in the high school population nationally. In the past decade, the schools of the NAIS have doubled their minority enrollments, while increasing their total enrollments by only 30 percent. Put another way, 15 percent of the increased enrollments in these schools in the decade have been minority students.

In the West, Catholic schools often enroll higher percentages of minorities than the public systems. The largest private school systems in California enroll larger proportions of either blacks or Hispanics than the public systems (see Table 12-3). Catholic schools enrolled a substantially higher proportion of Hispanics, slightly more Asians, and almost as many blacks as the public system, when this survey was taken in 1978. The proportion of minorities in the Catholic

**Table 12-2.** Change in Catholic School Enrollment, by Ethnicity, 1970-1980.

| | 1970-71 | | 1980-81 | |
|---|---|---|---|---|
| Elementary | Number | % | Number | % |
| American Indian | 18,000 | .5 | 7,300 | .3 |
| Asian American | 18,300 | .5 | 42,000 | 1.9 |
| Black (non-Hispanic) | 172,000 | 5.1 | 200,300 | 8.8 |
| Hispanic | 177,900 | 5.3 | 199,300 | 8.8 |
| All others | 2,969,300 | 88.6 | 1,820,400 | 80.2 |
| Total | 3,355,500 | 100.0 | 2,269,300 | 100.0 |
| Secondary | | | | |
| American Indian | 2,400 | .2 | 2,400 | .3 |
| Asian American | 5,200 | .5 | 10,100 | 1.2 |
| Black (non-Hispanic) | 37,500 | 3.7 | 52,600 | 6.3 |
| Hispanic | 38,600 | 3.8 | 56,700 | 6.8 |
| All others | 924,400 | 91.8 | 715,200 | 85.4 |
| Total | 1,008,100 | 100.0 | 837,000 | 100.0 |

Source: National Catholic Education Association Data Bank, *Statistical Report On U.S. Catholic Schools, 1980-81.*

**Table 12-3.** Percentage Distribution of Enrollment in California Public and Private Schools by Race and Ethnic Group, 1978-1979.

| School System | American Indian | Asian | Black | Hispanic | Other |
|---|---|---|---|---|---|
| Public | 0.9 | 4.7[a] | 10.1 | 20.8 | 63.5 |
| Catholic (statewide) | 0.6 | 4.9 | 9.5 | 26.3 | 58.9 |
| Lutheran (Missouri Synod) | — | 12.0 | 14.0 | 2.1 | 72.9 |
| Lutheran (American) | 1.0 | 2.0 | 17.0 | 5.0 | 75.0 |
| Baptist | 0.2 | 2.4 | 12.5 | 8.8 | 76.1 |
| Episcopal (Los Angeles) | — | 9.1 | 17.0 | 8.8 | 65.1 |
| Independent (NAIS) | 0.2 | 4.6 | 3.5 | 2.4 | 89.3 |

a. Includes Filipino.

Sources: California Executive Council for Nonpublic Schools; California State Dept. of Education; National Association of Independent Schools (NAIS).

Note: Figures may not add to 100% because of rounding.

schools has increased since then, and was 44 percent in 1980, compared to 38 percent in the public schools of California.

The 1978 survey found that all other private school systems except the independent schools enrolled substantially higher percentages of blacks than did the public schools. Even the independent schools do better than it may appear. Given their necessarily high tuitions, the independents must offer scholarships to attract high proportions of minority students, and they receive no outside help in raising scholarship funds. The 11 percent minority enrollment should properly be compared with the minority enrollments in the public schools in Marin County, Belair, Newport Beach, La Jolla, and similar districts serving high-income residents, districts with only a trace of minority students themselves.

The role of the private schools as minority educator seen in California appears to characterize the private schools in the West. In 1977, the National Center for Education Statistics found that in the thirteen western states (including Alaska and Hawaii) blacks were more likely to use private schools than were whites; 7.4 percent of all elementary-school-age blacks were in private schools compared with only 6.6 percent of all school-age whites.[9] In more than half the western states, private schools enrolled greater proportions of minorities than did public schools.[10]

*Minority Enrollments in Urban Private Systems.* The growing importance of private schools to minorities is most dramatically evident in the statistics for selected private systems serving cities with large minority populations. In several Catholic systems, the portion of the schools within the central city is approaching or has surpassed 50 percent minority enrollments. For example, the New York archdiocese's New York City Catholic Schools (in Manhattan, the Bronx, and Staten Island) are 53.2 percent minority and the high schools are 32.3 percent minority (see Table 12-4). The percentages would be higher were it not for the effect of near-white Staten Island. The archdiocese's Manhattan elementary schools, for example, are 79.1 percent minority. The Brooklyn diocese's schools, which serve Brooklyn and Queens, have lower proportions of minorities (as do those boroughs), but their elementary minority enrollments have been increasing and have reached 34 percent—18 percent Hispanic and 16 percent black. And minority enrollments have increased in absolute numbers even though the Catholic system has closed 28 schools since 1972.

Table 12-4. Ethnic Enrollments in New York City Catholic Schools, 1979-1980.

| | Elementary | | Secondary | |
|---|---|---|---|---|
| | *Number* | *%* | *Number* | *%* |
| American Indian | 75 | .1 | 19 | .1 |
| Asian American | 2,601 | 4.0 | 507 | 1.7 |
| Black (non-Hispanic) | 11,392 | 17.5 | 3,035 | 10.5 |
| Hispanic | 20,506 | 31.6 | 5,802 | 20.0 |
| All others | 30,406 | 46.8 | 19,630 | 67.7 |
| Totals | 64,980 | 100.0 | 28,993 | 100.0 |

Source: Unpublished tabulations, Archdiocese of New York.

Table 12-5. Ethnic Enrollments in Chicago Catholic Schools, 1979-1980.

| | Elementary | | Secondary | |
|---|---|---|---|---|
| | *Number* | *%* | *Number* | *%* |
| American Indian | 64 | .1 | 59 | .2 |
| Asian American | 2,584 | 3.2 | 481 | 1.4 |
| Black (non-Hispanic) | 22,469 | 27.5 | 5,888 | 16.9 |
| Hispanic | 12,723 | 15.6 | 4,175 | 12.0 |
| All others | 43,772 | 53.6 | 24,189 | 69.5 |
| Total | 81,612 | 100.0 | 34,792 | 100.0 |

Source: Unpublished tabulations, Archdiocese of Chicago.

The Catholic schools of Chicago have experienced similar concentrations of minority students. Chicago's Catholic elementary schools are now 46.4 percent minority; its secondary schools are 30.5 percent minority (see Table 12-5).

San Francisco has experienced an even higher concentration of minority students than New York or Chicago. The San Francisco Catholic elementary schools are 57.7 percent minority; its secondary schools are 37.7 percent minority.

The Catholic secondary school statistics in these cities show lower minority enrollments for several reasons. First, secondary schools

**Table 12-6.** Ethnic Enrollments in San Francisco Catholic Schools, 1979–1980.

|  | Elementary | | Secondary | |
|---|---|---|---|---|
|  | Number | % | Number | % |
| American Indian | 25 | .2 | 28 | .4 |
| Asian American | 3,359 | 24.1 | 787 | 11.4 |
| Black (non-Hispanic) | 1,718 | 12.3 | 556 | 8.0 |
| Hispanic | 2,939 | 21.1 | 1,243 | 17.9 |
| All others | 5,905 | 42.3 | 4,315 | 62.3 |
| Total | 13,946 | 100.0 | 6,929 | 100.0 |

Source: Unpublished tabulations, Archdiocese of Chicago.

increase their minority enrollments gradually, several years after their initial enrollments in elementary schools, as these students move up the grade levels of the system. Second, tuitions at the secondary schools in these cities average at least twice the elementary school tuitions, but can be as much as five times as great. Third—and most interesting for those concerned with racial integration—private schools have established a reputation for superior performance that attracts white students back to schools, even those in racially changing neighborhoods. For instance, Cardinal Hayes High School, which serves the South Bronx—a heavily Hispanic and black area of New York—has maintained a relatively stable 18 percent white enrollment for several years. In 1979, the school attracted 245 white students from areas as distant as middle and upper-middle-income Riverdale, Bronxville, and Pelham Bay. It is not surprising that a school with a reputation for quality can hold or attract at least some white students, since that theory is the basis for magnet-school desegregation plans that have been attempted in public schools. At least in some instances, it is the private school's success at holding white students and remaining integrated that keeps down the percentage of minority students attending. This is an important observation. Private schools, as well as public, can help a city to maintain an integrated population because they can hold racially mixed communities together.

Much of the concern that private schools are racially segregated comes from the experience with southern "segregation academies," which are often pointed to as examples of private schools' tendencies in this direction. These academies, however, are not traditional private schools. They are only a small, recent component of private education in the South, created by public authorities trying to shield public schools from the Supreme Court's desegregation order of 1954.

In the South, the "real" private schools have traditionally been far more integrationist than public schools in the region. State laws which required private schools to segregate were resisted until the Supreme Court, in the Berea College Case of 1908, ruled that states could constitutionally *force private schools to segregate.* When the Supreme Court turned the tables again in the 1950s, many private school systems in the South integrated *before* the public schools in their communities. (These include the Lutheran and Catholic systems of New Orleans and Lafayette, Louisiana; Montgomery and Mobile, Alabama; and St. Louis, Missouri.)

Whatever the segregating aspects of specific private schools, the available evidence does not support the argument that, in general, private schools segregate racially. The belief that private schools have always been and are elitist, segregating institutions is incorrect.

### New York City Schools:  An Illustration

The private schools play a far more important role in New York City than they do in most other American communities. The city has about 5 percent of all private schools in the United States and 7 percent of all private school students. (The city has 3 percent of all public and private elementary and secondary students.) In fact, the city has more private schools—almost one thousand—than public schools.

Unfortunately, there are no adequate data describing the family characteristics of New York City's private school pupils. Some data are available from federal programs—most notably the Elementary and Secondary Education Act's (ESEA) Title I (compensatory education). About 14 percent of the city's private school students are eligible for Title I assistance. Eligibility requirements include both residence in a low-income target area and a substantial reading deficiency. Private school students tend not to have as severe reading disabilities as public school students, so the 14 percent figure substantially understates the proportion of private school students from low-income areas.

As we have noted, some information on the income of families sending children to private schools became available for the first time in the U.S. Bureau of the Census's 1976 *Survey of Income and Education*, in which the bureau asked the same sample population questions about income and private school attendance. A sufficient number of responses were received from New York City families to permit the Foundation for Child Development to estimate the family income of New York City's school-age children. However, the foundation was unable to identify the incomes of the families with children in private schools because the sample did not include enough respondents in this category.

In order to compare the incomes of New York City families using public and private schools, we must therefore look at a larger portion of the sample, the Northeast region. (It is reasonable to assume that the Northeast data reflect the situation in New York City; indeed, they present a relatively conservative picture because of the greater proportion of high-income families in the region.) As expected, Table 12–7 shows that private schools have a smaller proportion of low-income families than the public schools and a slightly higher proportion of upper-income families. But note how similar are the income distributions of the families using the two types of schools. Public and private schools enroll children from families in the same economic spectrum.

As the critics of the tax credit approach suspected, there is some evidence that low-income families are priced out of private schools, but once the income threshold that permits families to pay for private school education is passed, there is a relatively even use of these schools across all income groups, with a slight increase for the highest-income groups. Tax credits would have eliminated the "priced-out" threshold, however, and let lower-income families use private schools almost as readily as lower-middle and middle-income families.

New York City continues to offer a greater variety of private schools than any other large city in the country. Even though, as Table 12–8 shows, the enrollment in New York City private schools has declined, the enrollment of minorities has increased dramatically.

*Catholic Schools.* Catholic schools account for one-third of the city's private schools and two-thirds of its private school enrollment.

Table 12-7. Elementary and Secondary Enrollment in Northeast Region Private and Public Schools by Family Income, 1975 (numbers in thousands).

| Family Income | Total | | Private | | Public | |
|---|---|---|---|---|---|---|
| | Number | Percentage | Number | Percentage | Number | Percentage |
| Less than $5,000 | 842 | 7.7 | 58 | 3.8 | 784 | 8.3 |
| $5,000–9,999 | 1,862 | 17.1 | 189 | 12.4 | 1,673 | 17.8 |
| 10,000–14,999 | 2,235 | 20.5 | 259 | 17.1 | 1,976 | 21.1 |
| 15,000–19,999 | 2,214 | 20.3 | 329 | 21.7 | 1,885 | 20.1 |
| 20,000–29,999 | 2,529 | 23.2 | 431 | 28.3 | 2,098 | 22.3 |
| 30,000–49,999 | 998 | 9.2 | 196 | 12.9 | 802 | 8.6 |
| 50,000 and over | 222 | 2.0 | 57 | 3.8 | 165 | 1.8 |
| Total | 10,902 | 100.0 | 1,519 | 100.0 | 9,383 | 100.0 |

Source: U.S. Bureau of the Census, Survey of Income and Education, as reported in the Congressional Record-Senate, March 20, 1978, pp. S4158–60.

**Table 12-8.** Elementary and Secondary Enrollment in New York City Private and Public Schools, 1970–1971–1977–1978.

| Category | 1970-1971 | | 1977-1978 | | Change | |
|---|---|---|---|---|---|---|
| | Number | Percentage | Number | Percentage | Number | Percentage |
| PRIVATE SCHOOLS | | | | | | |
| Roman Catholic | 325,620 | 21.1 | 222,968 | 16.5 | (102,652) | (31.5) |
| Brooklyn Diocese (Brooklyn, Queens) | 198,003 | 12.8 | 126,787 | 9.4 | (71,216) | (36.0) |
| New York Archdiocese (Manhattan, Bronx, Staten Island) | 127,617 | 8.3 | 96,181 | 7.1 | (31,436) | (24.6) |
| Jewish | 32,770 | 2.1 | 39,459 | 2.9 | 6,689 | 20.4 |
| Nonaffiliated | 6,053 | 0.4 | 5,663 | 0.4 | (390) | (6.4) |
| Conservative | 1,312 | 0.1 | 1,476 | 0.1 | 164 | 12.5 |
| Orthodox | 25,405 | 1.6 | 32,320 | 2.4 | 6,915 | 27.2 |
| Other denominational | 15,399 | 1.1 | 17,375 | 1.3 | 1,976 | 12.8 |
| Lutheran | 6,056 | 0.4 | 6,727 | 0.5 | 671 | 11.1 |
| Episcopal | 4,204 | 0.3 | 3,989 | 0.3 | (215) | (5.1) |
| Greek Orthodox | 2,403 | 0.2 | 3,001 | 0.2 | 598 | 24.9 |
| Seventh Day Adventist | 1,546 | 0.1 | 2,151 | 0.2 | 605 | 39.1 |
| Other[a] | 1,190 | 0.1 | 1,507 | 0.1 | 317 | 26.6 |
| Independent | 31,413 | 2.0 | 36,674 | 2.7 | 5,261 | 16.7 |
| PRIVATE SCHOOLS TOTAL | 405,202 | 26.3 | 316,476 | 23.4 | (88,726) | (21.9) |
| PUBLIC SCHOOLS TOTAL | 1,135,298 | 73.7 | 1,033,813 | 76.6 | (101,485) | (8.9) |
| TOTAL ENROLLMENT | 1,540,500 | 100.0 | 1,350,289 | 100.0 | (190,211) | (12.3) |

a. Includes Society of Friends, Baptist, Presbyterian, and Russian Orthodox.
Source: New York State Education Department, Information Center on Education, March 1979.

They report rapidly increasing minority enrollment, which should not be surprising for two reasons: (1) most Catholic schools—and virtually all Catholic elementary schools—are neighborhood schools and are influenced by the same population trends affecting the public schools; and (2) recent Hispanic immigrants are traditionally, if not actively, Catholic. Both the New York and Brooklyn dioceses' enrollments are now over 50 percent "minority." The New York archdiocese's minority student population rose from 41 percent in 1975–1976 to 60 percent in 1977–1978.

Catholic schools are heavily concentrated in the inner-city areas of Manhattan, the Bronx, Brooklyn, and Queens. The system identified forty-seven elementary schools as "inner-city" in Manhattan in 1977. Of the 18,421 students in these schools, 78 percent were from minority groups. The system identified an additional thirty inner-city schools in the Bronx, for a total of seventy-seven in the inner-city areas of these two boroughs. In sixty-four of these schools, more than half of the students were from families with incomes below poverty level. In slightly less than half of its inner-city elementary schools (thirty-six), the New York archdiocese reported that more than 85 percent of the students came from families with below poverty-level incomes.[11]

*Hebrew Day Schools.* The city's second largest group of private schools are the Hebrew day schools (including Solomon Schecter, Torah Umesorah, and yeshivas). These schools enrolled 39,459 students in 1977–1978.[12] Although reliable data are not available, school officials estimate that more than half their students come from low-income families. Although these schools have virtually no black or Hispanic children, a high proportion of their students are immigrants or the children of recent immigrants. (In recent years, virtually all the Russian-Jewish immigrants settling in New York City, estimated at over ten thousand and most with low incomes, reportedly have enrolled their children in Hebrew day schools.)

Only the most formalistic integrationist would argue that the integration of black and Hispanic children with these Eastern European and Middle Eastern minorities is a reasonable solution to the problems of racial integration in the city schools. The integration projected under the Constitution and the civil rights laws involves the minorities with the majority or dominant population.

*Other Denominational Schools.* Most of the city's other denominational schools are not neighborhood schools, even when they are attached to a parish. Typically, they are selective in their admissions and draw their students from a wide area of the city. These schools appear to enroll students from families with slightly lower than median incomes and to enroll slightly higher percentages of minority students than do the city's private independent schools. But neither set of schools has compiled and reported reliable family income data, so conclusions are tentative at best.

It is not necessary to enter a detailed argument about the segregative or integrative impact of the denominational schools enrolling large percentages of minorities or immigrants. Clearly, these schools cannot be characterized as racial havens when they enroll minorities. Further, those with high percentages of recent immigrants, such as many Catholic and Hebrew day schools, help stabilize the ethnic communities where they are located and deter families from leaving for the suburbs.

The more interesting questions concern the integrative impact on middle- and upper-middle-income neighborhoods of the denominational schools, especially the higher-tuition denominational schools, and the selective independent private schools. These schools do tend to enroll a lower proportion of minorities than the public system as a whole and often a lower proportion than are present in the schools' neighborhoods. Consequently, the independent schools often strike casual observers as encouraging the segregation of the city's school population. But it is misleading to compare the record of the independent schools with that of a neighborhood public or private school serving a population with a substantially different socioeconomic composition.

*Independent Schools.* The independent schools should be evaluated against the norm for their principal clients—upper-income families. Are wealthier children in independent schools more racially isolated than wealthier children in public schools? Have the schools taken steps to minimize the racial and economic isolation of their students, and how do their efforts compare with the efforts of public schools serving comparable families?

New York City's independent schools enroll only about 11.5 percent of the city's private school students. But these schools are perhaps the most important to our argument because they enroll the students from families with the highest incomes, and they pride themselves on their selectivity (which some critics often perceive as exclusivity). True to their label, New York City's independent schools are not a tightly organized group; they do not collect information for the group as a whole about scholarship aid, minority enrollments, and the like. Many of the independent schools, however, belong to the National Association of Independent Schools, whose recent survey found its members nationally had an average minority group enrollment of 7 percent.[13] In 1978, the forty-four member schools in New York City (with 56 percent of the city's independent students) had a minority enrollment twice the national average—13.9 percent (the figure is 25 percent or more in several of the schools)—and they devote a greater proportion of their school budgets to scholarship aid. Virtually all private schools in the city ensure that their enrollments include students from low-income and minority families.

The alternatives to these private schools are the public schools serving the highest median income districts in the New York metropolitan area. Only 11 percent of all minorities in the New York area live outside the city, and these are concentrated in a few Westchester communities like Mount Vernon, White Plains, Greenburg District No. 8, and some Long Island and New Jersey towns. Students from upper- and middle-income families who turn from the city's private schools to suburban public schools will be unlikely to attend schools with more than 2 percent minority enrollments, if that much, and with only a handful of students from lower-income families.

Fears of supporters of public schools that New York City private schools are havens for the wealthy trying to avoid racial and economic integration have not been supported by the statistics describing the socioeconomic characteristics of the private school population in the city. We have enough information from available sources to know that these schools are not elitist institutions. We have seen that private schools contribute to integration in the city but that the tax system makes it less likely that middle- and upper-income parents will remain in the city and select these schools.

## CONCLUSION: THE IMPACT OF TAX REFORM

The preceding statistics suggest that private schools serve a population more racially and economically mixed than the stereotypical view of such schools assumes. This characteristic comes through the statistical descriptions despite the problem that regional differences in the presence of lower-income and minority populations in the United States do not coincide with the distribution of private schools. Thus, if private schools enrolled precisely the same proportion of lower-income and minority students as public schools everywhere they were located, the national statistics would still show private schools with a lower proportion of minority and lower-income students. The national socioeconomic statistics reflect concentrations of lower-income and minority families in Appalachia and the rural South, for example, where there are relatively few private schools.

Nevertheless, when we look at regional statistics, we find a significant drop-off of enrollments in private schools for families below $10,000, which appears to be the income threshold for families to use private schools. That threshold is lower than most people have assumed, but it is present. For example, in the Northeast, families with incomes above $30,000 (in 1975 dollars) are a little more than twice as likely to use private schools as families with incomes below $10,000. Because there are more families in the lower-income category in the Northeast population, the region's private schools have almost an identical number of these lower- and higher-income families: 247,000 lower-income students compared with 253,000 higher-income students in both elementary and secondary schools. Elementary school statistics alone, if available, would show a higher proportion of lower-income families.[14]

Existing tax laws have a complicated effect on these statistics. Lower-income families are clearly less likely to use private schools than higher-income families. We must assume that this is a consequence of their economic circumstances. The existing tax system exacerbates the difficulties of lower-income families using private schools because it effectively increases the amount of money the family must obtain to pay tuition. Thus, more families fall below the income threshold a family must have in order to use private schools. Existing policies also tend to discourage the use of private schools by upper-income parents since the effective cost of education in a private school for these families is several times the nominal tuition.

This might suggest, on balance, that the tax system has a benign influence on the tendency of wealthy families to separate their children from poorer or minority children. However, that inference is not correct because the typical alternative for a high-income family is not the heterogeneous urban school but the homogeneous, elite public school. Because public school population statistics are lumped together, they hide the racial and economic isolation that exists within that system on a school-by-school basis. In the private schools, as we have seen, some efforts are made to integrate the student population both racially and economically. Hence, the existing tax system encourages upper-income families to take what is effectively the racially and economically isolating alternative in the education of their children. The effect is also to limit the number of lower-income children in private schools. However, the system has a stronger discouraging effect on upper-income families and, therefore, tends to make private schools more economically integrated, statistically speaking, than they would be if only market forces operated.

We cannot simply assume, however, that private schools would let market forces change their socioeconomic mix of students. Lower-income students in private schools are subsidized by the school or by a sponsor. They are present in private schools because the schools have adopted policies that *oppose* market forces. The existing tax system takes a neutral or hostile position toward these policies.

There are two principal types of subsidy to low-income students in private schools: subsidy to the school organization as a whole, which permits a lowering or complete elimination of tuition, and subsidy to individual families or students in the form of scholarship aid. Some schools follow both policies. Typically, scholarship aid is funded from a school's general revenues, including its tuition income. Existing tax regulations permit the deduction of contributions to schools, or to churches or other organizations supporting schools. But they do not permit the deduction of tuition, and recent changes have attempted to limit the deductibility of contributions to churches by parents enrolling children in church schools. To the extent that these proposed changes become effective, the tendency of churches and other organizations to support schools will be discouraged, and therefore the subsidy of lower-income and minority students will be reduced. Under existing policy, the proportion of tuition which supports scholarship students is not deductible, and therefore the ability of private schools to offer tuition aid is reduced. Increasingly, existing tax policies inhibit scholarship aid to lower-income and minority students in private schools.

Several reforms of the tax system would both change the impact of tax regulations on private and on public schools and advance the national ideal of a racially and economically integrated student population at no great cost. In the late 1970s, the Internal Revenue Service proposed new regulations to encourage the racial integration of private schools by denying tax-exempt status to segregated schools. The regulations proposed were far reaching, but created potentially serious difficulties for schools which were not segregated, and Congress eventually intervened to prevent implementation of the proposals. The most serious difficulties occurred in two areas of the regulations. The Internal Revenue Service suggested, in order to determine whether a school was segregated, that its minority enrollment should be compared to the minority presence in the broad area in which the school was located, or of the public school district in which the private school was located, or in the general surrounding area of the school. The first option was obviously a poor choice, since that would mean that all black private schools in cities like Washington, D.C. would be considered integrated, and schools in Washington with 50 percent minority enrollments would be considered segregated. Similarly, all-white schools in virtually all-white districts outside Washington would be considered integrated. The standard ignores the problem that public systems in the North, Midwest, and West are becoming increasingly segregated among themselves. The alternative standard also presents difficulties. What is the general area surrounding the school? The precise attendance area boundaries, or the drawing area, of many private schools are difficult to establish. The schools would always be vulnerable to the charge that they did not reflect the composition of the area they served, since there would be debate over that area.

The second problem area concerned the remedy the proposals required. The Internal Revenue Service suggested that private schools falling below the appropriate proportions of minorities in their school population could avoid the loss of their tax-exempt status by offering scholarship aid. Thus, the school would have been caught in a double bind: the regulations would have required it to increase its budget and therefore its tuition in order to offer scholarships but would not permit individuals to deduct from their tax liability the proportion of tuition supporting that scholarship aid.

Despite these difficulties, this policy could have extremely beneficial social impacts if it were applied to public as well as private schools. Private schools in cities or suburbs must compete for students with public schools. The proposed tax regulations, if applied only to private schools, will raise private school costs and make their competition more difficult. As they stand now, the reforms would not analogously affect public schools. The tax regulation could require integrated private schools to increase the proportion of lower-income and minority students even when nearby segregated public schools are unaffected. However, if the tax deductibility of public school education expenses—that is, taxes levied by the school district, local government, or state for the support of the local schools— were made contingent upon the integration of the public school, the Internal Revenue Service measure would greatly benefit private schools and the integration of American public and private schools. Public school districts without minority or low-income families would be required to offer scholarships to recruit those students from other areas. Thus, public schools would be subject to the same standards as the private.

A second reform would also indirectly benefit private schools, as well as public schools in districts unattractive to wealthy families: the complete elimination of deductions for education expenses from calculations of tax liability. As we have seen, the tax deductions of education expenses (however charged—as tuition, local or state taxes, or any similar scheme) provide a kind of transfer payment from the taxing body to the school. However, the school recovers this transfer only if the taxpayers supporting it itemize their deductions, which most families in lower-income school districts do not do. Eliminating the deduction will raise the cost of public education for wealthier families, without changing the costs for lower-income families or for families using private schools. Such a reform will lessen the incentive for the wealthy to leave the urban systems and should therefore benefit city public school systems and private schools.

The measure will also increase the government's income from wealthier families. The increased income *could* be returned as state and federal aid to school districts. There would be greater political demand for this aid since wealthier districts would be more likely to call for such aid because of their new difficulties supporting the level of expenditure to which they had grown accustomed. But any federal or state program of distribution will be more progressive than the distributions of aid through the existing tax law. That is, any program of distribution will do no worse than give wealthy communities just as much as poor communities are given. Under existing law, the wealthy get much more.

Another reform would permit parents to deduct all basic education expenses for their children, whatever form those expenses take: tuition payments, local taxes, payments for specific services and supplies. This measure has the virtue of treating all forms of education neutrally, and it extends to individuals tax advantages on education expenses now enjoyed by businesses. This measure holds to a reasonable principle in a democratic society: that education of the population ought to be encouraged and ought not to be taxed, directly or indirectly, by the state.

Such a measure will become increasingly important because of the failure of our legislatures to index the income tax system in inflationary times. Roughly calculated for families close to median income, a 10 percent inflation rate will produce a 2 percent increase in the family's tax bracket—presuming that real income remains constant or, in other words, that the family's income increased with inflation. Thus, deductions become more important as inflation increases. Because of its tax system effects, inflation will make tuition at private schools more difficult for families, even when the family income has increased at the same rate as inflation.

Permitting the full deduction of education expenses will also make unnecessary the loan programs for middle- and upper-middle-income college students, freeing the money in those programs for lower-income students. But it will have no direct, positive effects on families at median income or lower who do not itemize deductions and for whom there are no programs of federal tuition assistance comparable with the higher education programs. It may have an indirect effect. The full deduction of education expenses could expand the market of families able to consider private school education and reduce the financial pressures on those families choosing private schools now. Tuition could be doubled for the highest-income families, and the family would still pay lower total education costs as a result of tax savings. Tuitions might more easily be pegged to family income since the tax benefits to the wealthiest families will be greater. In general, the schools will be able to increase the income available to provide scholarship aid to those who do not receive the tax benefits. Thus, lower-income families could be indirectly benefited.

Further regulations attached to provisions for total deduction of education expenses could increase these benefits. A school might be required to provide a certain proportion of scholarship aid before its tuition could be a deductible item for parents. Or families who take the standard deduction could be permitted to deduct education expenses from their taxable income. Or some version of a refundable tax credit for lower-income families could be added to the measure.

In sum, the system of tax deductions is an intervention in normal market decisions by which clients choose public and private schools. Existing incentives encourage wealthier families to choose public schools in racially and economically isolated districts and restrict the ability of lower-income families to make use of private schools. Existing policies inhibit schools from providing scholarship aid to minority or lower-income students from tuition-generated revenues. Proposed changes in taxation policy will further restrict subsidies for the private school education of lower-income students. Existing policies, and all currently considered reforms, apply different standards in establishing the tax deductibility of payments which support private and public schools and which determine the tax exemption of the school organizations.

Changes in the tax treatment of education expenses could substantially increase the egalitarian character of private schools and decrease the segregating tendencies of the existing systems of public education in metropolitan areas. Taxes, by their influence on the pattern of choices of wealthy and poorer families, shape the social characteristics of public and private education. Reforms should take into account the patterns of choice they will encourage.

The influence of the existing system of taxation is constantly increasing, as result of inflation and of the expansion of the reach of the Internal Revenue Service. Perhaps in its inception, when the tax system affected only the wealthiest and only to a small degree, the social impacts of the choices taxation encouraged could be ignored. But now its social effects have become quite important. The pandora's box has sprung its lid when no one was looking. While state and federal governments were concerned with governing education through direct regulations and aid programs, taxation policy quietly stole the game.

It is not that we should remove the tax system's effects that shape public and private schools—to do so would involve a major reform requiring the elimination of almost all deductions and the lowering of the tax rates, and would bring problems of its own—but rather we should acknowledge the effects the current laws have, take responsibility for them, and bring them under conscious direction. The current tax laws and regulations provide more aid to the wealthy than the poor, encourage the segregation of metropolitan districts or of suburban districts with lower-income residents, and encourage the economic and therefore racial segregation of private schools by discouraging lower-income students from attending at their own cost, and making it more difficult for the schools to offer scholarships from tuition revenues. None of these outcomes are intended products of the tax system. Some simple changes in tax regulations could substantially improve the effects the tax codes have on schools.

## RECOMMENDATIONS

1.  Despite the problems with the ill-thought-through, rigid, and rudimentary initial proposals for desegregating private schools through taxation policies, the direction is promising. It begins to follow the pattern typical in the Western democracies of providing full funding of government schools and variable partial funding of private schools adopting one or more state objectives. However, the approach should not be limited to the private schools. Congress should treat public schools by the same rules it proposes to apply to private schools: public schools which are economically or racially isolated (in comparison to the metropolitan areas of which they are a part) should be required to offer scholarships to lower income and minority students residing outside the district, and to develop other programs of minority and lower-income student recruitment, if they are to enjoy the benefits of the tax deductibility of the taxes that support the local schools. This single change in the rules would begin to undo some of the damage of the present system, though the massive incentives for the movement of upper-income families from lower-income districts would not be seriously affected. From that perspective, it is a modest change.

2.  For many middle- and upper-income families, private schools offer an alternative to the attractive suburban public schools that permit them to remain in the city. Parents choosing urban private

schools ought to be permitted the full deduction of their tuition from their taxable income, as that begins to equalize the competition with the suburban system, where they are permitted the deduction of their school taxes. Of course, the suburban system still has the edge, since its schools are free, but the competitive position of the urban private schools is increased.

It would be practically impossible to restrict the benefit of this deduction to parents choosing urban private schools and excluding those choosing suburban ones. These private schools could be held to the same requirements established for the public schools, if the first recommendation were adopted. In general, the private schools—such as those in the National Association of Independent Schools we have already discussed—outperform the public schools in the high income suburbs on economic and racial integration.

3. At the very least, current policies should be changed to encourage private schools to offer scholarship aid by eliminating the penalty on this aid. Parents should be permitted to deduct at least a portion of their school tuition that goes to provide scholarship aid to minorities or families in economic need. To avoid accounting complications and provide a reasonable incentive for scholarship aid, parents should be permitted to deduct a percentage of their tuition, equivalent to the percentage of scholarship students in the school, or the percentage of total school funds serving scholarship students.

4. In the absence of any tax benefits for the private schools, Congress should eliminate the deductibility of local school taxes on itemized returns. This would immediately increase the competitive position of the private schools vis-à-vis the suburban public schools, and would also substantially improve the competitive position of the urban public systems, which now receive little benefit from the system of deductions.

Any of these choices begins to redress the balance between suburban and city public schools, and public and private schools, and to reduce the segregating pressures within the tax system. But if present policies continue unchanged, the widespread and erroneous belief that private schools fail to enroll their proper share of the poor will become self-fulfilling; taxation policy will price the schools out of the reach of the poor and reduce the scholarship funds available to them. At the same time, it will increase the disadvantage suffered by urban public schools—and their communities, which include the urban private schools—versus affluent suburbs. As policies now stand, we encourage in public and private schools the opposite of what democratic ideology holds should be the role of schools in a democratic republic. There is no justifiable basis for providing a free education to wealthy families in economically and racially segregated schools, but our taxation policy goes further and offers an incentive to the wealthy to use these schools. There is no reason to discourage the wealthy and the lower-income and minority families from using integrated private schools, but our taxation policies discourage the integration of these schools and discourage wealthy and middle-income families from choosing them over segregated, exclusive public schools.

## NOTES TO CHAPTER 12

1.  These policy categories are taken from Theodore Lowi, "American Business, Public Policy, Case Studies, and Political Theory," *World Politics* 16 (1964): 677–712. Lowi sees the three categories of policy, defined in terms of their degrees of comprehensiveness and coerciveness and according to the characteristics of the political processes associated with their enactment and implementation, as "distributive, regulative and redistributive." I have chosen to use the more narrow and descriptive term of "redistributive taxation," and more specifically "tax deduction rules," in discussing the third type of policy to avoid too complex a discussion.

2.  The U.S. Office of Education has not studied the degree to which public school systems appropriately serve students enrolled in private schools with services funded under federal programs. As part of its congressionally mandated study of Title I, the National Institute of Education funded one exploratory study of private school students' inclusion in ESEA, Title I. The study found substantial indications that private school students were not being included properly in the benefits of ESEA, Title I, which is the most visible of all federally funded programs and the one arguably least likely to experience serious difficulties. See Thomas W. Vitullo-Martin, "On the Comparability of Services Provided to Private School Students Under Title I of the Elementary and Secondary Education Act (as amended, 1974) and on the Impact of the Act on Private Schools: A Report for the Education Equity Group, Compensatory Education Division of the National Institute of Education," U.S. Department of Education, National Institute of Education, NIE 400–76–0109, September 1979.

3.  I wish to acknowledge the valuable suggestions of tax consultants Harry A. Skydell, CPA, of Skydell, Shatz and Co., and of Warren Lieberman, CPA,

of Louis Lieberman and Co. Any errors in this report are solely the responsibility of the author.

4.  Grant McConnell, *Private Power and American Democracy* (New York: Alfred A. Knopf, 1965).

5.  Lowi, "American Business, Public Policy."

6.  Pocantico Hills has been singled out as a dramatic example of how wealthy districts benefit from the tax system. The district does, however, contain a development of more modestly priced homes and has, consequently, a 14 percent racial and ethnic minority enrollment, substantially above that of the average Westchester school district.

7.  The council's estimate of aid to private schools in 1977 was incorrect. New York City's public school system received direct aid of almost $300 per pupil; private schools received no direct aid. Most recent federal education aid programs—like ESEA Title I (compensatory education)—follow a child-benefit approach by which students are entitled to receive aid regardless of the type of school they attend. However, the federal funds for these programs are given to the public school district, not to individual private schools. The public system hires the teachers, plans the programs, and delivers the services to the private school students. Private schools have no direct control over the funds, teachers, or programs. In most cases, it is as if the private school students were enrolled in a public system's after-school program. So it is misleading to attribute the total value of services delivered to individual private school students as "aid to private schools."

    Furthermore, the $60 figure is not even an accurate estimate of the value of services delivered to private school students. The former U.S. Department of Health, Education, and Welfare could not state—based on any existing systematically collected data—the dollar value of services actually delivered to private school students. The new Department of Education has taken no steps so far to correct this incapacity. HEW simply assumed that a proportion of funds given to each state went to private school students, despite evidence that in a number of states and a number of programs, this was not happening. In three states, in fact, authorities refused to deliver *any* services to private school students. For a discussion of the record on the inclusion of private school students in ESEA, Title I, see Vitullo-Martin, "On the Comparability of Services."

8.  See U.S. Bureau of the Census, *Survey of Income and Education*, in U.S. Congress, Senate, *Congressional Record*, 95th Cong., 2d sess., pp. 4158–60.

9.  National Center for Education Statistics, "The Condition of Education, 1977" (Washington, D.C.: U.S. Government Printing Office, 1970), pp. 74, 77.

10. Ibid., p. 192, Table 4.05.

11.  Robert G. Hoyt, "Learning a Lesson from the Catholic Schools," *New York*, September 12, 1977, pp. 48–55. See also Edward B. Fiske, Catholic Schools Attain Stability in Urban Crisis," *New York Times*, October 9, 1977.

12.  Donald A. Erickson, Richard L. Nault, and Bruce Cooper, assisted by Robert Lamborn, "Recent Enrollment Trends in U.S. Nonpublic Schools," in *Declining Enrollments: The Challenge of the Coming Decade*, ed. Susan Abramowitz and Stuart Rosenfeld (Washington, D.C.: U.S. Government Printing Office, 1978), p. 86, Table 3.2.

13.  Ibid., p. 111. See also William Dandridge, unpublished memo, National Association of Independent Schools, May 23, 1979.

14.  U.S. Bureau of the Census, *Survey of Income and Education*.

# 13 EDUCATIONAL TAX CREDITS

*Roger A. Freeman*

Efforts to provide tax relief for parents who bear the burden of paying for their children's education have been active for about a quarter-century. They were and still are the subject of intense controversies in Congress, in state legislatures, in the courts, in the nation's press, and among the general public. Both houses of Congress and several state legislatures have passed tuition tax credit bills at some time or other, but judicial and other obstacles have intervened and prevented the plans from being carried out.

The core of the argument for financial relief is really not over money but over the role of nonpublic education, which, if aided, might expand and could threaten the near-monopoly position of the public schools. The basic question was and is whether all, or almost all, children should receive their education in government-run common schools or whether there should be diversity of offerings, giving parents a choice in the type of education they wish their children to receive and in the school they want them to attend. Although that choice exists in law, its exercise is severely restricted by the economics of the situation, by the penalty which parents have to bear who enroll their children in a nonpublic school. Finances make parental option largely hypothetical for the vast majority of families which cannot afford to pay the added expenses. As if the economic and ideological (public versus private schools) problems were not enough, the subject is further complicated by a constitutional question: most of the nonpublic schools are religiously affiliated, most of them connected with the Catholic Church. That brings strong emotions to the surface which divide positions on the constitutional issue and make both sides uncompromising. The religious issue has proven the rock on which past attempts to authorize tax credits have foundered.

The idea of educational tax credits, however, gained ground and became widely popular in the 1970s, and supporters grew increasingly confident that their drive would soon be crowned by success. Opponents are no less determined to keep educational tax credits from becoming a reality. The stage seems now set for fierce battles in the political and judicial arenas during the 1980s. Their outcome may decide the fate of educational tax credits, and of nonpublic education, for a long time to come.

With a national administration and a Congress significantly more favorable toward educational tax credits than any of their predecessors and with some of the top political leaders explicitly committed, prospects for approval appear to be better than they have ever been. The timing of personnel changes on the Supreme Court, a narrow majority of which has been the most formidable obstacle to educational tax credits, however, cannot be foretold with equal precision. Predictions should at this time be guardedly optimistic for the supporters of educational tax credits, though the ingenuity, dedication, and strength of their opponents must not be underrated.

## ISSUES AND TRENDS

Dissatisfaction with the educational results of the public schools has been growing for decades and reached new heights in the late 1970s, with no sign of a trend reversal. The schools are charged with failing to establish and uphold sufficiently high standards of behavior and curriculum. Untold numbers of parents have become increasingly irritated, perturbed, and alienated because they feel that schools do not teach and enforce the discipline which young people need to advance in life, that they do not transmit to students the skills and knowledge which they are able to absorb, and, last but not least, that they do not inspire pupils to acquire the proper attitudes without which their chances of becoming useful members of society are limited. When communities have tried to influence and change the direction of their schools, they have run up against a central bureaucracy—federal, state, and local—which has control of contents, methods, and pursued goals, often at variance with the local consensus. Frustrated in their efforts to improve their children's education in public schools, many parents searched for alternatives and found that nonpublic schools were their only available option.

Although the demand for nonpublic education has been expanding, the supply has been shrinking. Nonpublic schools found themselves increasingly unable to finance the gap between soaring costs and what they felt they could charge their patrons without becoming institutions solely for children of the rich. Some private schools resolved the dilemma by raising tuitions to whatever level their outlays called for and by trying to attract donations. The majority of systems reluctantly decided to close schools which ran intolerably high deficits and to restrict admission at most others. Nonpublic schools lost about one-third of their students between 1965 and 1980, not because they lacked applicants—they continued to be swamped—but because they could not afford to admit them. The nonpublic share of total elementary and secondary school enrollment shrank from nearly 15 percent in 1965 to 10 percent in 1980.[1]

Costs climbed steeply in public and nonpublic schools, much faster than the general price level. State and local governments supplied the required funds to the public schools by jacking up the rates of property, income, and sales taxes and were helped by small amounts of federal aid. The percentage of national income devoted to public education substantially more than doubled within the past two decades. With personnel accounting for close to three-fourths of total school expenditures, teachers are the main item of school costs. Most of the soaring school outlays can be traced to a shrinking teacher-pupil ratio (fewer pupils per teacher) and to rising teacher salaries. This is true in public as well as in nonpublic schools.

But nonpublic schools have special problems. Catholic schools, whose share of nonpublic education dropped from more than four-fifths to slightly over two-thirds within the past fifteen years, used to rely almost completely on members of religious orders to staff their faculty. Those teachers served for mere subsistence compensation. But the number of young people choosing religious vocations has been falling precipitously in recent decades, and Catholic schools have had to hire more lay teachers. Lay teachers accounted for 36 percent of the faculty in Catholic schools in 1965, for 70 percent in

1978. Lay teachers must be paid regular wages, usually less than public school teachers' salaries but far more than what members of religious orders were and are paid.

Catholic parochial schools used to run far larger classes than public schools, up to fifty pupils and more, in an effort to accommodate the largest possible number of children. This has been remedied. The teacher-pupil ratio in Catholic schools dropped from one to thirty-two in 1965 to one to twenty-two in 1978 (compared with one to eighteen in public schools). This means that a student body of constant size used 45 percent more teachers in 1978 than it did thirteen years earlier. The larger number of teachers required for a specified number of students and higher compensation because of the shift from religious to lay teachers forced the Catholic school systems to close 3,500 schools (a loss of 27 percent) between 1965 and 1978 and to reduce their student body by more than two million (a loss of 40 percent).

Secular nonpublic schools and schools affiliated with denominations other than Catholic—Lutheran, Baptist, Episcopal, Jewish, etc.—doubled enrollment between 1965 and 1976 and now account for close to one-third of nonpublic school enrollment. They could have grown even faster if they had been able to finance such an expansion. Current expenditures in public schools totaled $1,900 per pupil in 1978-79 and may be estimated to run above $2,200 in 1981. Very few nonpublic schools are able to charge their patrons that much or more. Most set their tuitions at between one-half and one-fourth of the cost of public schools, or lower, and thus find it extremely difficult to make ends meet. Most parents, however, particularly those with several children of school age, find it impossible to pay tuitions between $500 and $1,500 or more per child and avoid those expenses by sending their offspring to public school. They know that they pay for public school education in their state and local property taxes and income and sales taxes and feel that they cannot afford to pay twice for their children's education.

It is now generally recognized that thousands, and possibly millions, of additional parents would send their children to nonpublic schools if the penalty for doing so were not so heavy.[2] The number of parents wanting to transfer their children has undoubtedly risen in recent decades, whereas the number of children actually attending nonpublic school declined. Thus, the idea of governmental subventions of nonpublic schools gained increasing support. Each child attending a nonpublic school now saves the taxpayers an average of at least $2,200 for current annual expenses, not counting the cost of facilities. With about five million pupils in nonpublic schools, this equals a savings for taxpayers of $11 billion a year. With enrollment now shifting to public schools, that amount is likely to shrink. If part of the tax savings were used to subsidize nonpublic schools, more parents might be enabled to send their children there and taxpayers would still derive sizable benefits from the fact that millions of parents pay a substantial share of the cost of educating their offspring. In other words, a small subsidy to nonpublic schools could produce sizable reductions in the cost of public school education, with a resulting net gain to the taxpayer.

But direct governmental subsidies to nonpublic schools face obstacles which currently appear insuperable. Many nonpublic school systems do not want to become recipients of regular governmental appropriations because they know that this would subject them to governmental controls. Experience in recent decades has shown that beneficiaries of federal funds, as well as of state funds, thereby virtually lose the right to make their own policy decisions. In the end, there might be little difference between public and nonpublic schools.

Some of the nonpublic schools, those financially hard-pressed and facing possible closing, might be willing to surrender some of their independence in return for cash. But spokesmen for the public schools strongly oppose any aid to other school systems which would, in their opinion, encourage and aid unfair competition and lead to a gradual decline of public schools. They believe that all children should attend the common schools as a means of educating them as citizens in a democratic society where they must mix, deal, and get along with members of all other social and economic classes, ethnic groups, etc. Although attempts to make attendance in public schools compulsory for all children were turned down by the Supreme Court more than half a century ago and there is little chance that the issue will be raised again, public school forces demand that, at the least, nonpublic schools not be aided and abetted, that the economic penalty be kept so high that not many parents will be able or willing to pay it.

What has proven an insuperable obstacle to direct subvention is the fact that 85 percent of nonpublic schools, enrolling nearly 90 percent of the students, are religiously identified or affiliated. The

Supreme Court declared in 1947 that the nonestablishment clause of the First Amendment to the Constitution forbids spending of public funds for purposes that would advance religion and that attendance at church-affiliated schools would be so regarded.[3] When several state legislatures nevertheless enacted programs providing funds for nonpublic schools, the courts held most of those laws to be unconstitutional.

Attention then shifted to indirect forms of aid, such as financial assistance to students, vouchers, or tax credits. Federal or state grants and loans to students were held constitutional in higher education, not in elementary and secondary schools. Tax credits for enrollment in nonpublic elementary schools were enacted by several states but held unconstitutional by the Supreme Court. Several plans were developed which would have the federal government—or state governments—give parents of school-age children vouchers, which they could at their discretion use in public or private schools to pay all or part of the tuition. This would make public schools more dependent on vouchers than on appropriations. A voucher plan could establish closer economic equality between public and nonpublic schools, thus making the decision on whether to enroll in one or the other independent of, or at least less dependent on, financial factors. The choice of school would then be governed mainly or exclusively by parental preference for the standards, curriculum, or methods of the particular school, not its cost. Another plan would provide vouchers only for children in nonpublic schools, leaving the support of public schools unchanged.

Voucher plans have gained broader support but have so far not been able to gain acceptance by any state legislature nor been seriously considered by Congress. Moreover, a Supreme Court which declared tax credits to be unconstitutional is unlikely to view vouchers in a more favorable light. Vouchers would result in direct governmental payments, federal or state, to a school—whereas tax credits would mean only a reduction of the tax liability of individuals and not involve the expenditure of tax-raised funds, or any contact between government and the school. This suggests that vouchers may have a lower chance of passing court scrutiny than tax credits. The constitutional questions involved have become highly complex and call for close analysis. Were it not for the constitutional problem, tax credits would have been established years ago. As it is, constitutionality is the crucial consideration on which the future of tax credits depends.

## ARE EDUCATIONAL TAX CREDITS UNCONSTITUTIONAL?

In nearly fifty cases over the past three decades, the Supreme Court has been trying to interpret and apply the opening clause of the First Amendment. Most of the decisions were adopted with the narrowest of margins, and some of the decisions of the Court's majority were accompanied by up to four dissents in addition to one or several separate opinions. This enormous effort at interpretation by shifting majorities leaves some of the basic issues as complex, as unresolved, and as controversial as ever. This is why conflicts continue while state legislatures and the Congress search for solutions to urgent problems, which, it is hoped, can pass the Court's scrutiny.

### The Confusion of Major Court Cases

The governing constitutional clause is, in the words of Senator Daniel Moynihan, a leader in the fight for tax credits, "simplicity itself": "Congress shall make no law respecting an establishment of religion, or prohibiting the free exercise thereof."[4] At the time this was written, its meaning appeared clear beyond a doubt. Most of the states, while they were still British colonies, had established churches, as had virtually all European countries. Most of the churches established by the thirteen colonies were Anglican, Dutch-Reformed, or Congregational. The state's representatives, in drafting and approving the Bill of Rights, wanted to foreclose any possibility that the Congress might at some time want to establish a church of its own. Hence the nonestablishment clause, which caused little trouble for more than a century and a half.

In 1947, in *Everson* v. *Board of Education*, the Court, with a majority of five to four (which then became the rule more than an exception in this type of case), declared:

The "establishment of religion" clause of the First Amendment means at least this: Neither a state nor the federal government can set up a church.

> Neither can pass laws which aid one religion, aid all religions, or prefer one religion over another. . . . No tax in any amount, large or small, can be levied to support any religious activities or institutions, whatever they may be called, or whatever form they may adopt to teach or practice religion. . . .[5]

That the proceeds of taxes should not be used to "teach or practice religion" expressed then, as it does now, the belief in separation of church and state of an overwhelming majority of the American people. Did the decision forbid all types of action that might benefit religious denominations? In the *Everson* case the Court approved the expenditure of tax-raised funds to pay for the transportation of children to parochial schools on the theory that the outlay "was for a public purpose." The operation of church-affiliated elementary and secondary schools serves the public purpose of providing the education which nearly all state constitutions require children to receive, commonly between ages six and sixteen or eighteen. That those schools also teach religion does not mean that all or a majority of their activities serve to "practice religion." Most of their curriculum focuses on instructing children in the same basic skills and knowledge which public schools teach their students. The primary purposes of the school to which most of its own and the teachers' and students' time are devoted and to which most of the expenditures are allocated are secular.

It cannot be denied that the operation of denominational schools helps to advance religion and that it is so intended by their sponsors. That does not seem to run counter to the concept of the Court which in *Everson* authorized paying for the cost of transporting children to parochial schools. Speaking through Justice William O. Douglas, the Court stated in *Zorach* v. *Clauson*: "we are a religious people whose institutions presuppose a Supreme Being. . . . When the state encourages religious instruction . . . it follows the best of our traditions. For it then respects the religious nature of our people and accommodates the public service to their spiritual needs. . . ."[6]

The Court subsequently approved a few other incidental benefits for children attending church-connected schools but otherwise voided all state statutes which would have allocated sums for the general purposes of such schools. Legislative attempts in Pennsylvania and Rhode Island to earmark state funds for the secular activities of benefited schools were given short shrift by the Supreme Court in *Lemon* v. *Kurtzman* and *Earley* v. *DiCenso*. It declared the parochial school system to be "an integral part of the religious mission of the Catholic Church." [7]

The Court established a three-part requirement for the allocation of governmental funds. They must have (1) a secular purpose, (2) a primary effect other than the advancement of religion, and (3) no tendency to entangle the state excessively in church affairs. It can hardly be denied that church-affiliated elementary and secondary schools serve a secular purpose by providing a general education for millions of children. To avoid assisting a primary effect of advancing religion, the state would have to ban the schools' use of state funds for religious purposes; that is exactly what Pennsylvania and Rhode Island did. But to enforce this, the Court declared, would "require continuing state surveillance to ensure that the statutory restrictions are obeyed. . . . Historically, governmental control and surveillance measures tend to follow cash grant programs, and here the government's post-audit power to inspect financial records of church-related schools creates an intimate and continuing relationship between church and state." [8] The Court was, in effect, telling the states: if you appropriate unrestricted funds to church-affiliated schools, you are helping to advance religion, which is impermissible under the Constitution. If you restrict the funds to secular purposes, then you cause an excessive church-state entanglement, which also is unconstitutional. You might as well quit trying to give money to denominational schools because you can't win. We'll stop you coming or going. It's a case of heads I win, tails you lose.

But some states did not give up on trying to help nonpublic schools. If state funds could not be allocated to church-affiliated schools directly, the goal of aiding them could be approached indirectly through tax abatements. One year prior to *Lemon* v. *Kurtzman* the Supreme Court approved—more precisely reaffirmed—the tax exemption of churches. Speaking through Chief Justice Warren Burger, the Court ruled in *Walz* v. *Tax Commission*, with Justice Douglas a lonely dissenter:

> The legislative purpose of tax exemptions is not aimed at establishing, sponsoring, or supporting religion, and New York's legislation simply spares the exercise of religion from the burden of property taxation imposed on private profit institutions.
>
> The tax exemption creates only a minimal and remote involvement between church and state, far less than taxation of churches would entail, and it re-

stricts the fiscal relationship between them, thus tending to complement and reinforce the desired separation insulating each from the other.[9]

In *Walz* the Court traced the nonestablishment clause to the fact that at the time of the adoption of the First Amendment there existed an established church in England and in the colonies and that in other countries "establishment meant sponsorship by the sovereign." Trying to explain the zigzagging in its interpretation of the nonestablishment clause, the Court said:

> The considerable internal inconsistency in the opinions of the Court derives from what, in retrospect, may have been too sweeping utterances on aspects of these clauses that seemed clear in relation to the particular cases but have limited meaning as general principles. . . .
>
> The general principle deducible from the First Amendment and all that has been said by the Court is this: that we will not tolerate either governmentally established religion or governmental interference with religion. Short of those expressly proscribed governmental acts there is room for play in the joints productive of a benevolent neutrality which will permit religious exercise to exist without sponsorship and without interference.
>
> Each value judgment under the Religion Clauses must therefore turn on whether particular acts in question are intended to establish or interfere with religious beliefs and practices or have the effect of doing so. . . .
>
> The grant of a tax exemption is not sponsorship since the government does not transfer part of its revenue to churches but simply abstains from demanding that the church support the state.[10]

That seemed, at the time, to answer negatively the question of whether tax exemptions for religious purposes violate the nonestablishment clause of the First Amendment. The fact that churches undoubtedly and primarily "advance religion" and do not serve a primary secular purpose does not make tax concessions to them unconstitutional. The Court called church–state involvement resulting from tax abatement minimal and remote.

The door to aiding church-affiliated schools through tax abatement appeared to be wide open—until the Court three years later slammed it shut in *Committee for Public Education v. Niquist.* The case arose from a 1972 New York state law which authorized three programs intended to aid nonpublic school education. Two of the programs involved direct money payments, the third tax relief for parents with children in nonpublic schools. A three-judge federal court voided the first two programs and upheld the third. But the Supreme Court in a six-to-three decision, speaking through Justice

Lewis F. Powell, declared: "The system of providing income tax benefits to parents of children attending New York's nonpublic schools . . . is not sufficiently restricted to assure that it will not have the impermissible effect of advancing the sectarian activities of religious schools." To disabuse state authorities of the idea that they could correct the fault by inserting requisite restrictions, the Court warned them that such action "carries grave potential for entanglement in the broader sense of continuing and expanding political strife over aid to religion." If nonpublic school aid did not founder on the rocks of Scylla (aid to religion), it would surely be sunk when it hit Charybdis (church–state entanglement). In *Niquist*, the court de facto accepted Justice Douglas's dictum—in his *Walz* dissent—that "a tax exemption is a subsidy." It stated that "in practical terms there would be little difference. . . . The only difference is that one parent receives an actual cash payment while the other is allowed to reduce by an arbitrary amount the sum he would otherwise be obliged to pay over to the state."[11]

The thesis that there is virtually no difference between tax abatement and cash payments parallels action by Congress in the 1974 Budget Reform Act which provides that the annual budget list the revenue effects of selected tax exclusions, exemptions, deductions, credits, etc., under the heading "Tax Expenditures." If partial or total relief from taxation is legally equivalent to the spending of tax-raised funds, no tax concession can be allowed which is not clearly restricted to secular purposes and could be used to advance religion.

How then can churches—and schools sponsored by them—be exempted from paying property taxes and other taxes which everyone else must pay? How can contributions to churches and church-affiliated schools be allowed as deductions for income tax purposes? In *Walz* the Court in unequivocal terms upheld the tax exemption of churches. It never adjudicated the deductibility of charitable contributions to churches[12] because that deduction has never been questioned ever since its adoption in 1917. In *Niquist* the Court indicated in an oblique way that its negative decision on tax abatement for parents of children in religious schools should not be interpreted as questioning the constitutional status of tax deductions for charitable (religious) purposes ("We do not have before us and do not decide, whether that form of tax benefit is constitutionally acceptable.")[13] The Court left the implication, though it did not say so explicitly, that such deductions are constitutional.

Can anybody argue that tax exemptions and donations to churches and to schools affiliated with them do not advance religion but that tuition payments to those same schools do? Is there any special quality to money paid for tuitions that makes it different—and more apt to promote religion—than money paid in the form of a donation? What makes the latter constitutional and the former unconstitutional? Why did the Court in *Walz* with near-unanimity approve church tax exemptions and in *Niquist* take pains to dispel any doubt that decision could have raised about tax deductibility of contributions to religious institutions?

### The Politics of Court Decisions

It has been said that the Court—or at least, some of its members—sometimes holds a wet finger in the wind before proclaiming the latest version of Ultimate Wisdom. The Court knew that a decision declaring the tax exemption of churches or the tax deductibility of contributions to them unconstitutional would generate a national uproar, which, in short order, would sweep away that decision. To overrule such a verdict would not, as did *Dred Scott*, require a civil war; it would be done expeditiously by constitutional amendment. Such an outcome was, of course, the last thing the Court's majority wanted. To void the tax benefits under review in *Niquist*, while upholding church tax exemptions and tax deductibility of donations to them, it resorted to a twisted logic and contorted phrasing which the judges dissenting from the decision acidly criticized as running contrary to settled doctrine and to the words and spirit of a long list of Court decisions.[14]

The utter confusion created by *Niquist* was highlighted in *Wolman* v. *Walter* when seven of the nine justices disagreed with parts of the decision and agreed with other parts of it. It resembled a judicial lottery more than a judgment by the highest court in the land. Justice Powell remarked in his part-dissent: "Our decisions in this troubling area draw lines that often must seem arbitrary."[15] To others they appear worse than arbitrary: illogical, inconsistent, making a mockery of "equal justice under the law."

The above-mentioned case of *Wolman* v. *Walter* offers an illustration. A three-judge federal court upheld an Ohio law authorizing the purchase of secular textbooks, instructional materials, and auxiliary equipment (called "book substitutes" in the statute) for loans to students of nonpublic (including sectarian) schools. It was the judgment of the Supreme Court that loans of textbooks are constitutional but that loans of other instructional materials violate the Constitution.

The Supreme Court reaffirmed *Niquist* in *Byrne v. Public Funds*.[16] When New Jersey imposed a state income tax in 1976, it allowed parents of children in an elementary-secondary school "not deriving its primary support from public moneys" a one-thousand-dollar deduction for tax purposes. That, the Court ruled, was not neutral because parents of children in public school were given no such deduction. An appeals court judge, in a concurring opinion—bowing to *Niquist*—remarked:

> I have great difficulty, however, in understanding why the exclusion here is more of an aid to religion than a direct contribution to a church, synagogue, temple or mosque which is deductible under the Internal Revenue Code. . . . The state's financial burden is lessened whenever parents send their child to a nonpublic school. There is, therefore, more justification for permitting the school tax deduction than the charitable deduction, at least from the standpoint of advancing governmental interest.[17]

It is significant that neither *Niquist* nor *Byrne* voided a tax benefit for paying tuition to a sectarian school. The New York and New Jersey statutes had granted a deduction for *enrollment* at a nonpublic school, not for *paying tuition* to it. Deductibility of tuition has yet to be resolved and may be decided when an act of Congress allowing a deduction or credit for tuition payments reaches the Supreme Court. In his dissent with the Court's decision in *Meek v. Pittinger*, which paralleled *Niquist*, Chief Justice Burger wrote:

> One can only hope that, at some future data, the Court will come to a more enlightened and tolerant view of the First Amendment's guarantee of free exercise of religion, thus eliminating the denial of equal protection to children in church-sponsored schools, and take a more realistic view that carefully limited aid to children is not a step toward establishing a state religion.[18]
> . . .

Why did the Court deny the tax benefits which the New York and New Jersey laws intended to confer while upholding similar, far broader tax abatements aiding religious institutions? Deductibility of church contributions and the tax exemption of churches affect a majority of American taxpayers whereas tuitions at nonpublic schools are of major and direct concern only to a minority. Some minorities seem to fare better at the hands of the Supreme Court than others. The *Niquist* decision referred to the "narrowness of the benefited class." The meaning of the term "narrowness" may be clarified by comparing the role of governmental aid at the elementary-secondary level with conditions in higher education.

## A Constitutional Difference Between Higher Education and the Lower Schools?

Several large programs of grants and loans to students have long been in operation at public as well as at church-connected colleges and universities, but not at the precollege level. In *Tilton* v. *Richardson*, the Supreme Court upheld the constitutionality of construction grants to church-affiliated institutions.[19] But in *Niquist* it voided grants for the maintenance and repair of dilapidated buildings of parochial elementary and secondary schools. The Senate six times passed tax credit bills for tuitions paid to institutions of higher learning but balked at bestowing similar benefits for attendance at the subcollegiate level. We may wonder what the constitutional difference is between elementary-secondary education and higher education in a country whose Constitution does not even mention the word "education."

In *Lemon* v. *Kurtzman* the Court referred to "the impressionable age of the pupils" which makes parochial schools "a powerful vehicle for transmitting the Catholic faith to the next generation." No evidence was presented that impressionability disappears or sharply diminishes at eighteen and that reaching that magic age arms students with nonimpressionability. But the cited remark brings another consideration to the foreground. A majority of the religiously identified colleges are affiliated with Protestant denominations; well over two-thirds of the denominational lower schools are connected with the Catholic church. Because this is a delicate subject, judicial references to the fact that most of the benefits in the lower schools would redound to Catholics have generally been couched in careful phraseology. But they state a known and undeniable fact. That, of course, is not to say that anti-Catholic sentiment is the major motivating factor of opposition to educational tax credits. Most opponents are acting from a concern that any encouragement or type of aid to nonpublic schools would harm the public schools in whose advancement they have a strong ideological interest and/or material stake. Expansion of nonpublic schools—as a result of governmental aid—could not only diminish public enrollment but undermine the dominant position and importance of the public school system in American education.

We then must conclude that some of the opposition to tax credits is directed less against the growth of nonpublic schools generally as against Catholic schools or, more precisely, against aiding the Catholic church. It was no coincidence that when a tuition tax credit bill was pending in the Ninety-Fifth Congress, the two leaders in the Senate debate on an amendment to exclude elementary and secondary schools represented Bible Belt constituencies. Nor was it an accident that in the critical roll call on August 15, 1978, virtually all senators from that region—with but few exceptions such as the senators from Louisiana which has a large Catholic population—voted to allow tax credits only in higher education. House votes showed a similar picture.[20]

In summary then, there appear to be three possible interpretations of the nonestablishment clause.

(1) If any type of government action, whether in the form of direct payments or through tax abatement, has the effect of advancing religion, then it will be held impermissible. This means that tax exemption of churches and tax deductibility of church contributions are unconstitutional.

(2) If direct payments for purposes which advance religion are violative of the First Amendment but tax relief which may have a similar effect is constitutional, educational tax credits may be in the same category as charitable deductions and church tax exemptions and are constitutionally safe.

And (3) a literal interpretation of the First Amendment would rule out the *establishment* of a church under governmental auspices but would allow the spending of tax-raised funds as well as the granting of tax benefits, under whatever safeguards appear needed. Prospects for such a liberalization appear poor. The second interpretation probably best carries out a national consensus of friendly neutrality toward religion. It was well expressed by the Supreme Court's 1952 dictum: "When the state encourages religious instruction . . . it follows the best of our traditions."[21]

## ARE EDUCATIONAL TAX CREDITS GOOD PUBLIC POLICY?

Authorization of educational tax credits is, in the opinion of its protagonists, the most promising method to widen the diversity of school offerings and to improve the quality of American education. It could bring freedom of choice among several types of schools and programs to within the economic reach of millions of parents, would permit them to select from a range of curricula and standards those best suited to their children's individual capacities and aspirations, and would motivate schools, public and private, to compete with each other for the reputation of giving their students the best education they can absorb.

In the opinion of opponents, however, tax credits would lead to a mass exodus from the public schools and thereby lead to the destruction of the system which over the past two centuries has lifted American education to excellence and has been a key factor in the rise of the United States to leadership in the free world. Many regard common schools with at least near-universal attendance an essential element in preparing children for life in a democratic society, which is composed of many people who are diverse in ethnic background, culture, tradition, social class, religion, capacity, interest, and other characteristics, who must learn early in life how to live and work together. They believe that a splintering of the educational process keeps a distance between groups and tends to aggravate tensions and conflicts between them, that they will not get to know and like each other, that they will not adjust to each other because they were not given an opportunity to mix.

Let us look more closely at some of those claims and counterclaims. Both sides agree that a major consequence of tax credits would be a sizable shift from public to nonpublic schools. In the words of one of the leaders of the opposition: "[Tax credits] would lead to the destruction of public education by giving parents a financial incentive to remove their children from public schools and place them in private and parochial schools."[22] Yet we may wonder how tax credits could conceivably offer a financial incentive for shifting to a nonpublic school as long as parents would be reimbursed for only part of their additional expenses. Tax credits could, at best, *lower* the penalty for attending a nonpublic school, but they could never offer a financial advantage over enrollment at a public school.

For sending children to a nonpublic school costs parents money, whether or not there are tax credits, and they will send them only if they prefer significant features of an available nonpublic school over those of their public schools and if the differential cost can be fitted within their budget.

Discipline ranks tops among the features close to parents' hearts. Albert Shanker, head of the American Federation of Teachers, AFL/CIO, wrote: "Parochial schools are able successfully to have larger classes because of a tight discipline system. I doubt that many Catholic schools will indefinitely retain a student with chronic discipline problems, one who repeatedly disrupts the class or commits more serious infractions."[23] That may well be true. In fact, it may be a major reason why the income and the outcome of public school education have been moving in opposite directions: while funds and expenditures of public schools multiplied—on a per pupil *constant* dollar basis—the measurable results in terms of the pupils' skills and knowledge have been going down. Lack of discipline is responsible, to a good part, for dissatisfaction with the public schools and their results.

But public schools will not get tough by insisting on proper behavior or by upholding curricular standards as long as they enjoy a de facto monopoly in education. Their administrators know that most parents have no recourse and no alternative. If parents had a choice, public schools might start having second thoughts about permitting their institutions to be turned into blackboard jungles.

Is it proper for government to force parents to send their children to a school which they would not choose if they had an option? Why should an option be available only to affluent parents? Is it good public policy and is it educationally productive to make alternative schools—whose spirit is more conducive to learning—inaccessible to most children? If millions of parents prefer the discipline enforced in nonpublic schools, why should they not have an opportunity to send their children there even if their economic circumstances do not allow them to pay high tuition charges?

### The Effect on Public Schools

The United States Treasury on January 19, 1978 presented testimony to the Senate Finance Committee in opposition to tax credits and asserted that they would place further strains on the public school systems. When enrollment was rising rapidly in the 1950s and 1960s, we were told that the extraordinary influx was straining school resources. When over the past fifteen years over two million students shifted from nonpublic to public schools, this also put a burden on the latter. If that shift were to be reversed with enrollment in public schools declining by two million, would not that be a relief to their finances to the extent of at least $5 billion a year rather than a strain? Would cutting their payrolls by over one hundred thousand teachers really be a strain on the public schools? It could be a strain on those teachers who might have to seek jobs in nonpublic schools which typically pay lower salaries but demand more work.

It seems then that a shift to nonpublic schools would be a relief to the taxpayers who support the public schools. Taxpayers are now saving about $11 billion a year because five million children are attending school at their parents' expense without cost to the taxpayers. It would be an equally good investment to devote a fraction of the per pupil cost in public schools, now estimated in excess of $2,200 per year, to tax credits. That would encourage a shift from public to private schools. If nonpublic systems must continue to close schools because of the increasing financial pressure, the added costs will be placed on taxpayers. A closing of all nonpublic schools would boost state and local tax bills by at least $11 billion a year. But if, say, one-fourth of the per pupil cost was applied to a tax credit, the taxpayers would save three-fourths of the cost they now bear. That would seem a rather lucrative proposition for the taxpayer. In plain words, educational tax credits are not a cost, they are a productive investment. Budgetary arguments against tax credits— that they would cause heavy government revenue losses—are misleading. Tax credits would cause public expenditures to drop several times as much as revenues. Tax credits come at a profit to public treasuries not at a loss.

Demand for tax credits has been called "a church raid on the treasury," and some have asked: "Must the taxpayer contribute to the support of a religious institution, the doctrines of which he cannot accept?"[24] The question can be answered very simply: taxpayers are not forced to pay for a child's education at a denominational school or would be so forced by tax credits. They get a *net reduction* in their aggregate tax liability from a child's nonattendance at a public school. Their tax reduction would be even greater if tax credits enabled more parents to shift their offspring to a nonpublic school.

Similar opposition to tax credits is directed at more than merely preventing aid to nonpublic schools. Opponents resent the very existence of those schools as an infringement of the monopoly which the common schools ought to be granted as the only proper institution to educate children in a democratic—and egalitarian—society. They aim to eliminate nonpublic schools, if possible. Yet this monopoly is not recognized by the courts. For example, a massive drive to make enrollment at public schools compulsory for all children succeeded in Oregon in 1922. But the Supreme Court, in the landmark case of *Pierce* v. *Society of Sisters*, declared that attempt to establish a legal monopoly for the public schools and to eliminate nonpublic schools from the general education process to be unconstitutional: "The child is not the mere creature of the state; those who nurture him and direct his destiny have the right, coupled with the high duty, to recognize and prepare him for additional obligations."[25] The *Pierce* doctrine has since been cited in numerous relevant court decisions, including some of recent date, and is now beyond controversy. Forces opposed to nonpublic schools no longer hope to obtain a legal monopoly in education. But they aim to maintain and strengthen the de facto monopoly which the public schools enjoy by keeping the economic penalty of exercising the *Pierce* option as heavy as possible—beyond the financial reach of all but a small fraction of American parents.

Some hold that the existence of nonpublic schools impairs and threatens the educational mission of the common schools: to process all, or at least almost all, children through the same educational machine in order to produce a uniform, "one best" product. That, of course, could not be accomplished as long as local communities were able to control their public schools. But local school control has become but a fond memory as a nationally organized bureaucracy, federal, state, and local, gradually has taken command and has been increasingly tightening its grip. Nonpublic schools are the only means by which diversity can be offered to those dissatisfied with what is happening in and to the public schools.

The aim of the common schools is egalitarian. That, to many, is its virtue. It also is its downfall in terms of educational quality. The exodus from the public schools, which their supporters fear would result from the granting of tax credits, would be powered mostly by the burning desire of many parents to get for their children a better education than they can get at most public schools.[26]

How could the public schools be motivated to move from focusing on the lowest common denominator as their primary goal to the pursuit of excellence? By the necessity of competing with other schools for students. They do not now have to compete because most parents have no access to an alternative. Tax credits might succeed in forcing public school systems to strive for the high standards they could boast of a long time ago. In an editorial in August 1978, the *Washington Post* called the pending tax credit bill "a fundamental assault on the public schools. Any vote for it in the Senate is a threat to the public school system."[27] Why would tax credits be a threat to the public schools? Because without the crutches of a de facto monopoly, the public schools might have to change from their fixation on the lowest common denominator to a pursuit of educational standards—or lose many of their students. The necessity to compete on less unequal terms with nonpublic schools, to have to play with a deck that is less heavily stacked, could do wonders for the quality of education in many public school systems. We need a diversity of schools because we have a diversity of people whose abilities and proclivities range from one end of the scale to the other. To try to force them all into an educational Procrustean bed is self-defeating and cannot but produce calamitous consequences.

### The Tax Issue

Some oppose educational tax credits because the federal income tax is already riddled with too many loopholes. Such "backdoor spending" hides true costs from the public and exempts "tax expenditures" from the annual appropriations scrutiny by Congress. Why open another loophole? Let us view this matter in its proper perspective. Personal income in 1977 amounted to $1,532 billion, of which $731 billion appeared as taxable income on federal income tax returns—after exemptions, exclusions, deductions, credits, etc. This suggests that 52 percent of personal income was not taxable. Counting items which are not included in personal income (as defined in the national income accounts) but are taxed under the Internal Revenue Code, we may estimate that at least 55 percent of all personal income, equal to $850 billion in 1977, was not taxed. Itemized deductions accounted for $138 billion. Deductions for charitable contributions amounted to $17 billion, a fraction of which was accounted for by donations to religious institutions. A tuition tax credit averaging $500 for each pupil in a nonpublic school—assuming that 80 percent of the current five million students pay regular tuitions—would total $2 billion, which equals less than one-fourth of 1 percent of all nontaxable income, surely a tiny speck in the overall picture.

Congress prefers to accomplish certain objectives through tax concessions rather than expenditures for a variety of reasons. The most important among them is that direct appropriations, as a rule, mean stricter and more detailed governmental control through an expanded bureaucracy whereas tax credits or deductions usually grant greater discretion and freedom of choice to individuals, providing incentives for private initiative to act rather than for government to take over. On the other hand, appropriations often achieve the desired purposes more directly, more precisely, and possibly more quickly.

Many or most of the deductions for educational, scientific, and charitable purposes could be replaced by appropriations for the benefited institutions, and this could greatly strengthen governmental influence on their policies. But this could not be done in the case of religious institutions. Congress could not make appropriations to churches instead of letting individuals deduct their donations from adjusted gross income. This is equally true for church-affiliated schools. Donations to them are tax deductible. Tuitions could also be made deductible (or allowed as credits). But direct appropriations could not be substituted for the tax benefits. Therefore, if diversity is to be maintained or widened and if nonpublic schools are to be prevented from further diminishing and gradually fading from the scene, aid must be provided in indirect form by tax benefits—deductions or credits.

Still others have asserted that it would be unfair to grant tax credits for tuitions paid to a school because large numbers of people have no income tax liability and thus would derive no benefits. If this line of reasoning were correct, all deductions, exemptions, credits, etc., would have to be called discriminatory. If, for example, a person's income consists only of excludable items such as social security, veterans' pensions, or fellowships, he or she derives no benefit from personal exemptions or deductions. If a person's exemptions and deductions exceed his adjusted gross income, he gets no benefit from the excess. He gets no benefit from a casualty loss if he has no tax liability. Twenty-two million *non*taxable income tax returns were filed for 1977. Their exemptions, deductions, and proportionate amounts for credits exceeded their income. Many of them derived only partial benefits from exemptions or deductions. Does this mean that deductions and exemptions as such are unfair or discriminatory?

It has been proposed that if a tax credit for tuitions were to be enacted, taxpayers who have not enough tax liability to make full use of the credit should be paid their credit claims by the Internal Revenue Service. Otherwise, it is held, tax credits for tuitions will benefit only persons in the middle- and high-income brackets but penalize those with a low income. The authorization of tuition tax credits would lead to higher tuitions, which poor families would have to pay without a possibility of an offsetting benefit.

This problem seems unreal and contrived. It has always been the practice in schools to reduce or waive tuition for some students who are otherwise qualified and meritorious but cannot afford to pay the full or even partial tuition. Especially in parochial schools, tuitions are reduced or waived for students from low-income families with many children. If after the authorization of a tuition tax credit, tuitions are generally raised and the schools' income substantially increases, those schools will be more able to forego tuitions, wholly or partially, from students whose families lack sufficient tax liability to take full advantage of the tax credit.

To authorize payment by the Internal Revenue Service of tuition tax credits which exceed an individual's tax liability, or to persons with no tax liability, could jeopardize a system of tax credits for tuitions to nonpublic schools. It would involve payment of tax-raised funds to parents, which under Supreme Court decisions would be unconstitutional because it could be used to advance religion.

Opponents charge that while tax credits are being demanded as tax relief for parents, the funds would actually be passed on to schools through higher tuitions. They would thus aid nonpublic schools, not parents. That is mere semantic obfuscation. Tax credits would help parents send their children to nonpublic schools. It makes really little difference at which point in the pipeline the funds are added which are needed (1) to enable schools to finance their operation or (2) to enable parents to pay the required fees. Tax credits are a technique by which we can avoid contact between the school and the government which could raise the specter of church-state entanglement and lead to possible control of the school.

## Class and Racial Issues

Some assert that tax credits would benefit mostly the rich. While high-income families can easily be excluded from eligibility by inserting upper-income limitations in the program, as some proposed bills do, I do not believe this to be necessary or advisable. A few hundred dollars are not a critical element in rich families' decisions about their children's school attendance. By far, the overwhelming majority of families with children in nonpublic schools belong to the middle class—and will so continue if tax credits are authorized. Tax credits would lower the income level at which many parents might find it possible to afford doing what they have wanted to do—send their children to a school of their choice, a school that is more consonant with their concepts of the type of education they want their offspring to receive.

It may well be that tax credits would provide relief not so much to parents with children in nonpublic schools as to all taxpayers. Nonpublic schools now account for about 10 percent of total school enrollment. Supposing tax credits helped to raise that to 20 percent. That would mean that savings to taxpayers on the cost of public schools would go up from the current 10 percent to a future 20 percent. In other words, taxes for school purposes—on property, income, sales—for all taxpayers could be reduced by 10 percent, minus the cost of the tax credit, which surely would be less. Estimating current per pupil cost in a public school at $2,200 a year and a tax credit of $500, the taxpayers' savings would amount to $1,700 for every pupil who transfers from a public to a nonpublic school. If recent trends are an indication, most of the increase would probably occur in secular schools.

Concern has been expressed that tax credits might help the "white flight" and thus increase segregation. The fact is that laws and rules forbidding racial discrimination apply to public and private institutions alike, in education as well as in business generally, with regard to employment, admissions, housing, etc. Tax-exempt schools under the Internal Revenue Code must obey the same rules as public schools.[28] Many parochial schools now have sizable numbers of black and Hispanic pupils; some black organizations, such as the Congress for Racial Equality, run their own schools and support tax credits.

Would funds for public schools diminish if tax credits were enacted? There is no reason to assume that one dollar less would be spent *per pupil*, though the total amount might decline if many children were transferred. But an exodus of any size could motivate public schools to tighten discipline, lift their sights with regard to educational standards, and generally adopt policies, programs, and features which currently make nonpublic schools attractive to many parents. As long as public schools on the average spend at least three times as much per pupil as do nonpublic schools, the former should be able to offer a program that compares favorably with those of nonpublic schools.

Some regard the granting of tax benefits to be equivalent to the spending of treasury funds. That may be true if we assume that the government has a prior claim, that it owns all income but magnanimously permits an earner to keep a fraction of it. This leads us to the question whether it is preferable that government expand its functions and obtain the necessary funds from heavier taxes or whether we would rather have government do less—in fields in which individuals can take care of themselves—provided the government leaves them enough of their earnings. The decision on educational tax credits thus is a good test of whether we prefer freedom or equality. We cannot have more of one without having less of the other.

Public schools are not an end in themselves. They are only a means to an end—to have the next generation properly educated. Can this best be accomplished by forcing students to mix or by enabling each individual to develop his capacity to the fullest and according to his own leanings and aspirations? Why should it not be left to parents to decide which schools they deem best suited to help their children advance? Why should the power of government be employed to force children to attend a common school system if their parents cannot afford to pay the whole cost of their education? Is mixing in the schools essential? Has it led to greater harmony, or has it fostered animosity, friction, and conflict, which is haunting the public schools and weakening, if not destroying their effectiveness?

The state must support education to assure that all children, regardless of their parents' economic status, have an opportunity to be educated. But that does not mean that the state has to provide that education in its own institutions unless it is its purpose to force uniformity on the students. Diversity is an essential element in giving the maximum opportunity to an enormously diverse student body. It could be brought within the reach of many by the authorization of tax credits.

## EDUCATIONAL TAX CREDITS – WHY AND HOW?

From its inception in 1913 the income tax law has permitted a number of deductions whose range has since been somewhat widened. The major deductible items are interest paid; state and local taxes; medical costs; contributions to certain nonprofit institutions such as religious, educational, and scientific organizations; and casualty losses. Standard deductions, to substitute for itemizing, were replaced in 1977 by zero bracket amounts.

Deductions (and exemptions) are subtracted from adjusted gross income to establish the taxable income, to which the rates of the tax scale are applied to compute tax liability. Tax credits are commonly granted as a percentage of a particular item of expenditure or income and may go up to 100 percent. They have come into wider use in recent decades and include credits for retirement income, productive investment, taxes paid to foreign governments, state inheritance taxes against federal estate taxation, state unemployment taxes against federal employment taxes, political contributions, child care expenses, earned income, energy conservation, hiring of workers through the Work Incentive Program, etc.

The basic difference between a deduction and a credit is this: if a taxpayer contributes $100 to a charitable purpose, he may be entitled to subtract $100 from his adjusted gross income – if the total of his itemized deductions exceeds a certain amount, depending on his status. That means that if he is in the lowest taxable bracket, he gets a *net* reduction of $14 on his tax liability. He must bear $86 of his gift. If a taxpayer in the top income bracket contributes $100, he reduces his tax liability to $70, and the net cost of the gift to him is only $30.

That, of course, is simply the result of our progressive rate scale, but it does not seem quite fair and has been called an upside-down subsidy. The main effect of this system, which has long been criticized, is a lopsided concentration of gift-giving in the top income brackets and heavy dependence of educational and other institutions on a small number of wealthy individuals and families.

Tax benefits now available to schools, public or private, consist of the exemption of their income and property from income and property taxes, exemption of certain transactions from sales or excise taxes in some jurisdictions, and the deductibility to donors of their contributions. Exemption from taxation of their own income and property is, of course, very helpful to the benefited schools. It reduces their expenses, but it does not help them increase their income, which is what they urgently need. This cannot be done from governmental sources directly. But government can provide incentives which could substantially boost the schools' revenues from their major private sources, gifts and tuitions. Deductibility of donations is of tremendous value and often essential to the schools' survival. But it is a far less effective stimulant than tax *credits* for donations would be.

A shift from deductions to credits would be of great help to taxpayers in the lower brackets. For example, a property tax payment of $1,000 costs a taxpayer in the lowest tax bracket $860, a taxpayer in the highest bracket only $300. A 50 percent tax credit would save a taxpayer $500, regardless of the bracket he is in. This explains why Congress has for some years often shaped new tax relief measures in the form of credits rather than as deductions. This is also why in the field of education emphasis has shifted from tax deductions to tax credits.

It has been asked why Congress permits so many deductions, exemptions, credits, etc., instead of taxing all personal income. But many question whether it would be fair to disregard the special burdens which many bear due to circumstances or by their own volition. The principal author of the Internal Revenue Code of 1954, under which we still operate, Dan Throop Smith, then deputy to the secretary of the treasury, declared in 1957: "Most, if not all, of the allowed deductions are intended to increase the fairness of the tax."[29] Subsequently, Smith wrote: "All of the deductions allowed in computing the taxable income of individuals are designed to give relief to the taxpayers benefiting from them and thereby make the law fairer."[30] C. Harry Kahn of Rutgers University, author of a standard work on tax deductions, defined two purposes: (1) to provide greater equity and (2) to promote desirable activities.[31]

Congress tried for many years to reduce deductions and close tax "loopholes." But whenever it attempted such tax reform, nontaxable income accounted for a larger percentage of total personal income afterwards than it had before. At the present time, at least 55 percent of personal income is beyond the reach of the federal income tax; most of the untaxed income is in the low- to low-middle-income brackets.

The law provides a financial incentive to engage in or expand activities which are regarded to be in the public interest. Some of them are of the type that would have to be undertaken and financed by government if they were not provided by voluntary action. Hospitals, schools, libraries, and museums are in that category. Congress may find that it is less costly to the taxpayers if government offers individuals or organizations an incentive to devote their own funds for such purposes than to have to underwrite the entire cost through taxes. More important, it may deem it preferable that certain activities be carried on under private auspices, partially or fully, and not be under direct governmental control or become a governmental monopoly. A greater diversity is often desirable so as to permit the widest range of individual freedom, consistent with the obligations and purposes of government.

Some deductions are allowed for activities which are regarded to be in the public interest but could not be carried on by government. This applies particularly to donations to churches and church-affiliated schools. Government cannot, under the Supreme Court's interpretation of the First Amendment, expend tax-collected funds for religious activities. To what an extent and in what form tax benefits may be made available to denominational schools is not entirely clear because of inconsistent Court decisions. In 1917 Congress first authorized tax deductions for contributions to religious and other charitable purposes up to 15 percent of an individual's income, subsequently raised the limit to 20 percent, then to 30 percent, and finally, in 1969, to 50 percent, where it now stands.

Efforts to make tuitions to educational institutions a tax-deductible item go back at least thirty years but were not successful. In the later 1950s the emphasis began to shift from deductions to credits as a more effective and fair method of accomplishing the same ends.

As it becomes increasingly clear that the courts would not permit direct grants to church-connected institutions, their supporters focused efforts increasingly on tax credits, especially in the field of higher education. The Senate passed tuition tax credit bills for colleges on six occasions between 1963 and 1978. None of those bills managed to get through the House because the powerful chairman of the Ways and Means Committee, Wilbur Mills of Arkansas, was strongly opposed to the idea of tax credits, as was, at least until some years later, his successor, Al Ullman of Oregon. Public school forces, led by the National Education Association and the American Federation of Teachers, strongly fought tax credits in higher education because they were afraid that their approval might set a precedent for the lower schools.

In the elementary-secondary field a drive was underway in the 1950s and 1960s for a major program of federal financial support of public schools. Catholic school forces were hoping to obtain tangible benefits in return for agreeing to far larger amounts going to public schools. The outcome of lengthy negotiations over nonpublic participation in programs of the Elementary and Secondary Education Act of 1965 made it clear to denominational schools that they could at best expect a few crumbs. Faced with a toughening attitude of the Supreme Court regarding public funds for nonpublic schools, they directed their efforts at tax benefits but were rebuffed in 1973 by the *Niquist* decision.

The leaders in the congressional drive for aid to nonpublic education—Daniel Moynihan of New York and Robert Packwood of Oregon in the Senate, Charles Vanik of Ohio and Bill Frenzel of Minnesota in the House—finally decided that their best strategy for overcoming arguments that their proposals were unconstitutional would be to take the bull by the horns—to bring an act of Congress, authorizing tuition tax credits, to the Supreme Court for a clearcut yes or no. They managed to get a bill on tuition tax credits at all levels of education through the House in June 1978 but ran into a stone wall in the Senate. Led by Ernest Hollings of South Carolina and Robert Hodges of Arkansas, the Senate eliminated participation by elementary-secondary schools in tuition tax credits while approving them for colleges.

Some members of Congress were influenced by President Carter's repeated threat that he would veto any tax credit bill that reached his desk. His heavy political commitment to the National Educational Association (Senator Moynihan called Mr. Carter a "wholly owned subsidiary of the N.E.A.")[32] made a compromise impossible.

Attempts at reconciliation through Senate-House conferences failed. The House would not accept a bill without the elementary-secondary schools, and the Senate would not accept it with them. The Senate rejected a proposed compromise, which would have included secondary schools but excluded elementary schools. The bills died with the Ninety-Fifth Congress.

## FUTURE PROSPECTS

Attempts are now under way to have tuition tax credits authorized by the Ninety-Seventh Congress. The Republican platform calls for them, and President Reagan has long been a strong supporter of educational tax credits and has stated on several occasions—before and after his election—that he would propose them to Congress. Congressional shifts in the November 1980 elections appear to give educational tax credits a far better chance than they ever had. The new chairmen of the congressional committees in whose jurisdictions such bills fall, the Senate Finance Committee and the House Ways and Means Committee, Senator Bob Dole of Kansas and Representative Dan Rostenkowski of Illinois, respectively, voted in favor of tuition tax credits at all levels of education in their respective houses in 1978.

The attitude of the Supreme Court remains a question. It never had the issue of tuition tax credits before it nor an act of Congress authorizing tax benefits for denominational schools. It has historically been reluctant to override action by a coequal branch of government without very compelling reasons. So there is a chance—but no better than that—that it may find a formula that permits it to uphold tuition tax credits without explicitly reversing some of its related earlier decisions. Moreover, changes in the Court's membership are likely to take place within the next two or three years which could lead to a shift in narrow majorities. But, of course, this is in the realm of speculation.

A strategy that might be worth considering would be to add tuitions to the currently allowable deductions instead of advancing tax credits at this time. The Internal Revenue Code's first item of charitable deductions is for contributions to churches. It might be difficult for the Court to declare that tax deductions for *tuitions* to denominational schools aid religion and are therefore unconstitutional but that deductions for *donations* to the same schools do not aid religion and are constitutional. Nor could the Court find that payments to church-sponsored schools aid religion but that payments to the churches they are affiliated with do not. There must be a limit some-where to the Court's ability and willingness to twist logic to suit the predilections of some of its learned members.

Tax deductions would not be a satisfactory means to accomplish the desired ends. But they could, within a reasonable time, be con-verted into credits. In the elementary-secondary school field, a 50 percent tax credit, with a maximum offset to tax liability of $500 — similar to the Moynihan/Packwood and Frenzel/Vanik bills in the Ninety-Fifth Congress—might be a good approach. In the higher education field a sliding percentage scale of credits—which I pro-posed to the Senate Finance and Welfare Committees in the early 1960s—might be preferable.

Related types of tax credits might be considered. If parents are to be helped in paying tuitions to nonpublic schools, there is no reason why others—friends, associations, employers, etc.—should not be equally encouraged to help. An effective way to stimulate charitable contributions and thereby motivate and expand voluntary action would be to permit a shift of donations from deductions to tax credits. That would, above all, reduce the concentration of donors in the high-income brackets and encourage large numbers of taxpayers in the lower and middle brackets to make donations to their favorite educational institutions. Those who feel that nongovernmental ini-tiative is generally preferable to government-direct operations might find that this would offer new prospects for wide-ranging shifts from the public to the private sphere.

## NOTES TO CHAPTER 13

1.  NOTE FOR ALL STATISTICS: All data not otherwise noted emanated from the National Center for Education Statistics, U.S. Department of Health, Education, and Welfare, and Department of Education (Washington, D.C.: U.S. Government Printing Office). The main sources were: *Digest of Education Statistics* (1979), *Projections of Education Statistics* (1976–78), *The Condition of Education* (1980), *Selected Public and Private Elementary and Secondary Education Statistics* (school years 1976 through 1978–79), *Bulletin NCES 80-B01* (October 1979), and from the U.S. Bureau of the Census: *Current Population Series P-20 #355* (August 1980).

2.  Dennis A. Williams, "The Bright Flight," *Newsweek*, April 20, 1981, p. 66.

3.  *Everson* v. *Board of Education*, 330 U.S. 1 (1947).

4. *U.S. Constitution*, First Amendment (1791).

5. *Everson* v. *Board of Education.*

6. *Zorach* v. *Clauson*, 343 U.S. 306 (1952).

7. *Lemon* v. *Kurtzman* and *Earley* v. *DiCenso*, 403 U.S. 602 (1971).

8. *Lemon* v. *Kurtzman.*

9. *Walz* v. *Tax Commission*, 397 U.S. 664 (1970).

10. Ibid.

11. *Committee for Public Education* v. *Niquist*, 413 U.S. 756 (1973).

12. *U.S. Code*, Title 26, par. 170 (b)(1)(A)(i).

13. *Committee for Public Education* v. *Niquist.*

14. Justice Douglas, when a freshman on the Court, was told by Chief Justice Charles Evans Hughes: "At the constitutional level at which we work, ninety percent of any decision is emotional. The rational part of us supplies the reasons for supporting our predilections" (William O. Douglas, *New York Times Magazine*, September 23, 1980, p. 39).

15. *Wolman* v. *Walter*, 443 U.S. 229 (1977).

16. *Byrne* v. *Public Funds*, 442 U.S. 907 (1979).

17. *Public Funds* v. *Byrne*, 590 F.2d 514, U.S. Court of Appeals, Third Circuit (1979).

18. *Meek* v. *Pittinger*, 421 U.S. 349 (1975).

19. *Tilton* v. *Richardson*, 403 U.S. 672 (1971).

20. It is impossible to close our eyes to the fact that the author of the *Niquist* decision comes from the Bible Belt—a judge who on other issues rather consistently has come down on the side of private initiative and in opposition to governmental action when proper alternatives were available. Anti-Catholic sentiment almost certainly is not the dominant factor in the opposition to educational tax credits for nonpublic schools. But it may at times be just strong enough to tip the scales on some crucial votes.

21. *Zorach* v. *Clauson.*

22. Albert Shanker, "Is the Opposition Anti-Catholic? A New Low in Debate Over Tax Credits," *New York Times*, January 18, 1981, p. E9.

23. Ibid.

24. D. L. Judd, *Saturday Review*, February 20, 1971.

25. *Pierce* v. *Society of Sisters*, 268 U.S. 510 (1925).

26. A self-appointed "semi-retired participant in the liberal consensus," Chester Finn, long-time education assistant to Senator Daniel Moynihan, recently made "preoccupation with questions of educational equity and equality and a pronounced lack of interest in the issues of quality" the subject of a brilliant article and incisive critique; Chester E. Finn, Jr., "The Future of Education's Liberal Consensus," *Change*, September 1980, p. 26.

27. "Tuition Tax Credits," *Washington Post*, August 7, 1978, p. A22.

28. Internal Revenue Code, sec. 501 (c)(3).

29. "General Policy Problems of Tax Differentials," in *Income Tax Differentials*, symposium by the Tax Institute of America (Princeton, N.J.: 1958), p. 6.
30. *Federal Tax Reform* (New York: McGraw-Hill, 1961). p. 90.
31. "Personal Deductions in the Income Tax," *Tax Revision Compendium*, U.S. House of Representatives, Committee on Ways and Means (Washington, D.C.: U.S. Government Printing Office, 1959), pp. 392ff.
32. Daniel P. Moynihan, *National Review*, February 6, 1981, p. 116.

# 14 EDUCATION AND CULTURAL REPRODUCTION
## A Critical Reassessment of Programs for Choice*

*Michael W. Apple*

## INTRODUCTION

The recent debate over what schools do has been quite intense. Sociologists, economists, and educators have begun to realize that the social role of the school is not at all simple, nor does the institution always act in a progressive way. Although our understanding of this complexity is not at all complete, most critical analysts of our educational institutions have focused on two basic areas of schooling. These have been labeled, respectively, the economic and cultural reproduction of class relations in our society.

This points, on the one hand, to the school's function as what has been called an ideological state apparatus,[1] one which produces agents (with the "appropriate" dispositions, values, and ideologies taught through a hidden curriculum) to roughly fill the needs of the social division of labor in society. On the other hand, it points to the place of our educational institutions in producing the particular knowledge and cultural forms "required" by an unequal society.[2]

*I wish to thank Geoff Whitty of King's College, University of London, for his help in shaping the arguments that appear in this chapter. An earlier version of the first part of this chapter appears in *Curriculum Inquiry* 10 (1980): 55–76. Additional research on this subject appears in Michael W. Apple, *Education and Power* (Boston: Routledge & Kegan Paul, 1982).

These two areas are interrelated, of course, but basically schools are seen to contribute in some very important ways to social reproduction. At the most basic level, schools are interpreted as reproductive agencies in that they help select and certify a workforce. But this is not all. They are sites for the production of cultural commodities (that is, technical/administrative knowledge) that are important to an economy.[3] And finally, they help maintain privilege in cultural ways by taking the form and content of the culture and knowledge of powerful groups and defining it as legitimate knowledge to be preserved and passed on. In this way, they act as agents of what Raymond Williams has called the "selective tradition."[4] Schools, hence, are also actors in the re-creation, and creation, of an effective dominant culture. They provide a site where important norms, values, dispositions, and culture are worked through and produced, a production that contributes to the ideological hegemony of dominant groups.

Notice that this listing of some of the major social functions of the school by necessity includes cultural as well as economic concerns. That is, we must talk about the control of *both* culture and economy if we are to understand what schools do. For we will miss a good deal about the institution and what it may accomplish if we only focus, as many people such as Samuel Bowles and Herbert Gintis have, on the political economy of the institution.[5] This has some significant implications for how we view schools and for thinking through some of the difficult issues surrounding the possibility of effective interventions to alter them.

In this essay, what I would like to do is provide some of the conceptual, methodological, and political tools for understanding the complex interrelationship that exists between schools and the cultural/economic dimensions of our society. This will entail, first, an overview of the basic conceptual framework needed to unpack the role of the school as a state apparatus in social reproduction. I shall point out the importance of examining both ideological as well as material determinations on institutions. Just as critically, I shall argue that social reproduction is by its very nature a contradictory process, not something that simply happens without a struggle.[6] After that, in the next major section, I shall then examine in some empirical detail the nature of the contradictions present both in the social order of the school and in the "needs" of the state. In so doing, I shall show how these very contradictions may end up supporting the institutions and ideologies that they seem to oppose. Finally, I shall analyze some of the major proposals that attempt to "de-determine," if you will, the determinants of schooling—proposals such as vouchers, tax credits, and the like. Here I shall assess the extent to which such proposals can serve the purposes intended or whether they too may ultimately serve dominant interests in the economy and the state rather than those disaffected groups for whom they are intended.

As we shall see, both aspects of Louis Althusser's phrase, "ideological state apparatuses"—ideology and the state—will be needed to unpack schooling and the current proposals being made to reform it. Not only political economy, but class, culture, ideology, and the state will be our guiding themes.

In my analysis of these themes, I shall adopt a neo-Marxist perspective. This implies that institutions are not seen as isolated but as fundamentally interconnected. These interconnections are organized in such a way as to generate structurally based inequalities in access to and control of economic and cultural goods and services. That is, they help some and hurt many others, and this differential helping and hurting is a constitutive part of the social polity.[7] In large part, it is "caused" or reinforced by the kind of economic order under which we live. Yet at the same time, this order is not only continually reproduced but is contested as well.

Finally, the perspective employed here reinstitutes class (and its accompanying conflict) as a fundamental dynamic to the issue of reproduction. Here "class" connotes not just "how much money you make" or "what kind of job you have"—the way most American social stratification researchers usually employ it—but one's relationship to the control and production of cultural and economic capital. It connotes a complex and creative cultural process as well, including language, style, intimate social relations, wishes, desires, and so on.[8] Class is something that is both a structural position (where you stand in the unequal processes of power, control, and reproduction) *and* something lived, not an abstract entity or set of determinations somewhere "out there" in an equally abstracted and totally separate economic sector of society.[9]

## UNDERSTANDING DETERMINATIONS

In order for us to proceed, the very question of how one construes the issue of determination, the basic concept behind the study of schooling and economic and cultural reproduction, needs further clarification. In this section, I shall limit myself to some rather general and relatively abstract points since the following portion of this chapter will provide concrete instances of the general arguments about the nature of determination I am making in these pages.

One of the most serious dilemmas in understanding the relationship between schooling and reproduction has been just this, the very concept of determination. Too many researchers have employed something of a base/superstructure model, where an economic base literally controls nearly every aspect of social and cultural life. A major danger here has been a marked tendency toward functionalism. That is, every important element of an ideology, a culture, the state, or of a social practice is thought of solely as a reflection or condition for the existence of a given mode of production or a set of social relationships. As Richard Johnson notes in his exceptional Marxist criticism of this approach, in these functionalist theories: "the whole sphere of the cultural/ideological . . . is subsumed within a single function, the reproduction of the conditions of capitalist production."[10] Nothing else of importance is going on. Struggle, disjunctions, and conflicts are suppressed in the analysis, and a model of one-dimensional control is substituted.[11]

In place of such a reflection theory and its variants, many investigators have constructed a number of considerably more sophisticated conceptual apparatuses to understand how cultural and economic forms interpenetrate one another. In their analyses, determinations can be thought of not only as functionally embodying a one-to-one correspondence between economy (understood broadly) and, say, culture and consciousness, where our social concepts and actions are totally prefigured or predicated upon a preexisting set of economic conditions that control cultural activity, including everything in schools. They can be thought of much more flexibly, as a complex nexus of relationships, which, in their final moments, may be economically rooted but which exert pressures and *set limits on* (rather than mechanistically determine) cultural practice.[12] The focus here, hence, is both on the kinds of limits set by social and material conditions and on the kinds of *partial* autonomy institutions and cultural processes might have within these limits.

There is yet another difficulty with the dominant models of determination we employ. Besides their functionalist orientation and their relatively less than flexible position, they also neglect an area of determination that cannot be ignored if we are more fully to understand the relationship between schooling and an unequal society, the area of ideology. For determinations are not simply social conditions external to a situation which "impose their will" or "force" people to become part of the reproduction of an unequal society. They are also complex sets of ideological practices and meanings which are internalized and which set limits back upon our actions and understandings. They are often constituted—that is, actively built—by our routine assemblage of needs, actions, and desires and by our individual wills as well.[13]

One of the most powerful ways of describing these "internal" needs and desires is that articulated by Antonio Gramsci. His most provocative insight into this problem can best be summarized by the concept of ideological hegemony. In essence, this is defined as "bourgeois domination of the thought, the common sense, the lifeways, the everyday assumptions" of large groups of people in a society. Thus, by making a distinction between coercion or the use of overt force or control (the strongest kind of determination) and hegemony, Gramsci called attention to the routine structures of everyday thought and action, routine structures that helped reproduce class domination and inequality.[14]

Thus, for Gramsci, an understanding of determination needs to include not just "external" social control, the structure of social rewards and economic determinants, and so on; it requires a concomitant analysis of the everyday routines and meanings themselves which provide the ideological support and justification for these external processes so that they seem natural.

A point of caution must be made here, one that will be of great importance to the next and more empirical section of this essay. Just as there is a danger in overusing economistic perspectives so that everything is reduced to its bald function of reproducing a given and static mode of production, so too do we need to be cautious of concepts such as ideological hegemony since they also can be employed in mechanistic and overly deterministic ways. For no assemblage of ideological practices and meanings and no set of social and institutional arrangements can be totally monolithic. As Gramsci was adamant in pointing out, there will be countervailing tendencies and oppositional practices going on as well. These tendencies and practices may not be as powerful as the ideological and material forces of determination which aim toward reproduction; they may in fact be inherently contradictory and relatively disorganized. But, they will exist. To ignore them is to ignore Johnson's points as well as Gramsci's, that in any real situation there will be elements of resistance, of struggle and contradiction, all of which will act against the abstract determination of the real life experiences of human actors.[15] Social and cultural life is simply too complex to be caught by totally deterministic models.

Notice the language I am using to talk about ideological hegemony. It implies that ideologies are not abstract ideas merely "held in the heads of people." As recent European social theorists remind us, ideologies are constituted by our whole array of commonsense practices and meanings that are lived out as we go about our daily lives. Furthermore, they may be internally inconsistent. These commonsense practices and meanings are often "deeply contradictory, shot through with [both] ideological elements [and] with elements of good sense."[16] Thus, side by side with beliefs and actions that maintain the dominance of powerful classes and groups, there will be elements of serious (though perhaps incomplete) understanding, elements that see the differential benefits and penetrate close to the core of an unequal reality.[17]

Now I realize that this brief discussion of the basic issues behind our understanding of how determinations impact on the school has been somewhat abstract. But we have a good deal to learn from the points raised by those who argue against mechanistic theories of economic and cultural reproduction. They suggest to us that a thorough analysis of the social and educational outcomes of the school and an understanding of how particular kinds of determinations bring them about necessitate an analysis of at least two kinds of determinations—"external" and "internal," material and ideological—that set limits on people's lives. It also involves a realization that there will be areas where such determinations at the level of real life are resisted or act in contradictory ways (for example, they both support and act against an unequal society at the very same time).

Therefore, a recognition of these points would lead us to interrogate complex social processes and institutions like the school and evaluate their efficacy in the following ways. What does our mode of production look like? What are its most significant characteristics? Which groups of people and classes benefit most and least from these characteristics? How do these *patterns* of class reproduction and differential benefit work themselves out in our day-to-day lives, for instance, in the actual curricular, pedagogical, and evaluative activity in which we participate and to which students respond in schools? If cultural and ideological forms are really dialectically related to material forces (they sometimes act back and mediate some determinations), how does this operate in these same schools? If determinations are at times contested, if reproduction is filled with conflict, what are the actual grounds of these struggles (for example, where are they found, what are they over, etc.)?

These are not easy matters to deal with, for the theory has to do two things. Not only does it need to be structural—that is, it must, at the level of theory, be general enough to provide fruitful explanations of how the social order is both organized and controlled so that the differential benefits are largely accounted for—but, at the same time, it should not be so general as to be unable to account for the everyday actions, struggles, and experiences of real actors in their day-to-day lives in and out of schools. It must account for where, how, and why people are caught, and where they may not be totally so. This requires a particularly sensitive perspective, a combination of what might be called a socioeconomic approach to catch the structural phenomena and what might be called a cultural program of analysis to catch the level of everydayness. Nothing less than this kind of dual program, one that looks for the series of connections and interpenetrations, not the one-way determination, of the economic and cultural "arenas" can overcome the previously noted problems of straightforward base/superstructure models. In essence, what is called for is a Marxist ethnography of life in and around our dominant institutions.

In the next part of my discussion, then, I want to provide an analysis of ways of integrating these elements together into a coherent approach that tries to go beyond theories of mechanistic determination. I shall draw upon a number of interesting studies, in particular Paul Willis's research reported in his volume *Learning to Labour* and Robert Everhart's analysis of an American junior high school in his *The In-Between Years.*[18] These investigations provide important first steps in building a conceptual approach for understanding what actually happens in schools and what the actual experiences of students are. And at the same time, they provide important correctives to the overly deterministic appraisals that some of us on the left have been too apt to embrace. In this way we can instantiate many of the arguments I made in this last section about the nature of understanding determinations.

## DETERMINATIONS AND CONTRADICTIONS

I stated at the very outset of this essay that there is no lack of evidence to support the claim that schools, at least in part, act as agents in the economic and cultural reproduction of an unequal society.[19] Nor is there any lack of evidence about the power of the hidden curriculum in schools in teaching norms and values to students that are related to working in this unequal society.[20] Yet my argument in the last section implies that one must contest a particular assumption—that of passivity—one which tends to overlook the fact that both students and workers are creatively acting in ways which often contradict these expected norms and dispositions which pervade the school and the workplace. In more analytic terms, the institutions of our society are characterized by *contradiction* as well as by simple reproduction.

As Stanley Aronowitz has shown, for instance, workers at all levels attempt to create informal conditions to gain some measure of control over their labor, to establish some serious sense of informal power over time, pacing, and the employment of their skills. Even on assembly lines, the archetypical example of the control of time and skill, many workers create their own unique culture, share jobs, work out ways to break the horrible monotony that confronts them, and establish alternative systems of informal control that counterbalance the formal system of authority on the factory floor.[21] At the same time that they are controlled, they also continuously attempt—often through cultural, not political ways—to articulate challenges to that control. These studies provide empirical support for the general theoretical position I argued for earlier, that economic form does not totally prefigure cultural form. The cultural sphere has some degree of relative autonomy. I shall have more to say about this below.

Similar things hold true for students, especially for some of those who are destined to become workers in these very same industries; and any evaluation of schooling must take this into account or risk failure. Students become quite adept at "working the system." Large numbers of them in inner-city and working class schools, to say nothing of other areas, creatively adapt their environments so that they can smoke, get out of class, inject humor into the routines, informally control the pacing of classroom life, and generally try to make it through the day. In these same schools, many students go even further. They simply reject the overt and hidden curricula of the school. The teacher who is teaching about mathematics, science, history, careers, etc., is ignored as much as possible. The covert teaching of punctuality, neatness, compliance, and other more economically rooted norms and values is simply dismissed as far as one can. The real task of the students is to last until the bell rings.[22]

Thus, any theory of the school's role in economic and cultural reproduction must account for the rejection of the norms which guide school life by many students. In fact, this very rejection of the hidden and overt curriculum gives us one of the major principles from which we can analyze the role of our educational institutions in helping to reproduce the social division of labor and inequality in corporate societies. For much of the way our schools function in roughly producing agents for a labor market is related not so much to a strong and unyielding correspondence between the characteristics companies think they want in their workers and what values schools teach, but, at least in certain segments of the working class, to a rejection of the messages of schooling and even our most creatively designed curricula by the students themselves. Analyses of this rejection can provide insights that can help us go a long way in seeing part of both the social function of and the values promoted by the school. Only with a more complete understanding of what schools actually do can we begin to grapple with the range of suggested reforms being proposed currently. But how are we to find this out? We must enter the school and see it first hand. We need to find out what meanings, norms, and values students, teachers, and others really act on in schools. Only then can we begin to see the layers of mediation that exist "between" the economic sector of a society and its other institutions. In essence, the school becomes a fundamental institution for seeing the dialectical relationships and tensions between what some Marxists have called (not unproblematically) infrastructure and superstructure.[23] And the school is the arena for working out these relationships and tensions that Willis, Everhart, and others have chosen to focus upon.

### Learning to Labour

Let us examine Paul Willis's provocative study first. His primary questions involve how major aspects of a working-class ideology are formed and how it is that hegemony is re-created. In short, he begins with an issue very much like that which concerns us here. How are values and interests made manifest in schools today? Whose values are they in the first place? Yet unlike a number of recent theorists of reproduction who argue that the ideological forms of capitalistic society are so powerful as to be total, Willis suggests something slightly more optimistic. He argues that even though the cultural and economic apparatus of an unequal society does have immense power to control the actions and consciousness of people, there are "deep disjunctions and disparate tensions within social and cultural reproduction." As he says: "Social agents are not passive bearers of ideology, but active appropriators who reproduce existing structures only through struggle, contestation and a partial penetration of these structures."[24]

*Learning to Labour* is an ethnographic account of a cohesive group of working-class boys in an all-male comprehensive secondary school in an industrial area of England. The "lads," as they are called, constitute a group of students who, like many of the students I mentioned earlier, spend a good deal of their time in school trying to maintain their collective identity and get through the day. They skillfully work the system to gain some measure of control over the way they spend their time in school, to have some free time and space, and to "have a laff." Most importantly, they reject a large portion of the intellectual and social messages of the school, even though the institution tries to be "progressive."

The lads are contrasted to another group of students—the "ear'-oles" (or earholes, so named because they seem to simply sit and listen). These are the students who have accepted the importance of compliance to educational authority, qualifications, and credentials. Nearly everything about the ear'oles provides a symbol to be rejected by the lads. The ear'oles' clothes, haircuts, conformity to both the values and curricula of the school, the teaching staff's more easy relationship with them, all of these are attributes of inclusion in a world the lads must reject. It is not real; it bears little resemblance to the familiar world of work, to making one's way economically in an industrial community, to the street. Instead, "the adult world, specifically the adult male working class world, is turned to as a source of material for resistance and exclusion."[25] For the lads, "real life" needs to be contrasted to the "oppressive adolescence" which is represented by the behavior of both the teachers and the ear'oles.[26] Whether it be the accepted social relations of the school, the formal teaching of what the school considers legitimate curricular knowledge, or the rules governing the physical facility of the school building itself, these are interpreted as both opportunities and challenges to increase one's personal mobility within the building, to meet each other, or basically to "have a laff."

But what about those aspects of the formal curriculum that attempt to be directly "relevant"? Even something like career education and associated curricula fare no better. In fact, such programs may even fare worse. Although the school curriculum attempts to portray jobs as offering opportunities for mobility, for personal gratification, for choice, the lads will have none of this. They have already experienced the world of work from their parents, their acquaintances, and in their own part-time jobs. This experience clearly contradicts the messages of the school, which are viewed cynically. Though only dimly conscious of it, the lads already "know" that they are being committed to a future of generalized labor. Thus, work is not something one really has a choice about (this is in essence a construct of middle-class consciousness). Rather, most semiskilled and manual jobs are the same. Choice is relatively meaningless. In the minds of the lads, nearly all work is "equilibrated by the overwhelming need for instant money, the assumption that all work is unpleasant, and that what really matters is the potential work situations hold for self and particularly masculine expression, diversions, and 'laffs.'"[27] These are all learned creatively in the informal culture—what Willis labels the counter-school culture—of the school.

In this way, physicality, masculinity, and manual labor all provide opportunities for confronting not the "false world" of the school but the real day-to-day existence the lads affirm. This process of affirmation and rejection illuminates one of the more important insights into the social reproductive role of the school.

By rejecting the world of the school, by rejecting what the ear'oles do, the lads also reject mental labor. They see it as effeminate, as not physical enough. *The seeds of reproduction lie in this very rejection.* The distinctions made and acted upon by the lads imply a strong dichotomy between mental and manual labor. The seeing of strength in the physical, the dismissing of mental "book learning," provides an important element in the re-creation of the ideological hegemony of the dominant classes.

How is this done? Consider this. In general, one of the principles guiding the articulation of social relations in our economy is the progressive divorce of mental from physical labor.[28] There are laborers who run machines, who work with their hands, or do menial paper work, and there are those who plan it and think it through. Planning is to be separated from execution whenever possible so that each process can be better standardized and controlled. In rejecting mental labor, hence, the lads are enhancing a distinction that lies at the roots of the social relations of production. Yet this is not a one-way operation. There is strength as well as weakness—paradox and contradiction—in the lads' action on this distinction.

Along with Willis, we can employ two major categories for analyzing the contradictions and paradoxes of life for these students and the economic class they represent: *penetration* and *limitation*.[29] By "penetration," he means those instances where students have developed responses to schools and work that see the unequal reality they will face. Their rejection of so much of the content and form of day-to-day educational life bears on the almost unconscious realization that, as a class, schooling will not enable them to go much further than they already are. The culture the lads create inside and outside their school actually constitutes a rather realistic assessment of the rewards of the obedience and conformism which the school seeks to extract from working-class youths. Along with scholars like Basil Bernstein and Pierre Bourdieu, Willis argues that the cultural capital employed in schools ensures the success of the children of dominant groups in society.[30] The repudiation of ideas of qualifications, diplomas, and compliance by the lads penetrates close to the core of this reality. Conformism may help the individual (but again not the working class in general); but the lads focus on their own informal group and not conformism to the model of individual achievement represented by the school. They, therefore, penetrate the ideology of individualism and competition that supports the economy.

This penetration is not a conscious option, an overt choice that represents the ideological solidarity of a working-class movement, of course. Instead, it is a response to lived conditions both inside and outside of the school, ones experienced by the lads at home, on the shop floor, within the counter-school culture, and elsewhere. It is an informal cultural response to the ideological and economic conditions and tensions they confront. And while it holds out the possibility of economic and political awareness, it remains relatively disorganized and unguided.

The conflict between the working-class culture of the lads and that of the school has another side, however, one that is properly called limitations. The cultural penetrations of the lads are repressed and prevented from going further (and in fact often paradoxically link the lads more fully to an unequal economy) by the contradictions built into their actions. For instance, as I noted, by dismissing mental labor, they heighten the division between the mental and the physical. Another instance is the way students like the lads tend to treat girls and women. Mental labor is effeminate; therefore, by preferring manual labor, and through it affirming their own subjectivity, they also affirm a sexual division of labor, as well. In Willis's words:

> We can see here the profound, unintended and contradictory importance of the institution of the school. Aspects of the dominant ideology are informally defeated there, but that defeat passes a larger structure more unconsciously and more naturalized for its furnacing in (pyrrhic) victory. Capitalism can afford to yield individualism amongst the working class but not division. Individualism is penetrated by the counter-school culture but it actually produces division.[31]

In short, the ideology of individualism is "defeated" but at the expense of increasing the power of more subtle and important economic and sexual divisions. Notice that no simple model of economic determinism or correspondence will do as an explanatory framework here. Reproduction is carried out as much through contradiction, through the relative autonomy of the lads at a cultural level.

Is this what the school consciously wants? Probably not. Nor does it want what else the institution latently brings out. The educational beliefs and pedagogic practices of many educators also act in a paradoxical way here. For example, we tend to picture certain elements of progressive pedagogy as being effective in "reaching" students who have been "unsuccessful" in more traditional classroom environments. More, and more varied curricular materials, guest speakers, films, more personal and caring teachers, greater student autonomy, and so on are often seen as answers in making education both more palatable and more rewarding to these students. If we could get students like the lads to listen and learn through better designed programs, then we could help large numbers of them get rewarding jobs, increase the chances of mobility for a large portion of them, etc. However, the tacit values which underlie the schools and our research are wholly at odds with those of the lads.

What actually seems to happen is that the somewhat more progressive setting sets limits on and enables students to develop within their own day-to-day lives in school an array of working-class themes and attitudes which give them strength and can act against the ideological values represented by the school. Resistance, subversion of authority, working the system, creating diversions and enjoyment, building an informal group to counter the official activities of the school, all of these are specifically brought out by the school, though all of these are the exact opposite of what the administrators and teachers want. Hence, if workers are interchangeable and work itself is undifferentiated and generalized, thereby looking about the same from job to job, the school plays an important part in enabling the lads to develop penetrations into it. At the same time, however, the limitations are clearly there, limitations that just as clearly end up tying such working-class youths to a labor market and preparing them for generalized and standardized work.

This is an essential point and needs to be gone into just a bit more. As Harry Braverman notes in his exceptionally important investigation of the role of workers in economic production, the use of labor in the modern corporation is increasingly guided by a number of needs.[32] First, the labor process itself must be focused, intensified, and made more speedy. Second, the control of this process needs to be removed from the workers themselves. And third, to create an even more efficient mode of production, complex skills and crafts need to be broken down into less complex components and then standardized. Thus, in general (though this varies by industry and "level of occupation" within the workplace), as control becomes centralized and more rationalized and as the scope and speed of production increases, a different kind of worker is required. Less skilled workers who are open to a greater degree of systematization become essential. Groups of people who can deal with a more intense working pace and who are flexible enough to allow for interchange between standardized labor processes also become more important. What is not needed is a craft ideology with its sense of personal control of one's job, pride in one's work, or personal meaning in work activity.[33]

Here one can see how segments of such a labor force may be produced in a *nonmechanistic way*. For, as we have seen, there is not necessarily a mirror-image correspondence between the economic and social needs of corporate production and the imposition of these needs on students in schools. Rather, the cultural response of these students is complex and both gives strength and yet prepares them to work in a job setting that can give them little sense of pride or craft.

This side of the argument, that involving the role of both the school and the informal culture which certain working-class students create within it in reproducing the social division of labor, can be seen in the following quote:

> The cultural and institutional processes [of schools] — taken as a whole — tend to produce large numbers of workers approaching this type. The nature of the "partial penetrations" we have looked at are precisely to devalue and discredit older attitudes towards work, feelings of control and meaning at work. In certain respects these developments are progressive with respect to monopoly capital and are likely to supply the instrumental, flexible, un-illusioned, "sharp," unskilled but well socialized workers needed to take part in its increasingly socialized processes.[34]

There is a real social contradiction operating here, as we have seen. The rejection of both the older attitudes toward work and the old skills must not go too far if a corporate economy is to maintain itself. If workers reject modern work, or have a complete understanding of the meaninglessness of so much of the labor they are called upon to do, then this could easily degenerate into a lack of loyalty and an erosion of the motivation to work in these increasingly centralized and rationalized industries. The modern monopoly's need for a less job-bound and less skilled workforce could also result in a group of workers who are susceptible to mass critical political perspectives. How is this critical sense of the reality of the workplace held by some workers prevented from becoming a sense of solidarity, from becoming a political and economic perspective on their own lack of power? It is *here* where the school plays such an essential role. As Willis concludes, while the informal culture of students like the lads allows them to penetrate almost to the heart of this reality, this same counter-school culture that they engender somehow acts against them as well. They ultimately become the workers needed by

an unequal economy, workers who are better able to cope with and
have some semblance of power on the shop floor, but workers who
ultimately employ categories and distinctions that are at root aspects
of the ideological hegemony required by the economy they started
out penetrating.

### The In-Between Years

So far I have focused on students, students whose backgrounds in a
particular industrial community and from a particular segment of the
working class resonate throughout their experience. Yet clearly the
lads are not the only students in schools. In working-class areas, as
Willis admits, a large portion of the students are members of that
amorphous group the lads call the ear'oles. These may be the children of parents who are slightly "higher up" on the economic ladder
within the working class, but still they constitute a large portion of
working-class people.

What of students like the ear'oles? Do working-class students who,
unlike the lads, seemingly generally accept the credentialing process
and the ethic of mobility simply sit still and listen? Is there a complex cultural form at work here as well, one that is also contradictory? Recent research seems to point to just this possibility. For like
the lads in Willis's English high school, similar things hold true for
students in the United States, though the specifics of class reproduction are somewhat more muted due to a different history and a more
complex articulation among the state, education, and an economy.
Here again students participate in the contested reproduction of the
ideological and material system of which they are a part. As Robert
Everhart shows in his investigation of a predominantly working-class
junior high school, the cultural world of these youth, youth like the
ear'oles, also re-creates, defends, and contests the hegemonic forms
which dominate the larger society, but again not in any mechanistic
way.[35]

Let us examine this more closely. While one might get the impression that such working-class youth sit passively by and both accept
and act on the formal ideological messages of the school, what one
finds is decidedly more complex. And, like the lads, the complexity
is filled with both penetrations and limitations. The vision we may
have of these "kids" (as Everhart calls them), like doing their work,

attending to school matters, and basically being taught the norms of compliance and relative docility that will equip them well for their particular rung on the labor market, is not quite as accurate as we might have thought.

As many other studies have shown, most of the time these students are in school is spent not on "work" (what teachers think school is for) but on regenerating a specific lived culture—talking about sports, discussing and planning outside activities done with friends, talking about the "nonacademic" things they do in school.[36] Like the lads, a large amount of time was spent finding ways to "goof off," to make class more interesting, to gain some measure of control over the pattern of day-to-day interaction that was so standard in school. In fact, as Everhart shows, nearly half of the time spent in school was not over "work" but in these other activities.

Unlike the lads, though, most of these groups of kids *did* meet the requirements of the school. They did this "despite a consuming interest in their own activities and the seemingly ambivalent manner in which they treated anything having to do with academics." However, because of its size and bureaucratic nature and because of the large numbers of students the school had to deal with, it actually demanded relatively little from these students. In fact, many of them could complete the required work in very little time (or could and did easily copy it from others), thus leaving a good deal of time for their own collective cultural activity. The students gave the school what relatively little was required, but certainly no more.[37]

This was true at the level of conduct as well. There were few serious instances of disrespect to a teacher or to an administrator, little evidence of maliciousness or vandalism.[38] Overt violations of the codes of the school were only acceptable if they did not put you in too much danger. While skipping classes, goofing off, and such things as fighting, swearing, drinking, and drugs were part of the cultural world of many of the kids, most of them maintained adequate or better grades. However, this does not imply that they had all totally accepted the formal ideology of the school or its hidden curriculum. Rather, it just as often seems to signify that a significant portion of these youth put up with this formal set of beliefs and practices "as a price to pay for their own activity to be generated."[39] Even for those students whose social class membership and expectations of the family created a sense that one should and would do well in school, having friends and having a good time was often more important than a very high average in their grades in school.[40]

The message seemed to be that in the daily routine of the school, one met the minimal demands of the institution—and tried to keep these demands as minimal as possible—and at the same time one's group structured its own agenda as well. This agenda centered around resistance to the regularities of organized school life and creating oppositional forms that often contradicted the emphases of formal educational practice. Again, where individualistic achievement and the ideology of individualism pervades the organizational properties of the institution, this is countered by the cultural life of the students where constant attempts at group humor, "bugging the teacher," sharing answers, and maintaining a cohesiveness in the face of the individuating practices of the school were the dynamic elements guiding the kids' lives.

For the students in this junior high school, since the school defines what is legitimate knowledge, what the appropriate strategies for gaining it are, how decisions should be made within the school itself, and so on—and this definition is pervasive throughout the institution—one has two choices (though of course these will not really be conscious decisions). As a student, you can either accept it and remain relatively bored a good deal of the time. Or you can find the cracks in the organizational control and exploit them to maintain some sense of power over your daily life. If overt rejection of the ideological messages of the school and of its authority is too threatening, then the cracks are still there to be used, expanded when possible, or even created.

In fact, those students who were most successful at mediating the demands of minimal work and exploiting the cracks were the ones who emerged as models for the others. Thus, most of the students who were highly regarded by other students were those who combined two attributes, attributes that are important for seeing ideology and its contradictions at work in this setting. "Kids who were 'smart' (that is, who could get good grades *and* who goofed off)" seemed to be the ones who fared best in the eyes of their peers. If you could do fairly well with minimum effort and still have time to goof off you did fine.[41] Hence, the ideal student seemed to accept on one level the goals and procedures of the school but at the same time was able to use them for his or her own purposes, purposes that were often quite opposite to those of the institution.

Notice what is happening here. While the kids clearly exercise a fair amount of informal power in the school setting—by goofing off, bugging teachers, and so on—like the lads they both participate in and at least partially reproduce hegemonic ideologies that may be less than helpful. In Everhart's words:

> As a form of knowledge, as a cultural system not unlike similar patterns in other settings, the exercise of power in this manner indicates how cultural forms are [often] reproductive and how participants, through opposition, actually participate in that reproductive practice.[42]

Not all of these kids are the same of course. For some students in this junior high school, the oppositional practices are massive. They spend all their time goofing off, "smoking dope," or simply skipping classes. Like the lads, these students are re-creating the conditions of their own futures as generalized laborers. On another level, however, while the culture has a differential impact on students, *everyone's* future is partly "determined" by the culture the students create. As Everhart goes on to say, the creation and emergence of these cultural forms tend to affect all students:

> and serves to reinforce the interpretation that systems of social relations are not meant to be confronted and critically analyzed, but rather resisted through these oppositional forms. And in the rise of the forms themselves, indeed the meaning attached to them, the basic system of social relations . . . remain unaffected, unexamined. . . . It seems then that the [actual cultural knowledge forms generated by the kids], while they are present in the forms of resistance, are also present as reproductive of that very system they oppose. As participants, as creators of those cultural forms, students are reproducing forms that will damn them to expressions of reaction but will not foster critical opposition. In this building of culture, students participate in the building of reproductive processes that make it likely they will suffer the same fate elsewhere, especially in the work place.[43]

Yes, there will be mobility for some of them, but not for all that many. Any real overt resistance is a threat to this possibility; but it is just this, only a possibility. This is already prefigured, "known," in the cultural sphere. It penetrates to the heart of the myth of the economy, yet clearly limits many of these youth to the blue-collar and low-level, white-collar jobs in which they will ultimately find themselves.

In essence, when a majority of American workers report that they would not work in the same job if given the choice again, yet continue to work in these conditions—while attempting to make them more livable through humor and the formation of an informal group culture—the ideological conditions which may foster this are produced out of the student culture in contradictory and complex ways in schools such as these.[44]

In ways that may be more masked than the lads, these American equivalents to Willis's ear'oles already "know" the norms of systematic soldiering on the job, looking for ways of generating fun and collectivity, and working the system to expand one's control of a situation. At the same time, they are also caught in the contradictions, the limitations, of their own lived cultural response. For the maintenance of some power and autonomy on the shop floor or in an office does not necessarily challenge the needs of capital *if the minimum requirements of production are usually met*. Thus, though many of these working-class students will go on to more skilled or higher-status jobs than the lads, they also are actively involved in the re-creation of the social relations which dominate the corporate production process.

Work need not be meaningful in this production process. It *is* just there to satisfy one's other needs, needs that are met when the work is done. One does it for money and because it provides opportunities for a collectively lived cultural response when it is engaged in. The seeds of ideological reproduction are laid. It will be a reproduction filled with contradictions, one that will be continually contested by the cultural response of these kids as they find their way into jobs, but it too will remain relatively unproductive as long as the penetrations into the nature of work and control generated by these working-class youth and their parents are unorganized and unpoliticized.

### Understanding Schooling as Cultural and Economic Reproduction

I have gone on at length here to document something of no small importance to our understanding of schools as sites of economic and cultural reproduction. Notice what is gained by entering into the debates over the social role of the school and, especially, by combining an analysis of the connections schools may have to other powerful social agencies with an attempt to go beyond correspondence theories to work out the intricate interconnections among schools, economy, and culture. A key here, obviously, is culture. The potency of the studies I have analyzed is their status as Marxist ethnographies. That is, they attempt to comprehend a concrete setting and do it by placing that setting within a larger framework of class and ideological and material forces, forces which set limits on, and actually help produce, the meanings and practices that one finds. At the same time that they go a long way in providing possible social explanations about why and how these conditions are produced, these studies do not lose the richness and variability of the experience of students of this class. They each have a rather strong commitment to the idea that, in the analysis of the social totality lived through in these microcosms, class is essential to the study of culture and institutions of economic and cultural organization, selection, and transmission such as schools. What makes this work so significant to an investigation of schooling and reproduction is the clearly articulated focus on class not as an abstract category but instead as a lived experience.[45]

Furthermore, and what must not be forgotten, they show that the real problem is to interrogate the social reality of schools to find out where our institutions are related, how these sets of relations are constituted, where there are contradictory elements, and, finally, where these elements are partly progressive and not totally reproductive. In essence, any analysis of the role of schooling in reproduction and any evaluation of the processes and results of schooling must remember that reproduction is hard and often resisted work.[46] Thus, the overriding concern with the economic outcomes of institutions, even those like the schools—with their contributions to inequality and their role in reproduction—tends to suppress "the fact that these conditions [for 'successful' reproduction] have continually to be won—or lost—in particular conflicts and struggles."[47]

The students in the extended instantiation of the earlier arguments I made about the nature of determination embodied these points. They helped produce the inherently contradictory outcomes of the institution, but only through struggle. They lived out class as an active force, one which is both creative and limiting at the same time.

The notion of consent, of self-creation if you will, is critical in this account. For, as Willis shows, for example, there is a moment of active appropriation at work in processes like these. We can see ideological hegemony in all its power and contradictions in the way the working-class boys in Willis's study nearly literally celebrate their future entry into manual labor.[48] Only by understanding this can we fully comprehend the outcomes of the school.

This point is quite important. While one could claim that my analysis here documents the process through which students like the lads and the kids ultimately lose, the process through which they are subtly determined, we must not forget the importance of the very nature of the determinations and contradictions I have sought to illuminate, using Willis's and Everhart's work here. For the hegemonic ideology of our society is "deeply and essentially conflicted" in a number of ways, ways which will continue to generate conflicts that may be difficult to resolve within existing institutional power relations and boundaries. As Todd Gitlin has pointed out, for instance, the ideological forms which dominate economies like our own urge people to work hard; yet at the same time these forms propose that real satisfaction is to be found not in work but in leisure, an area "which ostensibly embodies values opposed to work."[49] This conflict is clear in the lads and the kids and is what might best be called a structurally generated contradiction. It will create tensions and conflicts that, when they are lived through by large groups of people, will provide for the possibility of penetrations into social reality similar to those "seen" by the lads and the kids. Whether these tensions and conflicts will ultimately turn back upon those experiencing them, thereby linking them more fully to a corporate economy and ultimately benefiting those who control economic and cultural capital is, of course, not an uninteresting question given my arguments here.

But the realization that these tensions and conflicts are worked out in nearly every institution, especially including the school as we have seen, gives us an essential insight into the reality we as educators are called upon to face every day. Ignoring them or neglecting the socioeconomic and cultural sophistication needed to understand them will unfortunately not make them go away.

My discussion in the empirical section of this essay implies something else. If we find that our educational institutions do contribute something important to the reproduction of an unequal society, the question of personal action looms large. The painful question of "where do I stand?" emerges. Yet our more "intellectual" pains need at all times to be compared with pain of a different sort. We need only remember John Masefield's compelling lines:

> To get the whole world out of bed,
> and washed, and dressed, and warmed, and fed,
> to work, and back to bed again,
> Believe me, Saul, costs worlds of pain.[50]

A commitment to a set of values and institutional arrangements which would help eliminate this kind of pain is what we need to be about. And it is to a number of proposals for reforming these institutional arrangements that we shall now turn.

## REEXAMINING DETERMINATION AND WHO DETERMINES

The question of where one stands is not inconsequential since educational reforms are being currently proposed that would, it is argued, eliminate some of the economic and cultural conditions that we just saw were "reproduced" in the day-to-day life of the high school and junior high school students I analyzed. And a person must make sense out of these reforms if he or she is to decide whether to support or reject them.

One doesn't need to be a participant in the analysis of the school's role in the economic and cultural reproduction of the class structure in which the lads and the kids find themselves to realize that there is intense conflict among other groups over schools today. Industrialists and state bureaucrats wish to make schools efficient, to enable them to meet the ideological and "manpower" requirements of the economy. The tax problems generated by the fiscal crisis of the state contribute a good deal to the attempts of the same people to make education more efficient.[51] At the same time, there is pressure from "below," from many of the parents of students from racial, sexual, class, and interest groups, to make schools responsive to the often competing needs that each of these groups have identified.

One could go on nearly indefinitely, listing the claims upon school time, policies, and resources. And a similar amount of paper could be used to list the proposals for altering the way schools operate today to bring them into closer correspondence to these conflicting claims. Among the most prominent of these proposals, however, ones that are generating a good deal of discussion at the governmental level, are things like programs for voucher plans and tax credits.[52] If schools do all these social things people like Bowles and Gintis, Apple, Willis, and Everhart say they do and if they are not responsive to our competing interests, then open up the market goes the claim. If schools do act as important sites of the production and reproduction of culture and an economy, then give control back to, say, the parents. Reduce the control of the state by giving parents vouchers to pay for the kind of education they want for their children. In this way we can perhaps reduce the size and bureaucratic nature of the institution and make it more "relevant" to larger groups of children and parents. Here parents would basically be free to choose among nearly any educational and curricular arrangement (with some limits, of course) by paying public or private schools directly. The educational system would become a market, one regulated by the state but still open to all comers. This would eliminate many of the problems I focused upon in the previous sections of this essay. Or would it?

## Understanding Legitimation, Accumulation, and the State

In the introduction to this essay I noted that many investigators into the relationship between education and the larger society see the school as an ideological state apparatus. In the previous sections of this essay I focused primarily on one element of that phrase—ideological. Yet just as critical is the other element—the fact that it is a *state* apparatus. This is so commonsensical that we are apt to forget it. As the recent literature on the role of the state in social reproduction argues, however, to forget this means that we neglect the important functions the state itself performs in maintaining the relations of domination and exploitation in our society. Just as when we saw that if we wanted to unpack the daily lives of students in schools we had to relate those lives to class, culture, and economy outside of the institutions, so do we need to do that here. Without that we cannot fully appreciate the larger framework that reforms like voucher plans fit into.

As an aspect of the state, schools seem to engage, among others, in two fundamental activities. They assist in both *legitimation* and establishing some of the prior conditions necessary for capital *accumulation*.[53] On the one hand, as I argued earlier, schools are sites for the selection and production of a workforce that roughly meets the needs of the division of labor. They also produce, especially in higher education, the technical/administrative knowledge necessary for the expansion of markets, the stimulation of needs, the control of labor, and the production of technology in the economy. Accumulation refers to these activities of the school system. On the other hand, the educational apparatus contributes to inequality by legitimating an ideology of meritocracy (one that is inaccurate)[54] and by making the social relations in and out of schools seem natural. Although, as we saw, the school "produces" these outcomes in contradictory, unintended, and contested ways, it is important now to focus more directly on these elements as they relate to the state especially since the reforms being discussed are generated within it.

First, we should remember that these two functions of the state are often in conflict. For instance, as an aspect of the state apparatus the school needs to produce large numbers of credentialed workers who can be employed by a stratified labor market. However, as more and more workers get more and more credentials, the credentials themselves are devalued.[55] Because of this, the legitimacy of part of the state, here the school itself, is cast into doubt. Thus, the schools' role in accumulation may lead to an overproduction of credentialed workers and challenge the legitimacy of the way schools operate. One function of the state is almost necessarily in conflict with the other. These contradictions will be especially evident in times of crisis, like right now, in an economy. An economy plagued by inflation, unemployment, and recurrent recessions requires fewer credentialed workers. Like the lads and the kids, the school is caught in a structurally generated contradiction.

It is out of this conflict that we can begin to understand the current cry for tax credits and voucher plans. With a crisis in the economy and in many of its major institutions, the state itself begins to lose legitimacy. It cannot control the economy without entering more and more directly into that economy; nor under current fiscal conditions can it maintain these other institutions without entering more directly into their day-to-day operations as well.[56] This is a paradoxical, almost no-win situation. The state does not require merely control of what goes on; it needs *consent* as well. Without such consent, it loses its legitimacy in the process. Here, then, is the paradox. By directly intervening, the state itself becomes blamed for the general economic and institutional crisis. Since it cannot control enough of the variables—to do so would require an enormous amount of power vested within the state, something the American population would probably not stand for and something therefore that would create its own crisis in consent—it loses some of its legitimacy.

Given these contradictory functions, pressures, and paradoxes, how is the state to cope with this? It can generate consent and legitimacy by expanding the market of capitalist social relations and individual consumption and then regulating this market to ensure that the function of accumulation will be met. This is a prime element in comprehending the role of many state reforms.

This is very complex, but let me try and briefly lay out what it means. In order for the economy to continue generating profits and employment and in order for capital accumulation to go on, the consumer must be stimulated to purchase more goods *individually*. This is a primary way markets expand. That is, the ideology of what might be called possessive individualism needs to be strengthened. However, ideologies are not merely abstract ideas that remain in our economic relations. They tend to permeate all of our experience, sets of social relations, and expectations. And it is exactly here that we can see contradictions operating. By stimulating an ideology of possessive individualism, the economy creates a crisis in the school. The school, which under current financial and ideological conditions cannot meet the stimulated needs of competing individuals and interest groups, loses its legitimacy. The state, in order to maintain its own legitimacy, hence, must respond in a way which both continues to expand capitalist social relations *and* an individualistic market at one and the same time. This is exactly the place of voucher plans and tax credit systems.

The contradiction is relatively clear. A crisis is caused by the fact that the economy needs to sponsor an ideology of consumption on an individual not a collective level. In this way, more goods are produced and consumed. At the same time, however, this sets loose social forces which impact on nearly every sphere of social life. Individual groups will then focus on the consumption of *all* goods and services, including education, in a less collective way. General collective needs over, say, education will be seen in the light of what it can do for my own specific group, family, or self. To the extent that schools cannot meet these needs—and they really can't in many ways—the state apparatus will be caught in a crisis of legitimacy.

This makes any evaluation of "where should I stand?" and of the progressive potential of these kinds of proposals to reform schools difficult indeed. They are largely determined by the contradictory role of the state. They open up an area to capitalist social and market relations that once—even given many of the problems of existing schools—had been somewhat less open. They contribute to a relatively unchecked ideology of individual consumption. Yet as we shall see soon, they do in fact present the possibility of interesting interventions to create those alternative "institutional arrangements and values" that I mentioned.

So far I have outlined an argument concerning how we might interpret proposals to alter school and curricular control based on the fact that schools are part of the state. I have claimed that the contradictory pressures on the state create needs within it to propose reforms such as voucher plans which would enable it to more easily deal with its own internal and external needs. These proposals document something quite interesting. When there is a serious crisis in the state, as there now seems to be, one very effective strategy is for the state to attempt to export its crisis *outside* of itself. Thus, by reducing overt state control and turning over schooling to a market, one deflects criticism.

This performs an interesting function. By deflecting criticism away from the state and seemingly establishing a more pluralistic market, the crucial question of the differential benefits of our social formation may also be deflected. The symbolic benefit of choosing one's school may tend to be exactly that, symbolic. The material benefits may continue to recapitulate the structure of inequality.[57] As the sociologist of medicine Vicente Navarro has shown, for instance, slogans of pluralism aside, in almost every social arena from health care to antiinflation policies, the actual impact of state policies has shown a consistent pattern in which the top 20 percent of the population consistently benefit much more than the other 80 percent.[58] The question of such a pattern and the differential benefits that seem to arise from a pluralist or market solution to school problems needs to be seriously considered.

The negative possibility of this is clear enough if we see reforms of this type within the current resurgence of the right in the United States and elsewhere. One of the reasons the right is enjoying an advantage in arguments about how we should cope with the problems of the schools, the state in general, and the economy is partly because of the "skillful populist translation of its key themes into grievances about taxes, strikes, and bureaucracies." It has been able to restate the case for the expansion of capitalist social and market relations in a particular form, "as a market order which maximizes individual freedom and choice."[59] Thus, it is quite possible that supporting such things as voucher plans and tax credits—while enabling more, and more interesting choices for the lads, the kids, and others to evolve—will do something else that is less satisfying on the more general ideological and structural level. It may assist in the legitimation through the state of the "bourgeois ideal of the market," a model of all social relations based on "individual calculation and the pursuit of self-interest, and the accommodation and adjustment of interests through competition,"[60] thus partially reproducing the patterns of differential benefits Navarro describes.[61]

## Toward Political and Educational Action

So far I have been rather negative about reforms such as voucher plans, tax credits, and the like. However, I do not want to dismiss the possibility that such proposals do signify a partial breaking in the power of the state, a different balance of contending forces within the state apparatus itself, and hence can be used for progressive ends. Such a plan could in fact be employed to create models of socialist education. That is, it could create schools that would be laboratories for the development of socialist alternatives to our dominant educational models. This is not unimportant. We have lost our own history of socialist education and, in essence, are faced with starting anew. Alternative pedagogies and curricular models need to be developed in an atmosphere that fosters such a process. Voucher plans might actually provide some of these conditions if used carefully by committed groups of people.

I want to stress that the articulation and construction of serious democratic socialist alternatives are not to be taken lightly. As long as such a clear alternative does not exist, each segment of the working population will remain unlinked to the others in terms of its vision of education and will propose disparate plans and demands. These individual corporate demands (as Gramsci would call them) will not be effective in generating pressure for the restructuring of economic and cultural institutions and their control. Sassoon makes this point rather well:

> The working-class movement has not often been able to suggest a programme adequate to the needs of the mass of the population going beyond the corporate demands of various sectors. Because of this lack of objective unity around an alternative political proposal, various governments are able to play off one group against the corporate demands of another.[62]

As part of this development of a concrete alternative political proposal, the building of a clear pedagogic and curricular model that could be worked from and argued over by, say, parents, progressive unions, and others could be an important starting point in articulating a collective program.

Voucher plans might help in yet another way. Structural changes in our society need to be prefigured in local experiments. That is, the skills and norms of democratic control of one's institutions and the reorganization of them so that they benefit the majority of the population need to be learned and tested out in practice. The creation of tax credits and vouchers could provide a limited step in this direction *if* they enable people to become more deeply involved in the democratic day-to-day planning and operation of the institutions which surround them.

These are probably the most positive possibilities for the progressive use of such reforms. In many ways though they are a bit utopian and, I think, may not outweigh the differential power in the way our existing institutions are controlled and the patterns of unequal benefits that exist. Organizational change, no matter how interesting, may not be sufficient in the face of these conditions. Because of this, while we may and should explore the potential within these reforms, I think we need to be both honest about the other possible long-term negative consequences of these state-sponsored proposals and search for coherent alternative strategies for building a more powerful base from which to act.

Appropriate strategies include building allies, concrete political action, and altering curricular practice within schools. We need, for instance, to continue the slow and painstaking work of political education of teachers and other workers within the state as it is currently organized. I do not mean this as a utopian vision. Rather, as Wright and others have documented, the economic conditions caused by the fiscal crisis of the state and the increasing rationalization and control of state employees' day-to-day work provide the objective conditions that make political work and organization possible.[63] Thus, the budgetary problems of school systems in places like Chicago, Cleveland, and elsewhere where teachers are denied pay for their work or must work in increasingly underfunded facilities have important implications here. The growth of management procedures for the control of curriculum and teaching, procedures taken directly from the corporate sector where they have been used to deskill and better control labor, also points to what might best be called the "proletarianization" of these people. That is, more and more the content and conditions of their work are stipulated and controlled by managers and state bureaucrats.[64] It begins to look increasingly like the work of people who are employed in the rationalized offices and factories of industry. These conditions can allow for a more sophisticated politico-economic analysis among these state workers and can provide important opportunities for struggle at a local level.

However, it is possible that the voucher plan's fragmentation of schools could also lead to a fragmentation of teachers. That is, there may be less space for political education among teachers. The importance of winning teachers—many of whom are becoming disillusioned by the overall results and conditions of their work and the effect of their teaching—over to a more progressive political perspective is minimized here.

If I am correct that inroads can be made with state employees like teachers, then another idea becomes vitally important—linkages. These local struggles in schools and state agencies need to be connected with struggles for economic and political justice by other organized groups such as workers on the shop floor and in offices, women who are beginning to organize in offices and stores, minority parents, and so on. These linkages are essential to provide a basis of both legitimacy and strength. They are a critical part of the development of the collective program mentioned by Mouffe earlier. Since teachers are being treated increasingly like the employees in industry and the service sector of our economy, such conditions may be more attainable in the future.

Voucher plans and tax credits could hamper this strategy. If, as I want to argue, the hard political labor at the level of one's local institutions—in particular the school, welfare institutions, health care, the workplace, and so on—is essential for socialist politics, then proposals for opening schools to market relations could defuse this kind of struggle. One must ask, therefore, whether these reforms will make it that much more difficult to make linkages between, say, politically committed teachers and organized groups of workers and parents. Can they lead to a more collective appraisal? If not, are they worth our support?

So far I have talked about teachers, parents, and other organized groups and the potential of building coalitions among sets of class actors. But what of the students themselves? The investigations of Willis and Everhart that I analyzed earlier pose some rather significant issues and strategies that need to be taken seriously. The first concerns the level of content in schools.

The issue is not just to consider proposed reforms in organizational arrangements but what is and is not actually taught as well. As Anyon, for example, has documented, the history of labor that is taught in schools is less than accurate.[65] Whole segments of the American population are cut off from their past. Their own current conditions remain relatively unanalyzed in part because the ideological perspectives they are offered (and the critical tools not made available) defuse both the political and economic history and the conceptual apparatus required for a thorough appraisal of their position. The possibility of concerted action is forgotten. This points to the importance of concerted efforts at engaging in curricular change to make this history available to students like the lads and the kids.[66]

Obviously, we need to be realistic here. Simply getting more or different knowledge into schools is not enough (nor may it even be possible at times). However, we must conceive of a socialist strategy as being based on a broad front with both cultural and politico-economic action being necessary at one and the same time. Isolated attempts at curriculum reform will remain relatively inconsequential probably. But, again, if they can be linked with other struggles and with other groups, their chances are undoubtedly increased. As I argued before, no institution and no dominant ideology is totally monolithic. There will be "spaces" that can be worked in that will at least offer the chance of partial success even if this success concerns learning more about both the politics of organizing and the conditions necessary for further concrete work.

Held up to this light, to the extent that voucher plans and the like will have schools controlled by an individualistic market, it will be harder to exert pressure on school systems as a whole to remedy this imbalance in curricular content. Just as seriously, this may effectively remove a potent point around which a number of groups could organize. Thus, such plans may make it less easy to create the conditions for large-scale future work.

One final point needs to be made about the content and the students themselves, a point that is of considerable moment given my arguments about the constitutive elements of the lived culture of students from those segments of the working class we examined. It is essential that we remember that the reproductive process in which these students in schools—and their parents in the workplace—participate is not all powerful. It *is* contested.[67] There *are* elements of good sense within it. There are alternative collective practices generated out of it on what I have called the cultural level. Given that this is the case, it directs our attention to the potential of ongoing political education of both the students and their parents (and I think to the potential of their educating the educators as well). It may be possible to use these elements of class resistance for both pedagogical purposes (in reorienting our teaching practices so that they are more in line with the vital elements of working-class culture)[68] and for the purposes of focusing this discontent on the unequal structural conditions which dominate this society. Once again, the importance of coalitions among committed people is apparent here. Groups of activists in the black, Hispanic, Native American, and in the legal and health communities, as well as in a number of our more progressive unions, have begun to take this seriously. Clearly, a significant amount of collaborative work needs to be done on both the educational and political levels.

## CONCLUSION

I have briefly outlined some major criticisms of proposed reforms and what I perceive to be some of the strategies that need to be engaged in. I have noted that reforms such as tax credits and voucher systems are contradictory. They may lead to the growth of alternative institutions, ones which may help the development of interesting and workable socialist models of pedagogical and curricular arrangements. This is not to be dismissed lightly.

In saying this, I have also claimed that the actual planning, building, and running of such an institution can be important in enabling people to learn the economic, political, and organizational skills and norms that are required for more democratically run institutions. However, and this is of great significance, this presupposes that these progressive groups can actually control and organize the programs they desire. Hence, these groups should be extremely wary if they are not able to control the program that is being proposed.

If in fact voucher plans fragment specific movements rather than uniting them, acceptance should be strongly reconsidered. Furthermore, the issue of *how* these groups will gain more power through the use of voucher plans is a critical issue. For instance, in the proposals being considered in California and elsewhere, too much is left open. The actual mechanisms for giving disenfranchised groups control *and* ensuring it are unspecified. Given what Navarro and others have shown about the way lobbying and unequal power and benefits work in the state and local governmental arenas, such plans may lead to a re-creation of inequality, not the opposite. Again one should be very skeptical unless shown otherwise.

On a larger scale, I have noted that these proposals may enable the state to export its crisis of legitimacy and may open up a large area of our lives even more to reorganization around the principles of capitalist social relations. Because of this I have also argued that by enabling the state to export its crisis and by isolating small groups of teachers and "community" groups from similar class actors, such proposed reforms may make it much more difficult for political organization and action to go on. Finally, I have urged that organized political and pedagogical action, beginning at a local level but connected across various progressive groups involved in the struggle for a less exploitative set of institutional arrangements, is a prior condition for serious action.

In saying this, I am implying that there are no general principles, no easy answers, to the question of when and where one should support or oppose reforms of this type. *It is decidedly dependent on the balance of forces within a specific arena.* Only by analyzing the specificity of each individual location can one make a decision on appropriate strategies. In some locations, such reforms may in fact provide the first real opportunity for oppressed groups to organize and control their own institutions and to develop the organizational skills to transfer these principles and practices to other institutions within their community. In other locations, it may very well be the case that, say, tax credits or vouchers will have exactly the opposite effect. They may in the long run fragment progressive groups and make concerted and coordinated efforts that much more difficult. Only within the context of an analysis of the objective and ideological conditions and forces that actually exist in each location, and in the state in general, can one come up with a viable approach. In general, I would argue against supporting such reforms. On a less general level, there are times I could envision them as allowing progressive action to be initiated, but only if the prior conditions of guaranteeing real power and control are met. Thus, a very real skepticism should guide our appraisals.

Because of this, certain questions need always to be asked in evaluating state reforms. What reforms can we genuinely call *nonreformist reforms*, that is, reforms that both alter and better present conditions and can lead to serious structural changes? What reforms should be supported because of their possible contribution to the political education of a large group of people or to their learning strategies that may ultimately enable them to reassert control of their economic and cultural institutions? Which reforms contribute to coalitions that may alter the balance of forces? What kinds of coalitions will tend to be progressive in the long run? Are there elements within students and parents themselves, in their lived culture, that penetrate into the reality of dominant social relations? How can these be employed?[69]

These questions will not be easy to answer. They require a sense of history, a framework that points to the class configuration and relations of economic and cultural domination of local schools and communities (and then beyond that community), and, finally, probably a lived experience within that location.

Not only will answers not be easy, but action based on them will be "hard and contested" as well. As Gramsci argued, we need to see the struggle to create more just economic and cultural institutions as a war of position, as a struggle on a variety of fronts.[70] One of these fronts is certainly education. If the state—because of our economic crisis and its own crisis of legitimacy, the competing forces within it, and the reality of what is in store for the lads and the kids—offers possibilities for democratic socialist interventions, then they should be taken up. But, as I have tried to demonstrate in the last section of this essay, taking them up is not at all that simple. This may be one of the times we should look a gift horse in the mouth.

## NOTES TO CHAPTER 14

1.  Louis Althusser, "Ideology and Ideological State Apparatuses," in his *Lenin and Philosophy and Other Essays* (London: New Left Books, 1971), pp. 127–86.
2.  Michael W. Apple, *Ideology and Curriculum* (Boston: Routledge & Kegan Paul, 1979); and Michael W. Apple, *Education and Power* (Boston: Routledge & Kegan Paul, 1982).
3.  Apple, *Ideology and Curriculum*; and Apple, *Education and Power*, especially ch. 2.
4.  Raymond Williams, *Marxism and Literature* (New York: Oxford University Press, 1977).
5.  Samuel Bowles and Herbert Gintis, *Schooling in Capitalist America* (New York: Basic Books, 1976). See also, Michael W. Apple, "The New Sociology of Education: Analyzing Cultural and Economic Reproduction," *Harvard Educational Review* 48 (1978): 495–503.
6.  The difficulties with the more economistic models now in use to describe this process of reproduction are analyzed in considerably more detail in Apple, *Education and Power*. It is important to note an obvious but too often forgotten point here. Economic and cultural reproduction go on in other than corporate economies. The more important questions to ask about this are: What specific cultural patterns and social structures are reproduced? For whose benefit? And, to what extent is there a critical awareness on the part of affected groups of what is being reproduced?
7.  John Hill, "Ideology, Economy and the British Cinema," in *Ideology and Cultural Production*, ed. Michele Barrett, Philip Corrigan, Annette Kuhn, and Janet Wolff (New York: St. Martin's Press, 1979), pp. 112–34. As Hill puts it: "If the concept of social totality is to go beyond a mere sociology of the interconnections between institutions then it must incorporate within itself a notion of domination" (p. 116).
8.  For the importance of the relationship between class (and gender) and language, see Noelle Bisseret, *Education, Class Language and Ideology* (Boston: Routledge & Kegan Paul, 1979). This point is *not* to say that all issues of race and sex should or can be totally subsumed under class, but that class must be a fundamental aspect of one's approach. See also, Lucy Bland, Trisha McCabe, and Frank Mort, "Sexuality and Reproduction: Three Official Instances," in *Ideology and Cultural Production*, p. 78–111.
9.  This is not the place to enter into a discussion of whether class has lost its potency as a central category of one's approach to studying the United States. Needless to say, I am satisfied that it has not. For a thorough, though sometimes technical, discussion of many of the empirical and con-

ceptual issues involved here, see Erick Olin Wright, *Class, Crisis and the State* (London: New Left Books, 1978); and Erik Olin Wright, *Class Structure and Income Determination* (New York: Academic Press, 1979).

10. Richard Johnson, "Histories of Culture/Theories of Ideology," in *Ideology and Cultural Production*, p. 69.

11. Ibid., p. 70.

12. This discussion is expanded in Apple, *Ideology and Curriculum*. See also Williams, *Marxism and Literature*; and the excellent overview in Centre for Contemporary Cultural Studies, *On Ideology: Working Papers in Cultural Studies 10* (Birmingham: University of Birmingham, 1977).

13. Williams, *Marxism and Literature*, p. 87.

14. See Antonio Gramsci, *Selections From the Prison Notebooks* (New York: International Publishers, 1971). See also Todd Gitlin, "Prime Time Ideology: The Hegemonic Process in Television Entertainment," *Social Problems* 26 (1979): 251–66; and Chantal Mouffe, ed., *Gramsci and Marxist Theory* (Boston: Routledge & Kegan Paul, 1979).

15. See also Wright, *Class, Crisis and the State*, especially ch. 1; and Stanley Aronowitz, "Marx, Braverman and the Logic of Capital," *Insurgent Sociologist* 8 (1978): 126–46.

16. Johnson, "Histories of Culture/Theories of Ideology," p. 43.

17. Richard Johnson is again helpful in summarizing some of these arguments:

> There is no doubt that there are ideological conditions for the existence of a given mode [of production], but this does not, in any concrete society, exhaust all that belongs to the ideological instance. There are cultural elements to which capital is *relatively* indifferent and many which it has great difficulty in changing and which remain massively and residually present ("Histories of Culture/Theories of Ideology," p. 75).

18. Paul Willis, *Learning to Labour* (Lexington, Mass.: D.C. Heath, 1977); and Robert Everhart, *The In–Between Years: Student Life in a Junior High School* (Boston: Routledge & Kegan Paul, 1982).

19. See, for example, Apple, *Ideology and Curriculum*; Bowles and Gintis, *Schooling in Capitalist America*; Jerome Karabel and A.H. Halsey, eds., *Power and Ideology in Education* (New York: Oxford University Press, 1977); and Caroline Hodges Persell, *Education and Inequality* (New York: Free Press, 1977).

20. See, among others, Michael W. Apple and Nancy King, "What Do Schools Teach?" *Curriculum Inquiry* 6 (1979): 341–58; Philip Jackson, *Life in Classrooms* (New York: Holt, Rinehart and Winston, 1968); and Michael F. D. Young and Geoff Whitty, eds., *Society, State and Schooling* (Guildford, England: Falmer Press, 1977).

21. Michael W. Apple, "The Other Side of the Hidden Curriculum: Correspondence Theories and the Labor Process," *Interchange* 11 (3) (1980–1981): 5–22. See also, Stanley Aronowitz, *False Promises* (New York: McGraw-Hill, 1973); David Montgomery, "Workers' Control of Machine Production

in the Nineteenth Century," *Labor History* 17 (1976): 486–509; Richard Edwards, *Contested Terrain* (New York: Basic Books, 1979); and Susan Porter Benson, "The Clerking Sisterhood: Rationalization and the Work Culture of Saleswomen in American Department Stores," *Radical America* 12 (2) (1978): 41–55.

22. Often this takes the form of an almost unconscious cynical bargain between teachers and students; see Linda McNeil, "Economic Dimensions of Social Studies Curriculum: Curriculum as Institutionalized Knowledge" (Ph.D. diss., University of Wisconsin, Madison, 1977).

23. As I noted, these concepts are under considerable scrutiny today; see, e.g., Michael W. Apple, ed., *Cultural and Economic Reproduction in Education: Essays on Class, Ideology and the State* (Boston: Routledge & Kegan Paul, 1981); and Williams, *Marxism and Literature*.

24. Willis, *Learning to Labour*, p. 175.

25. Ibid., p. 19.

26. Elsewhere, I have criticized Willis for assuming that the ear'oles and the girls the lads interact with are, in fact, totally compliant. See Michael W. Apple, "What Correspondence Theories of the Hidden Curriculum Miss," *Review of Education* 5 (1979): 101–12, on which this section of my essay is based.

27. Willis, *Learning to Labour*, p. 10.

28. Harry Braverman, *Labor and Monopoly Capital* (New York: Monthly Review Press, 1974).

29. I am wary of employing a concept like penetration, given the role of sexist metaphors in organizing our linguistic usage. However, I shall continue to employ Willis's own terms here.

30. See Pierre Bourdieu and Jean-Claude Passeron, *Reproduction in Education, Society and Culture* (Beverly Hills: Sage Publications, 1977); Basil Bernstein, *Class, Codes, and Control*, vol. 3 (Boston: Routledge & Kegan Paul, 1977); and Apple, *Ideology and Curriculum*.

31. Willis, *Learning to Labour*, p. 146.

32. Braverman, *Labor and Monopoly Capital*.

33. This may increasingly hold true for more scientific and technical occupations as science and engineering are further organized under a corporate context; see David Noble, *America By Design* (New York: Alfred A. Knopf, 1977); and Apple, *Education and Power*.

34. Willis, *Learning to Labour*, p. 180.

35. Everhart, *The In-Between Years*.

36. Ibid., p. 116.

37. Ibid., p. 213.

38. Ibid., p. 218.

39. Ibid., p. 220.

40. Ibid., p. 260.

41. Ibid., p. 337.

42. Ibid., p. 446.
43. Ibid., pp. 451–52.
44. Ibid., p. 451. See also, Apple, "The Other Side of the Hidden Curriculum"; and Apple, *Education and Power.*
45. Lesley Johnson, *The Cultural Critics* (Boston: Routledge & Kegan Paul, 1979).
46. Johnson, "Histories of Culture/Theories of Ideology," p. 74.
47. Ibid., p. 70.
48. Ibid., p. 75. A very interesting study of working class girls that makes similar arguments is summarized in Angela McRobbie, "Working Class Girls and the Culture of Femininity," in *Women Take Issue*, ed. Women's Studies Group (London: Hutchinson, 1978), pp. 96–108.
49. Gitlin, "Prime Time Ideology," p. 264.
50. Quoted in Lilian Rubin, *Worlds of Pain* (New York: Basic Books, 1976), p. ix.
51. James O'Connor, *The Fiscal Crisis of the State* (New York: St. Martin's Press, 1973). See also, Manuel Castells, *The Economic Crisis and American Society* (Princeton: Princeton University Press, 1980).
52. John E. Coons and Stephen D. Sugarman, *Education By Choice: The Case for Family Control* (Berkeley: University of California Press, 1978).
53. Michael W. Apple, "Curriculum Form and the Logic of Technical Control," *Journal of Economic and Industrial Democracy* 2 (1981): 293–319. See also, O'Connor, *The Fiscal Crisis of the State*; Wright, *Class, Crisis and the State*; and Roger Dale, "Education and the Capitalist State: Contributions and Contradictions," in *Cultural and Economic Reproduction in Education*, ed. Apple.
54. Michael Olneck and James Crouse, "Myths of Meritocracy: Cognitive Skill and Adult Success in the United States," discussion paper 485–78, University of Wisconsin Institute for Research on Poverty, Madison, March 1978.
55. Randall Collins, *The Credential Society* (New York: Academic Press, 1979).
56. Wright, *Class, Crisis and the State*; and Apple, *Education and Power.*
57. Murray Edelman, *Political Language* (New York: Academic Press, 1977), p. xxi.
58. Vicente Navarro, *Medicine Under Capitalism* (New York: Neale Watson Academic Publications, 1976), p. 91.
59. Andrew Gamble, "The Free Economy and the Strong State: the Rise of the Social Market Economy," in *The Socialist Register*, 1979, ed. Ralph Miliband and John Saville (London: Merlin Press, 1979), p. 22.
60. Gamble, "The Free Economy and the Strong State," p. 22.
61. I do not want to give the impression that the state, anymore than hegemonic ideologies, is monolithic internally. In fact, exactly the opposite is the case and this presents another aspect that once again makes a cut-and-dried evaluation of state-sponsored reforms no simple matter. For the state

is the site at which classes and class segments contend. In essence, it is a seat of *conflict* as well as domination. The fact that the state apparatus might wish to export its crisis and reestablish market power over schools is indicative of the partial success of some groups—groups who have not historically been helped as much by schools—in challenging the legitimacy of routine operations within the state. It points to a partial breakdown of hegemonic control. On the nature and impact of contestation within the state, see Anne Showstack Sassoon, "Hegemony and Political Intervention," in *Politics, Ideology, and the State*, ed. Sally Hibbin (London: Lawrence and Wishart, 1978), pp. 9–39.

62. Sassoon, "Hegemony and Political Intervention," p. 39.
63. Wright, *Class, Crisis and the State*; and Apple, "The Other Side of the Hidden Curriculum."
64. See Apple, *Education and Power*; and Edwards, *Contested Terrain.*
65. Jean Anyon, "Ideology and United States History Textbooks," *Harvard Educational Review* 49 (1979): 361–86.
66. Apple, "The Other Side of the Hidden Curriculum."
67. Ibid.; and Edwards, *Contested Terrain.*
68. See John Clarke, Chas Critcher, and Richard Johnson, eds., *Working Class Culture* (London: Hutchinson, 1979).
69. See Willis, *Learning to Labour*, pp. 185–93; and Mike Brake, *The Sociology of Youth Culture and Youth Subculture* (Boston: Routledge & Kegan Paul, 1980).
70. Mouffe, *Gramsci and Marxist Theory.*

# CONCLUSION

The fourteen essays in this volume provide a variegated picture of the relationship between education and the state. Although diverse, the essays are united by their common examination of topics central to the relationship between education and the state. An issue of special attention throughout has been the extent to which the state monopolizes power, resources, and agendas that control the schooling process, thereby dominating formalized education in American society.

To review, we first consulted the historical record in order to understand better the increasing overlap between educational processes and the state. Examination of this interrelationship was carried forth into the next major section, where we examined both constitutional and philosophical issues relevant to state control. Next, we focused on some educational consequences of the involvement of the state in education, particularly through state schooling, and attended to cultural, political, and organizational consequences. In the last section, we discussed some possible reconceptualizations of the relationship between education and the state. Here, voucher schemes, taxation policy, tax credits, and the process of nonpublic school choice were given special attention.

In this Conclusion, we attempt to answer, based upon the information presented within this volume, that critical question posed in the Introduction, that is, *to what extent does the state monopolize educational processes within American society?* In answering this and attendant questions, we propose no "grand theory," nor do we expect that any highly complex variable analysis can be identified for immediate empirical testing. Those goals, worthy as they are, have not been our purpose. Rather, we have devoted our efforts to a description of the problem. Thus, our intentions here are more modest in scope and are based upon utilization of a variety of disciplinary, methodological, and epistomological perspectives in order to explore what some political scientists have admitted is a much neglected issue—the nature of the modern state, especially as it applies to one institutional domain, that of education.[1] Our exploration can best be concluded by drawing together the information presented in this volume as it provides answers to three basic questions:

1. What specific role does the state play in the education of its citizens?

2. In what specific manners or through what mechanisms does the state control education? What are the consequences of that relationship for various groups in society?

3. What conditions might be necessary for alteration of the relationship between the state and the educational process?

## ROLE OF THE STATE IN EDUCATION

In the Introduction we stated that "the actual role of the state in education is an empirical question that should remain open in the reading of these essays" and that this issue would be addressed again in the Conclusion. Although it would be pretentious to advance the claim that our word is definitive on this issue, we can summarize important conclusions relative to the role of the state in education in North America.

La Belle provides the framework in his description of the tension that exists between centripetal and centrifugal pressures within all institutions, education among them. This tension, varying as to scope among schooling systems in numerous societies, defines the manner in which the nation-state affects certain institutional regularities said to be necessary for social integration. For instance, to the extent that structural heterogeneity exists within a culture, centrifugation rather than centripetalism in the process of cultural transmission will be most evident throughout the nation-state. Yet, as La Belle so force-fully points out, even when a decentralized system of schools that takes account of cultural pluralism exists, its existence is at the dis-cretion of the state. La Belle indicates that "the local level generally assumes responsibility for only those aspects of schooling delegated and/or sanctioned by the central authority." From a cross-cultural perspective then, schooling is a process dominated by the state to the extent that the balance between centripetal and centrifugal forces and their effect on schooling exist largely at the convenience of the state.

This point concerns an argument advanced by Apple and Everhart in their essays. As a neo-Marxist, Apple suggests that schooling in-cludes both "cultural and economic concerns" (the latter being what La Belle calls "structural" concerns) and that it is necessary to exam-ine the interrelationship between the cultural and economic dimen-sions of society. As he writes, schools are sites for the "selection and production of a workforce that roughly meets the needs of the divi-sion of labor"—the structural dimension of society. Yet schooling also "legitimates an ideology of meritocracy" and thereby convinces students that their position of alienation and subservience in schools is natural and to be expected. In this latter sense, schools serve to legitimate the day-to-day social relations within them as an orderly part of the relationship between the individual and the state's insti-tutions. Schooling, then, in addition to being intimately connected to institutional structure, serves also to reinforce the patterns of cultural transmission most functional for the state, of which state schools play an important part.

Everhart discusses the "institutional parameters" of the state edu-cational system by further examining the cultural dimensions of schooling. Hence the state, by regulating structurally the legitimate dimensions of schooling, also regulates the ongoing experience of those who are part of and make the school's routine—teachers, par-ents, and the students alike. Once the state establishes a structural configuration (state schools) in line with its basic value system (pre-servation of state dominance) and as long as that configuration is not critically examined and/or transformed, then that structural config-uration will continue to predominate and channel experience within it. In the case of educational "innovation," activities that fall within that rubric fit precisely that condition which La Belle noted earlier—

innovation is limited to those activities delegated and/or sanctioned by the state and its representative agencies. In the case of the United States, those educational changes sanctioned by or productive for the system of state capitalism are those we can expect to see most evident.

This same point is supported by Spring, who traces the evolutionary nature of state political control of schooling during the nineteenth and twentieth centuries. When we examine the educational practices fostered by the state during this period, it is no accident that those changes receiving the most attention are those that provide the greatest potential for control of resource allocation by professional elites. Thus, career education, the accountability movement, and educational research are all areas receiving increased federal attention. They are also areas in which the creation of "experts," who form a small elite influencing the structure and ideology of state education, is assumed to be a necessary characteristic of such innovations.

What then can be said of the specific role of the state in the educational process, most specifically state schooling? Returning to the Introduction, we note the supposition by nineteenth-century reformers that a proper role of the state was to serve as an objective arbiter between competing, sometimes conflicting, interests. Indeed, such a role was viewed to be quite possible with the rise of state educational bureaucracies staffed by professionals schooled in the "objective" strategies of the new administrative sciences. The movement in this direction seems to be a phenomenon documented by the essays in this book. Furthermore, regardless of political persuasion, all the authors appear to support the basic supposition that the state has attempted to control and monopolize the education of its young people through the imperatives of state schooling, usually to the detriment of minority groups and those holding nonmajoritarian beliefs. Smith reviews the nineteenth-century opposition to this trend by his focus on "Voluntaryist" movements, and Edson documents this process at work in the education of Italian immigrant children in nineteenth-century America. Arons and Lawrence examine the same basic patterns of state domination (although under a more complex form) in their discussion of the education of black Americans. Katz examines state control in terms of "dominance" to the extent that those being educated (as well as those who educate) are subject to commands and directions from the state.

But to what do we refer when we say the state attempts to control and monopolize? We must stress again, as we did in the Introduction, that the state is more than just "government"; it is also symbolic of the complex web of majoritarian interests channeled partially (but not completely) into and through respective agencies of control, with such agencies facilitating the exercise of majoritarian power and domination. The state is not a "thing" but rather a relation of dominant interests—a "material condensation of class rule."[2] Sheldon Wolin notes that in the United States:

> there has been an evolution from a loose structure of "government" to something like a state system. A state exists when power and authority are centralized; when their scope and application are, in principle and for the most part, unlimited except for procedural requirements; and when the basic tendency is toward the integration of the various branches of the government rather than toward their separation.[3]

In such state systems, control will be of such a nature that it will serve to protect majoritarian class, racial, and ideological interests in whatever way possible and necessary. This control will be present in the area of education to the extent that education serves or can serve state interests. Anthropologist Yehudi Cohen feels that this is an aspect of all state societies and notes that "to expect that a state will allow its schools to serve aims other than those of the national political structure is to expect that the state will not behave like a state."[4]

Yet these essays do not portray this process of state intervention and control as a unidirectional, deterministic, conspiratorial process fostered successfully by an all-oppressive state bureaucracy, unmercifully grinding out the state's will despite opposition. Indeed, as Apple describes, the state may even support certain liberal educational causes that appear on the surface to provide additional power to those very same groups which the state ostensibly has disenfranchised through economic or social segregation. Edson, too, has described the apparently benevolent intentions of educational reformers in the nineteenth century relative to the vocational education movement. Erickson and West describe the current practices in Canada to grant greater determination to patrons of private schools.

However, in all cases, we must examine critically the extent to which such "liberties" are true extensions of self-determination or whether they are really "the secret power" in disguise. The movement of the state in educational issues is unlikely to be obvious and preplanned but more likely to occur through the manipulation of symbols produced by the very contradictions which the state itself has produced. It is very much like the political arena, where democracy is espoused but where "democratic" elections occur via massive political campaigns that rely on the manipulation of political symbols and not upon the explication of issues and the true involvement of citizens in those issues. So too will such subtle manipulation of cultural symbols be found as the state works through educational agendas. Again, as Cohen notes:

> the educational part of a state's bureaucracy has as its relevant and specialized tasks to implant politically meaningful and legitimating symbols and to elicit approved and appropriate responses to those symbols as one means among many for the maintenance of order and uniformity of response throughout the polity.[5]

Thus the mechanisms and the symbols reflective of state control often are difficult to identify, and their presence will require considerable attention and thought on the part of educators.

## INSTRUMENTS OF STATE CONTROL

It is one thing to argue that the state effectively regulates and monopolizes schooling both structurally and culturally; the extent to which this regulation affects students, parents, and teachers or, more generally, influences the manner in which schools operate is a separate issue. Thus, if we are to look "behind the classroom door," we must examine the specific *instruments* by which the state regulates schooling and identify the most prominent manifestations of that regulation.

Many authors here claim that state schooling shapes and orders the ultimate culture of those who come under its influence (Apple, Arons and Lawrence, Spring, and Smith). In this ordering process, the manners by which people perceive, choose, and go about solving the problems of everyday life are guided and affected in a manner that reinforces structurally based privileges and inequalities. State schooling thus serves to legitimate social processes by leaving unexamined the manner in which many social and technical processes of schooling extend state domination. This legitimating function operates to justify success for those who "make it" as well as to rationalize failure for those who do not. Because elements of state schooling camouflage the structural and cultural regularities that preserve privilege and accentuate disenfranchisement, it is not surprising that thinkers as diverse as Marx and Mill foresaw public education leading to what Mill termed "a despotism over the mind."

Yet the manipulation of consciousness works selectively and somewhat secretively. As Arons and Lawrence note, for example, blacks suffer more from consciousness manipulation not necessarily because they are black but, more importantly, because they are disproportionately represented among the poor and disenfranchised.[6] Within such a class of society, the state educational system continues its legitimating function through testing, tracking, and value inculcation, all the while extending such legitimation under the rubric of academic selection and learning. Other more subtle modes of consciousness manipulation exist as well. Apple demonstrates, for example, that it is through the contradictions of schooling that working-class students may "self-select" into class-related social patterns and employment practices. All the while, this self-selection appears to be a manifestation of individual self-expression and liberation. Spring claims that the fact that schools do *not* influence students with explicit political behaviors, while it may signal a presence of benign neglect, also is a condition functional for a society of "experts." For to have a citizenry that is politically illiterate or ambivalent makes that society that much more dependent on the "experts," thereby removing citizens from active self-determination. Such varied patterns demonstrate again the necessity of examining the instruments of control as veiled and symbolic as well as clear and manifest.

The second critical instrument of state control of schooling (and one related to that noted above) is the minimal emphasis on the development of critical thinking. For example, Katz states that an education that fosters democratic ideals must "include the capacity and inclination to think critically for oneself." In Katz's view the state has an obligation not only to foster an individual's economic and physical self-sufficiency but also to foster a "critical spirit" which alerts one to the "possibility that the established norms ought to be neglected, that the rules ought to be changed, and the criteria in judging performances modified." The extent to which state schools adequately fulfill this function is seriously questioned by many authors here.[7] Arons and Lawrence go so far as to claim that the absence of freedom in idea formation can be construed as a First Amendment issue, a point that runs parallel to the thesis of the Voluntaryists described by Smith. La Belle sees such control as "functional," in part, for the survivability of the state and doubts that any state system would permit such liberty. Everhart and Apple view such regulation of idea formation as specifically related to the extension of state capitalism into state schooling, although both are silent on what patterns of idea formation might be present in socialist societies. The regulation of critical thought is a dimension many authors here agree is predominant in state schooling.

The limitation of those activities that the state legitimates as formalized education is a final instrument of state control. State schooling is almost always the exclusive form of formalized education that is legitimated by the state. Within this institutional form, the state moves toward centripetalism. West documents this trend in his analysis of how the public bureaus control competition by manipulating agendas in such a way that the initiative of choice provided by the bureau to the public is paired against as few alternative sources as possible. Such a pattern "dilutes" the power of each individual vote, exacerbating voter apathy and facilitating monopoly control by the bureau over decisions and the funding of decisions. That educational agencies, once formed, tend toward self-protection means that the state will attempt to maximize educational experiences in the form in which it has defined them to exist. Conversely, the state will diligently oppose any movements that may result in client-sponsored educational choices being available, as the availability of these choices will increase the power of clients and decrease the ability of the bureau to control agendas (see La Belle).

The limitations on formalized education by the state indicate clearly that state education is not always what it appears to be. The common public school, for example, is an organizational form said to permit maximum flexibility and diversity because the interests of all constituents are present and represented. Yet, as Everhart notes, those interests are not represented equally in the decision making about public education (Arons and Lawrence make this point clear as well), and even those interests that do emerge triumphant often are so twisted by the need for political compromise that they please few. Hence, the pluralism that the supporters of common schools tout as the strength of public schooling often ends up to be little more than majoritarian domination of minority viewpoints. As those majoritarian interests become institutionalized through curriculum, staffing, and resource allocation, the bureaus which administer the programs that are fostered by majoritarian groups begin to pursue their own self-interests, thus resulting in the monopolization of agendas and resources described so carefully by West.

Vitullo-Martin describes still another manner in which state-regulated schooling does not accomplish its objectives. Designed originally to minimize the extent to which the wealthy would make use of private schools (thereby creating a two-tiered educational system of wealthy private schools and poor public schools), the system of federal tax codes has had the effect of creating two tiers *within* the public schools near many metropolitan centers. Because the tax laws encourage movement of relatively affluent citizens from the poor schools of the city to the "better" schools of the suburbs, suburban schools end up more heavily stratified and elitist than many private schools in the same metropolitan area. Tax laws promulgated by the state may serve the contradictory functions of further worsening the overall quality of those very same public schools that are administered by the state.

Many of these essays claim that the *consequences* of state control have and continue to illustrate the further erosion of the education of those citizens to whom the state is responsible. First, the latitude of the state educational system to provide appropriate education is severely limited by many of the parameters that define that school system's very presence and existence. Public schools, in general, cannot be adaptive organizations because they must serve too many interests through one uniform means. Furthermore, and in order to facilitate this perceived needed uniformity, the public school bureaucracy minimizes the choices provided constituents, a stance which engenders further apathy and lack of commitment on the part of those same constituents. Partially as a result of the contradictions generated within state schooling, increasing numbers of people do choose, as Arons and Lawrence point out, to "pay twice in order to preserve [their] First Amendment rights," thereby resulting in increased attendance in private schools, many of which "serve a population more racially and economically mixed than the stereotypical view of such schools assumes" (Vitullo-Martin). The legitimation crisis raised by the monopolization of schooling by the state has resulted not only in movements out of the system but also in a trend toward at least the structural decentralization of public schooling (as

Iannaccone points out) and, indeed, in movements fundamentally to alter the state-education relationship. We now turn to an assessment of those movements.[8]

## ALTERING THE RELATIONSHIP BETWEEN EDUCATION AND THE STATE

These essays serve as a foundation for our claim that the fundamental nature of state schooling needs serious reconsideration. Some authors have been more specific in their proposals than others, but the need to examine critically the monopolistic control by the state over the formal education of its children and youth is a common theme throughout. Now let us examine the assumptions raised by those who have challenged the basis and extent of that control.

Although it seems simplistic, the posing and reposing of the "right questions" must serve as the beginning point in any discussion of state education. "Right questions" are not proposed to be so in the normative sense but more particularly in the sense that the questions asked probe to the institutional root of the educational process. Questions such as "What is an educated person?" "Who defines it as such?" "What roles do schools play in defining that process?" "What are the consequences and for whom, for schooling to be so defined?" are the type that must be asked repeatedly in every generation.

These questions are particularly important in an era which has seen the rise of "policy studies" in education, where research theory and application are determined, in large part, by the presence and predominance of educational practice as it exists in the public sector. The danger here is to define public policy through social utility (a common practice in policy studies) and thus to focus on questions of the function or consequences of any educational practice. Questions on educational worth are then left to philosophers and critics. An abandonment of such questions by policy analysts and policy makers leaves education a practice bankrupt of moral vision.

That asking such questions will make explicit the role of values and ideological structure in schooling is not surprising, for as Everhart, Arons and Lawrence, and others point out, schooling and education is a valuing process that involves political, moral, and social choices. Those choices are made daily by teachers in classrooms, by school boards, and as Katz points out, by state legislators who pass legislation that determines the legal definition of such critical terms as "minimal education." Yet the institutionalization of formal education and the subsequent tendency not to think critically about it has led to a steady transformation of the term "education." Most of these essays support the premise that our conception of education is limited because we have come to accept as given the presence of state schooling and with it the assumption that the needs of the state and its citizens are best served through the continuation of such schooling. The importance of redirecting our attention to such issues cannot be minimized if any significant changes are to emerge.

To pose such fundamental questions also signals the importance of analytical frameworks that help us understand educational phenomena. One such framework is that noted by Katz, the proposed bivariate distinction between education as a "principle" and as a "rule." In viewing education as a principle, we might specify that there is some goal or condition that constitutes a reasonable education, but we may differ on the means by which that education is to be obtained or how specific aspects of an education are to be weighed over another. Viewing education as a "rule," however, leads to prescriptive outcomes in that such a conception "regulates specific conduct by permitting or prohibiting this conduct" (Katz). Education viewed as a "principle" emphasizes the ends but permits, at the same time, flexibility to determine the means whereas education viewed as a "rule" attempts to prescribe both the means and the ends.

It is precisely this distinction that Arons and Lawrence address in their discussion of the role of schools as active agents in the manipulation of beliefs. A First Amendment interpretation of the current process of schooling focuses upon the conception of education as a rule (with specific prescriptions about how that education is to be obtained, evaluated, and, indeed, even applied), the consequences of which lead to infringement upon the constitutional rights of minority groups (and others as well) to obtain freedom of belief formation. An equally critical limitation is the continuing pattern of viewing education almost exclusively in the form of state schooling. Viewing education as a rule does not serve as a useful guide for change because rules are restrictive rather than expansive.

Asking the "right questions" is necessary but certainly not sufficient in order to understand a system of state education with a political and cultural momentum of its own. Schooling in our society is part of the state system, and it is naïve to believe that the state will wither away, thereby freeing for all time the educational process to exist unfettered by restrictions. Yet, too, the absence of any criteria or restrictions on education—that is, the absence of a basic conceptualization of what people in the society should be capable of and some structure to implement that conception—surely would benefit the dominant classes to the detriment of the disenfranchised, the working classes, and the minorities, leaving them to compete for limited resources with even more limited educational resources of their own. Accordingly, the prime issue should not be the elimination of the state in its interrelationship with education. Rather, we must turn to a reconsideration of the extent of monopoly control currently held by the state in education and the process by which that monopoly control minimizes self-determination by disaffected groups.

We do not advocate any specific answers as to what this reconsideration might accomplish, although we have discussed such alternatives as tuition tax credits (Freeman), vouchers (West), and tax codes (Vitullo-Martin). In an age that cries for certainty, for predictability, perhaps such a stance will be seen as a derelection of responsibility. We think that is not the case, for in issues as complex as education and schooling and their interrelationship within state systems, the proposal of definitive solutions too often is not only simplistic but may lead to hardened political alliances, the maintenance of which becomes an end in itself. Because our purpose in this volume has been to sensitize rather than to prescribe, we prefer not to propose a recipe, one that might be construed as leading to a prize-winning product.

Yet we can provide some guidelines on how the further reconsideration of the monopoly control of schooling by the state should proceed. One issue raised by Apple cautions us that a deregulation of schools by the government (via tax credits, vouchers, local options, etc.) does not necessarily mean the concurrent removal of the *state* from educational matters. The state *is* more than government, although government normally is a significant agency within the state. The movement toward forms of deregulation, much of which is becoming more acceptable to government, may represent little more than a recognition by one agency of the state (government) that it is losing its legitimacy in a certain area, whereupon it transports the problem outside of itself (in this case, to the market) to other agencies of the state (majoritarian interests in the economic sector, political elites, etc.). Those agencies may reassert (albeit in a disguised manner) the structural inequality which preserves the state's very existence, thereby deflecting criticism away from "government" and toward the "new" educational configuration. We need to widen our conceptualization of the state, especially as it becomes reconstituted over time, and not fail to ask the hard questions necessary to minimize the possibility of well-intentioned reforms from turning into unintended failures.

A second related issue to be considered in all policy legislation can be stated in the form of a caveat: be aware of unintended consequences in all educational changes. There must be a greater commitment to the study of *all* alternatives before policy is adopted rather than the emphasis upon pragmatics as is present today. Surely, for example, the framers of the tax codes on income never anticipated the long-term effect of those codes on issues as remotely related as residential housing patterns and the eventual "elitification" of the many public schools as described by Vitullo-Martin. Yet one must wonder about the extent of critical thinking that goes into the decisions about annual alterations in the tax structure and further question why so many decision makers have lacked the foresight to realize that the tax structure in this nation is as much (if not more) a determinant of social policy as it is a vehicle for raising revenue. Such expansive thinking ought to be more evident in public policy decisions about education.

Finally, we must be willing to make the necessary and critical distinction between the legal and analytical *possibility* of reform and the political *probability* of that reform being instituted. It is one thing to discuss the philosophical possibility of an educational system that is democratic in design and optimally beneficial in outcome. It is another to usher in that system given the political situation at any one time. Such is the reason why caution signals must be raised and seriously examined and why political reality often must supersede philosophical or legal idealism. To favor massive deregulation of education, for example, without serious and deliberative examination of the political realities that will be or may be operative within such a deregulated environment is not only irresponsible but avoids that very critical view of education advocated in this book. This is not to say that a careful consideration of the political climate may not favor moves toward deregulation, for indeed it might. It is to say, however, that the disengagement and/or reconstitution of various state educa-

tional agencies must take into consideration the political environment within which that new educational system might exist, as well
as the prima facie strengths of such arguments. We all need remember
that education exists within a social-political context and be able to
anticipate how that context might affect educational practice once
revised. Such is a critical stance, the absence of which is a guarantor
of future frustration.

The world of educational change is to be found largely in the
political forum, where political forces interact to create/re-create the
educational institutions of the state. The power of political forces
and political interest groups (some of which are not directly related
to education) will increasingly affect the course of schooling in our
country while, at the same time, the exclusive role of educational
bureaucracies in the formation of policy probably will decrease (see
Iannaccone). British Columbia is an apt illustration of this political
power in action, for, as West has shown, the movement in British
Columbia's experiment of fiscal support for private schools was not
motivated so much by concern for educational reform as much as
it was for fiscal reform. We will witness similar changes elsewhere,
and we should expect to see educational practice increasingly being
affected by policy decisions in the arenas of taxation, equal protection, conceptions of "minority status"—indeed as a result of the
very contradictions generated within the state itself. Those who wish
to democratize schooling would do well to recognize the political
nature of their task (Everhart) and be open to a careful analysis of
the nature of any given reform (Apple and Arons and Lawrence).
Only through such an awareness can the changing relationship between education and the state emerge to be potentially reformist. We
hope that the information in this volume serves as a significant catalyst in developing that awareness.

## NOTES TO CONCLUSION

1.   Although not dealing explicitly with the notion of "the state," the role of
     "government" in education is a topic of recent growing interest, as evi-
     denced by the recent literature in the field. See, e.g., J. Myron Atkin, "The
     Government in the Classroom," *Daedalus* 109 (1980): 85–97; Mary Frase
     Williams, ed., *Government in the Classroom: Proceedings of the Academy of
     Political Science* 33 (2) (1978): 1–60; and Arthur Wise, *Legislated Learning*
     (Berkeley: University of California Press, 1979). The classic work focusing

on the state and education still is E.G. West, *Education and the State* (London: Institute of Economic Affairs, 1970), although a new book by Thomas Green, *Predicting the Behavior of the Educational System* (Syracuse: Syracuse University Press, 1980), shows conceptual promise.

2.  Nicos Poulantaz, "The Political Crisis and the Crisis of the State," in *Critical Sociology*, ed. J.W. Freeberg (New York: Irvington, 1979), p. 375.

3.  Sheldon Wolin, "Reagan Country," *New York Review of Books* 17 (December 18, 1980): 9.

4.  Yehudi A. Cohen, "The Shaping of Men's Minds: Adaptations to the Imperatives of Culture," in *Anthropological Perspectives in Education*, ed. Murray Wax et al. (New York: Basic Books, 1971), p. 41.

5.  Ibid.

6.  See also William Julius Wilson, *The Declining Significance of Race* (Chicago: University of Chicago Press, 1977).

7.  The same question is raised by a recent Rockefeller Commission appointed to examine the state of the humanities; see *The Humanities in American Life* (Berkeley: University of California Press, 1980).

8.  These are movements suggested during the past decade by a host of commissions on educational reform; see, e.g., *Report of the National Panel on High Schools and Adolescent Education* (Washington, D.C.: U.S. Office of Education, 1974); and National Commission on the Reform of Secondary Education, *The Reform of Secondary Education: A Report to the Public and the Profession* (New York: McGraw-Hill, 1973).

# INDEX

# ABOUT THE EDITOR

**Robert B. Everhart** received his B.A. from the College of Wooster (Ohio) and M.A. and Ph.D. from the University of Oregon. Currently Associate Professor of Education, Graduate School of Education, University of California at Santa Barbara, his major field of interest is the sociology of education.

Dr. Everhart has been Research Associate, Center for the Advanced Study of Educational Administration, University of Oregon (1972); Staff Associate, Experimental Schools Evaluation Project, Northwest Regional Educational Laboratory (1972–1976); Research Director, Drug and Alcohol Abuse Program, State of Washington (1976–1977); and Visiting Assistant Professor of Education, University of Washington (1978).

His articles and reviews have appeared in *American Educational Research Journal, Anthropology and Education Quarterly, Change, Contemporary Sociology, Human Organization, Interchange, Journal of Research and Development in Education, National Association of Secondary School Principals, ASSP Bulletin, Review of Educational Research,* and *Social Problems,* as well as other journals.

# ABOUT THE CONTRIBUTORS

**Michael W. Apple** is Professor of Curriculum and Instruction and Educational Policy Studies at the University of Wisconsin at Madison. He received his Ph.D. from Columbia University. Writing extensively on the relationship between education and social reproduction, his recent books include *Ideology and Curriculum* (1979), *Cultural and Economic Reproduction in Education* (1982), and *Education and Power* (1982).

**Stephen Arons** is Associate Professor and Director of Legal Studies, University of Massachusetts at Amherst. He received his J.D. from Harvard University in 1969, and has been Senior Attorney, Harvard Center for Law and Education, and a Fellow at the Center for the Study of Public Policy, Cambridge, Massachusetts. His main areas of interest include law and education, the history of law as a social institution, and the First Amendment. He is the coauthor of *Before the Law* (Second edition, 1978) and has been a contributing editor to *Saturday Review*. He has recently completed a book on conflict in education which will be published in 1982.

**Charles Burgess** is a Fellow at the Institute for the Study of Educational Policy and Professor of the History of Education, University of Washington. He received his Ph.D. from the University of Wisconsin at Madison. He is currently studying the historic relationships between the consolidation of schools and the promotion of learning. His articles and reviews have appeared in *American Educational Research Journal*, *Harvard Educational Review*, *Review of Educational Research*, and *History of Education Quarterly*, as well as other journals.

**C. H. Edson** is Associate Professor of Education at the University of Oregon. He holds M.A.s in both history and education and a Ph.D. in educational history from Stanford University. His primary research interests focus on ethnicity and work and his articles and reviews have recently appeared in *Educational Leadership*, *Educational Studies*, *History of Educational Quarterly*, *Urban Education*, and *The Urban Review*.

**Donald A. Erickson** is currently Professor in the Graduate School of Education, University of California, Los Angeles, and serves as a member of the Board of Advisors of the Pacific Institute for Public Policy Research. He received his M.A. and Ph.D. from the University of Chicago, where he became Professor and Director of the Midwest Administration Center. He has also taught at Florida State University, Simon Fraser University, and the University of San Francisco. Dr. Erickson is the author of *Super-Parent* (1973), *The Three R's of Nonpublic Education in Louisiana* (1972), *Issues of Aid to Nonpublic Schools* (1971), *Educational Flexibility in an Urban School District* (1970), *Crisis in Illinois Nonpublic Schools* (1971), *Community School at Rough Rock* (1969), *Public Controls for Nonpublic Schools* (1969), and *Educational Organization and Administration* (1977).

**Roger A. Freeman** is a Senior Fellow emeritus at the Hoover Institution. He has served as Chairman of the Advisory Council on Financial Aid to Students of the Department of Health, Education and Welfare as Assistant to Presidents Eisenhower and Nixon, worked on President Reagan's preinaugural education policy task force as well as serving on a variety of government and nongovernment advisory committees. He has written numerous books including *School Needs in the Decade Ahead* (1958), *Taxes for the Schools* (1960), *Crisis in College Finance?* (1965), *The Growth of American Government: A Morphology of the Welfare State* (1975), and *The Wayward Welfare State* (1981). He has also written over a hundred articles in professional journals and magazines, has given numerous reports to congressional committees, and has delivered hundreds of speeches before audiences throughout the country.

**Laurence Iannaccone** is Professor of Education in the Graduate School of Education at the University of California, Santa Barbara. He received his B.A. in history and government at the University of Buffalo, and his Ed.D. from Columbia Teachers College, and has served on the faculties of the University of Toronto, Harvard University, Claremont Graduate, Washington University, and New York University. He is currently Editor of the *Review of Educational Research*, and is the recipient of the 1980 Cooperative Professor of the Year Award of the American Association of School Administrators. His many books include *Politics in Education* (1967), *The Politics of Education* (1974) coauthored with Peter Cistone, and *Public Participation in Local School Districts: The Dissatisfaction Theory of Democracy* (1978) coauthored with Frank Lutz.

**Michael S. Katz** is Associate Professor of Philosophy and History of Education at the University of Nebraska at Omaha. He received his B.A. from Amherst College (1966) and his Ph.D. from Stanford University (1974). He is the author of *A History of Compulsory Education Laws* (1976) and articles which have appeared in *Educational Theory, Journal of Teacher Education*, and *The Proceedings of the Philosophy of Education Society*. He presently holds offices in The John Dewey Society and the American Educational Studies Association. His academic interests include ordinary language philosophy, literature, constitutional law, and American educational policy. His current research project involves an inquiry into the ethical dimensions of teaching.

**Thomas J. La Belle** is Professor of Education and Associate Dean of the Graduate Division at University of California, Los Angeles. He received his Ph.D. in education from the University of New Mexico in 1969 with an emphasis in educational anthropology and education in Latin America. He recently completed a term as President of the Comparative and International Education Society. He has authored or edited more than five books and some forty articles in the last decade.

**Charles Lawrence III** received his law degree from Yale University in 1969 and currently is an Associate Professor of Law, University of San Francisco. Mr. Lawrence's fields of interest include law in education, constitutional law, and the area of minority rights. He is the author of *The Bakke Case: The Politics of Inequality*.

**George H. Smith** studied philosophy at the University of Arizona, and is currently Research Fellow, Institute for Humane Studies. He is the author of *Atheism: The Case Against God* (1974), and *Education and Liberty: The Separation of School and State* (forthcoming) coauthored with J. High. His articles and reviews have appeared in the *Free Inquiry*, *Journal of Libertarian Studies*, *Libertarian Review*, and *Reason*. His special interests include the history of radical individualism in America and England, with special emphasis on Herbert Spencer and his influence.

**Joel Spring** received his Ph.D. from the University of Wisconsin at Madison in 1969. He is Professor of Education at the University of Cincinnati, where his specialty is the history of educational policy in the twentieth century. He is the author of *The Sorting Machine* (1976), *A Primer of Libertarian Education* (1975), *Education and the Rise of the Corporate State* (1972), *Educating the Worker-Citizen* (1980), *American Education: Social and Political Aspects* (1978), and one of six contributors to *The Twelve Year Sentence: Radical Views of Compulsory Schooling* (1974), edited by W. F. Rickenbacker. His articles have appeared in *Educational Theory*, *History of Education Quarterly*, *Libertarian Analysis*, *School and Society*, *School Review*, *Socialist Revolution*, and other scholarly journals.

**Thomas Vitullo-Martin** is Research Director of Metroconomy, Inc., a New York-based management consulting firm. He has been a member of the graduate faculty of political science and education at the University of California, Riverside, and at Columbia Teachers College, and has served as Visiting Professor of Urban Politics at the University of Pennsylvania. He has studied the impact of federal policies on private schools for the past several years and is now writing a book on the emerging federal role in public and private education.

**E. G. West** received his Ph.D. in economics from London University. He is currently Professor of Economics at Carleton University in Ottawa, and is a member of the Board of Advisors of the Pacific Institute for Public Policy Research. He has been Research Fellow at the University of Chicago, and Visiting Professor of Economics at Virginia Polytechnic Institute and State University. Dr. West is the author of *Education and the State* (1965), *Adam Smith: The Man and His Works* (1969), *Education and the Industrial Revolution* (1975), *Economics, Education and the Politician* (1968), and *Non-Public School Aid: The Law, Economics and Politics of American Education* (1967). A frequent contributor to economics journals, his special areas of interest are public finance, public choice, the economics of education and the history of economic thought.